O RARE DON MARQUIS

O Rare
Don Marquis

A BIOGRAPHY

BY EDWARD ANTHONY

DOUBLEDAY & COMPANY, INC.
GARDEN CITY, NEW YORK
1962

Library of Congress Catalog Card Number 62–7596. Copyright © 1962 by
 Edward Anthony

All Rights Reserved. Printed in the United States of America

First Edition

TO ESTHER
who helped the most,
eagle-eye Dick, the family copy-reader,
and Toby for being so good an audience.

O RARE BEN JONSON!
Sir John Young: Epitaph

O RARE DON MARQUIS
Chapter head,
Christopher Morley's Letters of Askance

ACKNOWLEDGMENTS

I gratefully acknowledge the help of friends of Don Marquis's—Homer and Mae Croy, Fola La Follette, George Middleton, Mell Daniel, Katherine Glover, Frank Sullivan, Howard Lindsay, Dorothy Stickney, Dana Burnet, Susan Prince, Edith McDonald, Richard H. Hoffmann, Lawton Mackall, Julian La Rose Harris, Julia Collier Harris, Herbert Ranson, Lyman Beecher Stowe, and Sophia Y. Stokes —whose files and recollections are responsible for a great many of these pages.

Acknowledgment is also made of the fine co-operation of the leading repositories of Marquisiana: the Butler Library of Columbia University, which has the largest collection; the New York Public Library; the Henry E. Huntington Library; the Walter Hampden Memorial Library of the Players Club; the library of the American Academy of Arts and Letters; the Houghton Library of Harvard University; the Library of Congress; and the Library of the University of Texas.

A special word of thanks is due Kenneth A. Lohf, Assistant Librarian, Special Collections, Butler Library; George Freedley, Curator, Theatre Collection, New York Public Library; Herbert C. Schulz, Curator of Manuscripts, Huntington Library; Mrs. Matthew Josephson, Librarian of the American Academy; and Patrick Carroll, Librarian of the Players.

I express my gratitude also to Porter Wylie, chairman of the Managing Committee of the Players; to Charles Connolly, now an honorary member, who joined the Club's permanent personnel shortly after the turn of the century; to Henry Fisk Carlton, a member of the Executive Committee; to Herbert F. Erb, custodian of the Club's records—and for the help of John C. King, Wade Arnold, Joseph Cummings Chase, Charles Coburn, George H. Tilton, Walter Trumbull, George Britt, Van Cartmell, Newman Levy, William G. Tachau, Harry Gilbert, Francis Stilwell Dixon, Brooks Atkinson, Frank E. Mason, Paul M. Hollister, Laurie P. Bruenn, Charles Francis, Thomas Hardie Chalmers, Nicholas Samstag, and other Players.

My thanks, also, to Carlos F. Stoddard, Jr., Director of Information, Yale University; to William J. Waugh, chief of the Atlanta Bureau of the Associated Press; to Abel Green, editor of *Variety*, whose fabulous files produced significant data; to the Atlanta Historical Society; to Angus Perkerson and William Cole Jones, associates of Marquis's on the Atlanta *Journal* more than fifty years ago; to Robert U. Brown, editor of *Editor & Publisher*, and Ray Irwin, conductor of "Ray Irwin's Column" in that publication; and to the following: Gordon M. Bruce, Nunnally Johnson, Rosamond Gilder, Robert McKee, George Cornish, Bernard Sobel, Berton Braley, James M. Kahn, Ed Bartnett, Eddie Dowling, Hudson R. Hawley, Frank Graham, Louis Untermeyer, Cyril B. Egan, Stanley Walker, Joan Walker Wenning, Edmund Leamy, Brigadier General Charles G. Stevenson, John T. Winterich, Lyle C. Wilson, Cornelia Otis Skinner, the Marchbanks Press (and especially its president, Emily E. Connor), Sophie Treadwell, Bradley Kelly, Harry E. Maule, Frank J. Starzel, Wilber Forrest, Maynard Craig, Sumner Blossom, Katherine Adcock, Eleanor V. McAvoy, Royal Daniel, Jr., Joey Rosenberg, John H. Gleason, the administrative office of Knox College, Myrtice Boyd, James Quigney, Malthe M. Hasslriis, Eric Sloane, Thomas W. Dewart, Margaret B. Taffender, Arthur Moynihan, O'Malley's Bookstore of New York, specialists in out-of-print books, for many remarkable finds, Leery's of Philadelphia ("Old Books"), for producing a book that had eluded me for almost a year; a special bow to Robert A. Hug, a retired employee of the New York Public Library, a professional researcher with the ingenuity of a first-rate detective; and a salute to the memory of three former Players who died while this book was being written: John V. L. Hogan, Forest Hills neighbor and close friend of Marquis's, William Morris Houghton, a former newspaper associate, and Alexander F. Victor, Players Club companion of Marquis's and an authority on his repertoire as a storyteller—all three of whom gave generously of their time and contributed valuable data and first-hand insights into the subject of this book.

And a most appreciative thank-you to *The Saturday Review* for its instrumentality in locating Edith McDonald, formerly secretary to Don Marquis, and one of this book's most fruitful sources. This was accomplished by an ad in its "Personals" column. And a salute to Joseph Marks, vice-president of Doubleday and Company, for making available the Don Marquis correspondence, etc., in the files of the progenitors of the present-day Doubleday firm: Doubleday, Page and Company and Doubleday, Doran and Company.

I am deeply obligated to the Special Services Division of United Press International and its director, C. Edmonds Allen (and his associate, Wayne C. Butler), for using its facilities to find elusive pieces of the Don Marquis jigsaw puzzle that had resisted other quests; and to the many newspapers that carried the productive Doubleday announcement that material for this book was being sought.

To my wife, Esther H. Anthony, a garland of roses for converting into an easily consulted research unit a vast accumulation of documents of all kinds—literally thousands of them, including photostats of Don Marquis columns, letters by, to, and about him, countless newspaper clippings (interviews, editorials, reviews of his books, plays, and movies, news items, incidental allusions, etc.), more than a hundred sets of magazine tear sheets, several hundred pages of unpublished manuscript, outlines of projected Marquis articles, short stories, books, and plays, a mélange of notes of all sorts (Marquis's), and the notes I made—they filled twenty-seven pocket notebooks and five large ones—in interviewing people in New York and on our travels around the country in quest of Marquisiana. And for her help in other important categories.

And, finally, a separate and very special word of thanks to George Shively, Senior Editor of Doubleday and Company, for a perceptive job of editing. Few have his extraordinary insight into the rare mechanism that was Don Marquis, and I feel privileged to have had the benefit of his advice and guidance.

Edward Anthony

New Milford, Connecticut

AUTHOR'S NOTE

In the introduction to her distinguished biography, *Thomas Wolfe*, Elizabeth Nowell stated:

"In writing this biography I have drawn heavily upon Wolfe's interpretation of himself—in his novels, in his strictly autobiographical writings such as *The Story of a Novel*, the Purdue speech, his letters, and his pocket notebooks. It would be ridiculous not to."

In writing this life of Don Marquis I have done the equivalent. I found that there was so much of this material—most of it straight autobiography and autobiographical fiction, some of it extravaganza with overtones of personal history, and even self-revelatory poems and aphorisms—that not all of it that is worthy of publication could find a place in these pages. But not to have sampled generously the best and most revealing of it would have been to deprive the reader of insights into the subject of this book that could not have been gained in any other way.

It is doubtful whether Marquis himself realized how often he was writing about Marquis. When Clem Hawley, the Old Soak, made his widely quoted prohibition-era comment on the nationally advertised "Bevo," a sadly deficient brew, "This here near beer is all right for a near thirst," he was merely summing up what his creator had said in letters to friends about "this libel on lager." Hawley was a device by means of which much that Marquis saw and felt—indeed much that happened to him—was recorded.

At the time of his death Marquis had almost completed an autobiographical novel and had written a sizable chunk of his autobiography. Both are prime sources.

Before "submitting his record of crime to the microscope of self-examination" he wrote an article for the *Saturday Evening Post* (May 17, 1930) spoofing the mass production of personal histories. In fact, in a letter to a friend he postulated that he and "an anthropoid ape of my acquaintance, a gorilla named Goo Goo," were the "only erect primates" he could name who weren't writing their memoirs. In the *Post* article he developed this point somewhat:

". . . Fortune tellers, burlicue hoofers, pearl divers, football coaches, traveling evangelists, head waiters, party girls, Panama Canal swimmers like Richard Halliburton, bank robbers, confidence men, prison wardens, hijackers and related racketeers, college professors turned taxi drivers, glass eaters, princes, divas, jockeys, human flies, old pitchmen, state vice-presidents of the Anti-Saloon League, hockey players, missionaries, police sergeants and murderesses in and out of vaudeville—these and many more are telling the stories of their lives." He decided to make it unanimous by persuading Goo Goo to write *his* memoirs and to take the plunge himself. For the purposes of this book it was a fortunate decision. I welcome its help as gratefully as did Miss Nowell the mass of self-interpretation she inherited from Thomas Wolfe.

Where there is more material than can be used on any given subject—for instance, the satires based on Marquis's Hollywood experiences—I had to make some arbitrary choices. I could use only one of these film-colony pieces and decided to draw upon the one that gave Marquis an opportunity to talk about his friendship with Will Rogers. I had to make similar decisions in other categories, and I hope those who went to the trouble of offering material that could not be accommodated will understand.

                                                              E.A.

CONTENTS

O RARE DON MARQUIS

1
Marquis Discusses Marquis—Boyhood Days in Walnut, Bureau County, Illinois—Violence in a Tiny Town—Dr. Marquis, Don's Father

In 1931 Don Marquis's publisher suggested that he write his auto-biography. He turned down the proposal in these words: "I'm entitled to a better subject."

Then, having had his little joke, he started work on the book. On January 22, 1932, he wrote his friend Christopher Morley as follows:

"I am writing my autobiography, from time to time. It is not exactly a story of what I did, so much, as what I thought about and was.

"Here is chapter five for your personal perusal. When you've read it, will you send it back. Toujours yours, Don"

It is evident from a study of the many manuscript pages found among Marquis's papers that have to do with this projected memoir that the author was finding it difficult to decide what to include and how to deal with certain aspects of a book about himself.

Before he had produced the first hundred pages of a manuscript he considered publishable he had written over three hundred typed pages and many pages in longhand.

One of the decisions he made was that he would write about himself in the third person, referring to himself as "Marquis" or "M." Since this book would be a history of his thoughts as well as his deeds, he decided on the following title:

M.: The Egobiography of Don Marquis

This project was something Marquis worked on intermittently, taking time off, as the spirit moved him, from the labors that bought the groceries, as he phrased it. He wrote, rejected, rewrote; and in many instances killed page after page—sometimes whole chapters. The chapter Marquis sent Morley in 1932 was barely recognizable by 1935.

In his various stabs at his egobiography Marquis wrote well over 100,000 words. Of this he set aside about one-third as "final copy"—material he considered in good enough shape for publication. Then, having done all this work, he abandoned the project in favor of an autobiographical novel, *Sons of the Puritans*, which he did not live to complete and which was posthumously published in 1939.

The importance of the egobiography is that, aside from fragmentary oddments gleaned from letters, it contains the only information available about Marquis's boyhood days and the early history of his family, in addition to providing self-portraits of the author that give the full flavor of stories he had told friends about some of the unlikely jobs he held as a young man—stories that now take on much more meaning.

Marquis concludes the first chapter of the egobiography with these paragraphs:

* * *

Marquis has always been trying to settle down, feel at home and comfortable, in the midst of human existence; and he has never quite succeeded. Existence races by, gets away from him and vanishes like a puff of smoke, before he is able to determine his relationship to it. If, for a moment or a year, he thinks he has been able to penetrate to the significance of some phase of it, that phase immediately resolves itself into something else and he stands once more wondering, lost, and bewildered.

How does one start to write the story of his life, or stories from his life, when all that he knows is that he somehow finds himself on the earth and deeply implicated in human existence, without being at all sure what the earth is, or what he himself is, or what human existence is?

* * *

The opening chapter of the egobiography—three thousand words of satiric fantasy—makes entertaining reading but contains no biographical data, nor does it contribute anything to the "ego" phase of the memoir, and is omitted here for those reasons.

In Chapter Two Marquis gets down to the business of writing a memoir. It is a rather long chapter and at least three-fourths of it is pertinent biographical data that is available nowhere else. It seemed, therefore, that these portions, or the gist of them, should be published here as an essential part of the Don Marquis story.

Lifting big chunks out of Marquis's story of himself and dropping them into this book seemed like a lazy device; so I prepared a transposed and sharply condensed version of what Marquis had said about himself. It didn't work. The juices had somehow leaked out of what he had written.

Marquis's story of Marquis spoke for itself. What it needed most was to be left alone.

Here, then, is about two-thirds of Chapter Two of the final draft of Marquis's autobiography, the 1935 version:

* * *

Marquis was born in a little town with muddy streets, called Walnut, in the northwestern part of Illinois; and this birth was on July 29, 1878, at three o'clock in the afternoon, during an eclipse of the sun—not merely on the same day, but *during* the eclipse itself. In the fifty-seven years since his birth he has had but little time for study or reflection, for somebody or something is forever interrupting him.

Evangeline Adams, the celebrated astrologer, once told M. exactly what being born during an eclipse meant, but he cannot remember the details. There was something about a dark man and a blonde lady. Or maybe it was a blond man and a dark lady. Or maybe M. has got the horoscope somehow mixed in his mind with Shakespeare's sonnets.

At any rate, M. has always been proud of his eclipse. To be born during an eclipse is a good deal more remarkable, and should be a good deal more valuable to a man, than being born with an ordinary caul. In fact, to be born with an eclipse over you is to be born with a kind of cosmic caul covering you. Marquis has always been grateful to the gods for this spectacular advertisement of his notability. He has felt that it prefigured extraordinary luck (of one sort or the other) and an unusual destiny; and even yet, at the age of fifty-seven, he cheers up when he thinks about it, and looks out the window and up and down the street to see if the luck and the destiny may not be turning the corner on the way to meet him. A caul would not keep a man cheered up for fifty-seven years like that.

In fact, being born with a caul is perilously near to being born a freak; but an eclipse is astronomical, meteorological, and historical. People save cauls, and use them in queer old-hokum medicaments, or semivoodoo incantations, and it must be uncomfortable to reflect that what is practically a part of yourself is being used in witchcraft of that sort; but nobody can get hold of an eclipse for such superstitious purpose. An eclipse is a good deal more important in every way than a caul; and M. is more than a little bit snobbish in his attitude toward persons who were not born during an eclipse.

* * *

Nearly everything about Marquis seems extraordinary to himself. A few years ago Christopher Morley asked Marquis for some information to be used in a biographical note, and M. wrote the following letter:

Dear Kit:

The name Marquis is not French, but Scottish in origin. The first of that name of whom I have any certain record came to Virginia from the North of Ireland in 1720, and settled near Winchester. They were Calvinists who believed in Infant Damnation, Calomel, and Scotch whiskey. Anything prior to 1720 must be purely conjectural with regard to this family.

But I have made some conjectures which interest me. In Argyll, Scotland, the name Marquis is almost as common as the name Jones is in Wales. They are somehow hooked up with the MacDonald outfit and entitled to wear the MacDonald tartan. I suppose that the ones who are found in the North of Ireland are descended from the Protestant plantation of James I. I found a copy of an Edinburgh genealogical publication when I was in England which gives something of the history of the name. It is sometimes given as Marquis and sometimes as MacMarquis. But I suppose it to have been Englished in spelling at the time when so many

Gaelic names were given a roughly approximate English orthography, and to have had a Celtic form previously. I found it in one place spelled "Marc Uis"; from which I conjecture that it may once have been Mac-Uis—which means, I believe, Son of the Waters.

The earliest known Marquis given in this genealogical article was one John Og Marquis—or John Oig, I have forgotten which—who was a tanner in Argyll about 1580. Angus Og, or Angus Oig Marquis, was also among the names given.

Now, there was a Celtic deity named Aengus Og, and it seems possible to me that the tanner was descended from this god.

This god Angus, or Aengus, was a beautiful god, and he used to come over the hills like a burst of sunlight between two rainy clouds in April, singing as he came; and birds circled his head as he sang and perched on the top of his harp, a harp with strings of ruddy gold. Angus was a terrible fellow with the women, too. The kind of god a god ought to be—no bleak Semitic god, nor any damned early Calvinist, either, but a god of song and laughter; and he could be frightful, too, when the notion took him.

And yet . . . he wasn't respectable . . . he couldn't have been. So if you publish this information, better not go back any further than the tanner.

To be descended from a tanner is a solid, respectable sort of thing. One can come down from a tanner and be reasonably sure that there is an unbroken chain of wedlock all the way along the line. But to claim descent from a god like Angus is to make what practically amounts to a confession that the family got started on earth by an act of bastardy. The morals of some of those pagan deities were something lamentable, I understand; and Angus was one of the most careless of them. I insist on respectability.

Few of those gods married, or were willing even for a space to complicate their lives with domestic matters. Being a god takes up all one's time, I suppose. Domesticity is always felt to be an interruption to anyone with a divine mission on earth.

There is the case of Jesus of Nazareth, for example. He never married, and he repudiated his mother. He had no father but a Ghost, and no mother but a Virgin, and no wife and children to worry about, and this left him free to be a reformer, and he was a great success as a reformer. It is true that he lost his life, but a good many of his ideas have persisted, and occasionally something he advocated has actually been applied to human existence—though not very often or very consistently.

Most of the pagan gods were bastards themselves, as far as I can find out. At the first flush, a person may be rather proud to be descended from a god, but when he comes to think of all the connotations of such descent he is apt to shy away from it, if he is a person of my staid and sober temperament.

Of course, if it could be proved that one was descended from a god by a Virgin Birth, that would remove all shadow of reproach. But in my case there is no documentary evidence of a Virgin Birth; nor even that the god married the girl afterward. If there had been a *succession* of Virgin Births, child after child being born without any grosser physical contact, throughout a couple of centuries—and a succession of Virgin Births should be as easy for a god to accomplish as just one Virgin Birth—that would be something worth bragging about. But failing that, better say nothing about the god whatever. Stick to the tanner.

I used sometimes to wonder why certain well-known religions did not feature in their programs this succession of Virgin Births. But it may have been felt that such a course would have about it a faint air of trying to prove too much. . . .

Anyhow, everything back of 1720 is conjectural. M. may hint at his own private beliefs, but there is nothing back of 1720 which he cares to be quoted as endorsing absolutely.

It was M.'s grandfather's grandfather who got here in 1720. M.'s great-grandfather was named Thomas Marquis, and he was a soldier in the Revolutionary War. Thomas crossed the mountains from Virginia and settled in eastern Ohio about 1798. He took with him his wife and two children, a millstone, a whisky still, and a Bible. M. used to hear his grandfather tell about this trek when he was five years old and his grandfather was ninety-five.

The trip started well enough. The party was making camp one evening on the Virginia side of the Potomac, intending to cross the river the next morning, when no less a person than George Washington himself came riding along the bank of the river. He recognized Thomas as one of his old Virginia soldiers, inquired where he was going, and was gracious with the wife and children. M.'s grandfather—he was about ten years old at the time and his name was William—told until his dying day that he had once shaken hands with George Washington. He used to encourage M., in fact, to shake the hand that had once shaken the hand of George Washington, which at the age of four and five and six became an occasional ceremony between M. and his grandfather. It seems silly that it should do so, but it has somehow always made Washington seem more like a fellow creature to M., a recognizable human being; although the other men of that period, the Jeffersons and Hamiltons and the rest of them, seemed to his youth to be as remote as Cromwell or Columbus or Caesar.

When Thomas and his family were well on their way, a difficulty arose. They ran out of salt. Their salt had got rained on and had melted away. They were in a wild country, and it was necessary for someone to go back to the last trading post along the line of march and get a sack of salt. There was no Indian war on at the time, but there were always Indians, and no one knew what particular Indian might want to add a paleface scalp or two to his trophies. Too many settlers were pouring into their hunting grounds west of the mountains anyhow, and the Indians were beginning to get the idea that sooner or later, if this kept up, the Indians were going to be pushed off the face of the earth—and they were right about it.

Either Thomas or his wife had to ride back sixty miles and get a sack of salt. After a good deal of debate, it was decided that the man had better stay with the children; he would be more protection for them than the woman would. So the woman—her name was Betsy—took her rifle and mounted one of the horses and went back for the salt. She made the hundred-and-twenty-mile trip without meeting an Indian. She was red-haired and high-colored, and M. seems to remember that her maiden name was Hogg; a handsome woman, her son told M.

William, M.'s grandfather, used to aver that he was no slouch with a rifle himself as a young fellow. He was a captain in the War of 1812—"Captain Billy" they called him when M. was a child, and after he died the G.A.R. veterans in the little Illinois village where M. lived used always to decorate his grave first on Memorial Days.

Captain Billy might not have liked that so well if he had known about it. For he remained to the end of his days a Southern sympathizer. He was seventy-three years old when the Civil War broke out, or he would probably have gone South and joined up with the Confederacy, he felt so strongly about the matter. One of M.'s earliest recollections is hearing his father, who was born in Ohio, call his grandfather "a damned old butternut." M.'s father, who was in his eighties when he died, was forty-six when the Civil War

started, with three or four small children to take care of, as well as
Captain Billy and a sister, so he didn't go to the war on the Union
side; he and his father took it out in argument for twenty years or
more.

Captain Billy quit work along about 1834, and lived fifty years
after that—and there was a family story to the effect that he had
never done much work during the first forty-six years of his life,
either. He had inherited a great deal of farming land in eastern Ohio,
and he was a preacher fancier. He liked to sit on the front porch of
his farmhouse and entertain ministers of the gospel, and preachers
came from scores of miles to sit around and eat chicken dinners
and argue theology with Captain Billy. He was a very convinced
Calvinist, but no matter how strong a Scotch Presbyterian's conviction may be he always seems to find a good many things to
argue about. Johnny Appleseed was one of Captain Billy's friends.

After about 1850 Captain Billy never made any concessions to
current styles in dress. M. remembers him as a tall old gentleman,
with long white hair to his shoulders, very erect, who preferred stocks
to collars, and carried individual walking sticks, which he cut in
the woods himself, trimmed, and polished and varnished.

M.'s grandparents on his mother's side came from Virginia, also,
near Natural Bridge. People always brag about coming from Virginia,
just as in old times they used to brag about being descended from
the gods, and M. has all the idle vanities. M.'s mother's maiden
name was Whitmore, and *her* mother's name was Perry, kin to the
fifty thousand Perrys who are cousins of the young fellow who cut
down the trees and built the ships and banged the British on Lake
Erie. Oliver Hazard Perry, the Commodore's grandson, who died here
in New York a couple of years ago, used to tell M. that the
Commodore's father was a pirate; but whether that was true, or
Oliver just said it because he was so tired of hearing all the Perry
outfit brag about the Commodore, M. never knew.

M.'s mother was a pretty woman, pretty up to the time she died
at the age of eighty-one, and a darling. It was terrible that she had
to spend so much of her life in a commonplace little village such as
Walnut, Illinois. M.'s mother had relatives in the Confederate army.
M. never heard anyone brag very much about having relations in

the Union army, but he has always bragged about his relations in the Confederate army. There is a glamor about lost causes which persists. And he has always had a strong feeling that Southerners are superior people—a feeling so strong, indeed, that it even survived seven years of residence in the South, which is quite a test.

*   *   *

When Marquis was five or six years old he received an unfortunate impression of the Christian religion through attending a Baptist Sunday School; an impression which he was a long time getting rid of.

There was an old murderer who went to that church, and to the Sunday School, by the name of Hank W. Hank had killed his wife about fifteen years before M. ever saw him, beating her to death with an iron stove leg when she was pregnant. When she was dying, M.'s father, who was a physician, was sent for, and discovered that the woman had been savagely maltreated. He searched the premises, and found a dismantled cookstove in the woodshed, and the leg which had been used. He had Hank arrested; Hank was tried, and given a life sentence in the penitentiary.

But Hank got "converted" in prison. He began to love Jesus, as the phrase of the time and place had it, with an extraordinary fervor which impressed everybody within earshot. To hear Hank tell about it, he became more pious than anybody had ever been before. A lot of "good Christian people," as the saying is, who had some political pull, got Hank's life sentence commuted to twelve years; and when M. was a small boy Hank was back at the scene of his crime, and a great leader in prayer. He used to get up in church and tell, on the slightest provocation or none at all, how wicked he had been, and how he had been saved, and how good he was now.

There was a false glitter across his face; across his teeth when he smiled—and he was always smiling—a glitter on the tight skin across his high cheekbones and his high narrow nose, across the bald forehead, and the wiry wisps of white hair above his temples; and this glitter was in his eyes, too. The bony formation of his face and head was curved and quirked in places, and the hair about the ears was curled and quirked, and he looked like pictures of ancient patriarchs and prophets which M. had seen in a big old illustrated Bible. There were cruel, crooked talons in the wrinkles about the man's eyes.

At that time frightful little colored cards were given out to the children in Sunday Schools, which pictured various Bible heroes in violent colors—flaming reds, and crude blues and greens and yellows. There were pictures of patriarchs with knives, getting ready to obey Jehovah and sacrifice their sons. There was a horrible lot of talk about sacrifice, and the blood of sacrifice, and there were songs and hymns about the Blood of the Lamb, and fountains filled with blood drawn from Emmanuel's veins. There were pictures of fountains on the cards, also. And there was the cannibalistic idea that the bread and wine of the communion service represented the body and blood of Jesus Christ. It seemed to the young mind of M. that there was a terrifying lot of talk about blood in Sunday School . . . blood, and lambs, and sacrifices, and slaughter, and the saving blood of Jesus Christ, who bled for us all, and those ghastly picture cards, which looked as if gouts of blood had coagulated on them.

And in the midst of all this disgusting mental mess was old Hank W., who had actually shed blood. And now the blood of Jesus Christ had somehow saved and redeemed old Hank, and he was better than nearly everybody else, and you must never call him old Hank, but Mr. W., and you must treat him nicely, because he had been saved. On top of all this blood would be a golden crown, when dear old Mr. W. got to heaven, and he would strum on a golden harp, and Jesus would be in heaven too, and very friendly with Mr. W. because Mr. W. had repented. And no doubt there would be a fountain there, and maybe Mr. W. would be helping to fill it with blood drawn right from Emmanuel's veins; Emmanuel being Jesus. And it would all be a gorgeous red and golden-yellow picture . . . and if you were a very good little boy you could go to heaven yourself, and get much better acquainted with Jesus and dear old Mr. W.

M. was quite young, and it was not until some years later that he began to wonder what Mrs. W. would be contributing in the way of blood to the reeking ensemble, or whether she had contributed all the blood she had when old Hank beat her to death with the stove leg.

Hearing how much Jesus loved Mr. W., and how much he was willing to overlook in the case of old Hank, nearly ruined Jesus permanently with M. It was only when he got old enough to understand how much hokum there is in all this sort of stuff that he began dimly to see Jesus as a human being, and understand how much his so-called friends have lied about him. Then M. began to get a respect for the Nazarene prophet. But the Baptist Sunday School, with old Hank in it, was a terrible obstacle to get over. The sickening way in which preachers and Sunday School teachers used to pronounce the name of Jesus—"Je*sous*" seemed to be a favorite way in that part of Illinois; Je*sous*, mushily, with burbling lips and watery eyes—was enough in itself to put anybody off Him for life.

In more mature years M. has begun to suspect that old Hank was a kind of subtle, savage humorist. He had repented, officially, and he enjoyed making the church people live up to the letter of their creed; he saw to it that the Repentant Sinner got all the glory which was coming to him. Hank liked the whole show. His old murderer's heart leaped in hellish glee when he saw how his hypocrisy succeeded. His children, who went to the same church, wouldn't have anything to do with him; but the professed Christians were helpless. They *had* to forgive him or acknowledge that they weren't really Christians. Besides the harm he did with the murder, he went on doing harm as long as he lived, as a focal point for all the maudlin sentimentality of which these half-baked little churches are capable. If he had been legally hanged, or lynched out of hand right after he had committed the murder, it would have saved a lot of disgusting circumstance.

* * *

Walnut was one of those little towns in which "nothing ever happens." But looking back at it after all these years, M. realizes that a good deal happened there; and that much was of a violent nature. One morning when he was about twelve years old he and another boy were going to school together, and they were taking a short cut through the woods, when they came upon the body of "Old Horse" Wolf swinging from the limb of a tree.

His name was Orson Wolf; Orson had been shortened to "Orse";

and as he grew older he began to be called "Old Horse." Old Horse
Wolf had hanged himself, and not done a very workmanlike job of it,
either. He had climbed upon a large log, which lay against the base
of a hickory tree, fastened a rope around his neck, and the other end
of it around a limb of the hickory tree, and had stepped off the log.

But Old Horse had reckoned without the elasticity of the hickory
limb. The step from the log did not give him drop enough; and the
hickory limb bent. His toes had just touched the ground, and he had
danced himself to death, strangling, as the limb went up and down.
When M. and the other boy found him he was dead, but still
dancing. There was a little breeze, and Old Horse did not weigh
much, and the breeze was enough to move him and the limb of the
tree and keep him pirouetting on tiptoe. He was dressed in brown
overalls, and there was a slant of sunlight down through the green
trees, and he fluttered in the sun like a dead brown leaf just settling
to the ground.

Why Old Horse hanged himself, M. never knew. Possibly it was
because of domestic troubles. M. has noticed that people frequently
hang themselves because of domestic troubles; whereas, if they are
going to kill themselves because of strictly financial troubles they
often take crude, painful poisons, or jump from high buildings. General melancholia and despair seem to lead to drowning. Why has no
man of science ever made a study of why certain types of suicide
prefer certain kinds of death? It should be an inquiry quite in accord with the spirit of current pseudo-philosophy.

Anyhow, there was Old Horse, dead as a clump of last year's
grass, dancing delicately on his toes. Possibly he had had no time
during life to indulge himself in such a frivolous occupation. And it
may be that his ghost was helping the wind and the hickory limb
to keep the brown figure agitated like a marionette. M. doesn't really
know anything about him except that he was Old Horse Wolf, and
lived on the edge of the woods. It would be a nice little bit to have
a squirrel or a woodpecker doing something while Old Horse
danced; but M. doesn't remember anything of that sort. This book,
where it pretends to relate facts at all, will be honest; but there will
be a fable in it, here and there, which will represent a state of mind
behind the physical facts.

* * *

Then there was Emmett Lamb. M. was going along the street one Sunday morning, when he was a lad of fourteen or fifteen, when he saw a small crowd in front of the "city hall," a one-story wooden building which was not only the seat of municipal government but housed the village fire engine also. There was evidently some early effort to make the place a kind of community center, or club-house, as well, for there were billiard tables in it, and the paraphernalia of other games.

Emmett Lamb was laid out on a billiard table, dead. There was a hole right down through his chest, just beside his heart, so neat and clean that you could look through it; it might have been bored through wood with an augur. He had been shot to death with a load of buckshot at close range, by a man whose name may be abbreviated to Mr. F.

Emmett was an immense man, about six feet six inches in height, extraordinarily strong, and anything but lamblike in nature. One of his favorite tricks, when excited by alcoholic beverages, and feeling himself a hero, was to take a heavy glass beer schooner in each hand and "clean out" the barroom. He was a Republican, and he liked to hit Democrats. On Saturday night he had gone down to Mr. F.'s house, at the edge of town, and demanded that Mrs. F. come out and yield herself to his passionate embraces. Mrs. F. was reluctant, claiming that she had never done such a thing, and never would—and anyhow, her husband was home. Emmett replied that such talk was all nonsense, and that if she did not hurry he would come into the house and get her, even if he had to tear the house down in the process.

Mr. F., who really was at home that evening, was listening to the colloquy and quietly charging his muzzle-loading shotgun with buck-shot. So when Emmett came up to the house and tried to tear the screen door from the hinges, to make good his amatory threats and promises, Mr. F. shot him through the screen. Emmett's brother came into the town hall while M. was there, looked down through the hole in Emmett, and pronounced his epitaph. "I always thought," said the brother, as he turned away, "that Emmett would get it sooner or later."

* * *

The F.s had been "swamp angels" before they moved to town. West of the town where M. lived, and with its outposts of slough and lake not more than a mile or two from the village, was a large swamp. It was sixty or seventy miles long in wet weather, and anywhere from fifteen to eighteen miles broad. Through the middle of it wound a big creek, or little river, called Green River, which drained westward into Rock River, which, in turn, emptied into the Mississippi, not far away. This swamp was wild at its heart when M. was a boy; wolves were still found there about 1890, and, once or twice, eagles. It was beginning to be crisscrossed with drainage ditches; now it has been pretty thoroughly drained; has, in fact, almost disappeared, and the land is among the richest farming land in the world, with cornstalks growing to incredible heights.

In this swamp were the remnants of a peculiar people, when M. was a lad. They were the descendants of some westward-trekking tribe of white trash who had stopped there, and stuck in the mud, from very early days. A backward, ignorant people, they seemed to bear little resemblance to the most respectable settlers in the farms and villages about the borders of the swamp. The swamp itself was dotted with hillocks, wooded islands, swales, and ridges and hummocks of higher land; and when M. was a lad it teemed with small game of all sorts.

The early swamp angels, before the Civil War, were criminals who preyed on the peaceful settlers round about, and on the covered-wagon travelers, who were moving westward. The swamp lay right athwart one of the most popular covered-wagon routes to a crossing on the Mississippi and westward. There were, in those days, corduroy roads through it, which wound around among the sloughs and islands, and were in dry weather barely passable; but at that the traveler needed a guide. The early swamp angels, who lived in the middle of the big fen, offered themselves as guides; and often robbed and murdered the travelers.

When M. was about nineteen years old he was teaching school in a country district on the edge of this swamp; and frequently he spent the weekend with a friend about his own age, who lived on a farm a few miles away, and drove to the schoolhouse for him on

Friday nights. W.S. were this friend's initials. One Friday afternoon when W.S. was driving M. to the S. home, they stopped at a place where an old man was having a fit in the barnyard.

Call him Mr. Fitts . . . Old Henry Fitts. M. doesn't like to use too many initials; and he doesn't like to use real names, for the children and grandchildren of these people are still alive, and probably some of them have learned to read by this time.

Anyhow, the Fittses were butchering hogs, and Old Henry Fitts, who was getting along toward ninety, had interrupted the butchering by having a fit. Young Henry Fitts, his son, who was about sixty, was present; and so was Little Henry Fitts, *his* son, a man of about thirty.

Young Henry was saying to Little Henry, "You dam' fool, why did you let your gran'-pap monkey around when you was butcherin'? Don't you know your gran'-pap always has a fit when he sees blood?"

W.S. and Marquis wanted to know why Old Henry always had a fit when he saw blood. They were told, with much sour profanity, to go along and mind their own goddamn business; which they did.

But when they got home—that is, to the S. farmhouse—W.S. asked his father, "Why shouldn't Old Henry Fitts be allowed to see blood?"

"I've got an idea," said Mr. S. "But go and get Bill Bradley. He can tell us, exactly."

When Bill Bradley, a neighbor, arrived, he said, "Of course Old Henry can't bear to see blood. His conscience gets after him, now he's getting old. It reminds him of all the men he killed and planted out in these islands in the covered-wagon days. One night my father came onto Old Henry burnin' three naked bodies on a brush pile. He said he'd just found 'em layin' around; but my dad knew darned well they was covered-wagon people he'd killed for their horses and outfits."

There was a cave in one of the islands, which W.S. and Marquis used to visit, which had been used by horse thieves in the early days before the Civil War. The swamp angels of the period would steal horses from the decent settlers round about on the edges of the swamp, hide out in the cave, and then take them over to the Mississippi some dark night and raft them down to Cairo or St. Louis and sell them. Just after the Civil War a posse of Vigilantes was formed, who lynched fifteen of the gang one afternoon, hanging them in the timber near the cave; and after that there was no great trouble.

When M. was a lad the swamp angels indulged in pig stealing, chicken stealing, and other petty theft; but nothing on a large scale. When the swamp was drained, there was a sudden flood of settlers from all parts of the country; among them many Scandinavians and Germans, who were after the good land. Land that had been worth $10 and $15 an acre, because it was flooded so much of the time that nobody could be sure of a crop, went to $50 an acre; to $90; to $150 and $200, and finally, to the absurd price of $300 an acre, for there was a boom.

The descendants of many of the early murderers and trash mixed with the better blood of later immigrant settlers, became wealthy; and it is a fact that most of them do not know anything at all of the early history of the swamp. A good many years later M. saw some people in the Reelfoot Lake district of Tennessee, when he was there reporting the Night Rider troubles, who reminded him of the swamp angels in this little corner of Illinois.

A few years ago, when M. was in London, he was having dinner at the Press Club; and there were several London journalists there— nice lads, most of them, English, Irish, and Scottish—and a couple of them asked him why there was so much crime in America. It was not the ordinary supercilious British query directed at Americans, but a question from members of M.'s own craft who were seriously seeking to understand; there was nothing personal or snooty about it. It deserved an attempt at an answer.

"We Americans *are* a homicidal people," M. was forced to admit. "And this is easily understandable. For we are largely derived from the three most homicidal peoples on earth—the English, the Irish, and the Scots."

With a shout, the English, Irish, and Scottish present seized M. and led him up to the bar, for they were good sports. But presently an English editor, who had been thinking in his thorough English way, perceived that M.'s answer was really no answer at all.

"Why is it then," he said, "that the English, Irish, and Scottish don't go in for crime nowadays in the way you Americans do? If you inherited the traits from us, it is reasonable to suppose that we still have them, isn't it? That we didn't get rid of them merely through the fact of your inheriting them!"

"The British still have these homicidal tendencies," said M., improvising a theory under the pressure of the moment. "But the British Empire has always had a war going on somewhere, in some outlying corner of the world, which took all the homicidal energies of its born killers—its adventurers, its indigent younger sons, its criminals. You go and kill in the far corners of the earth, and get it out of your systems that way. You keep these home islands all neat and tidied up, and the killer comes back home to rest and be peaceful and happy, before he goes out again on another killing spree. But we haven't had an empire of that sort. Our killers have had to do their killing right in the home country, and of course it looks bad. Wait until we get an empire like yours, and we will have an overseas outlet for our homicidal proclivities; and continental America will be much less homicidal."

That gave them something to think about. But M. has never taken the trouble to examine the theory since, and see if it will really hold water. Probably it won't. It's just an argument, of the sort you come through with when you are backed into a corner.

* * *

There was quite a cult of spiritualists in Walnut.

When M. was five or six years old the family moved to a tall green three-story wooden house, which sat on a green hill at the edge of the woods, and this house was owned by a spiritualist. It was one of the few houses in that neighborhood which had open fireplaces. Most of the houses were heated during the severe winters by "base-burners," stoves with magazines in them containing anthracite coal.

This house had many rooms, and many fireplaces. The top floor had been retained by the owner, an old lady named Mrs. E., who lived up there with a lot of ghosts. At least, she said she did, and she may have thought so.

She used to get M. and an older brother of his named David— he was five or six years older than M.—up to her rooms at the top of the house, and give them lemonade and cake and oranges, and

ask them if they didn't hear the spirits rapping. They didn't, but
they said they did; she was such a nice old lady that they didn't like
to disappoint her. She would surreptitiously flip an orange seed so
that it rattled about the room, and then say, "Did you hear that,
boys?" It was supposed to be a ghost getting warmed up to rap out
a message.

There were séances up in Mrs. E.'s rooms occasionally. M. had
another brother, Harry, who was about twenty-five years old at this
time; and Harry, and some other young fellows of his own age,
got converted to spiritualism—or pretended to, just for the lark of
the thing—and two or three of them speedily became mediums, and
used to have some remarkable trances, for the edification of the real
believers. One of these séances precipitated a community row. Mrs.
E. had a fine thoroughbred shepherd dog, which disappeared. Harry
had a trance one night in which, under the influence of a spirit, he
described the felonious assassination of this dog by one Dave Wolf.

Dave Wolf was a spiritualist too—an elderly, solemn dry man, and
the brother of the Old Horse who later hanged himself—and he,
with all the other spiritualists of the community, was present when
Harry's spirit described the alleged crime. Mr. Wolf cast the lie in
the ghost's teeth. Harry, upon being recalled from his trance, didn't
know what he had said; a medium never does, it seems. The spiritualists of the place divided into two hostile camps over the murder
of this dog. Harry and his companions, conscience-stricken, confessed
their deception. But their confession was not believed; only their
previous mendacity continued to be credited. Mrs. E. and her crowd
were going to have their ghosts, even if they had to make them up
themselves.

*   *   *

M. knew that Mrs. E.'s ghosts were not genuine ghosts, but for
years afterward that particular house—the family lived there only a
year or two—had a ghostly air about it for him, too. He hadn't been
afraid of Mrs. E.'s ghosts, when they rattled around in her apartment,
because he knew how she made them rattle . . . and yet, there might
really be ghosts.

And that house was a good place for them. Back of it the woods were high and thick and green and gloomy; it was a shadowed place on the brightest summer days, and in the autumn and winter the wind moaned through the trees and about the chimneys and on moonlit nights the moon struck the windows on the third floor in such a way that you could imagine pale faces were looking out of them.

There were always noises about that house, and in the woods, and how did you know that the ghosts of dead Indians were not wandering about? A little way off, in the woods, was a creek; and you could find Indian arrowheads all along the creek, and it seemed reasonable to suppose that an Indian who had been killed by one of those arrows might be interested in coming back and looking about a bit, now and then. And then there were all the people who had been killed in the swamp, west of town, who might want to come to town and tell somebody the details of it. And there was old Mrs. E., up in the top of the green house, like a witch, just hoping for a real spirit, and rattling orange seeds.

* * *

When M. was six years old his grandfather died; and M. began having a dream about him so vivid that there were times, to his childish imagination, when it seemed like something that had really happened the night before in his waking hours, and no dream at all. In this dream M. would be in his aunt's house, where his grandfather had died. His aunt ran a millinery shop; and the shop part of her building was on Main Street. Back of that was the living room; back of that the dining room; back of that, the kitchen. There was a corridor, with bedrooms on each side. Back of all, was a rear porch.

M., in his dream, would be sitting in the living room, alone, at a small table, on which was a kerosene lamp. It would be night. M. would know something was to happen. Then he would hear a step on the back porch. Then the back door would be unlatched—it didn't have a knob on it, that back door, it latched and unlatched with an iron gadget. There would be footsteps crossing the kitchen, coming nearer. Then the door into the corridor would be opened. More footsteps, and the tapping of a cane. The footsteps would approach, while M.'s heart beat faster and faster. He would hear a hand on the knob of the dining-room door. He would know, now, who was coming; and be both eager and frightened.

Then the door of the room in which he sat would open, and his grandfather would be standing in it, tall, very tall, and erect, with his stick in his hand, and his long white hair down upon his shoulders. He would stand and look at M. in silence; kindly, too, for M. and his grandfather were very fond of each other.

"Why, grandfather, I thought you were dead!" M. would cry, eagerly.

Grandfather would make no immediate reply. He would come slowly to the little table with the lamp on it, where M. sat, before he spoke.

"But I thought you were dead!" M. would cry again.

Grandfather would lean over and speak, then.

"I *am* dead," he would say.

Then M. would scream, and wake up. He began having that dream fifty years ago, and he still has it from time to time. It is probably one thing which makes his grandfather so vividly remembered, after all these years. M. can remember further back into his youth—and into his infancy—than anyone else he ever knew or heard of. One day a cousin of his mother's, who was living with the family at the time, showed him a lot of little animals, about two inches high, which were running about on the dining-room table—dashing into holes and hillocks and out again, frisking about. She called them "little bears," and the child was charmed with them. She was really hypnotizing him, for her own amusement.

His grandfather was at the table, taking this procedure in. It must have been an amusing picture, the child of two years old, the old gentleman of ninety-two, and the woman—she was a beautiful and brilliant woman, haggard, mesmeric, and disappointed—of about forty. Suddenly grandfather realized what was going on.

"Abhominable!" he exclaimed, and drove her from the room with his stick, repeating the word. He did not say "abominable," but "abhominable." This cousin he always referred to as "The Witch," and "The Critter," and imputed occult powers to her; which she probably had to some extent. Her name was McColloch, she was from Columbus, Ohio, and she was related to the Zanes who had

Indian blood in their veins. One of her ancestors in the early days had been captured and killed by the Indians, who cooked and ate his heart on the theory that it would make them brave, for he had been one of their boldest foes.

But M. can remember back a good deal further than that. He can remember a trip to Columbus, Ohio, on which his mother took him, in most of its details; and he was just a trifle over a year old at that time.

* * *

M.'s father was a doctor; a graduate of Starling Medical College at Columbus, Ohio, and he had also a post-graduate degree from Rush Medical, at Chicago. He made a mistake when he went to Illinois, after the Civil War, and settled in Walnut, dusty in the summer and muddy in the spring and autumn—a place in which The Doctor, as he was always called, never found much intellectual companionship.

He had a big library, not only his medical books, but scientific works of every sort. M. got acquainted with Darwin, Herbert Spencer, *et al.*, in his home when he was a lad; and besides these there were hundreds—perhaps thousands—of other books of all sorts lying about, cluttering up every room; and M. read all of them, particularly the poets.

M.'s eldest brother, Harry, wanted M. to be an actor, and taught him dozens of speeches from Shakespeare when M. was little more than a baby—when he was only four years old Harry would have him spouting whole scenes from one play or another. M. quit school at fifteen and never went to college more than a few months, and he was startled then, and has been startled from time to time ever since, by a lack of general all-around literacy in college people; they seem to have read so very little, except along a few special lines, and this is true of a good many of them who have degrees of one sort or another. They are not really educated, in any broad sense, many of them.

There were very few families in Walnut who had more than a half-dozen books, or took in such magazines as the *Century, Harper's, Scribner's*, etc. M., at a very early age, noticed that when he spoke to a good many boys, he was not understood, merely because he

was literate. This made M. snobbish in his attitude toward his contemporaries in the place he lived in, and this snobbishness was unconsciously encouraged in his home; it is not a good quality for a boy
to have, either. It was years before M. got it knocked out of him.

The Doctor had a strange, paradoxical attitude toward preachers.
He had been brought up straitly by a Calvinistic mother, who whupped
him if he whustled on the Sawbath Day, so he never made any of
his own children go to church or Sunday School at all, and never
went himself.

But he was forever giving things away to preachers. He always
had a very large garden—almost a small truck farm, in fact, for he
was really more interested in growing things, experimenting with
fruits and vegetables, than in anything else. M. used to have to hoe
potatoes when he would rather have been going swimming or playing
baseball, knowing all the time that when the vegetables were grown
the preachers and their families would descend and garner the fruits
of his labor. . . .

*   *   *

2   "A Shark at Repentance"—His Brother Dave Dies—Don Learns about Anarchists at Ten—Assorted Jobs: Delivery-Wagon Driver, Drugstore Clerk, Life in a Clothing Store, Poultry Plucker, Lunchroom Cook, Sewing-Machine Agent

At this point we leave the egobiography briefly to give Marquis a chance to tell a few things about his early days in other media. He once told a newspaper interviewer that if he could remember all the things he promised never, NEVER to do again he would be able to comply with the request that he give some idea of how a boy passed the time in Walnut, Bureau County, Illinois, his birthplace. Most vividly he recalled that he had solemnly vowed never to steal another of Old Man Pendleton's watermelons. Actually he had not intended to swipe a single one. He wasn't sure himself how it kept happening.

First he found himself gazing at the melons and the next thing he knew there he was in the melon patch sizing up the assortment and telling himself that since he was already there he might as well take one. He never could quite remember the actual transition from the road to the field. But he must have made it. Else how could he have come by that beautiful watermelon? Etc., etc.

Marquis, in the *American Magazine,* managed to put together a list which throws additional light on how he spent his time as a boy. It seems that before he was ten he had had occasion (in addition to renouncing watermelon-stealing) to foreswear the following forever:

Picking his teeth at the table;
Breaking the windows in the village
  calaboose with a slingshot;
Putting mustard into the ice cream
  at the Baptist lawn social;
Throwing spitballs in school;
Catching Mrs. Nettie Kelly's chickens
  with baited fish-hooks let down from the
  roof of the hardware store;
Putting sand burs in the curls of
  the little girl next door;
Pitching pennies at August Keithahn's
  livery stable on the way to Sabbath-school;
Introducing bluing into the baptismal
  font at the Baptist Church;
Fastening a board over the chimney of the
  Village Opera House, so that the smoke would
  interrupt performances of *East Lynne*, *The Hidden
  Hand*, and *Uncle Tom's Cabin*;
Pulling loose teeth during school hours, so
  that the flow of blood would earn a holiday;
Putting ticktacks up at the windows of Mrs.
  Epperson, the village spiritualist.

Such pranks, lapses, and misdemeanors, or somewhat similar ones, Marquis declared, were standard practice among small-town boys when he was a kid. Where he was different from most of the others was that he was a Great Repenter. "There are few boys," he wrote in the *American Magazine*, "who have sworn off as many things as I had at the age of ten. I was what you might call a shark at repentance."

So moving was his Repentance Act, as he called it, that sometimes his mother tearfully told him she was sorry she had Brought Up the Subject. He thought it odd, though, that she never made this touching statement until after she had whacked him and he had started repenting all over again.

At twelve Marquis "learned, with great tribulation, to smoke a corncob pipe." In this particular case his father "provided the first impulse toward reformation."

As a result of these early parental "suggestions," Marquis went on to say, "I have always been passionately in favor of reforming myself, and from time to time other persons near and dear to me have tactfully agreed with me that improvement was possible. . . ."

Getting back to the egobiography, in a rough draft of that work
Marquis tells how he came by his "four-part name," an account
that supports the following briefer version published in the New
York *Herald Tribune*: "Mr. Marquis, who was baptized Robert Perry
Marquis, used to say that when he was a baby his brother Dave had
a dog named Don, of which he was inordinately fond. One day the
dog disappeared and Dave, who had to have somebody to love,
named his baby brother after the dog. The name stuck when the
boy went to school and finally fastened itself on him."

Marquis is responsible for a number of stories about the family's
decision to name him after a dog, none of them, judging by their
tongue-in-cheek sound, meant to be taken too seriously. In one version the dog's name is given as Don Pedro but after a big family
conference it is decided that Don Pedro Robert Perry Marquis is too
long a name, so the Pedro is dropped. This, according to Marquis,
appealed to a relative who hated Spaniards because they had given
the world the Spanish omelet.

Perhaps this is as good a time as any to introduce the following
from "Codex A" of the 1932 version of Marquis's egobiography:

Any biographer of Don Marquis is assailed at once by the initial
difficulty that Mr. Marquis has always taken a perverse delight in
mystifying people with regard to himself. Christopher Morley charged
him with it, ten or twelve years ago, when Mr. Morley was preparing a biographical essay concerning him, and Marquis wrote in
reply:

It is quite true that I have invented for myself a good many
experiences which I never really had. But they were all experiences
which belonged to me by right of temperament and character. I
should have had them, if I had but had my rights. I was despoiled
of them by the rough tyranny of Circumstance. On the other hand,
I have suppressed a number of incidents which actually happened,
because I did not, upon mature reflection, find them in consonance
with my nature as I like to think it is—they were lies that were
told about me by the slinking facts of life.

In an undated document found among his papers—thirteen handwritten pages headed "Autobiography," written on extra-long sheets—
Marquis declares:

"I shall die and go to hell—at least, a number of eminent divines
have assured me that I will go to hell—in a few years; so I intend
to indulge myself in the luxury of being honest in this autobiography.
And I must begin being honest by telling you that I shall lie a little
here and there. It is impossible not to lie in an autobiography. Some
persons are unconscious that they are doing it. But I shall lie consciously; I shall take control of my lies, and try to weave particular
lies through a pattern in such a way as to make a fabric generally
more truthful. Usually, I shall represent myself as being better than
I am; but at times, if I should think it more picturesque to do so,
I shall represent myself as being worse than I am. I do not mean
that I intend to invent incidents; but I shall arrive at the essential
truth involved in the incidents by a species of minor falsifications
calculated to make . . ."

That is the end of page thirteen and the end of the document.
A careful search for further pages has yielded nothing.

Chapter Three of the egobiography confines itself entirely to the
"ego" aspect of the projected work. It contains some passages that
are worth preserving and these will be worked into the book later.

Marquis, no respecter of chronology, opens Chapter Four with a
scene in a once famous hangout for newspapermen, Lipton's Bar,
which he frequented in his early days on the *Sun*. Then the chapter
flashes back thirty years to the days when he was a small boy in
Walnut, Illinois. It is a well-integrated piece of writing, more concerned with significance than with sequence, and with making a
point where it has the most impact; but if published here as written
it would merely confuse the reader.

The scene in Lipton's Bar will be reserved for later. The following
excerpts are from the chapter in which it appears:

* * *

When M. was five or six years old his father—The Doctor—sold
a hotel which he owned, and some other property—nearly everything
he had—and went down to Florida and bought an orange grove.
About the time the oranges were to have been picked there was a
big freeze. It froze farther south, that season, than it ever did before
or since. Even the trees were frozen. The Doctor, pretty well cleaned
out financially, went back to Illinois and resumed the practice of
medicine. If he was discouraged, he never gave any sign of it. He

was well into his sixties then, and he had to start over again with nothing more than he had when he left medical school as a young man, except experience—and a houseful of dependents.

The family considered themselves rather poor; and there certainly never was any surplus of money lying around loose. But looking back, M. has the impression that they weren't really poor at all, for they lived extraordinarily well. For some years they lived in a place which had attached to it a garden so large that it was almost a small truck farm. M. doesn't know how large it was; but years later it was cut up into building lots, and three or four houses were built upon it, each with its own adequate garden. There was a somewhat remarkable orchard; some liberal spirit had planned and planted it so that apples of different varieties were getting ripe in rotation, all the way from late June until the russets arrived with the frosts of autumn. There were also cherry trees, peach trees, plum trees, pear trees, a grape arbor, elderberries, blackberries, gooseberries, huckleberries, raspberries. The cellar was always full of barrels of potatoes, turnips, carrots, apples, etc., and there were long rows of shelves filled with glass jars of preserved fruit, tomatoes, etc.

There were hundreds of chickens around the place, which wintered in a barn with a stone basement; there was a cow or two, so the family made most of its own butter; there was a pen full of pigs, and The Doctor smoked his own hams and side meat. In the winter there was usually a quarter of beef hanging in the cellar, with which some farmer had paid his doctor's bill.

There was the better part of a good living on that place, without spending a cent except for sugar, flour, etc. The whole region teemed with small game, and M.'s brother Harry used to go out with his gun and bring in bags of duck, wild pigeon, snipe, prairie chicken, quail, squirrels. M.'s mother had an immense iron baking dish, and a potpie containing prairie chicken, quail, snipe, with maybe a squirrel or two thrown in, is a meal fit for the gods. Poor? Yes—but if M. knew where eating like that was to be had nowadays, he would drop everything else and go there and sit down and eat till he died.

Harry went west when M. was eleven years old, and M. never saw him again. He went to the Puget Sound region, in what was then the territory of Washington. It is M.'s private opinion that, consciously or unconsciously, he had got tired of prairie chicken and wanted some venison. From Washington he went north with the first gold rush; and died at Whitehorse, in the Yukon, twelve or fourteen years ago; he ran a trading post for a concern called the Arctic Trading Company, buying furs and selling supplies to the Indians. M. saw a friend of Harry's in New York a couple of years before Harry died, who said, "Harry will never come outside again. He likes the game up there too well; he says he can't get anything fit to eat anywhere else." He disliked cities, and loved books, solitude, and hunting; and he was wise enough to go out after what he wanted and get it, and stay with it till he died; which is what M. calls a successful life.

* * *

Dave, M.'s other brother, died when he was twenty, and M. was fourteen. He was a handsome and poetic youth, but he was crippled; a fall on the ice when he was a child of six fractured one of his hips. The knob of the ball-and-socket joint was broken, and ankylosis resulted; later, tuberculosis of the bone. He was in love with a very beautiful girl, but he never told her about it, because he was crippled; he never told anyone but M.

He was taken to Chicago for a surgical operation when he was twenty, and through the carelessness of a trained nurse in a hospital took a cold after the operation, which finished him. He was brought home in a delirium, but just before he died his mind cleared, and he sent for M.

"Bring the dog in," he said. Jack, a beautiful black dog with a white throat, who worshiped him, was brought in.

"Now cook a beefsteak," he ordered. Jack was a pampered animal, who preferred his beef cooked. "I want to feed Jack once more before I die."

The meat was cooked and cut up. Dave was propped up in bed; and Jack stood up on his hind legs by the pillow and was fed a bite at a time. The dog seemed to have a queer realization that something unusual was going on.

"I want to see Don alone," said Dave.

Everybody else went out.

"Listen," he said. "We've all laughed at it, at home here—all this silly church stuff. But I don't know; maybe there's something real behind it. You'd better give it a chance. Good-by."

Then he died.

* * *

M. was naturally much impressed, and for two or three years did try to give the churches a chance. He tried on several occasions to join one or another of them. The trouble was that when he asked sincere and honest questions, the preacher—and people of that sort with whom he talked—seemed to feel insulted; seemed to feel that he was being deliberately offensive, which was not the case at all. After a while he learned that with most preachers you have to be so darned tactful all the time—just as you have to be with so many women—that discourse with them becomes wearisome.

There is no doubt about there being something real behind the churches—behind any and all of them. Unfortunately, it is in many instances a long way behind. And the way to get to this something real is not always through the churches for all people; they hamper and impede some of us; others, no doubt, find them helpful.

* * *

When M. was nine or ten years old, one of his sisters was going to school in Chicago—at the Cook County Normal School. It was located in Englewood, way out in Chicago's South Side, and presided over by one Colonel Francis W. Parker, a pioneer in education who originated many of the advanced ideas which others have cashed in on in the fifty years since.

M.'s sister, Maud, kept writing home that she couldn't get what she wanted to eat in the boarding house where she lived, and finally M.'s mother roused up and said the girl *must* have the right kind of cooking. So she went to Chicago, rounded up a number of the other students, likewise suffering, and started a boarding house. M. went with his mother. [Note—*But he apparently remained in Chicago less than a year*—E.A.] The Doctor stayed down in the country, and sent up crates, boxes, hampers, and packing cases filled with chickens, ducks, turkeys, hams, sausage, etc., etc. There probably never was a more pampered, or more appreciative, set of boarders in existence. . . .

* * *

M. never . . . got along in Chicago. The place intimidated him. . . .

This all goes back to a lowering November day in 1888—M. thinks that was the year, but is not certain. M. is sitting in school in Engle-wood, and whisper goes about the schoolroom: "Today the an-archists are going to blow up the whole city with dynamite."

This begins about nine in the morning, when school takes in, and the psychic panic spreads and increases by the quarter hour. The teachers are affected. They speak in subdued voices.

During the forenoon recess, nobody goes out to the playground. There are little spits of rain, out of low sullen clouds, and there is a cold wind drifting in from Lake Michigan. At recess M. asks another boy why the anarchists are going to dynamite the city today.

"Don't you know? It's for revenge. Some of them are being hanged downtown in the jail today."

"Why are they hanging them?"

"Because they threw bombs and killed those policemen. Didn't you hear about it?"

"No. Why did they throw bombs?"

"Because they are anarchists, of course. Where did you come from? Don't you know that anarchists throw bombs?"

"But why?"

"Well, to kill people. They're anarchists! One of them killed him-self in jail with a bomb, to keep from getting hanged. Didn't you hear about it?"

"No. Are there many of them?"

"Thousands and thousands of them. Say, I guess you haven't lived in Chicago very long. You must be from the country—you're a rube, ain't you?"

"I guess I am. Why do they want to kill people?"

"Haven't I told you why—they're *anarchists!* Foreigners, from the old country. They said unless this hanging was stopped they'd dy-namite the whole city."

There was a thousand thousand years of that day, with the frowning skies outside, and the growing hysteria within the schoolhouse. Every-body listened, listened, listened. Every now and then someone would break into hysterical sobbing, and have to be quieted by a teacher. After a few hours several teachers visited the various rooms, and made little talks to the students. But there was nothing very sedative in them, for the teachers were just as apprehensive.

That interminable, terrible day graved something so deeply into M.'s psyche that he was never able to efface the marks. Chicago has meant to him ever since a chill paralysis of his powers.

When he was about fifteen he went to Chicago—(a little over a hundred miles by train from Walnut)—to see the World's Fair, and stayed with a cousin whose husband ran a grocery store somewhere out on the West Side. He took a job driving the delivery wagon for the grocer. Again Chicago licked him. Although he was a country boy, M. was not a good driver. That delivery wagon existed for some weeks in an almost constant state of collision. It was always getting more or less bumped by cable cars, grazed and crashed into by other trucks, colliding with fire hydrants—it seemed to be the Sore Thumb of Chicago's West Side, the way it stuck out—and M. was so continuously bawled out by unsympathetic Irish cops all day long, that the nights were too short to recover in. He went back to Walnut, defeated, and went to work in a drugstore.

Years later, M.'s mother and sisters were living in Chicago, where the sisters were both teaching school, and he used to make three or four trips a year to see them. They lived out at Woodlawn, near the University. . . .

M. was not a success as a drug clerk. He might have developed into a competent pharmacist, but he was never very good as a salesman. The proprietor of the drugstore, a very well-informed and intellectual man, Mr. O. C. Nessle by name, who kept up with modern ideas generally, was always very kindly and lenient with his lapses and mistakes, and encouraged him to study chemistry; but the fact remained that M. was indifferent and inefficient.

The clerks of the various stores on Main Street had laid out a tennis court on waste ground back of several of the shops, and M. was more interested in tennis than he was in the drugstore. His only resounding achievement in this job was an explosion which he accomplished while engaged in a chemical experiment. The explosion wrecked one end of the drugstore, and injured another boy who was kindly holding steady a large Wedgwood mortar in which M. was pounding with a pestle at a mixture of chlorate of potash and sulphur. The chemistry textbook had intimated that an explosion would follow such a procedure, and the book was right about it. M. lost the hearing of one of his ears, and it was thirty years before it came back to him.

The Doctor looked grave—but patched M. up medically as well as was necessary without any comment. He did not even remind M. that a few months before he had had to pick some hundreds of powder grains out of M.'s face, one at a time, as a consequence of the bursting of a toy cannon employed in some amateur theatricals in a corncrib, but he must have wondered if his son was not turning out to be a fool.

* * *

At this point it seems appropriate to interrupt the egobiography with the following, which Christopher Morley wrote some forty years later:

The drugstore in Walnut, Illinois, where Don Marquis once worked, has modernized itself and put in attractive new showcases and furniture. But toward the back there is still one old mahogany prescription counter, in the style of the '90s. There, though concealed from casual view by the display of the moment, you may discover an area of deep scars and fractures. It is where young Don . . . was showing off some chemical stunt to impress his cronies. . . . There was an explosion, with effects of violence upon himself, the onlookers, and the store. The village still cherishes this sentimental souvenir of its distinguished son. As the druggist said to me, "It'll be a sad day for this town if we ever have to get rid of Don's old counter."

I suppose they will, eventually, for if I remember correctly the pharmacy is now one of a chain; and chain stores are precise about standardized equipment. . . .

And now to let Marquis resume his egobiography:

* * *

M. next went to work in a clothing store for a man named Goldstein, a very good-natured Jew. M.'s employers had to be goodnatured, or M. wouldn't have lasted a week with any of them at this period. Goldstein was a pathetic little figure, kindly, charitable, and bewildered. He was a new arrival in the village, and was astonished to perceive that there was a prejudice against him merely because he was a Jew. Where he had come from, M. doesn't know; but evidently it was his first serious experience with an anti-Jewish prejudice, and it puzzled him. In natural refinement and manner he was superior to the majority of the people in his new environment, but he spoke with a very marked accent.

"Why don't they like me, Don?" he used to ask M., wistfully.

"I don't know."

"Is it because of this here, now, crucifixion of Jesus Christ, already?"

"Maybe. I don't know."

"He wasn't no relation to them, neither. It is more likely he could be some relation of mine, ain't it? He was a Jew himself. You could tell 'em that, for me."

"All right, Mr. Goldstein."

"And you could maybe be brushing the edges of them stacks of pants on the shelves a little more often than you do. I don't want people to be looking in here and seeing Goldstein's clerk is idle. It looks like we got no business."

"But we haven't, Mr. Goldstein."

"We'll never get none, neither, when you go out every afternoon and play tennis a couple of hours. How does that look, I esk you?"

"What do you want me to do? Go out on the sidewalk and pull people into the store?"

"That's exactly what I was doing when I was your age, and you could do worse, maybe, than start learning the clodings business the way I done."

The chief trouble was, M. didn't want to learn the clothing business.

"You could maybe make yourself stop drawing pictures of the people that comes in here all over the wrapping paper. How does it look if a man carries away a suit of clothes wrapped up in paper that has got pictures of himself all over it? Does he get mad? Of course he gets mad, and who should blame him? Or maybe they are pictures of me, and because I got a big nose he says when he gets home that is one of them big-noses Jews what killed Christ already, and he'll never buy nothing more at Goldstein's store, even with *two* pairs of suspenders thrown in. You should be around town telling these people, which you know 'em all personal, that a Jew could be a good feller the same like everybody else—and Gott, but I am eating into my capital all the time!"

He *was* a good fellow, too; one of the best ever, poor perplexed little man. But he never really got his business started in Walnut, and he went bankrupt and died there. First, he fired Marquis; although he kept M. on for months after he really ceased to need him, out of sheer good nature.

* * *

M. went to work in a poultry house for a brief period. This was an establishment which sent out buyers, who scoured the farming country for chickens and ducks, which were butchered, picked, dressed, and shipped to the Boston market—why not the Chicago market, M. never knew.

It was the lousiest place imaginable; and when M. uses the word lousy, he means lousy. It crawled with lice; hundreds of millions, billions and billions of lice.

At one end of a big room was a row of troughs, or mangers. Hanging down above each manger was a loop of cord or leather. This was fastened around the chicken's feet. Then its wings were interlocked on its back. The operator then took a slender knife, with a blade about four inches long and sharp as a razor, thrust it into the chicken's mouth, cut the arteries in the throat, and then jabbed it through the brain. The chicken was picked before its death struggle had ceased. The feathers come off easily while the bird is dying. Once *rigor mortis* sets in, and the chicken is stiff, the chicken has to be submerged in scalding water before the feathers can be removed. This spoils the looks of the skin, and chickens which have been picked after scalding are not preferred goods in the market.

An expert chicken picker worked so rapidly that often a chicken was knifed and plucked and laid on a rack before he really knew he was dead. He would often get down from the rack and start to walking about the room, making queer gurgling noises in his cut throat, after he had been entirely denuded of feathers. Sometimes as many as three or four of these ghastly creatures, technically dead birds, and completely bald, would be wandering grotesquely about at the same time, clucking indignantly to the deaf gods to witness the unspeakable savagery of mankind.

So much blood was spurting in every direction all the time that it reminded M. of his early lessons in Sunday School. The professional chicken picker of the time and place was not usually an aesthetic character. Many of them were foul-mouthed drunken bullies —though not all, of course—and a favorite joke was to hit a man over the head with a hen as she was dying. She usually laid an egg, which broke in his hair and ran down the back of his neck. The retort courteous to this exquisite jest was to plaster the jester in the face with a gob of blood and feathers.

One day a gawky inarticulate Scandinavian by the name of Dahl, who had received more than his share of such hazing, attacked a bully with his chicken knife. Dahl—whose persecution had culminated in an indescribable filthiness—stabbed at the bully's throat, but unfortunately only succeeded in stabbing him in the shoulder, instead of slicing his jugular as he deserved.

Usually the fights which broke out were settled in a large half-empty room where the chickens were packed for shipment, and with boxing gloves in a regulation ring. On Saturday nights there were sometimes a half-dozen fights, saved up during the week, and these went to a finish. M. learned to box a little in this place. There was also a shower bath in this big room, where you could clean some of the lice and blood off yourself before you went home.

These chicken pickers were for the most part a wandering tribe, who drifted from place to place where this work was most plentiful. The more expert could make $3.00 a day. M. never made more than $1.50 a day. He lost his job through calling one of his bosses a son-of-a-bitch and kicking him in the stomach, or thereabouts—both laudable actions considering that person's character, but scarcely tactful behavior in an employee.

It was about this time that M. began to try to write poetry. He had been reading *The Origin of Species*, and *The Descent of Man*, and it occurred to him that the men of science and the men of religion were a great deal nearer together than either side perceived, and he tried to say so in a long limping poem. It must have been

awful tosh. Another one, written about this time, he had better luck
with. He had been reading somebody's book on comparative religions
—Fisk's, maybe?—and Carlyle, on how heroes get changed to gods in
the human consciousness—and he wrote some verse which he called
"The God-Maker, Man." It wasn't bad. He rewrote it a few years
later, and Dr. Paul Carus published it in *The Open Court*. He
has been rewriting it at intervals ever since, and publishing the
variations. It always goes pretty well, so M. thinks it is probably
a good poem.

* * *

The poem to which Marquis alludes first appeared in 1908, in
Uncle Remus's Magazine, edited by Joel Chandler Harris. The title
was then "In the Darkness, a Light." Six years later Marquis reprinted
it in "The Sun Dial," his column in the New York *Sun*, using the
title "The God-Maker, Man," under which title it also appeared in
his first book of poetry, *Dreams and Dust*, published in 1915. The
changes Marquis refers to were not organic, involving mainly the
substitution of one word for another. For instance, in his final version
he changed the word "skull" to "forehead," to achieve a more precise
meaning and better rhythm.

Since this poem, which is too long to quote entire, contains a
point of view Marquis expressed over and over again in prose and
verse, it seems appropriate to quote the final stanza, which sums up
his theme:

> For all of the creeds are false, and all of the creeds are true;
> And low at the shrines where my brothers bow, there will I bow, too;
>> For no form of a god, and no fashion
>> Man has made in his desperate passion
>> But is worthy some worship of mine,—
>> Not too hot with a gross belief,
>>> Nor yet too cold with pride,
>> I will bow me down where my brothers bow,
>>> Humble—but open-eyed.

Characteristically, Marquis some time later sought to make humorous capital of his experiences as a chicken plucker. He abandoned
the idea, perhaps realizing that this experience had been too real
to serve as a humorous device. He got as far as a title: "The Memoirs
of a Feather-Yanker; or, It's Pluck That Counts."

He also started a piece of light verse whose theme was that he

had had an opportunity as a chicken plucker to gather enough quills
to supply him with quill pens for the rest of his life. Psychologically,
it seemed to him that a poem would have a better chance of becoming a classic if written with a quill. Here are a few lines from
that unfinished effort:

> Wing and tail feathers by the gross I could have garnered free,
> And guaranteed myself a life of quill-pen poetry,—
> Unending music, bubble light, a golden jubilee
> Of lyrics with a feathery touch,—and immortality!

And now to go on with Marquis's egobiography:

* * *

After M. got kicked out of the poultry house—or kicked his way
out, to be more accurate—he had various other jobs, which he doesn't
recall clearly. He seems to remember something about a jewelry store;
and then he became cook and waiter in a bakery lunchroom. This
was a hot kind of job, for the cookstove was in the same room as the
bakery ovens, and he was doomed to the society of a German baker,
named Fritz, who had immense arms, covered with a thick growth
of red hair.

M.'s impression of this job narrows down to cooking thousands
of beefsteaks for Fritz, who ate from five to ten pounds of beef
every day, talking incomprehensibly with his mouth full about the
rights of labor. He was a lazy oaf; and M. had to do most of the
dirty cleaning-up work which Fritz was supposed to do himself, while
Fritz spouted about the oppression which was the lot of the workingman. M. doesn't remember why or how he lost this job; probably
because something caught afire. The cookstove was an inch deep in
grease when M. inherited it from Fritz, and he left it that way,
having his own ideas about the rights of labor, and it was forever
catching fire and endangering the whole building.

M. became a sewing-machine agent. You put a machine into a
buggy and drive out to the country and plant it on some farmer's
wife, and then her husband comes in from the field and says they
can't afford it. She asks you to show her how it works, and everybody
laughs when it turns out that she really knows more about it than
you do. It pleases her. But her husband says again they can't afford
it. She tells him they can afford it just as well as they can the new

reaper and binder he bought last week. They get into an argument, and ask you to stay to dinner, which they don't charge you for, because the woman has got so interested in showing you how to work your own machine. They don't charge you for feeding your horse either; and then the farmer gets sore at you, because now that damned thing is in the house the chances are that he'll never get it away from her, and he *really* can't afford to buy it. He can't afford it, probably because he leaves his own farm machinery out in the rain, and it has rusted into uselessness before he gets it paid for. They still do it. The last time M. drove from Hollywood to New York he saw farm machinery sitting out in the weather from coast to coast. It will take another hundred years of adversity to hammer the American farmer into being a businessman; there is a pull of the soil at his soul, which wants to drag him back into being a peasant.

M. wasn't a success as a sewing-machine agent. He could get machinery *set in* all right; but he found it difficult to get the name on the dotted line, and escape with notes or cash. Somebody else had to go out and "close the deal." He got fired.

3

More about Dr. Marquis—Don in a Fight for His Life—Near-Hobo Days—From Schoolteacher to Printer-Editor

For a long time I despaired of being able to add to my fragmentary information about two of Marquis's main conversation pieces—the last days of his father and a dramatic hand-to-hand encounter with a bully, which latter he called, with no little irony, the turning point of his career.

Then the egobiography came to light. Here is how Marquis tells the first of these stories:

* * *

The Doctor (M.'s father) was getting along toward eighty years old, and possibly he thought M. wasn't worth a damn. M. was beginning to feel that way about himself. He didn't seem able to hold a job; besides the ones enumerated, there were others. He didn't seem able to get interested enough in any of these jobs even to learn *how* to hold them. He was interested in reading the novels of Victor Hugo and Alexandre Dumas, the poems of Keats and Swinburne, and the plays of Shakespeare, and very little else, besides trying to draw pictures of everyone he saw.

M. believes that many of these sketches had a lot of character in them—and a knack of caricature, too, perhaps. He went to an art school a few years later, for he wanted to be a portrait painter. They set him to making charcoal drawings from plaster casts; plaster casts of all the fragmentary ugliness of ancient Greece. The idea, evidently, was to use the charcoal so as to get something that looked as sleek as a halftone reproduction of a photograph in a newspaper or magazine. If M. ever had any ability, this effectually blanketed it. The plaster entered his soul. If he tries to draw now, the result always looks like a plaster cast of something.

If the Doctor thought M. was no good, he never said so. He was uniformly lenient, kindly, encouraging, and sympathetic. He was so with everybody. He was interested in M.'s efforts to write verse, and encouraging. He never laughed at his bad drawings. One day something a little touching happened. He had been looking at one of M.'s attempts to write poetry.

"I used to write a good deal of verse myself," he said, almost timidly.

"You did?"

"Fifty years ago—more than that, maybe."

M.'s mother then produced some faded manuscripts which The Doctor had given to her more than half a century before. The two old people waited on the verdict of the boy almost tremulously, and when he said the verse was good, they exchanged shy, gratified glances. It seems they had never shown it to anyone before.

The Doctor was a good doctor, too. One day a girl was brought in who had been kicked and knocked down in the stable by a horse; the horse had then trampled upon her face, breaking every bone in it, reducing it to a pulp. He set about building her a new face. There was no hospital anywhere near; such a thing as a modern trained nurse was quite unknown in the locality; he had no help of any kind. Skin grafting was not generally practiced then; probably his chief antiseptic reliance had to be carbolic acid. But he built the new face, straightening out the bones, grafting skin as he needed it from her arms and legs, holding it all in a mask he made for her and feeding her through tubes till everything healed. She had been a pug-nosed girl before the horse stepped on her, but The Doctor, indulging a rather pretty humor which he possessed, declared he was going to make her good-looking enough so she could get a husband.

So he gave her a fine Roman nose; she wasn't pretty when he got done with her, but she was rather handsome, because of the profile with which he endowed her, looking somewhat like the head of the lady on the U.S. silver dollar.

Animals worshiped him—dogs, horses, birds. There was always a pet crow or pigeon trying to perch on his shoulder. All about the place, wherever he lived, he had drinking places, cans and pans, for the birds, which he kept filled with fresh water in dry weather; and in his calls upon his patients he was usually accompanied by one or more dogs, and often a crow. He had a knack of making things grow; he loved experimenting with fruits and vegetables; he developed a new variety of potato and a new variety of strawberry, but they lapsed when he died, for M. was too lazy to keep them going.

When he was getting along toward eighty, The Doctor announced he was tired of living in rented houses, and was going to build one. Probably the thought in his mind was that he wanted to die in his own house. He had owned a good many houses in his life; had been pretty well-to-do at several periods; but had lost it, in one way or another—had given a good deal of it away, in fact—and now, getting along toward eighty, he was still practicing medicine. If he ever felt downhearted, he never showed it; he never whined or complained about anything.

He built his house, on a lot which was still left to him; and there were so many people in the community who owed him doctor bills that he had to pay very little money for labor.

When William Jennings Bryan came out of the West in 1896, M. took it badly. Bryan set the prairies afire, and M. had no doubt that the Republic was doomed if Bryan were not elected, would cease functioning at once, almost automatically.

He shot off his mouth a good deal around town. This made him unpopular, as the Republicans were in the majority among the responsible people in the township and the county. M. still thinks there was something queer about that election. There was a normal Republican majority of about a hundred in the township. But in September of that year this had been reversed, and there was a slight plurality of votes pledged to Bryan. M. with some companions went all over the township and talked with every voter in it.

But in October and November the dirty work was done. Farmers, laboring men—everybody in the debtor class—would be called in to the bank, or to the creditor's office, whatever his business was, and some conversation of this general nature would take place:

"Well, Pete, it looks like we have a spell of hard times ahead of us."

"How do you mean, Mr. Gazokus?"

"If Bryan's elected, we're bound to have 'em."

"Do you really think so?"

"I'm certain of it. If Bryan should be elected, I wouldn't feel justified in extending that mortgage of yours which matures next January—(or renewing those notes, perhaps)—I'd have to have the money, or I'd be forced to foreclose."

The debtor, conscious of the coercion, but more thoughtful, would go away, his ardor dampened. That sort of thing went on in thousands of little towns and villages. A cousin of The Doctor's, who ran a bank in an Ohio town, and had been a delegate to the convention which nominated Bryan, told M. that numerous bankers in his locality had received instructions—from their important big-city correspondents presumably—to apply just such pressure.

M. shot off his mouth about certain incidents of this nature. Finally, a number of influential Republicans called on The Doctor; old friends of his; old conservative wheel horses; and suggested that he make the boy shut up, or kick him out of the house.

The Doctor was furious. He went and voted the Democratic ticket for the first and only time in his life.

A few months later he died—in the new house which he had built. The preacher who had charge of the funeral tried to start a sermon, but broke down. He went to the open window and pointed out at the birds; at the birds, and the drinking places he had made for them.

"There," he said, "is his sermon."

A little girl who lived next door tried to go to the cemetery and dig him out of his grave with her hands and nails; it didn't seem right to her that he should be put in the ground.

When he was dying, M. tried to cheer him a bit by telling him that he had got a job teaching school, and this time intended to stick to it and make good. But he was too far gone to understand; he probably died thinking M. was no good for anything at all.

* * *

Here is the "turning-point" story, as told in the egobiography:

* * *

A contemplative way of life was once within M.'s grasp, and he let the opportunity slip by him, and ever since then he has had trouble trying to adjust himself to a quick and noisy world which will not quiet down and let him think. As this was the turning point of Marquis's career, the matter must be narrated in some detail.

It was in the summer of 1899, shortly before M.'s twenty-first birthday, that he found himself working on a railroad job on the main line of the C., B. and Q. about eighty or a hundred miles west of Chicago. He was one of about five hundred men employed at what was known as "straightening track." The pay was $1.35 a day for only ten hours steady work at a quick pace in the broiling sun. The boss of the job was a big, handsome, crooked, lying, foul-mouthed Irishman whose name M. has forgotten. Let us call him Shag.

Shag was about six-feet-four in height, as strong as four Italians or two Swedes, with a chest about the size and shape of a keg of railroad spikes but a good deal harder, as quick as a train wreck, and a born bully. He loved to get into altercations with occasional hoboes whom he hired, and beat them nearly to death, after having cheated them out of two or three dollars on their pay checks. There were a couple of hundred Italians on the job, and he let them alone, for he knew one of them might slip a knife into him; and he was careful about bullying Swedes, for while a Swede is not particularly quick to anger, he may be subject to a sullen, slow, cumulative rage which takes no account of consequences once it reaches the boiling point, and the Swedes, like everyone else, had plenty of shovels, spades, pickaxes, and crowbars at hand. He particularly "picked on" other Irishmen, and plain American laborers, and, especially, as has been noted, on any hoboes whom he could get hold of.

Marquis, hating him and being afraid of him, resigned from his job. Shag, who needed all the men he could get hold of, as common labor was scarce that year, reviled M. in terms that could not be used even in a modern novel of the so-called "realistic" type, and M. came right back at him in similar terms. The quarrel was embittered by the fact that Shag was determined to beat M. out of half a day's pay, which came to sixty-eight cents.

The words "bastard" and "son-of-a-bitch" are freely employed nowadays on the stage and in many works of fiction which receive the endorsement of some of our most knowing critics; but they were mild in comparison with some of the epithets exchanged by Shag and M. on this occasion. If you know any words worse, you may fill the blanks below, and arrive at some approximation of the trend taken by the dialogue.

SHAG: You lousy—— —— —— —— ——bum, you; I don't owe you no sixty-eight cents.

M.: You flannel-mouthed—— —— —— ——crook, you do too owe me sixty-eight cents.

SHAG: —— —— —— —— —— —— ——!

M.: And what are you, you—— —— —— —— ——, you!

At this point in the conversation, Shag began to feel himself seriously insulted, and started for M.

Marquis ran. To have faced Shag would have been tantamount to facing a charging rhinoceros. Being sixty pounds lighter than Shag, Marquis was soon twenty yards in advance, his heart filled with the desire to murder which arose from a combination of fear and hatred.

On the right of way in front of M. he suddenly perceived an old-fashioned coupling pin, for this was before automatic coupling devices had been introduced on all types of trains.

M. grasped it and whirled on Shag, with the intention of killing him. It was now Shag's turn to face about and run, and Shag ran far more fleetly as the pursued than as the pursuer. M.'s overwhelming desire was to get near enough to Shag to beat out his brains from behind with the coupling pin, for he was possessed with the lust to murder this man who so richly deserved killing—and this is an opinion that has not changed in the thirty years since. But Shag fled like a winged mastodon, and after a hundred yards of this chase Marquis was still fifteen paces in the rear.

So he flung the coupling pin, aiming it at the base of Shag's skull. Unfortunately, his aim was a trifle faulty. It tore through and crushed the brim of a stiff straw hat which Shag was wearing, hit his left ear and tore it almost off his head, but did no further damage.

M., disarmed, turned and ran again; this time down off the embankment, and through a barbed-wire fence into a cornfield which bordered the railroad property. How he ever got through that barbed-wire fence without tearing himself to pieces he does not know to this day; he can recapture no reasonable picture of himself doing it. Shag brought up at the other side of the fence, and M. had picked up a rock in a field by that time. Shag, obviously, could not stoop to get through the fence without exposing himself to the rock.

And Marquis, through some failure of the moral faculties which he has regretted ever since, did not throw the rock. The rock might have accomplished what the coupling pin had not been able to, if the rock had been delivered squarely between the eyes.

The trouble was that at the moment M., who has always been somewhat the prey of a quick imagination, suddenly saw himself arraigned for murder. This image had not come to him in the instant when he flung the piece of railroad iron; that action had been instinctive and entirely proper. He had had a few seconds for reflection, and reflection, as is so often the case, led him wrong.

Later, M. realized that this had been the turning point in his career. If he had killed Shag he would probably have got twenty years in prison for manslaughter. He had enough political influence —having been editor of a country paper, and knowing the leading politicians of the district—so that he could readily have obtained an appointment as the prison librarian.

Imagine what that twenty years would have meant to M.! Twenty years of quiet and seclusion, out of the hurly-burly of the world, with no need to worry about food, shelter, or clothing! Twenty years in which to educate himself through books and reflection! Twenty years in which to speculate on God and write sonnets! It was a priceless opportunity; it was within his grasp, and he did not have the sense to take it. Added to which is the reflection that someone

should have killed Shag, and just as likely nobody has. The conversation that ensued, across the barbed-wire fence, was merely a
repetition of the one previously hinted at; and Marquis never got his
sixty-eight cents.

At that time he needed it badly, too. His entire worldly possessions
at that moment consisted of a straw hat, a coat—which he left behind him then and there and never went back for—a black shirt of
some material which faded onto his hide when he perspired, a pair
of blue-jean overall trousers, a pair of socks, a pair of grain-leather
plow shoes, and a corncob pipe. Underwear is not enumerated because he didn't have any that summer.

* * *

Living was pretty easy that year. The country was full of work. M.
went away from there (without his coat), flipped a freight train,
and rode a short distance—not more than ten or fifteen miles—to a
spot where they were digging a canal, and got a job at $1.75 a day
driving a pair of mules hitched to a big-wheeled scraper. Just exactly what and where this canal was he cannot recall now; but he
thinks it was what they called a "feeder" which connected the Rock
River—or perhaps it was the Illinois River—with either the Hen-
nepin Canal or the Chicago Drainage Canal. He never saw either
end of it; only a little stretch six or eight miles long somewhere near
the middle; he didn't know where it ran to, or from, nor what it was
being built for.

This job was very nearly the destruction of Marquis's habits
of industry. He got board at a farmhouse a mile or so from the
diggings for $3.00 a week. It became his custom to work two days
a week at the canal diggings—they were so eager to get men that
they let him do this—and accumulate $3.50, which was all he wanted.
This $3.50 would pay his board for a week, and leave him fifty cents
over for his tobacco. This was all he needed. The rest of the time, for
the next two or three months, until the weather became too cold,
he spent loafing up and down the right of way, lying in the woods
and writing poetry, or getting acquainted with the dozens of interesting characters, laborers, hoboes, who drifted along. He would
like nothing better now than to spend the rest of his life that way,
but he no longer has the physical stamina.

* * *

At this point we leave the egobiography and will not return to it until considerably later.

When Marquis, sensing that his father regarded him as a ne'er-do-well, promised the old gentleman on his deathbed that, having landed a job as a schoolteacher, he would stick to that profession, he meant to abide by this resolve.

It will be recalled that when he had that job driving a pair of mules hitched to a big-wheeled scraper, he worked only two days a week, spending the rest of his time "lying in the woods and writing poetry, or getting acquainted with the . . . interesting characters, laborers, hoboes, who drifted along."

Marquis didn't realize that what he was doing—working a few days a week and loafing the rest—followed the pattern by which most hoboes lived. He was taken aback one day when in conversation with a group of hoboes one of them, addressing him, used the expression, "us 'boes."

"Damn you, I'm no hobo!" exclaimed Marquis.

This was the beginning of a decision to find work of a different nature, perhaps a job that didn't depend on brawn. That hobo's remark had shaken him up because it made him realize how much he enjoyed the company of the ambitionless. He liked the company of drifters; he enjoyed hearing them tell about their experiences and secretly admired their philosophy of letting the world go hang; and he began to wonder whether, if he continued to live the life of a hobo—which he now realized he had been doing despite his protestations—he might wind up as a professional roustabout.

The more he loafed the more he wanted to loaf; and while he kept telling himself that some day he would get down to business and set up shop as a writer, he believed—as he looked back years later on those days as a near-hobo—that he might have wound up as a tramp poet or a chronicler of hobo life. Since he wrote better than most hoboes, he thought he might have become the "poet laureate of the waifs and strays," adding characteristically, "And who knows? It might have been a good life."

His hobo days behind him, Marquis, now a country schoolteacher, had every intention of sticking to that profession, in accordance with his promise to his father. He had not had much schooling himself but he had read widely and the man who hired him to teach in a

small country schoolhouse decided that he had been "born educated." In Illinois in those days they didn't bother with such formal-
ities as examinations or college degrees. If you struck the head of the
school board as having some "book learning" and as being an "upright young man"—(in telling the story years later Marquis remarked
that it's good the school superintendent didn't know that in his
roustabout days he was more frequently horizontal than "upright,"
preferring to lie on his back in the woods and dream)—you stood
a good chance of being hired.

Marquis had not been a schoolteacher long when he realized that
he had overpromised. What he had not reckoned with was a steadily
growing desire "to get into the writing game." Someone had told
him that the way to get started was to get a job on a weekly newspaper, first, if necessary, learning to be a printer. He had once worked
on a country weekly but not long enough to learn anything. Now he
decided to try it again if he could make another connection.

Marquis's father had died not many months before and the young
schoolteacher realized that this urge to forsake teaching, which he'd
promised the old gentleman would become his lifework, proved what
people had been telling his parents: that he didn't have the tenacity
to stick to anything. But the impulse to make a change—now almost a compulsion—was too strong and he decided not to fight it.
Here is the story, as Marquis told it many years later in an article
in the *Saturday Evening Post*:

"I was inoculated in early youth; when I was a kid I read, every
day, Eugene Field's column in a Chicago paper; and later, George
Ade's sketches, and I decided that I wanted to do something like
that. After teaching a country school—an occupation into which
I naturally drifted because I had very little education—clerking in
a drug store and other haphazard makeshift jobs, I finally went into
a country printing office. The owner and editor was good-natured,
and before I had learned to be a really competent printer I was
helping to edit the weekly paper. Besides the local news and editorials, I started a column, consisting of verse, sketches, jokes, character
studies, and so forth. I didn't get paid anything for this work; I was
more than gratified to get the opportunity of doing it. I even illustrated some of the things with sketches of local characters. These
were woodcuts; I first drew the pictures on a block of white wood
with a lead pencil, and then gouged away with a penknife. And to
make sure that they would be recognized by our subscribers, I care-

fully labeled the portraits, 'Uncle Peleg Higginbotham,' or whoever it was supposed to be. But the proprietor of the paper discouraged this after a while; he said too many people were coming in and complaining bitterly that they had been libeled by my portraits.

"It was during this earlier period of my aspirations that I developed a bad habit of inventing Lincoln stories. Lincoln was still a very lively personal memory thirty years ago to some of the older people living in that part of the Middle West, and they were forever repeating anecdotes about him or stories that were attributed to him. When I couldn't find anything better to fill up my column with, I used to invent a story and attribute it to Lincoln, and some of these, I believe, are still in circulation. I was young and irresponsible in those days, with no perception that this might contribute to the falsification of a great historical character; I thought most of the Lincoln stories were invented by somebody else and I might as well have a hand in it, too. And, indeed, I still wonder if as many as a quarter of the anecdotes attributed to Lincoln were really his. He couldn't have had much time for anything else if he told all of them.

"It was during this same period that I attempted to make an important change in one of the standard forms of verse. The sonnet has always contained fourteen lines. I composed a great many sonnets, but most of what I composed at that time went right from my head into the printer's stick in my hand without having been first committed to paper. I found this method saved a good deal of labor. I don't remember whether I used to set my sonnets in minion type or in nonpareil, but, whichever it was, I do remember that the printer's stick would contain but thirteen lines of iambic pentameter verse. So I habitually produced thirteen-line sonnets. A white mule couldn't be found dead or a three-legged calf born in that county, but that I made a sonnet about it. I even wrote sonnets in favor of William Jennings Bryan. I watched for a good many months to see if other bards throughout the English-speaking world were going to follow my lead with regard to the thirteen-line sonnet, but they all resisted the temptation; the official sonnet remains today just what it was before I took it up in a serious way.

"The man for whom I worked owned several country weeklies in that part of Illinois, and he transferred me to another town and put me in charge of one of them. I had to collect all the news, write all the editorials, solicit the advertisements and write them, set about half the type myself, saw boiler plate to fit holes in the columns, make up the paper, run off part of the edition myself on the old flat-bed hand press, fold and wrap the papers and take them to the post office. But this was incidental, in my mind, to the main thing, which was writing and printing a column; the other work was really the price I paid for the privilege of seeing my verse and sketches and paragraphs and fables in print.

"It was from this country weekly that I worked myself, in a round-way, into daily journalism. . . .

"The way in which it happened amuses me when I think of it; for quite without knowing I was doing it, I put across a political coup. The paper I was running was a Republican paper. But I was a Democrat; I was so firm and fixed a Democrat that I used to wake up and wonder every morning that the country, lacking William Jennings Bryan for its president, had not yet gone all to pot. It chafed me to have to get out a Republican paper. I paid as little attention to politics as I could. But now and then the boss would write me that he thought I ought to pay more. There was a Mr. Jones, let us call him, a Republican congressman from that district, who had had three or four terms in the House of Representatives and who was a candidate for renomination and reelection.

"So, one day, thinking that I ought to do what the boss had been urging me to do, and pay more attention to Republican politics, I wrote an editorial that began about like this: 'Is the Hon. X. Y. Jones the only Republican who merits office in the umpty-umth Congressional District? He's had three or four terms and what has he ever done with them? Isn't it about time he stepped aside and made room for some younger, more progressive Republican, who is in touch with the thoughts and feelings of the plain people in this part of Illinois?' And so forth. It wasn't that I had anything against Mr. Jones; I didn't know him; I didn't care a whoop, really, whether he went to Congress again or not. I was just being as good as gold, and obeying my boss' injunction to pay a little more attention to Republican politics.

"But it soon appeared that, ignorantly, I had started something. Six or eight other little country weeklies took it up. I wrote another similar screed. And in three weeks there were the beginnings of a very lively revolt against the organization in that district. One day the Republican boss of that county asked me to come over to the county seat and have dinner with him.

"I will call him Mr. Mack Clark. Mack was an old friend of my father's and of my elder brother's; they had been close friends, indeed, for many years. So I was not at all surprised, nor did I think of politics, when he said to me: 'Don, how would you like to go down to Washington and work in the Census Office? I can get you an appointment if you'd like it.' I immediately saw that if I got to a big town like Washington I'd have a chance to work into daily journalism. I took the job at once and went away from there. It never occurred to me at the time that I was being lifted out of the district. About three years later I lunched with Mack one day in the Great Northern Hotel in Chicago, and he said to me: 'I suppose you know that as soon as you left the umpty-umth district all those other fool little papers dropped their opposition to Mr. Jones and he was renominated and reelected.'

"'I'd never connected the two things before,' I said, beginning to think. 'Was what I said as important as all that?'

"'Well,' he said reflectively, 'it was getting pretty important—pretty important! Some people had been thinking it before you said it without thinking. I'd always thought you ought to have your chance on a daily paper, and when that thing came up it struck me that you'd put in about all the time on country weeklies that you could afford to, if you were ever going to get started on a daily paper.'

"As soon as I got into the Census Office I began trying to get onto one of the Washington dailies, but it was nearly a year before I succeeded. And then I discovered that I was no nearer to getting a signed column of my own than ever. In addition to my straight reportorial work, they let me do any other kind of writing I wanted to, however—verse, sketches, fables, paragraphs, anything and everything—and they would sign my name to it and play it up on the editorial page and in the Sunday paper. But they only let me do it; they didn't pay me for anything but the reportorial work, and they wouldn't let me have a signed column all my own that I could do what I pleased with."

4   *Boarding-House Days in Washington—Don Marquis as Census-Bureau Clerk, Newspaperman, Art Student, Beer Bibber—No Luck in Philadelphia—Atlanta Beckons*

Those were the days when Marquis didn't believe in sleep—when, in fact, he seemed to regard it as a needless intrusion—so, about eleven months after his arrival in Washington, and while he was still working for the Census Bureau, he accepted a second job: as a reporter for the Washington *Times*. Many years later he discussed his Washington newspaper experiences in *Everybody's Magazine*, citing the following as his low point in those cub-reporter days in the capital:

"'Monsieur Beaucaire' was being tried out in Washington, and Booth Tarkington, who had written it, was on hand to see it.

"I had never interviewed a playwright before. The city editor had said: 'Go and interview Booth Tarkington about his play,' and I went. But when Mr. Tarkington received me, I didn't know what to ask him. Finally I broke a silence that was becoming distressing, to me at least, by saying:

"'This is your first play, isn't it, Mr. Tarkington?'

"'Yes,' he said, 'this is my first play.'

"The silence gathered again, and after a while Mr. Tarkington offered me a cigarette. . . . By the time it was consumed I had thought of another question.

"'Do you *like* the play, Mr. Tarkington?' I inquired, brightly and cheerily.

"'Oh, yes, I *like* the play.'"

Marquis decided "to make one final effort to redeem himself." So, with what he described as "a false vivacity," he asked:

"How did you happen to write this play, Mr. Tarkington?"

Tarkington replied that he really didn't know.

Marquis, returning to the office of the Washington *Times*, was afraid he hadn't gotten much of a story. His city editor concurred.

In addition to running two jobs, Marquis managed to find time to attend the Corcoran Art School. Echoes of those days are to be found in magazine articles written by him years later, and in newspaper interviews. In one of these interviews he tells about an exhibition of Hubert Vos's paintings at the Corcoran Gallery. Vos was showing his work to Wu T'ing-fang, the Chinese Minister to the United States.

Reported Marquis:

> A lot of art students—I among them, replete
>   with Windsor tie—were trailing along.
> "Who's this?" says Wu, pausing in front of a
>   picture.
> "Li Hung Chang," says Vos.
> "It doesn't look like him," says Wu, sniffing.
> "It's only a three-quarter view," says Vos,
>   apologetically.
> "It doesn't look three-quarters like him,"
>   says Wu, and passes on.

In addition to the egobiography, in which Marquis wrote about himself in the third person, he left some manuscripts of a straight autobiographical nature, written in the first person. One of these— nineteen typed pages in length—gives a close-up of Marquis and the young men with whom he lived in a Washington boarding house at the turn of the century. It is, among other things, a picture of carefree youth, a study of the interdependence of the pawnshop and the saloon, and a good example of Don Marquis in a reminiscent vein. The following six of those nineteen pages show the home life of our protagonist not long after he had left Bureau County, Illinois, never to return:

"I was a young fellow. And there were a lot of other young

fellows at that time, strange as it may seem. It appears that there always are. Am I right in thinking that the young fellows of about 1900–1902 were the grandest young fellows who ever spurned this planet beneath their rapid feet? Probably wrong! In the thirty years since, I have learned one thing although I have muffed a thousand others—I have learned that I am often wrong.

"Well, anyhow, five or six of us young fellows were sitting in a large room on the third floor of a Washington boarding house one hot summer night in 1900, or 1901, in our pajamas, drinking beer out of a large tin bucket which circulated rapidly from clutch to clutch. Somebody had had thirty-five cents—or more likely, all of us put together had had thirty-five cents; or, possibly, somebody had hocked somebody else's scarf pin or cuff buttons and acquired thirty-five cents. Neckties, scarf pins, tobacco, pipes, cash, socks, shirts, books, beer, were considered communal property in this little Soviet. Even food. We were always all of us hungry. The usual Washington boarding house of the period never seemed to know how much food young fellows of from twenty-one to twenty-four really needed to keep the damask bloom of health upon the rosy cheek; but these caravanseries, as I remember them, were liberal in the matter of space. The rooms were each about the size of a modern New York apartment, with high ceilings and big windows. Six of us always took three rooms in a row whenever we changed boarding houses, which we did on an average of every four months, either by request or in the well-nigh hopeless search for more nourishment.

"Nourishment! What a part it played in our young lives! I said we were always hungry. More properly, always famished. There was, at that time, somewhere on Pennsylvania Avenue, that queer cluttered street of perennial tarnish, a three-cent lunchroom. Things which cost five cents at more aristocratic and exclusive resorts, cost three cents there. We used to go there in a body, when the state of the Soviet finances permitted, and fill up on vast quantities of cheap, plain (I wish I could add the word "wholesome") food. For twenty-seven cents you could eat yourself into a mild indigestion; for sixty-three cents you could eat until a coma overtook you and you fell from your stool into the sawdust on the floor.

"We were all government clerks and all students, and a couple of us had even a third occupation besides. I worked on a Washington evening paper from seven-thirty or eight o'clock in the morning until two in the afternoon; then I hastened to the Corcoran Art

School where I was, or fancied I was, studying art, and tried to sketch, draw, and paint, with results which never set the Potomac on fire. At 5 P.M., I reported at the Census Bureau and worked until midnight. From midnight until time to go to work on the paper again, I frolicked. I don't remember having slept for at least two years. I acquired in this way a constitutional insomnia which has been a great boon and blessing to me ever since. It has enabled me to work all day and play all night, and thus get twice as much out of life as most people.

"It is true that the old nervous system has sometimes observed, more or less mildly, that it isn't as spry as it used to be, but I always tell it: 'Go lie down. There's a dance or two in the old dog yet.' Is a man going to be boss, or is his nervous system? I ask you. From a person of any spirit there can be but one answer: I am the master of my fate, I am the captain of my solar plexus.

"Old Doc March (of whom more anon) was at this time a government employee, a medical student, and assistant dramatic editor of a Washington paper. We may not have looked it or talked it but we were all ambitious youths. While the tin bucket circulates, I like to look back on that little bunch . . . and heaven help my chilly middle age! There are two or three of those boys whose names I would not trust myself to spell today. Any one of them would have given me his last quarter—yes, and often did it, and now . . . Oh, what an imbecile is time . . . what a doddering, criminal old fool, to filch so much bright gold from the pouch of memory, and leave so many leaden counters . . . only thirty years, and they would have given me their shirts. And often did, taking better ones of mine in return—and now I'm not sure of the way to spell their names! (But you, J.F., the day that I forget your kindly face, I shall expect to forget my own father's and my own son's.) . . .

"The tin bucket went 'wham!' on top of somebody's head, which was the conventional signal that it was empty. Speculative glances went around. Could it be filled again?

"'Leave it to me,' said a long, subtle young man named Charlie.

"He left the room, and was back in a moment with something which he put into that container. Nobody knew at the time that it was Jim's watch. He tied the tin pail to a length of clothesline, let it down into the alley out of the back window, and banged it against the kitchen door. The door opened, and a colored man named Humphrey untied the bucket and disappeared with it down the alley. On the street—(I forget the name of it, but this boarding house itself was located somewhere on K Street, N.W.)—into which the alley debouched, near the corner, was a beer emporium. And next door to the saloon was a pawnshop.

"I have always considered this a very convenient juxtaposition; it was undoubtedly worked out by some more thoughtful economist. You could go into the pawnshop and make a minor business deal of some sort, then step into the beer saloon and expend the proceeds until your waistcoat began to feel a little tight. It would occur to you after a while that a waistcoat was a nuisance. Then you took the waistcoat into the pawnshop, and hocked it for fifty cents. Then you went back to the beer saloon. These two great institutions, the saloon and the pawnshop, made business for each other.

"Another great economic institution in Washington at this date was known as the Loan Shark. This animal preyed upon government clerks, and had hundreds of them in such a situation that they need never worry about their future—they didn't have any future worth worrying about.

"Humphrey had his instructions never to pawn anything he found in the tin bucket of more than thirty-five cents. A ticket at that figure was possible to redeem. And he was faithful, and always saved the tickets for us. The bucket of beer cost twenty-five cents—how much good beer you could get for a quarter in those days!—and how you needed the beer!—and how hard it was to get hold of the quarter!—and the extra dime was for Humphrey to buy beer with himself. It was a theory that Humphrey would not drink out of the bucket on the way back if he had some beer before he started home.

"Presently Humphrey appeared in the alley again, and immediately a chant arose, out the back window: 'Hump! Humphrey, hump! Hump, hump, hump yourself! Hump, Humphrey, hump!'

"Humphrey was a very rhythmic person, and did a kind of dance down the cobbled alley with the bucket of beer held high in front of him, to the accompaniment of this chant. It was also the theory that while these bacchanalian and terpsichorean rites occupied Humphrey's attention, he could not pause to take a draught from the tin pail. He came down the alley, a procession of one, but with all the effect of solemn ceremonial, and he gave a certain dignity to his progress—you would have thought there were a hundred Humphreys with buckets of beer following him, in some central African celebration of mystic significance.

"Arrived at the back door, Humphrey attached the bucket to the clothes line, and we pulled it up. Steady, Charlie! Do not let your excitement cause your nerves to quiver! Never but once did this system go wrong. On that occasion, as the bucket passed the window of the second-floor back, a hand reached out, grasped the clothesline, and annexed the bucket. Inquiry of the landlady brought the information that the second-floor back room was vacant. She was a long, lean, dry-looking landlady, and she said she did not approve of beer-drinking, and we would have to stop it in her house anyhow, and Humphrey was not to be used as the messenger of Gambrinus any longer. J.F. and I suspected her; she looked as if she could absorb enormous quantities of beer and never show it. It was only a couple of days later that we revenged and recompensed ourselves. We went into the dining room earlier than usual, and we caught on to the fact that while the meals served the boarders were poor in quality and scanty in quantity, her own food was plentiful and excellent. She sat at the head of the long table—alone. A magnificent sirloin steak had just been set in front of her—large, thick, juicy, rich and rare. Such a steak as we had never seen in that establishment before. When *we* wanted something like that we had to go out and buy it. We sat down, one on either side of her. No words were exchanged between J.F. and me. Only a nod and a look. But I lifted the steak from in front of the landlady, cut it in two, and deposited one half on J.F.'s plate and the other half on my own. She arose in a silent rage too deep for words and left the room. And the next day we were all looking for another boarding house."

When Marquis's tour of duty at the Census Bureau came to an end he decided to try his luck in some other city. Without his salary as a government clerk he had only his salary on the Washington *Times* and that was not enough to sustain him. His appetite was increasing "alarmingly," as he put it. A reduced income meant short rations and no beer, a frightening prospect. One of his friends on the *Times* had told him that newspapermen were paid a higher wage in Philadelphia and he decided to try that city. He was still hopeful that if he kept trying he would find an editor who would "let me have a signed column all my own that I could do what I pleased with," an oft-expressed ambition.

Twenty-six years later Marquis wrote about his arrival in Philadelphia. He was practically broke. ". . . I knew but one man in the

city, and I didn't know where he lived. I didn't like to waste any of
my three or four dollars going to a hotel, so I decided to sit up the
rest of the night in the Broad Street station and hunt my friend up
the next day. I knew what paper he worked on. Along toward morning I put my feet up on the bench and stretched out for a nap, but
a policeman made me put my feet on the floor again. He did this
several times. The scrubwomen were at work and the floor was covered with lye water, and I didn't like to put my feet down because
there were holes in the soles of my shoes; but this cop was relentless.
I got two lye-water blisters on the soles of my feet about the size of
silver dollars before I could wake up sufficiently to get away from
that floor and the cop."

Marquis's friend helped him get a job. It was a lifesaver in view
of the anemic state of his purse but he found himself further and
further away from that column he wanted to conduct, "immersed
in the dreary routine of editing copy and writing headlines."

Marquis was full of ideas for that column: poems, humorous
and serious, which "kept racing through his head," and satiric commentary on the fads and foibles of the time, ranging from brief
paragraphs to "fables and skits running a few hundred words a
piece, with a sprinkling of aphorisms of a timely and general
nature." He wrote and rewrote this material when he was finished
with his regular job, and decided that when he had enough for
nine or ten good columns he would submit them and try to land
a job as a daily columnist.

This despite the fact that he wasn't sure he wanted to stay in
Philadelphia. A local bartender had given him a bad impression of
the city. You could generally tell what a place was like from the
conduct of the barmen. He had also been shaken up by the behavior of that cop in the Broad Street station. But that was different,
he maintained. Nothing can be done about a literal-minded policeman spurred on by a sense of duty. Or maybe he was just a mean
s.o.b. It didn't matter, he declared, contending that it was a cop's
job to be mean and/or literal-mindedly dedicated. It was different,
however, with bartenders, who occupied a more exalted station in
life. This was a noble calling and you expected sublimity of character and deportment from those who had taken it up as a life
work.

He professed to be shocked, pursuing his point in true Marquisian
fashion, that the erring bartender, who, it developed, had served

him a glass of beer in which a fly was awash, had shown no concern when the matter was called to his attention. He had merely flung Marquis a spoon and said, "Flip it out with this!" No remorseful, "Sorry, sir, I'll spill that out and draw you another." A shocking performance, Marquis decided. If this was the way they ran Philadelphia . . .

Years later, cartoonist George McManus, creator of the perennial "Bringing up Father," told Marquis that, without knowing it, he'd been served a St. Louis cocktail—a glass of beer with a fly in it—by that Philadelphia bartender. "When I worked in St. Louis as a young man," McManus explained, "the flies were so thick in the summertime that there was only one way of avoiding the St. Louis cocktail. The second the bartender served your beer you spilled a small pool on the bar for the flies, and while they dove for it, you drained your glass in one swift gulp."

Marquis said he'd have left Philadelphia at once because of that uncouth barman if he hadn't remembered that he hadn't even seen Independence Hall. Philadelphia gave him a sense of history, a spinal tingle as he thought of the drama that had been enacted here in 1776, an urge to do something big . . . like found the *Saturday Evening Post*. "But," he ruefully told his friend Clive Weed years later, "it seems that Benjamin Franklin had beaten me to the punch. It's thrilling, though, to contemplate that Ben and I had the same idea."

Marquis submitted the humorous stuff he'd been writing on the side and applied for that job as columnist. He was promptly turned down but his chief told him that the material was publishable and would be used. It was considered good "filler" and was scattered throughout the paper. When he received no extra compensation for it, Marquis inquired whether a mistake had been made, only to learn that his boss thought this special material had been written on the paper's time. He was told that he should have asked whether the paper wanted to buy the extra material instead of assuming it would. When he protested this decision Marquis was promptly squelched. "And in such unbrotherly language!" he commented. "I asked the boss whether he hadn't heard the rumor that Philadelphia was the City of Brotherly Love. He replied that he had but that he never paid any attention to rumors. He was a rascal but always good for a snappy retort and I admired him for it. . . .

"From Philadelphia I went to Atlanta, Georgia, lured by a title

and the persistent hope of getting a column of my own. John Temple
Graves had just started a newspaper, the Atlanta *News,* and through
an old Washington pal of mine he offered me the place of associate
editor. Associate editor sounded important, and I went. All I had to
do was write two columns of editorials every day, and after that I
could write as many columns of my own as I wanted to. They'd
let me.

"Well, I actually did it. I couldn't keep it going every day, with
two columns of editorials to toss off first, but I managed it two or
three days a week, sometimes oftener, and was happy. After a few
months I went to the Atlanta *Journal* as an editorial writer. They let
me have a column too—as often as I could manage it after two columns of editorials had been written—and if anything crowded one
of these columns off the editorial page it used to enrage me. Grantland Rice was sporting editor of the *Journal* then, and he still tells
gleefully of my cries of rage and grief at times when I was not permitted to write as much as I wanted to for nothing, after having
done all the regular work I was paid for."

Those paragraphs telling how Marquis got started in Atlanta are
from a previously mentioned article he wrote for the *Saturday Evening Post* years later.

The difference between writing free stuff in Philadelphia and
doing the same thing in Atlanta was that in Atlanta he was permitted
to sign much of it, which gave him identity.

5 A Job with the Atlanta News—Poker and
Corn Whisky—Don Meets Henry Grantland Rice and
Frank L. Stanton—Entertaining an Escaped "Carnie"
Lion—A Switch to the Atlanta Journal—The Lost
Poems—Joel Chandler Harris Starts Uncle Remus's
Magazine and Marquis Joins Him—Reina (Queenie)
Melcher and the Ice-Cream-Soda Romance—Next
Stop, New York

In a prosaic moment Marquis said that Atlanta was made to order
for him; in a more poetic one he declared that by comparison with
other places where he'd worked, it was a garden of Hesperides. The
golden apples were people: Grantland Rice, Joel Chandler Harris,
Harris's son Julian, Frank L. Stanton, Charles J. Bayne, Reina
Melcher, Colonel John Temple Graves (his first boss in Atlanta),
Joseph Hitt, and others—some of them destined to play major roles
in his unfolding career.

"I remember thinking, when I went to Atlanta in 1902, that I had
never before struck such a hospitable and entertaining town," Marquis wrote long afterward. "I got off the train and went immediately
to the News office, and I had not talked with Colonel Graves for
five minutes before he made me a major. 'Major Marquis,' he
said, 'is euphonious and alliterative. I do not think you are old
enough, or that you have been in Atlanta long enough, to be a
colonel yet.' As I had been in Atlanta about twenty minutes, I agreed
with him that I could well afford to wait for this promotion."

Marquis's first week in Atlanta was a memorable one—two of the
men he met became lifelong friends, Grantland Rice of the Journal
and Joseph Hitt, one of the News editors, to whom he dedicated a

book more than twenty years later. Here are lines from that dedication:

> You taught me how to think: to see,
> To fix the forms that to and fro
> Across the mind's proscenium go.

Marquis often said that there was something breath-taking about the way he was immediately accepted by his fellows on the *News*. Hitt, whom he described as "the sweetest soul who ever lived," had been delegated to introduce him to the staff and he did so thorough a job that an old precedent was set aside and Marquis was invited to join his new associates in a game of poker on his first day in town. "The game," Marquis wrote thirty years later, "started in the office towards evening. . . . Some person of authority came in and suggested that the newsroom was not the proper place for a poker game. One of the reporters spoke up and said to come on out to his house. I was never able to determine afterwards just where this house was. We learned the next day, anyhow, that it was not his house at all. It belonged to a preacher who was away on his vacation, but had left it in charge of his son. The son thought he would take a little vacation also, with papa well out of the way, and turned it over to the reporter.

"There were seven of us in this poker game, which was staged around the preacher's dining room table; and after a while some of the card-players began to get hungry and thirsty. Somebody went downtown and came back with a cab full of eatables and drinkables. It was before state prohibition had descended upon Georgia. I remember this as the evening I first got acquainted with Randolph Rose's famous corn whisky—a friendship that lasted for some years and has helped to make me what I am today. Relays of food and corn whisky continued to appear all during the night, and about five o'clock in the morning some kind of barbaric dance was started. It was extended from cellar to the attic. I seem to remember that the minister's piano tried to climb the stairs. I woke up about four o'clock Sunday afternoon, sticking out of a trundle bed somewhere at the top of the house, and as I went down through the house to the street, I remember saying to myself: 'Gosh, this is the town! Gosh, this is the life!'

"I heard later that the preacher's neighbors had wondered that Saturday night just what kind of church party was being pulled at the preacher's house. I do not remember where the house was, and I am not sure that I ever knew the preacher's name, but after a lapse of thirty years, I do feel that it is about time to apologize for my own part in the affair."

Marquis once told Keats Speed, his last managing editor on the New York *Sun*, where his "Sun Dial" column became famous, that one of the major events of his life was meeting Grantland Rice. In 1902, when they met, Rice was twenty-two years old, Marquis twenty-four. There are a few old-timers around Atlanta who still remember those days and they recall that Marquis and Rice gravitated toward each other "as if in obedience to some natural law," as one of them put it. In a few months the young men were good friends and it didn't take them long to decide to give up their separate living quarters—(Marquis had taken up residence in a boarding house)—and take a flat together, which, according to Rice's autobiography, the vital and engrossing *The Tumult and the Shouting*, cost them three dollars a week. Recalling those days when they lived together, Rice wrote: "We once tried living on ten cents a day—the cost of a huge mince pie for breakfast, guaranteed to induce acute 24-hour indigestion for two."

Rice also recalled: "Don and I used to spend a few afternoons each fall helping with the coaching at Georgia Military Academy, some 20 miles from Atlanta." This calls to mind a reminiscent letter Marquis sent a Galesburg, Illinois, newspaper friend, Walter Whipple, many years later, in which he mentions playing football at Knox Academy:

". . . I played on the scrub team. A couple of birds named Lathe and Thompson tackled me at the same time one day in practice and between them did something to one of my legs that put me out of the football candidacy. I always thought that leg was cracked. I couldn't walk on it for a couple of weeks and it still has a ridge across it; but I didn't have enough money to see a doctor. Which is probably lucky; he might have amputated it."

Marquis has confessed that in 1902 he needed someone like Rice to tell him he had the goods, that some day he would be entrusted with that daily column he so badly wanted to write. He had tried to sell the idea to Washington and Philadelphia papers and had failed, and though in Atlanta they took him more seriously as a newspaperman than in those other cities, Atlanta didn't want the

column either. He was pegged as an editorial writer and as a man to
use on major political stories.

Marquis was beginning to wonder whether, after all, he might be
mistaken in his notion that he was capable of producing a good
humorous column. Then he and Rice became close friends and Rice
urged him to stick to his objective. Atlanta, Rice contended, was not
the town to start such a column. All Atlanta read the column of the
beloved Frank L. Stanton in the *Constitution*. This was as much of a
local habit as it had been in Chicago to read Eugene Field's
column. Stanton's stock in trade was sentiment almost as much as it
was humor but he was the established local columnist and Rice
thought he had the field sewed up. Impressed by the verses, prose
travesties, paragraphs, etc., that Marquis showed him, Rice urged
him to keep turning them out, suggesting that he avoid making them
topical so that they could be used later when he got his big chance.

Rice, a shrewd young man, also thought that the mocking tone of
much of what his friend wrote in prose and verse was a negation of
the popular Frank L. Stanton, "the James Whitcomb Riley of the
South." Some Stanton fans, mistaking Marquis's purpose, might
resent it; others might simply be puzzled by Marquis's tongue-in-
cheek approach; and then, of course, there would be those who
would enjoy M.'s exuberant nose-thumbing but even so it would be
a long time before he could expect to develop a following.

The Rice-Marquis twosome became one of the city's more fabulous institutions. The two young men did a little drinking together,
which brought out the poesy in each. Either was good for a stanza,
or at least a couplet, with the first or second swallow, and they
probably composed as much barroom poetry as any two young men
in the history of American literature.

Rice was fascinated by Marquis's tales of his days as a sewing-
machine salesman, chicken plucker, track straightener, schoolteacher,
and near-hobo; and Rice in turn held young Don spellbound with
his stories of life at Vanderbilt University, where he had earned his
B.A. in 1901 at the age of twenty-one. Rice had played football
and baseball at Vanderbilt, and Marquis never tired of hearing his
friend, a good storyteller, reminisce about exciting or amusing things
that had happened in games in which he'd participated.

At twenty-two Rice was sports editor of the Atlanta *Journal*, an
elegant way of saying that his job was to write the whole sports page;

and whenever his friend complained about having to write two columns of editorials a day, Rice (who first signed his stuff Henry
Grantland Rice, shortened it to H. Grantland Rice, and eventually
dropped the "H.") told him he had a cinch and offered to swap
jobs. Rice declared that an old football player like Marquis should
be at home as sports editor. The allusion was to the few months
Marquis played football when he was a student, briefly, at Knox
College's prep school. This fact stuck in Rice's mind and was mag-
nified with the years so that fifty years later when his autobiography
appeared, there was a reference to Marquis as a "heavy-set ex-athlete."

Rice, whose gregariousness began as a young man, had covered a
lot of ground in the brief period since his arrival in Atlanta. He
seemed to know everybody. One day he asked Don if he'd like to
meet Frank Stanton, "the melodious music-maker," and a meeting
was arranged. Stanton and Marquis liked each other instantly, became good friends, and kept in touch with each other until the
former died in 1927.

As a versifier Marquis thought Stanton had a virtuoso command
of technique, and that his work was characterized by "an eye for the
small miracles of growing things and a love of the average man that
stopped short of oversweetness." Once he referred to the *Constitution* columnist's "fatal facility," believing that if Stanton hadn't
established a format that called for his writing at least one poem a
day for his column, he might have developed importance as a poet.
Stanton had to turn 'em out so fast he didn't have the time to do
much polishing. But the fact that he had "a great verse ear," as
Marquis put it, was apparent even in his poems that needed more
work. Even so, several of Stanton's poems have survived as songs,
including his popular "Mighty Lak a Rose."

The new trio—Stanton, Rice, and Marquis—became one of Atlanta's more thrilling sights to local newspapermen, whose admiration
for the established Stanton was unanimous and who agreed with
him that his two young companions were comers.

In 1902, when this was happening, Stanton was forty-five, Marquis
twenty-four, Rice twenty-two. Most of Stanton's playmates were
older men but he had taken a shine to these youthful newspapermen
whose burgeoning talents he recognized and whose appreciation of
his column in the *Constitution* was something more flattering than
the same old fan mail from his readers.

Stanton was a fabulous storyteller, a man who could read a line of poetry like a professional actor, and an all-around good companion. His books were well known in the South—(several volumes of his poetry had been published)—and he was a big man around Atlanta. He enjoyed the company of "those tender striplings," as he sometimes called Don and Grant, although these meetings sometimes caused complications in the Stanton household and occasionally a ruse had to be devised "to get Stanton out of the house." Stanton thought that both Rice and Marquis had "displayed ingenuity in shaking him loose."

Their favorite meeting place was the bar of the Aragon Hotel, where singly, doubly, and sometimes trebly they turned out barroom poetry, according to how the spirits moved them. There were Rice-Stanton, Stanton-Marquis, Rice-Marquis, and Stanton-Rice-Marquis poems, and occasional solo flights. Some of these poems have survived. One has to do with a kidding match between Rice and Marquis about their respective names. Occasionally, to taunt H. Grantland Rice, Marquis called him Henry or Old Aitch. Rice retaliated by addressing his friend as Donald.

When Stanton heard that Rice and Marquis had declared a truce in this name war he pleaded with Don to reconsider his decision to drop the "H." in Rice's name. The *Constitution* columnist claimed that the crash of a dropping "aitch" always got on his nerves, and let his highball glass slip to the floor to illustrate his point as he remarked, "See what I mean?"

Fragments of a ballad on this subject said to have been written by Stanton have been handed down, including the couplet:

The jarring sound of a falling "aitch" as it hits the barroom floor
Is worse on the nerves than a thunderous belch or a shrill falsetto snore.

When Stanton discovered that, like himself, Marquis had worked as a printer, the two had a good time talking about their former jobs. Both had served in the print shops of country weeklies and had in common the experience, as practicing poets, of setting up poems they had composed and had not had a chance to commit to paper. This was what Marquis called the Tripe-to-Type-in-One-Operation School of Poetry.

When Rice discovered that Marquis had quit school at the age of fifteen and had had no further formal education except a few months at Knox Academy, and that Stanton had had "a common school education," he reminded them of his Vanderbilt University degree and suggested that henceforth they address him as Professor Rice. He also offered to tutor them, for a consideration, suggesting that they attend night school until they qualified for a degree of some kind. With a mock gravity that some of Rice's Atlanta contemporaries still recall, he expressed fear that it might hurt his social standing around town to be seen with such an unlettered pair, and the sooner they got an education the better.

Stanton's services were in demand as a lecturer who gave "poetry readings." Despite this extra source of income he was frequently broke. Once he offered to trade the bartender at the Aragon a poetry reading for a drink. Stanton had a copy of one of his volumes of verse in his coat pocket and was about to begin when a grumpy patron said he'd buy him a drink if he promised *not* to read. "Bartender," directed Stanton with simulated seriousness, "remove this boor." The disgruntled customer became resentful and a fight might have resulted if Marquis and Rice hadn't arrived before the situation got out of hand.

Rice had an endless fund of stories about the rollicking times he and Marquis had as young men in Atlanta. The following, from *The Tumult and the Shouting*, is a typical anecdote—typical also is Rice's comment at the end:

As two demon reporters, we shared a flat. . . . It was Christmas Eve of 1902 that I wandered in about midnight and found Don high as two kites and lathered with red ink and oil from a battered old hand letter press.

"Grant," he roared, "I'm putting out Page One of my Christmas issue—the way Hearst would do it!" Screaming across the top half of his front page, in red, 40-point letters was "CHRIST IS BORN!" By the time I'd added my four cents, we were both loaded on Georgia corn likker. We finally crawled into bed, smug in the feeling that we had indeed saluted the Lord.

How Marquis could write! An unaffected genius, at times he was a black brooder, but his physical and mental courage were magnificent.

. . . There I stood at the gate of God,
Drunk but unafraid.

That closing line of one of his verses mirrored Don's scorn for any human soul lacking the courage of its convictions.

Rice's book clears up a minor mystery in Don Marquis's life. In 1922 when he had a big comedy hit on Broadway he gave his friend Grant Rice credit, in a newspaper interview, for getting him interested

in the theater. There was no amplification and the reader was left
with the impression that Rice's enthusiasm for the theater had somehow communicated itself to his friend.

Marquis had something more specific in mind, as Rice's book
reveals:

"In those days (1902), the great from New York's Broadway would
make one-night stands throughout the cities of the South, with such
marquee'd names as John Drew, Richard Mansfield, the Barrymores
et al, all putting in their licks for the culture of the Confederacy.
The theater beat was handed to me. I can't tell you how many
nights . . . Don Marquis and I had two on the aisle as theater
critics for the Atlanta *Journal*."

Rice continued to write the whole sports page and to handle the
theater assignment on the side. Sometimes he wrote the reviews,
sometimes Marquis.

Early in 1904 Marquis left the Atlanta *News* for the *Journal*. The
News was a congenial place to work—Colonel Graves, Joseph Hitt,
and others saw to that—but the *Journal* offered him more money,
it was a better show window, and its staff was equally friendly. In
fact, he knew most of the *Journal* staff and was on as friendly a
basis with them as he was with his associates on the *News*.

Marquis was relieved when, before he made the switch to the
Journal, he talked things over with Joe Hitt, who had made life so
pleasant for him on the *News*, and Hitt expressed the opinion that
the move was logical and would prove stimulating.

By an odd coincidence, Charles J. Bayne, who succeeded Marquis
when he left the Washington *Times*, succeeded him again when he
left the Atlanta *News* for the *Journal*. The young men had become
friends in Washington and now they were to renew that friendship
in Atlanta.

Bayne devotes many pages in his memoirs, *Coming of the Crow's
Feet*, to Marquis. Here are some excerpts:

"Don Marquis and I often took long walks together while we
talked of poets dead and gone. . . . Our rambles often led to the
leafy solitude of Grant Park and Don gloried in revealing to me the
depravity of the animal kingdom by feeding plug tobacco to the
innocent-looking fawns in the zoo and, credit it or not, they ate it
ravenously, although we were careful to conceal our ministrations
from the keepers, who might not have understood. . . .

"Don Marquis and I were sometimes guests at dinner in the home of Mr. and Mrs. Joel Chandler Harris, where the head of the family radiated a quiet humor while dispensing typical southern hospitality. In that environment the birds themselves knew they were welcome and life, indoors and out, reflected the joyous pattern of host and hostess."

Many years later Marquis referred to Joel Chandler Harris as "one of the great before-, during- and after-dinner conversationalists." He never forgot the day his host revealed so many facets of his knowledge of natural history that it was apparent that here was a man who, if he had so chosen, might have achieved eminence as a botanist, zoologist, or ornithologist. Harris attached no importance to the knowledge he had acquired in these fields. He thought of himself as "an observer of nature" and once wrote: "A creature hunted, and a creature at play in the undisturbed freedom of the woods are not the same. . . . A hunter must have blood and a naturalist must have specimens, whereas an observer needs only patience and sharp eyes." It was in developing this theme, with specific examples, that Harris, according to Marquis, was as interesting as any man he had ever listened to on *any* subject.

What Bayne has written in his book suggests that the quotation "The birds themselves knew they were welcome" is intended as a reference to a story—familiar to Atlantans—about Joel Chandler Harris: when a wren started building her nest in his R.F.D. mailbox, which had somehow flipped open, he let her continue undisturbed, permitting her and her family to live there, and setting out another mailbox for the Harris family.

As a consequence the Harris home came to be known as the Wren's Nest. The next time you are in Atlanta, should you tell your taxi driver, "Take me to the Wren's Nest," you will be driven to the house where Joel Chandler Harris lived—now a public museum—and one of the first things they will show you when you enter is that same mailbox with that nest still nestling inside, just as it was when those wrens decided to occupy it.

Marquis's main job on the Atlanta *Journal* was to write two double-measure columns of editorials a day, seven days a week. Occasionally the paper used him as a reporter on a big story.

According to Homer Croy, one experience that Marquis had in Atlanta achieved a permanent place in his repertory as a raconteur. One day he was seated at a circular table in an Atlanta bar when a lion—one of the attractions at a "carnie" show that was playing in town—wandered in. Don's back was to the door and it took him a few seconds to realize why his drinking companions had jumped up and scattered.

According to Don's account of what actually happened, the lion must have been bored by his new surroundings, for he yawned, revealing an almost toothless set of gums. The great cat, having strolled quite a distance from the carnival grounds, was tired; or, at any rate, he stretched out on the floor, yawned a few times more, and seemed about to fall asleep.

But Marquis felt that when you find yourself alone in a room with a lion, toothless or not, you ought to make the most of your opportunity. And he did. His story—that is, stories—of what took place when he and the animal faced each other became quite a saga by the time he had put all the different versions together. In Version One he grappled with the animal, which struggled vainly to get one of his arms or legs between its "great flashing white teeth." By a Superhuman Effort he managed to clamp its jaws together with his hands, which had grown powerful through his labors as a poultry plucker and a track straightener for the C., B. and Q. Railroad. He made quite a thing of this struggle with the Fiendish Cat from Hell, demonstrating the hold the animal could not break. At the first sign of incredulity or heckling he would say, "After about twenty minutes of this, I said to the critter, 'How about a drink?' But of course with my hands clamped over his jaws, he couldn't talk, so he replied by means of a great affirmative nod which broke my grip and sent me flying in an arc against the wall behind the bar. "That's where you belong, anyway," exclaimed the lion, "if we're to have that drink."

Marquis said he then picked himself up, and, producing a bottle of whisky, poured drinks for himself and the lion.

"No, no!" cried the King of Beasts. "You're giving yourself as big a drink as you've poured for me. I'm used to the lion's share." With which he picked up the bottle with his forepaws and drained it— and then opened five others and drained those too. After which he slipped a paw under Don's arm and the two exited together, the lion saying, "Let's go find some women."

By the time Marquis got through telling this story nobody believed any part of it. It was assumed that it had all been invented. Yet the basic situation has a good oral history—i.e., the toothless "carnie" lion that wandered into an Atlanta bar while Marquis was having a drink there with some friends.

For some years Marquis told another story which, by the time he'd developed different versions of it, was accepted by his friends as pure invention. So fantastic were some of the embellishments that his listeners assumed that they were not expected to believe a word of what he was saying. The basic situation had to do with the time his friend Charles Bayne was alleged to have flagged down and stopped a fast express train on the Southern Railroad to ask the engineer for a match to light his pipe.

Marquis's friends assumed that this was a tall story to which he (Marquis) had lent verisimilitude by attributing it to an actual person. In *Coming of the Crow's Feet*, published after Marquis's death, Bayne states that he *had* stopped that train to ask for a match, and tells the story in considerable detail. Some of the stories Marquis told *were* inventions—extravaganzas he expected people to recognize as Munchausenism—and to this day there is a difference of opinion among those who knew Don as to what was fact and what was fancy.

In 1905 the Cleveland *News* offered Grantland Rice $50 a week. He had started on the Atlanta *Journal* at $12.50 a week and while he was appreciated and had received pay increases, he was still far from the $50 mark. He accepted the offer, though he was understandably reluctant to leave.

"To know Grant Rice is to like him," Marquis had often said, sometimes adding that to walk down one of Atlanta's principal thoroughfares with Rice was quite an experience. "He seemed to know everyone in town."

Marquis once offered to be his campaign manager if Rice decided to run for office. In fact, he urged him to do so as a service to Georgia newspapermen who complained that good political stories did not happen often enough. "From sportswriter to governor" was a copy-laden theme, Marquis thought. And if, on being elected, Rice could be persuaded to issue a proclamation disqualifying for state jobs all except athletes or ex-athletes, that would start a lively controversy and the reporters would have something to write about. Rice promised to think it over.

The Three Poets—Rice, Marquis, and Stanton—staged a farewell party that was said to be one of the most hilarious in Atlanta journalistic history. All records for writing barroom poetry were broken that night. Rice said a line count revealed that Stanton won in a driving finish by the margin of the first six lines of a sonnet; but he and Marquis were thinking of lodging a protest with the judges.

In his book Rice describes the Stanton technique of writing barroom poetry: "All Stanton needed was a pencil and a sheet of wrapping paper." Rice and Marquis, on the other hand, wrote their tavern rhymes on regular copy paper, which put them at a disadvantage with a man like Stanton who, working on one great big sheet, didn't have to take time out to grab a fresh page every few minutes.

The next day as Rice left the Aragon Hotel, where he and Marquis had lived and had so much fun together, the Cleveland-bound sportswriter predicted that some day he and Marquis would have a reunion in New York, a prediction that came true. Marquis began his New York newspaper career in 1909 and they had that reunion when Rice came to New York in 1910 to work for the old *Evening Mail.*

The Atlanta race riots of September 1906 imprinted themselves indelibly on Marquis's mind.

Years later, in telling the story to his friend Clive Weed, Marquis stated that he never could "quite forget that incubus." He had made several attempts to build a short story around those riots but his efforts never seemed to jell. He said he would keep on trying. He finally wrote the story and in 1916 sold it to *Harper's Magazine.* When in 1921 his publisher asked him for his first collection of short stories, the one that had as its background the Atlanta race riots of 1906 was liked best and it became the title story of the book, *Carter, and Other People.*

It seems appropriate to forget chronology for a moment and quote a few passages from that story in this chapter dealing with Marquis's Atlanta days:

"Carter began to learn that he was a nigger very early in life. Nigger children are not left long in doubt anywhere, and especially in the South. Carter first saw the light—and the shadows—of day in Atlanta. . . .

"When Carter grew up he went North. He went to New York. But the North, which affects to promise so much to a Negro, in a large, loose, general way, does not perform in the same degree. . . ."

No attempt will be made to give the theme of Marquis's story.

The purpose of these paragraphs is merely to show the lasting impression those unbridled outbreaks made on Marquis:

"There was a riot in the streets, a whirlwind of passion which lashed the town and lifted up the trivial souls of men and spun them round and round, and passed and left stains of blood behind. White men were making innocent Negroes suffer for the crimes of guilty Negroes. It had been a hot summer; scarcely a day had passed during July and August without bringing to the newspapers from somewhere in Georgia a report of a Negro assault upon some white woman. A blind, undiscriminating anger against the whole Negro race had been growing and growing. And when, on that Saturday afternoon, the newspapers reported four more crimes in rapid succession, all in or near Atlanta, the cumulative rage burst into a storm. . . .

". . . Carter . . . stood in a doorway, in the heart of the business district of the town, and watched the wild work that went on in a large, irregular plaza, where five streets come together and all the car lines in the place converge. From this roughly triangular plaza leads Decatur Street, at one time notorious throughout the South for its Negro dives and gambling-dens.

"Now and then Carter could hear the crack of a pistol, close at hand or far away; and again some fleeing Negro would start from a place of temporary concealment, at the approach of a mob that beat its way along a street, and make a wild dash for safety, as a rabbit startled from the sedgegrass scurries to the brush. There was not one mob, but several; the different bands united, split up, and reunited, as the shifting winds of madness blew. The plaza, with arc lights all about it, was the brilliantly illuminated stage on which more than one scene of that disgusting melodrama was played out; from some dim hell of gloom and clamor to the north or east would rush a shouting group that whirled and swayed beneath the lights, dancing like flecks of soot in their brightness, to disappear in the gloom again, shouting, cursing and gesticulating, down one of the thoroughfares to the west or south. . . .

". . . A crowd . . . swept past . . . from Decatur Street in pursuit of a panting Negro. The fleeing colored man was struck a dozen times; he fell at the street corner near them, and the mob surged on again into the darkness beyond, already in full chase of another quarry—all but one man, who left the mob and ran back as if to assure himself that the prostrate Negro was really dead."

Bayne's autobiography, in which these disturbances are described in detail, clearly indicates that in "Carter" Marquis, within the framework of fiction, had written a factual account of the Atlanta race riots of September 22, 1906.

When a man is as flamboyant as Don Marquis it is hard to visualize him as a hard worker; yet that he was, in Atlanta and throughout his life, as the record abundantly shows.

His wall mottoes proclaiming the folly of toil are so convincing that to those unacquainted with the facts it would be easy to think of him as one who loafed his way through life.

To a friend who (in his columning days) protested when weeks had elapsed without one of those antitoil manifestoes—written in verse, set as prose, and frequently intricately rhymed—Marquis complained that by the time he'd rewritten the last one about a dozen times he'd just about decided that deriding labor was too much work. But he resumed the series shortly afterward.

Marquis never lost his love of picturing himself as a loafer. He once said in his column that his pose of indolence was important; it kept reminding him that one of his goals was to be able some day to lead a lazy life. If he stopped talking about it he might lose sight of his objective.

With the publication of his twenty-seventh book—many years after his Atlanta days—we find him as actively engaged as ever in the business of presenting himself as an idler, this time by requesting of his publisher that the dust jacket of the book, a collection of short stories called Sun Dial Time, depict him comfortably ensconced in a wicker rocking chair with his feet propped up on a sun dial. The publisher complied.

Marquis managed to have a lot of fun in Atlanta; but he also found time to chain himself to his typewriter. The foreword to his contribution to the fiftieth anniversary edition of the Atlanta Journal, published in 1933 and written by a former associate who knew the facts, said: "In his days on the Atlanta Journal Marquis was a prodigious worker, filling trunks and packing boxes with manuscripts. . . . Some of these manuscripts were destroyed by janitorial mistakes and other calamities, but much of the fruit of that early labor was later revised and published, to form the basis of some of his most important work."

Among those who knew Marquis in his Atlanta days is Angus

Perkerson, one of the best-known Southern newspapermen since the early 1900s.

Mr. Perkerson writes:

"I started work on The Atlanta Journal in 1905 as a very young reporter. Don had already been on the paper for about a year as editorial writer. There wasn't any other on the paper then, though I think there are four or five now. He wrote all the editorials, seven days a week. I remember once he got tired of the grind and asked to be assigned to the capital run, and for several weeks he wrote political news, mostly from a feature angle, and then went back to doing editorials.

"Once I got together a feature story of sorts—some odd facts about the weather, I think it was. There wasn't a place for it in the news section—news was news then—but somehow my story fell into Don's hands and he used it as an editorial. Maybe he was having trouble that day filling up two columns of editorial space, set wide measure. Anyway, I was amazed and delighted.

"I was talking recently with William Cole Jones, the editorial writer who succeeded Don Marquis when Don left The Journal to join the Joel Chandler Harris venture, *Uncle Remus's Magazine*. Cole told me that Don had the walls of his small office literally covered with rejection slips from various magazines; that he took considerable pride in his papering job and also felt that he had one of the largest collections of rejection slips in existence. I never saw inside the office."

Years later Marquis recited to a friend a piece of verse he'd written about those wholesale rejections. The title, he recalls, was something like "Marquis, Go Back to Chicken Plucking," and it concluded approximately as follows:

> He may be rejected
> But is he dejected?
> The answer is yes!

Mr. Perkerson also writes:

"According to a story that a professor of English at Emory University told me, Don had decided one New Year's Day that he would write a poem every day of the year that was just beginning. This he did, and as he wrote the poems he dropped them into a box. Then on next New Year's Eve he decided to see just what he had done, so he got out all the poems and arranged them in a neat pile on the floor. About that time he was called out of the office, maybe to join in some celebrating that was being done in a neighboring office. When he got back a janitor had swept up all the poems and carted them off with the trash."

The story of the lost manuscripts appears also in letters, magazine articles, and newspaper interviews. On December 2, 1932, George Britt of the New York *World-Telegram* did a lively interview with Marquis from which the following is taken:

"I remember nearly thirty years ago when I was working seriously at poetry," he said between puffs at his pipe.

"Under my desk in the Atlanta Journal office was a wooden box, and whenever I wrote any verse I'd put it there. I wanted it to pile up before I sprung it on the world. I wrote a lot. At that age, if you're inclined, you just gush poetry.

"And every week I'd bump the janitor's head on the box and say, 'This is not a wastebasket and you're to leave it strictly alone.' He was very careful. But one day they got a new janitor.

"Well, it happened. And I went to the cellar and opened up a dozen bales of waste paper and sorted all through them. But I never found a trace of my poems.

"You know, even to this day, when I write anything that seems any good I think I am remembering from then. That loss really flattened out my spirit for two or three years."

Marquis was so constituted that usually he did not dwell long on misfortune. He was a man who felt deeply but who had an instinctive dread "of being caught telling hard-luck stories." There were not many sorrows that he kept mentioning. One of them was the lost poems.

A quarter of a century later we find him saying in a reminiscent article in the *Saturday Evening Post*: "One of the great tragedies of my life occurred while I was on the Atlanta *Journal*. For nearly three years I wrote poems, which I never printed, and threw them into a wooden box under my desk. They were my best work. For three long golden years I threw poems into that box, stamping them down from time to time, and there must have been, without exaggeration, two or three hundred of them. They were all about love and starlight and the red morning of the planet, and the young gods rampaging across the young umbrageous worlds, and the sudden ghosts that go whizzing through the moonlight—all the things one writes poetry about when one is twenty-five." Then he tells in considerable detail the story of how Henry, the janitor, threw them out, and of the vain search to recover them.

It seems clear that on those occasions when Marquis elected to joke about the thrown-out poems—("Maybe that janitor was one of those intuitive editors who instinctively did the right thing")—he was merely resorting to an old device of his for concealing his un-happiness.

You would have thought that Marquis would use up his creative energy writing two double-measure columns of editorials a day, seven days a week; but in those days he seemed inexhaustible and he frequently acted (as Grant Rice once put it) as if his office chores were just a tune-up for the night's creative work.

The years 1906 and 1907 were ones of fierce creative activity. He wrote and wrote, and precisely what he produced in those days will probably never be known. He did say that it was in Atlanta that he got the idea for his first novel—*Danny's Own Story*—and that he wrote "some of it" there. There are no other clues.

Publisher Gray had occasion to visit the *Journal* office late one night, and, finding Marquis at his typewriter pounding out copy, commended him for taking his job so seriously but wondered whether he wasn't working too hard. When Marquis explained that he was "working on his own stuff," Gray professed to be upset, declaring he would have to make a charge for typewriter rental and for wear and tear on the furniture.

Gray, in subsequently telling the story, said Marquis could easily have bluffed him into believing he was working overtime for the paper, adding that he liked his young editorial writer better than ever for not trying to fool him.

In 1907 Joel Chandler Harris made an announcement that was big news in Atlanta and throughout the South. He had decided to start a monthly publication to be called *Uncle Remus's Magazine*.

One of Harris's first moves was to offer Marquis a job as associate editor. Marquis accepted. He enjoyed life on the *Journal* but he wasn't learning or doing anything new. For three years he had been pounding out fourteen double-measure columns of editorials a week, the work was becoming monotonous and he'd been growing restive. The offer came at a good time. Most important of all, it had come from Joel Chandler Harris, "the first great man he'd ever met."

Marquis's admiration for Harris was unbounded. He considered him the best thinker in the South and, next to Mark Twain, the country's greatest living humorist; moreover, he respected him as a person, having designated him several times as "that great golden soul." He believed the Atlanta *Constitution* was making literary history with the Uncle Remus stories, folk tales that would find a permanent place in American literature. It gave his morale a great boost to be picked for a major job in this new publishing venture by a man he held in such esteem.

In a public announcement of "the principles and scope of the new magazine" Harris said:

". . . It will be a Southern magazine by reason of its environment, as well as by reason of the fact that the South is a part—a very large and definite part of this great Republic of ours—but all its purposes and intentions, its motives and its politics will be broader than any section and higher than partisanship of any sort. It is purposed to issue a magazine . . . genuinely representative of the best thought of the whole country. . . .

"The new generation in the South has been largely educated in Northern and Eastern institutions, with the result that a high appreciation of all that is best and worthiest in those sections is spread further and wider than ever before and is constantly growing in extent. On the other hand, in the North neighbor-knowledge of the South is confined almost entirely to those who have made commercial explorations of this section, and who have touched Southern life at no really significant or important point.

"It shall be the purpose of the magazine to obliterate ignorance of this kind. It will deal with the high ideals toward which the best and ripest Southern thought is directed."

Harris went on to say that while *Uncle Remus's Magazine* would be a Southern publication, it would be more than a medium for Southern writers. "It will have behind it," he also stated, "a sufficient amount of capital to secure the best writers of the country at large."

The name *Uncle Remus's Magazine* suggested a children's publication to many, which Harris was able to counteract by an expanded version of the policy statement quoted earlier. Believing that even in a magazine for adults there was room for children's stories, Harris announced that he would publish Uncle Remus stories in the new magazine, which was as good news for adult readers as it was for children. Throughout the South (and elsewhere) parents had found Br'er Rabbit as much fun as did their youngsters, so the Uncle Remus stories would be a good circulation builder.

A passage in the statement of Editor Harris about the "principles and scope" of the new publication that especially appealed to Don Marquis was one to the effect that *Uncle Remus's Magazine* would seek "to encourage the cultivation of the rich field of poetry."

The editorial names on the masthead were listed in this order:

> Joel Chandler Harris, Editor
> Don Marquis, Associate Editor
> Edwin Camp, Managing Editor

Marquis's chief responsibility was the editorial page, or pages. More frequently than not they were published as a two-page spread. The page size was approximately that of the *Saturday Evening Post*. A word-count of a typical spread—published under the standing head "A Glance in Passing"—came to a total of about two thousand words, or a little more, for about eight to twelve editorials. This was a romp for the facile Marquis, whose daily output of editorials on the Atlanta *Journal* usually exceeded that.

However, for *Uncle Remus's Magazine* he would have to select subjects that would stand up in a monthly—national problems, for instance, that had been around a long time and were not likely to disappear overnight. Harris wanted the page to have solidity but he also sought the light touch where that was indicated. Marquis's work on the *Journal* convinced him that his young editor could produce what was wanted.

The belief held by some that the public had no real interest in editorials Joel Chandler Harris considered a myth. It was dullness that people resisted, whether it took the form of an editorial, an article, or a piece of fiction. A vital editorial page had followers— and he cited the following Marquis had developed on the *Journal*. His editorial columns had become known as informative and entertaining, which is why he (Harris) and so many other Atlantans regularly read them.

In addition to the editorials, the book reviews were to be Marquis's responsibility. He was also to have a voice in the selection of fiction, articles, and the rest of the magazine. Marquis was also encouraged to make special contributions of his own—short stories, poetry, etc.—these to be passed upon by Editor Harris.

The new publication got off to a lively start. In a single early issue there were stories by Jack London, O. Henry, and George Randolph Chester, who had achieved fame as the author of the Get-Rich-Quick Wallingford tales, as well as contributions by the two staff regulars, Harris and Marquis. Among the well-known names represented in subsequent issues were George Ade with his Fables in Slang, James Whitcomb Riley, Herbert Ravenel Sass, Grantland Rice, Witter Bynner, and William Jennings Bryan.

In the spring of 1960 I called on Julian La Rose Harris, son of Joel Chandler Harris, at his home in Atlanta, to discuss *Uncle Remus's Magazine* and Don Marquis's part in it. Julian had played an important part in the new enterprise. His official title, as listed on the masthead, was business manager; but since he had shown editorial ability he was also consulted on the contents of the magazine. (Julian Harris subsequently became a newspaperman, and a distinguished one, winning a Pulitzer Prize in 1926.)

Julian Harris recalls his father's enthusiasm for Don Marquis's work, also his one reservation. Ribald touches had a way of creeping into Don's editorials, and, while the elder Harris enjoyed them himself, he had to edit them out, regarding them as inappropriate for the type of publication he was issuing. Fearing that sometime, when he was not around to act as watchdog, something too risqué might creep into Marquis's copy, Harris decided to caution Marquis in a memorandum.

He wrote this memo but never sent it, fearing that the formality of an official communication, however friendly its approach, might have the wrong effect. Marquis attacked his work with a zest that Harris admired and Harris was loath to do anything that might dampen his young editor's enthusiasm or check his spontaneity. What he wanted to get across was that it was possible to be robust without giving the reader too much of a jolt; and after much thought he decided he could do a better and friendlier job in conversation than in writing.

The elder Harris showed his son the memo he had decided to withhold. Julian, regarding it as a document worth preserving, kept it.

When I last saw Julian Harris he was sorrowfully pointing to the contents of his desk, which he had ransacked in an effort to find that unsent memorandum. But the great mound of papers that he had pulled out of that desk and piled up on top of it failed to yield what he was looking for.

The story illustrates what Grantland Rice meant when, in his autobiography, he described Joel Chandler Harris as the "unstuffiest" person he'd ever known.

Marquis's editorials in the Atlanta *Journal* had punch and point, and a sprinkling of humor when that was indicated, but in the main they were so local they would require too much explaining. A sampling of Marquis's work as editorial writer for *Uncle Remus's Magazine* seems more appropriate, especially as none of these editorials have been collected.

Marquis thought his best editorial for *Uncle Remus's Magazine*—perhaps because it was the most widely reprinted—was one having to do with the elder John D. Rockefeller. He frankly enjoyed the fact that this editorial, which carried the head, "According to St. John," had "gotten a rise out of one of Mr. Rockefeller's associates." The text:

"John D. Rockefeller's heart to heart talks with newspaper men are among the most entertaining contributions to current literature. This pious elderly gentleman, whose only ambition is to discharge with credit the great trust which it has pleased Providence (in recognition of his piety) to put into his hands, is at a loss to understand his own unpopularity. . . .

"Why should anyone grudge him his prosperity? Surely the world understands *why* he has prospered, does it not? Has not Mr. Rockefeller pointed out, time and again, that any young man now living is equally sure of prosperity if he will walk in the straight and narrow way, as Mr. Rockefeller did,—if he will conduct himself meekly, if he is neither froward nor contentious, nor yet intemperate nor incautious, but refrains from those evil communications that corrupt good manners? 'A good name is rather to be chosen than great riches,' Mr. Rockefeller agrees, but points out that the possession of the one does not necessarily imply a lack of the other.

"Indeed (we gather from his newspaper interviews) the best way to trap great riches is with the bird lime of piety. And if you are not rich, we infer, it is because you are not religious; there has been some little flaw in your behavior which the world, perhaps, sees not, but of which the Recording Angel (who is a kind of expert financial-religious accountant in the Scheme of Things according to Rockefeller) is shrewdly aware.

"Mr. Rockefeller's little sermons generally find their way into the papers just after some unusually wicked assault upon that divinely appointed organization, the oil trust, and coming so they serve to emphasize the sweetness of that unperturbed, forgiving spirit that loves the world in spite of the world's determined misjudgment. They must be very comforting to the smaller fry whom he has ruined, for they convey the cheerful message that Providence let Mr. Rockefeller crush them because Mr. Rockefeller is more righteous than they are. And for our part we never grow tired of the simple tale of his purity and worth as related by himself."

Another editorial that was characteristic of Marquis's work in those days stemmed from his having read that "an exposé of Newport society" by Upton Sinclair was based on Sinclair's having "penetrated into the homes he intended to expose in the disguise of a servant."

Marquis commented, in part, that "this does not strike the casual observer as being very good taste. . . . We feel no particular impulse to come to the defense of Newport any more than we do to the defense of Podunk, Pittsburgh or Dodd's Corners; and yet even Newport has a just cause for complaint when Newport is approached in this manner. There is no condition of society that does not include families and individuals that fall below the best standards. Stupidity and selfishness are old acquaintances. We may see them anywhere. We may see nothing else if we look for nothing else. And the person who enters a home in disguise by that token signifies the sort of copy he is looking for and means to have. . . .

"And yet what was Mr. Sinclair to do?—it must be obvious to anyone who has ever read *The Jungle* that it would be an impossibility for Mr. Sinclair convincingly to disguise himself as a novelist."

In a letter written many years later we find Marquis asking his publisher to send Upton Sinclair a copy of his latest book—*Chapters for the Orthodox*—pointing out that "Mr. Sinclair has shown a friendly interest in my work."

Once Marquis tried to devote the lead of his two-page spread to a page-long ballad he'd written about a long-time urge he'd had to slay a certain sea serpent—one of those hardy perennials, which may have been "the Loch Ness monster," though it was not so designated —that kept turning up in the news. When he learned that Editor

Joel Chandler Harris had asked for a prose editorial in its place, his spirits sagged. Later he learned the good news that Harris liked the piece well enough to pay him separately for it and run it as a special feature, with an illustration, on another page.

This ballad does not appear in any of the collections of Marquis's verse. Here is its opening stanza:

> I said to myself, "Not for glory nor pelf, but for Sweet
> Humanity's Sake,
> I will hie me forth to the south or the north and slaughter
> the great Sea Snake."
> So I talked and drank with many a crank grog-seasoned sailor-dog,
> And each one swore that he knew it of yore, and could prove it
> by the log.
> One said that the sheen of its hide was green and its tail was
> covered with scales,
> And another one said it had fins on its head which it flung to the
> breeze like sails;
> And each, as he talked, breathed hard and caulked the seams of his
> stomach with booze,
> And under his breath told tales of a death deep down in the
> ocean's ooze.

F. M. Krugler, the magazine's Eastern advertising representative, was pleased when this rollicking ballad was published opposite an ad from a new account, the National Biscuit Company. The burden of its message was: Uneeda Biscuit, 5¢.

"For years," Marquis declared in one of his most widely quoted editorials, "the critics have been seeking for, and sighing for, and laying down specifications for 'The Great American Novel', and it is possible they were overlooking a pretty good bet all the time. Just exactly what is meant by the great American novel we can't say; in the fullness of time there should be a number of great American novels, just as there are numbers of great English and great French novels, but if by the phrase is meant some book which exhibits the America of any particular period as Americans know and feel it to have been, the trick has already been turned in 'Huckleberry Finn.'"

Marquis, in developing his theme, pointed out that "while the critics were quarreling about whether Walt Whitman was a poet or not, and were rating Mark Twain along with such mere jesters as Artemas Ward, and were denying him the literary longevity they predicted for writers already half-forgotten," new thousands every year were discovering Mark Twain by themselves.

Today this sounds like Old Stuff. In 1907 it had novelty and was picked up and quoted.

Mark Twain was one of Marquis's favorite subjects. "In a recent number of his autobiography," he stated in another editorial in *Uncle Remus's Magazine*, "Mark Twain hints that he may devote some attention to the work of changing the fashion of modern masculinity's attire. He seems to lament the 'brave days of old' when color and fabric were as much regarded by men as by women."

He concludes with the thought that "if President [Theodore] Roosevelt will only take up dress reform for men with that enthusiasm with which he took up spelling reform something may be accomplished. He might begin by putting Secretary [William Howard] Taft into the costume of a toreador, and Vice President Fairbanks would look cute in bell-mouthed pantelettes and a Spanish ruff."

From twin editorials on a subject that explains itself:

"Now that the South is going dry, a whole army of Southern Colonel anecdotes must be mustered out of service. The survivor of an elder period, who spent the lazy days on his verandah drinking heavenly mint juleps, is a familiar figure—in fiction. . . . As a matter of fact, the juleps concocted in this part of the country are not a bit better than the ones that may be purchased in New York or Chicago barrooms. . . .

"And now that Georgia has got it, what is she going to do with it, this prohibition law? The few stills in the mountains untouched by the revenue officers will not be able to appease one-tenth of the unregenerate thirst still remaining in Georgia; besides it is not everyone who has been educated up to a liking for corn whiskey. The Rum Demon and the interstate commerce laws will probably form a working partnership to supply the greater part of the demand for Liquid Damnation."

Marquis was never happier than when the reaction to something he had written indicated that his words had struck home. In a fighting editorial he wrote: "The Russian government permits, if it does not directly encourage, the massacre of the Jews." This statement drew the fire of Russian officialdom. There was no denial that the massacres had taken place; it was merely represented that Marquis's passage, *"if it does not directly encourage,"* was inflammatory—

that it hinted that the massacres might have been government-inspired when as a matter of fact they had been unfortunate outbreaks beyond the control of the Russian authorities, etc., etc.

Julian Harris told me in Atlanta in the spring of 1960 that a Marquis editorial had gotten a hearty laugh out of President Theodore Roosevelt. The story had been told him by his father. The latter, a White House guest, was pleased when the President showed familiarity with the contents of *Uncle Remus's Magazine*. Marquis had written an editorial applauding a White House announcement that Roosevelt planned to launch a trust-busting campaign; but he cautioned T.R. that, what with countless mergers, it would not be easy. Unscrambling these industrial combines would be as difficult as separating the eggs in an omelet and restoring each to its original shell. "Don't say I didn't warn you, Mr. President," was the gist of his cautionary sign-off.

Some years later, when Marquis was conducting his "Sun Dial" column in the New York *Sun*, Theodore Roosevelt sent him a fan letter. There is no way of telling whether the former President connected the Don Marquis whose humorous column he regularly read and enjoyed with the Don Marquis who years earlier had signed the editorials in *Uncle Remus's Magazine*.

As a final sampling of Marquis's editorials, here is the lead of one of his most eloquent ones:

"Crucifixion is still the reward of the Christlike. Tolstoi loves the peasants of Russia, and would serve them. The peasants near his home lately showed their appreciation by shooting at him. And then Tolstoi excused the peasants to the authorities with the remark that 'it was only done in mischief'—a remark which sounds like that of the Master whom Tolstoi consistently emulates insofar as he is able: 'Forgive them, for they know not what they do.'"

Marquis's writings for *Uncle Remus's Magazine* were so diversified that the easiest way to describe them is to call them miscellaneous. There were many different Marquises—editorial writer, serious poet, humorous versifier, short-story writer, essayist, book reviewer—and Editor Joel Chandler Harris seemed to approve of all of them.

The editorials and some of the other pieces are signed Don Marquis; and there was an assortment of other signatures, including D.M., D.R.P.M. (for his full name, Donald Robert Perry Marquis), and Robert Perry.

Among the Marquis pieces that Editor Harris liked best were a
travesty on the blood-and-thunder plays of the period, called "The
Melodrama Child," a humorous fairy tale with an ingenious plot,
called "The Sixteenth Suitor," a serious poem called "In the Darkness a Light" which was published in Marquis's first book of
poems, *Dreams and Dust*, under the title "The God-Maker, Man,"
and "A Rhyme of the Roads," a travesty of the Songs of the Open
Road that had reached epidemic proportions in the early 1900s.

A few stanzas from "The Melodrama Child," which was published
as a full-page feature "in four acts" because of its timeliness in
1907 when two-thirds of the nation's "dramatic art" consisted of
melodramatic rantings:

> The Villain closer crawled, and stabbed
>   The Infant in the Back,
> While at the left the Midnight Train
>   Exploded on the track.
>
> His mother, and the Wicked Nurse
>   That stole The Child at Birth,
> Leaped from a Burning House nearby,
>   Expiring on the earth.
>
> The Scarlet-Robed Adventuress,
>   She seized him in her grasp,
> And, hissing out her hatred, wrenched
>   The Papers from his clasp.

"The Sixteenth Suitor," a hilarious fairy tale for children and
adults, appealed so strongly to Editor Harris that he ordered three
illustrations and asked Marquis to write more stories in the same
vein. This brief passage gives the flavor of the piece:

"The Prince of Morocco was a handsome man. And before proceeding it is just as well to settle this point once for all: there is no
one in this story who is not handsome."

Recalling his near-hobo days, Marquis decided he had as much right
as anyone to sing a Song o' the Open Road and to kid this whole
phenomenon with which so many poets were preoccupied that it
threatened to become a major industry.

Weren't these open-roaders too hermitlike? Marquis asked. In their
songs all they wanted for companions, like true ascetics, were the
sun and the sky and the moon and the stars and a road—any old
kind—under foot; or grass or wild flowers or weeds, if they de-

cided to travel cross-country. In his mind's eye he visualized two girls he knew as good hobohemians (a now familiar pun which Marquis seems to have originated in 1907) and after considering both—Lillian and Viola—decides to ask the latter, fearing the other might be "too intellectual" for such a test. Then he lets fly in a satiric ballad ("A Rhyme of the Roads") worthy of Charles Stuart Calverley.

Here are a few sample stanzas from this ballad, which is part of a lengthy lampoon called "The Tribulations of a Rhyme-Factory":

Pearl-slashed and purple and crimson, and fringed with gray mist of the
   hills
The pennons of morning advance to the music of rock-fretted rills;
The dumb forest quickens to song, and the little gusts shout as they fling
A floor-cloth of orchard-bloom down 'neath the violet-stained feet of
   young Spring.

To the road, gypsy-heart, thou and I! 'Tis that mad piper, Spring, who is
   leading,
'Tis the pulse of his piping that throbs through the brain with resistless,
   wild pleading;
Full-blossomed, deep-bosomed, fain woman, light-footed, lute-throated
   and fleet,
We have drunk of the wine of this wanderer's song, let us follow his feet!

Like ravelled red girdles flung down by some hoidenish goddess in mirth
The tangled roads reach from rim unto uttermost rim of the earth;
We shall weave of these far-scattered threads, thou and I, a sure snare for
   delight,
We shall make of these strands a sweet lute that will shame the low
   wind-harps of night. . . .

O woman, whose blood as my blood with the fire of the Spring is aflame,
We did well, when the red roads beckoned, that we laughed and we rose
   and we came. . . .

There are many clues to Marquis's likes and dislikes in literature in a department he conducted called "Under the Lamp with Books New and Old." This conventional standing head appeared over a decoration showing an ornate kerosene reading-lamp of the period, to the left of which was an inkwell in which reposed a long, full-feathered quill pen—a holdover, Marquis told Atlanta friends, from his days as a poultry plucker. These symbols were flanked by an assortment of books.

In this department Marquis, who was given plenty of space, wrote articles on books. Some of them were straight book reviews, others might be classified as literary essays. Since none of the latter have been collected, it seems fitting to quote from one of them by way of giving the reader the flavor of Marquis's work in this field. Almost any one of a score or more passages from these articles and reviews could be quoted as "typical" of the Marquis of 1907.

In an estimate of Rudyard Kipling's *Collected Verse*, published by Doubleday, Page and Company, he expressed the belief that there were "three poetical Kiplings." Here is an excerpt from that piece, in which he stated that "one of these poets is largely informed of the spirit, as well as very knowing in the ways of the world, the flesh and the devil, and the other two are not so morally awake.

"The first Kipling, who wrote *Departmental Ditties* and the first *Barrack-Room Ballads*, showed a deal of cleverness, much individuality, and some rather cheap cynicism. The third Kipling, author of some of the poems originally published in *The Five Nations*, was a master of the art of forceful statement in verse, but had looked so long and so hard at the British Empire that it had begun to seem to him the most important thing in the universe. In several of the poems in that volume, and included in the present collection, he shows himself so possessed of the imperial idea that all notions of right and justice in the larger sense are forgotten. It is the Kipling of this disappointing third period who has the effrontery to justify the British in kicking up a war with the Boers in order that the Islanders might steal the Dutchmen's country; and in Cecil Rhodes, who combined great intellect and vast capacity for hard work with the ethics of a pirate, this Kipling sees a demigod."

The piece is a long one, much too long to quote entire. What is here added is just enough to enable Marquis to round out the points he made in the foregoing: "But we would not judge Shakespeare by *Titus Andronicus*, nor Keats by the many lines in which he seems to whimper because the world is not made out of peppermint candy, nor Wordsworth by the intolerable dullness of many of his pages; and Kipling has a right to be considered at his best. It is the second Kipling who is the best as a poet; the author of much of the matter in *The Seven Seas* and of a small portion of that in *The Five Nations*; the Kipling who had not yet conceived himself to be a singing figurehead to the British ship of state, and who still possessed the ability to look at all men in a large and generous way."

Marquis was delighted with the word "blurb," which Gelett Burgess had coined shortly after the turn of the century. It was a felicitous invention, he thought, that in some mysterious way transmitted precisely the shade of meaning it was meant to convey.

During its first year of publication, *Uncle Remus's Magazine* carried a short article called "About Blurbs." It asserted that Mr. Burgess had performed a public service in creating this new word because of the need for an easy designation of the extravagant claims of publishers. The author of "About Blurbs" then went on to write a blurb about *Uncle Remus's Magazine*, pointing out its many distinctive features. The final paragraph called attention, as follows, to the publication's editorials:

"*A Glance in Passing*, by Don Marquis, the associate editor, is worth more than a passing glance. The department is as full of ideas as a porcupine is of quills."

The author of that piece was Don Marquis, who didn't believe in passing up an opportunity to have some fun.

The article Marquis wrote for *Uncle Remus's Magazine* that was most widely quoted in Georgia and other Southern states was one that dealt with "Billville," an Arcadia that Frank Stanton had invented for the purposes of his widely read column in the Atlanta *Constitution*. In those days practically everyone in Georgia knew about Billville. And it was almost as well known in other Southern states. This had been accomplished through the combination of Stanton's column, his books, his lectures, and publicity in the many Southern newspapers that regularly quoted Stanton, especially when he wrote about the bizarre doings of the wild bards of Billville.

When Marquis called on Stanton for an interview, he told his friend that he had always wanted to go to Billville. "Where is it?" he asked.

Stanton replied that he had no intention of sharing his secret with anyone. Marquis quotes him as saying, "I see myself letting you go there! First thing I know someone will be sneaking a railroad through Billville if I start letting outsiders in." He argued that that would stimulate an influx of tourists who would frighten away the inhabitants, all of them poets.

Stanton suggested that if Marquis wanted an article on Billville he'd have "to figure one out for himself."

Here are some passages from what Marquis "figured out":

Billville lies in a pleasant, wooded valley, which is traversed by tinkling streams, among the mountains of South Georgia. The fact that there are no mountains in South Georgia has nothing to do with the case, and is nobody's business anyhow. Billville *has* to be in South Georgia, very near the Florida line, because that is the only part of Georgia that is warm all the year 'round; and Billville is warm all the year 'round. And Billville has to be among the mountains, because the kind of streams that amble rhythmically through its environs could only have picked up their pure lyric gift in the clear air above the snow line. So Billville is in a musical, sequestered vale among the mountains of South Georgia. It is not to be found on the map. . . .

The Billvillagers, or shall we not say simply, The Bills?—The Bills, then, are a folk who have never got over what the Billville *Banner* would call "their primevalness." They are all poets. They sing all the time. They sing at their play. They would sing at their tasks, if they had any. But there are no tasks in Billville. There is no reason why anyone should work there. It is so warm that you may sleep outdoors all the time. Not many clothes are required. Food may be plucked ripe from almost any tree or bush. Some Bills lie in the shade and allow the songbirds in the trees above to shake down the ripe fruits into their open mouths. Possums are so accommodating that they come up to be killed and cooked, and a certain Billville genius, who aspires to do for the animal kingdom what Luther Burbank is doing for the vegetable kingdom, is trying to breed possums that will kill and cook themselves. The Bills are not lazy, but there is really no necessity for them to engage in what the world calls work. . . .

They are a timid folk. If a stranger strays "into their midst," as the Billville *Banner* would say, they take to the trees and the rocks, and may only be coaxed out when they are reassured as to his intentions. Few of them have any desire to wander beyond the limits of their valley. And it is well for them that they do not.

For, alas, even Billville is not altogether song and pleasant shadow and pleasanter sunshine. Never was there a sheaf of joy that wasn't tied about with a cord of sorrow. These brothers and sisters of the clouds, and kinsmen of the trees and streams, are too frequently made the victim of a community of sordid Humans who live just across the mountains from them. These Humans, when they run short of farm labor, or want hands for the cotton mills, organize hunting expeditions, raid the valley, and capture all the poets who do not succeed in scampering to safety. In some parts of Georgia it is no uncommon sight to see a ragged-eared mule and a captured poet yoked to the same plow.

Marquis added this comment at the end of the article:

Stanton did not tell me so, but I suspect that he himself was a Bill. He was stolen away and shut up in a newspaper office. Only he has not forgotten, as most of the captured Bills have, the music of that vale among the mountains. The mockingbirds of Billville sing to him still, and the creeks of Billville chirp and chuckle through his verse.

One day a girl called at the office of the Sunny South Publishing Company at 20 South Forsyth Street, Atlanta. This was the name of the company that published *Uncle Remus's Magazine*. The girl was a young writer named Reina Melcher, who said she wanted to meet one of the editors. She had just sold a story to the magazine and wanted to get some advice about future contributions. She was taken in to see Marquis.

Marquis remembered the name. He had read a story by a Miss Melcher, had liked and recommended it, and it had been bought.

Miss Melcher was blonde, slender, of average height, attractive. She was a poised, affable conversationalist and Marquis enjoyed meeting her. She told him how happy the acceptance of her story had made her. She wondered how soon she could submit another. Should she wait until after the first one had been published?

Marquis urged her to submit a second story whenever she had one that she considered good enough, adding with a smile that he had a secret notion that the real reason she had called was to look around and see what the headquarters of the new magazine and the inmates looked like. Miss Melcher insisted she had *not* called out of curiosity, that her purpose had been serious. Nevertheless Marquis continued to tease her (according to friends to whom he told the story years later). Would she like to meet Mr. Humphrey, treasurer of the company, or Mr. Meyer, the cashier? As a writer he had always found it profitable to know the men who handled the money.

Miss Melcher laughed and said she would forego that privilege. But she did have another question and she asked it: "What about poetry?" Would she be overdoing if she submitted poetry as well as short stories?

Marquis claims he laughed "sardonically" at this point and announced that he regarded all poets as his rivals. He planned to unload so much poetry of his own on Editor Joel Chandler Harris that there would not be space for the work of anyone else. It was his avowed intention "to discourage the whole kit and caboodle of Georgia poets."

He had been named Poetry Editor, he told her "meaningfully."

This was the one type of material he had authority to purchase without consulting anyone else. He planned to push this advantage for all it was worth, and God help any poet who thought his or her stuff was better than Marquis's!

Having said which, he informed his visitor that the Poetry Editor would be glad to pass on anything she cared to submit as long as she realized that she would have to be as good as Keats or Shelley at their best, or at least Elizabeth Barrett Browning, if she expected to sell anything. He considered himself qualified to produce all the *average* poetry the magazine could use. From *others* he was in the market only for masterpieces.

Falling in with the spirit of the thing, Miss Melcher said she "happened to have a poem with her." But she was afraid it wasn't a masterpiece. Would the Poetry Editor care to read it?

Marquis said he'd just remembered something that necessitated his shifting his position. He and Editor Harris had agreed that editorially the magazine should take an antimonopoly position. They were supporting Theodore Roosevelt in his trust-busting campaign and it could damage *Uncle Remus's Magazine* if it became known that he, Marquis, was the head of a poetry trust that was stifling the competition of other bards.

Whereupon Marquis read Miss Melcher's poem, pronounced it good, and announced he would buy it.

And that was the Beginning of a Beautiful Friendship. It was a hot day and Associate Editor Marquis invited Miss Melcher to join him in an ice-cream soda. She accepted.

From Homer Croy and others I have heard the story of that ice-cream soda and the other details of that first meeting with the girl Don Marquis subsequently married, as handed down from Marquis's own account. It was while he sat and chatted with Miss Melcher in what was known in those days as an "ice-cream parlor" that Don decided that he wanted to see more of this girl.

In time he grew accustomed to, and had appropriate replies for, the inevitable hecklers who observed that it saddened them to think of Their Hero drinking ice-cream sodas—a man who, in the best tradition of poesy, had seemed more at home invoking the muse at the Aragon Bar in the company of such kindred spirits as Rice and Stanton and Bayne. It seemed all out of focus. Years later, on hearing the tale, Rollin Kirby, distinguished New York *World* political cartoonist and close friend of Marquis, said he couldn't connect a soda fountain with poetry and he couldn't visualize "a man of Don's character in so unwholesome an environment."

"What women won't do to men!" he was heard to exclaim. "Can you imagine Don downing so depraved a drink?—or Frank Stanton saying to a soda jerker, 'I will pen thee a poem for a strawberry soda'? Ugh!"

It wasn't long before Reina Melcher and Don Marquis were good friends. She called him Tommy and he called her Queenie, a free translation of Reina.

Reina wasn't sure how or why she came to call her favorite editor Tommy. She offered no explanation beyond a spontaneous hunch she'd had that this name suited him. That is, she could think of him only as Tommy—from *her* point of view it was the right name for him. Others could go on calling him Don. That name had the right ring when his old friends used it. Just as Tommy had the right ring when *she* addressed him. Marquis described it as "one of those things." And once accused Reina of rechristening him in deference to the tommyrot he wrote for a living.

After that first meeting Don and Reina—i.e., Tommy and Queenie —spent a good deal of time together. Once they chatted until dawn. Marquis, telling the story, said that, as usual, they started by discussing poetry, then ranged far and wide until they'd covered the whole realm of conversational possibilities, "from peach ice cream to speculation about the hereafter."

In time the pair became inseparable. They were seen together constantly and there were reports that they were engaged to be married.

Before *Uncle Remus's Magazine* had been started Reina had sold stories to women's magazines and now, as a regular contributor to the new publication, she was encouraged to write the kind of fiction that had feminine appeal and would help Joel Harris's magazine acquire women readers.

Marquis thought Reina Melcher was at her best in fiction about teen-agers. He thought her best short story was one called "The Kiss Denied." It describes the problem of Christopher, a twelve-year-old boy who has never kissed a girl. He finally decides to make the plunge, selecting a little girl named Sylvia as the one he would like to kiss. Not knowing how to go about it, he consults his dad, as follows:

"Father, did you ever kiss a girl?"

This question, and the situation that developed from it, appealed greatly to Marquis. He liked Reina's treatment of the father, who chose to ignore the phony "indignation and blushes" of his wife, "a typical turn-of-the-century blusher and fainter," when the boy propounded his question. Marquis thought too many parents were overstrict about "the minor proprieties" and in the process sometimes stifled the spontaneity of their offspring—a subject on which he had editorialized.

One day when Don and Reina were having an ice-cream soda Don said he had bad news for her. When her last story came in it occurred to him that perhaps now that they were such good friends it was no longer ethical for him to pass on her work. He had told Editor Harris and Managing Editor Camp that for personal reasons he preferred not to read this particular story. Then, after they had read it, they had rejected it.

Reina (i.e., Queenie) reminded Don (i.e., Tommy) that she had sold a story to the magazine before she had met him. She thought he was being rather stuffy.

Marquis said he resented this. He was merely being honorable. When you no longer can be objective . . .

He began to laugh, unable to push his joke any further. Then he told her the truth: he had read and liked the story, had urged its publication and it had been accepted that very morning. Queenie said she couldn't decide whether to throw her soda at him or to give him a big kiss. She decided on the latter. Marquis claimed that the startled soda-fountain attendant nearly dropped a brace of sodas he was about to serve.

Of the poems Reina Melcher contributed to *Uncle Remus's Magazine* Don's favorite was one called "The House of Darkness," one of her earliest, whose theme is similar to Walter de la Mare's "The Listeners." Though well below that classical challenge to the terrors of the unknown, it creates a mood of its own, one of somber brooding, that appealed to the young editor.

It would be interesting to know whether Reina had been influenced by De la Mare's piece before she wrote hers. The only possible clue is a tenuous one, the dramatic use of the word "smote" in both poems.

Both pieces deal with a lone mysterious figure visiting a long-uninhabited house in the dead of night. In the De la Mare piece the

visitor, the reader will recall, knocks but does not enter; in the
Melcher poem we see the visitor moving along cautiously inside the
House of Darkness:

> Along the corridor I passed,
> And onward up the winding stair;
> Was that a footstep, light and fast?
> Or rush of wings that smote the air?

It is possible that Miss Melcher's poem was written before De
la Mare's and that this is one of those strange literary coincidences.

In 1908, less than two years after *Uncle Remus's Magazine* had
been started, Joel Chandler Harris died. Marquis was retained by
the new management but, with the passing of his friend and mentor,
he began to lose interest. What was once an adventure now became
just another job.

Uncle Remus's Magazine had gotten off to a flying start. It was
attracting important writers and its articles and editorials were being
widely quoted in the press. At the time of Harris's death it had
reached a circulation in excess of 200,000—unusual for a sectional
publication—and was growing rapidly. It had lived up to its promise
to keep its advertising columns clean. Advertising revenue was
showing encouraging growth and the publication was developing
prestige and seemed marked for success.

The death of Harris changed everything. *Uncle Remus's Magazine,*
while it was not a one-man show, was, after all, a regional publication—a Southern magazine whose original acceptance stemmed from
the fact that it had been launched by one of the great figures of the
South. When it was announced that he was starting a magazine,
thousands of people subscribed because the name of the founder was
considered a guarantee of a good product.

The passing of the founder did not mean the end of the property.
It continued for several years and fared reasonably well; but it was
inevitable that, in time, without the magic presence of Joel Chandler
Harris, it should become just another magazine.

Marquis wrote a tribute to his former boss (known to intimates
as "the Farmer of the Snap-Bean Farm") for *Uncle Remus's Magazine*. It was warmly received by the "farmer's" son, Julian La Rose
Harris, his wife, Julia Collier Harris (the "farmer's" biographer),
other members of the family, and close friends, who were unanimous
in their belief that Marquis had "caught the real Joel Chandler

Harris." Julia Harris called my attention to the following excerpt from that tribute, which she uses as a chapter head in her book, *Joel Chandler Harris, Editor and Essayist:*

The Farmer of the Snap-Bean Farm liked to take his whimsical fling at some aspects of modern science when occasion offered and he could never accept the rather sweeping conclusions of certain of its prophets. And yet he had one habit of mind in common with the most thoughtful men of science of his day, and had it in a degree not known to these men themselves: nothing appeared to him to be simply dead matter; his universe was all made of one stuff, and very much alive. It was a habit of mind, and more than a habit of mind; it was not so merely an intellectual trait as the essence of his personality—it was the feeling about which his whole nature was organized. This sense of the basic kinship of all the things which exist is very familiar in all his writings, it is the quality which makes his "creeturs" half human, sympathetic, understandable characters, instead of merely caricatures of animals or stories about animals; it underlay all his serious philosophy, and it put him in possession of all those delightful secrets about Brother Wind and Neighbor Tree. A child would not be so greatly astonished if a bush spoke to him; most of us lose what little wisdom we had as we grow older and duller; the Farmer kept on listening to the real world, and his wisdom gained in subtlety and grew.

Marquis frequently pointed out that Joel Chandler Harris was a great newspaperman before he achieved fame as the author of the Uncle Remus stories, that his widely quoted editorials and articles in the Atlanta *Constitution* and other publications were of salutary help during the long and difficult period of readjustment between the North and the South. Here is part of the Harris credo:

"An editor must have a purpose. He must have in view some goal beyond the mere expression of opinion or the publication of a newspaper. . . . I shudder when I think of the opportunities the editors in Georgia are allowing to slip by. It grieves me to see them harping steadily upon the same old prejudices and moving in the worn ruts of a period that was soul-destroying in its narrowness. . . . There never was a time when an editor with a purpose could accomplish more for his state and his country than just at present. What a legacy for one's conscience to know that one has been instrumental in mowing down the old prejudices that rattle in the wind like weeds."

On June 8, 1909, "the ice-cream-soda romance," as Marquis sometimes called it, culminated in marriage. Don and Reina were wed in Atlanta, and, not having enough money to furnish a home, took up residence in a local boarding house.

Marquis became more and more restive. *Uncle Remus's Magazine* was losing its character and what was once a stimulating job had become a dull grind. He began thinking of trying his luck in New York. He talked things over with Reina, who felt even more strongly than he that this was the next move. He showed some hesitancy at first because he didn't consider it fair or practical to ask his wife to leave Atlanta until he'd landed a job. She solved that problem by suggesting that he make the trip to New York alone and send for her when he had achieved that objective. Neither wanted to be separated from the other but they agreed this was a good time to keep expenses down. A few weeks before there had been a sudden decision on the part of *Uncle Remus's Magazine* to change his status to "half-time editor at half pay."

"I couldn't make out whether I was being fired or not," he wrote long afterward, "so I said 'Oh, hell!' and went away from there."

Ambitiously Marquis hoped to sell some New York editor the idea of letting him run a daily column. But he was a realist and planned to take the first job that promised a livelihood.

Here is Marquis's own account of how he got started in New York, as told by him nineteen years later in the *Saturday Evening Post*:

"When I got to New York I had $7.50 cash and my wife was ill in a hospital in Atlanta. To make the picture complete, I stepped out of the ferry station into a blizzard—it was Thanksgiving Day, 1909—and the blizzard cuddled up against my chest, which had grown used to the mild Georgia winters and turned itself into the prettiest case of flu you could imagine. I was in no financial condition to indulge myself in the flu, and so I hunted up the only man I knew in New York and told him that the first thing I wanted was an awful lot of whisky, and the second was a job. I explained that it would have to be his money which we spent for the whisky, as I only had enough to buy the quinine. He was the kind of bird who never cared whose money it was; so I put in my first two days in New York curing my flu, and we really cured it. At the end of that time he said that during those two days I had got a job, and I asked him: 'Where?'

"'On the *Herald*,' he said. He worked on the *Herald* himself, and it seemed plausible, so I sent a wire to my wife in Atlanta to cheer up, everything was all right, I'd landed a job at once, and would very soon have that daily column of my own.

"When we got to the *Herald* that afternoon nobody knew anything about my having a job there, and not only that, but they told my friend he didn't have any job there himself any longer. It seems he had devoted himself to curing my flu too assiduously to please his employers, neglecting his reportorial work in this human-itarian task. Then I went to all the other papers in New York to find out just where this job was that he was so sure I had, but all the editors pretended that they'd never heard anything about it. The Sunday editor of the *Tribune* said, however, that he would pay me five dollars a column for stuff for a certain section of his paper. I went to work at once, without looking at the columns in that section.

"I worked continuously for four days, and then he showed me proofs of what I had written. Those columns were wider than any other two newspaper columns I ever saw. The matter was set in five-point type, without leads. I believe you could have dropped the canonical gospels into one of those columns and still have had room for the *Apocrypha* and the *Lives of the Saints*. I was appalled. My four days' work at five dollars a column came to twelve dollars. 'I came to New York looking for a column,' I told the Sunday editor, 'but I don't think this is the column I was looking for.'

" 'I don't understand you,' he said.

" 'Give me the twelve dollars,' I said, 'and let me go away from here. I could work twenty hours a day on this job and still starve to death. I consider that it would be far more decent and self-respecting to jump in the river at once, while I still have bulk, rather than to wait until I get so thin I won't even make a splash. My intention in coming to New York was to make a splash of some sort.'

" 'Lots of people,' he said, 'make their living off these columns.'

" 'They must all be little people, with subnormal appetites,' I said. And I went and stood in the Nassau Street slush and thought it over. It dawned upon me then for the first time that I was starting in life all over again; that no matter what I'd been, done or written in other towns was of no particular interest to New York. I perceived the essential justice of this. New York hadn't invited my presence. I was attempting to force myself upon it and it wasn't interested. But if I could get it interested, I saw, the interest might amount to something. Interest and amuse Atlanta and other such towns, and you get friends and praise. Interest and amuse New York, and you get friends, praise and money. The cynics on the one hand, and the idealists on the other, may say what they like about money, but it has been my experience that it is a pretty good thing to have a little of it kicking around now and then. I began to like New York on account of what I intended it should do for me later.

"So I went and sent my wife a wire that New York was fine, and she had better pawn everything that I hadn't pawned in order to pay my railroad fare up here, and come on as soon as she got out of the hospital. I sent the wire from a telegraph office in the old Tribune Building at the corner of Nassau and Spruce streets, and went out and stood in the slush again.

"Diagonally across from me I perceived a building that interested me. It was wedge-shaped, situated in the triangle where Nassau Street and Park Row converge. There were swing-doors on the Nassau Street side, and high stained-glass windows. I went around to the Park Row side. There were swinging doors there too. A confused and jolly sound floated out into the foggy air. Something told me, instinctively, that within this particular barroom I would find newspapermen. I am psychic at times. It was just the kind of barroom where there would be newspapermen. I don't know how I knew, but I knew. At that time, New York was a great newspaper town. The *Globe*, the *Mail*, the *Post*, the *Press*, the *Sun*, the *Evening Sun*, the *American*, the *Journal*, the *Tribune*, the *World* were all down in that neighborhood, within a few blocks of one another, to say nothing of various press associations. I went in, and at a glance saw that there were at least fifteen newspapermen present. Again I say, don't ask me how I knew what they were; I just knew.

"This was Lipton's. It had two or three other names, and it had been long since anyone named Lipton had been connected with it, but the old-timers never called it anything but Lipton's. Not to have known Lipton's in the old days is never to have been a New York newspaperman. I cannot think of it yet without sighs of regret and twinges of conscience. Lipton's was the training camp in which a good many battlers left their fight; I very nearly left mine there in one of the high-backed booths under the stained-glass windows. But it is so intimately connected in my mind with my search for a column of my own in New York, and my first five or six years after I got one, that I couldn't leave it out of this exceedingly personal—perhaps too personal—narrative. Lipton's was not merely an eating and drinking place. It was a tavern, and more than a tavern; it was a club, and more than a club. It was an institution. Perhaps the Mermaid Tavern in Ben Jonson's day had more and better poets in it, more famous wits and more subtle philosophers, but there are a few of us left who would tell Ben to his face that it never had any better fellows or as much fun. There is a soda fountain there now, and—but I mustn't get bitter.

"Let the grouches say what they will. New York is a friendly place to struggling strangers, if they will only take its careless Brobdingnagian cuffs and unconscious kicks as cheerfully as they can, laugh when they get a sock in the eye, and realize there's nothing personal about it all; that the grotesque, half-human monster is just frolicking. And it was in Lipton's, that first afternoon that my instinct led me into it, that I began to realize how helpful, friendly, comradely and kind the best type of New York newspaperman could be to the stranger struggling for a foothold. Within an hour, in Lipton's I met two old newspaper friends who I hadn't known were in New York—Sam Small, Jr., whom I had worked with in Washington, and Wilson Burke, whom I had known in Atlanta—and within another hour I knew ten more newspapermen, and they were all eager and willing to put me wise to the game in New York—counsel which I badly needed. . . .

"The first afternoon that my feet led me into Lipton's made me at home in New York, but it didn't get me a column or end my struggles in New York, by any means. It got me, through Wilson Burke, a job as reporter with a news service, which I didn't like, because I naturally couldn't have a signature and write what I pleased, and wasn't what I came to New York for, at all. So I went away from there.

"Sam Small got me a job on the New York *American*. For a few brief weeks I deluded myself with the belief that now that signed column of my own was really on the way. For, in addition to my regular work, which was that of rewrite man, the *American* bought from me and printed a good deal of stuff which was essentially column stuff, which they paid me very well for and played up with my signature on the back page. I began to be a little known in New York. I was making pretty good money—for me—what with my salary and this extra stuff. I sent for my wife and we began to keep

house. I was doing the kind of work I wanted to do; I was getting a
pat on the back almost daily from some of the important people
on the paper; I thought I was one of the fair-haired boys in that shop.

"From this rosy dream I awoke with a jolt, and when I came
to I was in the slush and mud of a New York March, without a
job. I had been fired, just like that! I never ask why I have been
fired; when I get fired I just go away from there and let it go at that.
The result is always, for the moment, so much more immediately
interesting to me than the cause.

"The result was, in this case, that my wife and I went on a
starvation diet for about three months. I wish people, when they
fire me, would pick out a time to do it when I have a little money.
But every time I have ever been fired I have been broke at the time.
I once had a bit of money in the bank, which had accrued from a
play, and I tried my darndest to get fired, for I had the thought that
it would be a good idea not to do any work at all until it was spent.
But I just simply couldn't get fired that time, and I was on a contract
and couldn't quit. Not being able to spend the money for anything
valuable and reasonable like diversion, I wasted the entire sum by
putting it into real estate.

"When the *American* fired me I'd been using most of the money
to pay up some debts. My wife sold a story and we lived on that for
a while. I couldn't sell anything; I couldn't get a job anywhere. We
ate so many beef stews during that period that it was two years
before I could look one in the face again. And toward the end of
the period the beef stews got more watery and less beefy. We got
hold of $2.35. I don't remember how; maybe I borrowed it some-
where. I sent out three wires for jobs, one to Boston, one to
Washington, and one to Cincinnati.

"It took a good deal of money. But within twenty-four hours I
got answers and all three of the jobs. They would send money for
railroad fare.

" 'I don't like leaving New York,' I said.

" 'If we leave this way we're defeated,' said my wife.

" 'Licked,' I rejoined, 'to a frazzle. And licked for the rest of my
life, so far as the big time is concerned. I came here to make good,
and I haven't done it. If I'm licked here, I'll be licked everywhere.
At the same time, we've got less than a dollar now; we owe a month's
rent; we've got no credit; and we don't know anybody we can borrow

from; we haven't got the stuff we pawned out of hock yet; nobody wants what I write; our food hasn't been all that heart might wish lately, in the way of quantity or variety—in short, I think maybe we'd better be licked than starved.'

"'I think we'd better stay in New York,' said my wife, with a gentle decisiveness which was characteristic of her. I never had any backbone of my own; at times when I've acted as if I might have, it has been due to someone else in the background whose opinion I valued. I started for the *Herald* office and on the way there I thought up an idea for a serial feature for the Sunday editor.

"He liked it and he wanted four installments of five thousand words each—twenty thousand words in all—for which he would pay me two hundred dollars on delivery if the stuff held up to the idea. But he wanted to syndicate it and to get it illustrated before he sent it out, and could I have it in his hands by Monday noon, so he could start his art department right to work on it? This was on a Saturday afternoon, but, like a fool, I promised. I thought if he didn't get it then, he wouldn't take it.

"I sat down Sunday morning to knock out the twenty thousand words, and I wrote all day. It was specifically understood that it was to be funny stuff. Gay, you know. Humorous; light, easy reading. I worked all day Sunday and all night Sunday night, and about six o'clock Monday morning I collapsed across my typewriter in a kind of stupor, variegated with delirium; for in my mind I was still writing that story, although everything else about me had quit. My wife, who was the gamest person that ever lived, man or woman—and women are usually gamer than men when it comes down to brass tacks—got the janitor up and they lifted me into bed.

"Then she sat down at the typewriter and wrote the last three thousand words of the story herself. I had talked it over with her. I can't tell to this day where my work stops on that stuff and hers begins. She took it to the *Herald* office and came back with a check. It was afternoon before I came out of whatever darned thing I was in, and the first thing I did was make for the typewriter. I didn't know how long I'd been out, nor how she'd been working over me.

"'I finished the story and delivered it,' said my wife.

"'Did you keep it gay—the way he wanted it?' I asked her quite seriously.

"'Yes, it's gay right to the end,' she said; and she broke down a minute for one of the only half dozen times I ever saw her cry in the fourteen years we were married; and then we went down to the old Brevoort and had a swell dinner, and I worked my way outside of a bottle of sparkling Burgundy."

6

Broke in Brooklyn—"Reveries of a Bigamist"—"Don Marquis, the New Humorist"— Memories of the "Night-Rider" Excesses and of Riding the Rods—A Successful Column on the Evening Sun—Dreams and Dust, a Jinxed Book

Don and Reina took up residence in Brooklyn and lived there for a total of about seven years, though not continuously. Their first address was 151 Joralemon Street, where they occupied a small cold-water flat. They subsequently moved to 15 Clark Street, then to 64 Clark Street. Their last Brooklyn address was 129 Columbia Heights, their favorite neighborhood in the borough.

The year they took up residence in Brooklyn—1909—was the year Louis Blériot, inventor of the monoplane, made the first flight across the English Channel; and the year Robert Peary reached the North Pole. It was also the year Brooklyn abandoned its horse-drawn streetcars and began expanding its electrically powered car lines.

The cars were featured by overhead trolleys that made contact with live wires, and as more and more of these conveyances swung down the streets of Brooklyn, the local citizenry came to be known as trolley dodgers. Eventually this was shortened to "dodgers," and, as most New Yorkers are aware, that is how the Brooklyn Dodgers, the baseball team that for years represented the Borough of Brooklyn in the National League, acquired its name.

Don and Reina found the Brooklyn trolleys a great convenience and in later years enjoyed spoofing friends who lived in the supposedly more progressive Borough of Manhattan, where horse-drawn streetcars continued in operation for several years after Brooklyn had abandoned them. In their early days in the metropolitan area they took rides in these horse-drawn cars for the fun of it. There was one line that wove in and out of Canal Street and another on 28th Street that made the crosstown run, and they made trips on both. Don, though he joked about the horse-drawn streetcars, considered them one of New York's most charming phenomena, a last brave stand against the encroachment of the Machine Age. When their little flat on Joralemon Street gave them claustrophobia, they headed for what Marquis called the Wide Open Spaces of Prospect Park. When the weather permitted, Marquis wrote years later, they sat on a park bench and held hands and watched the children and squirrels cavort, discussed poetry (a subject of which the two poets never wearied), some new and exhilarating discovery about New York, how they planned to make their first million—not neglecting such short-range planning as ways and means of paying the rent on time that particular month.

One of Marquis's enthusiasms of that period is reflected in this passage from "The Almost Perfect State," a book he wrote several years later:

"I used sometimes to walk over the Brooklyn Bridge—that song in stone and steel of an engineer who was also a great artist—at dusk, when the tides of shadow flood in from the lower bay to break in a surf of glory and mystery and illusion against the tall towers of Manhattan. Seen from the middle arch of the bridge at twilight, New York with its girdle of shifting waters and its drift of purple cloud and its quick pulsations of unstable light is a miracle of splendor and beauty that lifts up the heart like the laughter of a god . . .

"But, descend. Go down into the city. Mingle with the details. The damned, dirty old shed from which the 'L' trains and trolleys pull out with their jammed and mangled thousands for flattest Flatbush and the unknown bourne of ulterior Brooklyn is still the same damned, dirty old shed. On a hot, damp night the pasty streets stink like a paperhanger's overalls."

It will be recalled that Reina had developed the knack of writing a type of fiction that had proved popular with the women readers of *Uncle Remus's Magazine* and she continued to contribute to that publication for three years after she had left Atlanta for New York, using the signature Reina Melcher Marquis and one other. (Her last contribution was a short story called "The Girl-Boy," published in the April 1912 issue. Marquis also sold the publication founded by Joel Chandler Harris, which went through a few changes in ownership, short stories and poems after he had moved to New York.) Occasionally Reina also sold an article or a short story to a newspaper syndicate, a Sunday magazine section, or one of the general magazines.

In Marquis's summary of his early jobs in New York he mentioned working on the New York *American* as rewrite man. One of his jobs was whipping into shape the copy of a man said to have exceptional sources of information on crime stories—Captain Herbert Rivet-Carnac. He was not a reporter but had been recommended to the paper as a man whose contacts enabled him to get stories not otherwise procurable.

Marquis considered Rivet-Carnac a latter-day Munchausen but had instructions to write these stories from the notes and supplementary comments of this "source" and he did, occasionally adding tongue-in-cheek embellishments of his own. One of Rivet-Carnac's "scoops" was an exposé of a counterfeiting ring. He told the story so forcefully and indignantly it sounded convincing to Marquis until he started asking questions. Rivet-Carnac even produced a counterfeit ten-dollar bill as a sample of the work of these malefactors. A man with a lively imagination, it developed that he had invented the story about the counterfeiters when someone had stuck him with the phony tenner.

A born swashbuckler, Rivet-Carnac lent color to his fabrications by inventing hand-to-hand encounters with the soulless wretches he was trying to bring to justice, though it was not quite clear after reading the resulting copy just who they were. There was something about this master of the whopper that appealed to Marquis—for one thing, he is said to have had an engaging personality—and, sometime after this "source" took to his heels, Don is reported to have sent him financial aid in answer to an urgent appeal.

Some of Marquis's friends thought that Captain Herbert Rivet-Carnac was the inspiration for Captain Peter Fitzurse, one of the most successful of the characters he subsequently created in "The Sun Dial," his famous column in the New York *Sun*. Fitzurse, a swaggerer in the grand manner, was wont to reminisce with relish about the days when he fought on both sides in the Civil War. When the Union cause bored him he switched to the Confederacy, and vice versa, in the best tradition of professional swashbucklery which demanded, at whatever the price, that a man keep up his interest in Life. When in the early 1920s, at the age of ninety-two or thereabouts, Fitzurse accompanied Marquis to Paris, he lost no time hatching a plot to overthrow the Republic and restore the French monarchy.

Like Captain Rivet-Carnac, Captain Fitzurse affected a sword-cane, and both men told thrillers about escapes from certain doom made possible by expertness in the use of this little-known weapon.

In Marquis's own account, quoted earlier, of his newspaper jobs in the metropolitan area, he neglected to mention the days when he was a reporter and rewrite man for the Brooklyn *Daily Eagle*, his last job before joining the *Sun*. Katherine Glover, whom he knew in Atlanta when they both had newspaper jobs there, recalls Marquis's days on the *Eagle*, as do H. V. Kaltenborn and other friends. In the columns of that no longer published newspaper there are to be found prideful references to the success of their former employee, one of which proclaims that he was known to his associates as a "mighty good reporter, the acme of praise among working news-paper people."

Until he landed his job on the *Sun*, Marquis made a practice of taking part-time jobs to supplement his income. For instance, when he worked for the *Eagle* he was retained by the Civil War Veterans of the 14th Regiment "to compile and write a history of that regiment, the bulk of which was devoted to the regiment's three years of service in the Civil War." The title page reads: "1861 to 1911—The History of the Fighting Fourteenth, Published in Commemora-tion of the Fiftieth Anniversary of the Muster of the Regiment into the United States Service, May 23, 1861."

Marquis was philosophic about the hack work he had to do to supplement his income. As he often pointed out, he would have preferred to use his spare time writing "the great American some-thing or other," but most writers had to piece out an existence as best they could.

A study of the record shows that Marquis undertook several strange spare-time assignments, a few of them for the New York

Herald. One of these, which seems worth telling as part of the story of his early struggles, he considered the most bizarre rewrite job of his career.

The *Herald* had come into possession of a crudely written manuscript allegedly dealing with the long-term incarceration of a notorious polygamist of the 1900s whose term was about to expire. Marquis was retained to write this man's reminiscences for serialization in the New York *Herald* as a Sunday feature.

The series was published under the title "Reveries of a Bigamist" and is full of examples of Marquisian tongue-in-cheek writing.

Each installment was accompanied by a "box" featuring some of the alleged "sayings" of this wholesaler in matrimony under the heading, "Vagaries of a Polygamous Philosopher."

The following is a condensed version of the announcement in the *Herald* that appeared as a foreword the day the series was launched:

"The author of these random reflections will be released from a certain penitentiary in about eight months. He refers to himself as a bigamist. . . . But the fellow has not merely had two wives simultaneously; it was brought out at his trial that he had married no less than thirteen in twenty years.

"It has often been noted by the learned critics of life and letters that some of the most despicable characters have their mouths full of the noblest sentiments. . . .

"The jailbird author is not only a villain, but a cad, since he kisses and tells. . . ."

When Marquis's fundamentally philosophic nature helped him accept the fact that writing the "autobiography" of a fraud was all in the day's work he began enjoying himself and even gave an occasional reading from the confessions of the master of polygamy in a saloon near his home where Brooklyn newspapermen sometimes congregated and where he claimed he could get the biggest schooner of beer in New York for a nickel. One of his favorite passages was:

"I have been called a monster. But I am not. No bigamist is. Nor yet a woman hater. The man who marries just once proves only his ignorance of women. The man who marries many times proves, in spite of his disillusionments, his faith in women. . . ."

It seems that this poor misunderstood creature had his feelings trampled when, as a mere youth of nineteen, he was trapped into marriage by a scheming woman of twenty-six. This gave him the wrong impression of women, embittered him, and eventually led to a determination to "get back at the whole sex this designing creature represented."

After the publication of the first installment, Marquis wrote a letter to the editor of the *Herald*, to which he signed a fictitious name, congratulating the paper on coming to grips with so vital a subject. He quoted the following, which he attributed to "anon.," as "too frivolous an approach to a serious question," and not nearly as effective as "The Herald's hard-hitting approach":

> A practice that's harmless is digamy,
> I'm not quite so sure about bigamy,
> > Which folks who are nice
> > Insist is a vice,
> And they say the same thing of polygamy.

In quoting the foregoing Marquis could not very well credit the author, and found "anon." a convenient device, since he had written it himself. Marquis was never happier than when carrying out a silly assignment, and making fun of it at the same time. He'd have preferred a better assignment, to be sure, but he was stuck with it, and he'd see it through and get a few inner laughs out of it. As a young man, that was Marquis's way.

After the publication of installment two, Marquis sent another letter to the editor of the *Herald*. He summed up his sentiments in these four lines and signed a woman's name:

> Oh, do not judge the man too harsh,
> > He has the human touch
> And cannot help it if he loves
> > We girls so very much.

On and on these confessions go, the "author" marrying a new wife whenever the spirit moved him, without bothering to have himself divorced from any of her predecessors. By this time Don Marquis, himself indignant over these affronts to American womanhood, wrote another letter to the editor in which he expressed these sentiments:

> You cannot trust a bigamist,
> > He causes naught but strife,—
> You turn your back and, lo! the scamp
> > Has grabbed another wife.

One can readily credit Marquis's statement that once he warmed up to this task it provided a lot of fun both for him and Reina, with whom he talked it over and who contributed a number of suggestions.

Earlier in this discussion of the imprisoned Lothario it was mentioned that he fancied himself as a coiner of philosophic aphorisms about love, women, marriage, and whatnot, and that each installment was accompanied by a box—a rather deep one, two columns wide—in which over a hundred of these sayings appeared during the life of the feature.

How Don Marquis handled this phase of his curious assignment, these "sayings and observations" reveal:

"The inconstancy of woman"—that is the most convenient phrase ever invented by man, for it condones in advance all his meditated indiscretions.

I have often been asked my opinion on female suffrage. . . . I can only present a poll in the nature of a straw ballot. Of my thirteen wives, seven I considered as worthy of being trusted with the franchise. All seven were bitterly opposed to female suffrage. . . . Five were not intellectually equipped for participation in politics. All five were wild for the ballot. The one not voting was a Christian Scientist. She saw no use in the argument, claiming that women already had the ballot if they only believed they had.

The temptation of St. Anthony was as nothing compared to the temptation of the woman who had been told that it was utterly useless to try to make the holy anchorite sit up and take notice.

The Queen of Sheba never told what she thought of King Solomon's proverbs warning young men against women.

Why should this be considered a sordid and unromantic age when the almshouses are full of the children of people who married just because they loved each other.

Coquetry is an art of the intellect; flirtation is a function of the senses.

Do not pity the unsuccessful lover of a woman of genius. Save your sympathy for the man who marries her.

After a few years of marriage a man and his wife are apt to be, if nothing else, at least the sort of enemies who respect each other.

Not every woman in old slippers can manage to look like Cinderella.

When a woman who admits that she is "unhappily yoked" holds long conversations about "the soul" with a man not her husband it isn't the soul either of them is thinking about.

These paragraphs, where they cause you displeasure, madam, were written about the traits of some other woman. I am quite sure that none of them apply to you. And equally sure that you can identify in an instant the woman to whom they do apply.

In a foreword to the last installment Marquis declares: "The scoundrel who wedded thirteen wives in twenty years brings his reveries to a close this week with . . . a final climax, in which, by the side of his last wife, he is confronted by his deserted first, 'aged, gaunt, haggard, implacable like an antique fury.' It is she who at last brings merited retribution, and the prison doors close upon him."

"Reveries of a Bigamist" is a work of some 25,000 to 30,000 words, giving perhaps the best available picture of Don Marquis as a man with the faculty for adjusting to whatever task confronted him. Faced by an assignment that could have been a grim experience, he made a lark of it by fulfilling it and at the same time imparting overtones that made it an effective burlesque of the confessional school of literature, probably the best early one. The fact that only he and Reina and a few friends knew he was kidding his subject made no difference. He had had his little joke.

One day Reina told Don she thought he should try his hand at fiction. That was precisely what he wanted to do, he replied, but he was convinced that at this stage of the game the right course was to pound out the stuff he was sure he could sell. He had an idea for a sure-fire Sunday newspaper feature—this one would run for five weeks, and he was confident he could get $250 for it.

Then Don confessed there was something on his mind that was troubling him. He had lifted Reina out of her pleasant surroundings in Atlanta, where life was comparatively tranquil and leisurely, and dropped her into a stuffy little cold-water flat in Brooklyn where she was under constant pressure. He had subjected her to the humiliation of stalling off the landlord when the rent was overdue and to other embarrassments. It was clearly up to him to concentrate on making life easier for her, and the most dependable way was by writing Sunday-feature stuff.

Reina reminded him that she "had never voted for the easiest way." She had persuaded him to remain in New York when he was jobless and had been offered employment out of town, convinced that if he left New York he'd be licked. She took full responsibility for their low standard of living and pleaded with him not to think about anything except his work. He had demonstrated on *Uncle Remus's Magazine* that he could write fiction and she thought he should devote himself to that whenever he felt equal to working in his spare time, instead of continuing to do Sunday-feature stuff that led nowhere. They would be able to get along on his salary at the *Eagle* and the occasional sales she made as a free-lance writer; and when he started selling fiction, which she felt confident he would, they would be able to pay back the few hundred dollars they owed and then head for a higher standard of living.

That was the clincher. Don promised to try his hand at a short story and to take a look at the notes for a novel he had started blocking out in Atlanta and see if he still liked the idea.

A few weeks later he completed a short story. It made the rounds of several periodicals and was finally bought by *Putnam's Magazine*.

The editor of *Putnam's* was greatly pleased with his new author. He asked Marquis several questions, including this one: "What is your real name?" Marquis replied that he had signed his real name to the story. But the editor was not quite satisfied and wrote back: "Since your real name sounds so much like a nom de plume, why not choose a nom de plume that sounds like a real name?"

In a newspaper interview a few years later Marquis told how people habitually asked him whether his name was real or a pseudonym, mentioning the incredulity of the editor of *Putnam's*. In this interview he supplied some details not mentioned in an earlier version of how he had acquired the "Don" part of his name. The stories add up to the same thing, but the details differ, illustrating Marquis's policy of helping a newspaperman get a good story even if it meant a little improvising. He had a standard reply for those who recognized the embellishments and embroidery: a man was entitled to have a little fun.

One day Don made Reina happy by announcing that he had decided to write That Novel—the one he had been puttering with in

Atlanta. A believer in synopses—a number of them were found among his papers, detailed blueprints of projected books and plays—Don produced several before he and Reina thought he had an outline that was "sure-footed." He didn't believe in sticking too literally to a synopsis but thought it was good to have a "map" showing where you were heading.

The novel was completed in the summer of 1911 and accepted by the first publisher to whom it was sent, Doubleday, Page and Company, progenitor of Doubleday, Doran and Company and of today's Doubleday and Company.

Entitled *Danny's Own Story*, the book was published in January 1912. It was enthusiastically reviewed and Marquis became news. Several newspapers interviewed him. One of the stories, a column and a half long and the most comprehensive of the lot—(unfortunately the aged clipping is cracked in places and the name of the paper is missing)—proclaims in its lead that "'Danny's Own Story' by Don Marquis has achieved a distinction unique in the publishing world by proving a success in January, the slowest month."

The story carries the headline:

DON MARQUIS, THE
NEW HUMORIST

It goes on to say:

A part of "Danny's Own Story" grew accidentally out of a visit as a reporter to Kentucky and Tennessee at the time of the "night rider" troubles in 1908. Mr. Marquis spent several months in the tobacco country as a correspondent and wrote a series of magazine articles about the disturbances." [Marquis was then with *Uncle Remus's Magazine*.]

Marquis enjoyed being interviewed and co-operated zestfully. When a reporter asked him about his hobbies, he said he liked to cook. "In fact," the story read, "Marquis believes he has in him the makings of a truly great chef.

"'There are lots of men who can write better than I can,' he says, 'But I claim to be as good a cook as Shakespeare was; disprove it if you can. I can roast a turkey or a chicken that would make your mouth water; my buckwheat cakes are dreams, and not long ago I designed and executed a deep dish apple pie that moved my wife to tears; she said it was better than her father used to make.'"

In observance of the publication of his book, Doubleday, Page and Company held a reception for Marquis at Garden City. He was asked to pose for a photograph with another Doubleday humorist, Ellis Parker Butler, author of *Pigs Is Pigs.*

The photographer, in posing Marquis, had failed to notice that he had placed him directly under an alarm clock that had been left on a bookshelf. When he received a copy of the photo, Butler wrote his publisher: "Why did you sneak my halo away from me and hang it over Don Marquis's mussy hair? Anyone can see that my 6¼ halo is a misfit on his 7¾ head."

When Marquis received a copy of the photo he also thought that his halo had reproduced nicely but insisted that the alarm clock had had nothing to do with what took place. Here, in part, is what he said to his publisher in acknowledging the picture: "I am sorry you have started this alarm clock theory. It is well known in my family and among my friends that I have a halo. It is not always noticeable to the naked eye but a sensitive camera unfailingly picks it up. When I was a kid and it was customary to show your sore toe for a bite of apple I always showed my halo to the other boys."

Danny's Own Story is a picaresque novel in which Marquis depicts some of his favorite rogues, including Doc Kirby, a pitchman with a colorful line of chatter who put on street-corner shows in country towns, featuring "gen-u-wine Injun tribal dances," and who when he'd collected a crowd, addressed them eloquently on the subject of Siwash Injun Sagraw, nature's own remedy for all ailments.

This cure-all, according to the story's narrator, Danny, a likeable young roustabout without a last name, "had been a secret among them there Injuns fur thousands and thousands of years. Any Injun that give away the secret was killed and rubbed off the rolls of the tribe and buried in disgrace upon the plains of Oregon. And Doc Kirby was made a blood brother of the chief, and learnt the secret of that medicine. Finally he got the chief to see as it wasn't Christian to hold back that there medicine from the world no longer, and the chief, his heart was softened, and he says to go. 'Go, my brother,' he says, 'and give to the pale faces the medicine that has been kept secret fur thousands and thousands of years among the Siwash Injuns on the plains of Oregon.'"

Since Marquis claimed that as a youngster he worked briefly for a medicine show as a "gen-u-wine tribal Injun," decked out in a gaudy turkey tail of feathers rainbowing down from his heard, a blanket even gaudier than the feathers, war paint, moccasins, etc., it is possible that Doc Kirby is fashioned after his former boss.

A character the reviewers liked almost as much as Doc Kirby was an assistant named Looey, who wearied of life with the medicine show. Looey was a man with a gloomy disposition who didn't like to be cheered up. He enjoyed being morose and was compelled to abandon Kirby *et al.* "one day when we was in the upper left-hand corner of Ohio" because of hilarious developments that offended Looey's melancholy nature.

For months Danny wondered what had happened to Looey and then . . .

But here it is in Danny's own words:

"One day Doc Kirby and me was walking along the main street of a little town and we seen a bang-up funeral percession coming. It must of been one of the Grand Army of the Republicans, fur they was some of the old soldiers in buggies riding along behind, and a big string of people follering in more buggies and some on foot. Everybody was looking mighty sollum. But they was one man setting beside the undertaker on the seat of the hearse that was looking sollumer than them all. It was Looey, and I'll bet the corpse himself would of felt proud and happy and contented if he could of knowed the style Looey was giving that funeral.

"It wasn't nothing Looey done, fur he didn't do nothing but jest set there with his arms folded onto his bosom and look sad. But he done *that* better than any one else. He done it so well that you forgot the corpse was the chief party to that funeral. Looey took all the glory from him. He had jest natcherally stole that funeral away from its rightful owner with his enjoyment of it. He seen the doctor and me as the hearse went by our corner, but he never let on."

Buried in the pages of this novel, published half a century ago and out of print for many years, are bits and pieces of a philosophy that stayed with Marquis all his life. A few examples:

One of his basic beliefs about love, as expressed by old Doc Kirby, the patent-medicine faker, in one of his serious moments: "If she's fool enough to love you, treat her well—treat her well. For if you don't, you can never run away from the hell you'll carry in your own heart."

And this, on another subject: "They is a lot of mean, stingy-souled kind of people wouldn't never lie to help a friend, but Doc Kirby wasn't one of 'em."

Throughout his life Marquis was preoccupied with the riddle of

identity. A few examples of it are to be found in this novel, as when
Danny says:

"If anyone will shut his eyes and say his own name over and over
agin fur quite a spell, he will get kind of wonderized and mesmerized
a-doing it—he will begin to wonder who the dickens he is, anyhow,
and what he is, and what the difference between him and the next
feller is. He will wonder why he happens to be himself and the next
feller *himself*. He wonders where himself leaves off and the rest of
the world begins. I been that way myself. . . ."

Reminders of what Marquis wrote as a reporter in 1908 about the
"night-rider disturbances" in Kentucky and Tennessee are to be
found in the pages of *Danny's Own Story*.

In the words of protagonist Danny:

". . . Miss Lucy and Bud, they tells me what them night-ridings
is fur. It seems this here tobaccer trust is jest as mean and lowdown
and unprincipled as all the rest of them trusts. The farmers around
there raised considerable tobaccer—more'n they did of anything else.
The trust had shoved the price so low they couldn't hardly make a
living. So they organized and said they would hold their tobaccer
fur a fair price. But some of the farmers wouldn't organize—said they
had a right to do what they pleased with their own tobaccer. So the
night-riders was formed to burn their barns and ruin their crops and
whip 'em and shoot 'em and make 'em jine. And also to burn a few
trust warehouses now and then, and show 'em this free American
people, composed mainly out of the Angle-Saxton races, wasn't going
to take no sass from anybody.

"An old feller by the name of Rufe Daniels who wouldn't jine the
night-riders had been shot to death on his own door step, jest about a
mile away. . . . The night-riders mostly used these here automatic
shotguns, but they didn't bother with birdshot. They mostly loaded
their shells with buckshot. A few bicycle ball bearings dropped out of
old Rufe when they gathered him up and got him into shape to
plant. . . .

"These here night-riders . . . can shoot up more law and order in
one night than can be manufactured agin in ten years."

From a long ironic passage dealing with the Ku Klux Klan and its
suppression of Negro rights:

"The old man says the Ku Kluxes was working for a principle—the
principle of keeping the white supremacy on top of the nigger race.
Fur if you let 'em . . . go around balloting and voting it wouldn't do.

It makes 'em biggity. . . . And next the hull dern country would be niggerized. . . . So they Ku Kluxed the niggers to make 'em quit voting."

On lynching:

". . . The habit of illegal killing," says the colonel, "grows when it gets started. . . . You'll lynch one for murder and the next for stealing hogs and the next because he's unpopular and the next because he happens to dun you for a debt. . . . You'll all be toting guns and grudges and trying to lynch each other. . . . You've got to stand pat on the law, or else see the law spit on right and left, in the end, and *nobody* safe."

"But," says Grimes, "there's a higher law than that on the statute books. There's——"

Marquis (through "the colonel") then takes a crack at "the higher law" and "the unwritten law," which he'd heard about *ad nauseam* in covering the night-rider disturbances and other stories in the South. The book contains many other evidences of his sensitivity to basic values and of his hatred of hooliganism and mob rule. In *Danny's Own Story* he does not confine himself to taking a crack at abuses in the South. We find him even more bitter in a reference to "a New York slum where they feed immigrants to the factories." Nowhere, he writes, is life held as cheap.

Not long afterward child labor aroused him and he wrote, in "The Child and the Mill":

    . . . these fools with their lies and their dollars, their mills
       and their bloody hands,
    Who make a god of a wheel, who worship their whirring bands,

    They are flinging the life of a people, raw, to the brute machines.
    Dull-eyed, weary and old—old in his early teens. . . .

    Dumb is the heart of him now, at the time when his heart should
       sing——
    Wasters of body and brain, what race will the future bring? . . .

In discussing his near-hobo days Marquis showed such familiarity with the subject of "riding the rods" that some of his friends assumed he had had this experience. A letter has come to light in which Marquis refers to his last day at Knox: "I sold my books, laid away one final enormous meal, and left Galesburg in an empty box car." The letter, written in 1930, was addressed to Edward Caldwell, chairman of a committee that had invited Marquis to attend a Knox dinner; and it contained no reference to "riding the rods."

In view of Marquis's skill as a young man in getting from place to place without spending any money—in that same letter to Mr. Caldwell he mentions having traveled free *to* Galesburg with the help of friendly brakemen on the C., B. and Q.—the following passage from *Danny's Own Story* is quoted:

"Riding on trains without paying fare ain't always the easy thing it sounds. It is like a trade that has to be learned. They is different ways of doing it. I have done every way frequent, except one. That I give up after trying her two, three times. This is riding the rods down underneath the cars, with a piece of board put acrost 'em to lay yourself on.

"I never want to go anywheres agin bad enough to ride the rods.

"Because . . . sometimes you don't arrive. Every oncet in a while you read a little piece in a newspaper about a man being found alongside the tracks, considerable cut up, or laying right acrost them, mebby. He is held in the morgue a while and nobody knows who he is, and none of the train crew knows they has run over a man, and the engineer says they wasn't none on the track. More'n likely that feller has been riding the rods, along about the middle of the train. Mebby he let himself go to sleep and jest rolled off. Mebby his piece of board slipped and he fell when the train jolted. Or mebby he jest natcherally made up his mind he rather let loose and get squashed then get any more cinders into his eyes. Riding the blind baggage or the bumpers gives me all the excitement I wants. . . . Others can have the rods fur all of me. And they *is* some people ackshally says they likes 'em best."

This is authentic hobo lore; and since there are many demonstrably autobiographical passages in the novel, it is possible that Marquis wrote about riding the rods from personal experience.

There are in print several versions of how "The Sun Dial," Marquis's column in the *Evening Sun*, came into being. He tells the story himself in an article previously mentioned, "Confessions of a Reformed Columnist," published in the *Saturday Evening Post* in 1928. After stating that in the spring of 1912 he found himself editing a magazine page in the New York *Evening Sun*, he goes on to say:

"It was probably, in some respects, the worst magazine page ever published in New York City. I couldn't get hold of enough money from the proprietors to buy what I wanted. It blew up, as it deserved to do, and they set me to writing editorials. . . . Then they gave me the short editorial paragraphs to do, as well as occasional longer editorials.

"I saw my chance at last, and—I don't know how else to describe it—I stole that column when they weren't looking.

"The editorial paragraphs in the *Evening Sun* had from time immemorial followed the editorials under a small separate headline: 'Notes and Comment.' I deliberately wrote more 'Notes and Comment' every day than they had ever had before, and, after a few weeks, suggested that the 'Notes and Comment' department be lifted to another part of the page. Nobody kicked. When I had got the thing settled over on the right-hand corner of the page, under the cartoon, I wrote still more of them. Then I gradually began to run in more and more verse, more and more comment and features of an entirely different character. Before the editor and proprietors were aware of what was going on I had a column of my own.

"But still it wasn't what I wanted. It was set in nonpareil type. It had this deadly dull headline over it, 'Notes and Comment.' It had no signature. I ran it for ten months in that fashion and as far as I could make out nobody ever paid any attention to it. It didn't catch on at all. It was too solid looking, too unattractive typographically; I was not permitted to do stunts with it: I was obliged to make it conform more or less closely to the editorial policy of the paper itself. What I wanted was my own editorial policy.

"One day the late George M. Smith became managing editor of the paper, and almost the first thing he did was give me the column I had been after so long, with a fixed spot on the editorial page every day, with an attractive heading, 'The Sun Dial,' with a signature, and with permission to go as far as I liked in the way of personal expression—within the limits of good sense, of course. For several years he stood like a rock in protecting me in all my idiosyncrasies and experiments.

"Whenever a writer makes a hit on some publication it will usually be found that there is some canny and forceful executive in the background encouraging him, supporting him, guiding him without his being altogether aware of it. George Smith knew exactly how to handle me; he always left me the feeling of perfect liberty. At the same time I was well aware that I couldn't put anything over on him, even if I had ever wanted to; he would have brought me up with a jolt that would have made my teeth rattle. In my professional career I have always had alternating periods of humility and vanity, self-depreciation and outrageous egotism. Sometimes I need encouragement badly; at other times I get so stuck on myself that I need— roughly speaking—a wallop on the nut to restore my sense of values; and I have always got plenty of both. . . .

"When I first got the signed column I had so long been struggling for, I was ready for it. As I saw it coming nearer, I had written for it and saved up for it some of the best general stuff I could do; and the day I got it, I began slamming into it the stuff I had saved. 'The Sun Dial'—that was George Smith's name and not my invention— caught on with the town almost from the first week. Before it had been running two months I began to get kindly letters about it from generous professional workers in New York with whom I was not personally acquainted—I remember, offhand, William Winter, the veteran dramatic editor of the *Tribune*; Robert Underwood Johnson, the editor of the *Century*; that versatile all-around genius, James Huneker; Bob Davis, the editor of *Munsey's*, and many others— men whose work and opinions I had admired and respected.

"Within six months I was overwhelmed with requests for work from every magazine in New York, and I was foolish not to have done more of it. But I had been after that column for a long time, and now I had it and I was putting all my time and energy into it. When the tide finally does turn in New York it turns swiftly and with a rush. . . .

"Showmanship figures in everything. The difference between failure and success is frequently the difference between nonpareil type and brevier. Nobody had noticed the 'Notes and Comment,' but 'The Sun Dial'—with no better stuff in it, really—got across at once. A column must have plenty of white space, a challenging make-up, constant variation in typographical style; not only must it catch the eye but it must have points and corners and barbs that prick and stimulate the vision, a surface and a texture that intrigue and cling to and pull at the sight. Franklin P. Adams, of the New York *World*, is the master hand at this sort of thing. . . . I used to have spells when I was very careful about it, like Adams; then I would get bored with the trouble and neglect it. . . . But it should never be neglected. It advertises to people that here is quick and easy reading, and people like easy reading. They will even take a difficult thought if you wrap it up in easy reading for them.

"I tried to get as much variety in the stuff itself as there was in its typographical presentation. So, besides the verse, paragraphs, sketches, fables and occasional serious expression of opinion, I began to create characters through whom I might comment upon or satirize current phases of existence, or whom I might develop for the sheer pleasure of creation."

In the early days of his career on the *Evening Sun*, Don Marquis's desk was a big packing-case. He claimed to like this arrangement. "No one expected me to tidy up a packing-case," he argued, "so my untidiness didn't bother anyone until I graduated to the formality of a desk. Things piled up so fast on that desk that more than once I was kidded about pulling down the *Sun's* neatness average. It was even suggested that I go back to my packing-case. Associates claimed that a disorderly packing-case wasn't as much of an eyesore as a disorderly desk."

In *Letters of Askance*, published in 1939, Christopher Morley wrote: "I remember that in the early days of the *Sun Dial* when the paper moved from Park Row to Nassau Street, Don's typewriter desk got lost in the skirmish; so for some years he rattled out his daily stint with his machine perched on an up-ended packing case. This box had stenciled on it the statement 1 GROSS TOM CAT, which meant Tomato Catsup, but became by legend the first suggestion of me-hitabel."

In *Shandygaff*, a collection of his newspaper and magazine pieces, Morley also wrote that "much of Marquis's best and subtlest work has been clacked out on a typewriter standing on an upturned packing box. When the *American Magazine* published a picture of him at work on his packing case the supply man of the *Sun* got worried, and gave him a regular desk."

Marquis's packing case fascinated Morley and other writers and a number of references to it are to be found, as for instance a story told by Maynard Craig, a friend of mine who has been a Don Marquis fan most of his life and who is conversant with Marquis's work as few people are. His mother, the family's original Marquis enthusiast, decided in those early days of "The Sun Dial" to drop in at the *Sun* office and try to catch a glimpse of her favorite contemporary humorist. Young Maynard accompanied her on this little adventure. When they located Marquis and found him working at a packing case in a dark corner of the office, Mrs. Craig told her son she would have preferred not knowing that her hero did not occupy a pedestal in the *Sun* office. "What an awful place to put that great man!" she exclaimed as she took Maynard by the arm and hurried away from the scene.

When Marquis graduated to the dignity of a permanent desk, to clutter as he saw fit, he found himself in a rather long, narrow room that accommodated three other members of the staff. One of them was Frink Dana Burnet, who in later years dropped the "Frink," and, as Dana Burnet, achieved distinction as a short-story writer and dramatist, and then as one of the movie world's most successful screenplay writers in the Golden Age of Hollywood.

Marquis and Burnet became good friends. Nothing could have been more natural. Both were wits and poets, both had an instinctive dread of the meretricious.

"Don," Burnet told me in 1959, "sat at a big oak desk that had a central drawer and drawers down the sides. It wasn't long before all the drawers were jammed with papers, thrown in willy-nilly. The top of the desk was stacked with papers too, and whenever Don wanted to find something he had to plow through all that stuff. His mail was heavy and he opened it all himself.

"Once, in an effort to make it easier for him to find things, I tried to straighten out the mess on top of his desk where the papers were piled up in disorderly mounds. But the very next day he started looking for something he'd mislaid and by the time he'd finished tearing through everything on top of his desk and inside it, and filling the air with papers as he discarded them one by one, the floor looked as if covered with king-size snowflakes.

"There was a period before he started his daily column when he edited a so-called magazine page that was published Saturdays. The back page of the paper was devoted to it. Until Don came along it had been customary for the management to wheedle contributions out of the staff for such special departments without extra compensation. Don immediately endeared himself to everyone on the paper interested in writing for that magazine page by announcing that he had worked out an arrangement with the managing editor whereby all contributions would be paid for. The pay was modest but it was most welcome."

Burnet said that one could see nothing more stimulating in New York newspaperdom than Don Marquis, clutching a fistful of copy, striding briskly across the city room—"a big cheerful man with a Santa Claus face."

Which reminds one of Frank Graham's description. Graham, one of the paper's outstanding sportswriters, once had an office near Marquis's on the *Sun*, though during a later period. "I remember him," writes Graham, "as a round, smiling, friendly man who lighted up the room every time he came in."

Not long afterward Marquis described himself in part as follows in a letter to Christopher Morley, who had requested the information for use in an article he was writing:

"Height, 5 feet 10½ inches; hair, dove-colored; scar on little finger of left hand; has assured carriage, walking boldly into good hotels and mixing with patrons on terms of equality; weight, 200 pounds; face slightly asymmetrical but not definitely criminal in type; loathes Japanese art, but likes beefsteak and onions; wears No. 8 shoe; fond of Francis Thompson's poems; inside seam of trousers, 32 inches; imitates cats, dogs and barnyard animals for the amusement of young children; eyetooth in right side of upper jaw missing; has always been careful to keep thumb prints from possession of police; chest measurement, 42 inches, varying with respiration; sometimes wears glasses, but usually operates undisguised; dislikes the works of Rabindranath Tagore; corn on little toe of right foot; superstitious, especially with regard to psychic phenomena; eyes blue; ruddy complexion; garrulous and argumentative; prominent cheek bones; wears 17-inch collar; waist measurement none of your business; favorite disease, hypochondria; walks with rapid gait; mark of old fracture on right shin; cuffs on trousers, and coat cut loose, with plenty of room under the arm pits; two hip pockets; dislikes Roquefort cheese, 'Tom Jones,' Wordsworth's poetry, absinthe cocktails, most musical comedy, public banquets, physical exercise, Billy Sunday, steam heat, toy dogs, poets who wear their souls outside, organized charity, magazine covers, and the gas company; prominent calluses on two fingers of right hand prevent him being expert pistol shot; belt strap on trousers; long upper lip; clean shaven; shaggy eyebrows; affects soft hats; smile, one-sided; no gold fillings in teeth; voice, husky; scar above the forehead concealed by hair; commonly wears plain gold ring on little finger of left hand; trousers cut loose over hips and seat; would likely come along quietly if arrested."

On Marquis's desk, according to Frink Dana Burnet, to whom we now return, there sat "an old beat-up Remington, one of those mammoth typewriters that looked like a small printing press. When in operation it didn't make quite as much noise as a printing press but almost."

Those were the days when the *Sun* was located at Nassau and Frankfort Streets. Nearby stood an establishment, previously referred to, that played quite a part in those days in the lives of New York newspapermen, Lipton's Bar. It was to this place that Burnet and Marquis repaired whenever their latest conversation designed to solve the world's problems bogged down and needed revivification.

One day Don, weary of pounding his massive typewriter and noting that Burnet had grown a bit restive too, said, "It's a nice day, Frink. Let's stroll over to Lipton's, split a bottle of champagne and found a new school of poetry." Burnet does not recall whether they ever started that new poetry movement, and if so, what its requirements were. But he does recall Don saying to him, "Frink, this morning there scampered across my desk the goddam biggest cockroach you ever saw. I believe he could damn near play my typewriter."

This was the beginning of archy, Marquis's famous lower-case cockroach, who made his debut in "The Sun Dial" not long afterward. archy, it will be recalled, could not work the shift key of the typewriter, consequently his product was devoid of capital letters, quotation and question marks, parentheses, apostrophes, and such other shift-key impedimenta as the dollar sign and the percentage symbol. Whenever archy dealt in percentages he had to do it the hard way, i.e., by laboriously spelling out the word. And since he operated by hurling himself, head first, at the keys, his practice, insofar as possible, of avoiding economics, mathematics, and other subjects that dealt in percentages is understandable. Blessed with an omniscience equating a genius I.Q., archy understood *everything* and regretted the necessity of having to duck *any* subject, but since it was bruising to his brains to make those head-first dives at the typewriter keys, he preferred to let the uninitiated think he knew nothing about subjects that involved the use of percentages.

All that archy asked of The Boss (Don Marquis) was that he leave a sheet of paper in the typewriter, since working the gadget that controlled the platen was beyond a cockroach's capabilities. In fact, archy once pointed out that if The Boss had not happened to leave a blank sheet of copy paper in the typewriter one night it would not have been possible for "the insect Voltaire," as Christopher Morley called him, to compose his first piece for "The Sun Dial."

As the building in which the *Sun* operated was known in newspaper circles as Vermin Castle, a Marquis series whose central figure was a *Sun* office cockroach merely served to focus attention on that fact.

There were some mutterings among the paper's high command but these were silenced by Managing Editor George Smith, who came to the rescue several times, according to Marquis in a magazine article written fifteen years later. Marquis quotes Smith as saying to William C. Reick, then owner of the *Sun*, "I think we've got to let Marquis do about as he pleases with his department." Reick backed down.

Lipton's, where Marquis made the remark to Frink Dana Burnet that indicated that archy was about to be born, was more than a spot where the columnist liked to drop in for a drink. It had a place in his affections. He devoted a whole chapter of his egobiography, from which the following excerpts are taken, to Lipton's:

"Stained-glass windows, on the Nassau Street side of the place, were a peculiarity of Lipton's. They led Christopher Morley to name this saloon 'the Gin Cathedral.' It was characteristic of Marquis at this period of his life that he did his serious drinking in a place with some resemblance to a church. Not only the essence of piety has always attracted him, but its external associations as well. There was no organ at Lipton's, but occasionally in the afternoon there would be a hoarse bawling of gospel hymns, usually led by one Harry Staton. (It was Staton, incidentally, who popularized the song about the daring young man on the flying trapeze.) Tom Crowley, the proprietor, used to become uneasy about these hymns and protested.

" 'It's unlucky,' Tom would say, 'to sing church songs in a barroom.' Whether he meant unlucky for the churches or for the barroom, M. could never determine.

"The place was infested at all hours with girls who collected money for various charitable organizations connected with practically all the religious denominations. They would bless your immortal soul to all eternity for a drunken dime. Many of them carried tambourines. Marquis used to think it would add something to the atmosphere and color of the place if they would swing into a ritualistic dance, banging their tambourines, while the hymn-singing was in progress; but he could never get them to do it, not even for a quarter. They were sincere priestesses, and humorless, intent only on salvation regardless of joy. . . .

"M. will take up Lipton's in more detail further along in his egobiography. Too many hours of his life were spent there (in philosophical speculations and other games of skill and chance such as gambling on how much liquor he could hold and not quite kill himself nor lose his job) during a period of several years."

Burnet recalls that one day he and Marquis were in Lipton's when a man who had just joined the *Sun's* staff—his name, he seems to recall, was Owens—drifted in. Lonely and ill-at-ease, he tried to start a conversation with someone at the bar. When the man proved uncommunicative, Owens looked around the room helplessly, made a feint at addressing someone else, changed his mind and started for the door.

Marquis quickly took in the situation, bustled over and introduced himself and invited Owens to have a drink with him. Owens didn't think he had the right to accept, since there was no reason why Marquis should spend money on a stranger. This remonstrance was Don's cue to get busy explaining the Marquis Law of Economics. Actually Owens would be saving him money. In Lipton's the drinks were two for a quarter. One drink cost fifteen cents. By buying two drinks Marquis was getting his own for twelve and a half cents, a saving of two and a half cents, he explained in deadpan fashion. Owens was puzzled by this kind of arithmetic and started to say so when he caught the twinkle in Marquis's eye and his amused look. With a laugh and a word of thanks he accepted the drink.

As loyal as Marquis was to Lipton's, he couldn't resist the temptation to drift occasionally into a saloon patronized largely by the mechanical staff of the paper—compositors, pressmen, etc. He'd heard about this place, had tried it and liked it, and patronized it when he was not in the mood for the Gin Cathedral.

One day Marquis found himself at the bar of this establishment with three members of the *Sun's* mechanical department, all named John. Recalling the three Johns of the New Testament, he said, "I don't know which of you is John the Baptist, which one is John the Apostle, and which is John Mark." When they laughed he regarded them with mock gravity and asked, "Which reminds me, what are you three Biblical characters doing in a saloon?"

Marquis was known for his knowledge of the Old and New Testaments, as reflected in his column, which contained frequent scriptural allusions, but even so the three Johns were flabbergasted. None of them realized until one of the trio looked it up that there *were* three Biblical Johns.

The conductor of "The Sun Dial" was never one to parade his knowledge. But he was so full of information that he was frequently consulted when a difference of opinion had to be resolved. Once, in the Gin Cathedral, two members of the *Sun* staff were arguing as to the genesis of the familiar "In God we trust." Each attributed it to a different American poet. Marquis was called away from a table where he was chatting with friends and asked if he knew the answer. In the soft, slow drawl that was so typical, he said he was pretty sure that "In God we trust" was an abbreviated version of a passage from the Bible and cited the psalm from which he seemed to recall it had been adapted. When the disputants got back to the office a concordance was produced and Marquis was proven correct.

The office in the *Sun* that Burnet and Marquis shared with two others was not the quietest place to work. "The printing presses were directly overhead and you could hear the floor groan as they clattered away," said Burnet. "Don and I used to joke about the possibility of us ink-stained wretches becoming even more so as the presses crashed through the ceiling overhead and landed in our laps."

There are echoes of this flamboyant thought in a poem in which Marquis describes such an eventuality, using as his refrain line, "I'm an Inka from Peru." He also wrote a versified supplication to the floor above, imploring it to live right and remain strong. It contained these lines:

> Floor, do not yield! A falling press
> Would be a nuisance, more or less.

When the presses weren't kicking up a racket, the huge trucks— some of them horse-drawn—that delivered the great rolls of newsprint took up the burden of shattering the quiet of that long narrow room where Marquis and three others worked. He once called it a miracle of co-ordinated unco-ordination. "The trucks never arrived while the presses were in operation. They seemed to be operating in separate noise-making shifts. Sometimes the boss trucker, directing the unloading of the paper, would shout more instructions than an old-time sailing master at the height of a storm."

"Because he was not a church-goer," observed Dana Burnet, "some people mistakenly thought Marquis was an unbeliever. Those who really knew him were aware of the very special kind of faith he had; it was not the kind you can pour into a denominational mould.

"He was too wise to have a fixed position on the great mysteries and was puzzled by those who professed to have the answers to what he considered life's riddles, including the riddle of identity.

"In all the time I knew him—and it covered quite a span—I never heard him express a preference for any particular religion. In fact,

he didn't seem to have much use for formal religion. Yet he was a
deeply religious man in the sense that he was a profoundly spiritual
person. People—that is, the voice of the human spirit—and poetry,
these were his religion."

In rummaging through articles written about Marquis and reviews
of his books I found a piece by Stuart P. Sherman, then editor of
the New York *Herald Tribune's* Sunday book section. The piece is
called "Don Marquis—What Is He?" Starting on page one of the
February 8, 1925, issue, it covers a total of six columns, exclusive of
space devoted to illustrations from Marquis's books; and amounts to
an appraisal (a most favorable one) of "the many Marquises"—poet,
humorist, novelist, commentator, playwright, short-story writer, light
versifier, etc.

A passage in Stuart Sherman's article reminds one of Dana Burnet's
observation just quoted. In this passage Sherman comments on the
"idealistic and religious" quality of Marquis's poetry, adding: "He
sees that man has 'at his noblest an air of something more than man.'
He is the receiver of mystical intimations. He speculates on the
mystery of Self. Disillusioned, he yet sees man as the god-seeker,
the god-maker, and he respects man's aspiration, in the face of
'the hissing hate of fools, thorns and the ingrate's scoff.'"

"You never knew what would come out of that wonderful mind,"
Burnet continued. "He wasn't joking when he said to me, 'Frink,
I get up in the morning with an idea for a three-volume novel and by
nightfall it's a paragraph in my column.'" Once in a discouraged
moment Marquis wrote a long piece for "The Sun Dial" about the
futility of writing poetry. There was something he wanted to say but
he felt it hadn't quite come off. What he had written emerged as
merely a plaint. He had not set out to write a plaint. He had tried
to say something in a semihumorous, philosophic vein, with overtones
of self-spoofery. Eventually he boiled down the piece he considered
unsatisfactory—it took more than half his column—into a one-sen-
tence aphorism and published that instead: "Writing a book of poetry
is like dropping a rose petal down the Grand Canyon and waiting
for the echo."

Burnet recalls that Marquis's chief abomination was pretense. "He
didn't spend much time sitting in judgment on his fellows. He could
even put up with rogues as long as they didn't try to pass as something
else. But he hated the masquerader."

His pseudo-literary Greenwich Villager, Hermione, the archpriestess of pretense, was a means of expressing his contempt for mumbo jumbo disguised as Art. But Marquis was not a man to foam at the mouth. So entertainingly did he satirize Hermione and Her Little Group of Serious Thinkers that only Marquis's close friends realized that these pieces were really editorials.

Burnet remembers Marquis as a man who liked to laugh. "But he was a chuckler, not a roarer."

Burnet conducted "The Sun Dial" when Marquis vacationed. It was an ideal arrangement since Don admired his office mate's work. The two men had many bonds and chief of these was that both were poets. Burnet, like Marquis, wrote both serious and humorous verse and in his prose pieces was an effective lampooner.

Don used to say to his office mate, "Frink, if I give 'em three good columns a week that's all they can expect." He also thought he couldn't possibly produce three good ones weekly unless he tried to make them *all* good; and that meant discarding, making fresh starts, and eternally rewriting.

Among the many Don Marquis legends is one to the effect that he used to pound out his column in an hour or so, then head for the nearest saloon.

Legends frequently have some basis of fact or *seeming* fact. I have talked with members of the Players Club who recall Marquis's banging out "The Sun Dial" in what seemed like record time for this kind of writing, so that he could join friends at the pool table—making one of the Club's typewriters hum as he performed this miracle. One member tells about the day Don sat at a table in the Club's bar and "dashed off his column in longhand in about a half hour." When it appeared, he was dumfounded because Don's lead-off piece proved to be a skillful piece of light verse, written in a difficult meter and full of intricate rhymes. Marquis never troubled to explain that in his paper's composing room he always had some "overset," including verses serious and humorous to be used as column leads. When complimented on "dashing off" one of these columns, he would say something like, "There was nothing to it," or "It was a romp," giving further support to Christopher Morley's remark that he liked to keep people guessing about himself.

And not only in connection with his column. Once when he told a *Sun* associate that he had "lasted" only a few months at Knox College his friend ribbingly asked, "What were you kicked out for?"

Marquis replied with a simulated shudder, "I'd rather not say." Which gave rise to a rumor that he had been expelled from Knox. This tale was still very much alive when I picked it up in 1958. A letter to the administrative offices of Knox College produced a reply that left not a scrap of doubt that Marquis had left of his own volition.

During the early years of "The Sun Dial" Marquis occasionally sent for a messenger at the Players Club to take his copy to the office. Usually it was a column he had written at home and given some finishing touches at the Club. The Players had one of those long-since-vanished signal systems by means of which you turned a little knob to notify Western Union that you wanted a messenger boy. More than one column that was dispatched to the *Sun* in this fashion was presumed to be the latest he'd written on the premises in jig time; which further helped build up those myths about the spectacular speed with which he produced his column. A dozen years later he told an audience of Yale University students that he had found news-paper-columning "an agony of effort."

Early in his career as a columnist Marquis wrote a narrative in verse called "Noah an' Jonah an' Cap'n John Smith." It proved pop-ular and not long afterward he was requested by readers who had forgotten to save the clipping to reprint the piece. This he was glad to do as the piece filled his column exactly.

Those readers gave him an idea. A few times thereafter when he had written columns that he didn't like he discarded them and sub-stituted this ballad, one of his most rollicking.

Dana Burnet recalls the day Managing Editor George Smith rapped Marquis's knuckles for overdoing the republication of this poem. Here is Marquis's own account of what Burnet told the writer:

"I had a poem exactly one column long, called 'Noah an' Jonah an' Cap'n John Smith,' which people were forever asking me to reprint. But when I wanted a day off, whether I had any current request or not, I used to put it in with the line above it: Reprinted by Request. One summer I must have taken a little more than the traffic would bear, for I got a note from George Smith, with the poem clipped and attached, as follows:

Dear Marquis: The next time you reprint this particular poem by request, won't you please be sure that the request is quite overwhelming?

                                                                 G.M.S.

"Smith always had my number."

Marquis laughed as he told Burnet the story. He didn't mind this spanking by a man he respected. His favorite comment on Smith was: "He protected me from all sorts of interference."

The evolution in its final form of "Noah an' Jonah an' Cap'n John Smith"—(which Louis Untermeyer considers one of the greatest of American humorous ballads)—seems worth relating. In an interview with George Britt of the New York *World-Telegram* published many years later—on December 2, 1932, to be exact—Marquis, after describing this versified narrative as "the most widely liked thing he'd ever written," said it owed its final form to the pressure of newspaper space. "It was merely a day's work," wrote Britt after Marquis had told him the story, "to fill his daily column in the paper. When the printers set it up in type, it was about four sticks too long. 'I had to take the proof down to the composing room,' Don said, 'and tell the printers what to kill. The extra type was thrown out and the proof was lost, so I never had any idea what was in those other twenty or thirty lines.'"

Marquis enjoyed poking good-natured fun in his column at the people with whom he worked. One of the best examples is to be found in the scrapbook of James Quigney, an office boy on the *Sun* in 1913. Marquis had published a poem a few weeks before Christmas of that year containing these verses:

> The Christmas list is going round
> And office boys with rapt, profound
> Devotion in their eyes
> And looks of glad surmise
> Smile on us—strange boys by the score—
> Strange boys we've never seen before.
>
> Where were they when we wanted proofs
> Aforetime? Gambolling on the roofs!
> Where, in our hours of need,
> Was this devoted breed
> Of young well-wishers—when we tore
> Our throat with yelling "Boy!" of yore?

Quigney and two other office boys—all about fourteen years old at the time—collaborated on a rejoinder, which they signed James Quigney, Poet; George Slane, Messenger Boy; James Doran, Esquire.

> O Mr. Marquis,
> You think your it.
> If you gave a dollar tip
> You would take a fit!

Marquis closed out the exchange with this comment:

"Shamed out of our Spugginess, we hereby notify James Quigney, George Slane and James Doran that we add fifty cents to our original contribution. But all efforts to obtain another fifty cents by another poem will be of no avail."

Jim Quigney, recalling his days as an office boy on the *Sun*, told me that when Marquis cried "Copeee!" you didn't know whether he wanted someone to run copy or put out a fire. "He smoked a pipe constantly at his typewriter in those days," said Jim, "and when deep in concentration on something he was writing, he would shake out his lighted pipe into his wastebasket without realizing what he was doing. That basket was always full to overflowing with rejected contributions, so the burning tobacco would start a fire. I can't tell you how many such blazes Marquis started." Quigney said that in time he and his young associates could tell from Marquis's voice what kind of service he wanted rendered when he yelled for a boy. There was more than a hint of anguish and frenzy in his tones when there was another fire to be extinguished, and whoever answered the call first armed himself with a pail of water.

Years later when Marquis was a frequent contributor to *Collier's* and the *American Magazine*, Quigney was in the employ of the Crowell-Collier Publishing Company, which published those periodicals. (He had become an authority on photographic illustration and at one time or another had served all the Crowell-Collier publications in such matters. He was eventually named Photography Editor of *Collier's*.)

Marquis occasionally called at the Crowell-Collier offices to see Charles Colebaugh, managing editor of *Collier's*, or Sumner Blossom, editor of the *American Magazine*, and when he did he invariably looked up Quigney. Quigney reminisced about this in conversation with me a few years ago. "There never was a friendlier man than Marquis," he said. "He was pleased that I was making progress in the magazine business. And his pleasure was the real thing. I'm sure you remember that way he had of beaming that made anyone in his company feel good. He enjoyed recalling some of his kidding matches in the early days of his column with those he worked with on the paper. He had a retentive memory and once as he was reminiscing about interoffice horseplay, he referred to the episode of the poem the two other office boys and I had sent him and laughed as he recalled the story.

"It meant a lot to be remembered by a man like Don Marquis. Looking up an old friend or acquaintance, no matter how unimportant the original relationship, and finding out how he was getting along, was second nature with him. I never knew anyone who loved old associations as Marquis did."

Years ago Christopher Morley wrote an article for the New York *Evening Post* on those early days of "The Sun Dial." Subsequently he expanded it into two long chapters on Don Marquis in a book of essays previously mentioned, *Letters of Askance*. Here is an excerpt that seems appropriate:

". . . Six days a week, bedevilled by a million interruptions and beclamored by all the agreeable rattles, the social rivetters who gang round a man trying to work, Marquis created something utterly his own. It was as racy of our day as Addison and Steele's *Spectator* of theirs. . . .

"I speak feelingly, for when I came to work in New York in 1913 as a boy fresh from Oxford—how fresh, you would have to have been a pre-War boy to realize—the *Sun Dial*, then less than a year old, was the first journalistic specialty I noticed. Its freakish pungency, offhand gusto, bewildering alternation of seriousness and buffoonery, of delicate lyric and prattfall slapstick, how different from the prim journalism I have been trained to esteem. Contagion was immediate. I had lately passed through the fevers of an early Stevensonian influenza, and was ripe for new inoculations. Literary beginnings are always imitative. At once I wanted, if not necessarily to write like Mr. Marquis, at least to get a chance to try to run a column of that kind. Eventually I did, and if anyone were to embarrass me by studying the matter they would see how admiringly I followed Don's technique. I don't think anyone noticed it, because I started in a Philadelphia paper, the most perfect form of secrecy."

A letter sent to the editor of the *Evening Sun* late in the summer of 1914 played an important part in Don Marquis's career. It was written by Robert Underwood Johnson and expressed his admiration of Marquis's work as a serious poet, with special reference to a poem called "They Had No Poet . . . ," based on Pope's couplet:

Vain was the chief's, the sage's pride!
They had no poet and they died.

This was no ordinary letter. When it was published in the letters column of the *Sun* it made a stir in writing circles. Johnson had just completed thirty years as associate editor and editor-in-chief of the respected *Century Magazine*. Known as a tough editor, Johnson's endorsement of Marquis carried weight.

Shortly after the letter appeared, Harper's asked Marquis to submit a book of poetry. On September 30, 1914, Marquis wrote Johnson as follows:

"Harper's have asked me to submit a book of verse—and I think you have done this, either directly or indirectly, through your letter in the Evening Sun.

"I'm going to trespass on your good nature further, if you'll let me. I have 80 to 100 possibilities for a book of verse. I don't think they'll want such a big one. If I could only enlist your mature judgment as a poet and a veteran editor in selecting the stuff that should go into the book I'd feel a good deal safer about it. I reckon they'll come down to 30 to 40 poems. I don't want to pile a lot of work onto you with this thing, but if you'll look at the dummy before it goes to Harper's and put an N. G. onto anything you think is too darned bad I'll hold the N. G. ones out—and feel safer about the whole thing.

"There were 15 or 18 in the bunch I sent you the other day. I was copying 'The God-Maker, Man' to send you also. But the dumb-waiter bell rang, and I stuck my head into the shaft to see what it was. At that instant the iron wheel fell from the top of the dumb-waiter shaft and hit me on the head and laid me out.

"The doctor said afterwards my head must be solid bone from the top to the chin. Anyhow, I had to use 'The God-Maker, Man' to fill the column, because the wheel jolted the humor out of me. Which is the reason you got the God-Maker in the paper instead of the package.

"The first thing I thought, after coming to, was: 'Here I am, getting some recognition as poet—and this lick on the head will probably make me an idiot, since it hasn't killed me.'

"The wheel escaped with a slight dent, which exactly corresponds to one of my bumps."

Much of the correspondence that followed is to be found in the files of the National Academy of Arts and Letters. (Johnson had

been an official of the Academy while it was being organized, was
its Secretary for several years after its formation, and played a part
later in Marquis's nomination and election as a member.)

Excerpts from some of Marquis's letters to Johnson:

"I have written quite a large number of serious poems. But, unfortunately, I have to make a living grinding out alleged humor for
newspapers and this stands in the way of my building up any sort of
reputation for serious verse. The light verse, bad as most of it is, is
rather popular and pays the rent and the grocery bill. I'd like to get
out a book of serious verse—but I wouldn't know how to go about it.
I understand the publishers aren't any too eager along these
lines. . . ."

"He [William Winter] is right about the artificial business. It
was a big idea inadequately worked out." (Mr. Winter, well-known
drama critic, had also written the *Sun* an enthusiastic letter about
Marquis as a serious poet. He and Robert Underwood Johnson
were friends and had agreed to pass on the manuscript of Marquis's
projected book of poetry. Winter criticized one of Marquis's poems as
"artificial" and Marquis apparently thought he was right.)

"I've been sending around to different places and digging through
newspapers and things trying to get my verse together. I start scrapbooks and then move and lose them. The more I look at it (my
verse), the more I wonder why in the deuce I didn't work harder over
it when I did it in the first place. But if you and William Winter
think there's a streak of the real thing running through it, I'm willing
to agree with you. . . .

"What he [Winter] says about the painful drudgery, though, is
only partly true. The newspaper column is only drudgery one week
out of three. The other two weeks I like it; I'd rather have it than
any other salaried job I know; I have an idea of gradually making it
into something rather vital in a critical way—getting away, bit by
bit, from the more obvious and cheaper type of wheeze into a kind
of comment with a little more thought behind it. Whether I can
carry a sufficient public over with me is the question. I think I can if
I don't tell either the public or my bosses what I'm doing.

"Your letter has really cheered me up a lot. I was quite sincere
when I wrote you that I often wondered whether it was worth while
to publish serious verse in the newspapers. As for the magazines,
Scribner's, the *Century*, the *Atlantic* and *Harper's* are still doing
their best to maintain a standard; as for the others, I don't care

whether I sell them verse or not; few of them know good verse when they see it. Perhaps that isn't altogether fair, either; at any rate, I should except the *Smart Set*; I've seen some good things in the *Smart Set*. But most of them try to shock. The real thing is not to shock, but to stir. You can shock a man by hitting him with a club. It's a very external kind of trick. But if you get inside of him, at the roots of his soul, the merest little flutter will stir him all through, and will be very salutary for him, too."

"Your letter has meant a lot to me."

In one of his letters to Johnson we see Marquis in his familiar role of trying to do something for a friend. In giving examples of poems he had read in "The Sun Dial" and thought suitable for the projected book, Johnson mistakenly named two that Marquis had not written. To Marquis this was an opportunity to tell his influential mentor something about the author of those poems. And now to quote: " 'The Builder' and 'Plaint of Pan' are both by F. Dana Burnet, of the *Evening Sun,* who wrote the Sun Dial column while I was on my vacation. . . . I think he has the real thing. I'll send you some of his stuff that I like even better than those. You see, you've stepped into a regular den of poets."

In this correspondence we find Marquis returning to the theme of the sorrow he couldn't forget: that box jammed full of his poetry that the janitor of the Atlanta *Journal* had mistaken for waste paper and thrown out—"a bushel of it," as he said in a letter to Johnson in which he makes some new points about his belief that the lost poems had qualities he didn't believe he could recapture. Supporting his own declaration that he never fully recovered from that calamity, we find him brooding over it in a detailed restatement from which the following is taken:

"All the Atlanta *Journal's* waste paper was tied up into big bundles to be sent back to the paper mills and worked over, and there were about a dozen of these big bundles in the basement. I went through the whole damned mess to get that poetry back, but I never found any of it.

"I had copies of five or six of them, and some more of them I remembered in part, and worked over again. But all the good verse I ever did was in that box in one form or another. Some of them, I suppose, when I worked them over from memory later, were better. Some of them were worse.

"Of course, I will always think that the best verse the world ever saw, ever will see, was in that box. And I am certain that my stuff now isn't as spontaneous or as lyrical in quality as it was then; when you are twenty-four or twenty-five years old it comes with more of a rush. And there was a warmer, more human kind of touch in some of that earlier stuff than I am able to get now."

The year 1915 was a good one for Marquis on the *Sun*, for his column was developing a following. It would have been a better year if his column had appealed as much to William C. Reick, then owner of the *Sun*, as it apparently did to the paper's readers. "Mr. Reick," Marquis subsequently wrote, "was always a little doubtful about me; he had a feeling that I was helping to make circulation for the paper, but he never quite knew why. Every now and then he would get vaguely alarmed at some of my propensities and speak to me about it."

Whenever Reick's fears took the form of requesting his columnist "not to write any more stuff like that," Marquis would consult Managing Editor Smith and Smith would call off the owner and tell Marquis to continue to be himself. The trouble with a situation like that, Marquis pointed out to friends, was that while he was reasonably sure he was not going to be fired, he also knew that he couldn't expect a raise until Reick showed some enthusiasm for his work. When he "stole" that column he started at a low salary, the same pay he was receiving for writing "Notes and Comment." He had counted on the management's generosity when, as, and if the column was a success.

It is true, as Dana Burnet has pointed out, that Marquis had "a magnificent contempt for money," but he liked to have enough of it to pay his bills. Reina had suffered a long illness following a miscarriage of unusual severity. A specialist had been called in and he stipulated two shifts of nurses when he found that Reina had been weakened by hemorrhages.

A few sales to magazines helped keep him solvent but Marquis still owed money he was anxious to repay. He was confident that eventually his column would be more liberally rewarded and his main concern continued to be Reina's health.

On October 23, 1915, we again find Marquis writing his benefactor, Robert Underwood Johnson. The letter gives a good picture of what was happening to Marquis at the time:

"Dear Mr. Johnson:

"I've been waiting until I got a perfect copy of 'Dreams and Dust' to send to you [Marquis's first book of poems]. The first ones that came out had a transposition in pages, which looked like the dickens. The publishers got as many of them back as they could, and rebound some of them. . . . The ones that went out to the newspapers were the mixed up ones. The whole thing has caused a delay. I didn't want you to get one of the punk ones, so I didn't send you any before.

"There is stuff in the volume that should have been winnowed out. I sent it to them last spring, in its present shape, more as a tentative than as a final thing; I expected them to say it was too long, or suggest changes, or something of the sort. And then I was coming to you with it and ask you which poems should be picked and which consigned to oblivion. But about that time things began to happen to me, and happened quickly and continuously for about two months; and I forgot I had a book on the way until I got the proofs; there wasn't any winnowing out or editing done, by them or by me or by anybody else; the tentative suggestion is the final thing, without even a line of acknowledgment to magazines or newspapers that hold the original copyrights on the stuff. As a matter of fact, I even forgot to ask anyone for permission to reprint the stuff—though I don't suppose they'll care. There was going to be a note dedicating it to my mother; she was sick, and I never wrote the note. I did get the line set up dedicating it to her, and took a dummy with the cover and that line to her. But I don't know whether she realized what it was or not, for she died a few days after.

"I think it very largely, if not altogether, due to your kindly interest in the verse that Harper's got it out in book form, and the volume itself should have contained an acknowledgment of your interest in it. But it was just at the time when all those things should have been . . . attended to that I was up in the air; my wife was desperately sick here while my mother was sick there; I was afraid to go to Chicago, where my mother was; I was afraid not to go; when I finally went I was afraid to stay on account of my wife's condition here; the situation was a nightmare that dragged on for weeks. My wife is getting well.

"I don't know why I should pass on all these depressing details to you—I shouldn't, if they were still continuing. But, after your original friendly interest in the book, I never made a sign to you, one way or another, during the time when it was being actually prepared for the press, and I did want you to know that my neglect of the whole matter wasn't due to any lack of appreciation of what you had done. With cordial good wishes, Yours sincerely,"

To a book reviewer who complained about the garbled copy he had received, Marquis wrote a letter of apology in which he mentioned that the title of a poem on page 43 of *Dreams and Dust* explained how he felt about the whole thing. The poem was called "A Nightmare."

Much about this book is personal. For instance, the poem based on Shakespeare's

> Golden lads and lasses must
> Like chimney-sweepers come to dust,

and dedicated to "D.V.M." is a tribute—a moving one—to his brother David, whose death he described earlier in these pages. Marquis had sent his mother a typed copy of this poem, which had meant a great deal to her, but she never saw it in book form. It was in a tentative dummy of the book he had shown her months later when she was dying in Chicago, but she was then so weak he didn't believe that she was equal to grasping the significance of anything in the pasted-up proofs.

One of the ironies of Marquis's first experience as the author of a book of poems was that "Unrest," one of his wife's special favorites —one which, in fact, she liked so much that she had committed it to memory—was printed upside down in that ill-starred first printing of *Dreams and Dust*, with the concluding stanzas preceding the ones that opened the piece and established the mood. Six years later Louis Untermeyer published this poem in *Modern American Poetry* and it is reprinted here to give the reader a picture of poet Don Marquis in 1915:

UNREST

A fierce unrest seethes at the core
  Of all existing things:
It was the eager wish to soar
  That gave the gods their wings.

From what flat wastes of cosmic slime,
  And stung by what quick fire,
Sunward the restless races climb!—
  Men risen out of mire!

There throbs through all the worlds that are
   This heart-beat hot and strong,
And shaken systems, star by star,
   Awake and glow in song.

But for the urge of this unrest
   These joyous spheres were mute;
But for the rebel in his breast
   Had man remained a brute.

When baffled lips demanded speech,
   Speech trembled into birth—
(One day the lyric word shall reach
   From earth to laughing earth)—

When man's dim eyes demanded light
   The light he sought was born—
His wish, a Titan, scaled the height
   And flung him back the morn!

From deed to dream, from dream to deed,
   From daring hope to hope,
The restless wish, the instant need,
   Still lashed him up the slope!

      .   .   .

I sing no governed firmament,
   Cold, ordered, regular—
I sing the stinging discontent
   That leaps from star to star!

One of Marquis's chief embarrassments in connection with the publication of his first book of serious poetry was that a poem he had written for *Uncle Remus's Magazine* as a satiric thrust at the "songs of the open road" that were enjoying a vogue in the days when he worked for Joel Chandler Harris emerged as a serious poem in *Dreams and Dust*. Lifted out of the article in which it had originally appeared—a gaily worded poke at the swarm of poets who engaged in wholesale lyric vagabonding shortly after the turn of the century —it became a paean of praise of the very thing he had set out to spoof.

There were periods when Marquis stopped writing serious poetry but there never was a time when he quit lampooning what he called "the mass production of poesy," which he ranked among the nation's leading industries, "not far below steel, automobiles, food, clothing and one or two others." In fact, an article in the *Saturday Evening Post* written some years later, called "The Poetry Business" (1931), was merely an updating—a livelier and more mature version, that is—of what he had said as a young man in *Uncle Remus's Magazine* in whose pages he had bemoaned with a wink of the typewriter "the tribulations of a rhyme-factory." In the opening paragraphs of that *Post* piece—one of his most entertaining magazine articles—he reported:

"The poetry business is not quite what it was two or three years ago. But at that it is a great deal better than it was twenty-five years ago. There was a great boom period of fifteen to twenty years, during which vast quantities of poetry were manufactured, sold and consumed by the American public. In fact, this public became almost verse-minded. Never again will the trade sink to the low levels of the time before the big boom, in my estimation. I look for a revival of business which will get us out of the present temporary slump, and will carry the peak of production and consumption to a higher crest than has ever before been attained in these states; and that within the next five or six years. The domestic market absorbs more and more poetry, and a small but active export trade has been growing up. Imports have always done well, sometimes to the prejudice of the home industry.

"I am writing from the point of view of the sympathetic outsider. I used to set the machines in my plant for verse and knock out a good deal of it at one time; but I have given up that line of goods and deal almost exclusively in various grades and brands of prose. Economic reasons governed my change in production policy. I have always found that it takes just as much time and trouble and hard work to manufacture and assemble a Class A-1 sonnet, which contains only fourteen lines, as to get a complete short story ready for a customer; and the difference in pay would astonish you unless you have had occasion to investigate this business. But if I ever get rich enough I shall go back to poetry. I shall get me a yacht and sit back all day long on the back porch of it and write poems, and cork them up in bottles—bottles which have been emptied in the process of producing the poetry—and throw them overboard. Hundreds of editors and women's clubs and radio people and little groups of serious thinkers will follow the yacht about and scramble for the poetry, and I shall turn machine guns on them from the yacht. It is the perfect way to spend a happy and contented old age."

7 A Copy-Reader's Dreams of Glory, "Beauty in Distress," and Things Like That—Hermione and Her Little Group of Serious Thinkers, and the Old Soak, Are Born—Maud Marquis, a Problem—God and Little Bobby

Ever since the publication of the successful *Danny's Own Story*, book publishers had tried to interest Marquis in trying his hand at another novel.

He really needed no coaxing; all he needed was time. He enjoyed writing fiction and had written and sold some short stories since the publication of his first novel. He found it difficult to free enough time to undertake a full-length novel but he had every intention of writing another as soon as he could.

During the early days of "The Sun Dial" he puttered with the outline of a satiric novel built around a character—Clement J. Cleggett—who was an amalgam of Thackeray's Barry Lyndon, his own swashbuckling Captain Fitzurse, Don Quixote, and Edwin Arlington Robinson's Miniver Cheevy, of whom Robinson had said in part:

> Miniver sighed for what was not,
> And dreamed and rested from his labors;
> He dreamed of Thebes and Camelot,
> And Priam's neighbors. . . .
>
> Miniver cursed the commonplace
> And eyed a khaki suit with loathing;

> He missed the medieval grace
> Of iron clothing. . . .

Marquis's Clement J. Cleggett merely resembled those other characters to a point. Like Miniver Cheevy he "sighed for what was not,"
like Barry Lyndon he never questioned his ability to cope with any
crisis that might arise, like Don Quixote he was forever tilting at
windmills, and like Marquis's Captain Fitzurse he was a medievalist
overtaken by the twentieth century and full of the tricks of four-
teenth-century swashbucklery. But, in spite of all those resemblances,
Cleggett was, in toto, an original. The minute you had him pegged
as Lyndon or Fitzurse or Cheevy or Quixote, he became—Cleggett.
Marquis had so completely given this character the stamp of his own
individuality that he had in effect created something new.

One night Marquis dug up that old outline, added some new
touches, and submitted it. It was enthusiastically received and the
following week he had another book contract; and shortly thereafter
he was engaged in writing his second novel, which he called *The
Cruise of the Jasper B*. It was finished in 1915 and published the
following year.

The Cruise of the Jasper B. was the story of the aforementioned
Cleggett, a copy reader on the staff of the New York *Enterprise*,
who, though he seemed drab and unimaginative to his fellows, was
actually a soaring romantic whose dreams of glory kept him alive.
His release from the monotony of the daily grind was his escape on
the wings of fancy to the dream world where he regularly saved
Maidens in Distress from the Foul Play of Black-Hearted Villains,
usually by fighting duels which he unfailingly won. He was a man of
many facets. For example, he also happened to be a master criminol-
ogist and solved baffling crimes with an ease that flabbergasted the
world's greatest detectives.

One day Cleggett inherited a fortune and decided to quit his job
to devote himself to a life of adventure. In resigning he Roundly
Insulted the Tyrannical Editor who had Made Life Miserable for
him for years. An altercation results and when the editor calls him
a name that No Gentleman Can Overlook, Cleggett challenges him
to a duel. The editor—dirty coward!—declines. Cleggett makes a
jaunty exit, feeling he has scored a Moral Victory. Here we see him
leaving the office of the New York *Enterprise*, never to return:

As he left the elevator on the ground floor he stabbed the astonished
elevator boy under the left arm with his cane as a bayonet, cut him harm-

lessly over the head with his cane as a saber, tossed him a dollar, and left the building humming:

> "Oh, the Beau Sabreur of the Grande Armée
> Was the Captain Tarjeanterre!"

With the money he inherited Cleggett bought an old scow and began converting it into a seagoing vessel. His plan was to sail it hither and yon in quest of adventure. The scow, which he named the *Jasper B.*, was completely remodeled and became the scene of much drama and romance although it never once left its moorings.

Here is a sampling of Marquis's chapter heads:

> A Bright Blade Leaps from a Rusty Scabbard
> A Schooner, a Skipper and a Skull
> A Bad Man to Cross
> Beauty in Distress
> First Blood for Cleggett
> A Flame Leaps out of the Dark
> The Man in the Blue Pajamas

Reina referred to 1915 as "the year we both were pregnant." She was with child and Don, as he had put it, was "with book." The child arrived first—Robert Stewart Marquis, born November 7, 1915 —and a few months later the book made its bow. Don and Reina gave their son ecstatic notices, and the reviewers, although they did not go that far, were kind to *The Cruise of the Jasper B.*

One of the critics wrote that the best way to get a picture of the character Marquis had created was to consult the author's description of "the astonishing clutter of books and arms" that one found in Cleggett's room:

Stevenson, cavalry sabers, W. Clark Russell, pistols, and Dumas; Jack London, poignards, bowie knives, Stanley Weyman, Captain Marryat, and Dumas; sword canes, Scottish claymores, Cuban machetes, Conan Doyle, Harrison Ainsworth, dress swords, and Dumas; stilettos, daggers, hunting knives. . . .

The first edition of *The Cruise of the Jasper B.* was dedicated "to all copy readers on all the newspapers of America." This was changed in subsequent printings. But perhaps Marquis ought to explain the switch himself:

"I reckoned that there must be thousands of copy readers in America, and that they would all of them be so pleased and flattered by the dedication that each would buy a book for himself, and then go and buy another copy to give to someone at Christmas. And this would happen Christmas after Christmas, I thought.

"More than that, copy readers who were bringing up their sons to be copy readers (and it is a strange fact which I present to the sociologists for what it may be worth, that all copy readers wish their sons also to be copy readers) would give their sons this book. It seemed to me that I was made, not only in a literary way, but financially, by this one happy stroke.

"But the copy readers of America have not responded. Other persons have read the book, thousands of them, but so far as I have been able to gather not one single copy reader has ever perused it. Or, if they have, they will not talk about it. Copy readers to whom I have actually given copies never mention it again.

"I am not angry about this, but I confess that I am disappointed. The book is a good book, and they ought to be damned glad it was dedicated to them, and make a noise about it. The truth seems to be—I have arrived at the conclusion reluctantly—that they are not, as a class, worthy of the dedication.

"Therefore, I strip it from them, as far as this second dedication is concerned.

"I dedicate 80% of this book as it stands to Mr. Christopher Morley, poet, novelist, essayist and Founder of the Three Hours for Lunch Club.

"I dedicate the chapter containing the account of the storm at sea to Capt. David Bone, of the Cunard-Anchor Line ship *Tuscania*. I did not have the advantage of a conference with Capt. Bone before writing it, but he tells me that the seamanship, while unusual, is interesting.

"I dedicate the chapter containing the duel scene to Mr. Richard Malchien, formerly champion fencer of America, and one of the best in the world. Mr. Malchien says he wishes I would consult him before I write another duel scene.

"'But, Dick,' I told him, 'the main part of that duel scene *must* be right. I stole it right out of one of Dumas's romances.'

"'Dumas didn't know anything about fencing,' said Mr. Malchien.

"I dedicate all of Chapter XVI, entitled Romance Regnant, to the Poetry Society of America and its heirs and assigns forever."

Marquis's kidding of the brotherhood of copy readers caused no little merriment in newspaper circles. He received letters of condemnation reminding him that he had been a copy reader himself

and calling him a traitor to his class. One copy reader challenged him
to a duel.

Marquis, over a drink at Lipton's with a copy reader he knew from
the days when they both worked at that specialty for the Brooklyn
Daily Eagle, confessed that there was a bit of himself in the character
of Clement J. Cleggett, although his own particular dreams of glory
took a different turn. The secret life of Clement Cleggett had to do
with the past, Marquis's with today and tomorrow. In the dream
world to which he escaped Marquis was acknowledged to be the
greatest writer of all time, and other writers came from all over the
world to pay homage to him. He was also the world's greatest pool
player, having defeated—with ease—the champion of every country
where the game was played. He had also achieved such proficiency at
his favorite card game—poker—that no one any longer would
play against him, preferring to pay him handsome fees for lessons.

If that brilliant actor Alec Guinness ever finds himself in need of
a motion picture theme, I suggest that he consider the possibilities
of *The Cruise of the Jasper B*. I recently reread it and found that time
has not played havoc with its inspired lunacy. Guinness would make
a fine Clement Cleggett. He would be especially effective in a scene
in which Cleggett, who has a good opinion of himself as a detective,
flies into a jealous rage when someone praises Sherlock Holmes.
Clement considers himself the world's greatest master of the kind of
deductive reasoning essential to the solution of clever crimes, and
will not even countenance complimentary remarks about fictional
sleuths. It's an affront, that's what, and if you want to be in good
favor with the owner of the *Jasper B*., don't provoke him. He's a wonderful host if you remember the ground rules.

Royal Daniel, Jr., now editor and publisher of the Quitman (Ga.)
Free Press, recalls the days when he and Marquis lived in the same
building on Clinton Avenue in Brooklyn and Don, after a day's
columning on the *Evening Sun*, worked late at night on "The
Cruise of the Jasper B."

Writes Daniel: "I had a job on the 'lobster trick' of a Manhattan evening newspaper . . . It meant leaping out of bed at one
a.m., catching the elevated train at about 1:45 and entering the
office at three a.m. . . . . On my way out of the apartment, when I
passed the door to Don's apartment, I frequently heard the clickety-
click of his ancient Oliver typewriter. A scratch on the door brought

a warm welcome . . . Usually Don would break off writing, spoon some baked beans from an earthen pot, pour coffee from a carafe and command: 'Sit down and I'll read you a new chapter.'"

By 1916 "The Sun Dial" was solidly established. Marquis had become a figure—a definite factor in the life of New York. When a big political story broke it was a cinch that Marquis would make comment through archy; and it was equally certain that his following, in reading what the Vermin Voltaire had to say, would have two objectives in mind: to be entertained and to learn what Marquis thought.

Magazine editors continued to ask Marquis for short stories and articles and he wrote and sold as many as he could find the time for. He was finding himself with less and less time; so he could not take advantage of these opportunities on an important scale.

In the earliest days of "The Sun Dial" he was able to write his column with little or no interruption. Now that he was well known —and had in fact become a local celebrity—the interruptions were frequent and it was becoming harder and harder to get out his column. He tried writing it at home but this clashed with front-office policy. Nevertheless he took a chance occasionally and worked at home. Once there was hell to pay when he couldn't be reached to explain a paragraph that had a few words missing, a typing error he had failed to catch in copy-reading that particular column. He didn't think much of this crisis since he had plenty of overset in the composing room.

In *Shandygaff* Christopher Morley explained in graphic detail the work problem that confronted Marquis at this particular time:

"The tragedy of the columnist's task is that the better he does it the harder it becomes. People simply will not leave him alone. All day long they drop into his office, or call him up on the phone in the hope of getting into the column. Poor Don! he has become an institution down on Nassau Street: whatever hour of the day you call, you will find his queue there chivvying him. He is too gracious to throw them out: his only expedient is to take them over to the gin cathedral across the street and buy them a drink. . . . How many times I have sworn never to bother him again! And yet, when one is passing in that neighborhood, the temptation is irresistible. . . . I dare say Ben Jonson had the same trouble. Of course someone ought to endow Don and set him permanently at the head of a chophouse table, presiding over a kind of Mermaid coterie of robust wits. . . ."

Marquis was eager to free as much time as possible for magazine writing. He needed the money, for one thing. Besides, as he confessed, he enjoyed being courted by the publications with whose rejection slips he had papered his office at the Atlanta *Journal* in the early 1900s.

His financial problem had become more acute because of an unexpected development. His sister, Bernice Maud Marquis, who was known to the family as Maud, had resigned her job as a teacher in one of the Chicago public schools and had no means of support. She was being helped by her older sister Neva, also a Chicago schoolteacher, but Neva—or Nev, as the family called her—earned only a modest salary and it was not enough to take care of the needs of both, especially as Maud was doing a lot of "doctoring."

As a comparative youngster Maud had decided that she had "heart trouble" and nothing could shake her from this belief. Her father, a reputable physician, had tried to convince her that she was wrong but up to the time of his death had not succeeded. When the serious approach failed, he tried to laugh her into a better frame of mind about her health, which he considered excellent. One of his suggestions was that she try eating less. He thought the "distress" of which she complained was due largely to overeating.

Both Maud and Nev were older than Don, and Nev was the oldest of the three. Temperamentally, Don and Nev were much alike —both were good-natured, friendly, laughed easily, and were slow to take offense. Maud was inclined to be tense and somewhat grim, and had a faculty for finding unkind meanings in the most innocent remarks. Several people described her as "snappish."

Maud was a woman of taste. She read good books and discussed them intelligently. Nev's reading was not on as high a plane but she had a contagious enthusiasm about what she read and liked. Don, who read and appreciated good books himself, preferred the company of Nev. They made each other laugh. He was never quite sure how to deal with Maud. In later years she became known as the only person who could taunt him into a rage. They had their good times together, too, but he freely confessed to intimates that there was nothing in the world he feared as much as Maud's tongue.

Nev is remembered by friends of the family as "the jolly one," Maud as "the chronic complainer."

"Any way you look at it," Clive Weed, at one time Marquis's closest friend, confided, "Maud was bad news. She was so concerned about what went into her stomach that she thought nothing of disrupting the whole family. Her father, a hard-working country doctor, was left to shift for himself. And, according to Don, it never occurred to Maud that her persistent whining resulted in the uprooting of her mother, who allowed herself—foolish woman!—to be talked into the back-breaking job of running a boarding house. She had grown accustomed to small-town life. Big cities terrified her. And here she was running a boarding house in Chicago!"

Don was now regularly receiving gloomy letters from Maud telling how hard it was for her and Nev to live on Nev's salary. It is ironic to note that the "heart trouble" that caused Maud to quit her Chicago teaching job did not prevent her from fulfilling her father's prediction that "she was the kind of healthy hypochondriac who was destined to live a ripe old age."

"As dull as duty" was one of Marquis's favorite expressions; but it never prevented him from honoring what he considered a family obligation. He agreed to send Maud a monthly check—not realizing at the time that he had assumed a responsibility that would continue for the rest of his life.

Marquis decided he would *have* to find time for more magazine work.

A few years later he observed that "there's nothing so habit-forming as money." It was shortly after he had cautiously suggested to Maud that, if her "heart trouble" was better, she might want to resume her work as a schoolteacher. "It was like trying to cut off a drug addict's dope supply. She damn near had a fit. This was a cruel time to bring up the subject, she pointed out, since I knew very well she was preparing to leave for Florida for the winter. Florida, she reminded me, was good for her heart. I decided then and there to take on still more outside work."

As has been pointed out, Marquis was free with his money. If his family needed it, or a friend, and he had it, he would help; there were also times when he didn't have it and he borrowed in order to be of help.

What bothered him about Maud—it was something he forgave but which he was incapable of putting out of his mind completely—was that her series of laments about the inadequacy of the food in that Chicago boarding house had worried her mother to the extent that she left Dr. Marquis to run the house in Walnut by himself so that she might look after her daughter. This had angered him; for since his boyhood days his father had been his hero, the kind of selfless country doctor whose one thought was to be of service to the community. He blamed his mother too for her poor judgment in leaving the good doctor's side. But mostly he blamed Maud for creating a situation that had deprived her father of the kind of home life he needed to carry on his work.

There is ample evidence in Marquis's work of his love and admiration of his father. In a short story characterized by a simple, almost matter-of-fact kind of eloquence, "Country Doctor," published in the *American Magazine*, Dr. Marquis emerges as a man of heroic proportions.

In this story the protagonist is a Dr. Stewart—(the author's father was James *Stewart* Marquis)—and the locale is undoubtedly Walnut, Illinois, and environs. This is made clear by the geographical details.

Here is a glimpse of Dr. Stewart—i.e., Dr. Marquis—taken from that story: "He was a country doctor and he did not know what it was to spare himself. He had been going hard all last winter and spring—battling through prairie blizzards, battling through flooded swamps, to some remote house of suffering, battling all night to save a life, and reaching home again in the dawn, to gulp down a pot of boiling coffee and take up the new day's work without an hour of sleep."

And here is another, especially pertinent as it gives a picture Marquis developed verbally in telling friends about the conditions under which his father worked:

"It was still raining; the water had been flung turbulently down out of the sky all day long. And now it was early dusk, an October dusk, and the world outside the Doctor's windows was a chaos of cold, wind-driven rain and lowering gloom and mud, the sticky black mud of northwestern Illinois which clings and clogs and overwhelms. Dr. Stewart peered out at the village street, or as much of it as he could see through the wind-slashed crevices in the murky wall of storm, and drew the heavy shawl tighter about his shoulders, and took another sip of his hot lemonade, and breathed a little prayer that he would not have a call, especially a call out to the Swamp.

"He shuddered when he thought of what the Swamp would be like tonight. Green River, which drained the vast tract westward to

Rock River and the Mississippi, would be up and roaring and tearing at its low clay banks; and the swamp roads—if you could call them roads at all when the spring and autumn floods were in spate—would be roiled and brawling creeks, themselves, in places, almost rivers. And here and there would be a melancholy twinkle of light, flickering through the mists and scrub timber across the bogs and bayous, from some lonely farmhouse perched on a wooded island. For scattered over the district, forty miles or so in length and half as broad, were many farmers; and even when the freshets left them only a third or a quarter of the crops they had planted, they still could live, for the land was incredibly rich.

"Dr. Stewart knew the Swamp and its people, none better; for day and night, winter, spring and fall, sick or well, he had had a good many years of it.

"'Always ague, malaria and influenza,' he murmured. And then, with grim self-irony, 'I've dumped enough quinine into that hole, myself, to pave a solid road from Dante's frozen hell to Timbuctoo, and still it shakes, shivers and shakes.'"

Marquis, a past master at self-reproach, used to upbraid himself for having jumped from job to job with bewildering frequency right up to the time of his father's death, leaving the old gentleman with the feeling that he would never amount to anything.

Asked how his father voiced his displeasure, Marquis invariably replied that The Doctor had never once criticized him: "He never said an unkind word to me in all his life." When the logical next question was asked, "Then how did you know he thought you'd never amount to anything?" Marquis would reply that he could read it in his eyes. This curious bent for self-reproach—at times it bordered on self-torture—never left Marquis. It was characteristic throughout his life that he didn't wait for others to accuse him. He accused himself.

Greenwich Village was very much in the news in those days. Marquis decided to see for himself. He had written that one of the wonderful things about New York was that everything was so neatly departmentalized—there was a cloak-and-suit area, a jewelry district, a big fish market, a neighborhood devoted to the fur business, etc., etc.—and if you wanted to look over the latest thing in pseudo-culture you could go to Greenwich Village.

Marquis induced Reina to join him on his first excursion to the

Village. This took considerable coaxing as she was loath to leave little Bobby alone. The word "baby-sitter" had not yet come into being but the practice *had*; and she succeeded in finding a friend—a neighbor who was a trained nurse—to look after her baby so that she and Don could take a look at Culture as practiced in some of the establishments that made up New York's Cognoscente Center (a Marquisism).

Reina was glad to get away from the flat in Brooklyn but, typically, told her Tommy—(as in their earliest days together, she still used that nickname)—that she was pretty sure he'd be able to pick up more stuff to write about if he visited Greenwich Village alone. The budding young poetesses, for instance, would feel freer to gather round and bare their souls if he didn't have a woman with him.

Reina was the ideal wife for a writer. She kept telling her husband that to keep his column fresh it was essential that he occasionally prowl around town by himself and look for things to write about —that inevitably he would be thrown in with "characters" who would quicken him to thought on possibilities for the column, and for extravaganzas of different kinds; and by getting the views of strangers on what was going on in the world he might get new insights on how to richen the humor of his comments on current happenings.

What Don and Reina saw that first night, with due allowance for Marquisian extravagance, is reflected in the following, which is taken from a column-long piece he wrote on the subject:

> I visited one night, of late,
> Thought's Underworld, the Brainstorm Slum,
> The land of Futile Piffledom;
> A salon weird where congregate
> Freak, Nut and Bug and Psychic Bum.
>
> There, there, they sit and cerebrate:
> The fervid Pote who never potes,
> Great Artists, Male or She, that Talk
> But scorn the Pigment and the Chalk,
> And Cubist sculptors wild as Goats,
> Theosophists and Swamis, too . . .
> Tame Anarchists, a dreary crew,
> Squib Socialists too damp to sosh,
> Fake Hobohemians steeped in suds,
> Glib Females in Artistic Duds

With Captive Husbands cowed and gauche . . .
I saw a Genius on the Brink
(Or so he said) of suicide.
I saw a Playwright who had tried
But couldn't make the Public think;
I saw a Novelist who cried,
Reading his own Stuff, in his drink . . .

A rat-faced Idiot Boy who slimes
White paper o'er with metric crimes—
He is a kind of Burbling Blear
Who warbles Sex Slush sad to hear,
And mocks God in his stolen rhymes
And wears a ruby in one ear—
Murmured to me: "My Golden Soul
Drinks Song from out a Crystal Bowl . . .
Drinks Love and Song . . . my Golden Soul!"
I let him live. There were no bricks,
Or even now that Golden Soul
Were treading water in the Styx.

After a few more trips to Greenwich Village Marquis launched a
series in "The Sun Dial" that was destined for fame—"Hermione
and Her Little Group of Serious Thinkers."

The Hermione series had none of the angry overtones of that introductory poem and therefore had more bite. Marquis returned to
the device that enabled him to achieve his most felicitous effects:
kidding. Occasionally the spoofing was rough-and-tumble but in the
main it was good-natured, doing its deadliest work when the writing was blandest. Which is another way of saying that Marquis, in
satirizing current fads and fancies, was at his best as a deadpan
comic.

Pseudo-intellectuals, Marquis thought and wrote, were Old Stuff.
There was nothing new about charlatanry in the arts; but never had
he seen it so lavishly practiced. And never had he known it to be so
accessible. It was as great a convenience, he told friends, as an established red-light district. If you were in the mood for a cultural
bordello you knew just where to go. Here in the New Bohemia the
seven lively arts daily grew livelier if not lovelier. The Poetry Renaissance, which reached full bloom in the 1920s, was beginning to
sprout and the town was alive with literary cocktail parties featured
by chanted versions of poetry then current—and some manufac-

tured on the spot. The word "recitation" had lost favor. Poems were
"chanted," not recited, and if you knew how to "chant" you were
good for several cocktail parties a month and all the alcoholic stoking
you needed to get up a good head of chanting steam. It made no
difference whether the poem you read required chanting, as did
Vachel Lindsay's "The Congo" or his "General Booth Enters into
Heaven"; in Greenwich Village you chanted because that had become the thing to do.

Marquis's timing was good. He created Hermione at the psychological moment. She was a much-needed antidote; and soon she was
being widely quoted. New Yorkers who had suffered through endless
stretches of the "futile Piffledom" Marquis described in his opening
blast hailed her and joyfully used her pet phrases as a device for
kidding the phony in every field.

It wasn't long before Appleton and Company, publishers of *The
Cruise of the Jasper B.*, asked for a book. It was published in 1917
and gratefully received by most of the reviewers. The title was the
same as the one Marquis used in his column except that it was split
into title and subtitle, as follows:

HERMIONE
And Her Little Group of Serious Thinkers

It was made up of sixty of the Hermione pieces that Marquis had
published in the *Sun*, each one making its own particular point. Here
are some typical chapter heads:

Vibrations
The Swami Brandranath
Aren't the Russians Wonderful?
Soul Mates
Literature
Mama Is So Mid-Victorian
Beautiful Thoughts
Will the Best People Receive the Superman Socially?
The Parasite Woman Must Go!
Fothergil Finch Tells of His Revolt against Organized Society
On Being Other-Worldly
Psychic Power
The Little Group Gives a Pagan Masque
The Bourgeois Element
The Japanese Are Wonderful, If You Get What I Mean

In the book-publishing world, whose editors, readers, and sundry other workers had suffered through so much of the New Literature, Hermione's pet expression, "if you get what I mean," became a shibboleth.

Hermione is still an impressive book. Flip it open almost anywhere and you come up with a reasonably good lampoon, though, of course, some of the things Marquis satirized have long since been laughed out of court. I tried the experiment as I worked on these pages and came up with the following:

"Isn't Heredity wonderful, though!

"We've been going into it rather deeply—My Little Group of Serious Thinkers, you know.

"And, really, when you get into it, it's quite complicated. All about Homozygotes and Heterozygotes, you know. . . .

"Don't you think the great lesson of Heredity is that Blood will Tell?

"Really the farther I go into Philosophy and Science and such things the more clearly I see what a fund of truth there is in the old simple proverbs! . . .

"Isn't the Subliminal Consciousness wonderful; simply *wonderful?*

"We're going to take it up in a serious way some evening next week, and thresh it out thoroughly.

"But I must run along. I have an engagement with my dressmaker at two o'clock. You know, I've really found one who can make my gowns interpret my inner spirit."

In *Harper's Magazine* for March 1950 Bernard De Voto, an all-out Marquis fan and the kind of critic Marquis never had in his corner during his lifetime, wrote: "A year or so ago I tossed an allusion to Hermione into a review of a silly book; at least one scarred veteran of her era was soothed by it, for he wrote and told me so. . . . Hermione is with us still, and Fothergil Finch, and her whole Group. Their stuff is in a different key now but no effort is required to transpose it to the original one; only the key ever changes, the melody is the same forever."

Subsequently Marquis had several looks at Greenwich Village, once in the company of a *Sun* reporter who claimed to be an authority on the subject. He knew all the places with names like the Green Canary, the Blond Zebra, the Grotto Euterpe, Pierian Walk, Rebels Rendezvous, Thalia Tea Room, Free Souls' Salon, etc., and Marquis agreed to make the Grand Tour with this office mate after they had highballed themselves into an adventuresome mood at Lipton's.

Before they set out they returned to the office, which was across the street, so that Marquis could slip into his pocket a free-verse pronunciamento he planned to ascribe in one of his columns to Fothergil Finch, Hermione's soul mate on the Cultural Front. Here is a quote from it:

> Look at Me!
> Behold, I am founding a New Movement!
> Observe me . . . I am in Revolt!
> I revolt!
> Now persecute me, persecute me, damn you, persecute
>   me, curse you, persecute me!
> Philistine,
> Bourgeois,
> Slave,
> Serf,
> Capitalist,
> Respectabilities that you are,
> Persecute me!
> Bah!
> You ask me, do you, what I am in revolt against?
> Against you, fool, dolt, idiot, against you, against everything!

On the itinerary was a gypsy tearoom, run by a poetic nomad from the Bronx in whose establishment it was customary for the patrons—mostly young Poets of Revolt—to read their own stuff, when they could get the floor. Marquis could visit such places without being recognized because, though his column was now well known, his picture had not appeared in the papers since the publication of *Danny's Own Story* about five years earlier.

Marquis and his *Sun* crony listened to these young bardlings read their stuff and thought their brand of nonconformity rather tame. They—Marquis and his guide—were sufficiently alcoholized to think it was time the audience heard something with a kick in it. They announced that they were about to do a two-part reading, Marquis's companion to open and he to close. Accordingly, they tore the poem in half and proceeded. When the *Sun* reporter reached the passage,

> Philistine,
> Bourgeois,
> Slave,

> Serf,
> Capitalist,
> Respectabilities that you are,
> Persecute me!—

there was wild applause. Marquis was applauded too when he took over but not as vociferously; and he remarked later that that was the last time he'd give a lousy reporter the best lines and let him steal the show.

When they had departed, Marquis told his companion that he was convinced that his vers libre manifesto lacked something. If it had been first-rate satire, he argued, they would not have been applauded; they would have been thrown out.

Marquis kept adding to his gallery of characters—among them Aunt Prudence Hecklebury, described by her creator as "the ancient and indubitably virgin reformer," and the "red-haired lady," to whom he addressed countless sonnets, from one of which this sample is taken:

> When I approach the chill Lethean river
> And stand, all astral gooseflesh, on the brim,
> Will your Red Head shine for me through the dim
> Damp shadows where I rub my soul and shiver
> As I await old Charon's hydro-flivver?

And this:

> O Lovely Griddle where my Cakes of Song
> Are baked! O Gulf Stream of my ocean deep!
> O Human Thermos Bottle! will you keep
> My love as hot as this our whole lives long?

He also launched a series of narrative poems called "Famous Love Affairs," most of them a full column long. Here are the opening stanzas of one of them, "Lancelot and Guinevere":

> King Arthur was a steady king,
>   Who loathed light talk or skittish,
> Respectable as anything,
>   Strong-'eaded, blond and British.

> His Queen beside him on the throne,
>   So golding-'aired and tidy,
> Would tip the beam at fourteen stone,
>   And every ounce a lydy.

Sir Lancelot was 'andsome, quite,
   The women all adored him—
He tried to bear it like a knight,
   But being worshipped bored him.

His big, bright shield was curved and bent
   And more tub-shaped than normal;
He'd often halt a tournament
   And bathe, all stern and formal.

The knights, they might 'ave bashed 'im then
   While 'e was coldly scrubbing,
But they were British gentlemen
   Respectful of his tubbing.

An important addition to Marquis's gallery of characters was the Old Soak—subsequently christened "Clem Hawley" after the matter had been put up to readers of "The Sun Dial." In later years Marquis spoke affectionately of Mr. Hawley as the character who had made him the most money.

The Old Soak summed up his philosophy as follows: "Three things I always held by—the old-time religion and calomel and straight whiskey."

Marquis's sisters—Maud and Nev—had moved from Chicago to New York and had taken up residence at the Hotel Irving. Nev had become eligible for a small pension from the Chicago school system. This was the only income the sisters had. Marquis supplied the rest. The *Sun* had increased his salary and he had become a fairly regular contributor to the magazines. Book royalties had also helped, though these had not yet become an important factor.

Reina continued to contribute to the family income. She had a monthly department in *Today's Magazine for Women*; and she also made an occasional sale to *The Delineator* and the other Butterick magazines, whose editor-in-chief in those days was Theodore Dreiser.

In 1916 Marquis arranged a summer vacation for his sisters at Seacliff, Long Island. One day Nev telephoned him to announce in a voice bursting with emotion that Maud was dying. Don telephoned Homer Croy (who tells the story), gave him the news, and asked Homer if he could drive to Seacliff with him. Homer grasped that his friend needed company and they made the trip together. Homer gives a graphic account of what proved to be a nerve-racking trip. Whenever traffic slowed him down Don fumed; he risked arrest by pushing his car for all it was worth. As they pulled up in front of the inn where his sisters were stopping, Don found it hard to credit what he saw through the glass-enclosed front porch—Maud calmly rocking herself! She was feeling better now, she announced; but she *had* thought she was dying when she asked Nev to telephone. This was one of the devices Maud used when she thought she was being neglected and felt the need for attention; she suffered several of these fictional deaths before her actual demise many years later at the age of eighty-one.

In those days before the dawn of the twenties Marquis had done his share of drinking. A member of the staff of the Players Club, which he joined in 1916 and which became his favorite haunt, said it was hard to classify Marquis as a drinker. This man—Charles Connolly, today an honorary member—stated that although Marquis sometimes "drank plenty" you wouldn't call him a heavy drinker because there were times when he drank lightly and stretches when he didn't drink at all. Once after he had announced his decision to quit drinking for a whole month he was found at the Players bar with a highball in his hand after only a week's abstinence. Heckled, he calmly said that he had *hoped* someone would mention it so that he could try out the following wheeze, and use it in his column in case anyone laughed, "even charitably": when you get jounced in a wagon long enough—a Water Wagon or any other kind—you develop a terrestrial *mal de mer* comparable to car sickness. He had found only one cure, the remedy which he held in his hand and which he recommended to members of the Club suffering from the same ailment.

Another time Marquis put it this way: he was a militant wet, as anyone familiar with his column knew. How would it look if he didn't practice what he preached? To complicate things, Hermione was forever preaching sincerity. ("Sincerity should be the keynote of a life, don't you think? . . . Sincerity, that is my watchword. . . . I heard such an interesting talk on Sincerity the other evening. . . . My little group of serious thinkers is taking it up in all its phases this week. . . . Sincerity is next to godliness, as the old 'saw' so aptly puts it. . . . I hope to make many converts to Sincerity . . . I *sincerely* do. . . . Ha! ha! The light touch helps, don't you think?")

Friends at the Players bar agreed completely and they joined Marquis in a toast to Sincerity.

One incident in this category became famous. Marquis, in one of his more remorseful moments, announced that he would never take another drink in all his life.

These were the circumstances: a former associate on the Atlanta *Journal* had looked him up and Don had shown him the town. They had done the job so thoroughly that the boss of "The Sun Dial" arrived home at about five o'clock in the morning minus his overcoat and with no recollection of what had happened to it. He developed a heavy cold that almost turned into pneumonia; and, until he was better a few days later, his good friend Dana Burnet ran his column for him.

This was Marquis's low point as a drinker. He said afterward that if Reina had given him hell, for which with typical self-reproachfulness, he thought there was justification, he would not have felt so badly. But, characteristically, she took the matter calmly and put "Tommy" to bed, and when he apologized and tried to explain what had happened she told him she understood, adding that it must have been quite a reunion. (She knew and liked the Georgia newspaperman with whom her husband had been pub-crawling most of the night.)

With typical Marquisian remorse he told Reina he would never "touch another drop." She wasn't sure that was a good idea, she said. She'd prefer to hear him say that from now on he would try to drink more carefully.

Reina seldom took a drink herself. But she had lived among newspaper people and writers most of her life and she didn't want Tommy to overpromise. She seriously thought that when he didn't overdo, drinking was good for him, that it provided necessary relaxation. She told friends that he was at his merriest after drinking a bottle or two of beer at home, and that an unending source of amusement for her was his latest discovery—there was a long series of them—of the "biggest schooner of lager in town for a nickel."

But Marquis, who often described himself as a "shark for repentance," was at his remorseful best that day and repeated that he would never touch another drop, by God, adding dramatically that, by all that was good and holy, he had the will power to do it, too.

Marquis usually wrote a serious poem after a spree. It was one of several ways in which his bent for self-castigation manifested itself. Of his "repentance poems" his favorite was "This Is Another Day," which he had written early in his career. He liked it best because he thought it the most philosophic—i.e., after wallowing in self-reproach he held out some hope for a bright tomorrow.

Because it illustrates better than anything else he wrote what has been described earlier in these pages as one of Marquis's most ingrained characteristics, this poem, to which he added new stanzas when he thought the time for self-chastisement had come, is reprinted:

> I am mine own priest, and I shrive myself
> Of all my wasted yesterdays. Though sin
> And sloth and foolishness, and all ill weeds
> Of error, evil, and neglect grow rank
> And ugly there, I dare forgive myself
> That error, sin, and sloth and foolishness.
> God knows that yesterday I played the fool;
> God knows that yesterday I played the knave;
> But shall I therefore cloud this new dawn o'er
> With fog of futile sighs and vain regrets?
>
> This is another day! And flushed Hope walks
> Adown the sunward slopes with golden shoon.
> This is another day; and its young strength
> Is laid upon the quivering hills until,
> Like Egypt's Memnon, they grow quick with song.
> This is another day, and the bold world
> Leaps up and grasps its light, and laughs, as leapt
> Prometheus up and wrenched the fire from Zeus.

One day, after fulfilling the first month of his pledge to stay on the water wagon forever and a day, Marquis was seen entering the taproom of the Players Club. Advancing to the bar he announced, "I've conquered my goddam will power. A double scotch, please."

Thanks to the management of the Players, in 1959 an announcement was sent to the full membership of the Club informing them that a fellow member was working on a biography of Don Marquis and that anecdotes, odds and ends of human interest, letters, and authentic memorabilia in any category would be gratefully received.

The response was excellent and a number of productive letters and interviews resulted. It might be worth noting, in support of the enduring quality of Marquis's conquest of his will power, that of those who responded to my appeal for biographical data, twenty-two recounted this anecdote, either orally or in writing.

The anecdote has also crept into an assortment of biographies, joke books, magazine articles, etc. The crispest versions of it are to be found in George Middleton's engrossing memoir, *These Things Are Mine*, and in E. B. White's introduction to the current edition of *the lives and times of archy and mehitabel*. A few passages from White's piece, a felicitous blend of biography and critique, are reprinted here as a significant tribute from one humorist to another:

"When the publisher asked me to write a few introductory remarks about Don Marquis for this new edition of *archy and mehitabel*, he said in his letter: 'The sales of this particular volume have been really astounding.'

"They do not astound me. Among books of humor by American authors, there are only a handful that rest solidly on the shelf. This . . . is one of those books. It is funny, it is wise, it is tender, and it is tough. The sales do not astound me; only the author astounds me, for I know (or think I do) at what cost Don Marquis produced these gaudy and irreverent tales. He was the sort of poet who does not create easily; he was left unsatisfied and gloomy by what he produced; day and night he felt the juices squeezed out of him by the merciless demands of daily newspaper work; he was never quite certified by intellectuals and serious critics of belles lettres. . . .

"I hesitate to say anything about humor, hesitate to attempt an interpretation of any man's humor: it is as futile as explaining a spider's web in terms of geometry. Marquis was, and is, to me a very funny man, his product rich and satisfying, full of sad beauty, bawdy adventure, political wisdom, and wild surmise; full of pain and jollity, full of exact and inspired writing."

One day Marquis and Clive Weed, a political cartoonist, discovered each other at Lipton's. Weed had come to New York from Philadelphia where he had worked for the *Press* and the *Record-Ledger*. In New York, over a period of years, he worked for the *Evening Sun*, the *Tribune*, and the *World* (achieving his greatest success with the last-named).

Both men had studied art, Weed at the Academy of Fine Arts in Philadelphia, Marquis at the Corcoran School in Washington. Weed had been a pupil and protégé of Thomas Anshutz, whose paintings are represented in the permanent collection of the Philadelphia Academy.

Weed said he had visited the Corcoran School once when he was in Washington and recalled that many of the students affected Windsor ties. "Remember those young idiots?" he asked. "We had a few of them at the Philadelphia Academy but Corcoran had a swarm." Marquis said he certainly did remember—in fact, he was one of "the swarm." What was wrong with being an idiot when you were young, Marquis wanted to know. Wasn't that normal? "Unless you've worn one," he told Weed, "you don't know how important a Windsor tie makes a young idiot feel—especially if he has no talent."

Weed had started life as a painter, had been unable to make a living at it, and had turned to cartooning. But he continued to paint as a hobby.

Marquis had studied art only briefly and never had a chance to learn whether there was anything to his hunch that he might have developed into a pretty good portrait painter. Since he had studied art for "only about ten minutes" this question would remain unanswered; but he *did* know, he insisted, that none of those other young idiots at the Corcoran School had his particular flair for wearing a Windsor tie. "I wore mine with an air," he insisted.

When they met for a drink a few days later Weed appeared in an extra-long, flowing Windsor tie. This was the kind of fooling that appealed to Marquis. They met frequently thereafter. Both were lively conversationalists and both liked to laugh. It was a friendship that was destined to last for years.

I became acquainted with Weed a few years later—an acquaintanceship that ripened into a close friendship; and, from this knowledge of the man, can understand why Marquis enjoyed his companionship. Weed was well-informed. And his views on books, art, and what was going on in the world were strikingly expressed. He was a flowing conversationalist; but, though he liked to talk, he was also a good listener. His impatience with stuffiness and cant was as real as Marquis's and they had a lot of fun shooting at the same targets. One of their favorite pastimes was reading aloud pompous excerpts from trite speeches reported in the press.

Although they agreed on most things, they had their disagreements too, and they enjoyed themselves most during the ensuing arguments in which each tried to outdo the other in the matter of mock insults. Once during one of these exchanges Weed exclaimed, "Do you realize, sir, that you are vilifying one who is descended from royalty? Which reminds me, who are *you* descended from?"

"I am not a descendant," replied Marquis, quoting a French wit, "I am an ancestor!"

Weed frequently alluded to this as his favorite squelch.

Inevitably there was a dinner foursome at which Reina and Weed's wife, Helen, met. The women liked each other and became warm friends, as revealed by the letters they subsequently exchanged.

The Weeds lived in New Jersey, within commuting distance of New York, and raised fruit and vegetables on a plot of land that went with their home. Clive frequently met Don at Lipton's with a parcel of produce, and when Don remembered to bring it home it was joyfully received by Reina, who missed the fresh vegetables that were so plentiful, and so inexpensive, in Atlanta. There always was a problem when Reina had to acknowledge a parcel that Don had left in Lipton's, the office, the subway, or a streetcar.

This called for ingenuity. Sometimes Don handled the matter himself—in a brief poem so constructed that it wasn't necessary to mention specifically what was inside the parcel. One was called "On Receiving a Present from Clive and Helen and Mother Nature." The phrase "earth's bounteous gift" was as close as Don dared go in referring to the contents of the package.

Once a missing parcel of fruits and vegetables turned up in Lipton's a week after Marquis had left it there. After opening it and surveying the contents, most of it rather sad-looking by then, he wrote an ecstatic note of thanks in which he referred specifically to every item. He apologized to Reina for his carelessness but forgot to mention that he had acknowledged the package; so Reina wrote an effusive note telling Helen Weed how much they had enjoyed her gift.

Mrs. Weed thought it was charming of the Marquises to send *two* letters of acknowledgment and promised Reina that the next bundle Clive brought in would be the biggest of all because of their enthusiasm. This package was rather cumbersome and gave Marquis an excuse to go home by taxi. He left the package in the cab.

Most of the letters the Marquises and the Weeds exchanged are undated or only partially dated. Several of Marquis's are signed "Darling Don," a signature he sometimes affected when he had been unable to resist the temptation to call Clive Weed by his Marquis-coined nickname—Old Fishface. Weed in turn had struggled to find a nickname for Don, who tried to help him out by suggesting various possibilities, including Darling Don, which signature he used only in his correspondence with the Weeds.

In a letter dated December 10 we find Don writing Clive and Helen and addressing them as "Dear Children." Reporting on his infant son Bobby, also known as the Bobber, he wrote: "The Angel Pup was weighed today, and he is now a great big hulking animal of 6 pounds and three ounces. This is a gain of 19 ounces since he was born, so you can see he is coming along fine. His mother is doing well, but he keeps her pretty tired. Especially because he gets a meal at 10 P.M., another at 2 in the morning; so you see her rest is broken. To do him justice, he is not much of a night howler, though one night he howled for 4 hours at a stretch. He does bite, kick, scratch, squirm, strike with his fists and yell when his ears are washed. He is certainly a job. The nurse has been gone a week, and Reina has been doing everything for him herself. I've been home from the office on a week's vacation. He has taken all her time and most of mine. (He gets fed every two hours all day). If he had 2 grand-mothers, 4 aunts and three nurses he would take all their time too.

"Reina has been frightfully busy. She meant to write again. With love from the three of us to both of you, Don."

In an undated letter Reina wrote to Clive:

"I'm ever so grateful to you for sending me the news about Helen. . . . It's a great relief to know the operation's safely over. You know I love her lots more than I've ever been able to tell her and it hurts me to have her hurt. But I'm sure this is the beginning of better health for her and happier days for both of you. . . .

"Bobby's been sick with intestinal indigestion ever since you were here, and I've had my hands more than full. He's about straightened out now, I think, so I'll get a few minutes for other folks.

"I'm glad you appreciate the Bobber. Of course I expected you would—but now and then someone fails to become eloquent enough about his charms and graces. Tell Helen that he's worth coming to New York to see and that she must do it as soon as she's able to stand a household that revolves around a baby. I admit it isn't restful.

"Tommy's grown sassy about my writing you and sends the en-closed to Helen—for you to deliver! Lovely situation, isn't it? Love to you both, Reina (Queenie)"

There was a standing joke among the four about Clive and Reina and Don and Helen being too fond of one another. There were several exchanges about this. In one Marquis delivered a tongue-in-cheek rebuke to Weed for showing "too much interest in Reina." The letter concluded: "And she a nursing mother too!"

Reina had been writing a monthly page for *Today's Magazine for Women*. When Bobby was born and developed illness after illness, she received permission from the magazine to do her work at home.

This made it necessary for *Today's*, as Reina called it, to send to her the letters that came in from readers of her department (excerpts from which she sometimes used). It also necessitated her conferring over the telephone with the editor to whom she reported. It was an awkward arrangement and Reina sensed that the management, although they had agreed to give it a trial, were not enthusiastic about it.

Because of the need to send a monthly check to Don's sister Maud, this job of Reina's occupied an important place in the Marquis economy. Recalling that Helen Weed knew the editor to whom she reported, Reina wrote her: "Please write my boss whenever it's convenient! I'll need all the help I can get in holding my job if I'm to be a semi-invalid long. Thanks!!!"

In another undated letter that was evidently written not long after the foregoing, Don thanked Helen Weed for a handsome gift of golden bantam corn, ginger cakes, and pears that she and Clive sent him as a birthday present. He declared that they'd never had "finer meals" than the ones Reina prepared with the aid of the Weed contribution to the Marquis larder.

That offering came at the psychological moment, Don pointed out, because with the arrival of every new birthday he was reminded that he was "galloping toward middle age," a thought that depressed him and affected his appetite so adversely that now he could not manage more than four meals a day.

Reina appended a postscript in which she said: "Here's *my* thanks too! *Today's*—in the person of Miss Splint—has just fired me. Nothing less than your ginger cakes and golden bantam corn could possibly have comforted me. A letter from you would also help, however. Lots of love, Reina—Queenie."

The Marquis-Weed letters reflect a warm friendship. Occasionally there are minor differences, as when Helen Weed good-naturedly refers to Don as "difficult."

In his reply Marquis declares that Helen is right but thinks his intractability can be explained. At any rate, he attempts it, calling

himself the type of difficult person who got that way through an
excess of refinement. When a man is as utterly refined as Don Marquis he develops an oversensitivity, with the result that he is sometimes annoyed by things that do not bother people of a coarser
strain.

Having disposed of that question, Marquis continues in another
vein. The letter is a long one. Toward the end it provides a good
example of how the columnist complicated his social life and how
he went about extricating himself. The following illustrates his technique:

"Well, Clive and Helen, I am in bad about something else, and if
you see Sam McCoy soon I hope you will tell him how it was and
that I do not wish to be misunderstood about it. Reina says Sam
probably sent me an announcement card to his wedding, and that
I left it at the office, and I am not saying whether I did leave it or
whether I did not leave it. But if I did leave it the reason was this:
I was very nervous, on account of the moving of the Sun from 170
Nassau Street to 150 Nassau Street being postponed so many times,
and it looked for a while as if we were never going to move.

"It was like this: they would say you must get all your papers
together on your desk so as to make the move easy, and tie them into
bundles, for we will move Saturday and we want the papers on the
desks in bundles, and every week when Saturday was coming around
I would tie all the papers on my desk into bundles and then they
would not move that Saturday after all, but would put it off to the
next Saturday, but there would be the bundles on my desk, and then
the next Saturday it would be the same thing again, with more and
more bundles piling on my desk week after week, and still no moving,
for weeks and weeks like that, Clive and Helen, and me not daring
to untie any of the bundles after I had tied them up, for fear just
the day I untied a bundle would be the day they finally moved.

"And so it went along like that with more and more letters getting
into bundles, and me getting more and more nervous, and intending
to open the bundles in the new building, only never getting into
the new building for weeks and weeks, and when I was not tieing
my own bundles the office boy would go over to my desk and tie
bundles, and it seems very likely to me that the day Sam's wedding
announcement came into the office was one of the days when the
office boy was tieing the bundles, and so I never saw it at all, and
the bundles are not all untied yet in the new building, and I am

nervous about some of them, and never after the bundles were tied could I tell which was the office boy's bundles and which were mine for he ties just like me. His name is Godfrey Rosenbaum, Clive,—he is the boy that was always trying to draw, so if Sam's wedding announcement came that is the reason I did not write him about it or bring it home, and it seems to me I have been misunderstood. When I told Reina, she was incredulous about those bundles, but I trust to make her understand.

"Now, Clive, here is what I want you to do: if you will talk about this and that with Sam, in an easy-going sort of way, and never let him know what you are driving at, maybe you can find out if he really sent me a wedding announcement. And if he did send me one, you tell him about the bundles, for that is my explanation of that, and I hope he will understand it. But if you talk with him in a roundabout, easy-going way and find out he forgot to send me one, then don't mention the bundles at all, but say you got a letter from me and I was very grieved because I got no wedding announcement, and wrote you so, and then *he* will have to do some explaining so I will not misunderstand *him*, because people are always misunderstanding me, and I don't want to misunderstand anyone else, if I can help it, but will go to a good deal of trouble not to, as it grieves persons, especially if refined. With love to all, Don."

In one letter we find Reina apologizing to the Weeds for not asking them over to see the latest of the several flats she and her husband occupied in Brooklyn: "This will seem a dreary hole to you when you come to it from the country. Tommy became very much excited over your imposing term—'crops.' I believe he now regards Clive with awe as a country gentleman."

In this letter Reina speculates on the advisability of moving to a better apartment, one that she had recently looked at. Because of the heavy medical expense they were under at the time she decided against it, explaining, "The rent—$55. a month—appalls me."

If not for the check that her husband sent monthly to his sister Maud, Reina would have been able to move her little family to more attractive quarters. Weed quoted Marquis as saying that Reina never once complained about this awkward situation. Marquis's way of putting it was something like this: Reina, when she wasn't feeling well, was capable of an occasional irritable comment on something of no importance but that where the big issues were involved—like a monthly check to his sister—she was incapable of embarrassing him.

There are many letters indicating that Bobby was a sickly child until the time of his death at the age of five years and three months. These letters reveal that a number of times the plans of the Weeds and the Marquises to get together were canceled because of Bobby's condition, reinstated, and canceled again.

In a typical letter to Clive Weed about his luckless little son, Don writes in part:

". . . Bobby has been very sick again. He went down to almost nothing. Reina now has a trained nurse to look after him, and a cook to look after the nurse. So all Reina has to do now is to look after the cook and the nurse and him. He has slept for several nights past, and during the last few days has taken a little food voluntarily again. For a while he had to be forcibly fed again. He will pull through but it has been the deuce and all. . . .

"Reina has been too near to collapse to write. . . .

"Outside of sickness, things have been about the goddamned same. Nobody getting anything done but their Christianful jobs and duty, and everybody getting older and a hell of a while yet before financial support can be expected of the younger generation so we can sit back in ease and tell what we might have done and been if things had been different."

The Weeds were plagued by illness almost as much as the Marquises and they had a standing joke about the desirability of retaining a doctor to look after the two families and to pay him, Chinese fashion, only when all members of both families were well, which was practically never.

When Clive pulled through a serious illness Don wrote him: "We are rejoiced to hear that you are pulling out of the hole. . . . I was afraid for a while that it was going to be tag for you. . . .

"I went to church with Reina the other night, but fortunately the preacher had bronchitis and the congregation was dismissed before anything religious happened. It's the closest call I've had in fifteen years, and I shall not tempt Providence again.

"I am writing in this irreverent vein to you deliberately. I know you must have been thinking so seriously of the hereafter, etc., on account of so nearly dying, that the thought that sacrilege is still possible will cheer you up and hasten your ultimate complete recovery. I always think I am going to die when I get sick—and it makes a Christian out of me temporarily; I get as good as gold. Then when a blasphemous thought comes to my mind, I know I must be on the road to recovery again, and it does me a lot of good. You probably have fifty years yet to repent your sins in, and I trust you will not use them for that.

"With these spiritual admonitions, my dear Clivie, I close, with love to you and Helen from all of us, Don."

The Marquis-Weed correspondence is so voluminous, and the Marquis part so characteristic, that one is tempted to go on and on. Much has to be left out, including material which, to at least one reader, is illuminating and entertaining.

Here is an oddity that is perhaps worth preserving—a postscript to a long letter from Don to Clive, in which the columnist reveals a hobby that few of his friends seemed familiar with:

"When you come over I will be able to shoot the bridge of your nose off at 60 feet. I went up to the cops' pistol range and practised with a pistol today and surprised myself. I hadn't fired a pistol twice before in more than twenty years. Well, I shot about 60 times and got better and better. I put about fifty shots into a space the size of a German's face at 65 feet. And I wound up by cutting a string thinner than a lead pencil at fifty feet—which is *some shot* with a pistol, though not much with a rifle, of course.

"War may now begin anytime. . . . I am going to quit boozing and smoking so as to steady my nerves a bit, and think I will really make a pretty fair shot." Marquis was referring, of course, to World War I. This letter was written not many months before the United States declared war on Germany. Marquis was nearing his fortieth birthday at the time and it is doubtful whether his draft board had any interest in him when war came. In addition to being overage, he had a wife and child, an important factor in those days. And the fact that he was overweight—he weighed about 210—didn't help his chances of being selected for military service. And, with an ailing wife and child—and two sisters also dependent upon him—he couldn't very well volunteer.

In 1918, when little Bobby Marquis was about two and a half years old, Reina gave birth to a daughter. She was christened Barbara.

By this time Marquis had adjusted to pram-pushing, for which he was available mainly on Saturdays and Sundays. But little Bobby was bedridden so much of the time that he was only occasionally pressed into service.

Bobby was now medically classified as a malformed child. He had shown such tendencies earlier but the doctors thought his chances of "outgrowing" them were good. When he was three years old he was wearing clothes intended for an infant half his age. An old friend of the family said "it was heart-breaking to see this undersized child drag himself around."

Those who remember Bobby describe him as precocious, one declaring that he was "almost alarmingly so."

Dana Burnet, office mate of Marquis on the *Sun*, told me:

"The boy inherited his father's brain. He was imaginative and poetic to an extent that was almost eerie in one so young. His brain, so far ahead of his years, was a compensation, you felt, for his physical deformity."

Bobby was known for his flights of fancy. Another friend of the family—also a writer—put it this way: "A dwarf, little Bobby always threw his head back and looked up at the people with whom he conversed, his big mop of yellow hair seeming to light up his face as he did so. He watched you so intently it almost made you feel self-conscious."

Bobby spoke a great deal about talks he regularly carried on with God. Burnet says that once in the office Marquis told him about one of these conversations.

At the time the Marquises lived in a Brooklyn apartment house that had a back yard where Bobby played when he was well. One day the tot, chatting with his father in this enclosure, which was crisscrossed with clotheslines, told him about a friend of his—God. Pointing to a garment on one of the lines, he said, "That's God's playpants over there." Apparently God was a little boy Bobby was fond of.

Once, after hearing him talk at length about God, whom he liked better than any of the other children, Marquis said he would like to join one of these conversations. He had always wanted to meet God, and now he could thank him for being so nice to Bobby. Bobby regretted that this could not be arranged. People expected God to be 'normous because he made the world and they thought anyone that made the world would have to be a great big giant. And if you asked them to meet a little boy and you said he was God they wouldn't believe you. They would only laugh and hurt God's feelings. This had happened once and he did not want it to happen again. Marquis promised to behave in God's presence but Bobby was firm and his father never met the owner of the playpants.

Bobby had an unusually deep voice for a child and Marquis told friends, including Homer Croy, who still tells the story, that when he pushed the child around in his pram—(which continued for some time after the normal age for such things)—passers-by would be startled by the near-basso that issued from that baby carriage.

Bobby's conversations with God became a fixture in the Marquis household.

"And what did God say to the Bobber today?" Marquis would ask Reina on returning from the office.

These conversations with God took place whether Bobby was well enough to be up and around and meet his playmate in the back yard or not. When he was unable to leave the apartment he would describe messages he had received from God "through the air" and replies he had sent back the same way.

Once he had asked God to make him new legs—longer and stronger than the present pair and better for playing. He had tried to play ball with some youngsters in the back yard but couldn't quite manage it. He was too slow and the other children had made fun of him.

God told him his legs would get better in time and not to mind what the other children said. But this time not even God could comfort the Bobber. Weeping, he had dragged himself back to the Marquis apartment.

When Bobby was four years old he was wearing the clothes of a two-year-old, according to Mrs. Homer Croy, who, with her husband, has been one of my best sources. The boy's mental growth, however, continued apace.

Bobby loved birds and they became one of his favorite topics. After God made all the birds he called them together in a great, big meeting on a great, big cloud and asked them please to fly around everywhere and sing all the time so that everybody would have music.

Dr. Richard H. Hoffmann, another old friend of Marquis's, tells a story about little Bobby that involves an incident that made a lasting impression on Marquis.

One day Bobby told his father that he wanted to see if he could write a column. He and God had been watching some birds that

usually sang but this day they just flew around and didn't sing a note.
He and God had talked it over and they decided that when it had
rained the day before they must have got their feet wet and caught
cold and got sore throats and that was why they didn't sing. Bobby
said he wanted to write this and some other things he'd talked over
with God and asked his father to place him on the chair at which
he sat and typed when he wrote his column at home. (Bobby, even
then, when he was four and a half years old, was unable to seat
himself in an adult's chair. He had to be helped up.)

Marquis placed the Bobber on the chair in front of his desk, put
a sheet of paper in the typewriter, and told him to go ahead. The
little boy was about to strike the keys when he looked up and studied
the top of the desk. He asked his father to put him back on the
floor.

Bobby then began to creep and crawl around the room, opening
a closet door and looking in, peering under sofa cushions and under
the sofa itself, and leaving no nook or cranny uninspected.

His father, looking on in bewilderment, asked him what he was
looking for. The boy replied, "A bottle of whisky." He had noticed
that when his father did his writing he always had one on the desk
beside him.

"That experience," Marquis told Hoffmann, "damn near crumpled
me." He took to the water wagon and stayed there for several months.

When he was nearing his fifth birthday Bobby began to fail
rapidly, losing interest in food completely. In bed almost constantly,
and kept alive in the main by forcible feeding, he no longer had the
strength for his favorite topic—God. Or for any other topic.

The Marquises called in pediatrician after pediatrician but it was
a lost cause. Bobby died on February 15, 1921, at the age of five years
and three months.

The grief of Reina and Don is reflected in the poems they wrote
on Bobby's passing. Here is the first stanza of Reina's:

> I laid my little child away
>   Within the fragrant earth;
> The world was sorrowful that day,
>   And heaven hushed its mirth.

A typed copy of the poem, which I found in the Don Marquis
Collection in the Butler Library, Columbia University, bears still
another of the Marquis addresses, 10 Orange Street, Brooklyn.

When Bobby was about four he was fascinated by his first look at the New York waterfront and kept talking about it until Don and Reina decided to move to a neighborhood—Columbia Heights, Brooklyn—where he could see it from his window. A letter from a first cousin of Don's, Miss Neeta Marquis, to Mrs. Homer Croy, dated September 5, 1953, says: "Bobby used to stand at the window and watch the light come on in the hand of the Statue of Liberty."

Bobby was cremated and his ashes scattered in the waters at the foot of the Statue of Liberty.

Marquis had written a poem about Bobby's death for publication in "The Sun Dial" but withheld it because it had failed to say what he had set out to write. Subsequently he told friends about a dream in which Bobby appeared—alive and happy. It was "painfully real" and inspired these stanzas which he published in his column the following April, under the title "In the Dawn":

> Was it a dream, or was I waking
>   When the dead came back to me?
> For when night waned, and the shadows shaking
> Told me the April dawn was breaking
>   My dead came back to me.
> Not as the ghosts of old tradition,
>   Doubtful, that waver and peer,
> Not with the wind of terror . . . terror . . .
>   Not with the wind of fear;
> But simply, boldly, in at the door,
> As a hundred times before.
>
> And I put my lips against his throat
>   And felt the pulse beat there,
> And I put my hand upon his head
>   And twined it in his hair;
> For that was always our way with each other,
>   To stroke each other's hair.
>
> Myself, with mine own hands, I gave
>   His ashes to the sea;
> For I said: "Let the whole wide world be his grave,
> The waters of all the earth are his grave,
> That the tides forever may say that the world
>   Means but his grave to me."

And how should his body be gathered together
  To run back home to me?
Out of the fire and the blowing wind
  And the vast dispersing sea?
For it seemed no mist that clothed a thought,
Nor a thin pale thing out of spirit wrought
  But himself that stood by me.

Oh, I know it was only a dream! A dream
  Out of my memory springing,
But I would that it came again . . . and again
Bringing him back to the ways of men
  Where his April birds are singing;

For when I am done with the buffoon's part
That I play lifelong with a burdened heart
  That gets no leave for breaking,
I may not see such visions then
Nor dream such dreams of him again,—

I may sleep a sleep that is far too deep
  For visions to be shaking,
Nor hear his birds, nor any voice,
  Where the April day is breaking.

The reference to "the buffoon's part" in the last stanza is typical.
Marquis accepted and rejected the role a number of times.

The subject was on his mind throughout his writing career.
Once when one of his satires angered Constant Reader he explained
that the offending item had been intended as a joke, in support of
which he wrote that, as his associates could attest, his standard attire
in the office—his writing habit, so to speak—was a clown's suit complete with cap and bells. Moreover, he wrote everything on foolscap.

Before he had written his poem on the death of Bobby, with that
allusion to the "buffoon's part," he wrote the following, which is an
excerpt from "The Jesters" in *Dreams and Dust*—a poem in which
he takes a happier view of the Harlequin role:

Then here's to the Fools!
Flouting the sages
Through history's pages
And driving the dreary old seers into rages—
The humbugging Magis

Who prate that the wages
Of Folly are Death—toast the Fools of all ages!
They have ridden like froth down the whirlpools of time,
    They have jingled their caps in the councils of state,
They have snared half the wisdom of life in a rhyme,
    And tripped into nothingness grinning at fate—
Ho, brothers mine,
Brim up the glasses with gooseberry wine!

Though the prince with his firman,
The judge in his ermine,
Affirm and determine
    Bold words need the whip,
Let them spare us the rod and remit us the sermon,
    For Death has a quip
Of the tomb and the vermin
    That will silence at last the most impudent lip.
Is the world but a bubble, a bauble, a joke?
Heigh-ho, Brother Fools, now your bubble is broke,
Do you ask for a tear?—or is it worth while?
Here's a sigh for you, then—but it ends in a smile!
Ho, Brother Death,
We would laugh at you, too—if you spared us the breath!

Marquis returned to the same theme over and over again, the
results proclaiming that he was a man of many moods who had no
intention of being bound by any of them. A version he wrote over
ten years after the one just quoted—and also called "The Jesters"—
was singled out for honorable mention by the reviewers when it
appeared in Marquis's second book of serious verse, *The Awakening,
and Other Poems*. It is here reprinted for that reason, and for the
more compelling one that it comes as close to being autobiographical
as anything he ever wrote, in terms of the ground rules he established
for his egobiography:

We cannot help it, we are cursed
With an incorrigible mirth:
Although we too have saddened with the clouds
    that shadow
The disconsolate Earth;
Although we too have mourned with all mankind
    the disillusions of the barren years;
Although with all mankind we drink the acrid tears;

Although we too have stolen cowering through the
    nethermost
Dim crowded hells
Where in the common terror of doomed multitudes
The vague ghost cringes, huddling toward his
    neighbor ghost,
And each finds each the mirror of his sins;
Although we too have sought beyond the outmost
    bounds of space
A god of our imaginings,
His will, his form, his face,
To sink again with baffled wings
For that we only found familiar riddles there;
Still, in our ultimate
Numb moments of despair,
Still, in our desolate
Bowed anguish here beneath the whips of fate,
Still, when we reach the dark way's darkest end
And by the blind wall droop with none to friend,
Then, of a sudden,
Some perverse humor shakes us, and we laugh!
Some tricky thought will grip us, and we laugh!
Some rebel mood will seize us, and we laugh!
Ho, Jove! loose all your peevish lightnings from
    the height,
And slay me, Jove!—but in the end some brother
    clown
With desperate mirth will laugh your foolish godhead down!

The death of Bobby was bad enough. It was made worse when Marquis's old bent for self-recrimination reasserted itself. Why hadn't he taken XYZ's advice and tried Dr. So-and-so when this was strongly recommended. After all, what did he have to lose? If he'd had a lick of sense he'd have grasped that Bobby was fighting a losing battle and that he had everything to gain by calling in still another specialist.

This despite the fact that four consultants had been called in— physicians of high professional standing—as Bobby developed crisis after crisis.

The Marquises did more than lavish affection on their sickly, poetic little boy; they did everything humanly possible to save his life. Nevertheless Marquis continued to torture himself by thinking of things he should have done for the Bobber.

Clive Weed was good medicine for Marquis in those days. He resorted to all sorts of dodges and devices to take Don's mind off Bobby's death.

One day at lunch—not many weeks after Bobby had died—Marquis told Weed how a *Sun* friend, in an effort to take his mind off his troubles, had dragged him off to a musical-comedy matinee. Marquis found the entertainment dull and couldn't keep his mind on it. One number in particular annoyed him. It featured the show's leading comedienne in a travesty, a rather crude one, he thought, of Anna Pavlova, the famous Russian ballerina who was very much in the news those days, and whom Marquis considered a great artist.

The columnist said he was tired of that kind of comedy—it had been done to death in vaudeville and now Broadway was taking it up.

He couldn't sit through the performance; told his host he wasn't feeling well and got up and left the theater.

This recital gave Weed a beautiful opening. He remembered that Marquis had written a poem about Pavlova in which he thought he had "caught" her. It was not easy to get Marquis to talk about his work, with one exception—his serious poetry. This explains why even his closest friends, except Christopher Morley and Clive Weed, did not know that he had written a sizable chunk of a projected autobiography.

Weed mentioned the Pavlova poem and said he would like to reread it. Marquis had published it in his column and had included it in his first book of serious verse, *Dreams and Dust*. Weed returned to the office with Don, who thought it would be too much trouble to locate the column in which the poem had appeared. He was pretty sure he had a copy of the book in the office but couldn't find it, which was normal. He seldom could find *anything* in that cluttered office. Weed telephoned a nearby bookstore. No luck.

Weed suggested that they stroll over to Harper and Brothers, publishers of the book, whose offices were downtown in those days and only a brief stroll from the *Sun* office. "I told him the walk would do us both good." So they walked over to the Harper office, picked up a copy of the book, and dropped in somewhere for a cup of coffee, which gave Clive an opportunity to draw out Don on his serious poetry. "He didn't get any work done that afternoon," Weed said afterward, "but he didn't do any brooding either."

The poem in which Marquis thought he had "caught" Pavlova follows:

The soul of the Spring through its body of earth
   Bursts in a bloom of fire,
And the crocuses come in a rainbow riot of mirth. . . .
   They flutter, they burn, they take wing, they aspire. . . .
Wings, motion and music and flame,
Flower, woman and laughter, and all these the same!
She is light and first love and the youth of the world,
She is sandalled with joy . . . she is lifted and whirled,
She is flung, she is swirled, she is driven along
   By the carnival winds that have torn her away
   From the coronal bloom on the brow of the May. . . .
She is youth, she is foam, she is flame, she is visible song!

He called the poem "A Mood of Pavlova."

The Mystery of the History of the Sun—
*Publisher-Owner Munsey Has a Plaint—Marquis
Publishes Three Books—Invited to Dramatize* The
Old Soak—*and Other Items*

In 1918 Appleton and Company published *The Story of the* Sun
by Frank M. O'Brien, who had served the paper in an editorial
capacity for many years. The book, originally inspired by the paper's
top management, had the blessing of the owner and was considered
"official."

Although "The Sun Dial" had caught on shortly after it was
started in 1913 and was a solid success by 1915, there was not a single
reference to Don Marquis in O'Brien's book, an omission that could
not have been more glaring. By 1921 schools of journalism were
beginning to take Marquis, Franklin P. Adams, and other major
columnists seriously. Since *The Story of the* Sun was considered
a "standard work" and since Marquis was not once mentioned in it,
the impression these schools got was that the *Sun* didn't consider
Marquis important. Some of them wondered why. O'Brien had to
answer a lot of questions. How he handled them is not known.

Marquis's friends were mystified. Some of them were also annoyed.

If Marquis was offended he didn't show it. He seemed amused.
O'Brien had saved him money. If he'd been mentioned in the book
he would have been tempted to buy a copy to remind Reina what

a big man she had married—not to mention copies for his sisters and his cousins and his aunts.

Nevertheless Marquis's friends—those who knew about the book—thought he had been slighted and wondered why. Leaving him out was made more noticeable by the inclusion of a number of *Sun* people who held minor jobs.

Marquis always contended that he got along with Frank A. Munsey, who bought the *Sun* in 1916 and who, on all counts, was probably the most unpopular newspaper proprietor in New York journalistic history. George Britt, who interviewed Marquis for the New York *World-Telegram* after Don had ceased columning, told me that Don's comments on Munsey were entirely friendly, which was characteristic. As Clive Weed put it, "He expected people to have shortcomings. He didn't give a damn whether those deficiencies worked against him or not. It had to be something big before he'd pay attention to it. I can imagine him saying something nasty to you if you set fire to his house or did something like that. But he ignored the mine-run of pettiness. He just couldn't be bothered."

Marquis has mentioned Munsey several times in magazine articles but never in disparaging terms. He had opportunities to get back at his former boss for O'Brien's failure to mention him in that history of the Sun. It was a Munsey project. But it would have been out of character for Marquis to bring it up. In writing about Munsey he preferred the device of good-natured banter on topics that lent themselves to his own special brand of kidding. Here is an example from an article in the *Saturday Evening Post*, written after he had left the *Sun*:

"It used to bother him [Munsey] that he could never find me about the *Sun* office at the infrequent times when he had something to say to me. I had found, after running a column about five years, that I could get more work done by not coming to the office every day, because so many persons always try to visit a columnist if they can corner him. Mr. Munsey had a theory, quite tenable from several points of view, that an employee should frequently appear at the office where he is supposed to be employed; in fact, if he could have put it over, I would have been there every day from nine in the morning until five in the evening. He sent for me one day and said:

"'I've been trying to get hold of you for nearly a week.'

"'What for, Mr. Munsey?' I asked him.

"'In order,' he said, 'to find out why you are never here. Everybody

else on the staff gets here in the morning and does a day's work in
office hours and leaves in the evening, and I don't see why you
shouldn't.'

"'The office hours on the *Evening Sun*,' I said, 'are not long
enough for me to do a day's work in. I'm ashamed to have people
know how many hours of intense labor I put in on that column of
mine. There's verse, for instance. You haven't any conception how
long it takes a conscientious poet such as I am to write a single
sonnet.'

"'How long does it take?' asked Mr. Munsey seriously.

"I unfolded the current copy of the *Evening Sun*, in which I
was then running a humorous series entitled: *Sonnets to a Red-
Haired Lady*.

"'That first sonnet,' I told him, 'has taken me ten years to bring
to its present state of absolute perfection. I'd like to have you read
it.'

"Mr. Munsey read it. He knew as much about sonnets as I did
about high finance—which is nothing. He said it struck him as a
pretty good sonnet.

"'It is one of the world's great sonnets,' I told him. 'Ten years
ago I wrote the first line, and it didn't suit me and I tore it up. I
worked seven or eight months getting it just right. I had to rewrite
the second line twenty times in twenty months to make it the
absolutely perfect thing it is. After that there were two years when I
made hardly any progress at all, and then five years when things went
along more rapidly and swimmingly. And the last six lines came with a
rush, all in one year. But if I had put in the ten years on novels and
short stories that I have put in on this sonnet I would have made
two hundred thousand dollars. I don't mean to say that all my sonnets
take that long; some of them I can write in a week. But the point
is that I couldn't put in the intense, prolonged inspirational work on
my column in the few brief hours each day the *Evening Sun* allows
me. I have to start at six every morning and work until midnight.'

"After that he never said anything more about office hours, but
he would send for me from time to time and say, with every outward
appearance of seriousness:

"'How is your health, Mr. Marquis?'

"'Very good indeed,' I would tell him.

"'You must be careful,' he would say. 'You must watch yourself;
you must not overwork.'

"Mr. Munsey was popularly supposed not to have any sense of humor whatever, but he really had a remote, deep, quiet appreciation of little comedy sketches of this nature."

I joined the Munsey organization in 1921, when it was known as the Sun-Herald corporation and operated at 280 Broadway, and worked for the *Herald* for about three years and briefly for the *Sun*. (The *Sun* and the *Herald* were housed in the same building and members of the staffs of both used the same facilities.) A heavy smoker at the time, I got most of my exercise in those days walking to and from the W.C.; and while these walks were bracing, the interruptions could not have done my work any good.

The temptation to sneak a few puffs in the office was great but when you learned that people had been fired for doing it, you decided that perhaps it wasn't a good idea. This antismoking rule was Mr. Munsey's own decree—that was made plain to all hands—and since he had demonstrated a bent for sacking people, everyone was careful to observe the rule, including the big man of the paper, Don Marquis.

Marquis liked to smoke while writing his column and this was one of the reasons why he contrived to work at home a few days a week. When Munsey's predecessor, William Reick, owned the paper, Marquis smoked constantly at his desk, and the switch to the no-smoking rule was hard on him. It will be recalled that, during the Reick regime when heavily preoccupied with his column, Marquis would absent-mindedly shake burning tobacco from the bowl of his pipe into his wastebasket, which was usually full of rejected contributions, and set them afire, as reported by Jim Quigney, his former copy boy. It was merely his way of "getting warmed up to his work" he explained to an associate who accused him of having the instincts of a pyromaniac. At one of the gents' room smoking sessions this fellow toiler in the Munsey vineyards accused Marquis of being responsible for the no-smoking rule. "Munsey *had* to get tough," he postulated, "when he heard that you used to set fire to the building on Nassau Street a few times a week."

Marquis replied that setting a building on fire was nothing; anyone could do that; when he really got going as a columnist he expected to set the whole world on fire.

That ended the discussion.

Munsey's proudest boast was that he ran a "businesslike organization"—in view of which it would have been fun to know how much it cost the Sun-Herald Corporation to enforce his no-smoking rule. Charles Lincoln, then managing editor of the New York *Herald*, once remarked that when he couldn't locate a member of the staff whom he knew to be on the premises, he tried the gents' room first.

In cold weather the editorial gents' room (also the smoking salon) was a pretty cold place, and Ed Bartnett of the New York *World-Telegram* recalls Marquis's comment—which will mean nothing to those unfamiliar with a certain robust story—that that W.C. was no place for a brass monkey.

Since the city rooms and offices of the *Sun* and *Herald* were better heated than the privy turned smoking lounge, there were those on the newspapers who believed that the office handy man had instructions to keep the steam heat low in the men's room as a means of discouraging what one of Munsey's business associates, Ervin Wardman, called "loiterers."

I once told Marquis a story about the Munsey no-smoking rule that seemed to amuse him. I had been writing crowd stories of the 1921 all-New York World Series (Giants *vs.* Yankees) for the *Herald* and before the start of one of the games was pushing my way through the mob at the Polo Grounds when a fan, spotting my press badge, said, "I'll give you a swell cigar if you put my name in the paper." "It's a deal," I replied, "every man has his price and mine is a good cigar." I had lighted the cigar on the way from the subway station to the office, meaning to douse it on reaching the Sun-Herald Building, but forgot and walked absent-mindedly into the city room smoking it. One of Mr. Munsey's stooges, a Mr. Ridgway, spotting the outrage, shouted, "Put that damn thing out!" No sooner said than done.

The next day I found on my desk a copy of my story, with a heavy, black-penciled ring around, "Every man has his price," etc., and this notation in Ridgway's hand, "And I don't think much of this joke either."

In an effort to find clues as to why Marquis didn't get a single mention in *The Story of the* Sun I consulted members of the Sun-Herald alumni and men who worked on other New York newspapers and knew the conductor of "The Sun Dial." None of them could throw any light on the mystery. Some of them advanced theories. One said, "Did you know that Munsey was a frustrated

novelist? He wrote imitations of Horatio Alger, Jr. The originals were
bad enough but the Munsey counterfeits were strictly in the oh-
my-God department. Bob Davis once told me that every time
Marquis published one of his wall mottoes, all of them flamboyant
negations of the Algerisms that Munsey lived by, the latter had a
fit. Munsey was too dull to realize that Marquis, a hard worker all
his life, was merely having fun when he wrote his down-with-work
manifestoes. In fact, it is doubtful whether Munsey grasped much
that Marquis wrote. The 'Sun Dial' was good box office—it was
talked about all over New York; and were it not for that Munsey
might have fired Marquis just as he'd fired so many others."

A check reveals that Munsey *did* write some Alger-like novels. One,
published in 1887, was called *Afloat in a Great City*. Another, published the following year, was titled *The Boy Broker*. Both were
grimly didactic and stiltedly written; and, as for the characters, they
had no relationship whatsoever to human beings.

A man who knew and liked Frank M. O'Brien, author of *The
Story of the* Sun, stated with complete seriousness that he thought
O'Brien might have been as baffled as Munsey by Marquis's success
as a columnist. "Frank was what you'd call a nice guy," he told me.
"He had a feeling for horseplay and obvious humor but I doubt
whether the satiric overtones of archy, mehitabel, and Hermione,
for instance, ever reached him. You drove me back to O'Brien's
book and I'm appalled, on reading it carefully for the first time, at
some of the things he wrote. It's a thoroughly bad book, loosely
constructed, sloppily written, with emphasis throughout on the wrong
things. It's so full of stuff that doesn't add up that I wonder if anyone ever gave it a good copy-reading before it went to press. If you
want to have a revealing experience, look up the pages in which
O'Brien praises the *Sunbeams* column of the 1870s."

Well, I looked up those pages and found O'Brien saying that "in
the *Sunbeams* column were crowded the vagrant wit and wisdom of
the world." Then he gives examples:

> The mules are all dying in Arkansas.
> A printer in Texas has named his first-born Brevier
>   Fullfaced Jones.
> Real estate is looking up in New Orleans.
> Translations from Hawthorne are becoming popular in
>   France.
> Venison costs six cents a pound in St. Paul.

> Queen Victoria says every third woman in Cork is
>   a beauty.
> Goldwin Smith is coming to the United States.
> The Pope denounces short dresses.

A former *Herald* associate of mine believes that the so-called "Max's Busy Bee incident" may have led to the exclusion of Marquis from O'Brien's book. In one of his archy pieces designed to satirize an established institution of those times, the Andrew Carnegie Medals for Bravery, which Marquis thought were being overpublicized, he gave a stirring account of how archy had saved another cockroach from drowning in a beef stew in Max's Busy Bee, a long-since-vanished downtown lunch counter, by throwing him a toothpick which he used as a life raft. In tossing the lifesaving toothpick archy had risked losing his balance and falling into the beef stew himself; and Marquis in a graphic citation urged the Carnegie Bravery Committee to consider archy for one of their medals. Munsey and Carnegie had known each other for years—so the story goes—and when the offending item was spotted in "The Sun Dial" by one of Munsey's top executives it was allegedly killed and the column remade for later editions. This was said to have started a row in which the normally mild-mannered Marquis reportedly used strong language.

One of those I consulted was Stanley Walker, who knew Marquis when they both worked for Munsey and when Marquis left the *Sun* for the *Herald Tribune*. Walker, who, as city editor of the latter, was one of the most respected men in his field, writes: "Frank O'Brien always impressed me as a thoroughly decent gentleman in every way. I have not read 'The Story of The Sun' for many years, and my copy has long since been stolen, but the idea that O'Brien intentionally slighted Marquis seems odd to me. But I simply don't know."

In a subsequent letter Walker says:

"On the O'Brien thing: I don't understand it. The evidence, from what you say, points strongly to the conclusion that Munsey was up to one of his cheap pranks. He had a way of getting strong prejudices on matters that a larger-minded man would have laughed off as inconsequential. God knows."

In 1919 Marquis published *Prefaces*, a collection of introductions to thirty-two imaginary books. Each reviewer had his own particular favorite. Christopher Morley's is indicated in the following excerpt from his review in the book section of the New York *Evening Post:*

In a riotously absurd piece of kidding, "The Preface to the Prospectus of a Club," Don was talking about Brooklyn:

"Walt Whitman used to live over there and edit the *Eagle* and go swimming in Buttermilk Channel, two points off the starboard bow of Hank Beecher's church. Once an old Long Island skipper sunk a harpoon into Walt's haunch when he came up to blow, and the poet, snorting and bellowing and spouting verse, towed the whaler and his vessel clear out to Montauk before he shook the iron loose. Is there a bard in Greenwich Village that could do that?"

What I'm suggesting, and the whole gist of this little tribute, is that this casual comic paragraph, in the very guts and gusto of its Munch-hausenism, contains more shrewd criticism . . . than many a whole serious tome about Moby Walt.

Marquis's own particular favorite was his "Preface to a Book of Literary Reminiscences," probably because it gave him an opportunity to return to one of his favorite pastimes, the ribbing of alleged witty exchanges recorded in some of the literary memoirs of his day. Here is a sample:

"They are tearing the old chop house down—the Eheu Fugaces Chop House—to build on its site a commercial enterprise. . . . So passes another literary landmark; mere business triumphs again over The Arts.

"It was in 1850 that Jack Whittier first brought me in to dinner there. Jolly Jack Whittier! There was a wit and a true Bohemian for you! His quickness at a repartee was marvelous. Mike Cervantes was drinking in the bar as we passed through.

"'Hello, Jack,' hiccoughed Mike, 'been snow-bounding lately?'

"'No,' said Whittier, with a sidelong look at Mike's glass, 'nor skating either.'

"'Ralphie Emerson has more humor,' Ollie Holmes used to say, 'but, after all, Whittier is wittier!' . . .

"Ah! the gay parties! The old days! The present generation does not know what Bohemia was! There are certain mechanical imitators, and imitations—but the *esprit*. Where is *l'esprit?* . . . Where, for that matter, is *l'empire des lettres?* Where? . . .

"Roaring Hank Longfellow and I, rather elevated one night . . . wound up at the Hippodrome . . . and seined from a tank a young woman, whose name I forget—she was the Annette Kellermann of that day—whom we brought back to Eheu's place with a demand that she be grilled at once. . . . 'Let her be stewed!' shouted Wash Irving, wag that he was."

Some of the best extravaganza in the book is based on actual occurrences. For instance, in "Preface to the Plays of Euripides" he tells a story that is a gaudy embroidery of something that happened during his Atlanta days. He had told it over and over again—never twice the same—and by the time he had narrated it for ten years he claimed he didn't know himself how much of it had happened and how much he'd invented. Several people have sent us versions of the story on which this "preface" is based, and since it was a fixture in his repertoire as a raconteur it seems appropriate to record it here:

"We approach a preface to the plays of Euripides with more confidence than we could summon to the critical consideration of any other Greek dramatist. We know more about Euripides. We have read more of him. We once read five lines of him in the original Greek. It is true that we did not know what they were about when we read them, and should not know now; but we read them thirty or forty times and something about the manner in which we read them saved a man's life.

"We were fussing around the office of the Atlanta (Ga.) *Journal* one morning about three o'clock, having just finished writing an editorial which we thought would likely elect Hoke Smith governor, if he were able to live up to it, when we ran across a copy of *Iphigenia in Tauris*. It was a new edition, and some trusting publisher had sent it along in the vain hope that it would be noticed. We happened to know the alphabet and could mispronounce a few words, and we turned over the pages wishing that we were able to read the thing—it might give us a chance to elevate our mind, which was suffering from the frightful strain of writing about Hoke Smith in such a way that even Hoke would believe himself a statesman. And thinking how great a man Euripides probably was, for all we knew, and how superior to Hoke Smith he must have been in many ways, we got very hungry.

"We went across the street to a little basement lunchroom kept by a fellow named George Stefanopoulous, who always put so much onion in his hamburger steaks one could not taste the beef. If one poured enough Worcestershire sauce over them so that one could not taste the onions they could be eaten. We carried Euripides with us, and George told us proudly that there is no more difference be-

tween the Greek of Euripides and the Greek written and spoken
in Athens today than between the English of Shakespeare's time and
the English of today. Inquiry revealed that George's knowledge of
Shakespeare was about as extensive as our knowledge of Euripides,
and so we cannot vouch for his statement.

"Interrupting our course in Euripides—someone or something
has been interrupting us all our life every time we seemed to be on
the point of really getting into the classics—in came a young man
named Henry.

"Henry roomed with us, and roamed with us at that time, and he
was a chronic sufferer from false angina pectoris. This is a disease
. . . which has all the effects upon patient and observer of real
organic affection of the heart; no one takes it lightly but the doctors.
In Henry's case it was aggravated by a fondness for Georgia corn
whisky and stuff he ate out of tin cans. This diet did things to his
stomach; his stomach kicked to his pneumogastric nerve, and his
pneumogastric nerve gripped his heart as with iron claws, squeezed
it to the size of a peanut, twisted it . . . and convinced it that it
would never beat again. The chief difference between real angina
and pseudo-angina . . . is that while both can kill you, the real sort
kills you more quickly and kindly.

"Henry pulled a spasm of it while George was telling us about
Euripides; writhed about, and fell to the floor semi-conscious.

"Heat, applied to the heart, and strychnine or aromatic ammonia,
if you can get hold of them, are (as Aesculapius would say) 'indicated.'

"So we sent George's assistant to telephone for a doctor and applied a hot hamburger steak, just out of George's frying pan, to
Henry's bosom. . . .

"We had frequently helped Henry die with his heart, but this time
we were alarmed.

" 'George,' said we, 'throw another hamburger steak into the skillet
at once. His pulse has stopped entirely. And this steak is cooling.'

"Just then Henry's eyes fluttered and he strove to speak. We
bent over the sufferer.

" 'I'm dying,' murmured Henry. 'Pray! Pray for me!'

"The request caught us unaware; we could not remember any formal petition. In desperation we took up Euripides, and, as the second
hamburger steak went hot and sizzling and dripping with grease from

George's frying pan to Henry's heart, we began to chant one of the choruses.

"There was something about a *Basileon* in it, whatever a *Basileon* may be. . . .

" 'Thank you!' muttered Henry. . . .

"The third steak was getting cool, and still George's assistant did not return with a doctor. Henry's chest was cooling, too. His feet and hands were cold. He had no more pulse than . . . one of the iron dogs in Hoke Smith's front yard. If we had known a real prayer we would have switched to it from *Basileon*. . . .

"And just as we were putting *Basileon* over the jumps for the eighteenth time George Stefanopoulous announced:

" 'Sir, I have no more hamburger steak to fry!'

" 'My God!' said we, 'Basileon—Basileon—dig up something else —Basileon—Basileon—fry an egg, George—Basileon—Basileon—and be quick about it! Fry two eggs!'

"It was at the sixteenth egg that the physician arrived and complimented us on our treatment.

" 'Heat,' he said, 'is the great thing in these cases, and it is well to remove all apprehension from the patient's mind if possible.' 'The prayer,' said Henry, who had been hypodermicked into something like an appetite for corn whisky and tin cans again, 'the prayer is what saved me!'

"Euripides did not live as long as Sophocles, but was, on the whole, more widely popular. And one has only to compare the *Iphigenia* of Euripides with the *Agamemnon* of Aeschylus to see their entire dissimilarity. They are products of practically the same period of Hellenic culture . . . and yet, what a difference!

"Henry married, Hoke Smith in the Senate, Euripides dead— how time flies!"

When Marquis lived in Atlanta he *did*, as stated in the foregoing, "room and roam" with a Henry—Henry Grantland Rice. And both subsisted for a time on a diet of "corn whisky and tin cans." It will also he recalled that to Marquis, years earlier, Rice was sometimes "Henry." No one remembers anything beyond this.

A Georgia newspaperman who is familiar with the pranks Marquis and Rice played on each other as young men in Atlanta hazards the guess that Marquis in this preface may have been trying to get a rise out of Rice with this allusion to "Henry." The men were now both in New York and when they met they reminisced and kidded each other about the old days in Atlanta.

Reina, Marquis's wife, whom he once called "my favorite copy reader," gave the manuscript of *Prefaces* a final look before it was sent to the publisher. She persuaded her husband to tone down a passage dealing with Tennyson, one of his favorite targets. He used to tease her about an overfondness for "the Rev. Alfred Tennyson," whose didacticism bothered him, as also did that of "the Rev. William Wordsworth." Marquis was aware of the magnificence of Tennyson's major work but enjoyed kidding what he called "the unctuous laureates" who made him yearn to fly to "the nearest bardello," a pun he abandoned when the printers kept changing his coined word to "bordello," making it necessary for him to find other ways of exaggerating the preachiness of Lord Alfred.

Reina thought he should be permitted to have as much fun as he pleased with Tennyson without working the subject to death. What finally emerged in *Prefaces* was:

"An elderly gentleman who found me a bore once asked me desperately, 'Are you fond of literature?'

" 'I dote upon it,' I said.

"He was a painter; we had met at a kind of tea where everyone was talking of Art and Literature and Things Like That; we hated each other at once because each had been told the other was interesting. . . .

" 'Sir,' I said, striving with all the rancor of my nature to be offensive, 'sir, are *you* fond of literature?'

" 'I am,' he said, putting on a pair of eyeglasses, and looking as if he might look like Whistler if he thought me worth wasting the look on.

" 'What *sort* of literature are you fond of?' I asked.

" 'I am fond of Lord Tennyson's Poems,' he retorted insultingly.

"I permitted myself a faint, superior smile. It maddened him, as I intended it should; his nose turned a whitish blue as the blood receded from his face."

Marquis had written a piece of verse about Tennyson which could not have been intended for his book of prefaces, and which, judging by eight unpublishable lines was one of those things—there were many of them—he wrote for the fun of it and for the amusement of his friends. The publishable part:

Alfie Tennyson,
Eat your venison,
And point no moral as you do.
Best not to chatter while you chew.

Alfie Tennyson,
You're a menace, son,
With your sermonizing ways.
Don't you have no wicked days?

Alfie Tennyson,
You've my benison,
Though I've limited abidance
When you offer Moral Guidance.

In 1920 Barbara, the two-year-old daughter of Don and Reina, began to show sickly tendencies. She caught cold easily and the colds lingered on. She was a cheerful mite despite her frailty. Unlike her ill-starred brother Bobby, who was now four years old and had for some time been classified as a malformed child, her frailty was not accompanied by any malformation. The family pediatrician assured her parents that, unlike Bobby's, her legs were sound and normal and that what she needed principally was "building up."

The strain on Reina was greater than ever; for now she had two ailing children to look after. And it became increasingly difficult for her to leave the apartment. There were times when, for weeks at a stretch, the borough of Brooklyn was her universe. She had found it relaxing to attend the theater occasionally but Broadway now seemed hundreds of miles away; and even when she had household help who were willing to stay on and look after the children at night, she declined to leave them. She was an authority on their needs and their moods, having discussed every phase of their problems with the doctor in charge, and the consultants who had been called in from time to time, and insisted it was her responsibility to "stick around at all times." Don was unable to budge her from this point of view.

Marquis used to say to Clive Weed, who was closest to him in those days, that it was hell to have an uncomplaining wife. Why didn't she squawk like other wives and give him a chance to beef about the load *he* was carrying? He considered it much less taxing than hers but, according to the marital code, husbands and wives were supposed to argue about their respective burdens. Why couldn't he and Reina have such arguments like other couples? It would give them a chance to blow off steam, something everybody needed.

Reina's "quiet assumption of responsibility" kept reminding Don that she had been "bogged down in Brooklyn too long" and that she saw only those few friends who found it convenient to drop in occasionally, among them the Weeds and Katherine Glover. She was a hospitable woman and liked to have friends in for dinner but it was seldom practicable. She had her "little hospital" to supervise; and when her patients were feeling better, which eased the strain, she tried to get some rest. Marquis's old friend, Dr. Harry March, whom he had met when they were young men together in Washington, had cautioned Reina that her heart had been "weakened by childbirth," and that it was important for her to get all the rest she could. The term quoted was the one the doctor used; he did not name any specific heart ailment.

Whenever Bobby and his sister had a few good days in a row, Reina dug into her desk for her notebooks and started thinking of things to write about. Don felt keenly that her career as a writer had been too long frustrated, that they must not let this go on indefinitely; and Reina made several efforts in those days to put a few short stories together and to plan another book. In 1914 Appleton and Company had published her novel *The Torch Bearer* and she had been encouraged to try her hand at another.

Marquis considered his wife a talented woman and nothing could have been more genuine than his unhappiness over the interruption of her writing career. He was determined to see it get started again somehow. And with that penchant for self-reproach which he never lost, he flogged himself for not having managed things so that they "could both have writing careers."

Reina had the perception to see that the best way to keep Don from tormenting himself was to try to write something, or at least go through the motions. It made him feel better to hear that she was "fussing with some ideas"—though actually she lacked the time and the energy for the sustained effort needed to produce a short story or a novel. As she told intimates—straightforwardly as a reporter, and with no element of self-pity—she was too tired at the end of her day's household chores to do any writing.

Don had volunteered to discuss any of her writing projects with her and to offer advice and suggestions, as he had in the case of *The Torch Bearer*, which she dedicated

TO
MY HUSBAND
for without his heartening faith in my
work, his genuine sympathy with it, and
his discerning criticism of it, this book
would never have been written

Reina was proud of the contributions she had been able to make
to the mounting expenses of their little household—(it will be recalled that the monthly check to Don's sister Maud was now a fixture
—and she wanted to contribute more. Her ideas on this subject
emerge in several things she wrote, including *The Torch Bearer*, in
which she says of one of her characters, "She had the modern
woman's desire to earn her living; to justify her existence by doing
something well."

She more than justified her existence by the way she ran her home
but the urge to write was still there—to a greater degree than she
permitted her husband to realize.

Don had set himself the goal of a trip abroad with Reina and the
children. This would make up in part, he said, for Reina's being
"interminably mired hub-deep in Brooklyn." It was an iffy proposition, this trip, but it gave them something to look forward to;
they would go the first time Don—whose magazine work was becoming a fairly profitable side line and who was now talking about
writing a play—made a killing . . . *if* Bobby and Barbara were well
enough to travel. Don kept telling Reina—who found the subject an
exciting one—that he would not rest until that trip abroad became
a reality. They studied travel books and decided what they wanted
to see and do in Europe long before their projected trip became a
reality.

Again and again Don expressed the belief that if he could "drag
Reina out of the flat for a few months" and give her a chance to
travel abroad, her health would be fully restored, her mind would be
stimulated, she would find herself getting her best ideas, and she
would be able to make a fresh start as a writer.

The year 1921 was a big one for Marquis. His column was at its
peak and now more than ever the characters he had created were a
part of the life of New York.

It was also a tragic time, the year little Bobby died—on February 15, three months after his fifth birthday. How Don and Reina

weathered that blow was described some pages earlier, for reasons which will become apparent.

It was also the year that the health of their daughter, now three years old, began to improve.

The year 1921 saw the publication of three of Marquis's books—a collection of short stories called *Carter, and Other People*, *The Old Soak*, in which the O.S., subsequently known as Clem Hawley, held back nothing in declaring himself on how the world should be run, and *Noah an' Jonah an' Cap'n John Smith*, a collection of humorous verse.

The year 1921—or most of it—was also the one that Don Marquis said he devoted to looking for the money that readers of his column had sent him, after deciding to turn his office into a bookshop, for autographed copies of one, two, or all three of the aforementioned volumes. Little did these enthusiastic readers realize what they were doing in mailing cash, checks, or money orders to the boss of "The Sun Dial," whose office Frank Sullivan once described in *The New Yorker* as an "oasis of disorder," adding: "His cubicle looked like a small post office that had been hit by a cyclone that in passing had dropped odds and ends from previously wrecked delicatessen stores, second-hand bookstores, and possibly a junk shop or two. Mail that had lain unopened for weeks strewed the desk and floor, and fragments of ham sandwiches lay about, in case archy and mehitabel got hungry."

Marquis told Clive Weed that by the time he found the money readers had sent in for autographed copies of his books—after losing it a dozen times—and after calling on his publishers for the purpose of signing the books and having them mailed out, 1921 was practically over.

It wasn't that Marquis was swamped with such mail. There was plenty of it, Weed stated, but not enough to disorganize anyone who was orderly. "Once when I called on him at his office," said the cartoonist, "I found him sitting on the floor sorting out a stack of mail that his letter-covered desk couldn't accommodate. He said he was looking for checks and finding nothing but bills and bum contributions."

He asked Weed to help him. The cartoonist sat down on the floor beside him—by this time the only chair in the room was covered with mail—and the two friends went through everything. Their special quarry that day was a letter from a reader who had sent a wire demanding to know why the check he had sent weeks before had not produced the autographed books he had "ordered."

Thereafter Marquis, at Weed's suggestion, returned money sent him by readers for copies of his books, enclosing an autograph scribbled on a gummed label, to be pasted on the flyleaf of the book.

Weed reminded Marquis that his fellow columnist, Franklin P. Adams, who was then appearing in the New York *Tribune*, had reported the following telephone conversation with a reader:

Reader: "Where can I buy your latest book, Mr. Adams?"
Adams: "Have you thought of trying a bookstore?"

Marquis shrank from this kind of bluntness, Weed said. He could be forthright but not under such circumstances. "Me, I'm busting with love and sticky baby-talk for people who want to spend money on my stuff. But I wish someone would tell 'em I'm a lousy shipping clerk."

Arthur Hopkins, successful and respected Broadway producer, had become acquainted with Marquis and enjoyed his company. He was a "Sun Dial" fan whose favorite Marquis character was the Old Soak, whom he considered "one of the great philosophers." He had bought the recently published collection of Old Soak sketches, had once again found them fun, and agreed with an associate of his who thought the character had stage possibilities. Did Marquis think he could write a play?

Marquis, in telling the story to Rollin Kirby, Clive Weed, and others, put it this way: what do you tell a producer who casually asks whether you think you can write a play? Answering his own question, he observed, "Of course what you say is: 'Yes, boss. When do you want it? Tomorrow? Or will the day after do?'"

There are a number of Hopkins-Marquis anecdotes in circulation. One is to the effect that that very night the creator of the Old Soak wired the producer, "When do rehearsals start?"

At a subsequent meeting Hopkins told Marquis that the only thing that bothered him was the columnist's apparent belief that it would be a cinch to transfer the Old Soak to the stage. "It's not as easy as you think," the producer said, indulging in a bit of whimsy based on a story the columnist had told him, "to write a bad play."

Marquis, in one of his conversations with Hopkins, had told the producer about a conversation he had had with an interviewer for a college publication. To what, the campus reporter had asked Marquis,

did the columnist attribute his success? Marquis, in his best deadpan
delivery, replied that he ascribed it to the public's lack of discrimination. "I've been writing a bad column for years," he said, "and no
one seems to get wise. Now go back to your editor, young feller,
and tell him you found Marquis the most modest genius you ever
interviewed."

Hopkins had picked up Marquis's little joke and had adapted it to
the proposed dramatization of the Old Soak.

Dana Burnet, who shared an office with Marquis on the *Sun*,
reports the following conversation between Hopkins and Marquis as
described by the latter:

Hopkins: You're sure, absolutely sure, you can write a bad play?
Marquis: Positive.
Hopkins: What makes you so confident?
Marquis: I'm resourceful.
Hopkins: Other writers I consider resourceful have tried it without
success.
Marquis: I've consulted the foreman of my Hack-Work Department and
he says we can count on him. He's never failed me.
Hopkins: Good! But never lose sight of the fact that it's hard to write a
really bad play—one so bad it's good.
Marquis: I'm your man. I'll write the worst play you ever read.
Hopkins: I'm banking on you. You mustn't disappoint me.
Marquis: If it isn't perfectly terrible I'll eat it.

Reassured, Hopkins stuck out his hand and they shook to seal the
bargain.

Was it a good idea to publish three books during the same year?
Some of Marquis's friends wondered. He wondered too. But the publishers had asked for them, and he took the position that if they had
no objections, why should he?

The first part of *The Old Soak* consisted of twenty-two chapters
in which the protagonist covered such subjects as:

> The History of the Demon Rum
> The Barroom as an Educational Influence
> Evils of Prohibition
> The Barroom and the Arts
> The Old Soak Fears for the Growing Children
> The Barroom's Good Influence
> Prohibition is Making a Free Thinker of the Old Soak

The second half of the book, a section called "Hail and Farewell," contains some of Marquis's sprightliest light verse. There are twenty-nine poems and each of them is dedicated to a friend, including Grant Rice, Ned Leamy, Loren Palmer, Clive Weed, Oliver Herford, Ben De Casseres, George Van Slyke, Christopher Morley, Jimmy Farnsworth, Charley Bayne, and Frank Stanton. (The last two were old Atlanta playmates of Marquis's, with whom he still occasionally corresponded.)

One of the poems, "Down in a Wine Vault," ranks with Marquis's best versified narratives. This introductory stanza gives the flavor of the writing:

> Down in a wine vault underneath the city
>   Two old men were sitting; they were drinking booze.
> Torn were their garments, hair and beards were gritty;
>   One had an overcoat but hardly any shoes.

Another favorite is "The Old Brass Railing," a rollicking ballad —all eighteen stanzas of it. These excerpts will convey the idea:

> Our minds are schooled to grief and dearth,
>   Our lips, too, are aware,
> But our feet still seek a railing
>   When a railing isn't there.
>
> I went into a druggist's shop
>   To get some stamps and soap,—
> My feet rose up in spite of me
>   And pawed the air with hope. . . .
>
> I do not seek for sympathy
>   For stomach nor for throat,
> I never liked my liver much,
>   'Tis such a sulky goat—
>
> But, oh, my foot! My cheated foot,
>   My foot that lives in hope,
> It is a piteous sight to see
>   It lift itself and grope!
>
> I carried it to church one day—
>   O foot so fond and frail!
> I had to drag it forth in haste:
>   It grabbed the chancel rail. . . .

> Myself, I can endure the drouth
> With stoic calm, and prayer—
> But my feet still seek a railing
> When a railing isn't there.

The piece adds up to seventy-two lines of entertainment—and one of the author's shrewdest satires on Prohibition.

Attacks on *The Old Soak* by members of the clergy brought no reply from Marquis. When a few years back he was under fire from churchmen for satirizing the Rev. Billy Sunday, the ballplayer turned evangelist who was touring the country and attracting huge crowds, he had replied to his critics and in so doing had accomplished nothing except start new arguments. "You can't defend satire," he told his friend and fellow columnist Franklin P. Adams, and Adams had agreed. If you do it humorously, Marquis argued, it sounds disrespectful to the church, or is so interpreted; and if you try the serious approach you merely touch off endless theological arguments.

In the Billy Sunday imbroglio Marquis had attempted to answer the following question from a clergyman's letter: "Even if he [Billy Sunday] is lacking in taste, don't you think he is doing good?"

Here is part of what Marquis said in reply in his column:

"I do not. And I am not greatly concerned about his lack of taste. . . . Nor do I worry about the amount of money he makes. . . .

"My detestation of what he is doing goes deeper than his surfaces and manners; it goes to the essential spirit of the man as revealed in his continual, morbid emphasis on the idea of Hell.

"The word Hell rings through his sermons like a clanging tocsin. It never seems to be far from his tongue. The thought of Hell seems to be ever present in his mind. Fear, fear of Hell, is the chief motif of his performance. . . . Directly or indirectly, but artfully and assiduously, he fosters the growth of this implanted fear until it bears its crop of hysteria. . . . A smack of relish goes with the utterance of his threats and warnings; this crude, effective psychologist of terror knows his power and exults in the exercise of it. . . .

"Fear is the most base and ignoble of motives. Men may be frightened into conformity, but never into virtue. We insult all the saints of all the creeds if we suppose that they sneaked and scurried into their Heavens with the curs of terror snapping at their heels. There are many myths concerning deity incarnate, but the instinct of humanity has always been too sound to imagine a Jesus or a Prometheus whose courage faltered. . . .

"The creeds that have endured have endured because of the truth in them; and this truth has always been a courage about life on earth and a high thought concerning the ultimate destiny of the spirit. . . .

"This unceasing talk of Hell is iniquitous, and the reek of it is an abomination beneath the clear and friendly sun; it is the last gabbling echo of the silly tales we gibbered when we were blue-lipped apes back yonder in the gray dawn of time; and one day it will fall on silence; there will come a language in which the thing is not. . . ."

Some years later—in 1928—Marquis had this to say about the Old Soak in the *Saturday Evening Post*: "He all but ruined my reputation. For a period of six years, after Lipton's closed, I never drank a drop; during that period the Old Soak was going strong in song and story, and it used to come back to me from every side that I was an old soak myself."

If after the word "never" in the second sentence of the foregoing paragraph one inserts the Gilbertian parenthesis "that is, hardly ever," the result is a reasonably accurate statement—one that makes allowances for the occasions referred to earlier in these pages when Marquis "conquered his will power." He did have a long period of comparative aridity when his physician—his old friend Dr. Harry March, who had counseled him to "take it easy"—remarked that he had never hoped to see the day when Don would permit himself "to be intimidated into overcooperation."

In the "Hail and Farewell" section of *The Old Soak* there is a poem—it was widely quoted when it appeared in "The Sun Dial" —called "The Battle of the Keyholes" which, in Marquis's opinion, contributed more than anything else he had written to the spreading notion that he was the Old Soak himself. It had been set to music and was being sung all over New York at gay parties A few sample stanzas:

> The keyholes to the right of me
>   Were dancing of a jig,
> The keyholes to the left of me
>   Were merry as a grig,
> The keyholes right before my face
>   Were drunk and winked at me,

And I stood there alone—alone!—
   With one
     small
       key.

They frightened me, they daunted me;
   I turned back to the stair,
And faced nine keyholes pale and stern
   That lay in ambush there.
Six keyholes on the ceiling sat,
   Eight keyholes on the door,
And seven saddened keyholes lay
   Hiccuping
     on the
       floor.

I crawled through one, I crawled through two,
   I crawled through keyholes three,
And then I saw a vistaed mile
   Of keyholes waiting me. . . .

Keyholes at the front of me,
   And keyholes on the flank,
And as they rushed at me I smelled
   The liquor that they drank;
Keyholes on my spinal cord,
   And keyholes in my hair—
And with a "Heave together, boys!"
   They rolled
     me down
       the stair.

Of the three books Marquis published that year his own particular
favorite was *Carter, and Other People,* a collection of short stories
that had appeared in *Pictorial Review, Putnam's Magazine, Harper's,*
the *New Republic,* and other periodicals. The book served as a reminder that the author, known principally as a humorist, could write
effectively in a serious vein. The title story, "Carter," is a moving
portrayal of the problem of the mulatto in America, and to Marquis
fans unfamiliar with his social-mindedness it came as something of
a surprise. So did "Old Man Murtrie," which despite occasional
flashes of humor, is the work of a mordantly earnest Marquis. Of the
story's protagonist he wrote:

"Old Man Murtrie never got any fresh air at all, except on Sundays on his way to and from church. He lived, slept, cooked and ate back of the prescription case in his little dismal drug store in one of the most depressing quarters of Brooklyn. The store was dimly lighted by gas and it was always damp and suggested a tomb. Drifting feebly about in the pale and cold and faintly greenish radiance reflected from bottles and show cases, Old Man Murtrie with his bloodless face and dead white hair and wisps of whisker was like a ghost that has not managed to get free from the neighborhood of a sepulcher where its body lies disintegrating.

"People said that Old Man Murtrie was nearly a hundred years old, but this was not true; he was only getting along towards ninety. The neighborhood, however, seemed a little impatient with him for not dying."

When "Old Man Murtrie" was originally published in the *New Republic* it had elicited warm praise from Franklin P. Adams, who in "The Diary of Our Own Samuel Pepys" (New York *Tribune*, February 11, 1920) had said: "Read 'Old Man Murtrie,' of Don Marquis's, the best piece, meeseems, any one ever wrote." Those who remember Adams's column will recall that its conductor, a hard man to please, reserved such extravagant praise for that which he considered first-rate.

One reviewer made the novel point that in *Carter, and Other People* Marquis had mastered the art of starting his stories with provocative lines and cited these opening sentences in support of his statement:

"There seemed nothing left but suicide."

"Looney had but one object in life, one thought, one conscious motive of existence—to find Slim again."

"See that old fellow there?" asked Ed the waiter. "Well, his fad is money."

"Merriwether Buck had lost all his money; also his sisters', and his cousins', and his aunts'."

"How I ever come to hit such a swell-looking house for a handout I never knew."

Part of the foreword of *Carter* is worth reprinting as a picture of Marquis's magazine market in those days; also because of a tongue-in-cheek passage in which he accuses himself of plagiarism:

"I wish to acknowledge my indebtedness to the editors of several magazines for permission to reprint the following stories in book form. 'Carter' was originally published in *Harper's Magazine* under the title 'The Mulatto.' 'Old Man Murtrie' was printed in *The New Republic*; others were first brought out in *Everybody's Magazine*, *Short Stories*, *Putnam's Magazine* and the *Saturday Evening Post*. 'The Penitent' was originally printed in *The Pictorial Review*, with the title 'The Healer and the Penitent.' The plot of this story is taken from two poems, one by Browning and one by Owen Meredith. Happening to read these two poems, one after the other, I was struck by the fact that Owen Meredith had unwittingly written what was in effect a continuation of a situation invented by Browning; the plot of the one poem, telescoped into the plot of the other, made in effect a complete short story. I pasted the two situations together, so to speak, inventing an ending of my own, and had a short story which neither Browning nor Owen Meredith could claim as his— and which I scarcely have the nerve to claim as mine. And yet this story, taken piecemeal from the two poets, gave me more trouble than anything else I ever tried to write; it was all there, apparently; but to transpose the story into a modern American setting was a difficult job. It is my only essay in conscious plagiarism—I hate to call it plagiarism, but what else could one call it?—and I give you my word that it is easier to invent than to plagiarize."

The third of the three books Marquis published that year was *Noah an' Jonah an' Cap'n John Smith*. The reader is familiar with Marquis's practice of "reprinting by request" the book's title poem. It filled his whole column and was a convenient device when he felt like a day off. This feeling, he said, seized hold of you fairly often if you happened to be a six-times-a-week columnist.

The poem was popular and readers *had* requested that it be reprinted but not as often as Marquis ran it. That story has been handed down for years and last appeared in an article by Frank Sullivan in *The New Yorker* in 1950.

A new anecdote dealing with this quaint practice of Marquis's has come to light. It has to do with a practical joke played on the columnist by one of his friends in the composing room as a means of getting a rise out of him. (Marquis was reasonably well acquainted with nearly everyone on the mechanical side, including the typesetters, and he and they occasionally swapped pranks.) This particular schemer, a veteran compositor who knew his way around the compos-

ing room, got hold of the standing proof of "Noah an' Jonah an'
Cap'n John Smith," with its "Reprinted by Request" under the title,
which was always kept handy for emergencies, as recounted by Sullivan in that *New Yorker* piece. He changed the line to read "Reprinted by Request of Mr. Marquis" and sent the proof to the
columnist with a note requesting him to proofread it. It hadn't
been published in recent months, the compositor pointed out, and
Marquis had not seen this latest proof. Characteristically, Don
merely glanced at the proof, okayed it, and sent it back. The compositor's next move was to return it with a note saying he'd noticed
a change in the line under the title. Was that the way Marquis
wanted it? It was not until then that the boss of "The Sun Dial"
noticed that the line had been altered to: Reprinted by Request
of Mr. Marquis. Marquis corrected the proof and sent it back with a
two-word comment: "Foul play!"

The popularity of the title poem overshadowed the rest of the
contents of "Noah an' Jonah an' Cap'n John Smith." The book is
a good cross section of Marquis as a light versifier. In its humor-
laden pages—157 of them—we find the author doing Pierian hand-
springs all over the place, with an occasional cartwheel for good
measure—a rollicking book that would have been better if Marquis
had dropped about thirty pages of only so-so stuff.

One is tempted to reprint "The Rubber Plant," which could only
have been written by a perceptive Brooklynite—one who knew what
this symbol of Mother Nature meant to Flatbush's early green-
thumbers. But, alas, it covers five printed pages.

"The Jokesmith's Vacation," a felicitous example of self-kidding,
begins like this:

> What did I do on my blooming vacation?
> I solemnly ate, and I frequently slept;
> But I chiefly live over in fond contemplation
> The days that I wept. For I wept and I wept.
>
> One making his living by humorous sallies
> Finds the right to be mournful a blessed relief—
> And hour after hour in the byways and alleys
> I sobbed out my soul in a passion of grief.

Here are four lines lifted out of "Spring Ode," as mad a hymn
to the vernaltide as anyone ever wrote:

> Out of the prison of Winter
> The earth and its creatures emerge,
> And the woodlouse sits on a splinter
> And flirts with the Cosmic Urge.

Throughout his career as a columnist Marquis wrote what he called "Sad Thoughts." Here are two typical ones from this book:

> I've never seen a pyramid
> A-standing on its head
> But what I've thought, "Some katydid
> Is underneath it, dead."

> I've never seen a dinosaur
> A-hanging out the wash
> But that I've thought, "He'd rather, far,
> Be eating Hubbard squash."

Of the so-called "poetry renaissance" Marquis had stanzas and stanzas to say—as, for example:

> There's a grand poetical boom, they say.
> (*Climb on it, chime on it, brothers of mine!*)
> 'Twixt the dawn and the dusk of each lyrical day
> There's another School started, and all of 'em pay.
> (*A dollar a line!*
> *Think of it, Ferdy, a dollar a line!*)

> Perhaps you're a shark with the "nuances," kid?
> (*Go lightly, go sleightly, brothers of mine!*)
> Tones, Colors, Gradations, and Didn'ts that Did. . . .
> (*A dollar a line,*
> *The vaguer the better, a dollar a line!*)

> But whatever you write, be sure you're Sincere.
> (*Carefully, prayerfully, brothers of mine!*)
> If you're chanting of Penitence, Passion or Beer,
> It's that deep Earnest Note that catches the ear.
> (*A dollar a line,*
> *You gotta have Soul for a dollar a line.*)

Before the year was over Don and Reina decided to move from Brooklyn to one of the suburbs, a decision that was applauded by the doctor who attended their three-year-old daughter. They considered several locations and finally decided upon Forest Hills, under the circumstances described by Homer Croy, their newspaperman-editor-novelist friend, in the Forest Hills-Kew Gardens *Post*:

"I claim to be the one who planted Don Marquis in Forest Hills, and this is the way it happened.

"He was working on the *Sun* and living in Brooklyn and thought Forest Hills was out around Montauk Point. One day I saw him at the office and invited him to come and see us, but he was vague about it. Awfully busy, he said; tinkering with a play too.

"I happened to mention that my wife had brought up from the South something new in this section in those days—spoon bread, for which Marquis had expressed a fondness in discussing his days in Atlanta with his New York friends.

"It proved to be the chink in the armor. In no time at all he was out to dinner, and we laid the glories of Forest Hills at his feet.

"'I don't want a house here,' he said sternly. 'I'm just curious.'

"Later he came out to see Burns Mantle, the drama critic, and Burns must have carried the banner, for it was not long until Don was actually talking to the real estate men. He settled on a house on Wendover Road, but quite a down payment was required and Don didn't have it. It runs in my mind that he had to raise the money in three days,—at least in some such short time—and it's not easy for a non-business man to rush out and put his hands on four thousand dollars.

"The next day I saw him and to my astonishment he told me he had got the money. I was flabbergasted at the speed with which he moved. 'Didn't you have to sign away your life?' I asked.

"Well, yes, he had signed some papers, he said; in fact, quite a few. The lawyers had requested it, he added.

"'Did you read the papers closely?' I asked.

"'Sure I did,' he replied, 'that is, all except the fine print. I was in a rush and didn't stop to go into that.'

"And that was exactly what happened. In three or four days a van from Brooklyn drove up in front, and he was living in the house. So now, when I see No. 51 Wendover Road, I say to myself, 'There's the house fine print bought.'"

Edward Wilde, who at this writing lives with his wife in the old Don Marquis house, recounted to me some of the stories they still tell in Forest Hills about Marquis's days as a commuter. "He had a habit of strolling in leisurely fashion to the railroad station, greeting people on the way and stopping to chat with them," said Mr. Wilde.

"Once when he stopped to greet a neighbor someone yelled from across the road that he'd better step lively if he wanted to catch the next train. 'Thanks,' Marquis yelled back, 'there'll be another.'"

None of the Forest Hills people who remember Marquis can recall his ever rushing to catch a train. He never carried a timetable. When asked one day as he strolled toward the station what train he was taking he replied, "The first one that gets there after I do."

This was not a pose, these friends insist. Marquis always had something to read with him, usually a book. He also carried a notebook. He once said that the most peaceful place in the world is a railroad station between trains. One morning when it was warm enough to sit outdoors he sat in front of the station and wrote most of the column he had to turn in that day. There is another story that one winter's day as he sat inside the station scribbling in his notebook the words poured out so freely he regarded the arrival of his train as an intrusion and went right on with his pencil-pushing while a solicitous neighbor tried unsuccessfully to get him to his feet.

A station employee, witnessing this performance, decided that Marquis was "queer." The ticket agent told him not to give it another thought, confiding, "What do you expect? He's one of those authors. They're nuts, most of them."

When on another occasion Marquis sat writing in the station through two trains, a railroad employee called his attention to a sign designed to discourage loitering. A few days later the following appeared in "The Sun Dial": "There are signs at all the stations of the Long Island Railroad that say: LOAFING NOT ALLOWED. But some of the Long Island trains can't read."

Talk to enough people who knew Marquis and Those Who Knew Those Who Knew Him, and the man who tended bar at the Such-and-such Grill in the days when the columnist dropped in occasionally for a drink, and you wind up with several versions of these and similar stories. But most of them follow a pattern based on some recognizable incident. And all of them begin or end with some such comment as, "He was a great guy," inevitable sign of the affection he inspired.

"I know he was a great guy," I told one of these sources. "But you knew him a long time and surely you can recall one of his caustic moments—perhaps some time when he took aim at someone who irritated him."

"I imagine he could get annoyed like anybody else," replied my source, "but it happens I never heard him say an unkind word. He was a great guy."

I got a little further with Berton Braley, popular light versifier of the 1920s and 1930s, who was a close friend of Marquis's, and saw him frequently at the Players.

Marquis, Braley pointed out, could be caustic in his own quiet way, but only on invitation. Once at the Players bar Braley heard a young actor turn to Marquis with a tale of woe to the effect that whenever he found himself in a group at the Club, and started to talk, the group would melt away, one by one. "Do you think I'm a bore or something?"

"Or something," replied Marquis.

Another time the same actor, conscious that he was addressing some companions in a rather loud tone, turned to Marquis and said, "Are you conscious of my voice?" To which Marquis replied, "Yes, but don't give it a thought. I'm about to be *un*conscious."

Braley described Marquis as "a ribald Christ."

"His ribaldry you're familiar with," he said, "so I'll confine myself to saying what you must be aware of yourself—that he could be inelegant—hilariously so—but never gross. He was almost Christlike in his eagerness to help others. Once, sensing I was having a tough time, he approached me and asked if I could use some financial help. I told him I could, which was an understatement. It was my worst year and I was earning next to nothing. Never did I receive help that was timelier, did more for my morale, or that I so thoroughly enjoyed repaying."

Braley departed from his main theme to point out that Marquis did not hesitate to publish in his column items of a controversial nature that might not "have found a home elsewhere." He cited as an example his "Mencken, Nathan and God," a parody of Eugene Field's "Wynken, Blynken and Nod." This is the extravaganza in which Mencken and Nathan insist there is no literature except Dreiser and a few plays from Germany. To quote Braley:

> When God protested, they rocked the boat,
>   And dumped him into the sea,
>   "For you have no critical facultee,"
> Said Mencken and Nathan to God.

The refrain line of this lampoon—"Mencken, Nathan and God" —was supplied by Marquis's good friend, Dr. Richard H. Hoffmann.

The piece amused Nathan, who referred to it in a magazine article as good leg-pulling. Mencken never made any comment.

It is interesting to note that Mencken and Marquis, contemporaries, began assaulting puritanism about the same time. But because Marquis used cap and bells and Mencken a sledge hammer, the results seem utterly different. There are a number of points of similarity in their careers. Marquis earned the brickbats of the clergy for attacking evangelist Billy Sunday at the peak of his popularity. Subsequently Mencken had a similar experience involving evangelist Aimee Semple McPherson.

To get back briefly to Marquis's ribaldry, which Braley mentioned, a favorite story about the columnist has to do with his mock criticism of a fellow member of the Players for using what he called a "certain unseemly four-letter word." He pointed to the following couplet he had written to illustrate the "delicacy" with which the subject could be handled:

It's more refined
To say "break wind."

Our apologies to Lawton Mackall for not using a more robust couplet by Marquis on the same subject; and to a half-dozen other members of the Players for stories in the same Rabelaisian category, all of them illustrating Marquis's philosophy that *anything* can be poetically enunciated . . . except, as he himself put it, "when you're in a hurry and you've got to get something said fast."

9

1922, a Big Year—The Old Soak, *a
Broadway Hit*—Don Publishes Three More Books and
Accepts a Handsome Offer from the New York Herald
Tribune—Enter Frank Sullivan—A Hymn to Bacchus
—Don, Reina, Their Daughter Barbara, archy and
mehitabel, and Captain Fitzurse Leave for Europe—
The Life and Times of Homer Croy—Don Enjoys
Himself in London and Makes a Confession—Tragedy
in Forest Hills*

Encouragement from a top-ranking producer like Arthur Hopkins
had a tonic effect on Marquis. It gave him the strength to work
when, as he put it, he had "earned the right to be tired." Night
after night he worked on his dramatization of *The Old Soak* until
he completed it. Hopkins read it and decided that it needed some
changes. So, continuing his earlier whimsy, he notified Marquis that
it was "not quite bad enough." It was *almost* a bad play but not
quite.

Marquis made the stipulated changes, the play was accepted for
production and Marquis received a contract and a check (advance
on royalties) to seal the bargain. The night Don came home with
the news that the transaction had finally been consummated he
grabbed Reina and danced her around the living room of their new
home in Forest Hills while little Barbara looked on in amazement.

The first thing Don and Reina decided was that if the play was a
success they would make that trip to Europe. Barbara, of course,
would accompany them. The doctor had said that the sea voyage
would be good for the delicate child. They discussed the trip as
though it were a *fait accompli*, making and rejecting itineraries. How
much time should they spend in Paris, in London, etc.? Marquis

thought they should visit Scotland and Ireland so that he could toast his ancestors on their native soil.

An important member of the Marquis household in those days was a full-time domestic named Agnes, a colored girl whose devotion to the Marquises is recalled by friends of that period. The Marquises were as fond of her as she was of them and they asked her to accompany them to Europe to look after little Barbara when they were tied up evenings, a rather iffy proposal since *The Old Soak* would have to make some money on Broadway before they could make the Grand Tour. Agnes said she would think it over; there was one thing about going to Europe that bothered her but she did not disclose what it was until some time later.

There is nothing to indicate that either Reina or Don at any time seriously considered the possibility that the play might not be a success. You wrote a play, it was produced, it made a lot of money and became the means of touring Europe and doing a lot of other exciting things. Neither Don nor Reina was that naïve; yet that's how they were thinking. They both seemed to have a hunch that Don was about to hit the jackpot.

When Marquis told his old friend Dr. Harry March about the proposed trip he urged it, again reminding Don that Reina's heart "was not strong"—diligent research has failed to disclose the precise nature of the ailment—and that such a change would do her more good than "doctoring." He also reminded his friend (who needed no reminding) that Reina had not recovered from the shock of her little boy's death.

Marquis, returning from work one day, found Reina in tears. When he had left her that morning she was in good spirits. Later in the day she had accidentally found at the bottom of an old hamper a favorite toy of Bobby's. She and the boy had hunted for it everywhere about six months before his death and now when she found it the memories of that fruitless search came back and she broke down and wept. In an article he subsequently wrote for the *Saturday Evening Post* Marquis said he had seen Reina weep "only a half dozen times." This was one of them.

It might be added that Marquis himself, though he usually had a good grip on himself, had not recovered from Bobby's death either— and never did fully, as the record shows. Years after the boy's death he was alluding poignantly to him in poems found among his papers.

At a meeting of the Three Hours for Lunch Club, a Christopher

Morley creation, Marquis, toward the end of 1921, met David Bone, master mariner and novelist. These luncheons were small affairs, the men around the table seldom numbering more than seven or eight. Marquis, known as a good storyteller and a good companion, was much in demand at these affairs but seldom attended. Morley used to chide him for not practicing what he preached. Wall mottoes, usually versified hymns to the glories of loafing, were featured in "The Sun Dial" but the column's author was actually a hard-working man who seldom made much of a ritual of lunch. A lover of good food, Marquis concentrated on dinner and was also known for his raids of the icebox between midnight and the early hours of the morning as a means of breaking up his frequent long stretches of night-writing, a habit he had acquired because of the need to bolster his income.

Marquis told friends that Morley's determination that he meet David Bone was an act of kindness he never forgot. Two or three times Marquis had been compelled to call off dates that had been arranged. But Morley, who had a hunch that the two men should know each other, kept trying; and finally Marquis and Bone met at what proved a memorable session of the Three Hours for Lunch Club. It went on and on and for a while Morley considered changing the name of the Club, substituting "Four" or "Five" for "Three."

David Bone, skipper of the *Tuscania* of the Cunard Anchor Line, and author of sea stories, including the well-known novel *The Brass-bounder* (which had been enthusiastically reviewed in the United States and in England and had enjoyed a good sale), was a jovial Scotsman. Well informed, a good talker, "a man with a humorous eye who enjoyed kidding people and being kidded back," he and Marquis hit it off immediately, as Morley had predicted.

Bone was a brother of the distinguished Scottish etcher and painter, Sir Muirhead Bone. Another brother was James Bone, London editor of the Manchester *Guardian*, and one of England's most respected newspapermen. An excellent writer, one of the fields in which he was considered an authority was literary London.

When Marquis mentioned that some day he and his wife expected to take a European vacation, the author-mariner suggested that they travel "under the Bone banner," explaining, "Mar-r-quis"—(Bone sometimes invoked a Scottish bur for comic effect)—"firrrst I'll take you over on the *Tuscania*. Then I'll send you to Glasgow to see brother Muirhead. You might manage to charrr-m him out of a painting or an etching. If not, perhaps you can pinch one. Then I'll have you meet brother James, who will show you around in London." Bone added that when he "ran out of brothers" he would send Mar-r-quis around to see some of his old cronies in England and Scotland. They shook hands on this proposition, which eventually became a reality.

According to Lawton Mackall, close friend of Marquis's and a charter member of the Three Hours for Lunch Club, Marquis and Bone subsequently met at one more luncheon of the Club. At this one, which was held aboard a steamship docked in New York harbor, Marquis ate haggis for the first time. A huge silver chafing dish filled with the steaming-hot Scottish specialty was "piped into the room with great ceremony by Scottish bagpipers in full regalia."

Marquis had a way of converting experiences of this kind into copy, and an idea was born when he learned that haggis is a kind of stew made of sheep's heart and liver with onions and suet, mixed with oatmeal and boiled in a sheep's stomach. He invented in his column a dish of his own made of old tennis shoes, cantaloupe rinds, beer-bottle tops, the left kidneys of female yaks, the right lungs of bull elephants, all generously mixed with grated chewing tobacco and boiled for three days and three minutes in an old traveling bag. He called it baggis.

The following year—1922—ushered in the period of Marquis's greatest financial success. Roughly, it covered the years 1922 to 1925 inclusive.

In 1922 three Marquis books were published, several short stories and articles in national magazines that paid well, the New York *Tribune* (which became the *Herald Tribune* in 1924) offered him substantially more money than the *Sun* was paying him, and he accepted; and, most important of all from the standpoint of income, Arthur Hopkins produced *The Old Soak*, which established itself quickly as one of the biggest comedy hits on Broadway in years. (It opened August 22, 1922, and ran for 423 performances, setting a new record for a run at the Plymouth Theatre. By today's standards this may not sound like a sensational run; but it was so considered forty years ago.)

The books Marquis published that year were *Sonnets to a Red-Haired Lady and Famous Love Affairs, The Revolt of the Oyster,* a collection of short stories that took its title from the lead story,

and a collection of verse entitled *Poems and Portraits* that was dom-
inated by a popular "Sun Dial" series called "Savage Portraits."

The sonnets to a red-haired lady survive today in several antholo-
gies. Three of them are to be found in A *Subtreasury of American
Humor*, edited by E. B. White and K. S. White (along with pieces
from other Marquis books). Commenting on his and Mrs. White's
experience in putting this anthology together, White, in his lively introduction to that perennial best-seller, Marquis's *the lives and times
of archy and mehitabel*, says: "I recall that although we had no
trouble deciding whether to include Don Marquis, we did have quite
a time deciding where to work him in. The book had about a dozen
sections; something by Marquis seemed to fit almost every one of
them. He was parodist, historian, poet, clown, fable writer, satirist,
reporter and teller of tales. He had everything it takes, and more.
We could have shut our eyes and dropped him in anywhere."

Here are a few typical passages from Marquis's lines to his red-
haired lady, which, according to the title page, were written by "A
Gentleman with a Blue Beard":

> When I grow older will you be my wife?
> Not now, Suzanne . . . in twenty years or more.
> Unless I change my mind, I'd like you for
> A Bonfire in the Autumn of my Life.
> —from Sonnet XIV

> Dante for Beatrice sang his solemn story,
> Dan for Beersheba all his poems wrote,
> Alpha in fair Omega's praises smote
> The lyre, and Petrarch jollied little Laurie . . .
> Suzanne, I'll make you famous, too, b'gorry!
> —from Sonnet XVII

> My Twentieth Wife had all too pallid lashes,
> And her thin eyebrows, too, were almost white.
> I shaved them off . . . some incidental gashes
> Made her to moan and murmur all that night,
> And with the dawn her spirit passed away . . .
> How fragile women are! Ah, welladay!
> —from Sonnet XX

In one of his articles on Marquis, Christopher Morley wrote:
"I assign you as home work the reading aloud of the sequence

called *Sonnets to a Red-Haired Lady*—where after 32 stinging cocktails of song he turns on us with four concluding sonnets that—as
William Rose Benét has said—might well have been written by the
earliest of our great sonneteers, Wyatt or Surrey——

> The poet blots the end the jester wrote:
> For now I drop the dull quip's forced pretence,
> Forego the perch'd fool's dubious eminence—
> Thy tresses I have sung, that fall and float
> Across the lyric wonder of thy throat
> In dangerous tides of golden turbulence
> Wherein a man might drown him, soul and sense—
> Is not their beauty worth one honest note?
>
> And thee thyself, what shall I say of thee?
> Are thy snares strong, and will thy bonds endure?
> Thou hast the sense, hast thou the soul of me?
> In subtle webs and silken arts obscure
> Thou hast the sense of me, but canst thou bind
> The scornful pinions of my laughing mind?

Commenting in *Harper's Magazine* on Marquis's light verse in
general and his sonnets to a red-haired lady in particular, Bernard De
Voto said: "It's just wonderful stuff to read. Throughout the *Sun Dial*,
throughout the books, you keep coming on verse that delights you
and frequently holds you breathless while you watch a jagged and
vertiginous imagination shoot through the air like a skyrocket, giving
off odd-shaped and slightly drunken stars of gold. . . . A clear, disturbing music comes through the oddest contexts, and maybe you
had better look up those contexts, and some crystalline images, and
the last four sonnets, before you decide what classification (as a
writer) Don Marquis fits. I'd be willing to waive taxonomy, if some
scholar would turn up fifty unpublished ones, or even two."

Pursuing further the theme of Don Marquis as a poet (humorous
and serious), De Voto had this to say: "The most innocent-appearing
start may presently pull the rug out from under your feet as 'The
Country Barber Shop,' or as 'Gog and Magog' may bump you dizzily
to the edge of mania. Or a trite line suddenly breaks in a curve and
gives you a glimpse of something dreadful or insane or damned, or
a glimpse of beauty from the murky fire-opal that was Don's mind."

To give the reader a fuller picture of "Famous Love Affairs," here

are the opening lines from a scattered sampling of the seventy
pages of his book that he devoted to this section:

From "Paris and Helen":

> Paris was a pretty gent,
>   His lamps were quite hypnotic;
> He used the most expensive scent;
>   His tastes were . . . well, erotic.

From "King Cophetua and the Beggar Maid":

> Cophetua was a merry King,
>   And slightly sentimental;
> His morals were, if anything,
>   What some call "Oriental."

From "Romeo and Juliet":

> Pop Montague's old brain was wried
>   Through all its convolutions
> With constant thoughts of Homicide
>   And kindred institutions.

> White-haired Giuseppi Capulet,
>   Although he liked his daughter,
> The pert, precocious Juliet,
>   Was fonder still of slaughter.

From "Hero and Leander":

> Leander in the Dardanelles
>   Had rather race a dolphing
> Than idle with the other swells
>   Or dance or go a-golfing.

From "Adam and Eve":

> Adam was a handsome lad,
>   Innocent and merry;
> Garden parties were his fad,
>   And he was honest, very.

> Eve was rather artless; she
>   Was also quite vivacious;
> She plucked her raiment from a tree
>   Elaeocarpaceous.

From "Dido and Aeneas":

> Aeneas was a cattle boy,
> And his career was checkered;
> Bull after bull, by roaring Troy,
> He threw, and copped the record.

Typically, in the final poem of the series—Marquis's version of the story of Harlequin and Columbine, from which the following is taken —he returns to the role of the serious poet:

> Harlequin
> Was a wind of the Spring that came out of the dawn;
> He was air, he was whim, he was fancy and mirth,
> And his feet on the earth
> Were as fleet as the feet of a faun.
> He was fickle as glimmers of starlight that shine
> On the waves of the rivers of dream; he was tricky as wine;
> He was pagan as Pan;
> A dancer, a lover, a liar, a wit,
> A poet, a satyr, an imp with the face of a man;
> And his heart was unstable as wings are that lift
> Where the dragonflies drift,
> His heart was as wings that turn, dartle and flit,
> And his loves were as swift.

Marquis thought that the best piece in his short-story collection *The Revolt of the Oyster* was the first tale, from which the book derived its title. As usual, Marquis introduces bizarre characters—one of them (in the title story) a mastodonic, prehistoric oyster that claims the evolutionary process began with him. This ancient bivalve was millions of years old when man discovered his edibility. With this discovery everything changed. As Marquis puts it, "In half an hour, mankind was plunging into the waves searching for oysters. The oyster's doom was sealed. His monstrous pretension that he belonged in the van of evolutionary progress was killed forever. He had been tasted, and found food. He would never again battle for supremacy. Meekly he yielded to his fate. He is food to this day."

In addition to the title piece, the best stories in the book are "The Saddest Man," "How Hank Signed the Pledge," and "Too American." The last-named is typical Marquis extravaganza, as this passage reveals:

"'Is it a real English cottage?' we asked the agent suspiciously, 'or is it one that has been hastily aged to rent to Americans?'"

"It was the real thing: he vouched for it. It was right in the middle of England. The children could walk for miles in any direction without falling off the edge of England and getting wet.

" 'See here!' I said. 'How many blocks from Scotland is it?'

" 'Blocks from Scotland?' He didn't understand.

" 'Yes,' I said, 'blocks from Scotland.' I explained. My wife and I had been trying to get a real English accent. That was one of the things we had come to England for. We wanted to take it back with us and use it in Brooklyn, and didn't want to get too near Scotland and get any Scottish dialect mixed up with it. It seemed that the cottage was quite a piece from Scotland. There was a castle not far away—the fifteenth castle on the right side as you go into England. When there wasn't any wind you didn't get a raw sea breeze or hear the ocean vessels whistle.

" 'Is it overgrown with ivy?' asked Marian, my wife.

"Yes, it was ivy-covered. You could scarcely see it for ivy—ivy that was pulling the wall down, ivy as deep-rooted as the hereditary idea.

" 'Are the drains bad?' I asked.

"They were. There would be no trouble on that score. What plumbing there was, was leaky. The roof leaked. There was neither gas nor electricity, nor hot and cold water, nor anything else.

" 'I suppose the place is rather damp?' I said to the agent. 'Is it chilly most of the time? Are the flues defective? Are the floors uneven? Is the place thoroughly uncomfortable and unsanitary and uninhabitable in every particular?'

"Yes, it had all these advantages. I was about to sign the lease when my wife plucked me by the sleeve in her impulsive American way. 'Is there a bathroom?' she asked.

" 'My dear Mrs. Minever,' said the agent with dignity, 'there is not. I can assure you that there are no conveniences of any kind. It is a real English cottage.'

"I took the place."

Most readers would probably agree that the longest story in the book, "The Saddest Man," is also the funniest. The plot is one of the maddest ever devised. It could only have been brought into being by an inspired madcap who had once worked in the Census Bureau, as Marquis had in 1900. There is method in the author's madness, the story having overtones of authentic political satire built around the Census Bureau's discovery that the "center of population" for the whole country is Brown County, Indianny.

The typical review of a Marquis short-story collection picks out certain stories as outstanding and criticizes the author for signs of haste in writing some of the others—which strikes me as fair. In *The Revolt of the Oyster*, for instance, the range is all the way from "Rooney's Touchdown," a satire on football whose possibilities are only partly realized—probably because it was rapidly written or gives that impression—to "The Saddest Man," in which an ingenious but intricate plot never gets out of control, the author having obviously done a great deal of work on it. Surely this tale will some day get the recognition it deserves—a place in anybody's collection of the best American humorous short stories.

Not far behind "The Saddest Man"—and perhaps on a par with it—is "How Hank Signed the Pledge," the story of how Hank Walters, the village drunkard, is baptized and made to join the church against his will. The protagonist is described as "a blacksmith in a little town in Illinois" and there is reason to believe that the story stems from happenings in Marquis's home town, Walnut, Illinois. (Here and there in this collection the author refers to "the little village of Hazelton," placing it in Illinois, a device he frequently used in referring to Walnut.) In the final paragraphs of this story Hank claims he was the victim of a ruse and puts it this way:

"That was a lowdown trick. You knowed I always made my brags that I'd never jined a church and never would. You know I was proud of that. You know it was my glory to tell it, and that I set a heap of store by it, in every way. And now you've gone and took that away from me! You've gone and jined me to the church! You never fought it out fair and square . . . but you sneaked it on me when I wasn't lookin'!"

The other book Marquis published that year was *Poems and Portraits*. Singled out for special commendation by the reviewers were "The Heart of the Swamp," "A Gentleman of Fifty Soliloquizes," "The Fellowship of Caiaphas," "The Jesters," "August, 1914" and "The Young Moses"—the latter a stirring tribute to the Jewish lawgiver: a long, majestic poem that reveals still another facet of the many-sided Marquis. The story of how Moses led his people out of capivity appears to have moved Marquis profoundly and one gets the impression that when he undertook to write "The Young Moses" he felt he was embarking on a major effort. The lines and accents of the poem are so interdependent that it is difficult to lift out a passage that does justice to the effect created by the whole.

This is the book in which Marquis's well-known "Savage Portraits"—a sequence of seventeen sonnets about types he didn't like—
appeared. Clive Weed, discussing his friend's "new toughness," said,
"I guess Don got tired of being taken for a good-natured slob." One
reviewer said he didn't like "the angry Marquis" but most of them
welcomed the "Savage Portraits" as something new in Marquis's bag
of prosodic tricks. In England the "portraits" were joyfully received
by some critics, unenthusiastically by others. F. L. Lucas, in the *New
Statesman*, picked this one out as specially meritorious and quoted it
in his review:

> Phyllida's young—but skilled in self-control;
> Phyllida's fair—of that Phyllida's sure;
> Phyllida's pure—notoriously pure;
> Phyllida's wise—when snaring men's her goal;
> Phyllida's innocent—when that's her role;
> With deft and silken craft, occult, obscure,
> She makes her proven purity a lure;
> Phyllida's virtuous, in all but soul!
>
> Phyllida's always outraged when she's played
> The very hell Phyllida planned to play.
> I spoke the latest fool Phyllida's made:
> "Were this," he mused, "a franker, elder day,
> Long since some amorous dagger had caressed
> The lovely hollow of Phyllida's breast."

The tireless Marquis had started his research on a play about the
Crucifixion, which he subsequently wrote. This is reflected in "The
Fellowship of Caiaphas," which appeared in *Poems and Portraits*, and
which follows:

The fellowship of Caiaphas were of good repute alway—
But Jesus tramped with beggar men and broke the Sabbath day.

The fellowship of Caiaphas, respectable were they!
But Jesus dined with publicans and He broke the Sabbath day.

The fellowship of Caiaphas would moan as they did pray,
But Jesus is a Human god and yearns to see men gay;
And He turned the water into wine one jolly wedding day.

The fellowship of Caiaphas were very strict alway,
But Jesus pardoned the harlot's sins—and He broke the Sabbath day!

The fellowship of Caiaphas, what righteous men were they!
Jesus they hanged between two thieves, for He broke their
   Sabbath day.

They slew the Rebel that broke their laws—what could they do
   but slay
This wistful vagabond whose love led men the Happier Way?
—And the fellowship of Caiaphas would slay Him again today.

When in that same year—1922—the *Tribune* offered Marquis
more money and a long-term contract (he had none on the *Sun*),
Munsey made no effort to keep his star. Managing Editor Keats
Speed, a friend and admirer of the columnist's, reported that when
Munsey heard about Marquis's offer he said, "Let him take it." The
M.E. expressed the belief that a raise—even a modest one—probably
would have held Marquis, that he had many friends on the paper and
had never shown any disposition to leave. Munsey, always affronted
when someone thought there might be a better place to work than
the *Sun*, instructed Speed to find someone to take Marquis's place.
And that was that.

There is considerable support for a story that Munsey came to the
conclusion that Marquis didn't have much sense when, before he
received the *Tribune* offer, Don turned down the editorship of the
Sun. Munsey, with his genius for miscasting people, had offered
Marquis that important post—at considerably more money than he
made running "The Sun Dial." Why would a man want to continue
grinding out a daily column in preference to running the paper? As
editor, Marquis could hire another man to run "The Sun Dial";
there were plenty of writers around.

Munsey, so the story goes, thought that Marquis had missed the
opportunity of a lifetime. To Marquis the offer of the editorship of
the *Evening Sun* confirmed his belief that Munsey did not grasp
the value of the following his column had developed.

Marquis made only one public reference to this situation. Six years
later, in the *Saturday Evening Post*, he wrote: "Mr. Munsey twice
offered to make me editor of the *Evening Sun*, but I didn't want
office hours or steady responsibility." Characteristically, he refrained
from saying in this article what he had told intimates—that if
Munsey thought his column had any special value to the paper he
would not have considered removing him from it and offering him
another job.

Marquis told me the following story shortly after he had left the *Sun* for the *Tribune:*

He was in the office of one of the *Tribune's* principals, who had just made him an offer. At that particular moment he was seized by an irresistible urge to visit the gents' room. "I told him," said Don, "that I had to make a telephone call. When he offered the use of his phone I replied, as I dashed out, 'This is personal and confidential.' There was a woman among those present and that kept me from saying I was heading for the toilet. Apparently they thought I was shopping around and perhaps reporting the Trib offer to another paper because when I returned the offer was upped considerably. In fact, you might call this the story of the $5000 bowel movement."

Newspaper columnists, even the topnotchers, didn't make much money in those days; and the more I thought about this the more strongly I felt that I ought to find out what Marquis's salary was when he joined the *Tribune*. The information itself would be interesting; also it would be fun to see if the figure sounded impressive enough to accommodate the $5000 b.m.

A letter addressed to George A. Cornish, then executive editor of the New York *Herald Tribune*, drew this reply, dated November 16, 1959: "Our business office informs me that Marquis joined the staff in September, 1922. His salary was $20,000 a year." Mr. Cornish expressed surprise that the salary was that high, regarding it as exceptional "by newspaper standards in those days."

So perhaps Marquis's story about the "phone call" he dashed out to make was not one of his impish inventions.

The *Tribune* contract was cause for rejoicing in the Marquis household. But of all the good things that happened to Don and Reina that year the most exciting was the success of *The Old Soak* on Broadway.

The reviews tell an interesting story. In an unsigned piece the *Evening Sun*, the paper Marquis had just left, said:

"Last night's audience ate up the comedy and pathos of Don Marquis's 'The Old Soak,' founded on his famous *Sun Dial* character. . . . And they forced a curtain speech from a shy and retiring author. It was a great night for the newspaper columnists, and most of them were in the audience applauding the success of their confrere."

Heywood Broun, reviewing the play for the *World*, wrote:

" 'The Old Soak,' by Don Marquis, is the first important play of the new season. . . . When it isn't merry it manages to be profoundly moving. . . . At the end of the second act Mr. Marquis, in his curtain speech, described it as an innocent play. This is a justifiable description. The play both suffers and benefits by its innocence. It is innocent enough to bring into the theater an enormous amount of material freshly and truthfully observed." Broun then goes on to criticize one of the twists of the plot, remarking that "only an innocent person" would employ so transparent a device.

After declaring that the laughs in the play are worth the price of admission, Broun points to an unexpected dividend, "a scene of melodramatic excitement much more thrilling than anything which has been done in a long time."

Broun concluded with this amusing paragraph:

"The play reveals the Old Soak not only in his negative phase as an anti-Prohibitionist but in the positive one of a good Darwinian. His is the observation, 'Heredity runs in our family.' If there is anything in the hypothesis of the survival of the fittest 'The Old Soak' seems destined to long life."

Reviewing the play for the New York *Times*, Alexander Woollcott gave it his enthusiastic endorsement. He also found fault with the plot, then dismissed this as unimportant and put the emphasis on "the rich and abundant and delightful overlay of humor and whimsicality that makes the plot . . . a mere prop for a genuine and hearty entertainment. . . . 'The Old Soak' is gorgeously entertaining. . . . An authentic comedy, it has the accents and overtones of a popular success."

Lawrence Reamer's review in the *Herald* carried this two-column head:

'THE OLD SOAK,' RICH IN HUMOR,
IS WELCOMED IN THE THEATER

— — —

Don Marquis Successfully Transports
His Column Character in The *Sun*
Into a Play

Toward the end of his long review Reamer wrote, under the subtitle, "Author Makes Speech," the following:

"The audience called Marquis after the second act with a compelling cordiality rarely heard in a New York theater. He responded amusingly, so amusingly that the spectators understood just why 'The Old Soak' had entertained them so much."

A reading of the playscript reveals characteristic Marquis touches, as for instance:

Scene: Shows the Hawley living room, a bourgeois and suburban interior. On the walls a couple of steel engravings and some cheap reproductions of Gainsboroughs or Romneys, a couple of crayon portrait enlargements and several pious wall mottoes, "God Bless Our Home," "What Is Home Without a Mother?" etc., these representing taste of Matilda (wife of the Old Soak).

The Old Soak distrusted bootleg liquor—even that produced by Al, his favorite bootlegger—and gave Nellie, the hired girl, instructions to "try out each batch" on Pete, the family parrot. This she did and the system worked well, keeping the parrot and the Old Soak reasonably happy until, toward the end of the second act, the bird became an Old Soak himself, pleading for more and more swallows of the bootleg whisky until, as the hired girl explained in a tearful speech, he had "deceased himself."

After his play had been running for about a month Marquis received a letter on the stationery of an organization of pet-lovers denouncing him for that disgraceful scene in his play in which a family pet is put to cruel uses by a soulless master.

This protest proved to be an elaborate hoax—the letterhead had been specially printed for this single use—which Marquis learned when his reply was returned with a post-office notation to the effect that there was no such address. Clive Weed, Rollin Kirby, and other members of the Players were under suspicion but Marquis never learned who had dreamed up this practical joke.

This reference to the parrot in *The Old Soak* is excuse enough to recount a story, which, according to Homer Croy, had gained currency. It seems that Marquis was visiting Arthur Hopkins at his home in one of the suburbs near New York City. The producer owned a pet parrot which kept squawking that day from his outdoor perch while Marquis was waiting breathlessly to hear Mr. Hopkins' final decision as to whether he would produce *The Old Soak*. To quiet the parrot, Hopkins reached for a T-pole and thrust it into some tall overhanging bushes nearby. The bird, which had been seeking attention, lighted on the pole and stopped squawking when Hopkins set it down beside him.

"That reminds me," the producer then said to Marquis, "of the parrot in your play. You've got a good character there, one that just about makes up my mind for me. I'll produce your play."

Croy does not tell this story "straight." He assumes it was part of the kidding match Hopkins and Marquis had been carrying on.

Complaints of a different nature that Marquis received about his play proved to be the real thing and not hoaxes, as he suspected when the first few came in. They were from clergymen who regarded the Old Soak's biblical allusions as a profanation—they also objected to such lines as, "Three things I always held by—the old-time religion and calomel and straight whiskey." But what proved most upsetting of all to the clergy was a situation in which the Old Soak's son, seeking his father's counsel on a vexing personal problem, is told: "I don't want to crowd any more advice into you than you can hold, but if I was in your fix I'd go get drunk myself."

The play eventually became an issue between Marquis and the Rev. John Roach Straton, pastor of New York's Calvary Church and author of several books, including *Church* vs. *Stage, Our Relapse into Paganism,* and *The Salvation of Society.* Marquis had previously angered Straton, a trustee of the Anti-Saloon League, by publishing a piece in his column called "The Barroom's Good Influence," attributing it to the Old Soak.

Marquis had also unconsciously outraged Straton by poking fun in his column at the so-called fundamentalists and their anti-Darwin tracts—this at a time when Straton himself was writing a book that was subsequently published under the title *The Fakes and Fancies of the Evolutionists.*

Eventually Straton exploded and in a statement that was published in the daily press predicted that Marquis was bound straight for Hell.

According to Marquis's sister Maud, Straton forgave Marquis after the publication, a few years later, of the latter's drama of the Crucifixion, which, ironically, was hailed by churchmen of all denominations as the work of a deeply religious man.

Many anecdotes about *The Old Soak* gained currency—a few of them so extravagant they sound as if Marquis, in a tall-story-telling mood, had invented them.

In going through the news stories that stemmed from Marquis's comedy hit, and odds and ends that columnists published on the subject, one finds frequent references to an expression that achieved popularity through Marquis's play and which was in common use in New York during several years of the prohibition era—"Al's here."

This is how the hired girl in *The Old Soak* invariably announced the arrival of the bootlegger.

Which reminds me that in those days the speakeasies that didn't issue admission cards frequently used passwords. There was one "speak" located in the west fifties—haunt of Claire Briggs, Clive Weed, Floyd Gibbons, Heywood Broun, and others—that had adopted the password, "Al's here," and you couldn't get in unless you knew it.

Royal Daniel, Jr., former New York newspaperman and now editor and publisher of the Quitman, Georgia, *Free Press* recalls attending the second performance of *The Old Soak* with Marquis. He writes me that Don found it hard to believe that his play was a success. Did his friend Royal *really* think the audience liked it? Mr. Daniel kept reassuring Don throughout the evening, remarking as they left the theater that his friend could relax and stop worrying since the audience had laughed uproariously throughout the performance. "I know," replied Don, "but was the laughter *spontaneous?*" He didn't fully believe that his comedy was an honest-to-goodness success until some days later when Producer Arthur Hopkins gave him a picture of the heavy advance sale, including that positive proof of success, the early use of the "Standing Room Only" sign.

Marquis joined the staff of the New York *Tribune* in September of 1922.

Some years later he wrote in the *Saturday Evening Post,* "From the *Sun* I went to the *Tribune,* but before I did so I took a six weeks' vacation and wrote as much good stuff as I could, so as to start in on the *Tribune* with a smash. They syndicated my stuff to twenty papers throughout the country, eight or ten being papers of the first importance. For two years and a half, on the *Tribune,* I did better stuff than I'd ever done before."

When his friend Frank Sullivan succeeded him on the *Evening Sun,* Marquis decided to send him a gift column and wrote the following, which was found among the Marquis papers at Columbia University:

Dear Mr. Sullivan:

I hear your name is really O'Sullivan, and that you have discarded the O because you did not want anyone to find out that you are Irish.

O'S.

Dear Mr. Sullivan:

From the picture I saw of you in Vanity Fair, where you are trying on the underwear, I know you are a kind hearted man, and just simply love Babies and Dogs, so I thought I would write you and ask your advice. Herbert and I have been married four years, and I would like a Baby, but Herbert says he does not think we can afford one yet, and in the meantime we have a dog. Of course, I love Dogs, too, everyone not an old grouch loves Dogs, they are so faithful and intelligent, but had I ought to let Herbert have his way about this matter and not have any Babies? I love the Wee Tots even more than I love Dogs, and if Herbert persists is it cause for a Divorce? You had such a kind, sweet look in the underwear ad I thought it could do no harm to put the question to you.

Thelma

Dear Frank, Old Scout, do you know that your name is being mentioned more and more frequently these days as a possibility for the next gubernatorial campaign? It's a fact! In Tim's Place and at The Old Hatrack Cafe, and elsewhere. The question has come up whether you are a sincere Wet, or whether you just pretend to be in order to keep on the band wagon. . . . A couple of dollars spent right now in the right places would do more towards crystallizing your growing popularity than hundreds spent later; I want to drop in and see you and talk over this situation, Frank, Old Scout.

Pud

My dear, *dear* Mr. Frank Sullivan:

I am sending you five of my poems, and O, Mr. Frank Sullivan, I shall hardly be able to breathe or eat or do anything but sit and tremble until you write and tell me that they are really and truly GOOD! I am sending you my latest photograph too—it was taken in May; my Understanding Dad, as I call him, gave me two dozen of them on my twentieth birthday.

(Over)

(page 2, you poor son of a bitch. You don't think I'd waste two sheets of paper on you, do you, Mr. Sullivan?

Don Marquis)

Oh, I do hope you'll like the poems and the photograph! Enough so you will ask me to come and see you personally! Dear Mr. Frank Sullivan, I do so need encouragement and recognition in my writing. . . . And you could introduce me to so many Literary People if you thought my work justified it!

I am leaving home, and getting a little flat of my own in town, for I think a Creative Writer should be free from all domestic entanglements, don't

you? Between now and October first, I shall be very busy choosing the
decorations and furnishings of my little flat . . . and would you think I
was terribly daring if I were to ask you to come with me and help make
the selections? There, now, it is out, and I feel relieved! I admire your
taste— Oh, how I WISH I could be certain that you would admire my poems
as much as I admire your literary taste! You see, dear Mr. Frank Sullivan,
I intend to give many little select parties this coming season, and I have
dared to hope that you would be a sort of guest of honor in every one of
them! It would help me immensely, of course, to get acquainted with your
little group of literary friends—and maybe I could be of help to you, too!
And if you help me decorate and furnish the flat, you may feel like making
it, in a way, your headquarters this next autumn and winter.

Oh, it all hangs on whether you like the poems, doesn't it? Even if you
don't like them so very well, but think they show promise, can't I still
come and see you, and chat with you about my literary career, and the
flat, and everything? . . . I hardly knew which poems to send you, dear
Mr. Frank Sullivan. . . . I hope especially you will like the one I have
called FREE, FREE AT LAST! . . . for that poem is from the heart.

I know from your pictures—especially one which I saw in Vanity Fair—
that I could TRUST you with any confidence I might make . . . and I
don't know of ANY confidence I could withhold from you!

I shall be in to see you some day next week, whether you like the poems or
not! So there!

Heavens, I hope your mail isn't read by a secretary before you see it! If
it is, I shall HATE her . . . I hate her anyhow! Maybe I could help you
in some secretarial work, dear Mr. Sullivan!

Diana V.

Now, there's a column for you; go out and get drunk!—D.M.

I sent Frank Sullivan a photostat of this column of imaginary fan
mail (originally typed by Marquis on both sides of a single sheet)
and received this reply:

"Thanks for letting me see this photostat. It is Don to the life,
taking a crack at all the pests who inflicted their shoddy contributions
on him. He was never much of a hand for contribs. It was easier
for him to do it himself. Frank Adams had the magic touch of
handling and attracting A-1 contribs. He let them do their stuff,
and stood aside while they did it. Don couldn't be bothered much
with contribs. And how he used to rail at those jokers who sent him
items that struck them as screamingly funny, like 'A dentist on
West 74th Street is named Dr. Payne' and so on. This is so funny
and so beautifully Don, I am going crazy because I CANNOT remember

having seen it before. There is a mystery here. Did he write it for me and forget to send it? If I had got it, it would scarcely have wound up in Columbia University. I never gave any mss. to Columbia."

Sullivan's guess that Marquis, after writing this column, forgot to send it to him is probably correct. There was no reason for not sending it to his friend and successor since it was in keeping with the kind of spoofing that was and still is the Sullivan trade-mark. The column was found among the Marquis papers—twenty-two sizable boxes of them and several scrapbooks—that Doubleday and Company presented to Columbia University after they had acquired the rights to them.

Marquis also wrote letters that he never mailed. Either he had second thoughts about them or simply forgot to post them.

Harking back to the question of how Munsey really felt about Marquis, Sullivan states in a letter to me dated May 8, 1958: "He [Munsey] was sore because Don had quit." Then declaring, "I couldn't stomach Munsey," Sullivan gives that as his reason for chucking his job as Marquis's successor on the *Sun*—not many months after he'd started running "The Sun Dial"—to join the *World*. Munsey did not understand men like Marquis and Sullivan and the miracle is that Marquis stuck it out as long as he did.

Before he left the *Sun* Marquis wrote a piece for "The Sun Dial" that proved to be one of his most widely quoted. Requests for permission to make reprints reached the newspaper from individuals, groups, and organizations. Some of these reprints are still in circulation, as for instance, one provided by Walter Trumbull, long-time friend and *Sun* associate of Marquis's, which carries this identification: "Done on his own press, by Elmer Munson Hunt, at Salisbury, New Hampshire." The piece, as it appeared in Marquis's column, follows:

After five years of almost total abstinence we are able to drink a little again—and, oh, the difference to us! That accursed, iniquitous, enforced, damnable, drab sobriety—that cautious, negative, elderly, tight-lipped, niggardly sanity—that slow-pulsed, even-ticking, calm and cowardly regularity—all that is gone, all that is done, and we have recaptured a sense of the richness and strangeness and mystic intricacy of existence; we have drink again, we have dreams again, we shall have again a laughing madness and golden maggots working in the brain, and poetry and opulent nonsense and the companionship of dancing stars and brief, sudden instants of unity with the careless gods. Middle age needs some impulse to fling it into sympathy again with youth and young love and the supersensual ecstasies, and drink is a sweet remembrancer of these. Defeat and frustration and a bitter self-knowledge come with the inevitable years; courage faces these things; intoxication soars above them and forgets them; drink has its glorious and triumphant instants when it wins for us all the old lost battles. Let others defend liquor; we praise it.

One of the paradoxes of this life is that in order to be normal we must have flashes of super-normality or extra-normality. Some persons are able to attain this state by way of religious emotionalism—a thing which we have often experienced but always distrusted, for it leaves its scars of dervishism on the character. An occasional drunk is healthier than permanent asceticism. And anchorites and flagellants are apt to get too proud of their itches and fistulas. But it is better to be drunken with sanctity than never to be drunken at all. It is better to go on a spree of religious emotionalism than never to transcend the tidy moralities. The main thing is now and then to stir the blood and move the spirit. If you are bidden to a wedding feast in Cana, do not stay at home nursing a dour superiority; be a little reckless of yourself; adventure your respectability, and who knows but that you may make the acquaintance of some necromancer happily turning water into the wine that makes the spirit leap and sing.

There was a mystery and a miracle—and the visible and tangible world, the solid and literal and customary world, is but a veil and a thin crust covering a reality that is all mystery and miracle. Drink helps us penetrate the veil; it gives us glimpses of the magi of creation where they sit weaving their spells and sowing their seed of incantation to the flowing wind. If you have a devil in you anyhow, drink can be a devil to you; make no mistake about that; your traffic is with a magic force that returns to you what it gets from you. But beasts and devils are always beastly and devilish. It is bad for Caliban; but Prospero lets Ariel have it now and then—and he knows that neither abstinence nor indulgence will change the one into the other.

We thank all our gods, both pagan and Christian, that we are able to drink a little again; we pour now a libation to Bacchus, and this coming Christmas we shall sit with publicans and sinners and make merry and drink with a reverent thought of the kindly magician of Cana.

The important words in the foregoing are these from the first sentence of the opening paragraph—"almost total abstinence." Those who saw Marquis often in those days—Lawton Mackall, for instance—call it a period when he didn't do much "important drinking." Discussing *all* periods, Mackall added, "I never once saw him drunk."

What Marquis has written about himself indicates that he did his "most sincere tippling" from 1900, when he worked in Washington, to 1917, which takes in his first eight years in New York. Marquis's 1922 hymn to liquor revived the notion that he was a lush himself.

It was inevitable that organizations eager for the overthrow of prohibition should see in Marquis a force that could be harnessed to their advantage. No one had so effectively ridiculed the 18th Commandment, as the Old Soak called it, or made out a more effective case, however humorously, for its repeal. Surely, thought a group that was organizing an anti-Prohibition parade, that man Marquis will be glad to co-operate. So they wrote him a letter suggesting that he participate, declaring that by marching in their parade and waving a whisky bottle as a symbol of defiance of the Volsteaders he would be striking a blow for the cause of repeal. This would give them an opportunity to announce that Don Marquis, well-known foe of Prohibition, had joined their fight against the Volstead Act. Marquis turned them down, stating that he never lent his name to causes, good, bad, or indifferent. Making another wrong guess, the organizers of the parade apologized for not inviting him to ride— (in an open car, with plenty of room to swing that bottle)—instead of suggesting that he participate on foot. This time he didn't bother replying.

Marquis also received requests to make speeches at anti-Prohibition meetings. His stock reply was that he'd been making speeches on the subject for years through the Old Soak. He told one overzealous press agent for a wet organization that if he didn't stop badgering him he'd turn Prohibitionist and take the stump for the drys.

A study of Marquis's column reveals that he thought the chronic drunk as much of a nuisance as the Prohibitionist. Such lines as these are typical:

"When a man gets along about 40 years old it ceases to be thrilling to act as a guardian for souse friends. . . . No one ever thought of himself as an immoderate drinker. . . . This drunken country must always be soused, either with alcohol or the dervish fanaticism of the puritan. . . . Work in New York is something they pad out the time with between booze parties."

Marquis admitted that, as a result of such paragraphs, he once received a fan letter from a Prohibitionist. Mortified, he addressed himself to his typewriter and launched a new series of "Prohibition Ballads," with this one (a favorite of William Rose Benét's) as a starter:

> The prohibition agents came
>   Unto a cabin door,
> Nine angel children played their games
>   And romped upon the floor;
> The agents laid a burly hand
>   On mother's hair so gray,
> For making hootch, you understand,—
>   And all the tots did say:

Chorus:
"Oh, do not take our mother's still, for she is old and worn,
What will she do if she can't make the moonshine from the corn?
Oh, do not lock our mother up! What will become of we
Without the hootch we learned to drink at dear old mother's knee?"
    (And eight more stanzas to the same effect)

The trip to Europe was now a reality.

When (in the spring of 1923) Don and Reina told Agnes, the colored girl who helped Reina run the house in Forest Hills, that the family was planning to sail that August, that they were thinking of remaining abroad ten weeks to three months, and that they had ordered a steamship ticket for her, Agnes announced flatly that she would be unable to make the trip and requested them to cancel her ticket.

Something would have to be done to get Agnes to change her mind. Don and Reina had grown fond of their girl-of-all-jobs who was as likeable as she was capable. Though she had had little education, Agnes was their favorite of all the domestics they had had; she was thorough, straightforward, had a lively sense of humor, and was completely devoted to the three Marquises. And she had just enough superstition in her soul, and a belief in old wives' tales, to be a "character." As important as anything was the fact that Barbara enjoyed her company. She made the child laugh with her little acted-out stories told with comic gestures. Agnes would be the perfect companion for Barbara abroad when Don and Reina had engagements that tied them up evenings.

At first Agnes would not say why she declined to make the trip, then she admitted that a friend had told her that the ocean was six miles deep and she wasn't Taking No Chances. Marquis claimed that he made her change her mind by convincing her that the ocean was only *three* miles deep.

Marquis said he had to overcome other objections too. The same friend had told Agnes that you couldn't get anything to eat in France except frogs and snails and she said it made her sick just to think about it. She'd also heard that the French had a way of sneaking absinthe into your soup or your coffee and the next day when you woke up you were in a den of robbers who made you work for them for nothing and if you tried to resist them they chopped your head off.

Don finally succeeded in calming these and other fears. "Never hesitate to resort to bribery in a situation of this kind," he told Clive Weed, explaining his discovery that Agnes had a boy friend she was loath to leave.

Marquis suggested that she and her friend have a bang-up farewell party at his expense. This won her over and she agreed to make the trip.

Don, Reina, Barbara, and Agnes sailed on the *Tuscania* in August 1923.

Don had piled up enough columns before leaving to make it unnecessary for him to do any writing en route. About the only work he did was to jot down such ideas as occurred to him. "You can make ironclad vows not to do any work," he said in a letter, "but you can't prevent ideas from popping into your head."

Marquis used to say that when he originally arrived in New York in 1909 his baggage consisted of a dozen books of poetry and a pair of old socks.

He and Reina had read poetry to each other during their courtship in Atlanta and now they resumed the practice. Nobody knows how many pairs of old socks Don took with him to Europe but it is known that he took many books of poetry and he and Reina lounged in their deck chairs and read favorite passages to each other. Among their enthusiasms were William Blake, Emily Dickinson, and Francis Thompson. Their enjoyment of Blake subsequently communicated itself to Barbara—the third poet in the family, who by the time she was a few years older was the author of many poems, including some that were accepted for publication in the then popular children's magazine *St. Nicholas*. At one time little Barbara carried a book of selections from Blake with her wherever she went. In a later chapter, and in another context, a letter from a former Forest Hills neighbor will be cited as an indication of the spell the eighteenth-century English poet had cast over the child.

One of the satisfactions Don derived from the trip was that at last Reina had a chance to travel and relax. For some time his easily invoked guilt complex had been working overtime about "all those years she was bogged down in a Brooklyn flat" and now he was able to take a much-needed vacation from nagging self-reproach.

Captain Bone, an attentive host, entertained the Marquises and the three became good friends. Don subsequently told Lawton Mackall that one of the deep satisfactions of the voyage was to see the cheerful skipper-novelist "stand foursquare on the bridge of his ship and exclaim, 'Don, I love my job!'"

According to Mackall, Captain Bone had his own ideas about what the interiors should be like on an ocean liner. He opposed the heavy formalism that decorators had brought to many of the best-known steamships of the period. Dispensing with stock furnishings and decorations—(having of course first won the support of the Cunard Anchor Line)—he had succeeded in giving his ship the feel of a comfortable home in good taste. "The *Tuscania*," declares Mackall, "reminded you more of a tastefully furnished private yacht than of a big impersonal ocean liner—and it isn't surprising that the Marquises fell in love with it."

Barbara became acquainted with many of the passengers, and she and Agnes, who was with her a good deal of the time, were constantly introducing Don and Reina to their new-found friends, all the way from children to elderly couples.

As the Marquises watched their daughter romp all over the ship, a picture of energy and high spirits, they decided that Barbara could no longer be classified as "a delicate child."

Even Agnes was enjoying herself. She had forgotten all her fears about the depth of the ocean and had overcome her fears about the possibility of seasickness by taking her boy friend's advice, which was to chew gum all the way over. Marquis said she had brought enough chewing gum aboard "to patch a thousand blowouts." He quoted her, in explanation of her preventive approach to *mal de mer*, "De motion ob de jaws offsets de motion ob de ocean," which sounds like a Marquis invention.

The big moment for Agnes came when Captain Bone invited her to visit the bridge, which she expressed a desire to see when Barbara, who had been "topside" with her parents, told her all about it. Agnes and Barbara, who wanted to see the view from the bridge again, called on the skipper-writer together.

The Marquis hired girl reported later that "Mr. Bones was very nice and showed her how to run a ship."

With an exaggerated gravity which he could turn on when the occasion seemed to warrant it, Bone told Agnes how glad he was to hear that she was feeling well and enjoying herself (having been previously apprised by Marquis of her concern about the depth of the ocean and the possibility of seasickness). Subsequently he gave Don a description of her elaborate explanation of the merits of chewing gum as a seasickness preventive, just how it worked, why she thought her particular brand was best for the purpose, etc. She was surprised that Captain Bone didn't know about these things and offered him some slabs of gum, which he accepted with a bow and a solemn word of thanks. He afterward told Marquis that this conversation with Agnes was one of the high spots of the crossing.

An amusing footnote to the stay of the Marquises in Paris is provided by Wilbur Forrest, a former associate of Don's, who writes:

"I was in Paris as correspondent for the *Tribune* when a tearful Don Marquis entered my office one day asking for help. Someone had recommended a *pension* on the Left Bank and Don, his wife, daughter and colored maid Agnes had landed there from the boat train to find that no one in the place spoke a word of English. They were completely befuddled and lost in an alien city and almost frantic. Don knew me, of course, and yelled for help. I moved them to the Hotel Laetitia on the Boulevard Raspail where every Frenchman spoke English. It was a job to detach them from the *pension* whose proprietor wanted to hold onto these four cash customers at a time when business was only so-so, but I finally managed it. Don actually cried with relief.

"Agnes got homesick a few days later and Don hired a cab and rode alone with her showing her the sights of Paris, of which he knew very little. Of every imposing building, including the Louvre, which they passed, Don would say in his soft drawling voice, 'Agnes, that's where the king lived,' and Agnes would reply, 'Sho nuff, Mr. Marquis.' Agnes got the idea eventually that the king had lived everywhere, including residence in the Chambre de Deputies. I saw a lot of Don in Paris. . . .

"When I was in the New York office we all read his column daily and got big laughs out of mehitabel the cat and archy the cockroach. . . .

"What impressed me most about Don was the constant realization that there were not many like him—gentle, kind, sentimental and companionable."

Marquis's column was now called "The Lantern" and it had been published in the *Tribune* for about a year when his stuff written abroad began appearing. One of his first gambits was the announcement of a movement headed by his renowned swashbuckler, Captain Peter Fitzurse, to restore the monarchy in France. This would not be easy, Marquis pointed out. But there were few difficulties that could not be surmounted by the fearless and resourceful adventurer who had fought on both sides in the Civil War and had made the North and the South cry "Uncle!" with equal pain and anguish. Throughout his spine-chilling exploits in pursuit of his Restore-the-Throne Campaign, Fitzurse was trailed by a secret agent of the French government; though, needless to say, Fitzurse proved More Than a Match for this pursuer, a character known as The Man of the Monocles.

Marquis, writing his column in Paris, gave a little of Fitzurse's early personal history designed to remind the reader of the old adventurer's hardihood and of the fact that he was no stranger to the French capital. As for instance:

"Capt. Peter Fitzurse, an old friend of mine who has run through three fortunes, four marriages and five depressions, says no country knows what hard times are until it has to eat horse meat and can't get any salt for it. 'As I did in the early seventies of the last century, in Paris,' added the Captain, 'when the city was besieged by the Prussians.' The Captain claims that he subsisted for four days on the roots of tulips, which had been planted by the Empress Eugénie with her own fair hands, which he dug out of the Tuileries gardens at night, Eugénie having sent him a map with crosses on it showing where the treasure was buried. I hesitate to express a shadow of disbelief, for the last man who called Capt. Fitzurse a liar was run through with a sword plucked from a cane which Fitzurse always carries."

In Paris Marquis also launched *The Old Soak's History of the World*, a work on which the author (Clem Hawley, the O.S.) did extensive research in bars and sidewalk cafés. For instance, he spared no expense—buying drink after drink—to determine whether Marie Antoinette was pushed off the Eyefull Tower or whether she jumped. In New York, when the Old Soak's findings were published, a pundit wrote Marquis to say that neither was correct, that actually Marie had been guillotined. It may have been one of the reasons why Marquis announced in his column, when the series had run its course: "The report that the Old Soak's History of the World will be used as a textbook in the New York public schools is premature."

Marquis was moved and excited by much that he saw in Paris, as reflected by several serious pieces he wrote and published in his column, including the following:

"There are a thousand adventures in the Louvre, and one could wander there for a dozen lifetimes and then thereafter haunt it as a ghost, and still keep feeding his incorporeal appetites. But for me the supreme spiritual adventure, always and recurrently, is the Nike of Samothrace, that victress over the rushing winds of Time who flings forever to the human soul a word of courage from the shadowy splendor of her wings.

"I fell under the dominion of this mighty being nearly twenty-five years ago, when I was an art student; I have worshipped her in plaster ever since, and to meet her now in marble is like coming one step nearer to the audacious dreamer, immortal and unknown, who was created by a god to the great end that he might create this goddess. There are legends as to what she was, and why she is— one of them that the statue commemorated the naval victory off Salamis about 300 B.C.—but these legends are concerned with the local and the temporal, and whatever event of whatever time she celebrates, that event was merely the spring that released the force of thought and emotion which rushed into this figure from the soul of its creator. Artists know things unconsciously that they cannot always speak with the lips of their consciousness, nor otherwise than through the medium of their art, and the sculptor of this Nike put into her wings and body the essence of all gleaming victorious flights of the human intellect against and through the clouds of chaos.

"And so it is that the sight of her lifts one up and bears one on; the heart that was downcast rises and goes with her.

"Whoever he was that made her, he was a great man of a great tribe, and as much as the Greeks have sent winging to us from antiquity, they have sent nothing nobler than this message and this messenger."

Perhaps the most important members of the columnar cast that accompanied Marquis to Europe were mehitabel and archy. As the boss of "The Lantern" put it, it's a cinch to find room in your luggage for a cat and a cockroach. The following excerpt is from a full-column piece called archy at the tomb of napoleon and can only serve to introduce the author's theme:

> paris france
> i went over to
> the hotel des invalides
> today and gazed on
> the sarcophagus of the
> great napoleon
> and the thought came
> to me as i looked
> down indeed it
> is true napoleon
> that the best goods
> come in the smallest
> packages here are
> you napoleon with
> your glorious course
> run and here is
> archy just in the
> prime of his career
> with his greatest
> triumphs still before
> him neither of us
> had a happy youth
> neither one of us
> was welcome socially at
> the beginning of his
> career neither one of
> us was considered much
> to look at . . .

archy wrote several columns about an affair mehitabel had with a creature that claimed he had been François Villon in a previous incarnation, describing him as:

a ragged eared tom cat
with one mean
eye and the other
eye missing whom
she calls francy
he has been the hero
or the victim of
many desperate encounters
for part of his tail
has been removed
to the spine
and his back has been chewed
one can see at a glance
that he is a sneak thief
or an apache . . .

Plainly shocked, archy reports that he saw the raffish pair—after they had imbibed too freely at the cafés of Montparnasse and the Boul Mich—return in a holiday mood to their temporary abode in the catacombs of Paris and . . . but from here on let archy describe it himself:

these cats
should have more respect
for the relics of mortality
you may not believe me
but they actually danced and
capered among
the skeletons while the cat
who calls himself
francois villon gave forth
a chant of which the following
is a free translation

outcast bones from a thousand biers
click us a measure giddy and gleg
and caper my children dance my dears
skeleton rattle your mouldy leg
this one was a gourmet round as a keg
and that had the brow of semiramis
o fleshless forehead bald as an egg
all men s lovers come to this

this eyeless head that laughs and leers
was a chass daf once or a touareg
with golden rings in his yellow ears
skeleton rattle your mouldy leg
marot was this one or wilde or a wegg
who dropped into verses and down the abyss
and those are the bones of my old love meg
all men s lovers come to this

these bones were a ballet girl s for years
parbleu but she shook a wicked peg
and those ribs there were a noble peer s
skeleton rattle your mouldy leg
and here is a duchess that loved a yegg
with her lipless mouth that once drank bliss
down to the dreg of its ultimate dreg
all men s lovers come to this

prince if you pipe and plead and beg
you may yet be crowned with a grisly kiss
skeleton rattle your mouldy leg
all men s lovers come to this

In writing to friends from Paris Marquis employed a technique that he discussed at length in his book of prefaces, which, appropriately enough, was reissued that same year—1923. In "Preface to a Book Withheld" he said: "The book to which this is the preface will never get into type. It consists, or would have consisted, of some eighteen hundred jests, short poems, anecdotes, etc., which have been considered too daring for newspaper publication. The 'art form' known as the limerick predominates.

"Most of them contain more wit than Boccaccio's 'Decameron,' they are more chaste than Balzac's 'Droll Stories'; they are more delicate than Smollett; they are more candidly what they are than the equivocal Sterne. . . .

"I have considered some of them daily for two or three years. . . . I do not quite dare to publish them in a newspaper which may finally line the pantry shelves and come to the attention of some young Finnish maid with an unformed mind. . . .

"There is, for instance, the one that goes:

> There was a young fellow from Frisco
> Who never had eaten Nabisco
> . . . .
> . . . .
> . . . . .the risk, O!

"Truly, it is a harmless thing. . . . I have been on the verge of printing it in its entirety a dozen times these last two years . . . and yet, now I am too cowardly and conservative. . . .

"We live in an age so remarkably pure, because it is so frequently reformed whether it likes it or not, that my apprehension of the iniquity in the minds of others has become almost abnormally acute. . . . This makes me cling tightly to appearances.

"Just another quotation from the slain book:

> There was a young fellow named. . . .
> . . . .
> . . . .
> . . . .
> . . . .

"Innocent, I swear! Innocent as the snow white hair that trembles beneath the halo of a saint.

"And yet could I trust you with it?

"For its innocence is of that sort of awakened innocence which is not by any means ignorant; its innocence moves daintily and delicately on the blushing feet of knowledge past a little area of less harmless sophistication, shrinking and mincing as the danger is avoided. One joggle from a thought less generously obtuse and the poem's pink toes might be stained."

Marquis had sworn off limericks. But in Paris he found himself writing them again. Once more he had conquered his will power.

His reason for abandoning the limerick, he wrote Clive Weed, was that there was no sense writing stuff you couldn't publish. There was something about the limerick form—an abandoned swing, he thought it was—that made him overstep. He thought there were plenty of offensive limericks but he also had a theory that the limerick, being a concentrate, sometimes *sounded* dirty when it really wasn't; i.e., he had said in his column in prose pieces, without being criticized, some of the things he had been told it would be wrong to publish in limerick form.

As to the limericks he wrote in Paris, though in a few cases he sent all five lines, usually he employed the "censored" technique with which he had so much fun in "Preface to a Book Withheld."

Among the censored ones he exported to the United States—some on postcards, some in letters—were:

> A madam whose name was Yvette
> Sought dignity through a lorgnette.
>   She lay claim to culture,
>   Pretentious old vulture,
> . . . .

> A charmer by name of Yvonne
> Could never stand being alone.
>   . . . .
>   . . . .
> . . . .

> Georgette had decided to charm
> An overly pious gendarme.
>   . . . .
>   . . . .
> . . . .

> A wonderful place is Paree
> For the Proper in quest of a spree.
>   Purveying of sex
>   Is approved by the lex
> . . . .

Here are a few examples of the ones he thought required no editing:

> There was a mam'selle from Montmartre
> Who objected when labelled a tartre.
>   "I'm as good as the next,"
>   She exclaimed, plainly vexed,
> "I'm merely pursuing my artre."

> A mademoiselle known as Claire
> Has the world's most tattooed derrière,—
>   It is something to see
>   All viewers agree . . .
> I heard it from one who was there.

> A limerick needn't be dumb,
> The work of a low-minded bum,—
>   And yet every time
>   I compose such a rhyme
> I feel like a dirty old *homme*.

Reina, it will be recalled, seldom took a drink. Don enjoyed teasing her and forged her signature to brief messages to friends in the United States indicating she was having a wild time. One read:

> Champagne is a drink I'd assess
> As liquid poetics, I guess.
>   Don says, "Have a fling,
>   Let the Muses take wing,
> You'll never become an *ivresse*."

Another to which he signed her name read:

> *J'aime* practically everything here,—
> The people, the French atmosphere.
>   The art is divine
>   And so is the wine,
> And ditto the brandy and beer.

With the aid of a French dictionary Marquis launched a series in his column which he called "French without a Struggle." It has been suggested by Marquis fans of that period that this was the starting point for the epidemic of books featuring Americans battling manfully—though without much success—to master the French language.

The series proved popular and inevitably Marquis was asked for a book to be called, like the column feature, "French without a Struggle." He decided it wouldn't make a good book—"too thin" —and turned down the offer.

Hudson R. Hawley, a former New York *Sun* associate of Marquis's, was in Paris for International News Service during Don's stay there in 1923 and saw a good deal of him.

In a letter dated October 28, 1959, Hawley writes: "In my opinion Don was a greater after-dinner story-teller than Irv Cobb, which is saying something. I well remember one luncheon of the Anglo-American Press Association of Paris at which he wowed a very distinguished company. . . . Unfortunately I haven't the clips on it."

Hawley also comments enthusiastically on Marquis's limericks, then ruefully reports that the ones he remembers are unprintable.

The writer had a chat with Hawley in which the former I.N.S.

man recalled an incident at another luncheon in Paris. The speaker of the day, a member of the faculty of a leading American university, had just returned from Russia and spoke glowingly of what the Soviets were doing for the Russian farmer. In support of his representations he pointed out that he had been afforded an opportunity to secure all his information firsthand, and cited the fact that the Soviets had made it possible for him to carry on a conversation through an interpreter with a Russian farmer whose enthusiasm was boundless as he described how the government, in accordance with established policy, had given him a generous parcel of land and the means of making it productive. When the speaker concluded, the guests were invited to submit questions to him.

Marquis apparently thought the speaker was naïve, although he did not say so. In the friendliest manner he asked whether—on second thought—the speaker wouldn't like to concede the possibility that the farmer who had testified so soulfully to the wonderful treatment accorded him by the Soviets might not have been a stooge for the Russian government. No, boomed the educator; he was sure that was not so. What he had witnessed was the real thing. But he had no facts in support of his strongly held views and seemed to resent Marquis's pointing this out. When the educator tried to put Marquis in the position of an ignoramus challenging an authority, Don, using his favorite weapon—kidding—routed his adversary; but, typically, Marquis was unhappy about the position in which he found himself. He didn't enjoy embarrassing anyone, not even an overbearing pundit.

It was in Paris that Barbara composed and shouted her first poem:

> Agnes is all the time washing my face,
> Paris is a pretty place.

Marquis's moodiness is reflected in his correspondence from abroad —it wasn't all gay limericks. Writing to his old friend, George Middleton, he said: "I have written the bloody guts out of myself, and don't know whether it is worth reading or not; probably not."

In a previous letter Marquis had written Middleton: "I have decided not to go to London on this trip." In the letter quoted in the preceding paragraph he announced: "Am leaving for London next week with a million things unseen and undone. A person needs to stay a year in Paris or else, while he is here, not to work at all."

In some of the letters of that period Marquis managed to combine the serious and the antic. For instance, the letter in which he complains of having written "the bloody guts out of himself" opens with as rollicking a bawdy limerick as he ever wrote—almost a classroom example of how the anapestic meter should be treated. Marquis's friend Brander Matthews would have applauded its technique and deplored its inadmissibility—on grounds of unpublishability—to the pages of his scholarly A *Study of Versification*.

Marquis also wrote Middleton (from the Tribune Bureau on the Rue St. Honoré): "I saw Lincoln Steffens and Jo Davidson shortly after I arrived; then they departed for Germany, and I don't think they are back yet.

"We haven't done a lot of sightseeing but, mostly, have been . . . letting the ordinary life of the place soak into us. . . . We keep the kid away from hotel and restaurant tables because we don't want her to turn into a Hotel Brat. . . .

"I find it hard as hell to get any work done.

"Give our love to your wife, and remember me to the gang at the club."

A study of his column for that period suggests that Marquis probably did more sightseeing in Paris than he realized. Captain Fitzurse, the Old Soak and his crony Al the bootlegger, and archy and mehitabel seemed to be writing about the French capital from firsthand information and it is to be presumed that when they decided to get acquainted with the city, which they apparently did rather thoroughly, they invited The Boss to join them.

Ever since I undertook this biography Homer Croy has been a prolific source. He supplemented our many long talks with letters—more than fifty of them. So it seems appropriate to reprint most of Don Marquis's column about his intimate friend Homer Croy, written in Paris and published in the New York *Tribune*, September 14, 1923. His news peg was the publication, not long before Marquis sailed for Europe, of Croy's *West of the Water Tower*, a novel that quickly leaped into prominence. Wrote Marquis:

"Homer Croy, author of 'West of the Water Tower,' has had the honor of my acquaintance for thirteen or fourteen years and is very proud of knowing me. I asked him, not long ago, to give me the material for a sketch of his life, for it occurred to me that such devotion as his should be rewarded with Fame. He responded with an alacrity which almost took my breath away and made me suspicious that he had been waiting eagerly to be asked for some time.

"Homer is between six and eight feet tall, and his head is bald all over the outside. But inside there is a fine luxuriant growth of brain. If you sawed off the top of Homer's skull and looked in you would probably find his brain all convoluted up, and the convolutions would have little extra twists and quirks that are not in the ordinary brain at all. . . .

"The differences between Homer and the ordinary person are all fortunate differences . . . they are the kind of differences that make a man admired and affectionately cherished. If I were not three thousand miles from the old coot at the present moment I wouldn't have the nerve to get sentimental about him and to print my sentimentality. But he may die before I get back, or I may die, or decide to spend the rest of my life in Paris or something, and so why not let the same sort of thing creep in that creeps into obituary notices? And then, if we both live, I can probably borrow money from him when I get back.

"I could borrow money from him anyhow, so far as that is concerned. If he didn't have it he would go and borrow it for me. And if he couldn't borrow it he would go and sell the brown corduroy suit which he puts on when he writes. . . . Homer has always been like that. . . .

"Homer was born in Junction City, Missouri, between forty and forty-five years ago, and at once the length of his legs attracted attention and comment. . . .

"Homer's legs reach from his body all the way down to his feet, and I have never seen another set of legs that could reach that far. Looking at his legs, his parents decided that he would either be a newspaper reporter or plow corn. Their prevision was unusually accurate; he has done both. His first job was gathering news items for the local paper, and he was paid three dollars a week . . . 'Every week, rain or shine,' he says. He turned in so many items about the Croy family that one day the editor called him in and said: 'I am afraid, Homer, that I will have to dispense with your services. There aren't enough Croys taking the paper to make retaining you profitable.'

"He went back to plowing corn for a while, and then took his legs with him to St. Louis. The editors of the Post-Dispatch looked at him and gave him a job as a reporter without a struggle. While he was reporting he used to write verse, humorous skits and so forth, and hand them to the managing editor, who always threw them into the waste-paper basket, snorting as he did so. (Homer didn't tell me this himself; I got it from an old St. Louis newspaperman.) Homer, waiting until after office hours, would dig his contributions out of the waste basket and send them to *Life, Puck, Judge,* etc., and these weeklies presently began to send him negotiable checks for them.

"Thus encouraged, he invaded New York about fourteen years ago, bringing with him a confiding smile, a straw suitcase and a brown corduroy suit of clothes, and all three of these things he has to this day. Being the only young man in America who knew nothing about baseball, and caring nothing about it, the first job he got in New York was that of editor of the *Baseball Magazine.* After he had been editor for a few months he went and saw a ball game, and found it, he says, much what he had expected it would be. He wrote short stories, without much financial success; he worked for various magazines, he started for Cuba with sixty-five cents and a safety razor and was caught in the coal bunkers and returned; he did all sorts of journalistic odd jobs, he started a magazine of his own on nothing and sold it at a profit, he went around the world for a motion picture company and he acquired an immense amount of human experience, a wide circle of friends who swear by him, a wife who is a helpmeet, a family and a load of debts. Homer has had a long, hard, continuous struggle in New York to keep going with all sorts of jobs and get the time to write novels, too. But 'West of the Water Tower' has pulled him through; it has established him. And I never saw a man whose success . . . was hailed with more genuine rejoicing on the part of his fellow workers; each member of the whole writing gang feels as tickled as if something good had happened to himself. And this is a tribute to the man's fine, loyal, game personality. For his is a nature that has permitted him to meet his own personal misfortunes and disappointments with endurance and gallantry and gentleness and a smiling exterior."

Once when the Croys were visiting the Marquises—this was after Homer had persuaded them to abandon Brooklyn for Forest Hills— Don complained about having a fireplace and matches but no firewood. The following night Homer raided some nearby houses that were under construction and collected a batch of firewood. Tiptoeing up the Marquis front steps, he deposited his haul near the front door and departed unnoticed.

A few days later an item appeared in Don's column thanking his anonymous benefactor but pointing out that, instead of carelessly dropping his offering the donor might have been a little more thoughtful and left his gift in a neat pile fastened together with a ribbon.

The following evening Croy stole more wood from the same source, this time stacking it and bundling it up with a bright red ribbon before leaving it on Marquis's doorstep.

A few days later Marquis ran an item acknowledging this new benefaction but expressing regret that the giver had used a ribbon that clashed with the blue décor of his living room (where the fireplace was).

"So I swiped some more wood," Croy told me, "and this time bound it round with a *blue* ribbon before leaving it, like a thief in the night, on the Marquis doorstep."

This elicited a comment in the column to the effect that the anonymous donor had now met all conditions. That is, *almost*. Marquis pointed out that there was one thing he had neglected to mention, alas. He and his wife had a particular fondness for perfumed wood. He hoped his princely almoner would take the hint and leave scented kindling the next time.

"So I went to a grocery store," said Homer, "bought some garlic and rubbed it all over the next batch before sneaking up Don's front steps and depositing it."

This drew a grateful comment from Marquis in his column. The odor was heavenly, he wrote—never had the house on Wendover Road been suffused with so agreeable a fragrance. But, as much as he liked to titillate his nostrils, something had just flashed across his consciousness that had been slumbering there—an old penchant for driftwood. Would the donor, when next dispensing his largess, confine himself to driftwood?

"That ended the exchange," said Croy. "I didn't yet own a car, so I was not in a position to drive to some shore-front point where I might have picked up some driftwood, which I would have been glad to do to keep the gag going."

Marquis and Croy had a lot of fun together. Each had his own bag of troubles—and his own bag of "wanton wiles." The first prank dates back to the days when Croy, before his marriage in 1915, was invited by the Marquises to join them in a steak dinner at their apartment. This was in the early days of "The Sun Dial," not long after the period when Don and Reina subsisted mainly on the various types of beef stew ("some with beef in 'em") served in cheap cafeterias.

A steak dinner was a big event for the hosts—and no minor event in the life of their guest, for that matter.

The Marquises had temporarily deserted Brooklyn—(they returned not long afterward)—for a small apartment near 110th Street and Central Park West.

When Croy arrived Don led him to the icebox—one of those tin-lined old-timers refrigerated by a ten-cent piece of ice—to show him the beautiful steak they were going to have for dinner. When the host opened the door of the icebox and looked in, he exclaimed in horror, "Good Lord! We've been robbed!" Croy looked in and saw no steak. It was missing.

Then Marquis searched the whole apartment. The steak was his responsibility, he having brought it home and threatened to cook and serve it. He looked everywhere, even among the papers on his desk, but it was nowhere to be found.

In the meantime Croy was having a bad time. His hopes were fading.

"Oh, I remember!" Marquis suddenly exclaimed when he thought Croy had suffered enough, "I put it away for safekeeping." He walked over to a wall safe and removed the steak.

Before Marquis left Paris for London he wrote a letter to the Manchester *Guardian*, whose London editor, James Bone, was a brother of David W. Bone, the mariner-novelist.

The letter tells its own story and was featured in the following news item which appeared in the New York *Tribune* on October 19, 1923:

London, Oct. 18.— The following letter from Donald R. P. Marquis, conductor of The New York Tribune's column, "The Lantern," appears today in the "Manchester Guardian":

"Can you put me in communication with one Mr. J. C. Squire, who announced in a recent issue of your paper that he is forming the Posthumous Exploitations Company, Ltd., for the purpose of selling the illustrious dead of England to America?

"I am a self-made American business man, with a great many millions, but with no ancestors—to speak of. I should like some ancestors—to speak of.

"I will pay Mr. Squire any sum within reason for a Crusader, so that he be normal and warranted entire. I should reinter him, with appropriate ceremonies on the part of the Ku Klux Klan, on my oil lands near Oklahoma City."

The Marquises found London, in its own way, as beguiling and stimulating as Paris. Little Barbara, after traveling around the city for a few days, remarked that they'd better change a rhyme her mother had taught her—the one about London bridges' falling down. She said she was going to write a poem telling a different story; it would say that London bridges were standing up. Without realizing it, Barbara frequently supplied her father with odds and ends of copy. To cite a brief example: "A child in a hurry to get out to play can sow a terrible crop of wild oatmeal."

Agnes, her homesickness over, settled down to enjoying herself. It dawned upon her one day that she was the only member of her set who had been to Europe, that she would have a thing or two to tell her friends about her travels on her return, and they would soon realize she was "somebody." For one thing, she would have a lot of correcting to do. Her boy friend, for instance, had told her that England was a little bitty country not much bigger than Harlem, and certainly no bigger than Brooklyn. When she learned the facts she decided that he didn't know about such things, because England was "easy three times as big as Brooklyn and ten times as big as Harlem."

James Bone, brother of skipper David, advised the Marquises on what to see and do. Drawing them out, he learned what interested them most, smoothed the way for them, and added suggestions of his own.

Bone himself took Marquis on a tour of literary London. Reina, Barbara, and Agnes had plans of their own that day.

Before the day was over Marquis saw Lincoln's Inn in Chancery Lane, where Ben Jonson, the inevitable book in his pocket, worked as a bricklayer; the rooms in Brick Court where Oliver Goldsmith lived; the old brick house in Gough Square where Samuel Johnson dwelt and where in an upper room he and his small staff compiled the first complete English dictionary.

Marquis saw churches, houses, and taverns that conjured up memories of Shakespeare, Chaucer, Fielding, Congreve, Defoe, Gissing, Blake, Byron, Dickens, Thackeray, Carlyle, and other great figures of English literature. When Bone pointed out the house in Villiers Street where Rudyard Kipling lived, Marquis said he'd al-

ways be grateful to the author of *Kim,* a book he liked so much he
tried to read it once a year. He was also grateful to the early Kipling,
who had made his life as a columnist easier by providing targets
for the parodist with space to fill. Marquis, at Bone's urging, quoted
a few lines from one of his Kipling burlesques—the one in which he
had written:

> The Cockroach stood by the mickle wood in the flush
>   of the astral dawn,
> And he sniffed the air from the hidden lair
>   where the Khyber swordfish spawn;
> The bilge and belch of the glutton Welsh
>   as they smelted their warlock cheese
> Surged to and fro where the grinding floe
>   wrenched at the Headland's knees.
>
> *Half seas over! Under—up again!*
> *And the barnacles white in the moon!*
> *The pole star's chasing its tail like a*
>   *pup again,*
> *And the dish runs away with the spoon!*

Bone warned Marquis that he'd better try to remember a few more
lines of his parody; he was sure they would amuse the London newspapermen, who were eager to meet him since the publication in
Bone's paper of Marquis's comment on J. C. Squire's plan for selling
the illustrious dead of England to America.

The next day in the course of their travels around the city Bone
told Marquis of his fondness for London's oldest shops. There was
something about them—atmosphere, tradition, the fact that they
dated back so far they seemed a part of English history—that drew
him to their counters and kept him out of many of the newer establishments. He invited Marquis to accompany him on a visit to one of
these ancient shops, a select grocery where Bone made a few purchases,
then mentioned to the clerk that he had asked his friend, a New
York journalist, to join him because he wanted the American to
see a 200-year-old grocer's shop. The clerk, who was wrapping Bone's
purchases, looked up and, precise soul that he was, remarked, "But,
sir, this shop is only 198 years old." Whereupon Marquis, grabbing
Bone by the arm and making a feint for the door, announced, "We'll
be back in two years."

Bone set up an opportunity for Marquis to have a drink with some

of his London newspaper friends. The first part of the conversation
was devoted to Marquis's ambition, as announced in the Manchester
Guardian, to acquire a Crusader as an ancestor. Then Bone asked the
columnist for a passage from his Kipling parody. Marquis, according
to his friend Clive Weed, quoted the following, though he didn't
remember it all and had to stumble through a few of the lines:

> The Cockroach spat—and he tilted his hat and he
>   grinned through the lowering murk,
> The Cockroach felt in his rangoon belt for his
>   good bengali dirk,
> He reefed his mast against the blast and he bent
>   his mizzen free
> And he flung the cleats of his binnacle sheets in
>   the teeth of the yeasty sea!
> He oped his mouth and he sluiced his drouth
>   with his last good can of swipes—
> "Begod!" he cried, "they come in pride, but they
>   shall go home with the gripes!"
> "Begod," he said, "if they want my head it is here
>   on top of my chine—
> It shall never be said that I doffed my head
>   for the boast of a heathen line!"
> And he scorned to wait but he dared his fate
>   and loosed his bridle rein
> And leapt to close with his red-fanged foes
>   in the trough of the howling main!

> *Half seas over! Down again and up!*
> *And the cobra is wild with her fleas—*
> *The rajah whines to the pukka's pup,*
> *And there's dirt in the Narrow Seas!*

To make it clear that he thought parodying the early Kipling was
no special feat, Marquis—characteristically—called attention to the
last two lines of his parody:

> *Honestly, fellows, this stuff is easy!*
> *The trouble's to tell when you're through.*

During this slightly alcoholic seminar Marquis took a few gentle
digs at one of Bone's friends, who had written an article on the bad
manners of Americans in London. He suggested that the author of
the piece should now address himself to an article dealing with the

bad manners of *Britishers* in London. He had had a distressing
experience that he disliked to mention, fearing it might undermine
Anglo-American relations; but on reflection he decided the English
were sufficiently civilized to stand the truth.

Marquis's audience was bursting with expectancy as he pulled a
slip of paper from his pocket and read a quatrain describing a *faux
pas* to which he allegedly had been subjected:

> A lack of control should not lead to expunction,
> A bodily function's a bodily function,
> Though I felt I was gazing at one who had sinned
> When a monocled, frock-coated Briton broke wind.

Amid the ensuing laughter, one of the company exclaimed, "Marquis, you're a damned liar! You made that up!"

"You mean," said Marquis, doing his best to look hurt as he sought
to reply, "that Britons never——"

"That is, hardly ever," interposed a hard-bitten Gilbertian.

"And certainly not in the presence of visiting Americans. It's
policy. You chaps can't keep a secret, Marquis, and we take no
chances."

"Marquis," repeated the first heckler, "you invented the whole
thing. Confess!"

Marquis confessed, which called for another drink.

Marquis's last columns from abroad were sent from Glasgow, where
he went to see what Scotland was like and to visit Sir Muirhead
Bone.

In Glasgow Marquis picked up some information which caused
him to say in his egobiography: "In Argyll, Scotland, the name Marquis is almost as common as the name Jones is in Wales. The Marquises are somehow hooked up with the MacDonald outfit and entitled to wear the MacDonald tartan."

Marquis also wrote in that same personal history that most people
assumed the name Marquis was French and therefore pronounced
it Mar-kee, instead of Mark-wis, the correct pronunciation.

Before leaving Scotland, the columnist decided to acquire Mac-
Donald kilts, which, as a Marquis, he claimed he was entitled to
wear. He had always wanted to make a spectacular entrance at the
Players and this regalia would be just the thing; but he became so
involved in Glasgow and other stops he made in Scotland that it was

not until he was on the way back home that he remembered his
failure to see this notion through to completion.

In one of his final "Lantern" columns from Scotland—the very
last to appear was dated November 8, 1923—Marquis paid tribute
to the United Kingdom for its thoughtfulness in providing the
traveling public with a happy combination of information in two
major categories—how to stay healthy and how to distinguish between English and Scottish territory. What he was referring to was
a two-arrowed sign, one arrow pointing toward England, the other
in the direction of Scotland. Atop this direction-finder was a message
from Beecham's Pills.

He celebrated this sign in a bit of verse:

> Beecham's Pills
> Will cure your ills
> And help you find your destination.
> Try the things,
> They're used by kings
> And others needful of purgation.

Those six lines were left out of Marquis's piece on Beecham's
Pills as it appeared in his column in the *Tribune.* Either he had a
second thought and dropped them himself or they were killed
by his editor in New York.

Back in Forest Hills, the Marquises were a happy, enthusiastic trio.
Their friends thought that all three had benefited by the trip.

Don, that master of self-reproach, appeared at last to have forgiven
himself for having "subjected" Reina to a bitter struggle for existence
in those early days in Brooklyn. Reina herself had always regarded
that period as something she had bargained for when she pleaded
with her husband to stick it out in New York at a time when he
was jobless and there was newspaper work awaiting him out of town
—firmly counseling that this was the course to take "or you'll be
licked forever." And she looked forward to the day when Tommy,
as she still called him, would grow up and realize that he had been
needlessly torturing himself. Now at last the promise of what he
would be able to do for Reina with his handsome *Tribune* salary
and the substantial royalties from the long run of *The Old Soak*
kept him off the theme of those days of constant financial stress. In
1923 the income tax was low—even in the high bracket in which

Marquis found himself that year—and he would be able to keep most of what he earned.

Don made many plans. For one thing, he wanted Reina to resume her writing career. She was to organize the household so that she would be able to do so. Abroad the *Tuscania*, a few days after they sailed for Europe, Reina began puttering with an idea for a new novel and by the time they had returned home these thoughts had crystallized into what Don thought was the outline of a good book —one that would establish her in the field of popular fiction.

Reina loved the theater but had seen only a few plays since her arrival from Atlanta in 1909. Even when Don had secured "comps" through the office, which happened occasionally, she had been unable to attend because of domestic responsibilities.

Now she would see all the good plays. This was a major plank in Marquis's new platform; and on theater nights he would take Reina to restaurants they had never been able to afford.

Marquis suggested that Agnes be switched from her role of girl-of-all-jobs to that of companion and nurse to Barbara. Someone else would be brought in to do the general housework.

Less than a month later, on December 2, 1923, something was to happen that would transfer the happy Marquis household into a place of tragedy—something destined to change the whole course of Marquis's life.

That night Don and Reina had dinner with the Marquis sisters, Maud and Nev, at their Gramercy Park apartment.

Before Don and Reina departed for Europe, Maud had reminded her brother that she and Nev had never been abroad, and now that he was doing so well, etc., etc. Characteristically, Marquis had responded by promising to send them on a tour of Europe, and Maud, who took the initiative in talking her brother into whatever plan she had in mind, was already at work on an itinerary.

Considering the fact that Maud disliked Reina, which the latter was aware of, the evening got off to a good start. Reina got along famously with Nev but normally she was ill-at-ease in the company of the sisters because Maud usually gave her an uncomfortable time. As a consequence, Reina did everything she could tactfully do to avoid Maud and when they did meet it was because she thought she couldn't very well put off a meeting any longer without the risk of offending her husband.

Tonight, however, everything was different. Maud was as cordial as Nev and the four had a gay reunion. Don and Reina took turns answering the many questions the sisters asked about their trip, Maud breaking in now and then to say that such and such was something she and Nev would do when *they* went abroad (which they did, a few years later).

It had been decided in advance that this was not to be a late evening. Don and Reina left New York for Forest Hills at an hour that brought them home about eleven o'clock.

Soon after their return, Reina drank a glass of cold milk, as had been her custom for years before retiring, and left for the floor above to prepare for bed, Don remaining below to organize his notes for the column he planned to write in the morning. Shortly thereafter she became nauseous. Seized by the urge to vomit, she headed for the bathroom. Now in severe pain, she called out to Don. He dashed upstairs, arriving as Reina slumped to the bathroom floor.

Don took in the situation at a glance and telephoned a Forest Hills doctor, explaining that his wife appeared to be seriously ill. (The regular family physician—Dr. Harry A. March—lived in New York City and had his office there.) The doctor said he would leave immediately. Returning to help Reina, Don found her breathing peculiarly, her face a chalky white. Although the doctor arrived only a few minutes later, Reina was already so weak she could do little better than gasp out a few words in answer to the doctor's questions, pointing to her heart to indicate pain there and in her stomach. The doctor, after a hasty examination, gave her an emetic, which failed to take effect. He decided on a second emetic and administered it. A few minutes later Reina suffered a violent convulsion and died on the bathroom floor.

Mell Daniel, a close friend of the Marquises, who then lived in New York, and still does, recalls Don telephoning him and haltingly transmitting the sad news, telling it a few words at a time as though pulling himself together between phrases to keep from breaking down. Daniel arrived a few hours after the tragedy occurred— he believes it was a little after 1 A.M., and remembers that a few other friends Don had called were there. "We slept on window seats," he said. "But I had a hunch that before retiring it would be good to get Don out of the house and suggested that we—Don and I, that is—take a stroll. We walked around aimlessly for hours. Don began pulling himself together but he couldn't keep off the subject of the illogic of Reina's death. What purpose did it serve in the over-all cosmic plan, if any? Was there any meaning to life after all? Wasn't it all just a scrambled mess? What was the use of making plans? Lightning suddenly hits you—a million volts—and in a twinkling your life has lost its point. He went on and on in that general vein, in that magnificent flow of language that I can't possibly recapture."

10
Marquis in Crisis—His Sisters, a Study in Contrast—Buried Treasure—Marquis, Grant Rice, and Golf—The Role of Tobacco—Maud Marquis, Now a Full-Fledged Martinet—Don's Escape Hatch, the Players Club—"The Struggle"—Clive Weed, an Intimate from Whom He Withheld Nothing— Courtroom Scenes

The suddenness of Reina's death left Marquis in a state of shock. Why, only yesterday he had discussed her new novel with her, the next play they would see together, the restaurant where they would dine before the theater. Things like that.

He kept walking in and out of the room where she lay stretched out on a bed. There must be a mistake. She couldn't be dead. Why, only last night—on the way home from dinner with Nev and Maud —they had discussed Barbara's interest in poetry, her ability to remember lines from poems that had been casually read to her, and the importance of encouraging this interest.

Like a stunned person coming to after losing consciousness, he suddenly became fully aware—in the late hours of the morning— of what had befallen him. And he broke down and wept.

His long-time friend George Middleton makes this observation in his memoirs, *These Things Are Mine:* "Don had one self-preserving quality. He had no repressions: he could suffer straight through his . . . many dark hours to release. No one otherwise could have dredged such depths as when Reina died. . . ."

At seven o'clock that same morning the telephone rang in the home of Mr. and Mrs. Homer Croy. It was Don. He told them what had happened. The Croys, who lived nearby, were in the Marquis house not many minutes later.

Don, reverting to that bent for self-chastisement that plagued him all his life, began blaming himself for Reina's death. This was the severest indictment of himself he had ever made, making past efforts seem trivial by comparison. Somewhere he had read that it was inadvisable to drink milk after eating shrimps. Maud and Nev had prepared a shrimp dinner and everything would have gone well if he had only remembered to caution Reina not to have her customary glass of cold milk before retiring. Why, O why, had he forgotten? She would be alive if he had been more alert and had instantaneously remembered, as he should have, the warning he had read in that article and insisted that she forego her glass of milk that night.

Dr. March, the regular Marquis physician, had by this time arrived from New York. It will be recalled that March and Marquis originally met in a Washington boarding house in 1900, when March was a medical student and a part-time newspaperman, and Marquis was working for the Census Bureau and the Washington *Times*.

March reminded his friend of Reina's heart condition and asked Marquis if he wanted to take the blame for that too. He also reminded Don that he and his sisters had eaten the same shrimp dinner and suffered no ill effects.

Marquis had asked March to pick up his sisters at Gramercy Park and they were also in the house when the Croys arrived. Mrs. Patience Bevier Cole, who lived directly opposite the Marquises on Wendover Road, was also there; and a few other neighbors.

Croy, fearing that Marquis would knock himself out if he went through another orgy of self-reproach, hustled him out of the house by a back door as other neighbors began arriving. Too shocked and bewildered to do anything but comply, Marquis followed his friend Homer into the Croy car and together they rode around aimlessly. Croy remembers driving through Jamaica, but where they went after that he doesn't recall.

With characteristic gentleness Croy tried to convey to his friend that if he insisted on continuing this business of blaming himself for Reina's death, he would knock himself out, and that wouldn't accomplish anything.

Croy would be the last one to claim it but it is nevertheless a fact that he helped Marquis pull himself together, just as Mell Daniel had several hours earlier.

When an hour later the two returned to the Marquis house, Don had figured out what to say to Barbara. That was the problem that haunted him during his first paroxysm of grief when, as he came out of his initial shock, he found himself thinking of what to tell a sensitive child in a crisis of this magnitude. He would tell her that Reina had gone to take care of Bobby (her five-year-old brother, who had died in 1921 when she was three and a half) and that she, Barbara, was to take care of her father. In the early stages this did little to assuage the child's grief; but it proved effective subsequently when she worked seriously at this little game Marquis had invented —that she now had a job: the business of taking care of her father.

On December 4, 1923, this item appeared in the New York *Times*:

"Mrs. Reina Melcher Marquis, wife of Don Marquis, columnist and playwright, died Sunday at her home, 51 Wendover Place, Forest Hills, L.I. She was born in Louisville, Ky., forty years ago, and spent most of her life in the South, receiving her education at Southern private schools. She married Mr. Marquis at Atlanta, Ga., June 8, 1909. In addition to her husband, who formerly conducted 'The Sun Dial' in The Evening Sun and now runs the column called 'The Lantern' in the Tribune, she is survived by a five-year-old daughter, Barbara. A five-year-old boy died two years ago.

"Mrs. Marquis was herself a writer. She wrote the novel, 'The Torchbearer,' and was at work on another book at the time of her death. She also contributed to magazines and had charge of a department in a women's publication, 'Today's Magazine.' The funeral services will be private."

The next day the following appeared in the *World*:

"Funeral services for Mrs. Reina Melcher Marquis, wife of Don Marquis, columnist and playwright, were held yesterday at the Marquis home, No. 51 Wendover Road, Forest Hills, Queens.

"Many friends in the newspaper, theatrical and other professions were present. The simple service was conducted by Miss Sylvia Loines and Miss Florence Frank of the First Church of Christ, Scientist, of New York.

"The pallbears included fifteen close friends of Mr. and Mrs. Marquis representing journalism, literary and theatrical circles. They were Dr. Harry A. March, George W. Seymour, Homer Croy, Dana Burnet, Edward F. Roberts, Christopher Morley, Royal Daniel and Grantland Rice. Honorary bearers were Geoffrey Parsons, William A.

Johnston, William Marshon, John Drew, John V. L. Hogan, Keats Speed and Franklin P. Adams."

It was not until the foregoing appeared that friends of the Marquises, with a few exceptions, knew what Reina's church affiliation was. According to her closest friend—the same Katherine Glover who was mentioned earlier—she had, during the last few years of her life, moved from church to church in quest of a spiritual prop, and had found contentment in Christian Science—her own adaptation of it. But Reina was so unobtrusive in matters of this kind, so fearful that her own enthusiasms might be interpreted as an effort to make converts, that only a few intimates knew that she had found great solace in a modified form of the teachings of Mary Baker Eddy.

Reina had written Miss Glover, on December 6, 1919, that "you are nearer and dearer to me than anyone in the world except my husband and babies." Marquis had known Miss Glover since they had met in Atlanta when he was an "old man of about 28 with something like 50 years of newspapering behind him" and she was a young cub, a number of years his junior.

Miss Glover played an important part in the lives of Don and Reina in their early days in New York. In fact, on February 4, 1912, he wrote her from Brooklyn, after the publication of his first book, *Danny's Own Story*: "I don't think I would ever have written said book if I hadn't stayed in New York. And I know I wouldn't have been able to stay in New York if you hadn't given me that boost onto the *Eagle* at the critical moment. . . . So you see you had a lot more to do with getting it written than you had any idea of."

In this same letter he wrote: "Reina has been kind of knocked out again; she is feeling pretty rocky today; she sends her love and says she will write soon."

Miss Glover wrote to Marquis after Reina's death, offering to make a home for Barbara and to look after her. In a long letter of thanks Marquis explained why this was unnecessary and why—under the prevailing circumstances—it would not prove the best course. For one thing, he now planned to make a daily habit of writing his column at home, which would enable him to be near the child during this critical period.

In a paragraph in which he developed the theme referred to earlier—that Barbara now had a job to work at, the business of looking after her father—he wrote: ". . . She clings to me. . . . I must foster in her"—(here a corner of the letter had detached itself, and is missing)—". . . continual, persisting spiritual presence of Reina as well as Bobby. I told her . . . that Reina had gone to take care of Bobby, for a long time, and that she (Barbara) was to take care of me. Every night when we pray together I get that into her prayers. At first I was afraid that she thought her mother, in the actual physical presence, would return soon; I no longer fear that disappointment for her; she knows that she is gone as Bobby is gone, I feel sure, now."

Then he continues:

"She is at times a very sad child—then turns and clings to me. . . . She must always find me in those moments. I am going to keep her in touch with her mother's living spiritual presence just as Reina kept her in touch with Bobby's. She can't talk of Reina yet, but I continue to give her opportunities.

"You see, old dear, nobody can do these things but I; and while I am doing them, Barbara is saving my life and my soul. Now, you will ask: where will I get the time for all this? I will get it. I can do a larger portion of my work right here at home, and with Barb near me. . . . I am writing this letter now with Barb drawing pictures at the same table. . . . Agnes is sick in bed just now, but I am managing. . . .

"Maud went south today. Nev remains permanently. Nev is a good cook, and I need not say how devoted. She will gradually break in to the housework end; she already knows exactly what Barb should eat, and has been cooking it excellently. Barb is now the big object of her life. We have a man who comes in two days a week and looks after the rough cleaning. . . .

"Barb must go through this thing in the same little house where she and her mother had happy times together. Barb loves the little house; no further slashing of continuities for her.

"Every so often Barb needs me—and here she has me. She takes me off alone, kisses me, and tells me how much she loves me. . . . She feels this thing too deeply and too maturely for anyone but myself to handle her through it. And I have an understanding of her mentality and spirit such as no one else but Reina had. I was next to Reina with her.

"I am not putting on her the burden of holding in her grief, for my sake. Neither am I forcing her to break down. She has a wonderful nature. . . .

"The big loss for both of us, nothing can ever replace. But I can give the child more than anyone else could, in every way, and I am doing it.

"I am sure I am doing just what Reina would want done. I feel that. I feel her spiritual presence here telling me to keep Barb. I will keep the child on at Reina's own church, and Nev will read to her from religious books that Reina used."

Over and over again Marquis thanks Miss Glover for offering to make a home for Barbara. But he insists that he must look after the child himself.

"I shall use you," he continues, "quite ruthlessly at times when I can. . . . I think I can bring her [Barbara] up . . . in conformity with Reina's ideas. I have the time, the energy, the money. . . .

"I am steady and sensible and efficient; I shall not, because Barbara needs every fibre of my being, allow myself to smash. I must be everything to her, and I shall be as much as it is in me to be. I have more things to atone for than anyone but myself knows; I shall not dilate on them; doing things for Barb, for Reina's sake, is to be part of my atonement. . . .

"You know I value your sweetness. . . . You will be used, all right, as I develop in detail my scheme of life from this outline."

Barbara began adjusting to her mother's death. Although she still had weeping spells, a few months after the tragedy they were noticeably less frequent. In time she was repeating her father's interpretation of her mother's leave-taking to the Forest Hills children with whom she played and she became known to their parents as that brave little Marquis girl who explained to her playmates how nice it was of her mother to join her departed brother Bobby so that she could tell him stories and sing songs to him to keep him from becoming lonesome.

Nothing could better illustrate the fundamental difference between Marquis's sisters than their conduct after Reina's death. Maud left for Florida, to spend the winter there; Nev volunteered to look after Barbara and Don and when her brother quickly accepted she was a happy woman. She moved into the house at Forest Hills and threw herself wholeheartedly into the task of doing anything and everything that had to be done. A constitutionally cheerful woman, she was good medicine for both Don and the child.

A self-described "homebody," Nev enjoyed this opportunity to be of service. The more there was to do, the better she seemed to like it.

At the time of Reina's death Nev was about fifty-six, Maud was fifty-four, and Don was forty-six. Short and stout, Nev was energetic, kindly, self-effacing. She loved children—(she had taught the lower grades in Chicago public schools)—and knew how to amuse them and keep their minds occupied. She was ideal for Barbara, a precocious child who as she neared her sixth birthday was more like a youngster of eight or nine. She had the experience and perception to understand that Barbara had outgrown the stories in the "baby books" that no longer interested her and to prescribe reading matter more in keeping with her mentality.

Nev told friends that it was wonderful to have a "job" again; to be doing something useful; and the enthusiasm reflected by the opportunity she now had to make a contribution quickly reflected itself in a more cheerful atmosphere in the house on Wendover Road.

In a sense Nev had a "job" before Reina's death—that of waiting hand and foot on Maud, who had established herself as the family invalid. It will be recalled that Dr. Marquis, her father, had told Maud when she was quite young that she had the makings of a "champion hypochondriac." He predicted that she would live to "a ripe old age" and would outlive the people she was destined to use as an audience for her never-ending tales of her aches and pains. When this healthy hypochondriac died at the age of eight-one she had written countless letters describing her imaginary maladies, a generous sampling of which I have read.

Nev had been around so many times when Maud was "dying," and had summoned so many doctors to her bedside before she "breathed her last," that she couldn't very well take her sister's induced invalidism seriously; but philosophically she took the position that anyone who regularly imagined herself to be desperately ill or expiring was a sick person in another sense; and with characteristic cheerfulness she took orders from Maud and acted as her nurse and maid-of-all-jobs for years. Because she had been so willing a slavey there were those who wondered if Nev wasn't a clod. Yet there is ample evidence to show that Nev had no illusions about her sister. She simply felt that her sister needed a prop and she had elected to serve in that capacity.

One doctor who had served Maud for three or four years—(he was finally compelled to drop her)—told me that he had never once seen her on her feet. When, in response to an unfailingly dramatic summons, he called on her, she would either be in bed or on a sofa, propped up by more sofa cushions than he knew existed—"a mountain of them," he observed. "It was an established routine in time," he added. "I would examine her and find nothing wrong. Then I would have to listen to a lengthy recital of symptoms that she considered significant. Occasionally I would re-examine her at her insistent urging, just to shut her up. When I pronounced her well for the second time she would change the subject and I would have to listen to a lot of neighborhood gossip. A visit usually killed two hours. It was agony."

Maud specialized in "breakdowns." Several of them are mentioned in her letters. There is no evidence that any of the doctors who attended her thought she had had an actual breakdown. She seemed to prefer her own diagnoses, hence the dramatic versions of minor illnesses reported in her letters.

Marquis financed a long series of vacations that Maud insisted she needed, and not infrequently something would happen on these excursions that would necessitate a vacation to recover from the last one.

Once, six years before Reina died, Maud had felt the need for a trip to California. The holiday was blighted by the inevitable mishap that prevented her from enjoying herself: "I had a sunstroke which incapacitated me for the rest of the summer. When I arrived here a couple of weeks ago I made the mistake of going out in the country among the hills to visit some friends. The visiting and the heat combined proved too much for me and I had another breakdown."

Complaint, complaint, complaint—that is the story of Maud Marquis. Once, when her brother had a Hollywood contract to fulfill, she persuaded him to let her accompany him. She had urged that they return by ship, through the Panama Canal. She had looked into the matter thoroughly, had discussed it with friends who had made the journey, and was delighted with what she had found—the trip home would amount to a wonderful vacation.

Here is what she wrote a relative when the trip was over: "Well, we stood the fourteen days of heat and poor food, no green vege-

tables to speak of. Don't go by way of the Canal ever!" Oddly
enough she reported in that same letter that this trip, which was a
total loss as far as she was concerned, had "set Don up in spite of
the heat."

Not long before Reina's death, Marquis's *Prefaces*, which had
been out of print for a few years, was reissued. Marquis had become nationally known since its original publication in 1919 and
the publisher, in a bid for a new harvest of publicity, sent the new
edition to some of the book editors for rereview. In an unsigned
critique in the Boston *Transcript* a point was made which, to me,
seems important. The reviewer pointed out that some of Marquis's
best humorous pieces were "buried" because he had dropped them
into books where they did not belong and where their inappropriate-
ness had a tendency to take the edge off them. The tortured "explanations" of their inclusion merely served to emphasize their ir-
relevance; a reviewer was usually too busy to try to appraise these
items as entities divorced from their awkward frames of reference. In
support of his point this reviewer cited the chapter "Preface to Hoyt's
Rules," into which Marquis had dragged, by means of the loosest
kind of connective, a rollicking ballad about a castaway on a tropical
island who for years had had nothing to eat but cockatoos and
monkeys—a diet which had had a surprising effect on him.

Because it is one of the liveliest of Marquis's "buried" pieces, and
virtually unknown, this ballad, which originally appeared in his
column as a parody of Gilbert's *Yarn of the Nancy Bell*, is here
reprinted:

> As I was passing the Seamen's Rest
>   There skipped across the street
> A sailor who screamed like a cockatoo
>   And used his hands for feet.
>
> "Now, wherefore, mariner," quoth I,
>   "Confuse the foot and hand?
> And why you crew like a cockatoo
>   I cannot understand."
>
> Then he swung himself from a fire-escape,
>   And he hung there easy and free
> Like a tropical monk from a pine tree trunk,
>   And he spun this yarn to me:

"On the *Reuben Ranzo* I set sail,
    And I was the larboard mate,
And a nautical guy you will never spy
    More orderly nor sedate;

"I never used my feet for hands,
    Nor yet my hands for feet,
I never screamed like a cockatoo
    For biscuits for to eat.

"But I eats as other humans does,
    And my tastes is nowise quaint,
And I never springs no caudal swings
    With a tail which really ain't;

"But I drinks my grog and I stands my watch,
    And I eats my normal duff,
And I was engaged for to marry a gal
    Which her name was Nancy Huff;

"But the *Reuben Ranzo* hooked herself
    As she rambled around the Horn,
And she foundered and sank on a lonely bank—
    A mournful coast forlorn!

"And I am alone in a jungle wild,
    And all I gets to eat
Is cockatoos, and monks what use
    Their little hands for feet;

"I mourns and mourns and I eats and eats
    Upon that sorrowful strand.
Till a gradual doubt arises in me
    As to whether a foot is a hand;

"I eats and I eats, and I mourns and mourns—
    And my beard like feathers grew,
And my nose to a peak like a parrot's beak,
    And I screamed like a cockatoo;

"And I eats and eats, and I mourns and mourns
    Till a ship sails over the blue—
Which they lassos me from a cocoanut tree
    And sells me into a Zoo;

"Alas for love! My Nancy seen
    Me frolicking in my cage
And all of her love turns into scorn,
    And she says to me in rage:

" 'I never will marry a man who screams
    With a voice like a cockatoo!
Nor a man who swings from bars and rings—
    You are changed, you are changed—adieu!' "

And I left him alone with his grief, and passed
    Sadly along the street;
But I flung him some peanuts to pay for his tale—
    And he picked them up with his feet.

Barbara continued to miss her mother and still had her weeping spells but these became less and less frequent as the resourceful Nev found new books and games to hold the child's interest.

Marquis had his bad moments too. There was no gainsaying the remark he had made in his letter to Katherine Glover: "The big loss . . . nothing can ever replace." Five years later, in an article in the *Saturday Evening Post*, we find him paying tribute to Reina. It is one of those eulogies in which the author heightens his effect by being stingy with his adjectives and relying on the overtones of his anecdotes to provide the eloquence. The result is strangely, beautifully moving.

But though memories of Reina continued to haunt the occupants of 51 Wendover Road, the trio of Marquis, Barbara, and Nev settled down to harmonious living.

Agnes, the domestic who had accompanied the Marquises to Europe, and who had been ill at the time Nev took over in Forest Hills, was well again. An exuberant soul herself, she enjoyed working for the ever cheerful Nev.

Barbara now had three adults whom she loved—her father, her Aunt Nev, and Agnes—to take turns at cheering her up when she showed signs of brooding.

Dr. March dropped in often to see how things were going. He thought Don was becoming "house-bound" and urged him to get out more and see something of his friends. In the presence of Nev and Agnes he ribbed Marquis about his lack of confidence in "the staff." If he had more faith in them he would pick up where he had left off at the Players Club. He had heard reliably that the members missed the laughs they'd grown to expect as Don performed ineptly at the pool or bridge table.

When Maud Marquis returned from Florida in the spring she gave up the apartment she and Nev had shared in Gramercy Park and moved into the house in Forest Hills. She had grown accustomed to being waited on by her older sister; therefore living alone in the apartment was unthinkable.

Maud mentions in one of her letters that she had never learned to cook and that the wages asked by cooks were excessive. Nev had done the cooking during the many years they had lived together.

When Maud moved into the house on Wendover Road she brought a number of problems with her. They might have created enormous difficulties if Nev hadn't seen the wisdom of letting Maud be "the boss." Maud considered herself an "executive," as she explained in a letter to her cousin Neeta. Nev did the best she could, Maud generously pointed out, but she had no "executive ability," and therefore needed someone to steer her. So Maud stipulated that she, and she alone, was to be in charge of the household. Which meant, she made it clear, that she—Maud—would supervise all purchases and handle the money for all expenditures having to do with the running of the house.

When Nev and Maud had lived together, Maud had issued the orders and Nev had tempered them with her own notions when she considered that necessary. The wielding of authority meant nothing to Neva Marquis. Her main interest was to see her brother and her niece through this tragic period. If she had to take a little bossing from Maud in the process, well, she could overlook that. There was a plank in her platform about the folly of making an issue of a minor matter. The chances favored Barbara's hearing any angry exchanges. There would be none if she could help it.

Things had run smoothly at 51 Wendover Road during Maud's long winter vacation in Florida and apparently it never occurred to her that the household could survive without her talents as an "executive." But Don and Nev fell in with her demands as a means of "keeping peace in the family." This was the motivating factor in many a move he made involving kinfolk. A few intimates thought he would have been wiser to have a showdown with his recalcitrant sister early in the game and let her go packing if she elected not to fall in with his own notion that the household didn't need a "boss." But if he had done this he would not have been Don Marquis, a man who would do battle over the slightest invasion of his rights as a newspaperman, as he had in the early days on the *Sun*, but who shrank from clashes with members of his own family.

At the same time Dr. March was urging Marquis "to get out of the house" more, his old friend Grantland Rice was trying to get him interested in golf. He thought a new interest would help Don over the rough period following Reina's death.

There was nothing in the world that Grant Rice would not have done for Don Marquis (the reverse being equally true). When Don's first book, *Danny's Own Story*, was published in 1912, Rice was running a sports column in the long-since-vanished New York *Evening Mail*. Since Marquis's novel had nothing whatever to do with Rice's specialty, and in fact did not anywhere in its 333 pages make a single reference to anything even remotely connected with the world of sport, Rice accomplished a minor miracle in working an elaborate recommendation of the book into his column. He remembered that Marquis had played football for ten minutes, or thereabouts, of his two-month career at Knox Academy of Knox College and this was his excuse for referring to the author of *Danny's Own Story* as a former football player turned novelist!

Rice had previously taken a stab at interesting Don in golf and had even succeeded in steering him into a sporting-goods shop, where his former Atlanta roommate bought a set of clubs and supplementary impedimenta, including a pair of outsize knickers. (It will be recalled that knickerbockers were extensively worn on the links in those days.) As mentioned earlier, Marquis was a big man—height five feet ten and a half inches, weight anywhere from 200 to 215 pounds, according to how much attention he was paying to the advice he gave himself in a magazine article called, "Eat, Drink and Be Merry, for Tomorrow You Diet"—and he thought it would be fun to drape those roomy trouserlings over his ample rump just to see how much time would elapse before the first person inquired, "When does the balloon go up?"

But Rice had been unable to get Marquis to take golf lessons or to go anywhere near a golf course.

Rice did not give up. He kept after his friend to set a date for the first of his golf lessons. This proved to be quite an undertaking, but Rice persevered. A date would be made, only to be changed when Don telephoned to ask that it be put forward a few days. After this had happened a few times, Grant called Don the world's champion procrastinator, mixing in a few friendly cusswords for effect. Marquis's response was that he didn't know he was The Champ but he agreed wholeheartedly that he was a procrastinator. In fact, you couldn't accuse Marquis of anything that he hadn't already accused himself of in his column or in a magazine article. Accordingly he sent Rice an article about himself that had appeared in the *American Magazine*, in which he had said:

"Procrastination, I must explain, is one of my favorite vices. There are other vices that have almost as strong a hold on me, such as Black and White Lying, Hypocrisy, etc., etc., but there is no vice that I like as well as Procrastination. When my House of Being was builded, it moved in. It has dwelt there ever since in perfect contentment. If I had been Adam, the Human Race would still have been living in the Garden of Eden, for I would have put off eating the fruit of the tree until the apples rotted.

"I am so complete an example of what Procrastination can do to a man that I am even a little bit proud of it. The only way I ever get today's work done at all is by pretending it is yesterday's. I even put off getting older from year to year. I am gray-haired and my hearing is a little bad, and my arteries aren't as elastic and zippy as they used to be; my eyes and my memory drop a stitch now and then; nobody but my dentist knows the truth and nothing but the truth about my teeth . . . but I am *not* getting older. I have just simply kept on putting age off. . . .

"I love Procrastination because it makes me feel so aristocratic. 'Darn your old train,' I say to the railroad companies, 'there's no law that can make me catch it.' . . .

"One day my Will Power said to me:

"'You've got to cure yourself of this Procrastination of yours!'

"'All right,' I said, 'I'll start tomorrow.'"

Marquis told Rice that he had taken a few practice swings with his driver at apples, onions, and the like but that was the only use to which his golf equipment had been put except for the day Agnes couldn't find the carpetbeater and he had permitted her to use one of his clubs.

Rice eventually succeeded in getting Marquis to take a few golf lessons and to take up the game in a haphazard way. But Don always had an excuse ready when Grant offered to take him out for his first day of golf. His favorite one was that if he couldn't hit a good-size apple or onion—he claimed he had never once connected—how would he ever be able to hit anything as small as a golf ball? The only dividend golf had paid so far came the day he had swung so hard at a tennis ball that he had lost his balance and fallen down. Barbara, his gallery, had laughed heartily and exclaimed, "Do it again, Daddy!"

Rice finally got Marquis to agree to meet him at a golf club. Marquis showed up without his golf bag. Said he had forgotten it in the office. Grant accused him of having deliberately left his equipment behind, of being a big sissy who was "afraid" of the game. Rice offered to borrow a set of clubs to get Don started but he declined—said he felt in the mood for a little more procrastination. They had lunch together in the club's dining room. All around him Don heard impassioned conversation about golf. "You're right, Grant," he confessed. "I *am* scared. In fact, these guys take the game so seriously I'm downright terrified."

Marquis might have dropped golf then and there if not for two things. First, Nev joined Dr. March in urging him "to get out more." The second factor involved Maud, who unconsciously contributed to the process of making him less and less house-bound.

When Don was ten years old and living in the Marquis home in Walnut, Illinois, Maud was attending school in Chicago, where she eventually qualified as a schoolteacher; and they had gone their separate ways ever since. Actually he did not know what it was like to live with Maud until she moved into the house at 51 Wendover Road.

He was familiar, of course, with her hypochondria. *That* he understood, explaining that at times he thought he had a touch of it himself. As for her bent for running things—for being the "executive"— Marquis deluded himself into believing that Maud's "intelligence" would take care of that and that as time went by she would exercise something less than the complete authority over the whole household that she had requested.

Marquis was inclined to confuse bookishness with intelligence. Maud, a tireless reader, read good books. This impressed Marquis, who thought there couldn't be much wrong with a person who had good taste in literature. He subsequently amended this view, learning that when Maud dismissed a book as "trash" it was not necessarily bad. Some of the books she so classified were precisely that; but, as he became more familiar with her views, he realized that a good book could wind up in the "trash" category if it dealt frankly with sex. In the main, Maud confined her reading to the classics, avoiding such "trash" as *The Scarlet Letter* which, she thought, overexploited "physical passion."

Maud had a genuine appreciation of fine writing but her views were so tinged by the spinsterish, as her letters reveal, that she had insufficient patience with many a good book.

The big secret in the Marquis family was that Maud had been married when she was in her twenties and had left her husband in a huff after spending one night with him. She never saw him again. The person who supplied the details of this story—several people know it—asked not to be identified. "I don't want to get mixed up in any family arguments," he explained. The possibility of this is slim, as there aren't many Marquises left, but I agreed to abide by his wishes.

"Maud," my informant said, "was pathetically afraid of sex. I once heard her say that she did not see how a sensitive bride ever survived the shock of her husband's premarital tenderness translated into 'animal passion'—that was the phrase she used and repeated. I have seen letters in which she voiced somewhat similar sentiments. Perhaps some of them are still around."

I am in possession of many letters written by Maud Marquis. They ramble from subject to subject and much of the text has no bearing on this book. But there are passages here and there that are revealing; and the collection, on the whole, has been helpful in establishing chronology. With a few exceptions, when Marquis wrote a letter himself he did not date it. Most of the dates his letters yield are available through carbon copies of dictated correspondence covering the periods when he had secretaries. The Maud Marquis letters have proven an aid in unscrambling sequences involving Marquis's undated letters to his friends.

In one of Maud's letters, made available by the Huntington Library in California, she says: "Did you ever think how long it took for Emily Bronte to be appreciated? Even Charlotte did not appreciate her work until after she died. I never saw the moving picture. You know there are things the 'movies' can't do. I think this the greatest love story . . . because there was no *sex* in that love."

The underscoring of sex is Maud's, as are the quotes around the word "movies." Schoolmarmishly fearful of seeming uncouth, she placed quotes around many a colloquialism that had long since achieved dictionary status.

There is a surpassing irony in Don's living under the same roof with the sex-shy Maud—Don, the author of much witty unprintableness, including the side-splitting saga, in galloping verse, of the sex life of Methuselah, covering nine and a half centuries of the patri-

arch's 969 years—Don, of whom George Middleton said in his ab-
sorbing autobiography, *These Things Are Mine:*

"Don's life was a coat of many colors. It warmed with robust, Rabelaisian mirth; for no Anglo-Saxon I ever knew had the Frenchman's
gusto, except possibly Waldo Peirce, the painter. Many of Don's
letters, like those of Eugene Field, are unprintable. Each of our
valued sheaf is a *tour de force.* He would send Fola [Middleton's
wife] a most profound and profane letter, telling her to read it
first to see whether she thought 'it proper for George to hear.'"

Marquis was aware of the irony of his living under the same roof
with his hide-bound sister when he wrote:

> A blemishless lady named Maud
> Considers her brother a bawd.
> She couldn't say truer
> About that he-whuer
> Who ever at Virtue has clawed.

Don Marquis was not a dirty-joke man. The typical barroom story
left him cold. If he repeated a story in that category—which he
seldom did—it was because he considered it exceptional. Usually he
backed away when some eager beaver pounced on him and inquired
if he'd heard the latest wow about the traveling salesman and the
farmer's daughter, or what you will. He appraised most of these
stories as obvious and lacking in wit. His own reputation as a storyteller rested on a repertoire of yarns that stemmed from his days back
home in Walnut, Illinois—stories about local characters that he kept
embellishing as he retold them, adding new touches and situations
until it was literally true that Marquis never told the same story
twice; or, to be more accurate, he never told a story the same way
twice. Then there were his stories of early newspaper days, such as the
one, recounted earlier, about the escaped carnival lion that strolled
into an Atlanta bar where Marquis and some friends were having a
drink.

Some of these stories were pretty robust; others could be told in
the presence of children if Marquis remembered not to punctuate
them with profanity, which seldom had anything to do with the
tales themselves. Mostly they were tall stories, a kind of modern
Munchausenism.

Because of those occasions when Don forgot himself and seasoned
a story with an oath or two, Maud was apprehensive when he began

yarn-spinning, especially if there was someone in the house she was fearful of shocking. On one count Maud found his behavior reliable: when Barbara was around he refrained from telling any of these stories, afraid that he might forget himself and say the wrong thing.

It was no surprise to Don that Maud was outspoken. He even had a few favorite stories about his sister's candor and bluntness.

Now that they were occupying the same house and really getting to know each other for the first time, he began to take a different view of Maud's outspokenness, realizing that it was merely an early manifestation of a quarrel in the making. For Maud Marquis was a contentious woman with a genius for making issues out of minor matters. There is no doubt that the quarrels she provoked took a great deal out of him.

As understanding a person as Fola La Follette, an old friend of the Marquises, who is known for going out of her way to find good things to say about people, told me, "There was something evil about Maud."

Marquis prided himself on his avoidance of arguments. He once said that no one had ever won an argument—that when a verbal battle is over the adversaries think as they did when they started trading insults. The one that backs down is merely trying to protect his eardrums.

But this philosophy went for naught when Maud taunted him sufficiently. When a friend and/or associate kidded him about the creaselessness of his trousers he took it good-naturedly, usually responding with a sermon on the vacuousness of the clothes-crazy dandies who notice such trivia; when Maud told him that he dressed too sloppily "for a man in his position" it infuriated him.

There was no pose in Marquis's wearing a suit until it practically fell apart; the man simply hated to shop. Moreover, he was ceaselessly preoccupied with something he was writing or planning to write and it never occurred to him to devote any serious thought to his wardrobe. In the morning you reached for whatever was handy and put it on—and that was that.

As Berton Braley put it, "He was no George Buchanan Fife. He dressed like a newspaperman."

Clive Weed said that Marquis's idea of being presentable was to be well-scrubbed and shaved and to wear a clean shirt, and to hell with ministering to clothes that lost their well-pressed look as soon as they were called upon to cope with his portliness.

As to his cluttered desk, which Maud considered a "disgrace," Marquis was aware—without any reminders—that he was no model of neatness. He once said that he could have written two or three books in the time he spent during the first twenty years of his writing career looking for things—notes, letters, and other papers he'd misfiled or mislaid. He had turned this liability into an asset by writing magazine and column pieces about it—variations on the theme of how to be sloppy without half trying. When Maud told him to stop boasting publicly about his disorderliness he lost his temper and there were angry words. No one else could cause Marquis to lose his temper. There was something about Maud's taunting manner that enraged him. In time he made a practice of checking himself and saying nothing in response to his sister's needling . . . until he could take it no longer and exploded again.

Poor Maud! This probably makes her sound like a monster. There are those who thought she was approximately that. A few defend her, including Mrs. Homer Croy, a woman of many accomplishments, who thought at the time and still thinks that Maud did an efficient job of managing the Marquis household and was on the whole a good influence, and that she has been overcriticized.

Mrs. Croy's husband takes a different view, likening Maud, who was short and slight and sharp-featured, to a small feist-like terrier that enters a room snapping and snarling at those who try to befriend it. Completing the metaphor, he likened the roly-poly Nev—"the one who had a kind word and a smile for everyone"—to a big, good-natured, overfed collie that bounces into a room wagging its tail and ready to take on anyone that wants to play. There is no doubt that the tense, unsmiling Maud suffered by comparison with her genial, easygoing sister.

One observer of the Forest Hills scene believes that the reason Maud irked her brother so much was that she was a reformer at heart, the line of reasoning being: here was a man who had no illusions about himself, who had laid bare his own shortcomings in writings serious and humorous. He did the best he could and he resented it when his sister put him on a rubbing-table and tried to massage the faults out of him.

He had no use for reformers, amateur or professional. He had made that clear countless times in prose and verse. Why didn't the woman take the hint?

Maud Marquis thought her brother smoked too much—cigarettes, a pipe, cigars. Dr. March also thought so; so did Marquis. But when Maud tried to ration him—suggesting how many cigarettes he should smoke a day—and gave him a tally sheet to keep on his person so that he could keep track of his consumption, and did a lot of moralizing about Will Power, it angered him. It was the wrong approach to a man who had written extensively in his column and in magazine articles about his comic-opera resolve, of long duration, to take on the Demon Nicotine in a finish fight and send him sprawling through the ropes.

Since its jovial approach to the problem illustrates the folly of "lecturing" a man like Don Marquis, and also because it was one of Reina's favorite pieces, one that she once spiritedly read for the amusement of guests at a party, the following excerpt from an *American Magazine* article on Marquis's plan to annihilate all his faults in one grand assault, is here reprinted:

"I have been Swearing Off the use of tobacco for thirty years. I learned, with great tribulation, at the age of twelve, to smoke a corn-cob pipe. My first impulse toward reformation from this Disgusting Vice was furnished by my father; but after he gave up the job my Conscience took the thing in hand. After thirty years, I am still hopeful, still enthusiastic, still looking forward to the day when tobacco will mean absolutely nothing to me.

"Indeed, at the present moment, I am puffed up with pride—I have sworn off pipes and cigars altogether, and now I only smoke thirty or forty cigarettes a day. This is only twenty-five or thirty-five more than my physician says I may smoke, hence my boastful spirit.

"The thing I like about the Human Race is this beautiful hopefulness, this recurrent optimism, this childlike faith that it is going to put across something that it never yet has put across; this willingness still to believe in success after a thousand failures. . . .

"Have you ever waked up at two o'clock in the morning, off in the country somewhere, miles from a store or hotel, and wanted to smoke when there was no smoke to be had? You look for cigarette butts in order to crumble them into your pipe, but you don't find any. You go through all your coat pockets in the hope of garnering a few grains of tobacco that may have spilled out of a can or package, but you don't find any.

"You feel pretty sure there is a broken cigar in the pocket of your overcoat. But your overcoat is packed in the bottom of a trunk with camphor balls in and around it, and you can't find the key to the trunk. Probably your wife knows where the key to that trunk is, but you don't feel like waking her.

"You sit and chew your pipe stem for a while, and wish that you dared to wake her. But she has heard the doctor tell you that tobacco is getting next to your heart, and she agrees with the doctor.

"As you sit and chew the stem of the empty pipe you begin to get sore at your wife for being imposed on so easily by doctors. That is a trait in her nature that you never did like. And as the gnawing agony of the desire to smoke eats deeper and deeper into you, you begin to think of other traits your wife has that you don't like.

"Indifference is one of them. There she lies, in her bedroom, sunk in selfish slumber, while you are undergoing the agonies of the damned. It is true that she doesn't know what you are suffering—but if she were in complete accord with you, your sufferings would penetrate her sleep and speak to her heart, and she would leap from her couch and minister to you.

"She has become a cold and indifferent woman, you decide. And you are martyring yourself for *her* sake. She will never know all that you have gone through, to spare her; because you will be too fine and big and noble ever to tell her.

"Finally you wake her up, and *demand* the key to that trunk. You don't say anything about the hope of finding a crumpled cigar in the breast pocket of your overcoat. You tell her there is a receipted bill there that you *must* have, for you are being dunned unjustly for an account that you have already paid, or something of that sort. And when she finds the key you hasten to the truck, trembling with eagerness and get the overcoat out—and of course there isn't any crumpled cigar in your pocket.

"Just why this almost makes you hate your wife is something I leave to the psychologists, but it does. You are so bitter with her that you drop the mask; you tell her frankly what you wanted from that overcoat. You ask her where that cigar is. You remember feeling it there last March. She says that of course she threw the nasty thing away when she packed your clothes, and——

"Well, before you are done with it another marriage vacillates on the verge of dissolution. That is what the tobacco habit does."

Maud was the key to Marquis's next three years. He began figuring ways and means of spending as little time as possible in the house without neglecting Barbara. The child went to bed early—she was now a little over six—and her father organized his working habits so that they would be able to spend some time together daily. They took little walks together and shared all kinds of "secrets."

When they returned home Marquis would make a point of conferring further with Barbara in the living room regarding these secrets, which they discussed in whispers. When he heard approaching footsteps he would caution the child, "Quiet! Here comes someone!" As soon as they were alone again, he would say, after he had cast his gaze all over the room and even looked into the fireplace for spies, "The coast is clear!" and they would put their heads together again and resume their whispering, both of them tiptoeing to the nearest door to look for eavesdroppers when the spirit moved them.

Barbara and her Aunt Nev spent a good deal of time together. This worked out well for Maud, who kept busy exchanging letters with friends around the country, checking on her latest symptoms through medical books, and making notes dealing with books, plays, and poems she planned to write. Maud had writing ambitions—a few samples of her work will be given later—although she had never displayed any talent in this direction. In her letter to her cousin Neeta Marquis, who lived in California, she frequently complained about the responsibilities that prevented her from getting any writing done.

Maud was also interested in puppetry, a field in which she displayed genuine talent. People in show business who knew something about marionettes thought the ones Maud made were of professional caliber. Had she found a collaborator to help her organize this talent and steer it into some specific channel, she might have achieved success in this field. She had ideas for puppet shows that sounded good in the telling but she never committed them to paper.

As far as producing an actual manuscript was concerned, Maud didn't seem to understand what the requirements were in any of the writing categories. For instance, subsequently when she decided to try her hand at a play for the Broadway stage—(this time she had live performers in mind, not puppets)—she turned the resultant manuscript over to her brother and asked him to help her get it produced. Purporting to be a full-length play, it proved to be only twelve pages long! At first Marquis thought this was probably Maud's idea of a synopsis, but no. According to Homer Croy, she thought she had written a full night's entertainment!

Marquis did everything he could to help and encourage Maud

with her marionettes. Once he offered to find her a collaborator, a professional puppeteer who might be able to devise a story that she could execute—something appropriate for children. But she did not want a collaborator. An extremely suspicious woman, she was afraid some stranger might be tempted to steal her ideas for bizarre characters, of which she had many.

Puppet shows had quite a vogue in those days. Some of them had been lavishly produced in the long-since-departed Punch and Judy Theatre and had settled down to respectable runs. Then there were the seasonal opportunities. Marionettes had developed a substantial following among vacationing school children—and their parents—during the Christmas and Easter holidays. Marquis reasoned that if Maud could gain enough acceptance to be recognized as a professional, it would tone up her morale; an interest of this kind might transform her into a reasonably busy and perhaps even happy person.

But Maud Marquis was hard to advise. She would make attractive, ingenious figures without giving any thought as to how they might be woven into the fabric of a story. It was as practical as making an assortment of good-looking pieces for a jigsaw puzzle that didn't fit together.

Maud enjoyed being the center of attention and several times produced her puppets when there were guests at the house on Wendover Road. This would swing the conversation around to her and her marionettes and there would be much chitchat about these little figures—how cleverly they had been designed and executed, which was indeed a fact—and wasn't it too bad Maud couldn't make capital of this unusual talent? Suggestions would be made by one and all as how she could get started on Broadway; and Maud, happy to have an audience, would have a wonderful time. When the guests left she would put the puppets back in a closet and forget or ignore the advice she had received—some of it from people of the theater, among whom Marquis was widely acquainted.

Marquis spent very little money on himself—next to nothing on clothes, for instance. Clive Weed once mentioned that Don had not visited a haberdashery in over two years until the day he saw in the window of a cheap men's furnishing shop a pair of bright red arm garters similar to ones he had seen on the shirt sleeves of a bartender of his acquaintance. He had offered to buy them from the barkeep, who declined to sell, pleading that he didn't know where he could be sure to find another pair in exactly the same color: fire-engine red. Those arm garters were his trade-mark, they had caused him to become known as "Red" and he thought it would be bad luck to sell them.

Occasionally Marquis blew himself to a long taxi ride. It was one of his few extravagances.

"In those days," reports Lawton Mackall, a member of the Players Club since 1917, "there was a taxi stand in front of the Club. The starter and the drivers on the line all knew Don and when he was in the Players and he hadn't emerged by a certain hour, he would be due, according to their calculations—(they were familiar with his habits)—to come tearing out, jump into a cab, and ask to be driven to the Long Island station or all the way to Forest Hills, according to his mood. The drivers all liked him—he was a generous tipper and they could all recount amusing stories he had told them—and they considered it a privilege to drive him. When he visited the Players, Don spent most of his time at the pool table, his coat removed and his bright red arm garters showing, with a group known as the Poolist Fathers (Rollin Kirby, George Bellows—who, incidentally, was the only member who had the nerve to turn up at the Club in a turtle-neck sweater—Frederic Dorr Steele, myself, and a few others). Don's favorite excuse for starting another game was, 'I haven't earned my cab fare yet.' As we played for small stakes Don would have had to keep playing until breakfast to earn his cab fare to Forest Hills. Don was not what you'd call a good player, though no one enjoyed the game more or heckled an adversary more entertainingly. He was a lucky player and occasionally he won. When he made a good shot that obviously was more the result of accident than design, he would explain in elaborately scientific lingo how he had brought it off."

Maud thought the aforementioned taxi rides from the Players to Forest Hills were a needless extravagance and told her brother so—once in her best snappish delivery in the presence of neighbors. Don made no reply. He continued to return home by taxi whenever the spirit moved him.

Maud decided to teach her brother a lesson. One day when she had some shopping to do in New York she took a taxi from Forest Hills, retained it all day as she went from store to store and then made the return trip to Wendover Road in this same cab, which was now loaded with parcels. She had had no success for some time in dragging Don—who had grown weary of "scenes"—into an argument,

and possibly she figured that this would do the trick. If that was the
case, she had miscalculated. When she told her brother that this taxi
excursion had left her short of funds, he gave her the money she
needed and made no comment. This new policy was the lesser of two
evils; the arguments, Marquis had found, threw him off stride and
interfered with his work. Even when Maud repeated her return trip
from Forest Hills to New York City by taxicab, and made a point
of letting him know about it, he said nothing. He had decided that
there would be no more angry exchanges and he was living up to it.

Lyman Beecher Stowe told me that now and then Marquis made
no effort to conceal that Maud wasn't one of his favorite people.
Once when Don was a weekend guest at the Connecticut home of
the Stowes the conversation turned to Maud. Marquis made a remark
that his host considered significant despite the frivolous terms in
which he couched it. What he said follows, a verbatim quotation: "I
suppose I ought to knock her [Maud] on the head and bury her
somewhere. But that would be indiscreet, possibly even wrong."

If Neva Marquis had been less tactful, there would have been more
stresses and strains at 51 Wendover Road. While Maud was in Florida
during the winter of 1923–24, Nev and Barbara had developed a free-
and-easy camaraderie. The child felt completely at home with her
Auntie Nev and they developed an understanding, a warm relationship, that never existed between her and her Auntie Maud.

Children as a rule haven't the time or the guile to be studiously
diplomatic. If Maud also happened to be in the room, Nev would
send the child over to greet her. This was purely perfunctory and
Barbara would usually wind up in Aunt Nev's lap a half minute later
to ask the roly-poly ex-schoolteacher to tell her a story or to read to
her from a book.

Maud and Nev differed on the question of what Barbara should
eat. One of Maud's pet theories was that "heavy meats" (Homer
Croy's phrase) were helpful in "building up" a child. According to
Croy, Barbara did not take kindly to this type of fare and had to be
coaxed to eat it. On the other hand, she ate with relish the meals
Aunt Nev prepared for her.

Aunt Maud prevailed, as she usually did when she put her foot
down. And as a result Barbara had more solid chunks of meat placed
before her than she cared to eat. Occasionally the child, weary of this
heavy diet, would push her plate aside and refuse to eat. When this

happened Nev would feel the lash of her sister's tongue. It was all her fault. She had a "hold" on the child and had failed to teach her to obey.

Nev learned to take these things in stride. That kindly soul would point out that Barbara wasn't much of a meat-eater, that there were plenty of other foods that could give her the basics she needed for a balanced diet. But Nev was no match for Maud and more than once she was ordered to leave the room while her sister "talked some sense into the child."

Maud also had her gentler side in dealing with Barbara. She designed and made a handsome puppet for her—a character that figured in one of her "secrets"—but exercised the right to tell the child when she could play with it, and how long.

Reminding one of Rollin Kirby's wry comment: "I wish people would stop misrepresenting Maud Marquis. She's by no means an ogre—she's a bossy bitch, which is even worse."

Aunt Maud strove for Barbara's affection but never quite won it. Nev achieved it without trying. Intuitively the child sensed the devotion of this warmhearted woman who was so unobtrusive about her good works that only a few insiders realized that it was she, not her dictatorial sister, who kept the Marquis household functioning. Some of her defeats were only temporary. She accomplished her main purpose, which was to see that Barbara constantly developed new interests that would leave the child with less and less time to brood over her mother's death. Because Barbara was a sensitive, emotional, poetic child, Nev gave these considerations priority over everything else.

Barbara settled down to reasonably happy days in Forest Hills. Needless to say, she still missed her mother, and occasionally was found weeping in her room, but such occurrences were becoming less and less frequent.

Nev's days as a schoolteacher had taught her that imaginative children need an audience; that when you tell a child a story and he or she wants to reciprocate by telling *you* one, it's important to listen and to ask questions to show how seriously you take what the youngster is saying. Nev was a good audience, which is what Barbara, who liked "to make up stories," needed. Her father was a good audience too—he was also a pretty good actor—and Barbara loved it when in pleading tones he said, "Barb, tell me a story." As she improvised and invented "adventures" she had had, Don could be

counted upon to register joy, sorrow, astonishment, horror, or whatever the situation called for. In describing one of these storytelling
sessions with his daughter to an actor friend at the Players, he remarked that he never realized that being a ham could prove so useful.

Don was now spending more and more time at the Players, occasionally writing his column there. How he felt about the Club is
best reflected in a sonnet which is to be found today—in the author's
own hand and framed with his photograph—in the Club's bar, where
he tossed it off one afternoon when, as he put it, "the spirits moved
him." He had published it in the verse section in the back of his
successful book, *The Old Soak*, capitalizing the names of those mentioned in it and dedicating it to his friend Winfield Scott Moody of
the *Sun*, who had originally proposed him for membership. Entitled
"A Certain Club," this tribute to his favorite haunt reads:

> Ah, dead and done! Forever dead and done
> The mellow dusks, the friendly dusks and dim,
> When CHARLEY shook the cocktails up, or TIM—
> Gone are ten thousand gleaming moments, gone
> Like fireflies twinkling toward oblivion!
> Ah, how the bubbles used to leap and swim,
> Breaking in laughter round the goblet's brim,
> When WALTER pulled a cork for us, or JOHN!
> I have seen ghosts of men I never knew,—
> Great, gracious souls, the golden hearts of earth—
> Look from the shadows in those rooms we love,
> Living a wistful instant in our mirth;
> I have seen JEFFERSON smile down at DREW
> And BOOTH pause, musing, on the stair above.

The Players almost became a religion with Marquis. There he
found good conversation, heard good stories, swapped banter with
kindred spirits, discussed books, plays, and contemporary art with
George Bellows, Rollin Kirby, Franklin P. Adams, Oliver Herford,
Brian Hooker, Clive Weed, Gelett Burgess, and others whose wit and
lively-mindedness appealed to him.

Marquis, as ebullient and popular a member as the Players ever
knew, made his own contributions to the Club's cherished mots. To
Frank Adams, a father for the first time, who was passing around the
cigars and seeking advice on how to raise his son to be a genius and
a millionaire, and loudly proclaiming how wonderful it was to be
"a new-born papa," Marquis casually remarked that it *could* be

wonderful if Frank remembered certain fundamentals, such as, "Never change diapers in midstream." The author is indebted for this anecdote to Harry Gilbert, a long-time member of the Players. (In most cases the crediting of anecdotes would be cumbersome since they come from so many sources.)

Lawton Mackall, gourmet *extraordinaire*, and author of books on wines and comestibles, tells a Marquisism at his own expense. After a long session at the pool table during which billows of cigar, cigarette, and pipe smoke enveloped the players, Mackall says he suddenly made the remarkable discovery that the air in the poolroom was on the tainted side; and forthwith registered a complaint. Marquis, who was about to address his ball, heard the remark and looked up to say, "Lawton, this air was good enough for Edwin Booth," then took a deep breath and beamed as though he had just filled his lungs with atmospheric nectar straight from Mount Parnassus.

Marquis, Frank Adams, and others indulged in the pastime of composing limericks, mostly unprintable, as they played Kelly pool, each man contributing a line at a time. One of the few publishable ones that survives is the following:

> There's a certain club known as The Players
> Frequented by guys who ain't prayers,
>   Excepting at pool,
>   When they pray as a rule
> That their conquerors fall down the stayers.

Adams and Marquis collaborated on a gloriously unprintable limerick about newspaper publisher Frank Munsey. The following adaptation, designed merely to suggest in a general way what the authors had in mind, preserves none of the inelegant splendor of the original:

> There was a lank feller named Frank
> With barrels of coin in the bank.
>   He purchased some papers,
>   Which died of his capers,
> The poor misbegotten old crank!

A study of some of Marquis's unpublishable limericks leads me to the conclusion that the sharp limitations of the form make some of them sound more soiled than they really are. He manages to be just as robust in the Villon ballade but because there is no need for iron-clad compression in a twenty-eight-line poem, passages culled from these ballades, while not exactly nursery rhymes, are publishable.

(A stanza from one of them appears later, in a letter from Marquis to George Middleton.)

Marquis considered the limerick an overrated verse form. For every good one there were hundreds of indifferent ones. He regarded the writing of limericks as a diversion which only rarely produced anything worthwhile but which invariably provided fun for those struggling to put them together—ideal sport for a man waiting his turn at a billiard table. He expressed himself on one phase of the subject in "On the Making of a Limerick":

> It needn't have ribaldry's taint
> Or strive to make everyone faint.
> There's a type that's demure
> And perfectly pure,
> Though it helps quite a lot if it ain't.

At the Players Marquis occasionally played bridge, but according to William G. Tachau, a member since 1906, he wasn't good enough to join the better players, who held forth in the bar. Marquis played upstairs with a group known as "the minor league."

This worked out perfectly for Don, who played what he called, according to George Middleton, "conversational bridge." Merely to sit and stare at cards was unendurable to Marquis, who would try to draw out the other players on whatever subject caught his fancy at the moment.

The writer also discussed Marquis as a bridge player with John C. King, retired actor who joined the Players in 1903 and is its oldest living member. With a broad smile King said, "We always knew what to expect when we let Don into the game. There wouldn't be any serious bridge but there *would* be fun. Everybody loved him, so we'd allow him to ramble on. You'd find yourself trying to ignore him and concentrate on your cards but he had a way of being so darned entertaining that sometimes, against your better judgment, you'd put your cards down and get into the conversation yourself— and the first thing you knew, nobody was playing bridge. Only Don, with that contagious smile and those innocent blue eyes, could have gotten away with it."

Once when Clive Weed asked him why he went to the trouble of playing bridge in the first place, Marquis replied that his motives, as usual, were purely mercenary. Weed couldn't figure this out; for Marquis and whoever teamed up with him almost invariably lost.

The puzzled Weed, caught off guard, asked for an explanation. How could a steady loser benefit in a "mercenary" way?

Marquis replied that a writer had to have new subjects. He thought there was something pretty funny about bridge. He wasn't sure what it was but he was going to find out. When he had the answer he would sell articles about it, materialist that he was, making capital of what he had learned at the expense of his fellow members. He hoped no one would move to have him thrown out of the Club.

Marquis was as good as his word. On and off over the years he used bridge as a theme—in his column and in magazine pieces. His major effort was a tongue-in-cheek piece in *Collier's*, in which, parodying the experts, he told how to win at bridge by means of the Marquis System. This system, by the way, is the only one that shows any concern about the health and well-being of bridge addicts, stipulating as it does, that "no table of bridge is complete without a physician in attendance, or a registered trained nurse, competent to take the blood pressure of players."

Every time Marquis played bridge at the Players he reaffirmed the conviction of his fellow members that he was a great conversationalist and a lousy bridge player.

Much has been written about Marquis as a conversationalist. In the *American Mercury* for March 1947 Rollin Kirby, after discussing his friend's "beguiling personal charm," said: "To spend hours with Don was to become convinced that that which he threw away in conversation was better than a great many writers' life work. He loved to pick up an idea and embroider it, sometimes seriously, sometimes in Rabelaisian fashion, sometimes in the lowest plane of verbal slapstick. No matter what the subject was, he left it, like Thoreau's borrowed axe, sharper than it was when he got it."

Marquis had promised his publisher an archy and mehitabel book for 1924 but felt impelled to beg off. He had more than enough material for a book—pieces that had proved popular in the *Sun* and the *Tribune*—but he considered too many of them topical and he thought it best to hold up publication until he could write more pieces that had no connection with current happenings.

Moreover, he was already committed to one humorous book that year, *The Old Soak's History of the World*, an expansion of the Clem Hawley columns he had written during his travels abroad. This he completed and it was published and joyously received by a majority of the reviewers. There was only one dissenting argument, that perhaps there had been too much of the Old Soak.

Among the pieces that were singled out for special applause were: "Men Are Not Dessended Off Of Monkeys," "The Founding of Rome," "Marie Antoinette," "Jonah, and Jed Hawkin's Wife" and "The Taking of the Basteel."

As to whether there had been too much of the Old Soak, once in reply to a reader of his column who took the same position, he wrote that the reader was probably right but that the matter was out of his hands. He had once asked Clem Hawley (the O.S.) how long he planned to continue his writing career and Clem had replied that in the best interests of the country he thought he ought to keep it up until he had killed off Prohibition and brought back the saloon, which, it will be recalled, he considered a molder of character and in many other respects a fine influence in American life. Marquis had accepted Clem's recommendation, he informed his critical reader, and having given his word he felt himself irrevocably committed.

A study of his column and other writings reveals that Marquis took criticism good-naturedly. Nine years after the publication of *The Old Soak's History of the World*, in a retrospective article in *Harper's Magazine*, he made a comment that typified his happy-go-lucky attitude toward criticism: "Three generations of young newspaper critics have cut their teeth on me; and it has sometimes made me feel as if my books were a box of puppy biscuits."

A few times Marquis kidded the reviewers a little more broadly than he did in that *Harper's* piece. Among his papers there are some notes and fragments indicating that he planned to write a lampoon called "An Encyclopedia of Hedges for the Busy Yes-and-No Critic."

Occasionally Marquis was his own severest critic. It will be recalled that when he was asked for a book of serious poems in 1914 he prepared a dummy—a comprehensive paste-up of verses from his column—to indicate the possibilities, informing the publisher that he was submitting much more material than he thought belonged in such a book. He reasoned that an editor to whom the material was new, and who could thus appraise it objectively, was best qualified to weed out the dispensable material.

When the book, *Dreams and Dust*, appeared as a 183-page opus containing every line that had appeared in his dummy he was both surprised and dismayed. It was not until he saw his book in type that he realized which were the poems that should have been dropped. He never fully liked that book because it contained pieces that he did not consider worthy of book publication.

It is hard to say why Marquis was not a better judge of his own work in manuscript and why his critical faculties did not click into place until he held the finished book in his hand. There were times, according to Clive Weed, when his own estimate of the finished product was approximately that of the reviewers.

At any rate, we know that he was a tough audience for his own work. One is again reminded of E. B. White's essay on Marquis— the most searching of all the tributes—in which he said: "He [Marquis] was left unsatisfied and gloomy by what he produced."

Little Barbara Marquis enjoyed the company of both children and adults. The children were her Little Friends, the adults her Big Friends. After Reina's death Marquis decided that Barbara should have as many Big Friends as possible. She had a way of losing herself in conversation with new people, especially grownups; and Marquis, whenever he could, threw her in with friends who liked children and knew how to amuse them.

Thus we find Franklin P. Adams writing in his column in the New York *World* not many weeks after Reina's death: ". . . So to catch up R. Kirby, and with him to Forest Hills, and had luncheon there with D. Marquis and his daughter Barbara, as sweet and merry a little girl as ever I saw, and we had a great bond, because she misliked carrots also." This appeared in one of Adam's Saturday columns, the day he devoted to "The Diary of Our Own Samuel Pepys."

Barbara confided to these new Big Friends that some day she planned to publish a newspaper. Adams volunteered to write a column for it and Rollin Kirby, political cartoonist for the *World*, offered "to draw pictures." Not many years later Barbara *did* publish a paper—a mimeographed monthly. But by that time she was a big girl of ten, so she wrote it all herself and decided to get along without pictures. Among her subscribers were Grantland Rice, Christopher Morley, Clive Weed, Donn Byrne, Benjamin De Casseres, Franklin P. Adams, Rollin Kirby, Brian Hooker, John Barrymore, Otis Skinner, Homer Croy, and other friends of her father.

Marquis was proving himself a good child psychologist. Not long before Adams had found Barbara "as merry a little girl as ever I saw" she had had one of her crying spells; and now for days she talked about "Daddy's friend who doesn't like carrots either."

"By Christopher Morley and Don Marquis" reads the title page of *Pandora Lifts the Lid*, a novel published in 1924, but it was really the work of Morley without benefit of collaborator. It was a tongue-in-cheek tale cooked up one day by Marquis and Morley at the Players.

Marquis had so many writing commitments at the time that he had to beg off. It was a friendly dissolution of what had been a nebulous arrangement, neither writer having more than the haziest idea of how they would go about writing a novel together.

Marquis agreed to the publisher's suggestion, seconded by Morley, that his name be used since the book had been widely publicized as a collaboration and since it *was* partially, Marquis having contributed a number of flamboyancies to the mad plot.

The author of the blurb on the dust jacket of *Pandora Lifts the Lid* wrote so enthusiastically about this "collaboration" that one wonders whether he knew about its dissolution. Here is part of what he wrote:

"Imagine the morning paper headlined with the news that six of America's richest and most fashionable families had lost their daughters by kidnapping! . . .

"With this as a starter, think what the author of 'Where the Blue Begins' plus what the author of 'The Old Soak' would weave out of such a situation. You will not be disappointed; the deft hands of both are here. . . ."

As soon as advance copies of the book were ready, Morley sent one to his "collaborator." On the title page he had written, "With the compliments of the author."

Interest in Marquis was developing in England. Some of his articles, short stories, and poems had appeared in British publications. It was hardly an overwhelming interest—it heightened considerably after archy and mehitabel made their London debut, and Hilaire Belloc, Rebecca West, E. V. Knox, and others prominent in the literary life of England hailed these characters—but there *was* a curiosity about him and this led to the publication in Great Britain, in 1924, of *The Awakening, and Other Poems*. It was published in the United States the following year.

The London Times, in reviewing *The Awakening*, said:

"Don Marquis has much of the pungent unrest of John Davidson. . . .

"He is too militant towards the mysteries of life. He tries to seize them and finds himself fighting the impalpable, and in a remarkable poem called 'The Struggle' seems to recognize this."

The Awakening was a combination of poems that Marquis had published in earlier volumes in the United States and a group that were appearing in book form for the first time. The poems were all of a serious nature with the exception of the author's "Savage Portraits," a series of eighteen sonnets—candid-camera character studies—previously mentioned in another context.

There was an amusing difference of opinion between the London *Times* and the *New Statesman* regarding this section of the book. The *Times*, behaving as if it had caught the author red-handed, grimly proclaimed, "The savagery of his [Marquis's] impulse is most apparent in the series of satirical sonnets with which this book concludes." The *New Statesman* took this contrasting position:

"At the tail of the book comes its sting, and its real individuality, in the satire of 'Savage Portraits.' "

In the United States the *Bookman* had this to say about *The Awakening* in a review signed "J.F.," the initials of John Farrar, the editor: "Some day the world at large will awake to the fact that Mr. Marquis is one of our truly great literary figures. In these verses there are his gusto and his sense of musical phrase, his mysticism and his great humanity. 'The Jesters' is a great poem. It has majesty, irony, beauty. Mr. Marquis has the gift of writing the graceful lyric; but it is never a lyric too sweet with sentiment or too lush with color. Nor is he a cautious poet; he has not been afraid to be lowbrow. Now, as he reaches middle age, he discovers that he is admitted to the paths of the great. I quote one of the least important of the poems, but a lovely one—'A Mood of Pavlova.' " (The poem Farrar quoted, a short lyric, originally appeared in *Dreams and Dust* and was reprinted earlier in these pages.)

The Awakening is one of the most autobiographical of Marquis's books. A goodly percentage of its total content stems from environmental factors, the author's ceaseless preoccupation with the incorporeal, a magnification of his bent for self-reproach to a deep dissatisfaction with himself, and from nostalgic recollections.

For the purposes of this biography, the poems that throw some light on Marquis—not necessarily the best ones from a literary standpoint—would seem to serve the reader's interests most satisfactorily. There is, for instance, a poem based on the Shakespearean lines:

> King Pandion, he is dead;
> All thy friends are lapped in lead.

Marquis revealed in the *Saturday Evening Post* in 1928 that he wrote the poem when Lipton's Saloon, famous rendezvous for newspapermen, went out of business.

Here is one verse of several he wrote about the passing of Lipton's, as quoted from the *Post* article and *The Awakening*:

> Dreamers, drinkers, rebel youth,
> Where's the folly, free and fine,
> You and I mistook for truth?
> Wits and wastrels, friends of wine,
> Wags and poets, friends of mine,
> Gleams and glamours all are fled,
> Fires and frenzies half divine!
> "King Pandion, he is dead." . . .

It will be recalled that when Marquis worked in Atlanta his first boss was a man named Joseph Hitt, whom he once called "the kindest and gentlest soul" he'd ever known. In time he and Hitt became close friends and when Hitt was stricken with tuberculosis Marquis regularly visited him—in fact, to the time of his ex-boss's death. Marquis dedicated *The Awakening* to Hitt, in a thirty-line poem from which the following is taken:

> You taught me how to die; when Death
> Moved in between us, mute and grim,
> You smiled and made a friend of him . . .
> God grant to me a smile like yours
> When blurred day lessens and grows dim.

The reader will recognize Reina Marquis in "Only Thy Dust":

> Only thy dust is here, thy dust . . .
> But when chill May uncloses
> Her petals and is June, I feel
> A heartbeat shake the roses.
>
> Earth and the sun were sweet to us,
> Green grass and brooks and laughter . . .
> And I cannot think of thee a ghost
> Within some strange hereafter.

Dawn and the hills were glad of us,
   Tossed corn and windy meadows . . .
And I should not know thee as a shade,
   Pallid among pale shadows.

Stars and the streams were friends to us,
   Clear skies and wintry weather . . .
And it was not wraith and wraith with us,
   But flesh and blood together.

Only the dust of thee is here . . .
   But when mine own day closes
I will lie down beside thee, love,
   And mingle with thy roses.

In letters to friends we find Marquis trying to probe the great mysteries. One of these letters—it comes to five pages of solid typewriting and is addressed to Christopher Morley—begins: "Are there gods? Is there a spirit which controls life, to some purpose? Or is there only life?"

He then tries to answer his own questions. This letter (like the others referred to) has its brilliant moments but is confusing on the whole and hard to follow. This is because Marquis, a mystic in the throes of a struggle, can't make up his mind what he is fighting. In a poem in *The Awakening* he has made this decision and the result shows that at last Marquis is beginning to understand Marquis. It is a long poem but so searching a piece of self-analysis that it becomes required reading. It is the one entitled "The Struggle," which the London *Times* called "remarkable":

I have been down in a dark valley;
I have been groping through a deep gorge;
Far above, the lips of it were rimmed with moonlight,
And here and there the light lay on the dripping rocks
So that it seemed they dripped with moonlight, not with water;
So deep it was, that narrow gash among the hills,
That those great pines which fringed its edge
Seemed to me no larger than upthrust fingers
Silhouetted against the sky;
And at its top the vale was strait,
And the rays were slant
And reached but part way down the sides;
I could not see the moon itself;
I walked through darkness, and the valley's edge

Seemed almost level with the stars,
The stars that were like fireflies in the little trees.
It was the midnight of defeat;
I felt that I had failed;
I was mocked of the gods;
There was no way out of that gorge;
The paths led no whither
And I could not remember their beginnings;
I was doomed to wander evermore,
Thirsty, with the sound of mocking waters in mine ears,
Groping, with gleams of useless light
Splashed in ironic beauty on the rocks above.
And so I whined.

And then despair flashed into rage;
I leapt erect, and cried:
"Could I but grasp my life as sculptors grasp the clay
And knead and thrust it into shape again!—
If all the scorn of Heaven were but thrown
Into the focus of some creature I could clutch!—
If something tangible were but vouchsafed me
By the cold, far gods!—
If they but sent a Reason for the failure of my life
I'd answer it;
If they but sent a Fiend, I'd conquer it!—
But I reach out, and grasp the air,
I rage, and the brute rock echoes my words in mockery—
How can one fight the sliding moonlight on the cliffs?
You gods, coward gods,
Cone down, I challenge you!—
You who set snares with roses and with passion,
You who make flesh beautiful and damn men through the flesh,
You who plump the purple grape and then put poison in the cup,
You who put serpents in your Edens,
You who gave me delight of my senses and broke me for it,
You who have mingled death with beauty,
You who have put into my blood the impulses for which you cursed me,
You who permitted my brain the doubts wherefore you damn me,
Behold, I doubt you, gods, no longer, but defy!—
I perish here?
Then I will be slain of a god!
You who have wrapped me in the scorn of your silence,
The divinity in this same dust you flout
Flames through the dust,

And dares,
And flings you back your scorn,—
Come, face to face, and slay me if you will,
But not until you've felt the weight
Of all betricked humanity's contempt
In one bold blow!—
Speak forth a Reason, and I will answer it,
Yes, to your faces I will answer it;
Come garmented in flesh and I will fight with you,
Yes, in your faces will I smite you, gods;
Coward gods and tricksters that set traps
In paradise!—
Far gods that hedge yourselves about with silence
And with distance;
That mock men from the unscalable escarpments of your Heavens."

Thus I raved, being mad.
I had no sooner finished speaking than I felt
The darkness fluttered by approaching feet,
And the silence was burned through by trembling flames of sound,
And I was 'ware that Something stood by me.
And with a shout I leapt and grasped that Being,
And the Thing grasped me.
We came to wrestling grips,
And back and forth we swayed,
Hand seeking throat, and crook'd knee seeking
To encrook unwary leg,
And spread toes grasping the uneven ground;
The strained breast muscles cracked and creaked,
The sweat ran in my eyes,
The plagued breath sobbed and whistled through my throat,
I tasted blood, and strangled, but still struggled on—
The stars above me danced in swarms like yellow bees,
The shaken moonlight writhed upon the rocks,—
But at the last I felt his breathing weaker grow,
The tense limbs grow less tense,
And with a bursting cry I bent his head right back,
Back, back, until
I heard his neck bones snap;
His spine crunched in my grip;
I flung him to the earth and knelt upon his breast
And listened till the fluttering pulse was stilled.
Man, god, or devil, I had wrenched the life from him!

And lo! even as he died
The moonlight failed above the vale,—
And somehow, sure, I know not how!—
Between the rifted rocks the great Sun struck
A finger down the cliff, and that red beam
Lay sharp across the face of him that I had slain;
And in that light I read the answer of the silent gods
Unto my cursed-out prayer,
For he that lay upon the ground was—I!
I understood the lesson then;
It was myself that lay there dead;
Yes, I had slain my Self.

In 1923 Heywood Broun was writing a weekly sports article in a light vein for *Judge*, the humorous weekly. In addition to his daily newspaper column, the *Judge* feature, and other magazine commitments Broun was writing books and delivering lectures. He had over-committed himself and decided to drop *Judge*.

I knew Broun, who asked me whether I would like to undertake the *Judge* assignment. He had notified that publication that he would be unable to continue, had been asked to suggest a successor, and had recommended me. I had written pieces for the New York *Herald* that were not far removed from what *Judge* wanted. Broun was refreshingly frank when I thanked him for the compliment. He said that *Judge* was in trouble financially, which was the reason why he had decided that this was the most dispensable of his commitments. Sometimes they were weeks late in making payment. He thought I should know that; also that occasionally when you made so bold as to ask for a check you were told by one of the editors that, on second thought, that last article of yours that had been approved was unsuitable, and would you mind writing another in its place?

I had a steady job with the Crowell Publishing Company, so I would eat whether *Judge* paid me or not; and I decided to take a chance and accept this dubious post if my boss at Crowell, editor George Martin, had no objection. Martin gave his approval, so I accepted.

Broun commented approximately as follows: "I think you're wise to take a flier. It'll be good experience—and you'll collect *some* of your money, possibly all of it in time."

All of which leads up to the following: the art editor of *Judge* assigned Clive Weed, at that time Don Marquis's closest friend, to providing the humorous illustrations to accompany the pieces I was to write—two-page spreads, sometimes self-contained, sometimes with runover. The trick, as it was explained to me, was to write the kind of pieces that gave the illustrator opportunities—"picture writing," the editor called it.

I had a lot of fun working with Weed on the *Judge* assignment (and subsequently in connection with a book of mine that he illustrated). Kindly and thoughtful, he made many suggestions, based on his familiarity with the humorous weekly's policies, which were most helpful to a newcomer.

At our first meeting—(Weed was thirty-nine, I twenty-seven)—the artist was amused by my "sirring" him, and later, when we were well acquainted, he would occasionally cut in to say, "You forgot to 'sir' me, you young upstart!" His two favorite topics were Don Marquis and Heywood Broun.

It wasn't hard to see why Marquis would find Weed good company. Well-informed and fundamentally of a serious turn of mind, the cartoonist didn't know how to be "heavy." He was not far behind Marquis as a conversationalist, was just as refreshingly open-minded and was blessed with a lively wit—though as to the latter he was more inclined to be caustic when aroused. Marquis relied more on kidding in slapping down bores and pests. He reserved the tart remark for extreme situations.

Weed, who had studied at the Academy of Fine Arts in Philadelphia under the distinguished artist Thomas Anshutz, and who was considered a good painter himself, was teaching Heywood Broun to paint. He had a room in Broun's brownstone in the West Eighties, which he used when the spirit moved him, and a key to the house. Several times, after late parties, Weed invited me to use one of the beds in his room in the Broun house and I accepted. On one of these occasions the two of us talked far, far into the night about Marquis, Broun, and other interesting personalities of that time. He mentioned Marquis's early interest in art and expressed the belief that Don would probably have wound up as a first-class portrait painter if he had elected to continue the art studies he was able to pursue only fitfully in Washington at the turn of the century when he found it difficult to maintain his classes at the Corcoran School and run two full-time jobs.

In time Weed would talk himself out on Broun but he always had

some new slant on Marquis. One of his pet themes was the problem
of the professional humorist in general and Marquis in particular.
One of his remarks jolted me so hard I never forgot it: "How'd you
like to try to write a funny column the day after your wife dropped
dead?"

Weed was looking for ways of supplementing his income. George
Martin, editor of *Farm & Fireside,* had asked me to help find a
political cartoonist. I recommended Weed for the job. He had served
in that capacity on the *Press* and *Record-Ledger* in Philadelphia;
and subsequently distinguished himself in his chosen field in New
York on the *Evening Sun,* the *Tribune,* and the *Evening World.*
Martin knew Weed's work, liked it, and hired him. It meant only
one cartoon a month—a full-pager—but the pay was high. Bob
Dumm, the magazine's art editor, also gave him assignments as an
illustrator. Weed's work for *Farm & Fireside* was well received by the
readers of that rural monthly; it also attracted interoffice attention
and it was not long before he was given assignments by *Collier's,*
published by the same company.

Weed and I became good friends. We met frequently at some
speakeasy at the cocktail hour; and during the next few years also
lunched and dined together many times. Weed, an authority on
New York's speakeasies, had volunteered to complete my education
in this field, which he thought inadequate for a native New Yorker
with newspaper experience. He had a standing joke that he was helping me gather material for a thesis on the Prohibition Era for Ale
University and when I got my degree—(Weed had long since
matriculated)—we would do graduate work together.

Once Weed and I were guests of Heywood Broun at a "black-vel-
vet" party at Charley Murphy's speakeasy on West 54th Street. I confessed that I didn't know what black velvet was and Weed explained
that that was why he had added it to our curriculum. It was a subject
in which Professor Broun specialized, conducting special classes at
this particular "speak."

Black velvet, it developed, was a mixture of champagne and stout.
I thought that either the champagne or the stout would have tasted
better alone but as a freshman who was getting a free education I
didn't have any right to have such thoughts and didn't express them.

Weed, an accomplisher needler, reminded the social-minded Broun
that he was supposed to be a friend of the proletariat—what would
the workingman say if he heard that the friend of the people was

buying champagne like Diamond Jim Brady instead of contributing
the money to some fund for the downtrodden? He threatened to
expose Broun in Don Marquis's column.

Weed thought that Marquis, who was a contributor to both
Collier's and the *American Magazine* (Crowell publications, as was
also *Farm & Fireside*), would be a good subject for one of those so-
called "personality stories"—(part interview, part straight biography)
—for either of the Crowell magazines in which his fiction and articles
appeared. The *American*, which specialized in such pieces, seemed the
better prospect. I took the matter up with Merle Crowell, the editor,
who immediately expressed interest and asked for an outline, which
was submitted (based largely on material supplied by Weed). Mr.
Crowell approved the project. But Mr. Marquis—and quite
understandably—did not. Some day he would welcome the opportunity to help in the preparation of such an article; it would give
him an opportunity to pay tribute to the late Mrs. Marquis, who, he
felt, was largely responsible for any success he had had. But he did
not feel equal to discussing that for publication so soon after her
death.

Marquis, as the reader knows, was considered an extraordinary
conversationalist. One night after he and some friends had dined in
a midtown chophouse there was a discussion of courtroom scenes
which stemmed from a widely discussed murder case that was then
being tried. The range was all the way from actual cases that had
been reported in the press to courtroom scenes from plays and books.

Marquis, according to Weed, sat sucking his corncob pipe and
listening. When everyone else had had his say Marquis said he
thought the greatest trial scene he could recall had taken place in a
British court. The drama was heightened by the fact that the judge
also happened to be King of England. This created a problem.
Should the monarch wear his wig over his crown or his crown over
his wig? The latter course was adopted since in the true spirit of
monarchial symbolism the crown could not be superseded by anything.

It was a most unusual case, Marquis pointed out. For instance,
before any testimony had been heard, the king, addressing the jury
had said, "Consider your verdict!"

When the king was reminded that this was highly irregular he
consented to hear some witnesses. One of them was rebuked by the

king for appearing on the witness stand with a teacup in one hand
and a piece of bread-and-butter in the other. "You ought to have
finished," complained the king. This so unsettled the witness that he
bit a large piece out of the teacup instead of the bread-and-butter.

The trial was characterized by many developments that made it
unique in the true sense of that oft-misused word, Marquis continued. For instance, on several occasions the judge—the king, that is
—threatened to have witnesses executed for fidgeting or showing
nervousness in any other way, also for failures of memory.

"There was never such a case before," stated Marquis, "and probably there'll never be another. For instance, one of the witnesses, an
exceptionally tall female, bumped into the jury box and upset it,
spilling the jurors in all directions. The king threw the offender an
angry look but feared to threaten her with execution, as he had
threatened other witnesses, because she was so big and strong she
could have broken him across her knee like a piece of firewood."

One of Don's auditors reminded him that he had not yet mentioned who was on trial, and for what crime. "The prisoner at the
bar," Don replied, "was the Knave of Hearts"—then he recited the
following from *Alice in Wonderland:*

> The Queen of Hearts, she made some tarts,
>   All on a summer day:
> The Knave of Hearts, he stole those tarts
>   And took them quite away.

"Only Don," was Weed's concluding comment, "would have
thought of enlivening a discussion of courtroom scenes by turning to
Lewis Carroll. He had that kind of mind."

Later that same evening, according to Weed, the conversation
turned to the subject of American reporters and their most outstanding work. Everyone present named what he considered a great
example of reporting. Exceptional stories by Richard Harding Davis,
Frank Ward O'Malley, and other great reporters were cited. When
Marquis's turn came he agreed on the excellence of the stories that
had been mentioned, then said he considered Mark Twain's *Life on
the Mississippi* the greatest example of reporting by an American he
could think of. He asked the group to forget for a moment that this
book was a great literary work—not far behind the same author's
Huckleberry Finn—and to consider it as an example of the reporter's
art.

"In about twenty minutes of the most engaging conversation I ever listened to," said Weed, "he developed the theme that much of the authentic information we have today about steamboating on the Mississippi derives from Mark Twain's classic—beginning with his days as an apprentice pilot." Marquis pointed out, among other things, that the book is full of colorfully presented factual information that gives the clearest kind of picture of the problems of a Mississippi pilot and the vast fund of information about the river he had to have. Where else can one find, he postulated, such reliable data on the formation of the Pilots' Association, one of the first labor unions organized in this country, by means of which the pilots brought the riverboat owners to terms and created a wage scale that was fantastically high for that period? And where is there so graphic and thrilling an account of the *Pennsylvania* disaster, in which a hundred and fifty lives were lost when the steam boilers of that de luxe riverboat exploded?

"This was no gag with Don," said Weed as he wound up his story. "There was no question that he considered Mark Twain the greatest reporter this country had produced, and by the time he'd finished documenting his argument, punctuating that soft drawl of his with picturesque phrases, the rest of us were ready to accept his verdict."

One of Weed's favorite anecdotes involved both Marquis and Broun. It has to do with the decision of friends of the columnists— newspapermen, mainly—to determine which of the two was the worst pool player in New York. Surely, they thought, it must be one or the other. To put it mildly, Marquis and Broun played with considerably more enthusiasm than skill and it was felt that there was a good opportunity for fun in pitting these duffers against each other.

It was decided to stage the match at Doyle's Billiard Academy, a famous establishment that was then New York's favorite haunt of the pool-minded. Those who made the arrangements consulted Mr. Doyle on the best method of playing a practical joke on the contestants. That resourceful entrepreneur said he would see to it that the columnists played their match with balls that were just a trifle too large to enter the pockets. To the naked eye they seemed like any other billiard balls but they weren't; and consequently they were pocket-proof . . . by the tiniest fraction. Mr. Doyle promised to provide these slightly oversize balls; he had once had some specially made, to enable him, when the occasion arose, to get a little extra fun out of his business.

Even poor players like Marquis and Broun occasionally made a good shot—but not that day. Every time a ball seemed headed for a pocket it would carom off to one side; and when, after Marquis and Broun had been playing for some time and hadn't pocketed a single ball—their highly vocal gallery heckling after each miss—they decided to investigate.

Broun picked up a ball and tried to push it into a pocket by hand and when he was unable to do so he and Don realized that they had been duped by friends. With this discovery the game broke up amid general laughter and everyone retired for a drink. One of the reporters present did a mock interview of the contestants, asking if they cared to make a statement. Marquis whispered in Broun's ear, then announced a plan whereby he and Heywood would pool their billiard talents so that between them they'd make *one* good player— a man who, according to Marquis, could lick anyone in the crowd.

Approximately the same story is told by my friend Walter Trumbull, well-known newspaperman of that period, who knew both Broun and Marquis intimately. In Trumbull's version the match at Doyle's Billiard Academy was played on an English table, which Doyle had installed for the benefit of his British clientele—a table that only an expert could tell at a glance from the American type. Such tables have pockets that are a tiny fraction of an inch narrower than the standard U.S. table; and the balls used are correspondingly smaller. American billiard balls, slightly larger than the English type, had been provided; and this, according to Mr. Trumbull, was enough to make trouble for the contestants.

11

*Publication of a Serious Play—Few Sales,
Much Acclaim—"Don Marquis—What Is He?"—
Golf and the Grandfather's Clock—An Important
Discovery about Maud—Enter Harold Winney, Who
Years Later Robbed Ross of* The New Yorker—
Marquis Quits Columning

Before Reina's death Marquis had begun work on *The Dark Hours*,
a drama based on the betrayal, trial, and crucifixion of Jesus Christ.
Reina had been moved and excited by her husband's plan to synthe-
size from the four Gospels the last earthly hours of the Saviour. She
had often said that there were many Marquises, and here was one that
only intimates—Frank Sullivan, for instance—knew.

Reina was a churchgoer, Don was not. Having lived most of
her life in a world of newspaper people, authors and the like—few of
them churchgoers yet most of them people she respected because of
their fundamental belief in what she called "the decencies"—she
realized that a sensitivity to life's finer values was possible without
churchgoing. It was a matter of individual choice, she thought. She
admitted that she would have liked to have her husband accompany
her to church but, believing as firmly as she did that he was a deeply
spiritual person, she defended him when he was criticized for letting
her go to church alone.

Reina postulated several times that it was hard to pour her husband
into the mold of any particular denomination. He himself tried to
point out the difference between religion and religiosity. Typically,
when asked, as he occasionally was, to define this difference, he de-

clined, fearful of getting into arguments in this sensitive area. Once he suggested to a persistent woman who pressed him for a definition of "religiosity" that she look it up in the dictionary.

Once the wife of a friend put on a campaign to make a church-goer of Don. Realizing he was up against a determined woman—one of those point-by-point arguers—he decided to rely on his most dependable device: kidding. In accordance with which he asked the woman's husband, an old crony, to explain to his wife that "Don Marquis was a hopeless case, no better than Hennery Withers." (Hennery Withers, one of Marquis's most felicitous creations, was a friend of the Old Soak's. The O.S. regularly referred to Hennery as "that damn little athyiss."

The Dark Hours, published a year after Reina's death and dedicated to her, appeared late in 1924 and was reviewed early in 1925.

The publication of an unproduced play does not usually result in much review space. *The Dark Hours* proved an exception. The following is taken from a lengthy review by John W. Crawford in the New York *Times:*

"The author has chosen to respect the Anglo-Saxon sentiment against the representation of Jesus in the theatre. Although Christ is never seen, his voice and his words are recorded by the little groups of watchers in the various scenes, and by them transmitted to the presumptive larger audience. The effect, oddly enough, is to heighten the passion of the Saviour. . . .

"The magnetic power of Jesus is conveyed in a sort of telepathic reponsiveness between him and Judas. . . . In the Garden of Gethsemane, Mr. Marquis makes this bond visible and graphic in a daring but beautiful flight of fireflies between the praying Jesus and the fearful, helpless, hostile, yearning Judas. . . .

"The trial before the Sanhedrin filters out to the crowd in the courtyard, is registered and diffused by them and converges in a new concentration beyond the footlights. It is an interesting experiment in oblique presentation of events, which seems to enrich the model afforded by the stylized choruses of the Greeks. . . ."

In a review signed "A. McS." the *Bookman* said:

"A revival of the mystery play of the Middle Ages seems again imminent: and it could have no more fitting herald than *The Dark Hours,* a drama based on 'The Betrayal, The Trial and Calvary,' written by Don Marquis which has overleaped many intermediate grades of excellence and touched a surprising height of power, reverence, and beauty. . . ."

The *Saturday Review of Literature* said:

". . . The venom of the priests, the cries of the crowds, tossed this way and that as their fears or their gratitude are worked upon, the witness given by the men and women whom Christ has cured or raised from the dead, and whose evidence is perverted into charges of witchcraft and deviltry, can nearly all be referred to their authentic source in one text or another of the four evangelists. But the skill in marshalling all this material and fusing it to a white heat of dramatic climax is Mr. Marquis's own. Whether the play will ever be presented on the stage the future alone can tell. . . . For the reader, at least, a rarely moving and wholly reverent Passion Play has been the result of Mr. Marquis's meditation upon the greatest tragedy in history."

The New York *World's* review said, in part:

"*The Dark Hours* is a play that, at least in book form, reproves criticism. By its concordant beauty it compels remembrance.

"Only one point in which it might have been further perfected comes to mind; that is the part of the third scene where a twofold action is going on, and the reader's attention must needs be divided."

The book was also enthusiastically reviewed in Chicago, San Francisco, St. Louis, Philadelphia, Cleveland, Boston, and other important cities.

In terms of feature stories, interviews, and review space *The Dark Hours* achieved—by a wide margin—a greater volume of publicity than any other book Marquis had published. This publicity, especially the consistently enthusiastic reviews, naturally came to the attention of the clergy.

Many churchmen had previously taken a dim view of the writer who in "The Sun Dial" and now in "The Lantern"—and through 423 performances of *The Old Soak* at the Plymouth Theatre—had made a laughingstock of Prohibition. The Anti-Saloon League and organizations of a similar nature had great strength in the clergy; and Marquis had been attacked from the pulpit for "irreverent motives" in putting quotations from the Gospels in the mouth of a "mocking unbeliever," the Old Soak.

It will be recalled that Marquis had previously been assailed by members of the clergy for making a negative report in his column on Billy Sunday, the ballplayer-evangelist, whose taste, methods, and cupidity he challenged. He had also expressed sharp disagreement with churchmen who took the position that "regardless of what you may think of Sunday's methods it must be conceded that he gets results." Marquis "conceded" nothing, contending that all that Billy Sunday had achieved was "a big fat zero." For this he had been lambasted as "an incurable cynic" and "a doubting Thomas who had no faith in anything except his own doubts."

It will be recalled that of Marquis's critics in the ministry, the severest was the Rev. John Roach Straton of the Calvary Church in New York. A trustee of the Anti-Saloon League, the winner of a five-hundred-dollar prize for an essay on the evils of drink, and the author of *Our Relapse into Paganism*, Straton at one time took it upon himself to single out for attack from the pulpit or in prepared statements to the press those he thought were "destroying the moral fibre of the country." In one of his manifestoes he declared that Sinclair Lewis, Heywood Broun, and Don Marquis were bound straight for hell. When the press asked him to comment, Marquis had a chance to counterattack but, characteristically, he did not seize the opportunity, confining himself to the bland statement that it would be an honor to go to hell in such distinguished company.

Now Straton was reading in the newspapers that Marquis had written a moving and reverent drama about the last earthly hours of Christ and he was puzzled and confused. To add to Straton's confusion, laudatory reviews of *The Dark Hours* and supplementary articles of an equally complimentary nature were appearing in church publications.

Straton reportedly read the play, was impressed by it, and made overtures to Marquis, who is said to have responded gracefully. This, the story goes, resulted in their patching up their differences. In a letter which is in the Huntington Library collection, we find Maud Marquis writing her cousin Neeta about this reconciliation.

The publication of *The Dark Hours* proved to be a major development in Marquis's career as a writer. That it enhanced his reputation is unmistakable. He considered it the best job of writing he had done in any category but, as indicated earlier, he did not expect an unproduced play to get much attention in the book pages. He was not indulging in false modesty when Doubleday's enthusiastic acceptance of *The Dark Hours* for book publication took him by surprise. Having previously had twelve books published, Marquis now knew something about the book business, and had prepared himself for a letter informing him that his play was too much of a publishing risk. He himself couldn't figure out much of a market for it; and his only reason for submitting it was that it came closer to satisfying him than anything he had previously done.

When Marquis made his prediction that *The Dark Hours* would get the briefest kind of reviews he also expressed the hope that some day a producer might be tempted to take a chance and put it on—(it called for a big cast and would be an expensive production)—and, assuming it succeeded, it might sell enough copies to enable his publisher to make some money.

As things worked out, the book of which he had expected the least had made the biggest stir!

Marquis apparently did not realize that he had become news. Not many months had elapsed since his successful *The Old Soak* had played on Broadway; and the announcement of the sale of the motion-picture rights had been widely publicized. The transition from Clem Hawley, the Old Soak, to Jesus of Nazareth was so sharp that it started a wave of re-examination. Several of the reviews were more than reviews; they were in fact comprehensive analyses designed to find the key to this many-sided writer and his wide variety of interests.

Stuart P. Sherman, editor of the Sunday book section of the New York *Herald Tribune,* reviewed *The Dark Hours* himself, making it the occasion for a recapitulation of Marquis's literary career from the very beginning. Starting on page one of his book section dated February 8, 1925, Sherman reconsidered the twelve books that preceded the Passion Play, the runover covering four columns. Accompanying this summing up of Marquis's writing career were a two-column photograph of the columnist and two illustrations by Stuart Hay, one from *Sonnets to a Red-Haired Lady,* the other from *The Old Soak's History of the World.* It is a good blueprint of Marquis's writing career from 1912 when his first book was published, and whether one accepts Sherman's judgments or not, I believe it helps the reader reconstruct what happened from the publication of the picaresque novel *Danny's Own Story* to the drama of the Crucifixion *The Dark Hours.* Here is what Sherman wrote:

"'Don Marquis, you know,' Mr. Brander Matthews remarked to me the other day, 'is essentially a poet.' I didn't know it! I doubted it, on general principles. I regretted it, thinking the country overpopulated with essential poets on part-time, Apollos in the press room and that sort of thing. Instantly I linked him with the melancholy company of Charles Lamb, Thomas Hood and Mark Twain, three gloomy men who, it is now suspected, secretly yearned to add to the world's woe, yet were hopelessly condemned by chance and circumstances and fatally unwise marriages and the economic theory of history and the depraved state of public taste—were hopelessly condemned to contribute to the sum of human happiness.

"Tragic maladjustment!

"I don't know—nobody knows—just how it came to be accepted as axiomatic that it is better to be even the worst kind of poet than even the best kind of humorist. Probably it is connected in some way with our deep-seated northern European conviction that there is no virtue where there is no suffering. And, confidentially, I think it is nonsense. All the same, when I was told that Don Marquis is essentially a poet I elevated my eyebrows in the conventional way and said, 'Alas!'—meaning that what a pity that a man who is essentially one thing should be devoting himself, however successfully, to something else.

"My curiosity, however, was aroused, for I had sat once within eyeshot of Don Marquis for an hour or so; and having in surreptitious sidelong glances studied his bulk—I like to see letters represented by men and women whom the wind won't blow away—the silvery grizzle of his solid head, his tawny temperamental skin, and a certain gravity of the ensemble—a gravity illumined by occasional lambencies of smoldering eyes—I had wondered then what *else* he was besides the creator of the aspiring Hermione, the Red-Haired Lady and such Falstaffian poetry as the Old Soak. Something else, I was sure; for he was a visible reminder of George Meredith's discovery that all the great wits have been grave men. Several feet away one could feel that there was someone there. If I had possessed the *sang froid* of the representative of the press who interviewed the sanguinary Cleopatra, in 'Famous Love Affairs,' idly flicking a slave, from time to time, from her roof garden to the crocodiles below as she chatted with the journalist, I might then and there have boldly accosted the daimonic mask and have plucked at the heart of his mystery, saying, 'What are you, *essentially?*'

"That sort of pike and cutlass boarding of a personality might have been attempted by Mme. de Stael or by Miss Amy Lowell; and, of course, if they had attempted it they would have got away with it. But I was deterred from the attempt by two considerations. In the first place, the natural savage intrepidity of my character has been mollified by contact with *belles-lettres:* I have read 'Hermione,' and know what arrows its author has in his quiver for persons who go about inquiring with earnest frivolity into the mysteries of art and into the natures which 'we best give the clouds to keep.' In the second place, I doubted whether Don Marquis could have answered my question if I had ventured to put it to him, and if he had cared to try.

"He interests me, indeed, because he is, I suspect, like most modernized and well sophisticated men, a good bit puzzled himself by what he is. In several of the most striking of his personal poems he exhibits a kind of desperate amusement and bewilderment over the classical task of self-knowledge. Something—what is it?—has knocked our tight, snug little personalities to pieces. We see our fragments strewn all about us; but where is our core? In 'Heir and Serf' Don Marquis speaks of his Self as 'a chance loose knot in the skein of life where myriad selves combine'; he feels his heart quivering 'with hatred not mine own'; he thinks of his Self as a house haunted by old doubts, old lusts of the blood, unreconciled, and he ends his rummaging from basement to garret of that ancestral dwelling of spirit and flesh which he inhabits with a blank question —'What is this Self of mine?'

"If the occupant of the tenement doesn't know, what should I learn by knocking at his door? Shall I turn to another poem called 'The Struggle?' It describes a terrific combat with a spirit in a Dantean 'dark valley' under frowning cliffs, a combat terminating in the death of the fell adversary, but—'He that lay upon the ground was —I!' That suggests much. So does the poem called 'The Jesters,' which speaks of disillusions and acrid tears and numb moments of despair, drowned in an 'incorrigible mirth.' So does the poem called 'A Gentleman of Fifty Soliloquizes,' which bids affection stand a little farther off:

'Give me your mind, and I will give you mine.
    Then, should it change, no heart will bleed or burn.
Give me your wits. I want no heart of thine.
    You'll ask too much of life-blood in return.'

"We foiled self-seekers, we shattered fragments of personality, have devised ways to conceal our frustration and to keep impertinent curiosity from ascertaining whether the inner chamber of our lives contains a shrine or a tomb, or whether it is merely vacant. As for Don Marquis, he walks habitually in a defensive cloud of the humorous butterflies that his brain gives birth to; behind his whimsy moods and his satirical laughter he is, you will find if you pry into the matter, reticent—for a lyric poet, very reticent—about himself.

"The only way to get at these reticent authors is to sit down before their complete works and read them straight through. It is infinitely better sport than cross-word puzzles, I conjecture, never having tried the latter. It is like big game hunting, when you get a soul at bay. When you have done that, you are in a position to tell the author all sorts of things about himself which he doesn't know —some of which may be true. I have tried this method with Don Marquis, and shall report my discoveries presently. But first let us consider the immediate occasion for subjecting a humorist to treatment so cruel and so unusual.

"The occasion is this: Don Marquis has just proved by the severest of tests that he is a poet of very nearly the rarest sort. He has published a drama of poignant beauty and memorable reality on the betrayal, trial and crucifixion of Jesus. Whether any other poet in America could have approached his achievement on this theme, I do not know. No one has. He has accomplished what I had thought was impossible: he has thoroughly dramatized the chief narrative of the New Testament, developing with marked originality several of the principal characters, notably Judas, and freely inventing incidents and speeches for subordinate figures, yet—to my sense, which is reasonably sensitive—without striking a single note which is not perfectly in harmony with the tone and atmosphere of the Gospels. In the case of the central figure, he attempts no interpretation that deviates a hair's breadth from the Christian tradition. The character and personality of the Son of Man, the Son of God, are left quite inviolate; and this makes the more marvelous the utter congruity of his own developments. His feeling about the delicate ethical and artistic questions involved in handling this material he discusses with admirable taste and insight. In my judgment, his feeling has led him absolutely right.

"I have almost nothing strictly parallel to compare with the effect of 'The Dark Hours' except a Passion Play which I saw a few years ago solemnly presented in a canyon of southern California, with the Crucifixion dim on the hilltop above it. With its elaborate reproduction of Palestinian dwellings, costumes and scenery, it was pictorially correct, like the colored illustrations in a modern Bible, of which it constantly reminded me, and the lines were gravely and eloquently recited, yet somehow it seemed remote and it left me cold.

"'The Dark Hours,' on the other hand, even silently read, is of a seizing and transporting reality. Its tremendous dramatic stress is intensely felt. It puts one there—in ancient not modern Palestine. I am there—with Judas, with Peter, with Lazarus. I feel within myself the suspicious spleen of the high priest, the impotent deprecation of Pilate, the anguish of Procla, the nonchalance of the Roman soldiers gambling for the seamless garment, all the troubled confusion of blind men, lepers and possessed men healed, the mocking scoffs and panic blood-lust of the rabble—and the stark solitude of one crying: 'It is finished.' As for the dreadful question whether this was indeed the Son of God who was crucified, at the end of the play one is facing it again with fresh astonished mind and senses, like the centurion standing there aghast at the foot of the cross. I believe this to be a great tragedy, greatly conceived and written with austere sincerity. When it is adequately produced, as I hope it may be, it should affect us as the tragedies of Aeschylus and Sophocles affected the Greeks.

"Socrates argued all night on one occasion to prove that the type of mind best adapted for tragedy is also the type of mind best adapted for comedy. If you reflect just a little about 'The Dark Hours' you recover from your first surprise at the thought of its coming out of a mind which had just produced 'The Old Soak's History of the World.' In a sense which Charles Lamb understood when he shocked Carlyle by expressing regret that the Royalists didn't hang Milton, the Crucifixion, the execution of Socrates—all such incidents in history may be conceived of as tragic and stupendous jokes. In order fully to appreciate them one must be endowed with a comic poet's comprehension of the immensity of human folly, which is the prime source of all tragedy. To put the matter in more familiar terms, no one can adequately know how dreadful the World War was who does not at the same time adequately know how absurd it was, how ridiculous, what an inexhaustible subject for the unsparing laughter of gods and men. In Don Marquis the tragi-comic spirit is very strong. He respects gods because he knows fools so well, so intimately; indeed, he knows them so affectionately that, as he suggests somewhere, he will be found fighting on their side 'against the millennium' till the Judgment Day.

"But it is time we had a little more information about the author of this notable religious drama.

"Don Marquis is a typical New Yorker—that is to say, he was born in Walnut, Bureau County, Ill.—some sixty miles southwest of Franklin P. Adams and three years earlier. Where and when he was educated I do not know. The book with which he seems to be most familiar is the Bible. Next to that, I should say the most obvious influences traceable in his prose and poetical styles and in the form of his humor are Mark Twain's 'Huckleberry Finn' and 'Tom Sawyer,' the various yarns of Frank Stockton, O. Henry, perhaps H. C. Bunner, and the poems of Swinburne, Kipling and Arnold, and an extensive study of prosody.

"His first published book, 'Danny's Own Story,' 1912, is a picaresque narrative with an earthy Mid-Western flavor, Illinoisian, and much in the vein of Huck Finn, whose domain lies in the same rich humor belt, to the south. . . .

"In 1915 Don Marquis made the first collection of his serious poems, under the title 'Dreams and Dust.' In 1916 he uttered a farcical Stocktonian yarn, 'The Cruise of the Jasper B.,' which relates the adventures of a romantic journalist attempting to sail his schooner, scow or canal boat—it isn't clear which—from her moorings on a brick pier in Long Island. In the same year appeared Hermione and Her Little Group of Serious Thinkers, asking themselves at bedtime many heart-searching questions. In 1919 a volume of 'Prefaces' —thirty-two of them, introducing A Check Book, A Cook Book, The Works of Billy Sunday, etc. In 1921 appeared the first records of 'The Old Soak'; also a notable collection of short stories, 'Carter and Other People,' and a volume of humorous verse, 'Noah an' Jonah an' Cap'n John Smith.' Next year, 1922, a second collection of serious verse, 'Poems and Portraits,' in which Don Marquis takes the war seriously, and adds thirty-three satires with teeth. In 1922, 'The Revolt of the Oyster,' containing some capital stories of dogs and boys and the ripe tale of 'The Saddest Man'; also 'Sonnets to a Red-Haired Lady.' In 1924, 'The Old Soak's History of the World' and 'The Dark Hours.'

"There are a few things among these thirteen volumes of a sort which I never read except in the line of duty. With me, a very little Stocktonian extravaganza goes a long way. So does a very little of the ordinary run of humorous verse. Practically all the rest goes very well with me, including the satires in 'Savage Portraits,' which are as neat and sharp as those of the Roman masters. But I enjoy Don Marquis most when he is enjoying himself most, and that is obviously when his imagination is at work and he is creating something, if it is only a prolific cat, a loquacious cockroach or a special kind of thorough-bred dog: 'Any dog can be full of just *one* kind of thoroughbred blood. That's nothing! But Spot here has got more different kinds of thoroughbred blood in him than any dog you ever saw.' I admire the creative energy with which Don Marquis steers his elderly inebriate through his barroom reminiscences; I prefer the Old Soak's gorgeous, blowing historical style in his account of Ancient History to that of Gibbon, Wells or Van Loon, and I admire immensely the masterly poetizing stroke in the invention of 'that damn little athyiss, Hennery Withers.' That is Shakespearean—no less.

"But previous to 'The Dark Hours' I suspect the most memorable writing that Don Marquis has done is in eight or ten short stories: 'Old Man Murtrie,' 'Never Say Die,' 'McDermott,' 'Looney the Mutt' and 'The Locked Box'—in 'Carter and Other People'; and 'The Saddest Man' and the dog and boy stories in 'The Revolt of the Oyster.' In reading this group of stories I have no compunctious feeling that I am enjoying humor by the sacrifice of a poet; for in the wider sense of the word these stories *are* poetry. Several of them are, I think, the kind of poetry in which Don Marquis expresses himself most adequately, that is, tragi-comic poetry.

"Take Old Man Murtrie dying behind his prescription counter in a Brooklyn drug store, with God and the Devil disputing as to which of them has got to take his miserable soul; first neither of them wants him; then both of them want him, and Death peevishly urges them to settle it somehow—pure poetry! Take the story of the man who has killed his wife out of jealousy set in motion by the Locked Box, finds that it contains only a tender letter to him, marked, 'Not to be opened till after my death,' confessing that now, after five years of marriage, she has begun to love him passionately; she has sealed the confession only because she did not wish him to know there was ever a time when she did not love him. Take the story of 'Looney the Mutt': a half-witted tramp who has lost his pal seeks him, seeks him, following false clues, scoffed at, mocked at, fondly, eagerly, hungrily—seeks him as a man seeks a God who forever eludes him.

"We are on the main trail that runs from 'The Dark Hours' back to 'Dreams and Dust.' In 1915, when this volume was published,

Don Marquis was both technically and essentially a poet. I am struck by the sort of poet he was then. There is in this first collection little indication of historical passions, little indication of locality, no very particular or specific attachment to 'Nature,' and no significant love-interest. The dominant note is an almost Arnoldian concern about God and the soul and their relations in a world which has lost faith in supernatural guidance.

"Whenever he turns from polishing a rondeau or a triolet, which he does very nicely, to grappling with a theme, he is idealistic and religious. He sounds the silver trumpet to 'paladins, paladins, youth, noble-hearted.' He scornfully bids farewell to the 'lost leader.' He sees that man has 'at his noblest an air of something more than man.' He is the receiver of mystical intimations. He speculates on the mystery of the Self. Disillusioned, he yet sees man as the god-seeker, the god-maker, and he respects man's aspiration, in the face of 'the hissing hate of fools, thorns, and the ingrate's scoff'——

> For all of the creeds are false, and all of the creeds are true;
> And low at the shrines where my brothers bow, there will I bow, too;
> For no form of a god, and no fashion
> Man has made in his desperate passion
> But is worthy some worship of mine;
> Not too hot with a gross belief,
> Nor yet too cold with pride,
> I will bow me down where my brothers bow,
> Humble—but open-eyed!

"The only trouble about bowing down 'open-eyed' is that presently you notice every one else has his eyes open, too; and you see such funny things going on around you, that the first thing you know you are conducting a Column. And if you *will* insist upon giving people a choice between Jesus and the Old Soak—well, you know what people are."

The Stuart P. Sherman summary of Marquis's career as a writer appeared under the headline:

DON MARQUIS—WHAT IS HE?

One of Marquis's friends clipped the article from the *Herald Tribune* and tacked it up on the Players Club bulletin board. Subsequently someone added this handwritten comment under the above-mentioned headline; "A lousy bridge player."

The handwriting looked suspiciously like a disguised version of Marquis's.

No writer of his time had produced so bewilderingly miscellaneous a spate of books as Marquis, and I believe that the Stuart P. Sherman recapitulation of the columnist's literary career from 1912 to 1924 will help the reader to a better understanding of the subject.

By and large Marquis's friends thought Sherman had dealt generously and understandingly with the columnist. A few of them voiced dissent but nothing of major consequence. One of the few invariables is that friends seldom qualify as objective critics. Clive Weed thought Sherman had not paid enough attention to Marquis's humorous verse, notably "Noah an' Jonah an' Cap'n John Smith"; he also thought that *The Cruise of the Jasper B.* was not so much a "Stocktonian" book as a lampoon of the melodrama-crammed romances of the period.

But such considerations didn't matter. What *was* important was that the busy and respected editor of a major book-review section had taken the trouble to review Marquis's whole career.

The Dark Hours was the supreme effort of Marquis's years as a writer, and when Stuart P. Sherman wrote that it was "a great tragedy," he did more to hearten its author than anything that had happened since 1900 when he decided that the Census Bureau would not do as a career and he would try to make a living by putting words together.

Cyril B. Egan, who as a contributor to "The Sun Dial" became acquainted with Marquis, writes me:

"Not long after its publication, *The Dark Hours* was performed by the young men of the little seminary in Cathedral High School for Boys, New York City.

"An audience of proper parents and relatives, tense with the solemnity of the occasion and with their concern for their member-of-family on stage, at length found a bit of relief when the voice of an adolescent Judas cracked in fluting falsetto. Giggle, snicker and chuckle . . .

"'Well,' said Marquis, an attentive standee with an ear for reactions, 'we got a few laughs out of them anyway.'"

In the spring of 1925 Grantland Rice, now nationally known as a sportswriter, resumed his efforts to get his friend Don to take up golf. Marquis pleaded that he would not make a good golfer. Rice said he couldn't agree more but insisted that that was not the point; Marquis needed to get away from himself and the links was the place to do it. It was no secret among Don's friends that periodically he had "black days," when he even avoided intimates. And though he would be himself again when his "incorrigible mirth" came to the rescue, there was concern about him in the inner circle of his friends.

Marquis's troubles with his sister Maud were mounting and though his ever reliable sister Nev, that self-described "homebody," kept the household running smoothly even though she wasn't supposed to be "the boss," the tenseness that had developed between Don and Maud had an unsettling effect on him. Once when he had managed to avoid discussing one of her minor complaints with her he was congratulating himself on missing an argument as he headed for the Forest Hills railroad station; but it developed that all he had won was a breathing spell. She telephoned him at the office and harangued him at such length he found it difficult to write his column that day.

Grantland Rice got nowhere in 1923 when he first tried to get Marquis interested in golf. He persisted and the following year he persuaded his friend to buy a set of clubs and submit to a briefing on what you were supposed to do with "those sticks and that little white ball."

Grant reminded Don that he was part Scotch, which made it a natural thing for him to swing a golf club. Marquis's retort was that he was also part Irish and that it was just as natural for him to swing a shillelagh.

As Rice explained the different clubs, Marquis gave them names of his own. His driver he called Patrick. Marquis, a habitual user of taxis, liked the men who drove them, his favorite being a driver by that name. His putter became Don, in recognition of himself as the world's champion putter. His irons he named after people he thought had some of that metal in their souls, his number one iron becoming Maud; his number two, Munsey, proprietor of the *Sun*.

Marquis had his moments when he feared he would never learn to do *anything* right in golf; and then he would behave something like the Backslid Baptist in the Hugh Wiley stories. On such occasions he would retreat to the position that golf must be a good game or so many people wouldn't play it; but he was afraid "it was not for him." Rice would remind him that when he and Winfield Moody, some years before, first offered to put him up for membership in the Players he had expressed fears, before joining, that "clubs were not for him." Now he was finding the Players a never-ending source of good companionship. Rice predicted that he would wind up discovering that golf also was "for him."

In 1924 Marquis got around to buying knickers, which were popular on the links in those days, a tweed cap and the other habiliments of the well-dressed golfer. But he didn't get a chance to use them with any degree of regularity until 1925.

When Marquis was told that his knickers made him look as big as a house he replied that that was the effect he was striving for. He doubted whether he could outplay anyone but hoped he could frighten someone into losing through sheer Bunyanesque size and bulk. An echo of this is to be found among the miscellanies he left, the following written in the familiar third-person technique of his projected egobiography:

> Marquis, in thy vasty knickers
> Thou'rt an item for the tickers.
> Overlook the witless snickers.
> With accentuated beam
> Like Paul Bunyan dost thou seem.
> Where can mortal man be found
> Whose dimensions are so round?
> 'Tis a sight exceeding rare,
> That protruding derrière!

Marquis told Rice that what he liked best about golf was that it gave him something new to write about. "Two or three weeks ago," he wrote in "The Lantern" for August 25, 1924, "we read an article on how to play golf which began: 'Imagine yourself to be a grandfather's clock, and the club the pendulum.'"

Marquis proceeded to develop that item into a whole column, from which the following is taken:

"We have the sort of imagination that can take a hint . . . but it was a little difficult at first. By the second day, however, we were able at will to induce the hallucination that we were a grandfather's clock, and the driver the pendulum, and the thing worked so well we reduced our game from 187 strokes to 168. . . .

"Naturally we kept it up. . . . Our score came down to 164. . . .

"So far, so good. But we had started something we could not stop.
It is dangerous to fuss with this psychic stuff; self-hypnosis is easy
to begin and hard to control. . . . One day after playing 36 holes in
320 flat, we left the links weary and worn to try to get a night's
rest . . . and found we could not quit imagining ourself to be a
grandfather's clock. . . .

"We had to stand in a corner and sway a club all night. And by
three in the morning . . .

"We hesitate to go on with this. The world is full of levity and
incredulity. . . .

"By three in the morning, such is the force of the imagination, we
could hear ourself ticking, regularly!"

William G. Tachau, a member of the Players since 1906, recalls
playing golf with Marquis. It was sometime during the 1920s.
They were going around the course in leisurely fashion and when two
golfers who had been moving along briskly behind them asked
for permission to "play through," Marquis and Tachau told them
to go ahead.

The first of these golfers stepped up to the tee and with no pre-
liminaries drove his ball a tremendous distance. "It traveled straight
and true, the kind of shot a good professional makes," said Tachau.
"I was curious to know who had hit that ball and asked Don if he
knew."

"Sure," he replied. "God."

Dana Burnet, former *Evening Sun* associate of Marquis's, recalls
meeting Don decked out in knickers and tweed cap, on Broadway
in the Forties. "He was beginning to bounce back from the shock of
Reina's death and seemed his old cheerful self," said Burnet. "He
looked well. He mentioned that he had taken up golf and was
getting some fun out of it." He also told Burnet that the Broadway
run of *The Old Soak* had made considerable money for him. (Marquis had made over $100,000 from the run of the play and the
motion-picture rights. The exact sum is not known. The royalties
have been estimated at $85,000, other estimates run as high as
$100,000—not impressive by today's standards for a run of 423 per-
formances. Playwrights fare better today, thanks to George Middleton and the Dramatists' Guild. It is not known how much Marquis
received for the movie rights. Those were the days of silent films
and most of the records connected with them are gathering dust in
warehouses.)

Pirie MacDonald, Hon. F.R.P.S.

DON MARQUIS

Early photo of Don Marquis.

Courtesy of Katherine Glo

(Right) Snapshot
of the typical Don.
(Below) Don Marquis at work
at his typewriter.

W. H. Langley

(Left) Marquis
as he appeared on stage
as The Old Soak.
(Below) Don Marquis,
summering in Skowhegan,
Maine, where he was
appearing in the title role
of *The Old Soak*—1926.

W. H. Langley

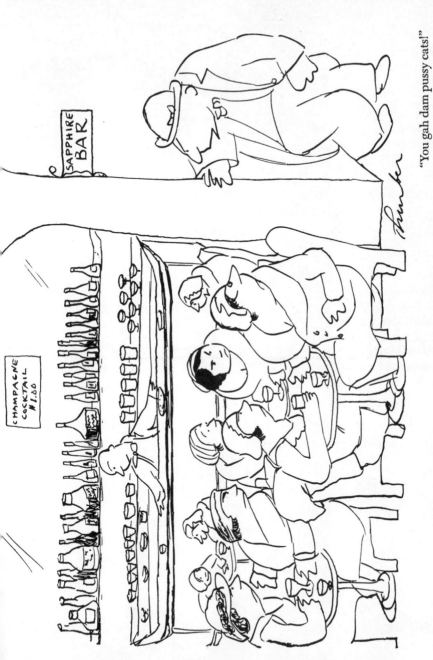

"You gah dam pussy cats!"

Drawing by James Thurber;
Copyright © 1934 The New Yorker Magazine, Inc.

(Right) Marquis with
his son Bobby.
(Below) Mrs. Reina
Melcher Marquis
(Don's first wife)
with their son Bobby.

Courtesy Players Club

Courtesy of
Katherine Glover

Mrs. Reina Melcher Marquis with the two Marquis children,
Bobby and Barbara.

Marquis's second wife, Marjorie Vonnegut Marquis, as she appeared in
the Theatre Guild production of Eugene O'Neill's *Ah, Wilderness!* in 1933.

Burnet was reminded of what he called "Don's magnificent contempt for money." To him money was something with which, after you'd made your family comfortable, you did what you could for friends who needed a helping hand. This was his philosophy throughout his life, when he had little money and when he had lots of it. Several people who knew him have cited examples of his having borrowed money to help a needy friend.

There are many stories about Marquis and his Volunteer Loan Association (Rollin Kirby's phrase). The Marquises were the dinner guests of the Burnets one night—this was about 1916, only a few years after Don and Reina had graduated from insolvency—when Don said to his friend Dana, "You're looking tired. Why don't you go to Europe for a rest?" Burnet recalls that in those days Marquis was systematically overworking and could have used a good rest himself. But all he said to Marquis was, "What would I use for money?"

Pausing for a moment to address the writer, Burnet said, "What with a wife and a young child and an English nurse, I was under heavy expense. When I think of it now, I wonder how I ever managed to pay the bills."

Marquis told Burnet not to worry about the money. He had a thousand dollars in the bank and his friend could have that as a starter. The main thing was to get away.

Burnet turned down the offer but never forgot Marquis's generosity.

There are many stories that illustrate Marquis's open-handedness. One of them is told by George H. Tilton, a member of the Players Club since 1916, the year Marquis joined. In a letter sent from his home in Littleton, New Hampshire, Tilton informed me:

"One night I was dining at the Players with Don and Pat McNutt. Pat was producing a play and was running out of money and was most unhappy. We listened to his woes for some time. Don reached in his pocket, took out a check from the Saturday Evening Post for $2,000. and said, 'Take this, Pat, I don't need it at the moment.' Those were the days when a couple of thousand bucks meant something. The play was a hit. Whether Don was cut in I haven't the faintest idea."

In an earlier letter Tilton describes Marquis as "one of the great gracious souls of the world." In the one in which he relates the McNutt incident he also reminisces about some of Don's mots that have been handed down. Tilton was unwittingly responsible for one of them. Some of the older members were kidding him. He doesn't remember what it was all about but he does recall exclaiming as the leg-pulling continued, "At least I've got this on you bastards—I have youth." Whereupon Marquis, who was within earshort, observed, "Yes, and you've had it a hell of a long time."

Tilton also recounts a Marquis anecdote which has reached me in different versions, all with the same punch line, and only the details varying. The majority version places the story in the Players bar, where a member, in an excess of virtue, was drinking a glass of ginger ale, telling how much better he felt since he had stopped boozing and proclaiming as though he were addressing the whole membership that it was "great to be off the stuff." Marquis, who from time to time had been on the wagon for months at a time (doctor's orders), was unimpressed. The imbiber of the soft drink said to Marquis, who was sipping a whisky and soda, that he had reached the point where he was beginning to wonder why people drank alcoholic beverages at all. Surveying this member, a one-time drinking companion, Marquis remarked, "I drink only to make my friends seem interesting."

Some time during 1925 Marquis's attitude toward his sister Maud suddenly softened. There had to be a compelling reason since the change came at a time when that combative woman was at her most contentious. She found fault with much that she read in her brother's books, columns, and magazine pieces, recommended subjects to him, and showed annoyance when he made his stock comment, "Let me think it over." Marquis was known as open-minded about criticism and suggestions but didn't believe Maud had much to offer in either category.

She continued to nag him about his use of taxicabs, which she considered excessive. She also thought he was spending too much time at the Players, where he now dined about twice a week, in addition to dropping in during the day when he could find the time. One day she telephoned him at the Club and insisted that he return to Forest Hills for dinner after it had been understood that he was dining with friends at the Club that night. After explaining several times why he could not change his plans he told her that he would now have to join his friends, said good-by, and hung up. She claimed he had cut her off. He maintained that he had not, that he had merely prevented her from berating him further, which to Maud was the same as being cut off.

Maud was at her most rambunctious but instead of being angry, Don was deeply concerned. He had learned reliably that his sister was struggling with a drug addiction. When it originally developed, and how, he did not know and apparently never learned; but he was able to establish that she had been taking narcotics and grown accustomed to them.

This "family secret," with which many people seem to be familiar, proved one of the hush-hush aspects of my task. Several friends of the family urged me to investigate this situation but only one was willing to be quoted. Reluctance to be quoted in a matter of this kind is quite understandable. One of my sources said, "Don't use my name but *do* look into this. If you dig long enough you'll get the confirmation you need, and this should give the readers of your book a better idea of what Marquis had to contend with."

I had no peg on which to hang this addiction story until Homer Croy said, "It's a story that has to be told. It explains so much. If necessary, use my name." Croy added that it was known to insiders at Forest Hills that Maud had contracted the drug habit. In fact, Marquis told him that Dr. Thompson Sweeney, a member of the Players and a close friend, "was handling the matter for him." Marquis now regarded his sister as a sick woman and began treating her accordingly.

Croy made it clear that in recommending that the story be told he was not giving vent to personal feelings. In his days as a newspaper reporter he had learned the folly of suppression unless there was a compelling reason for it. It seemed to him that in this case there were compelling reasons why the story should be told. Nothing better illustrated the continuing ordeal of Don Marquis—the man who had lost his son and wife and was now confronted by the problem of controlling the erratic behavior of a drug-addict sister. "I've often thought," Homer observed, "that Don might have rivaled Mark Twain if life had not clobbered him so."

I had a chat with one of the physicians who attended Maud Marquis. (She flitted from doctor to doctor and eventually she consulted a goodly percentage of the medical men in the Forest Hills-Kew Gardens areas.) This doctor declared that Miss Marquis asked him for Pantipon pills, a morphine derivative—in fact, one of the most powerful. When he turned her down and she became insistent, he

had some placebos made that resembled the real thing. He also gave
her distilled-water injections when she asked for morphine injections.
Her case was well known to the local medical profession and there
was an understanding among the doctors in Forest Hills and nearby
towns that made this standard practice.

How Maud acquired "the stuff" is not known. It must have taken
resourcefulness, which she had in abundance—perhaps it would be
more accurate to call it cunning. Besides, it must have been expensive. In those days Marquis had plenty of money, and although he
was sometimes puzzled—until he learned the facts—by Maud's inability to live within a generous household allowance, he gave her
any additional funds she requested.

Maud, a diligent correspondent who in writing friends and relatives frequently discussed the most intimate matters, makes only one
reference to this narcotic problem in the letters that have been recovered. In one addressed to a California cousin (Huntington
Library Collection) she wrote, "Have had to fight against becoming
an opium addict. Did it with will power and the grace of God."

Medical authorities with whom I have discussed the matter are
loath to offer opinions based on nothing beyond secondhand information and the pattern of Maud's letters as to whether the unfortunate woman had actually won her fight. One of them pointed
to the asperity of her verbal and written gibes at people who had
unfailingly treated her with kindness and consideration.

The fact that Maud, in her contacts with people and in her letters,
alternated between snappishness and what for her almost amounted
to friendliness, caused a second authority to express doubts as to
whether she had been "cured." "I haven't enough information on
which to base a hard-and-fast opinion," he said, "but it seems to me
that the irritability might reflect the presence of what we call 'with-
drawal symptoms,' induced by inability to get 'the stuff,' while the
show of friendliness might mean that she was temporarily at peace
with the world, having reestablished contact with her source of supply.
It is risky to speculate about such things. All we can be reasonably
sure of, on the strength of what we know, is that this woman had an
addiction problem."

Marquis brought in a nurse to keep an eye on Maud, so that Nev
would be free to run the household. Nev was aware of Maud's
problem, and, warmhearted soul that she was, sympathized and did
everything she could to make life easier for her sister. One of her tasks

was to mail letters, which wasn't as simple as it sounds. Maud wrote many and sometimes was seized by an urge to have each one mailed as soon as it was written. When it didn't interfere with her household duties, Nev made as many trips to the mailbox as her sister's eccentric nature demanded.

She once told her brother that she had developed the faculty of occupying her mind with "other thoughts" when Maud nagged or scolded. What makes this ironic is that, many years later after Nev's death, Maud wrote a letter indicating that she regarded her sister as rather dull and insensitive.

I am indebted to Frank Sullivan for the information that Harold Winney, before he achieved notoriety by defrauding his employer, Harold Ross, editor of *The New Yorker*, served as secretary to Don Marquis. To bring Winney into focus, the following is quoted from the chapter, "The Secret Life of Harold Winney," in James Thurber's *My Life with Ross:*

"Harold Winney . . . was Ross's private secretary from 1935 until the middle of August, 1941. In his years with Ross, the pallid, silent young man steadily swindled the editor out of a total of seventy-one thousand dollars. His multiple forgeries, his raids and inroads upon Ross's bank account, expense account, salary, and securities, belong in McKelway's 'Of Crime and Rascality.' . . . Bankers, tax men, and accountants still shake their heads in wonder and disbelief over the case history of Harold Winney, which has become a part of the folklore and curiosa of American capitalism."

Marquis did not pursue very seriously the business of knowing how much money he had in the bank. He never filled out check stubs, according to Edith McDonald, a much later secretary. He considered this practice a waste of time. Of course, if you had all the time in the world it was probably the thing to do; but he was not gaited for it. When he wanted to know what his balance was, he called the bank. This method he called the Marquis System of Strainless Accountancy.

Miss McDonald will be heard from later at considerable length. She is worth listening to, this woman who began her career as Marquis's secretary under unusual circumstances. The day she reported for work and tried to sort out the mountains and hillocks of papers on his desk, stuffed into drawers, etc., she found nestling among them a pair of socks long needful of rinsing, the remnants of a sandwich that had seen better days, and other oddities. Undismayed, she fell to and "straightened him out," serving him devotedly and happily for several years. The combination of an excellent memory and her foresight in jotting down certain reminders, and a generously co-operative nature, make her a major source.

To return to Harold Winney: if he had elected to forge a Marquis check it is doubtful whether his boss would have known anything about it. Clive Weed tells of seeing stacked up on Marquis's desk, and overflowing onto the floor, dozens of unopened envelopes from his bank containing canceled checks. When Weed asked him why he didn't open them his friend replied that he found this necessary only when he needed a canceled check to establish that he had paid a bill. The statements accompanying the canceled checks weren't a good index to his balance, he said, as some people didn't deposit his checks promptly. There was the added complication that usually when he lent a friend money he would predate a series of checks, spreading them out over a period of time. He kept no record of these beyond a notation on a slip of paper which he never could find when he wanted it. So, when he wanted to know his bank balance, he continued his practice of calling his bank.

It is not known whether Winney had access to Marquis's money, as he had to Ross's.

In 1925, one of Marquis's most prosperous years, and the year Winney worked for him, it is doubtful whether Don knew within $5000 how much money he possessed. Considerable money was coming in, and considerable was going out, including unforeseen outlays. For instance, word of Marquis's success had reached his older brother, Harry, in the remote village in Alaska where he had settled. Don had not heard from Harry for years until Harry wrote him saying that "if convenient" he hoped Don could send him some money. Characteristically, Don found it "convenient" and sent his brother a substantial sum.

Winney *had* persuaded his boss to do other things that were *out* of character—for instance, to buy a Dictaphone and dictate his column. Winney said it would lead to "greater efficiency." The spectacle of Marquis being sold the philosophy of "efficiency" in connection with anything creative is enough to make the gods laugh. But Don had little or no sales resistance, and he knew it, once describing himself as "the roundest-heeled of round-heeled push-overs."

Since Winney, as reported by Thurber, was a first-class stenographer, it is not clear why he did not suggest that Marquis try dictating his column to him instead of recommending the purchase of a Dictaphone.

Here are a few excerpts from Marquis's column of March 13, 1925, which he devoted to telling about his efforts to make Winney's suggestion work:

"Ladies and gentlemen: Introducing the new Dictaphone.

"The idea is to save labor by the installation of this very modern efficiency device. I talk my airy nothings into the machine, and Mr. Winney, my efficient secretary, removes them in chunks and puts them in the shape of a column. . . .

"I should say the thing was the misbegotten child of a sewing machine which had an illicit affair with a dentist's chair. All I have been able to do with it is to foster a kind of copiousness of voice together with a sort of poverty of intellectual output."

During Marquis's career as a columnist he wrote approximately four million words, among them countless items of an autobiographical nature. The Winney column is a good example.

Marquis had no set device like Franklin P. Adams' "The Diary of Our Own Samuel Pepys," in which the diarist recorded his goings and comings, discussed the people he met and gave the highlights of his colorful meanderings. But Marquis's philosophy of regarding anything interesting that happened to him as grist to his mill, however irregularly he reported it, was the equivalent. Sometimes he handled these developments reportorially, with an overlay of extravaganza, as he did in the case of the Dictaphone; or, when he considered such an approach more appropriate, he would use an actual occurrence as the starting point for a flamboyant spoof that read like pure invention and seemed to be just that except to those who knew the facts.

It has been taxing but rewarding to wade through this endless stream of words. In addition to valuable clues that could be tracked down, they contain specific information that has proven invaluable to the writer.

Buried among those millions of words is a certain amount of treasure that never found its way into Marquis's books. A remark De Quincey made about the press seems peculiarly appropriate:

"Worlds of fine thinking lie buried in that vast abyss, never to be disentombed or restored to human admiration. Like the sea, it has swallowed treasures without end, that no diving-bell will bring up again."

That same year—1925—Marquis wrote the introduction to the published text of the Broadway hit, *The Poor Nut,* a play by Elliott Nugent (co-author with James Thurber of the successful comedy *The Male Animal*) and J. C. Nugent. It is worth reprinting in part because we find Marquis taking advantage of the opportunity to express himself on something he felt strongly about—"the notion of the American writer that he must imitate the European masters; that he must always find Life as discouraging as the most melancholy Scandinavian or Russian of them all, or he is not real, he is not honest—he is not Significant. . . . Anything joyous must be untrue and trivial, any episode that is triumphant and unclouded must falsify existence; there must be defeat somewhere, there must be the sense of shadow encroaching upon even the lighter moods and moments . . . or else a lie has been uttered in the teeth of the Cosmos and an insult has been offered to the Norns. Even in comedy, we must feel Urth, Verthandi, and Skuld in the background, looking askance at human endeavorings for a space of light-hearted happiness, and smiling cynically at the human hope that there has been or is or can be anything continuingly fortunate and victorious in the past, present or future of any individual. Such is the creed of the boneheads known as the intelligentsia. . . .

"The European masters are honest—they have represented the life about them truly, they have been faithful to its letter and its spirit; I do not doubt it; and what they have seen and felt and responded to these many decades has been, when it has been more than superficial, predominantly hopeless. For the common man of Europe, millions and millions of him, has been in a devil of a mess in one way or another for scores of years, for centuries. The immigrants who come hither will truly tell us as much, even if we do not read the literature of the masters.

"The discovery of many honest American writers of the past century is that life is not hopeless in America for the common man. I know that there are thousands, hundreds of thousands, even millions, in America affected by poverty, and disease, and social and industrial injustice, and victimized by many oppressions, and denied the fulfilment of the promises made by the optimistic founders of the republic—but I also know, and you know too, if you are honest about it, that here and now in America for the great majorities of the ordinary inhabitants there really does exist the fuel and food for such hopefulness as nowhere exists in Europe, and there exists a spirit of hopefulness generally that is not found there. In short, the blither and more victorious outlook upon life and its problems spiritual and material which has been adopted by certain of our popular American writers is justified by the life which they find about them.

"The false thing, the inartistic thing, the unreal thing, would be to suppress the utterances of this more optimistic mood in American life. The outlook upon heaven and earth on this continent is different, and the artist who fails to respond to such differences is not honest.

"I am not saying that life in American does not have its sordidness, its tragedies and disillusionment, its ghastly frustrations, its terrors for the sensitive and discerning soul, its problems of maladjustment and wickedness, its martyrdoms and tyrannies and crucifixions, its failures and despairs and futilities and perversions, its grotesqueries and ironies, its acrid comedies, its lacerating stupidities, its lies and defeats, its humours too bitter for either tears or laughter. But I do say that there exist, besides all this, great wide stretches of life played upon and suffused with a cheerful native sunlight of hopefulness and success; and that these stretches also are legitimate settings for stories and dramas that need not be untrue because they are not unhappy.

"The contribution of this play is that is shows several millions of American young men and women, from Maine to Oregon, at a glance, living joyously and youthfully in the midst of this fortunate environment and breathing and floating in this atmosphere, and shows them truly, and with an understanding that is both penetrating and genial. It is not uncritical of their obvious faults, but it does not falsify their essential spirit. The particular problems of the hero are in themselves a criticism of the life in which he finds himself; it would have been possible to predicate the same set of facts and turn the story into a soul's tragedy—but it would have been no truer to the things that are. Personally, I like it better for not ending with a vista of wreck and ruin or having anywhere in it the suggestion of the corpse of an illegitimate baby carried out in the ash-can."

In bits and pieces Marquis had been saying the same thing in his column and he evidently welcomed the opportunity to make an all-out statement on the subject in his preface to *The Poor Nut*. In his column he had also gibed at the cloyingly sweet, and the author of a book he had placed in this category accused him of joining the "despair school." This gave him another excuse for stating his position.

From time to time during the spring of 1925 Marquis mentioned to intimates that he was thinking of quitting his column. Naturally they wanted to know whether he was having any trouble on the paper. No, the *Tribune* (which had become the *Herald Tribune* on March 17, 1924) was the pleasantest place he'd ever worked. He'd never known such unanimous appreciation or been treated with such consideration. On the *Sun* there were men who had been in his corner—first "Boss" Smith, his managing editor in the old Nassau Street days, then Keats Speed when the paper moved to 280 Broadway—but on the *Herald Tribune everyone* seemed to be rooting for him. And this created a problem. How do you tell an employer who is compensating you generously and thinks you are doing a good job, and is quite vocal about it, that you want to resign?

When after Reina's passing Marquis thought it advisable that he work at home much of the time as a means of being constantly near his little daughter Barbara, who had been jolted into a state of near-shock by the suddenness of her mother's death, the paper had told him he could do *all* of his columns at home, that it wasn't necessary to come in at all. He couldn't help contrasting this with the philosophy of Owner Munsey of the *Sun*, who had said to him, "Everybody else on the staff gets here in the morning and does a day's work in office hours and leaves in the evening, and I don't see why you shouldn't."

Several times Clive Weed had talked Marquis out of resigning. He thought that Don would miss his column—that his desire to quit was due in large measure to his being emotionally used up. Reina's death, followed by his unending series of difficulties with Maud, had him in a daze and his nerves were close to the surface, old friends noting an edginess that gave them concern. In that frame of mind his friend could not make a sound decision. If, after a period of tranquillity, he still felt the same way, well, he could always quit.

But Marquis was determined to resign. He said there were several reasons, some of them hard to explain. He hadn't realized until after Reina's death to what an extent he was writing the column for her. He missed their talks about it. He went further, admitting he missed her "applause." Reina, a professional writer herself and a woman of discrimination, didn't like everything her husband wrote. She had a good analytical mind and didn't hesitate to put it to work when Marquis asked for criticism. She loved his column and the characters who peopled it but when in her opinion he had written a piece carelessly or hadn't thought an idea through she told him so. In the process she was of considerable help to him, which he acknowledged publicly several times.

Marquis missed both Reina's plaudits and her criticism. Many a time, he said, he found himself putting in extra licks on a piece of verse or a skit about one of his characters to be sure Reina would like it. Not until after her death did he realize fully how much her interest in the column had done to keep him interested in it.

And then there were other reasons. Year after year went by without his finding the time for books and plays he was eager to write. Some of them would never materialize, he feared, if he didn't cut loose from columning. There was, for instance, an autobiographical novel that was taking shape in his mind and which he couldn't possibly write in less than a year. It would probably take longer. And there was a play about Henry VIII that he had been putting off and putting off, and all sorts of other things which he described as "long-pull jobs."

What disturbed Marquis most about his desire to quit his columning job was that he had a contract. He believed strongly in the sanctity of agreements and did not enjoy the prospect of asking to be released from one. He was afraid he would not sound convincing when it came time to call on Ogden Reid, owner of the paper, and ask him to void the agreement. This was probably due to the fact that friends with whom he had discussed quitting told him frankly that one of the reasons why they had advised against it was that they didn't think he had made out a compelling enough case for so drastic a move. Rollin Kirby, a blunt man, had asked him why the hell he didn't get away from Forest Hills and Maud for a few weeks, think things over, and then make his decision—arguing that Marquis couldn't afford to make a decision of such importance until he could see things in perspective. Not the type to spare anyone's feelings, Kirby reminded his friend of his inclination to self-reproach, predicting that if he quit his column he'd "spend the rest of his life bemoaning it."

But Marquis had made up his mind. He would see Mr. Reid and tell him he wanted to be released. He would have preferred to explain his position to one of the editors. Mr. Reid, owner of the paper, seemed remote to him—in fact, they had seen very little of each other in the approximately three years that had elapsed since he and Reid had signed the agreement that moved his column from the *Sun* to the *Tribune*. Ogden Reid, to Don Marquis, was a more generous Frank Munsey; he was not "a real newspaperman." When Reid, at the urging of his top editors, had sought Marquis's services, he had not displayed much familiarity with the work of the man he was signing up. Reid had given him the best job of his career, and for that Marquis was grateful; but there had never been any warmth of feeling between the two men.

If Marquis could have convinced himself that Reid, who occasionally used the title, *was* an editor, he would have felt more confident about approaching him for a release. Whereas he was instinctively at ease and articulate with honest-to-goodness newspapermen, he didn't know how you went about asking a newspaper proprietor to tear up a contract.

He was nervous during his first talk with Reid on the subject and the meeting was a failure. By his own admission his approach was wishy-washy, reflecting a feeling of guilt about breaking an agreement. He remembered telling Reid that he "had run out of gas and didn't see how he could continue." This he repeated several times, forgetting, in his agitated state, the more specific reasons he had planned to give.

Reid reminded his columnist that his contract had three more years to run. Marquis said he knew himself better than anyone else and didn't see how he could go on. Reid suggested that he take a vacation, following this up with a generous, if impractical, offer to provide Marquis with an assistant to help him get out his column. When Marquis turned this down Reid was puzzled and hurt.

The conversation wound up with Marquis agreeing to withdraw his request for a release. If he felt the same way in a few weeks, suggested Reid, they would have another talk. In the meantime he hoped Marquis would make a real effort to recapture his interest in the column that had become so popular with readers of the *Herald Tribune*.

Lyman Beecher Stowe, close friend of Marquis's and subsequently his editor at Doubleday, was one of those to whom the columnist confided his desire to quit his job. Stowe, a meticulous reporter, from time to time jotted down things Marquis had said to him and has a typewritten record of some of these conversations. The following was copied from Mr. Stowe's typescript:

"Don told me he was deathly sick of his column, 'The Lantern,' which he was writing for the *Herald Tribune,* and that 'he wished to hell he could chuck it.'

"I said, 'Why don't you?'

"He replied, 'I can't because I've got a contract.'

"'Won't Mr. Reid let you off?'

"'No, he won't,' Don answered.

"'Is he such an admirer of your work that he feels they can't get along without it?'

"'Oh, no, he doesn't like my work. But someone in whose judgment he has confidence has told him it's geat stuff.'"

In accordance with his promise to Reid, Marquis made a determined effort to re-establish interest in his column.

A month passed and Marquis's urge to quit had not left him—if anything, it was stronger than ever and he decided to have another talk with Mr. Reid and tell him how things stood.

Marquis believed that he was no longer capable of writing six humorous columns a week. He could not sustain the mood. He was not turning his back on humor; but as a daily stint he could no longer face it. If he forced himself to write light stuff—anything that purported to be in the category of humor—the chances are it would turn out to be heavy. He could vouch for this because it had happened to him—and he dreaded the thought of having it happen to him with any degree of regularity.

Marquis asked for another appointment with Reid and this time did a better job of making his position clear. The owner of the *Herald Tribune* was loath to lose the biggest "name" on the paper but he agreed to release Marquis from his contract and they parted on a friendly note.

Marquis was asked to stay until August of that year—1925—to which he assented. After that he would devote himself to writing books and plays, and articles and short stories for the magazines. The leading magazines paid him top prices but he had never been able to avail himself fully of this market. Now he would be able to do so; in fact, he had queried some of the editors and the response was so satisfactory that he felt justified in counting on this for what he designated as "eating money."

Even sadder than Mr. Reid when Marquis quit was the staff of the *Herald Tribune*.

In an article in the *Saturday Evening Post*, Marquis told the story of his decision to abandon daily columning:

"For two years and a half, on the *Tribune*, I did better stuff than I'd ever done before.

"Then I struck a spell where I couldn't go on. I told the editors and proprietors. They were very liberal; they offered me as long a rest as, and any assistance, I wanted. I was nervously ill; it became an obsession with me that I must quit or die. I got to seeing that column as a grave, twenty-three inches long, into which I buried a part of myself every day—a part that I tore, raw and bleeding, from my brain. It became a nightmare. Finally Mr. Ogden Reid, the proprietor of the *Tribune*, seeing that I really couldn't go on, and was not being stubborn about it, very kindly canceled my contract, which still had three years to run, and I went away from there.

"Within two months I wanted to do a column again, and was able to, and I've had to fight against the craving ever since. But it grows less with time—and never will I yield, so help me!"

In the same article Marquis wrote:

"So many people used to say to me, when I ran a column in a New York newspaper, 'I don't see how you fellows can keep it up every day!' and otherwise express their curiosity concerning the columnist's job, that I am forced to the conclusion that there must be a good deal of public interest in the matter. I have been out of the game for more than three years, and I can look back upon the thirteen years when I was chained to a column—like the well-known Prisoner of Chillon—almost as if that overwhelmed and struggling journalistic captive had been someone else. I have, in fact, been encouraged to turn in evidence for the state and split on the old gang.

"I never knew but two columnists who said it was easy. One was the late Frank L. Stanton of the Atlanta *Constitution*, and the other is Franklin P. Adams of the New York *World*.

"One day, in 1904, Mr. Stanton told me that he had turned in a column of his verse, paragraphs, character studies and aphorisms almost every day for thirteen years. He said it had always been pretty easy for him, and was getting easier all the time. He did it every day for twenty years after that, until he died, and I understand that until the very end he continued to maintain that it was easy. Mr. Adams, whom I have known for eighteen years, has always maintained publicly and privately during that time that it is the easiest job he ever struck. It may be that I quit too soon; perhaps the first thirteen years are the hardest.

"Perhaps Mr. Stanton was, and Mr. Adams is, quite on the square. It may always have been easy for them. At the same time, I remember that while I was at it I always told people it was easy too. For the fact is, that while it ruined me, I loved it. It sapped my vitality, made corns and bunions on my brain, wrecked my life, and I adored doing it. During the three years since I have quit it I have had four or five terrible struggles not to go back to it. I am apt to walk into any newspaper office in America at any hour of the day or night and hand in half a dozen columns if I don't watch myself, and give them away for nothing but the pleasure of seeing them in type. I loathe, hate, abhor and dread the column-writing game; I think of it as the most poisonously destructive vice to which any writer may become addicted, and the hardest work to which any human being might contract himself; and at the same time I love it and adore it and yearn for it and have to fight against it."

In that same article Marquis again refers to Lipton's Bar and Restaurant, that storied hangout for newspapermen that closed its doors forever when Prohibition became the law of the land. He would never forget the carefree days in that vanished Utopia, he wrote, "with Harry Staton and Paul Thompson singing 'The Flying Trapeze' by the brass rail, with Frank O'Malley and Benjamin De Casseres arguing cosmic philosophy at a table, with Kit Morley or Dana Burnet dragging me into a booth to read his latest poem, and with a boy from the *Sun* composing room sticking his frowzled head through the swinging door and bawling with one intake of breath:

"'Mr. Marquis, it's only an hour before that page has gotto be locked up, and the foreman he says, where the hell's that column of yours—he can't find the type nowheres, he says; where the hell is it?—ain't you wrote it at all yet?—and it takes a little time to set type even if you don't believe it!—and he says some of these days you're gonna look at the paper and wonder why you ain't in it!—that's what he says, Mr. Marquis, and where the hell is it?'

"On such occasions one gets up a column in thirty minutes, depending largely upon contributions; at other times I have worked twelve and fifteen hours on one of them."

Also in that article is Marquis's own version of a famous anecdote that has reached the writer in a dozen different forms—all of the same approximate components but as a narrative not quite clear because some of the step-by-step developments are missing. Here is Marquis's version, a yarn he was frequently asked to tell, an example of why he was known as a good storyteller:

"One thing that amuses columnists is the way they are confused with one another. If one of them says a good thing in print, it will as like as not be attributed to one of the others; I have been congratulated time and again for something that Franklin Adams has written, or Kit Morley, or Roy K. Moulton, or Heywood Broun; they, no doubt, have had the same experience with regard to one another and me. Of course, in the end, everything good that is said in New York is finally attributed to Irvin Cobb or Oliver Herford; and that is easy to understand, for they say more good things than anybody else.

"This confusion of identity among columnists almost led to serious results for a nice old German woman who was cashier and manager of a barber shop which was in the Spruce Street side of the old Tribune Building. I used frequently to go there to get shaved when I was on the *Sun*. She conceived herself to be a kind of hostess and liked to converse with her guests; and often she tired one intolerably. She knew I was a columnist, but thought I was Franklin Adams— who never went in there, as far as I knew—and I let it go at that; she always called me Mr. Adams and I never corrected her.

"One day Paul Thompson, the photographer, was in there when she called me Mr. Adams.

"'See here,' he said; 'that isn't Mr. Adams. That is Mr. Roy Moulton.'

"So she called me Mr. Moulton for six months. One day Clive Weed, the cartoonist, was there with me and heard her call me Mr. Moulton.

"'That isn't Mr. Moulton,' he said. 'That is Mr. Heywood Broun.'

"She didn't speak to me for about three weeks, but she would look at me darkly when I came in, with something unexpressed moving in her mind. And then one day she said:

"'Why are you sometimes one of them and sometimes another?'

"'I am always all of them,' I said. 'In one paper I sign myself F.P.A.; in another Heywood Broun; and in another, Roy K. Moulton.'

"She went and sat down and thought. Everytime I saw her for

two months thereafter she was still slowly thinking. In the spring of 1916 she asked me:

"'You draw pictures for the papers too? Yes?'

"'For all of them,' I said. 'Sometimes I sign them Goldberg, and sometimes I sign them Tad, and sometimes Briggs, and sometimes Webster. I draw all of them.'

"'It should keep you busy—all these newspaper writings and drawings. No?'

"'Yes and no,' I said.

"She thought that over until the autumn of 1916. And then one day she said: 'And what do you think of the war now? Eh?'

"I didn't want to converse that day, so I said: 'What war?'

"'What war?' she cried. 'Gott! He asks me what war! Two years it has been going on, and he yet asks what war! Gott! Why, the war! The war! The war in the newspapers!'

"'I haven't heard of it,' I said. 'I have been so busy writing and drawing that I never read the news.'

"And then the thing took a turn that made me ashamed of myself. The poor soul said: 'I wish to tell you one thing, mister: I cannot believe that you have not heard of the war—not for a minute can I believe that! And thinking about everyone you are, and all those newspapers, hurts my head in the same place where I fell off a street car on it!'

"I saw then that I had been cruel, and I straightened out her mental confusion for her and we became very good friends. For months she told me twice or thrice a week all about her head, and it was a great comfort to her to have anybody listen, and seemed to relieve her."

One notable phase of Don Marquis's work as a columnist was his facility as a paragrapher. In the early 1920s when I worked for the New York *Herald* (which was also owned by Frank Munsey and quartered with the *Sun* at 280 Broadway) I frequently saw the boss of "The Sun Dial" and once heard him refer to the aphorisms he published in such profusion as "fillers." There were times when he ran from five to ten of them in sequence, sometimes more; at other times he would run one or two to separate a piece of verse and a long item featuring a member of his cast of characters—the Old Soak, archy, mehitabel, Hermione—depending on what his mood happened to be.

It is interesting to note how many of those brief sayings—which he seemed to treat so casually—have crept into books of maxims, for instance, *A Little Book of Aphorisms*, collected by Frederick B. Wilcox and published by Charles Scribner's Sons twenty-two years after Marquis had ceased columning. Here are typical lines that have been collected:

A pessimist is a person who has had to listen to too many optimists.

Bores bore each other too; but it never seems to teach them anything.

The art of newspaper paragraphing is to stroke a platitude until it purrs like an epigram.

Some persons are likeable in spite of their unswerving integrity.

In all systems of theology the devil figures as a male person. . . . Yes, it is women who keep the churches going.

Science has always been too dignified to invent a good back-scratcher.

When a man tells you that he got rich through hard work, ask him: "Whose?"

A Pharisee is a man who prays publicly and preys privately.

Middle age: the time when a man is always thinking that in a week or two he will feel just as good as ever.

Even Olympus needed the corrective of laughter. When they kicked Momus out, the deities degenerated into sots and jades.

Writing in America is largely a matter of plastering pink peppermint candy over the realities of life.

We pay for the mistakes of our ancestors, and it seems only fair that they should leave us the money to pay with.

Pity the Meek, for they shall inherit the earth.

A hypocrite is a person who—but who isn't?

A demagogue is a person with whom we disagree as to which gang should mismanage the country.

Occasionally Marquis voiced an aphoristic notion through his favorite spokesman, archy the cockroach. Here are a few examples:

> honesty is a good
> thing but
> it is not profitable to
> its possessor

> unless it is
> kept under control
> if you are not
> honest at all
> everybody hates you
> and if you are
> absolutely honest
> you get martyred
>
> boss i believe
> that the
> millennium will
> get here some day
> but i could
> compile quite a list
> of persons
> who will have
> to go
> first

It had been suggested to Marquis many times that he compile his best aphorisms for book publication. To a reader who made such a suggestion, expressing the view that the columnist had been too modest about this aspect of his output, he replied: "Modest? Dear, no! Our reluctance to publish 'The Aphoristic Wisdom of Don Marquis,' or some such book, is based on compassion for the hard-working geniuses—all the way from part-time wits to world-famous writers—who are represented in Bartlett's Familiar Quotations and whose saws, epigrams and sayings would suffer by comparison."

Even if such a book had appealed to Marquis, the job of rummaging through the back files would have been too time-consuming. It would have entailed, in addition to a combing of the back files of the *Sun*, the *Tribune*, and the *Herald Tribune*, an examination of thousands of aphorisms Marquis wrote for his unsigned column "Notes and Comment" before the *Sun* gave him a signature. This department, which he ran for a few years, became known for its bite and sparkle. Walter B. Pitkin once called it "bright as new tin."

"Notes and Comment" was widely quoted by other newspapers and played a significant part in Marquis's appointment as conductor of "The Sun Dial." These unsigned paragraphs, which flowed steadily from his typewriter early in his career on the *Sun*, were about evenly divided between timely comment and maxims of a general nature. In the last-named category there was a sprinkling of serious items, among them "definitions." One of the most pungent was: "Poetry is what Milton saw when he went blind," which I called to the attention of Louis Untermeyer, who commented, "I think that line would have pleased Milton himself." Marquis, Christopher Morley reports in "John Mistletoe," subsequently sent that line to "some idiot society" that had offered a prize for "the best definition of poetry." Marquis did not win the prize.

Here is another of Marquis's lines from "Notes and Comment" that has been frequently picked up: "Happiness is the interval between periods of unhappiness," which Marquis considered a pretty good summing up of his own life.

Franklin P. Adams once told me that he thought Marquis could "pack more into a line" than any of his columning contemporaries, citing the following as an example of "telling a whole story in a sentence":

"By the time a bartender knows what drink a man will have before he orders, there is little else about him worth knowing."

In a review of Harry Leon Wilson's *Oh, Doctor!* published in the New York *Herald Tribune* in October of 1925, Homer Croy wrote:

"It is not so good as one of Mr. Wilson's earlier books. I suppose that is a cruel thing to say, when that other book was published twenty years ago. I refer to 'The Seeker.' Don Marquis and I seem to be the only perons who have read it. But we have organized a little club for its promotion—the Lull Club. When the conversation dies down we leap in and say, 'By the way, have you ever read The Seeker?' Of course, no one has, so we have the floor."

Which calls to mind a passage from a magazine article in which Marquis told, among other things, the story of how he went about resigning from the *Herald Tribune* and getting Ogden Reid, the owner, to cancel his contract. It begins with an experience involving Harry Leon Wilson and moves on to a few related anecdotes:

"Whatever success I have had, I owe a great deal of it to the extraordinary generosity of other writers; they were always trying to help me. Here is one little incident: one day I met Harry Leon Wilson, the creator of Bunker Bean, Merton of the Movies, Ruggles of Red Gap, and other immortal characters, at the Players Club, and after we had played a game of pool he said to me:

" 'Say, why don't you drop this newspaper column and write fiction entirely? You are wasting stuff in newspapers that should go into fiction.'

" 'I can't stop to start,' I said. 'It would take me eight or ten months to get established as a fiction writer, and I need every week's salary.'

" 'Any time,' he said, 'you want to start, let me know. I'll always have a couple of thousand at your disposal.' And a couple of hours later he reiterated the offer. I should have taken him up too; it would have saved me ten years of toil that exhausted me nervously. . . .

"For sheer generosity, can you beat it? He'd known me only an hour when he made the offer. And this generosity is common to editors and publishers as a rule: I have never got into a bad hole that some editor or publisher hasn't pulled me out of. The late Joseph Conrad told me one time that, during many lean years when his books were not profitable, his American publishers had, nevertheless, carried him along financially. This generosity was eventually justified in a business way; nevertheless, the thing at the root of it was admiration for the work of that great man.

"These same publishers—Doubleday, Page & Co., the firm was then; it is now Doubleday, Doran & Co.—once invited me to a garden party at their plant on Long Island.

"I wrote them that I didn't like to ride on Long Island trains, but if they'd send me enough money to buy an automobile I'd come. They sent it at once, and later it struck me I ought to own something besides a car, so I wired them to send me enough money to buy a house, which they did the next day. They gambled on some books I was going to write as soon as I could think up what they were to be about."

It will be recalled that when Marquis decided to buy the house in Forest Hills he didn't have the money to consummate the deal. This was before he had written his comedy hit *The Old Soak*, and before the money started rolling in from that and other sources. Homer Croy, a resident of that Long Island community who had found life there pleasant and had become a sort of one-man Live-in-Lovely-Forest-Hills Association, had persuaded Marquis to move there from Brooklyn, the family doctor having urged the Marquises to move their then sickly daughter out of the city to the country. In those days—it was forty years ago—Forest Hills was regarded as being "in the country."

It will also be recalled that Croy said that Marquis "had to raise the money in three days." Croy said also that "it was not easy for a non-business man to rush out and put his hands on four thousand dollars," the sum Marquis needed.

Croy never could figure out where Marquis got that money so quickly. Now he knows. The money was advanced by Doubleday, Page and Company, which subsequently merged with George H. Doran's book publishing house and became Doubleday, Doran and Company.

Continuing, in the same magazine article in which he reported how Doubleday, Page and Company helped him buy a car and a house, Marquis wrote:

"George Doran, who recently combined forces with the Doubledays, is equally capable of these fine gestures.

"I went into his office one day and said: 'Mr. Doran, Christopher Morley and I are going to write a book together.'

"'Fine!' said he. 'I'll publish it! It's all settled but signing the contract.'

"'That and the advance check,' I said; 'as there are two of us, we'll need twice the usual advance royalties.' And within an hour, Mr. Morley and I went happily shopping together."

12
Christopher Morley's Theory—Mystic Meets Mystic—The Second Mrs. Marquis—Landlord Marquis and Tenant Ethel Barrymore—"See Here, Don, You've Got to Stop Stalling"

Marquis, no longer a newspaper columnist, had no office to go to; and he found this had its advantages, chief of which was that he now saw more of his daughter Barbara. It also had its disadvantages; for he now saw more of Maud, too.

The *Herald Tribune*, it will be recalled, imposed no restrictions on Marquis, letting him come and go as he pleased. But it didn't take him long to discover that he couldn't write his column at home for more than a few days at a stretch without feeling the need for outside stimuli—an exchange, for instance, with some associate on the paper who might quicken him to thought, perhaps unwittingly, of some humorous potential in the news. He had said that such conversations had at times primed the pump and got him started.

He was not the type who enjoyed going to an office daily; he didn't do his best work that way. But neither was he suited to having *no* office to go to. It was nice to know you had "a place to light" when working at home began to pall, and you felt the need for dropping in at the paper even if only to have lunch with a few associates and get the stimulation of their company. And to go through the mail in the office for a change. When he worked at home one of the office boys bundled up his mail and sent it to him. And every once in a

while he was seized by an urge to switch from the typewriter he used
at home to the one in his office at the *Herald Tribune.* He had some
curious notions about writing, one of them being that when the
words were slow in issuing forth from one typewriter they might flow
more freely from another.

Christopher Morley had a theory, which he once expressed to me,
that Marquis didn't realize himself why it had become necessary
for him to quit as a columnist. The idea was that Don didn't know
how to get rid of people. In *Shandygaff* he had expressed that notion:

"The tragedy of the colyumist's task is that the better he does it
the harder it becomes. People simply will not leave him alone. All
day long they drop into his office, or call him up on the phone in
the hope of getting into the column. Poor Don! he has become an
institution. . . . Whatever hour of the day you call, you will find
his queue there chivvying him. He is too gracious to throw them
out: his only expedient is to take them over to the Gin Cathedral
across the street and buy them a drink. Lately the poor wretch has had
to write his column out in the pampas of Long Island, bringing it
in with him in the afternoon, in order to get it done undisturbed."

In another book, *Letters of Askance,* he described Don's struggle
at the *Sun* office (before he decided to risk offending Proprietor
Frank Munsey by working home occasionally) to produce six columns a week "bedevilled by a million interruptions."

Morley thought Marquis underrated his column. Commenting on
this in the last-named book, he observed how "ironical" it was that
"when we deliberately sit down to tackle the annunciated masterpiece, how often it goes wooden in our hands. The journeyman job
we drudged at day by day, and grimly estimated as potboiling, perhaps was the big thing after all. I'm sure dear old Dr. Johnson,
as he ground away at his *Lives of the Poets,* cursed them as hack-
work; yet in every paragraph they show the volume and pressure of
that leviathan intelligence, breaching in the white foam of humor.
So it was with Don Marquis . . . who created something utterly his
own. It was as racy of our day as Addison and Steele's *Spectator*
of theirs."

Morley thought Marquis should continue his column but "since he
didn't know how to get rid of pests and couldn't hire a bouncer to
do it for him," abandoning it was preferable to letting it wreck his
health.

After Marquis had resigned his columning job Morley tried to sell him the idea of renting a small office and alternately working there and at home. Don, he thought, needed a workshop to which he could retreat when, through the process of working at home, he became overinvolved in the machinery of the household.

But Marquis thought he had not been seeing enough of Barbara and that proved the overriding factor in his decision to do his writing at 51 Wendover Road. One of the ironies of his decision to work at home was the opportunity it gave Maud to unburden herself at length about her writing ambitions, which she had mentioned many times before. She thought that she had exceptional writing talent but that she would not be able to show what she could do until she had "the right subject." When she found one big enough she would show the world. In the meantime she sought Don's advice on some oddments she was working on—a sheaf of poems and a story about a mustache cup. She kept issuing bulletins to friends and relatives about the latter. At first it had been her intention to write in a serious vein but Don's success in the humorous field convinced her that this was the better prospect. She was still working on her mustache-cup story several years later. In fact, in a letter to her cousin, Neeta Marquis, written long afterward, we find her announcing: "Am rewriting my moustache cup story, making it more of a burlesque love affair."

Marquis now, in addition to being a free-lance writer, was a writing instructor—Maud's. He was to learn that if he did not produce sufficient stories and articles for the magazines he would not have enough income to meet current expenses. Sooner or later he would have to deal realistically with Maud's writing ambitions. But for the moment he would have to humor her on the recommendation of the doctor— an authority on narcotic addiction—he had retained when he learned of his sister's problem.

Maud was showing improvement and the physician who was keeping an eye on her for Marquis recommended that she would make even faster progress in licking her "problem" if she kept her mind constantly occupied. An opportunity to help his sister do precisely that developed unexpectedly and Marquis, against his better judgment, seized upon it.

In line with the advice of the doctor who had recommended that he "humor" her, Marquis discussed this question of a "subject" with his sister and it developed that she had long wanted to try her hand at a motion-picture version of the escapades of archy the cockroach (which would include mehitabel and her raffish entourage). Her idea was to do this with puppets of her own design—it will be recalled that this was the one field in which she had clearly displayed talent—and these puppets would act out their roles in a screenplay that she would write. There was also talk of a stage version of the antics of Marquis's philosophic cockroach and amoral alley cat.

Maud had sought the advice and guidance of Helena Smith Dayton, well-known and highly regarded sculptress, who had had some Hollywood experience as a special consultant, on the types of marionettes that would photograph best, etc. Miss Dayton, a friend of Marquis's and an archy and mehitabel fan of long standing, was enthusiastic and agreed to participate in the project if Maud could secure her brother's permission and get him to promise to make himself available for consultation when his advice was needed.

To this Marquis quickly assented. He gave Maud the permission she needed; and when she indicated that she would feel freer to proceed with the enterprise if she had the dramatic and motion-picture rights to archy and mehitabel in written form, he signed these rights over to her.

Marquis thought the enterprise had real possibilities, although he confided to intimates that it would have a much better chance if a professional writer undertook the screenplay and Maud confined herself to producing the puppets needed to interpret the script. But there were other advantages in having Maud work on the script. Even if nothing of a salable nature resulted, she would keep busier if she functioned as both writer and puppet-maker than if she merely designed and executed the marionettes—and her doctor wanted her kept as busy as possible. So the dramatic and motion-picture rights to archy and mehitabel were sacrificed to Maud's need for occupational therapy. In a newspaper interview Marquis said: "What, archy on the stage? Well, as a matter of fact my sister (Maud) is doing a scenario of archy for Helena Smith Dayton, the sculptress, to make a movie. You know her work? She really is a wonder with animal caricatures and animated puppets for the films."

There was still another writer in the family—Barbara. She and her father resumed the walks they used to take and on these excursions she returned to something she had mentioned to him before—"the poems that were jumping around in her head." Marquis was pleased that the child had returned to this interest and encouraged her to keep at it, and, as they strolled along, drew out of her bits and pieces of those poems that were playing hopscotch in the playground of her mind. Absorption in a creative hobby was good for her, he thought; though she now brooded less about the death of her mother, occasionally something would unexpectedly happen to bring back sharp memories of that searing calamity, to which she had never fully adjusted because of the suddenness with which the blow had descended, and there would be unhappy repercussions. As she developed new interests these relapses lessened.

Barbara was now developing a preoccupation with words—with the business of putting them together until she had "made" one of her poems. Sometimes she wrote out her creations in her crude hand; at other times she dictated them to her father or Aunt Nev (Marquis's idea).

He enjoyed feeding this interest. He discussed poetry with her, drawing her out and encouraging her to express her likes and dislikes. And he and Nev took turns reading to her poetic selections that seemed in keeping with her elfin spirit and imaginative make-up. In dealing with children Marquis believed in the philosophy of shooting a little higher than your audience. Suppose some of the overtones *were* lost? If need be, they could be explained.

Among Barbara's favorites were William Blake, Robert Louis Stevenson, Ralph Waldo Emerson (she loved "The Mountain and the Squirrel"), Emily Dickinson, and Henry Wadsworth Longfellow. And he had made the discovery that he could make his daughter laugh loud and long by reading to her from Edward Lear (she loved "Uncle Arly") and W. S. Gilbert. Although she was a precocious child she probably could not follow all the satiric nuances of the last-named but the combination of felicitous rhymes, the music of the flying meters, and her father's comic delivery appealed to her sense of the ridiculous and she squealed with delight over excerpts from the *Bab Ballads*; and from *Pinafore, The Mikado*, and some of the other operettas.

One day Barbara, who was now nearing her eighth birthday, sent a poem to the newspaper published in Forest Hills. It appeared a few days later but, according to Homer Croy, when she saw it in print she burst into tears. One of her lines, as she originally wrote it, had read:

I was born on a dusty rock.

Through one of those freakish typographical errors the word "dusty" had emerged in print as "dirty," and all that day poetess Barbara was inconsolable. Her father brought her around eventually with exaggerated versions—designed to make her laugh—of typographical errors from which his own work had suffered. "We poets have to get used to such things," he told her.

In a letter to her cousin Neeta, Maud announced a new policy: "I'll love everyone and grin like a Cheshire cat." By way of amplification she composed the following, called "Lines to a Cheshire Cat":

> Pretty kitty, don't get spitty,
> Hide your awful rage within,
> It's rather raw, you know, to claw,
> Slyly eat the bird, then grin,
>   and grin and grin.

Miss Marquis was proud of her quatrain about the Cheshire cat and showed it to some of her brother's friends. To one of them to whom she sent it she wrote that her brother knew what cats were really like and had once written a poem showing "the jungle in them." This aroused my curiosity; I hunted until I found the following—probably the poem Maud had in mind—which originally had appeared in "The Sun Dial" and was subsequently published in *The Awakening, and Other Poems* and from which I quote a couple of stanzas:

> At midnight in the alley
>   A tomcat comes to wail,
> And he chants the hate of a million years
>   As he swings his snaky tail.

> Malevolent, bony, brindled,
>   Tiger and devil and bard,
> His eyes are coals from the middle of Hell
>   And his heart is black and hard.

Marquis kept busy writing articles and short stories, which he sold to the magazines at good prices—top prices, in most instances. His earnings from *The Old Soak* had put him in a good financial position but that bonanza was beginning to dwindle. He still had a substantial part left but he was under rather heavy expense and the money was going out faster than it was coming in. Maud had a nurse to look after her, there was also Agnes's salary and that of a

part-time handy man. Marquis usually had to badger Dr. March before he could get that old friend to send him a bill, and, when he
succeeded, it didn't amount to much. March, however, had had to call
in specialists to look after Barbara and Maud and these items were
substantial, especially in the case of his sister who was under constant
medical care.

Marquis had started sending Maud and Nev checks more than
ten years earlier, when his sisters were living together in a Gramercy
Park hotel. At times, in order to send his sisters the monthly allowance he had had to borrow. Dana Burnet is one of those who recall
that Marquis was constantly in debt in those days.

When *The Old Soak* hit the jackpot he repaid those debts.

Marquis believed that borrowing was a two-way street. He was most
receptive when approached, particularly by those who had helped
him and now could use some help themselves. When it got around
that Marquis was a soft touch, people who had no call upon
him—some of them panhandlers—got in line. Little of the money he
lent the latter was ever repaid.

Homer Croy, strictly a nonborrower, recalls the joy with which
Marquis volunteered to act as his banker in an emergency. Mrs. Croy
was hospitalized and it was necessary to produce fifty dollars in a
hurry to pay for a blood transfusion. Homer, who claims he can't add
or subtract and is therefore compelled to shun accountancy, had long
before persuaded his wife to handle the family funds. In her ailing
condition he didn't want to trouble her to write out a check.
Marquis, who had accompanied his friend to the hospital, didn't have
fifty dollars on him but said he knew where he could get it fast.
Beaming like Kris Kringle about to embark on his annual good-will
tour, Marquis led Croy out of the room and announced that their
destination was the Plymouth Theatre. There Marquis asked the
box-office man for the money, signed a chit for it, and handed Homer
the fifty dollars.

"You may use that anecdote," Croy warned me, "if you mention
that I promptly repaid the money. Otherwise you'll hear from my
lawyer."

Franklin P. Adams told me that the greatest thrill Marquis got out
of the success of *The Old Soak* was the opportunity it gave him to
step up to the Plymouth Theatre's box office and ask for some cash
whether he needed it or not. Don told him so. Ever since he'd read
fairy tales as a tot he'd wanted to make something happen by waving

a wand. A signed chit, waved at the man in the box office, produced as magical a result as any of those Hans Christian Andersen wands, and he thought, therefore, that every writer should have a hit show running on Broadway.

It was with this in mind that he started giving serious thought to a sequel to *The Old Soak*, a new play that would present the same characters in an entirely different setting.

This was an odd decision, since Marquis's writing credo contained an antisequel clause—in fact, he had once burlesqued sequels in his column—but he turned his back on his own philosophy because it seemed to be pretty generally accepted that the most hilarious of all the Old Soak columns had been those he wrote abroad describing the adventures of Clem Hawley (the O.S.) and his friends: Al, the bartender; Jake Smith, the "public-spirited rum-runner from Baycliff" who Made Good during Prohibition and became a millionaire; and Hennery Withers, "that damn little athyiss." In Paris they probably attained their all-time laugh-provoking peak, their excited preoccupation with sidewalk cafés "and other customs of the French" monopolizing their thoughts to such an extent that the Old Soak, who professed to be religious, having once shaken the hand of Henry Ward Beecher, and Withers, the free-thinker who had once gone through the same ritual with Robert Ingersoll, temporarily forgot their long-standing argument—which, over the years, they had pursued hither and yon—as to whose hand had been more signally honored.

So Marquis decided to try to hit the jackpot with a sequel to the comedy that had contributed so much to making the Volstead Act the laughingstock of the land. In the beginning all he was sure of was that in the new play most of the action would take place in Paris and that there would be a scene in a sidewalk café in which Clem, Al, Jake, and Hennery would dominate the action. Life would not be fully exciting, he told Frank Adams, until once again he could waltz up to a box office and exchange a small piece of initialled paper for some U.S. currency.

Marquis was getting a lot of advice from his friends in those days. He did not seem to realize that, in discussing his problems with intimates, he was inviting it; and as a consequence he was occasionally testy when, after he had unburdened himself to an old crony, the result was a recommendation or two or a bit of counsel.

Marquis had an unorthodox approach to this business of unburden-ing oneself. He didn't believe that one man could advise another; but that when one is in a troubled state it helps to have a friend handy to tell his troubles to. Through the process of "talking it out" he sees the problem in better perspective and is thus in a better posi-tion to advise himself. The reason why no man could advise an-other, Marquis postulated, is that only rarely can anyone bring him-self to "tell the whole story" to another. Whether he realizes it or not, he slants things in his own favor.

Maud was constantly upsetting him and retarding his work, which he had not hesitated to mention to intimates; he had even gone further, having bluntly stated that he disliked her. Yet he was capable of defending her, contending that "She can't help what she is. Life has twisted her mind out of shape."

Inevitably Marquis's "incorrigible mirth" came to the rescue. It was the day it occurred to him that he had never written a screen-play himself and that his attempt to teach Maud the fine points of scenario-writing was a case of the blind leading the blind. He vowed he would urge her to find a teacher with experience but admitted that he had never had the nerve to do it.

For over a year Marquis's publisher had been unable to get him to put together an archy and mehitabel book, the one they thought would outsell by a good margin anything he had published before. Those characters—whose popularity in "The Sun Dial" and "The Lantern" had even exceeded that of the Old Soak—had been the sub-ject of hundreds of columns during the eleven years he had written about them. Exclusive of the pieces that were too topical for book publication, there was enough material for *several* books, not just one. When the publisher mentioned this, Marquis took the position that that was the trouble. He couldn't decide which of these stacks of archy and mehitabel skits and sketches to put between covers and to what extent they should be edited or rewritten. He had addressed himself to the task several times but he simply couldn't concentrate on it. The last time he started wading through a pile of archy and mehitabel columns something in one of them re-minded him of a short story he wanted to write and he started work on *that*. And he would defend himself, the next time the publisher pushed him for a manuscript, by stating that he was tem-porarily sick of archy and mehitabel. He loved them dearly but he needed a vacation from them; he thought they would make money for him and the publisher but he had lived with them so long he'd lost his perspective on them and had made up his mind to wait until he could approach the task with a fresh slant.

Clive Weed once told Marquis, with the candor for which he was known at the Players and elsewhere, that he and Barbara ought to get out of "that goddam house" and move into a New York apartment. He argued that this would enable his friend to get much more work done. Marquis said this would offend Maud and Nev; besides, Forest Hills was better for Barbara than New York. That had been decided long ago. Weed lost patience, made some caustic remarks, and a row resulted, the first they had ever had—but not the last.

Irritability is always more noticeable in a man known for his joviality and when Marquis showed signs of mounting testiness his friends tried—unsuccessfully—to get him to take a vacation. It was then suggested that he take a room in a New York hotel for a few weeks, where he could work undisturbed. At least that would be a vacation from Maud. He turned that down too. He didn't want to leave Barbara.

I could find only one reflection in Marquis's work of his annoyance with "too damn much advice." It was when he reported that archy had left him this message:

> everybody has two kinds of friends
> one kind tries to run
> his affairs for him
> and the other kind
> well i will be darned if i can remember
> the other kind

Marquis, to create more writing time for himself, decided to work at night "when the household was asleep." He felt good about this new resolve as he had always enjoyed working late. He had done a great deal of it in his younger days and he didn't think that at forty-seven he was too old to return to it. By sleeping later than usual he would minimize the morning skirmishes with Maud and get himself well rested for the night's work. With plenty of coffee in him he could keep going indefinitely; he would keep a pot going constantly. There was something so peaceful about working in the stillness of the night, a serenity he seldom experienced as he sat putting words together with all sorts of daytime activity going on around him. He thought of those uninterrupted hours at the typewriter, a novelty in that household, and he couldn't wait to start. And when he did he quoted, "Ne'er saw I, never felt, a calm so deep."

He had placed himself on a writing schedule and he was living up to it. He kept himself flexible, seldom starting work at the same time on any two days, and providing for plenty of night hours to produce the quota of words he assigned himself as his daily stint. After sleeping until ten or eleven he might start the day with lunch at the Players, followed by a game of Kelly pool with any of the Poolist Fathers that happened to be around. Or, if that happened to be his mood, he might return to Forest Hills directly after lunch and try to get in a few hours at the typewriter in the afternoon too. He sought to schedule himself so that if Barbara felt like taking a stroll he would be free to join her and resume their chats about poetry and a monthly paper she kept talking about and which she said she would publish when she was a year or two older and could spell a little better.

When Marquis planned to have dinner in New York, which he did occasionally, he would sleep until noon or later so that he would not be too exhausted to do his night-writing when he returned to Forest Hills. On such days he called up Barbara before she retired, discussed the day's doings with her, and kissed her good night over the telephone.

Marquis's friends thought he was now more cheerful and relaxed than at any time since Reina's death.

After that tragedy several friends of Reina's offered to look after Barbara. One of them, it will be recalled, was Katherine Glover. Marquis told Miss Glover that he had been compelled to turn down all such offers and in the process hoped he hadn't offended any of the kind people who had made them. "I shall be quite brutal in not using you . . . or Marjorie, or any of the rest of you, when it comes to a place where I know more about Reina's ideas than you do. . . . This sounds frightfully mean. . . . You know I value your sweetness and loyalty and devotion."

The Majorie to whom Marquis had alluded was Mrs. Walter Vonnegut, a talented actress whom Reina had met through her activities in the First Church of Christ Scientist. The two couples—the Marquises and the Vonneguts—had become good friends as a result of the religious activities of the two women.

The Vonneguts had two children, one a boy younger than Bar-

bara, the other a girl who was a few years older. They had offered to
take Barbara into their home, believing that the companionship of
their children would prove beneficial to the child during the critical
period immediately following her mother's death. Marquis had declined the offer as he had all others of a similar nature.

When Marquis was elected to membership in the National Institute
of Arts and Letters he was asked to fill out a form giving the names of
friends he desired to receive invitations to functions of that body that
nonmembers were eligible to attend. He submitted this list:

> Mr. and Mrs. Christopher Morley
> Mr. and Mrs. Dana Burnet
> Mr. and Mrs. Walter Vonnegut

A few years later the Vonneguts were divorced and Mrs. Vonnegut was sharing an apartment in midtown New York with Miss
Mildred Dilling, distinguished harpist and teacher, who has given
concerts all over the world and who taught Harpo Marx the instrument responsible for his acquiring his well-known sobriquet.
Among her other students was Laurence Olivier.

Marquis remained on friendly terms with both Vonneguts—
Walter and Marjorie—after their divorce. Walter, an actor, was experiencing difficulty in finding a role that meant steady employment, and sought Marquis's advice. As a member of the Players Don
frequently heard about new plays that were going into production
and he introduced Vonnegut to producers and directors. Vonnegut
was a good actor but he had not had much luck in getting into
long-run productions and was not as well known as his talents merited. Marjorie appreciated what Don was doing to help her ex-
husband, as he had assumed certain obligations regarding the support
of the Vonnegut children.

We know from Miss Dilling that Don and Marjorie began seeing
each other. They met with increasing frequency at the apartment
the two young women shared.

During the period of almost three years after Reina's death Don
had occasionally chatted with Walter and Marjorie over the telephone but had seen very little of them. He was said to have had a
feeling of embarrassment because of his rejection of their repeated
offers to take Barbara into their home and he may have avoided
them for this reason.

Miss Dilling speaks rapturously of Marquis's visits to the midtown apartment where she and her friend Marjorie lived. Don, normally gregarious, had been tied down in Forest Hills by the problems that had accumulated there, and he saw little of his old friends except the men he met on his visits to the Players (whose severely masculine portals excluded women) and a few friends in Forest Hills.

Not until he had found himself in the company of two lively and attractive women—they were both about thirty—did he realize how drab was the routine that he had established for himself since Reina's death. With this duo as an audience he was his old storytelling self again. It was like the old days when he found himself in a group and one of his friends—Christopher Morley, Donne Byrne, or one of the others—would say, "Tell them the one about old lady Epperson and her home-made ghosts"—the last-named was the local spiritualist in Walnut, Illinois, Marquis's birthplace—"or the one about the German woman in the Park Row barbershop who mistook you for Frank Adams." The only difference was that, instead of a group, he had an audience of two, and instead of being urged by others to spin some yarns, he acted as his own prompter.

Marquis had several devices for getting such conversations started. One of them was this gambit: "If someone doesn't ask me to tell a story I'll be compelled to ask myself." Another was: "I'm about to be reminded of a story by *anything* anybody says." He maintained that a neglected phase of the storyteller's art was the chance to exploit the endless possibilities of the *non sequitur* in a parody of the professional master of ceremonies who is always being reminded of a story by something wholly irrelevant.

Miss Dilling recalls the hilarity occasioned by some of Marquis's stories. In the days when the Vonneguts and the Marquises met for dinner Marjorie may have heard some of these same tales; but that would make no difference. Don, a nimble improviser, never told a story the same way twice, and it was fun, if you had previously heard one of these yarns, to see what new twists the narrator's inventiveness would contrive *this* time. Homer Croy recalls Reina saying, before she learned that her husband's improvisations were chronic and deliberate, "Tommy, your stories keep getting bigger and bigger." Homer remembers this remark as an astonished comment on the fourth or fifth version she had heard of the one about the toothless and clawless carnival lion that had wandered into the Atlanta bar where her husband was having a drink with friends. The transition from a harmless, bored-looking creature that was no more of a menace than the timorous lion in *The Wizard of Oz* to a raging beast that bared its great teeth and claws had taken Reina unawares. From that time on she was prepared for anything.

So, too, were Marjorie and her friend Mildred when Don went on a storytelling bender.

On those visits Don also had his serious moments and Miss Dilling remembers one evening—she calls it "unforgettable"—when after dinner he stood before the lighted fireplace in the living room and read some of his favorite passages from Homer. (The reading was from *The Odyssey*, she recalls.) "He read beautifully," she said, "in that pleasant, soft voice into which he could put so much feeling. It was a wonderful evening."

Soon Marquis was seeing Mrs. Vonnegut frequently. These repeated visits to New York aroused Maud's curiosity but her searching inquiries yielded no information. That poor misguided woman, seemingly unaware that her possessiveness was betraying her into treating a middle-aged adult as one might a ten-year-old brother who needed looking after, was agog with curiosity but Marquis knew better than to tell her anything. One day she said to him, "You weren't at the Club last night." That was correct, he told her. She said she was pretty sure something fishy was going on; for he had clearly implied, she insisted, that when he didn't return to Forest Hills for dinner he would be dining at the Players. He had implied no such thing, he stated; and that ended the conversation.

Marjorie and Don had many common interests—the theater, a preoccupation with the riddle of identity (what Marquis called the "Who am I?" theme), survival after death, and the other Great Mysteries. And they discussed miracles—the "small miracles of daily life" and the Biblical ones.

Marjorie was fundamentally a serious-minded woman; and though she respected Marquis as a humorist, it was his serious work that impressed her most—*The Dark Hours*, his drama of the Crucifixion, and his books of poetry: *Dreams and Dust*, and *The Awakening*. Among her favorites, too, were verses of a serious nature that had not been collected (and which she had read in "The Sun Dial" and "The Lantern").

The Dark Hours was a great play, Marjorie thought, and some day she would like to see it produced in the theater. Had he done anything to bring that about? He had, of course. In fact every producer in New York had received a copy of the play not long after Doubleday had published it. But it called for a big cast; the costumes, décor, and direction would entail heavy expenditures, and all in all the producers thought it would be too costly and risky a venture. It would take a great director, he had been told, to fuse the different elements of the drama into a flowing entity. No one seemed to know who he should be; there was agreement, however, that his services would come high.

Marjorie, a woman who had a lot of faith in herself, expressed the belief that she could direct *The Dark Hours*. While her stage career had been devoted almost exclusively to acting, she had been experimenting with play direction and hoped to make a career of it some day. She thought that anyone with a good working knowledge of the theater, and an appreciation of the sweep and grandeur of Marquis's drama, could do an effective job of directing it.

The effect on Marquis of an exceptionally attractive young woman—the words "handsome" and "beautiful" had been used by reviewers in describing her—focusing so much attention on Marquis's special favorite of all his books, should not be hard to guess.

Marjorie was impressed with the dramatic simplicity of Don's treatment of the scriptural miracles in *The Dark Hours*. She herself, she told him, had experienced one as a girl of twelve or thirteen. Her childhood had been marred by a clubfoot, and when the medical profession had been unable to do anything for her, her mother had taken her to a Christian Science practitioner. After several of these consultations Marjorie had an experience that changed the course of her life, since it started her on the road to a proper appreciation of things of the spirit. It seems that one morning she had walked into her mother's bedroom before she had thought to put on her stockings and shoes. An astonished look came over her mother's face as she looked down at her daughter's feet. "Look, Marjorie!" she exclaimed. "Your clubfoot is gone!" She looked down and to her joy saw that the ailing member was normal.

There are references in Marquis's writings to "the need for believing in miracles" but the man had his cynical moments too, and if he had heard the story under different circumstances and from a less charming source, he might have scoffed; or, if not, the reporter in him would have precipitated some rather searching questions.

Miss Dilling, in telling me Marjorie's account of the healing of her clubfoot through Christian Science, said that there was something so compelling about this story as narrated by her friend that it simply didn't occur to you to question it. If you had any doubts you would be incapable of expressing them in the face of a faith so movingly enunciated.

That night Marjorie was reaching Marquis the poet and mystic, and as such he was the perfect audience. There was something about this woman that appealed to the imagination of the man who, in a poem called "The Mystic," had expressed his own preoccupation with miracles:

> And would it be so strange a thing,
> Among the rainy hills of Spring,
> A veritable god to see
> In luminous reality?
> To see him pass, as bursts of sun
> Pass over the valleys and are gone? . . .
>
> And would it be too strange to say
> I see a dead man come this way?
> Like mist the houses shrink and swell,
> Like blood the highways throb and beat,
> The sapless stones beneath my feet
> Turn foliate with miracle;
> And from the crowd my dead men come,
> Fragrant with youth . . . and living mirth
> Moves lips and eyes that once were numb
> And blinded in the charnel earth.

And in "The God-Maker, Man" he expressed the belief that to keep going one has to have faith in that which seems "illogical, reason-defying." Then, addressing himself to the miracle of survival after death, he had this to say:

> Yes, nothing seems changeless but Change.
> And yet, through the creed-wrecking years,
> One story forever appears;
> The tale of a City Supernal—
> The whisper of Something eternal—
> A passion, a hope, and a vision
> That peoples the silence with Powers;
> A fable of meadows Elysian
> Where Time enters not with his Hours—
> Manifold are the tale's variations,
> Race and clime ever tinting the dreams,
> Yet its essence, through endless mutations,
> Immutable gleams. . . .

> Insistent, persistent, forever
> Man cries to the silences, "Never
> Shall Death reign the lord of the soul,
> Shall the dust be the ultimate goal." . . .

A favorite line of Marquis's, in his serious moments, was that we "must let the spirit weave its spells." He admired Marjorie for letting her spirit do precisely that, a philosophy he had expressed in a poem called "The Singer," published in the earliest days of "The Sun Dial," from which the following is taken:

> A little while, with love and youth,
> He wandered, singing.
> He felt life's pulses hot and strong
> Beat all his rapid veins along;
> He wrought life's rhythms into song:
> He laughed, he sang the Dawn!
> So close, so close to life he dwelt
> That at rare times and rapt he felt
> The fleshly barriers yield and melt.
> He trembled, looking on
> Creation at her miracles;
> His soul-sight pierced the earthly shells
> And saw the spirit weave its spells,
> The veil of clay withdrawn. . . .

Marquis had found a fellow mystic, one with whom he could range far and wide in the uncharted realm of the great riddles. He had not had much success in discussing the impalpable with his cronies at the Players. Once, when he had tried to draw out a group in that stronghold of good fellowship on the subject of a finite God, on which he had speculated in his poetry, Pat McNutt had asked him to climb down from the sky and tell some funny stories. "What we all need, Don, are some belly laughs." Marquis took such things in stride. McNutt was a friend of his and his friends could do no wrong.

Yet, over the years, Marquis had taken a number of pot shots at the philosophy represented by that squelch. In one of them he wrote:

> The fates this gibe have lessoned us:
> There sups tonight on earth
> No madder crew of wastrels than
> This fellowship of mirth . . .

To make it clear he isn't preaching he gets this idea across:

> What else is there remains for us
> But make a jest of care
> And set the rafters ringing in
> Our Tavern of Despair?

But in this particular poem he is more convincing when he writes:

> We're grown so fond of paradox
> Perverseness holds us thrall,
> So what each jester loves the best
> He mocks the most of all;
> But as the jest and laugh go round,
> Each in his neighbor's eyes
> Reads, while he flouts his heart's desire,
> The knowledge that he lies . . .
>
> If God called Azrael to Him now
> And bade Death bend the bow
> Against the saddest heart that beats
> Here on this earth below,
> Not any sobbing breast would gain
> The guerdon of that barb—
> The saddest ones are those that wear
> The jester's motley garb.

The foregoing is not cited as an example of Marquis at his poetic best. He had done much better. It is reprinted merely as another one of those autobiographical bits that show mirth and care at war in the man's mind. In this case, the serious Marquis won; it will be recalled that in other conflicts of a similar nature his "incorrigible mirth" prevailed.

It was to the serious Marquis that Marjorie Vonnegut addressed herself; and the serious Marquis responded.

One day at the home of W. O. McGeehan, famous sportswriter of that period, Don blurted out, "Bill, I'm going to marry a noble woman." McGeehan's widow—the playwright and novelist known professionally as Sophie Treadwell—recalls the incident well. The two men habitually ribbed each other and Bill saw an opportunity in his friend's remark. He thought for a moment, then said, "That's a hell of a reason for getting married." McGeehan, an unabashed skeptic, subsequently told his friend that if Marjorie was as noble as he claimed, canonization might appeal to her more than matrimony.

Miss Treadwell, who knew Marquis mainly from her husband's designation of him as a bubbling wit, observed that that night he sounded more like the hero of an old-fashioned melodrama than a humorist—tense, excited, unconsciously funny.

"This was my only meeting with Marquis, whose work I had long admired," said Miss Treadwell. "He and my husband were good friends and I had heard Mac—you fellows always called him Bill but he was Mac to me—repeat some of the salty sayings for which he was known around the office." (At one time Bill McGeehan and Don Marquis both worked for Frank Munsey's Sun-Herald Corporation, Bill for the *Herald*, Don for the *Sun*.) In conclusion Miss Treadwell said she had always regretted having met only Marquis, the lovesick humorist, and never the Marquis her husband rated so highly as a wit.

To another friend Marquis confided that Mrs. Vonnegut was "a high-minded woman." In passing this tidbit on to me this old friend of the Marquis family said, "No one should be permitted to see a humorist in the early stages of a romance. He should be kept under lock and key until the first tiff with his inamorata jolts him back to reality."

Mildred Dilling recalls with amusement the evening Don started pacing up and down in a curious kind of agitation that seemed a combination of the comic and the serious. Imagine a man biting his finger nails with a grin on his face and you have the picture.

"It's happened again!" was his opening remark, and since this meant nothing to either Marjorie or Mildred, he was asked for an explanation.

Marquis began with the statement that the sins of his days as a fledgling newspaperman were beginning to catch up with him. As the greenest of beginners on a country weekly some inexplicable urge had impelled him to let his fancy roam and improvise anecdotes about Abraham Lincoln. Some of them had crept into biographies of the martyred President which, fortunately for his troubled conscience, had not achieved prominence. That very day, however, he had picked up a more recent book on Lincoln, a major work that was being acclaimed, and in it he had found some of his fables. His first reaction to the discovery was to laugh, then he had some sobering thoughts and found himself wishing that he hadn't succumbed to the temptation to fatten up the Lincoln legendry. He was only twenty years old at the time but still he should have known better.

Marquis had done a lot of thinking about this youthful indiscretion and finally decided to Tell All in an article in the *Saturday Evening Post* in which, among other things, he discussed his early newspaper days in considerable detail. At the risk of repetition I take the liberty of excerpting this part of his confessional as a means of bringing the story into focus: "It was during this earlier period of my aspirations that I developed a bad habit of inventing Lincoln stories. Lincoln was still a very lively personal memory in those days (1898) to some of the older people living in that part of the Middle West, and they were forever repeating anecdotes about him or stories that were attributed to him. When I couldn't find anything better to fill up my column with, I used to invent a story and attribute it to Lincoln, and some of these, I believe, are still in circulation. I was young and irresponsible in those days, with no perception that this might contribute to the falsification of a great historical character; I thought most of the Lincoln stories were invented by somebody else and I might as well have a hand in it, too. And, indeed, I still wonder if as many as a quarter of the anecdotes attributed to Lincoln were really his. He couldn't have had much time for anything else if he told all of them."

Marjorie observed that it was generally accepted that confession was good for the soul and she was glad he had confided in her about this matter. If anyone else had uttered that platitude Marquis might have exclaimed, "Nuts!" But, coming from the woman he loved, there didn't seem to be anything wrong about it.

Marjorie thought Don should make amends, advocating that he write the authors of the books that contained the Marquis myths, explain the situation, and suggest to them that future editions be corrected. Whenever there was an opportunity to do so, Marjorie proclaimed, anything in any category of life that wasn't strictly true should be expunged from the record. That was the Road to Serenity. She was indeed a noble woman.

Marjorie—quite understandably—didn't know enough about book publishing to have any concept of the complications that could arise from a suggestion such as hers and he thought it best not to try to explain. To terminate the conversation, which he regretted having started, he made a vague promise to "straighten the matter out after giving it more thought."

In some respects Don and Marjorie were miles apart. For instance, although she had a quick intelligence she could, in certain situations, be quite literal-minded. Normally Marquis and literal-mindedness found each other incompatible.

But these weren't normal circumstances. So this wasn't of any consequence; nor did he consider any of their other dissimilarities, if he was aware of them, significant. All that mattered was that Marjorie reciprocated his love for her.

The key to Marquis's philosophy in affairs of the heart is to be found in the previously quoted advice of Old Doc Kirby to the protagonist of *Danny's Own Story*, Marquis's first novel:

"If she's fool enough to love you, treat her well—treat her well. For if you don't, you can never run away from the hell you'll carry in your own heart."

The phrase, "if she's fool enough to love you," embodies Marquis's dominant thoughts on what he called this "man-woman business." Sentimental? Yes. Old-fashioned? Probably. But it is pure Marquis. Only a part-time sentimentalist—and at times in full rebellion against the emotions the role demanded—he still clung to the if-she's-fool-enough-to-love-you credo. It was responsible for a number of decisions—far-reaching ones—that affected the rest of his life.

On February 2, 1926, Marquis and Mrs. Vonnegut were married in the rectory of the Community Church in New York City. "The ceremony was performed by the Rev. John Haynes Holmes," reported the New York *Times*, "and immediately after it the couple left on a wedding trip of two weeks in the South."

The item in the *World* mentioned that "the wedding was attended only by witnesses."

"Mrs. Marquis," this story said, "appeared in productions of The Stagers, an organization which began a few years ago at the 52nd Street Theatre and more recently operated in the Princess Theatre. She began her professional stage career with the Washington Square Players and later appeared in productions of the Theatre Guild. She will continue to appear on the stage.

"Both the bride and bridgroom have been married before. Mrs. Marquis's first husband was Walter Vonnegut, actor, whom she divorced. The decree gave her custody of her two children, Walter, Jr., and Ruth.

"Mr. Marquis's first wife was Reina Melcher Marquis, novelist, poet and short story writer. She died in 1923, and left one child, Barbara, now seven.

"The bride's age was given as thirty-four and Mr. Marquis's age as forty-seven."

On their return from the South Mr. and Mrs. Marquis moved into a furnished apartment in midtown Manhattan while they made their plans for the future.

Mrs. Marquis favored their taking up permanent residence in New York and owning their own home, and through a real-estate agent she secured a list of houses for sale in Manhattan's East and West Sixties, Seventies, and Eighties. After inspecting a number of these dwellings she narrowed the choice to two or three brownstones in the East Sixties. Eventually she and Don decided that a brownstone at 125 East 62nd Street best suited their needs. There were three floors and a basement. Two of these floors and the basement would take care of their needs—including a room for each of the three children—Marjorie's daughter Ruth, her son Walter, Jr., and Don's daughter Barbara—which would leave them free to rent one floor. This, they figured, would not be difficult as the neighborhood was good—what was known in those days as a "quiet section"—and the rooms were spacious and well laid out. Taking in a tenant would enable them to recapture some of their outlay, an important factor in their planning since the house was an expensive one that called for a large down payment, and the carrying charges would be substantial.

Reportedly Marquis was not daunted by these considerations. Sure, he would be under heavy expense but his "backlog of bucks," as he once called it, though not as impressive as it was a few years ago, was still pretty good. He seems to have been more preoccupied with such factors as that this house would give him two places to work. He would have an office on the first floor and he would do his writing there during the day. There no longer would be the need to work late at night to make it possible to have several hours at a stretch without Maud interrupting. But there were times when it was necessary to work at night in order to meet a deadline, so he would also have a desk on the third floor for such emergencies, where he could pound his typewriter without disturbing the sleeping family two floors below. He took the position that if anyone was to be disturbed it should be his lessee on the second floor. Having observed the villainies of landlords in melodramas, he would know just what to do if his second-floor occupants complained.

Marquis freely acknowledged that he didn't like to make decisions. In the beginning he wasn't sure he wanted to commit himself to owning a house in New York and undertaking the responsibility for its maintenance. Marjorie's confident belief that this was the thing to do had settled the matter. "A good push" from someone who believed strongly in his or her recommendation was a great thing, he had said in his column; this saved the wear and tear on the cerebellum entailed in weighing the pros and cons of any given situation. He had even speculated on how much a "pro" weighed, also a "con." If one could put this on a scientific basis, he contended, one would know precisely how much weighing and considering the human brain could comfortably accommodate, and thus how much indecision.

When the painters and paperhangers had finished their work and the plumbers and steamfitters had completed checking and repairing everything that needed it, the resultant bills—a not inconsiderable total—gave Marquis his first taste of the joys of urban home-owning.

Next came the problem of furnishing the house. Marjorie had some furniture of her own but not nearly enough for this big dwelling. A considerable amount of furniture and furnishings would have to be purchased.

Maud and Nev were in Florida when Don and Marjorie were married. Maud had convinced herself that she could not stand the winters in the North and had no trouble convincing Don that the thing to do was to go south. It was an annual respite for him—he had once called it an "armistice"—though a rather expensive one. Nev, the self-designated "homebody," wanted to remain in Forest Hills and look after Barbara, but the doctor had convinced her brother that Maud needed a companion. She still had those moments when a minor ache convinced her that she was severely ill— perhaps dying—and on such occasions she would seek relief through narcotics. Progress had been made in connection with her "problem" but it was still considered important to have someone with her— someone close to her who understood the situation—to see her through the erratic pattern of these seizures.

Don thought he had done a good job of keeping his romance a secret, forgetting how many times he had told intimates about the "noble woman" he was planning to marry. There is always the inevitable leak to be reckoned with—almost a certainty in the case of one as well known as Marquis.

Maud afterward claimed that before she and Nev sailed for Europe the preceding summer she knew that Don "had a woman up his sleeve"—a neat trick, he thought, if you could bring it off. It seems unlikely that Maud had any knowledge of her brother's developing interest in Marjorie Vonnegut as early as that.

There is no indication that Maud knew anything about Marjorie until shortly before she left for Florida. It is not known how she learned but we do know that she asked him to confirm or deny the report that he "was mixed up with some woman" he planned to marry.

It seems not to have occurred to Maud that her brother, who had been her benefactor for years, should be permitted to run his own affairs. She seems to have had no realization that he had done anything unusual for her in underwriting, within a period of eight months, long vacations in Europe and Florida. In only one of her many letters does she mention her brother's generosity, and this she quickly qualifies. The reference is in a letter to her cousin Neeta in which she says: "What he [Don] gives us we have more than earned and he thinks so. You know he is a big-hearted child."

Through the process of assumptive thinking, one of my sources has arrived at the conclusion that Marquis was "probably repaying" Maud for "something"—unnamed—she had done for him in the past. There is no evidence to support this; but there is ample evidence that she had been a burden to him during most of his adult life.

Nev, because she was easygoing and unfailingly cheerful, was mistakenly thought by some to be phlegmatic. These people were unaware that only a few days after Reina's sudden death that gracious soul had been shocked and dismayed to the point of tears when her sister announced her intention of spending the winter in Florida, offering her brother no help in this crisis. To make matters worse, Agnes, the domestic on whom Don had relied for years, was too sick to work, which, she thought, might result in an alteration in Maud's plans for an early departure. But Maud was a woman with a fixed idea: to get to Florida; and she took off for the South with a harrowing account of the aches and pains that would respond only to a warmer climate.

It will be recalled that Don and Marjorie were married February

2, 1926. A few weeks later—on the 28th of that month—we find Maud writing to her cousin Neeta from Florida:

"Much water has passed under the bridge since I last wrote you. . . . I have been living in a mental haze. . . . You may have heard that my brother is married again. I knew before we sailed for Europe that he intended this. You can imagine how I felt over it for it meant taking Barbara away from us and into an environment that I do not like, for the woman has two children of her own. I determined not to let it mar my trip but it did make a difference nevertheless. Now that it has happened I really feel better. You know you can't live with tragedy forever. . . . In the meantime my sister and I are to live in Forest Hills. Barbara is with her father in town but we hope will be with us often."

In this letter Maud, who did her own housework until she decided that leaning on her brother was easier than teaching school, complains bitterly about "the everlasting servant problem."

In that same communication Maud reported many other things, including the following: "Don is now bending all his energies toward getting enough support, financial and otherwise, to produce his play 'The Dark Hours' next fall. The Rev. John Marquis, the one you told us of when you were in New York, has made Don's acquaintance. They have become quite good friends. The Rev. likes the play and is using his influence to get his friends behind it. Augustus Thomas and other old veterans of the stage think it will be a sure-fire sort of a thing. But one never knows. . . .

"There will be no chance of your ever seeing us as a family any more. We will have to be taken in scattered segments now.

"Before this marrying mania struck Don he had intended taking us all over to England, had even made some arrangement about a house. I am not, as they say, 'crazy' over living with my relatives beyond my sister. That is not always exhilarating but it is something I am used to, like a bunion. It doesn't hurt all of the time." Maud's appraisal of Nev, who had done so much for her, as more or less of a necessary evil, would have dismayed Don—just as the bunion analogy, an adaptation of a passage from one of his short stories, would have amused him.

In one of her rare enthusiastic moments, Maud had this to say about her European vacation: "It is hard to communicate the joy that one gets from seeing what I did." While Maud was enjoying this and other trips, her brother was systematically overworking, passing up vacations in the process, in order to meet his obligations without cutting into his surplus any more than necessary.

Poor Neeta Marquis! Teaching was also her career but, unlike Maud, she worked at it. In her spare time she did a little writing and sought Maud's advice from time to time. It will be recalled that the latter had secured her brother's permission to adapt archy and mehitabel for the motion-picture screen. This had deluded Neeta into the assumption that Don thought Maud had writing ability, so she sought her cousin's advice on her manuscripts, which Maud had a knack for losing irretrievably. In that same letter she announces, apropos a "scenario article" that Neeta had sent her for criticism: "Something happened to it before I got to read it. I laid it down and never could find it again. My room is the dumping place for everyone's things. It takes me an hour every morning to pick up garters, shoes, etc., etc. I'm so sorry. I don't suppose you have another copy, have you?"

Nothing ever came of Maud's scheme to make a motion picture of archy and mehitabel. When Clive Weed criticized Marquis for ceding these valuable rights to his erratic sister, Don declared that as far as Maud was concerned, he was a peace-at-any-pricer—a prelude to his familiar argument that if you behave like a jellyfish in such matters you at least have the satisfaction of saving wear and tear on your vocal cords.

Don and Maud, before they stopped exchanging views on the subject of writing, frequently disagreed on what was and wasn't funny. In that same letter—a long one—Maud refers enthusiastically to a talk she had heard in which the speaker gave "a highly humorous account of his experience with a convict at San Quentin." The "experience" is so vaguely described it is hard to say whether it was "highly humorous" or another example of Maud's capacity for finding humor in subjects and situations—speech defects, for instance—that her brother habitually avoided.

That same year—1926—saw the publication of the playscript of *The Old Soak* in New York and London in Samuel French's Standard Library of the Theatre. As recently as January 1960 I was able to buy a copy at the office of the publisher in New York. There were only a few dozen copies left and they weren't sure whether this old stand-by would go into another printing. Inquiry yielded the information that over the years a great many theatrical organiza-

tions—amateurs, summer-theater professionals, etc.—had availed
themselves of the right to produce the play at twenty-five dollars
for each performance.

Marquis had been the victim of more practical jokes through *The
Old Soak* than anything else he had ever written, and now this
phenomenon started anew. Faking his signature, one of Marquis's
friends autographed a copy of the play and sent it to one of the
clergymen whose fire it had drawn when it was running at the
Plymouth Theatre. This cleric sent Marquis a blistering letter saying it was bad enough to flout the law of the land (Prohibition)
but that it was in bad taste and needlessly provocative to add this
kind of taunt. Marquis deplored what he considered a bad joke
and sent the clergyman a letter of explanation and regret. It was
another example of how even those close to him did not always
read Marquis's mind correctly. In explaining why he disapproved of
the prank he remarked that he didn't believe in "rubbing it in."

Another friend sent Marquis a letter, on stationery invented for
the purpose, purporting to come from the pastor of a small suburban
church. The alleged author of this letter called Marquis's attention
to "deliberate distortions of Holy Writ" in *The Old Soak*, citing
as examples of the recklessness of his perversion of the Scriptures
such passages as the following:

"The Good Book says to beware of the bob-haired woman, for in
the end she biteth like a serpent and stingeth like an adder."

"The Good Book says for the weary husbandman to toil not, neither
for to spin, for all such is vanity, vanity, vanity, and vexation of the
spirit."

Marquis, thinking the letter was genuine, sent a reply to the fictitious clergyman in which he explained that the garbled quotations
were merely a comic device; and when his letter was returned with
a notation on the envelope that there was no such person at that
address he knew that the pranksters were at work again. But this
time he enjoyed the joke.

Marquis was an occasional contributor to *Collier's*. The magazine
had tried, without success, to get him to contribute regularly. When
Charles Colebaugh, managing editor of *Collier's*, learned that Gertrude B. Lane, editor of the *Woman's Home Companion*, was a
friend of Don's, Colebaugh tried to accomplish his purpose through
her. She wrote Don a letter to which he replied on March 12, 1925.
His letter, made available through the Manuscript Division of the

Library of Congress, is typical of the airiness with which he put off
editors:

Dear Gertrude:

I certainly will come in and see you,—not because I am doing some
work for Collier's, which I am not, but because I want to see you.

With regard to the work for Collier's, I have been intending to do it
for at least a year and there must be a considerable portion of Hell rejoicing
in a new pavement. And yet they say, 'While Hell is paved with good intentions, Heaven is certainly not canopied with bad ones.' I say, 'they
say,' but as a matter of fact this epigram is my own and I print it at
least three times every year and have for the past ten years.

That letter was written about six months before Marquis resigned
his job as columnist for the New York *Herald Tribune*. A year and
a half later the expense of running two households made itself felt—
the one in New York and the one in Forest Hills—and from then
on, and with stepped-up frequency for a period of seven or eight
years, he appeared often in *Collier's*. In fact, when Colebaugh asked
him to revive archy and mehitabel, those characters and their raffish
companions began appearing regularly in that weekly. Christopher
Morley subsequently called attention to the fact that they proved as
popular there as they had in the *Sun* and the *Herald Tribune*.

Marquis established his office on the first floor of the brownstone
at 125 East 62nd Street in the room facing the street. He and
Marjorie adhered to their original plan to use for themselves and
the children the first and third floors as well as the ground floor
(referred to as "the basement" in the papers covering the sale of
the property) and to rent the second floor. They planned to advertise
its availability in the classified advertising columns of one of the
newspapers but it became unnecessary to do so. Ethel Barrymore,
who had been living in a hotel and had wearied of hotel life, heard
that the Marquis apartment was available and asked Marjorie, with
whom she was acquainted, to show it to her. (She had also met Don,
having been introduced to him by her brother John. Marquis and
John Barrymore were good friends.)

A few days later Miss Barrymore, having inspected the apartment,
declared it satisfactory, and a mutually agreeable rental was fixed.
The apartment was unfurnished at the time. Miss Barrymore
indicated that she wanted to rent it furnished and the transaction
was worked out in those terms. Miss Barrymore moved in and Marquis became a landlord for the first time in his life.

Marquis had writing commitments calling for articles, short stories, and books. He had also promised a Broadway producer a sequel to *The Old Soak*. He claimed that it took him time to adjust to new surroundings. Moreover, having been on a payroll for more than thirty of his forty-eight years, he had not yet adjusted to the idea of being a free-lance, a man who was his own boss. He had been operating on this basis only a little over a year and he claimed he had a lot to learn about bringing the whip down on his own back.

Several times he mentioned conversations with himself that went something like this: "See here, Don, you've got to stop stalling. Now that you no longer have a daily column to write there is no reason why you shouldn't write the great American novel, the great American play, and about a dozen great American short stories. . . . Put down that newspaper. Never mind F.P.A.'s column. Read it when you're through working. . . . See that typewriter over there? Well, park your big broad bottom in that chair and address yourself to the keys. If you hit the right ones often enough you'll have something to send to the market-place. . . . Don't ease up just because Miss Barrymore has moved in at a respectable rental. You still have loads of expenses. Maud knows how to spend money, and Nev is beginning to learn. There's that check you're committed to send them monthly—no small item. And with three children and a wife to support, and the people who've grown accustomed to borrowing from you an ever-present problem, you'd better bestir yourself. . . . That's better. . . . You're now bending over the typewriter, deep in thought. Good. . . . Now don't jump up to get another drink of water. You're water-logged now. . . . That's better. . . . Keep typing." This was merely an adaptation of a piece he had once written for his column describing Donald Robert Perry Marquis at work.

Marquis finally got down to working hard as a free-lance. He said he kept himself going with bribes, promising himself lunch at the Players if he had a productive morning—and perhaps an hour or two at the pool table before he returned to his typewriter. And he still dropped in at the Club for dinner, though not as frequently as in the past. He had told Marjorie about the Players Club before they were married, had mentioned that he had friends there whose company he enjoyed, and she had delighted him by declaring that these friendships must not be neglected. Besides, this would give her more time to keep in touch with her friends in the theater. She planned to return to the stage and there was no substitute for maintaining your contacts with people in the profession and thus assuring yourself of being *au courant*.

Little Barbara was a precocious child; her thoughts sometimes startled those around her—but there was one subject on which her thinking was uniformly predictable: Don Marquis. She loved her father and it never occurred to her to question anything he did. When it came time for her to move from the house in Forest Hills to the one in New York she accepted it matter-of-factly; it was her father's plan, so it must be right. He had told her that she would like her new mother, and if she had any doubts about this, she gave no sign.

Marjorie Marquis was a kindly woman who knew something about children, having raised two of her own. She knew that she must do nothing to favor, or even seem to favor, her own son and daughter—Walter, Jr., between five and six, and Ruth, nine or ten. She wisely decided that before any of the children were assigned to rooms, Barbara should have first choice.

Marquis's daughter thought the matter over carefully and selected a room overlooking the back yard (referred to also by the family as "the garden" or "the court"). Barbara loved dogs, her father had promised to buy her one, and she had decided that the back yard would be the ideal place for it. When she wanted to leave the dog in the garden she would be able to watch it from the window facing that enclosure. The room she picked was a large, cheerful one, with plenty of room for her things and ample space for a romp when other children visited her.

Aunt Nev had been like a mother to Barbara ever since Reina's death and the child might have had a tearful parting with that warmhearted woman if her father had not reminded her that Forest Hills was only a short trip from New York, and Aunt Nev and Aunt Maud—for diplomatic reasons both had to be mentioned—would visit her from time to time and she would visit them.

From all accounts, Barbara got along well with the Vonnegut children. There is general agreement that they had been carefully reared and had "good manners." Marquis had been quoted as saying that they "knew how to seem impressed with adults" but that, like the normal, healthy youngsters they were, they bubbled over with fun and were good company for Barbara who, as she neared her eighth birthday, was showing a tendency to be more bookish than her father wanted her to be at that age, and not enough interested in games. He even once expressed the hope that she would develop a mischievous side, which would give her a better understanding of the pranks of other children.

Ruth Vonnegut was a little too old for Barbara, Walter, Jr., a little too young, but nevertheless the three managed to have good times together—in the back yard or in the house, whichever they chose to use as a playground. Like all children, they had their quarrels but only Aunt Maud took these seriously. When the tiffs were over and the trio were happily playing together again, they never could quite remember what had started the trouble.

Aunt Maud had heard Barbara, in a moment of pique, tell how Walter enjoyed teasing her, and, with spinsterish determination, had tried to make an issue of this, but Marquis discouraged that combative woman's efforts to act as his daughter's champion.

Marquis figures in many an anecdote involving life at the Players during that period. His old friend Lawton Mackall, for instance, reports the following in a letter:

"One evening at a table for two alongside the veranda rail overlooking Myrtle-the-Turtle's pool, Don and I both ordered cherry pie. The first mouthful of mine yielded a pit, which I parked on my plate. Presently, Don had a similar experience, crying: 'Ha! Even with you! We've got us a game here. What do you say to fifty cents high man?'

"We went at it like Forty-Niners out for nuggets, Don ending up with a row of three, I with one.

" 'Good game,' said Don pocketing my fifty cents. 'We should play it more often.' "

There are many other anecdotes about Marquis's bent for making small bets on amusingly unimportant propositions. For instance, one day he and Clive Weed were standing at the then well-known long bar of the second floor of Charlie's on West 54th Street, a speakeasy patronized by an assortment of people connected with newspapers and various aspects of writing and publishing—and among them Heywood Broun, Floyd Gibbons, Clare Briggs, Frank Buck, Ray Long, Courtney Ryley Cooper, and Albert Payson Terhune.

Don, noting what people were drinking, said to Clive, "I'll bet you a dollar that two of the next three orders are for martinis." Clive took the bet.

At that moment four or five known martini drinkers stepped from a nearby table to the bar. Marquis laughed. "Kiss your dollar good-by," he said to Weed. It was Weed's turn to laugh when these mar-tini men switched to Scotch. They had overheard the bet and thought it would be fun to put one over on Don who, as he paid off Clive, re-marked that it was a sad day when a man was double-crossed by his bosom—beg pardon—boozin' companions.

It was during this period that *The New Yorker* was experiencing its early struggles. It had been operating less than two years when its editor, Harold Ross, in a chance meeting with Marquis at the Players repeated an earlier offer he had made the latter, whose work he ad-mired and wanted to publish.

According to Lawton Mackall, who witnessed the encounter, it developed into a kidding match, Marquis representing himself as an indigent author with three wives and a dozen children to sup-port. Now that he was no longer on a payroll, said Don, he had to get more money for his work than Ross could afford to pay. (It was well known in writing circles that the editor of the new magazine had a sharply limited editorial budget.)

Ross deplored Marquis's placing money above prestige and said that since he was dealing with a mercenary he would raise his price to twenty-five cents a word. "How about it?" he asked.

Marquis deliberated for a moment, then said, "We can do busi-ness but I can let you have only one word as a starter. Got a quarter?" Ross produced one.

Marquis, pocketing it, said, "Thanks."

Ross threatened to see his lawyer. Marquis maintained he had let him off easy. If he'd wanted to be greedy he could have offered Ross *two* words as a starter: "*No*, thanks." *That* would have cost the editor *fifty* cents.

Mackall's story calls to mind a letter I received from Frank Sul-livan, dated February 24, 1960, in which Sullivan, one of the oldest contributors to *The New Yorker*, and an authority on that publica-tion, says: "I wonder why Don Marquis never wrote for *The New Yorker*," and then tries to answer his own question.

"I should have thought he [Marquis] would have been one of those writers Ross would have coveted dearly. Maybe Don didn't want to. I can't believe Ross didn't want Don. Ross was too good an editor to overlook him."

Occasionally an anecdote of a more serious nature turns up. Sitting around with some friends one night, Marquis was asked if he had

had many restrictions imposed upon him during his days as a newspaper columnist. He replied that there had been virtually none—a
few on the *Sun*, none on the *Herald Tribune*. He said that people
commonly thought that a conservative newspaper like the *Herald
Tribune* would be inclined to be overcautious but such was not the
case. He cited a paragraph he had once written about the elder Henry
Ford that might have been killed in many a newspaper office since it
dealt with a touchy subject, Mr. Ford's anti-Semitism. The *Herald
Tribune* published it exactly as he had written it.

This story aroused my curiosity. After determining, through newspaper records, the approximate years during which Mr. Ford was a
controversial figure for the reason given, I started combing Marquis's
columns in an effort to find the provocative paragraph to which he
had alluded in that conversation. The following, from his column
dated November 20, 1924, would seem to be the item in question:

"Mr. Henry Ford's anti-Semitism, while it may never elect him
President, will always keep him from putting a longer nose on the
well known car."

One of Marquis's favorite topics in conversation with Christopher
Morley and other friends was the freedom he enjoyed as a columnist,
which is reflected in several things Morley wrote, including the following: "I have said before, the American press has much to apologize
for—more all the time with its increasing elements of what Lewis
Carroll called Uglification, Distraction, and Derision—but much can
also be forgiven when you think of the newspapers, the *Sun*, and the
New York *Tribune*, that saw Don's quality and gave him free hand."

Marquis was to learn that it was one thing to be a landlord and
another to collect the rent. Several months elapsed and he had not
yet received a month's rent from his distinguished tenant. He consulted Marjorie, who thought a friendly reminder slipped under the
door would get results. She was convinced that Miss Barrymore's
delinquency had no significance; undoubtedly the matter had slipped
her mind. People of the theater live in a world of make-believe, are
inclined to be absent-minded, and sometimes have to be jogged back
to reality.

So Marquis left a reminder for his tenant—a pleasant little note
that was said to be almost apologetic. To his astonishment she tore it
up and deposited the pieces on the floor outside her door.

Marquis was puzzled. When he and Reina lived in Brooklyn and from time to time found themselves a few months behind in their rental payments, they were never offended by dunning letters, usually peremptorily phrased; or by a rap on the door and a crude reminder from the janitor or some other representative of the owner of the building. The note he had left for Miss Barrymore couldn't have been more courteously worded, yet she had resented it.

A second reminder, a polite little note more or less like the first, elicited no response. Prose having accomplished nothing, Marquis decided to try verse and addressed this message to his famous tenant:

> Were I a wealthy codger
> You'd be a rent-free lodger.
> But since I'm not, Miss Barrymore,
> In case you'd like to tarry more,
> Please heed the message of my lyre
> And be a paying occupier.

Again there was no response.

Marquis decided to try personal solicitation. Miss Barrymore, it will be recalled, occupied the second floor. In order to leave the house she had to use the stairway that led to the first-floor's front door. Marquis used as his office the room that was directly to the right of that door. And when he kept his own door open he could hear everything that was going on.

One day Marquis heard Miss Barrymore close her door and start down the stairs. He stepped into the hallway and when Miss Barrymore saw him she retreated back to her room. This cat-and-mouse game went on for some time.

Once Miss Barrymore tiptoed down the stairs and was out the door before her landlord, preoccupied with a job of writing, had a chance to confront her. The humor of the situation appealed to him and it became one of his favorite topics.

A number of amusing side lights developed in the researching of this Marquis-Barrymore contretemps. A former *Sun* man, an associate of Marquis's in the "Sun Dial" days, reports having heard that Don sought the advice of Miss Barrymore's brother John, a fellow member of the Players. John is alleged to have commented wryly that, like all good Barrymores, Ethel hated to pay her bills; but that Marquis must persevere. According to this scuttlebutt, John is said to have predicted, "If she's badgered enough she'll pay, although she won't like it."

The situation was such common knowledge that at the Players members asked Don, "How're you making out with Ethel?"

One day Marquis, knowing from a message that had been left for his tenant that Miss Barrymore would be leaving the house at a certain hour, waited for her until she had almost reached the front door, then stepped out of his office and confronted her. There was something so ludicrous about the situation that he was compelled to laugh, Miss Barrymore breaking out into laughter almost simultaneously. "I completely forgot to ask for the rent," Marquis confessed afterward.

It is not known how the matter terminated. Did Marquis ever get his rent? No one knows.

Miss Barrymore moved out a few months later. The apartment was rented by John Dewey, celebrated philosopher, and Mrs. Dewey.

Bernard Sobel, publicity consultant to Florenz Ziegfeld and other famous producers, and author of many books on the theater, told me that Marquis's problem was an old story. He said that when Miss Barrymore lived at the Hotel Algonquin she frequently ignored her bills and had to be dunned with persistence before she would pay them. Frank Case, the proprietor, had told him so. "She was a great actress and a wonderful person on balance," he stated, "but she happened to have that failing." To understand the psychology of the Barrymores one has to read George S. Kaufman's *The Royal Family*. It throws light, however oblique, on the problem with which Marquis struggled as a novitiate landlord.

While it is not known whether Marquis and Miss Barrymore terminated their landlord-tenant relationship on an amicable note, it *is* known that he and John Barrymore continued to be good friends. In fact, if the Players Club ever appoints a historian he will have to weigh and consider many a Barrymore-Marquis exploit. For instance, the night John and Don visited New York City's Aquarium. Miss Edith McDonald, secretary to Marquis for five years, tells that story in a letter dated September 15, 1960, sent from her home in Atlanta, Georgia:

"I remember hearing Mr. Marquis talk about John Barrymore. He spoke very warmly of him and said that John Barrymore was the most charming person he had ever known, and quite unpredictable. One night when he had been at the Players Club, Mr. Barrymore and Mr. Marquis left together. John Barrymore decided that he wanted to go down to the Battery to the Aquarium and see the fish. Of course the Aquarium was closed, but they found the night watchman, and

Mr. Barrymore charmed him into letting them in and turning on the lights. They stayed for a while, discussing the specimens, and then took their way uptown. Perhaps some of the men at the Players will remember hearing Mr. Marquis tell about this, and can give you more of the details."

I tried to get "more of the details," as suggested by Miss McDonald. My early inquiries elicited nothing beyond inquiries from others, along this line, "I imagine they were plastered, don't *you?*" One can only hazard a guess. If they *were*, would the trusted watchman of a treasured city institution have let them in? Who can say?

Further probing turned up a story that has a reasonably good oral history. Peering hard at the display in which a phosphorescent fish was swimming, Barrymore is reported to have pointed dramatically and exclaimed, his voice echoing through the deserted exhibition area, "Ha! a kinsman! The piscatorus Barrymorus!"

Pressed for an explanation by the puzzled watchman, Barrymore allegedly replied, "Look! He's all lit up!"

It is no secret that Barrymore was known for his drinksmanship. So was Marquis, although his reputation in this field has been much exaggerated, due in large measure to his having created the nation's best-known lush, Clem Hawley, the Old Soak. Marquis was not the man to deny that he had done his share of tippling. He wrote about it freely, as the reader will recall. But he maintained that most of his "sincere drinking" had been done by the time he was nearing forty. Writing in the *Saturday Evening Post* about the characters he had created as a columnist, he said: "For me, Clem Hawley, the Old Soak, was the luckiest find,—Clem and his friends Al the Bartender, Jake Smith the Bootlegger, and so forth. I have got two or three books of prose and verse out of him, a dozen short stories, a play and a moving picture, and I discover even yet a certain public unwillingness to allow him to lapse into his ultimate alcoholic coma. Incidentally, he all but ruined my reputation. For a period of six years, after Lipton's closed, I never drank a drop; during that period the Old Soak was going strong in song and story, and it used to come back to me from every side that I was an old soak myself."

The indications plainly are that that *was* a dry spell . . . interrupted only for something very special like the arrival in New York of a former Atlanta newspaper associate or the need to lift a glass in celebration of an important birthday. Those six years he mentioned in the *Post* piece span the months when Marquis was traveling in Europe.

Hudson Hawley, former Paris correspondent for International News Service, who saw a good deal of Marquis abroad, told me early in 1960 that Don did not begin to live up to his reputation as a toper. "In fact," said Hawley, "he drank very little." (This was on the advice of his old friend Dr. Harry A. March and his fellow Player Dr. Richard H. Hoffmann.)

13 *Professor Marquis at Yale; or, Merriment on the Campus— Enter Howard Lindsay—The Stage-struck Days—The First archy and mehitabel Book—Maud Declares War on Marjorie Marquis— Two Views of the Latter—Acclaim for* The Almost Perfect State—*Spectacular Debut as a Dog Trainer— Christopher Morley and "The Marquis Semi-Centennial"*

Marquis, at a time when he was writing short stories and articles, assembling and editing the first archy and mehitabel book, working on still another book, *The Almost Perfect State*, and writing two plays simultaneously, surprised his wife, his friends, and himself, for that matter, by accepting an invitation to deliver two talks— the so-called Bromley Lectures—at Yale University. The invitation had come from a committee consisting of Professor Seymour, Chairman (Charles Seymour, later president of Yale), Professors Dudley, Tinker, and Johnston, and Secretary Hutchins of the University (later president of the University of Chicago). The unpredictable Marquis's excuse for dropping his antilecture rule was that this would give him a chance to mingle with young people, which, as a writer, he always found stimulating.

Correspondence with Carlos F. Stoddard, Jr., Director of Information of Yale University, yielded the following story from the *Yale Daily News* for May 18, 1926:

"Speaking before a large audience at Sprague Hall yesterday afternoon, Don Marquis, columnist and man of letters, told his listeners the reasons for his assertion that King Solomon was the first columnist of any repute. The lecture was the first of the Bromley Foundation, the fund for which was given by Isaac H. Bromley, '53, for many years an editorial writer on the staff of the New York *Tribune*.

"'I got so many inquiries as to the origin of the column,' said Mr. Marquis, 'that I finally began an investigation a few years ago. The results of my searching shows that the first columnist to emerge from obscurity was no less a person than Solomon himself, and I think we are lucky that so many of his wise and witty sayings and comments on life have been preserved for us.

"'He was in a sense not merely the father of his country but the father of the art of paragraphing. I imagine that Solomon really got more fun out of his job than any other columnist has ever gotten out of it since. He was in a strategic position. It was dangerous not to applaud, for Solomon was king in Jerusalem.

"'Those of you who are students of ancient journals and ancient journalism must remember that there were two pillars before the temple in Jerusalem. The right-hand pillar as you stood in front the temple and faced the street was called Jachin, and the left-hand pillar was called Boaz. When King Solomon after great cogitation in the midst of his hundreds of wives and concubines—and he was especially strong on matrimonial stuff and was probably the originator of the mother-in-law joke—produced a quip of which he was especially proud, he would have the wheeze graven right royally on a tablet of brass five cubits square and it would be stood over against the base of one of these columns that were before the temple.

"'If it were a serious, or poetic, or moralistic paragraph, it would be set over against the right-hand pillar, Jachin, and if it were a humorous one it would be set over against the left-hand column, Boaz. If the people saw something on Boaz they knew at once it was to be laughed at and so they laughed. In the course of time it became the custom in Jerusalem and thereabouts, when a man had made some especially witty remark to say, "Ha-ha, that is one on Boaz."

"'It sometimes happened that a Perrizite or a Hittite, newly from the provinces, would look upon the brazen plate set over against the pillar Boaz and wonder what it was all about. Then Solomon would indicate him with his scepter, and would murmur to the Captain of the Guard:

"'"There goeth one void of understanding; yea, a fool; he hath not an understanding heart. He is an abomination to my land. Shall there not be a rod for the back of him that is void of understanding? Yea, and an arrow shall strike him through the liver!"

" 'The Captain of the Guard was always a man chosen for his ability to take a hint without a kick, knowing exactly what to do without more conversation, and he would do it muttering: "Good understanding giveth favor; but the way of the transgressor is hard."

" 'I do not know whether you have the sort of woman in New Haven that is referred to in the quotation, "As a jewel of gold in a swine's snout, so is a fair woman which is without discretion." I do know that she is rather prevalent on Manhattan Island. Yes—when I was young and full of curiosity I used to see a good many varieties of her in the section of New York City known as Greenwich Village, and out of a combination of various individuals I made a character called *Hermione*, the modern young woman. *Hermione* knew a little about everything in the universe, but a great deal of what she knew was not true. Whether she was taking up social welfare, or the latest theosophic subtlety, or eugenics, or whatnot, she always vibrated in harmony with the Cosmic All.

" 'As for my first-hand knowledge of colleges, or the sort of lives that undergraduates lead, I must confess that I am totally ignorant. Most of my information has been gleaned from the perusal of various works of fiction. A few years ago I was familiar with the works of Owen Johnson. Currently, my information is gleaned from the opi of F. Scott Fitzgerald. From the latter's writings one is apt to gather that the Effort of Puritanism to reassert itself by the Prohibition amendment, for instance, has not been uniformly successful at our seats of learning—that is to say that there is an active minority —I trust it is a very small minority but my sources of information dwell upon its activity—who do not regard this renascence of Puritanism with the reverence which it deserves.' "

The following is taken from one of the letters graciously written by Mr. Stoddard, dated November 23, 1959:

"You may be amused at how sure I was that you were right in thinking that Don Marquis had appeared at Yale, if not in 1925 at least near then. Lucius Beebe, a member as I am of Yale '26, used to love to tease the great enthusiast and optimist William Lyon Phelps, our beloved Professor of English. If Billy Phelps liked a man, anything he did short of first degree murder was pardonable if not positively commendable. Don Marquis was at Billy Phelps' house during his Yale visit and, as so often happened in those Prohibition days, the talk turned to alcoholic beverages. Mr. Marquis is supposed to have said, 'Why, Mr. Phelps, I drink a bottle of brandy a day, and relish it!' And Billy replied—and this I can believe—'Bully for you, Don Marquis! Bully for you!'

"It became a byword among some of us in the Class of 1926, and it is still with a few of us. For example, if I am thinning out my woods, and hang one tree on another instead of cutting it so that it falls cleanly, there is no occasion for oaths. The obvious comment takes care of it: Bully for you, Don Marquis! Bully for you!"

The New York newspapers carried the story of Marquis's appearances at Yale. The following is culled from the piece carried by the *Herald Tribune*: "Don Marquis raised high merriment by pointing out the intellectual similarity between Solomon's column and his own. He recited poems comparing the warnings in the Songs of Solomon and his own."

The following day Marquis delivered his second Yale lecture. This item from the New York *Times* of May 19, 1926, tells the story:

"Good writing is agony to the writer, Don Marquis today told an audience at Yale University, lecturing in Sprague Memorial Hall on the Bromley Foundation.

" 'It is, isn't it?' he asked Professor William Lyon Phelps. Mr. Phelps agreed with him. Mr. Marquis, in telling of his work on The Atlanta Journal, half sobbed when he mentioned the name of James R. Gray, once editor of that paper. After recovering his poise, the speaker asked his audience to excuse him, saying Gray who is dead, was a personal friend of his.

"Mr. Marquis said the assertion so often made that newspaper policies are controlled by big business was 'all bunk.' He said that in his thirteen years as a columnist he had never been told what to write so long as he kept within the limits of sanity and decency. He said reporting was a good preparation for any kind of work, even dramatic criticism. He said his journalistic training had made it difficult for him to write leisurely, but it had been the best of training in helping him to think coherently and express himself intelligently."

Marquis, despite his heavy work schedule, found the time to write a great many letters in those days. He regarded sleep as "a habit most people overdo" and seldom spent more than six hours in bed. When the mood was upon him he returned to his old habit of working at night "when the household is asleep."

The letters Marquis wrote in those days were mostly gay. They were an outlet for his natural bent for ribbing, almost a substitute for the

spoofery forum his column had provided. Here is a typical one on
Players Club stationery to his friend George Middleton, well-known
playwright of that period, who had suffered an accident at an ocean-
side resort:

"The story going the rounds here is that in one of your periods of
helpless intoxication you were thrown out of a hotel and your back
hit upon a coral reef, injuring the coral reef and doing God-knows-
what to your back.

"My sympathy with the coral animals, who work so patiently and
obscurely to such great ends, leads me to hope that the reports have
been grossly exaggerated.

"Incidentally, I trust that the back is better, too. I have always admired your back—it is so long and architectural. It is a back that we
would all hate to lose."

Marquis had been joshed at the Players—by actors and others—for
his oft-repeated assertion that as a youngster he was stage-struck and
that he'd never quite got over it; that the only people he envied and
stood in awe of were members of the acting profession. His friend
John Barrymore once told him he didn't believe a word of it; that any
one with a lick of sense knew that actors were a lowdown, shiftless lot;
and that Don must have some ulterior motive for making gods of
them. Was he running for president of the Players?

During the summer of 1926 Howard Lindsay, who as actor, director, and playwright subsequently became one of the greats of the
American theater and whose achievements need no enumerating here,
decided to produce *The Old Soak* at the Lakewood Theater in
Skowhegan, Maine. He offered the title role to Marquis who, true to
his old declaration that he had the soul of a ham and had never
quite conquered his urge to be an actor, accepted.

I discussed these developments with Howard Lindsay at the Players Club, of which he is president. (Lindsay once said that he would
rather be president of the Players than President of the United States
and there is no doubt that he meant it. Being president of the Players
is much more fun.)

Lindsay, in harking back to Marquis's days as an actor, recalls that
Don had some vague notion that acting was a cinch, that all you did
was walk on and start talking. He was soon to learn that, in fact, it
was hard work. He also learned that he wasn't as familiar with his
own play as he had thought. In the four years that had elapsed since

The Old Soak had opened on Broadway, Marquis had become involved in so many other writing projects that the acting requirements of his hit comedy had slipped out of his consciousness, assuming he was ever aware of them.

Lindsay reports that, although Marquis studied hard, he found it difficult to remember his own lines—that is, in the presence of an audience. In many categories the man had a fabulous memory—Franklin P. Adams once called him his favorite Shakespeare concordance, and Will Rogers, Clive Weed, and Homer Croy as well as many churchmen had marveled at the impromptu appositeness of his quotations from the Scriptures—but there was something about that audience out front that made it a problem to remember lines he had repeated over and over again to himself until he could have bet they would never slip his memory. But elude him they did, reports Lindsay who, in addition to directing the production, played the part of Clem, Jr., the Old Soak's son. One night in a scene with Junior, Marquis, having forgotten his lines, remarked by way of conveying his predicament to his friend Howard, "At this point I don't know what to say to you, Son." It was a scene in which Clem, Jr., had sought his father's advice in a troubled situation. Lindsay, a resourceful trouper, managed to pull Marquis through the scene.

Lindsay reports that he and his associates took measures to make things easier for their author-actor. It was arranged that in one scene that gave Marquis trouble he was to carry in the palm of his right hand a slip of paper bearing the key words—typewritten—that would help him remember his lines. One night as he began to flounder he opened his hand and to his dismay found that the typed reminder wasn't there. His fellow players came to the rescue and somehow "carried" him. He got through the scene but he found it a nerve-racking experience.

Another device was a folded newspaper that Marquis carried in one of the pockets of his jacket. This represented him as the casual type who sometimes whipped out a newspaper during a conversation for a glance at the news and was very much in keeping with the character of the Old Soak. Pasted inside the newspaper, which he held away from the audience, were lines from the play that he had found it hard to remember.

Once, Lindsay said, Marquis strolled onstage and drew a big laugh from the audience before he had a chance to speak a line. It

developed that the fly of his trousers was most noticeably unbut-
toned.

During another performance when Marquis was onstage, one of
the crowded balconies in the theater started to break loose from its
supports. Lindsay reports that Don quickly took in the situation and
made a speech that calmed an audience that might otherwise have
panicked. Marquis tells this story himself in an article called "Stage-
struck" (*Saturday Evening Post*, March 5, 1930). Characteristically,
he is casual about his part in keeping that audience from losing its
collective head. In Lindsay's account of Marquis's coolness in quiet-
ing a frightened audience, the author-actor emerges as much more of
a factor in preventing a possible stampede than he does in his own.

If Marquis had lived to complete either an out-and-out autobiography or the egobiography—(he was experimenting with the former
and had more or less committed himself to the latter)—in all
probability he would have included "Stage-struck." It is quite possible that he wrote it with one or the other in mind. In a straight
autobiography he could have published it as written; and by trans-
posing it to the third person it would have fitted the formula of
the egobiography. It catches Marquis in a reminiscent mood on one
of his favorite topics, the theater, with which he became enamored
before the turn of the century, a love affair that lasted a lifetime. A
chunk of this article is here appended as basic Marquisiana:

"I was born stage-struck. I have had many years to get over it in.
But I can't. The stage to me is still the most glamorous thing in
human life. And nearly every actor wears a kind of halo. I've known
dozens, scores, hundreds of them; some of them I've known pretty
well—and still they're not like ordinary people to me.

"I can get used to novelists and poets and painters and sculptors
and musicians—I can even get used to playwrights—but the actor has
to take the most extraordinary measures to keep me from admiring
and envying him just simply because he's an actor. The glamor
clings.

"I know I can't act myself. I found it out by trying it. But even
now, at my middle-aged time of life, I'd rush from my cell with a
heluva yell and go on the stage, if I were not occasionally subjected
to restraint.

"In fact, once I did rush from my cell. Before the turn of the century, it was. I was working on a little weekly newspaper in a country

town in Northern Illinois, and a touring repertory company came
into the office one day and blew up right in my face.

"I was, at the moment, kicking off some dodgers on the job press.
The manager of this rep outfit—a burly, fat man he was, just simply
full of vocal cords—had come in to get some handbills printed and
a notice in the paper, and his troupe had followed him, wanting to
know querulously why they hadn't been paid. A terrible question to
ask anybody. The altercation reached its height right beside the job
press where I was standing with my mouth and ears open, and in a
few hundred well-chosen phrases the company resigned and were
fired.

"Only the fat man's wife and another lady stuck to him—I suppose they couldn't think of anything else to do. He sat down and
mopped his fat and troubled head until the external friction stirred
up an idea inside it.

"'Horace,' he said to me—and to this day I don't know why he
called me Horace, but I liked it better than Rube or Giles, which
people from the great outside world were apt to call me in those
days—'Horace, don't you tell me that there isn't a home-talent dramatic club in this town!'

"He'd nicked the mark; there was. I was—need I say it?—one of
them, specializing in bucolic comedy and low villains. He got us together; he gave a home-talent show with us and the two actresses
who had stuck, for the benefit of something or other and—

"Wonder of wonders! Ambition of my youth! He told me I could
act! He was a fat liar, but I believed him. Four or five other youthful inspired hicks like myself credited the same mendacious statement about themselves—oh, how readily! He organized us into a
traveling company!

"Napoleon never felt any more swell-headed after crossing a
bunch of Alps or kicking a scuttleful of kings off his front doorstep
than I did when I became a professional. An actor!

"This beautiful dream lasted just ten days, and we got as far
away from my home as the third village down the branch line of the
railroad before the company busted up again.

"I got home in a box car and asked mother if there was anything
in the ice box.

"We played several plays. I remember but one of them. It was
called *Tony the Outcast*, or *The Convict's Daughter*, and I played
James Barclay, the villain. I had a little black mustache, which I

twisted, and riding boots, which I assiduously switched with a riding whip. At the end of every act I rushed at the hero, pulling a dirk, and he pointed a revolver at me, and I dropped the dirk and slunk off, cursing, left upper entrance.

"The experience was not utterly wasted. The sort of wholesome American sentiment which dripped from this play always appealed to me; it appealed to audiences. There was a mother in it; there was a sweet daughter in it; the noble outcast was not all bad. I learned lessons from it. Twenty-five years later I wrote a play called *The Old Soak*, which had the same sort of wholesome sentiment, and a mother, and a daughter, and an outcast who was not all bad—and I made about seventy-five thousand dollars out of it.

"People have always liked that kind of play, and they always will. They like it better nowadays when the Russians do it, but it has always been the same play, and it will always go. Critics change—they tell people what they should like—but there are only three or four kinds of plays. The movies have this sort of thing in ten thousand theaters at the present moment.

"There was one pathetic incident about this little traveling company, although at the time I did not realize how dreadfully pathetic it was. With the thoughtlessness and inexperience of youth, I thought, at first, that it was funny. One of the professional actresses who had stuck with the manager had the longest, thinnest, boniest neck that was ever on a human being; you would have thought her father was a giraffe and her mother an ostrich.

"The manager, out of the wreck of his fortunes, had retained a veteran feather boa. It was molting, it was scrawny, it was all but bald, but still it was a boa. No matter what the scene was supposed to be—outdoors or indoors, summer or winter—he insisted that the actress wear this feather boa, wrapped twice around that remarkable neck to mitigate, in so far as it was possible, its incredible length and boniness. The poor woman resented it, and would get onto the stage without it if she were not closely watched, whereupon the manager, stamping and puffing in the wings, would cry out, cursing: 'Damn that woman! She's chucked her boa again!'

"I realized later that the girl was dying on her feet—and keeping her mouth shut about it, too, with the unconquerable gameness of the dedicated trouper. For, take them all in all, actors are the gamest bunch I've ever come in contact with. The real trouper gives the last atom of his strength to the show; no matter what's happening inside himself or off stage somewhere, it's the show with him, the performance, the intangible, inexpressible, ephemeral thing that he has lived for and that has led him on.

"This experience didn't cure me. A few years later I was working as a cub reporter in Washington at the princely salary of fifteen dollars a week, still stage-struck. Otis Skinner, who I thought then and who I still think is one of the best actors America ever produced, was in town. The dramatic critic of the paper saw Mr. Skinner in my behalf and Mr. Skinner said to send me around—he would give me a tryout; I could be assistant property man, and walk on in one of the scenes. If I made good walking on, maybe before long I could have a line to speak.

"I was elated. Life seemed to be opening up, indeed. But one of those things came along—the very same day!—that change the entire course of a man's life. The city editor called me to his desk and informed me that my salary on the paper was to be raised to eighteen dollars a week—in those days they used to look twice at a whole five-dollar bill before they hung the entire sum onto a reporter's salary every week.

"I pondered. The stage? Or literature? A couple of years previously I would not have hesitated a moment. But I had grown wiser—cynical, if you will have it so. I was at the parting of the ways. I realized it. Finally I said to myself, 'I guess I'd better stay where the big money is,' and took the eighteen-dollar job. But with this mercenary choice, a kind of bloom left my youth; I've never been the same ingenuous, artistic spirit, since.

"Ten or fifteen years later, when I met Mr. Skinner, he had forgotten this transaction—an actor has so many things to think of—and he didn't realize how he had let the lure of gold drag from the drama one who might have been——

"But maybe not. In fact, not.

"Just two or three years ago, I rushed from my cell once more. There's a stock company up at Skowhegan, Maine, that attracts some of the best actors in New York every summer. They have a pretty good vacation up there, and act and try out plays at the same time. I've seen shows put on up there with all-around casts so good that the average Broadway production couldn't compete with them.

"They played *The Old Soak* the summer I was there, and I played the leading part. The rest of the cast were experienced New York professionals, but they all happened to be personal friends of mine, and they helped me through. . . .

"But during that one week when I played the Old Soak as many things happened to me as happen to the average real actor in a couple of years experience.

"The second night I made a bust. There's a scene in the play where the chief character represents by pantomime that he is suffering terribly for a drink of some alcoholic beverage. After some moments of this, he has the despairing line: 'And yet, they say there's a lot of good stuff coming off these here foreign ships.' It never got much of a laugh—there isn't anything in it. That afternoon I heard that some prominent local man had come over from Canada with a few bottles of whisky in a new car, and that dry agents had taken the whisky from him and confiscated the car as well. So that night, when I came to the line, I read it: 'And yet they say there's a lot of good stuff coming in from Canada in these here cars.'

"The shout of laughter that went up exceeded anything I've ever heard in a theater. It all but knocked me over. And it kept on and on. It stopped the play, and grew and grew.

"When I got off the stage, there was the manager waiting in the wings, and he was wringing his hands and I believe—or else it was something about the lighting effects—that he was sweating blood.

"'That man,' he moaned, 'is my principal financial backer in this amusement enterprise, and he's out there in front now with a theater party! I'm ruined! I'm ruined!'

"But I saved him. I told him the line was in the script, and before I went to bed that night I fixed up a script with the line in it, so that he could show it to his backer if necessary.

"The next night I got one of the real jolts of my life. Robert Hudson, a most resourceful and distinguished actor, and I were on the stage together. It was about twenty minutes before the end of the play. Suddenly, from the darkened house in front of us, there was a loud crash, and then another and another. One of the crowded balconies, we could see, had started to break loose from its supports.

"There was a scream from the balcony, and a half-grown girl tried to throw herself over the balcony railing into the orchestra. A man caught her by the legs as she jumped and hauled her back. There were screams and cries and the beginnings of a panic from the body of the house.

"Then somebody had the presence of mind to turn on the house lights. But before they were turned on, I have never had such a moment of fright in my life—the audience was beginning to mill out there in the darkness. In another second that most dreadful of things, a theater panic, would be under way, with heaven knows how many people crushed and maimed and killed in the stampede.

"Hudson and I went down to the footlights and roared reassurance at the crowd—a reassurance which neither of us felt. The house lights came on and we continued to roar. We quieted them.

"The awful part of it was that we quieted them and reassured them too completely. With the house lights on, we could see what had happened to the balcony. It was a new wooden building. The balconies were hung to the wooden walls by long iron rods. These rods were secured by bolts. Some of the bolts had torn loose from the threads with the weight of humanity imposed—we found next day that careless workmen had put nuts a sixteenth of an inch too large over the threads at the end of the bolts—and the balcony had torn loose from its support and was sagging.

"We got most of the people to leave the sagging balcony, but as it did not continue to sag any farther, we could not get them all to leave. They were too easily reassured. And we played the last twenty minutes of that show with deadly terror in our hearts, for fear the balcony on the other side of the house, which was equally crowded, would tear loose and fall. The balcony was fixed up the next day, and the next night that courageous population filled the house again.

"There was something every night that week, and if I ever write the complete history of it I shall call it: Reminiscences of Fifty Years on the American Stage. For I lived at least that long between the first crash and the moment when we got them into their seats again —for half the people in the orchestra had risen and were shouting. Hudson and I literally bellowed them and bullied them down.

"The next week I almost ruined several performances of a show by Howard Lindsay and Bertrand Robinson by bad acting. I would have ruined it entirely if I had been on the stage oftener. It was during that week that I finally learned that I wasn't an actor.

"In spite of which, I keep right on being stage-struck. Don't anybody dare, even now, to offer me a part in his show. I'll take it, and I'll ruin his play for him.

"And one of the greatest thrills I get today is when Otis Skinner sometimes refers to me facetiously as 'my old property man.'"

In the foregoing, Marquis states that *The Old Soak* made $75,000, the reference apparently dealing only with the Broadway run of the play. In conversation with friends and in letters, etc., he gave higher figures—(usually in a jocular frame of reference in which he alluded to himself as the latest member of the *nouveau riche*)—the range being all the way from $85,000 to $135,000. Sometimes, as in "Stage-struck," he was confining himself to play royalties. Another time the figure was meant to take in the earnings of the play and his share of the rights to the first of two movie versions, a silent film. Another figure was meant to convey the total earnings of the property, which would embrace the short stories he wrote for national magazines based on the Old Soak's antics in his column, the play royalties (including the revenue from the many theater groups around the country that produced it, in summer playhouses, etc.), and Marquis's share of the silent film plus his cut of the subsequently produced "talkie" version featuring Wallace Beery.

Anyone familiar with the Marquis School of Accountancy, which was based strictly on guesswork, would be safe in saying that Don himself didn't know within several thousand dollars what his earnings had been from this property.

A special significance attaches to the passage in "Stage-struck" in which Marquis pays tribute to "the unconquerable gameness of the dedicated trouper," a quality he came to admire even in tenth-rate performers such as the bony-necked actress (of the feather-boa incident) who was "dying on her feet."

The middle-aged Marquis who wrote that piece was parting company with the younger Marquis who years before, in his war on what he then considered the stickier aspects of American folklore, had used as one of his targets the familiar shibboleth of the entertainment world, "the show must go on."

The earliest sign of this new philosophy came in a talk with Clive Weed after the death of Marquis's five-year-old son. In this conversation, which has a good oral history, Marquis said that he didn't realize how tough columning could be until he found himself trying to be funny in the period immediately following little Bobby's passing. This was the heyday of archy and mehitabel, the Old Soak, Hermione, Captain Fitzurse, Aunt Prudence Hecklebury, and others. He lived by writing humor, he had to keep these characters going and he did just that with the "unconquerable gameness of the dedicated trouper."

The reference to the death of Marquis's son calls to mind a letter that throws further light on Marquis in the role of "the show must go on" philosopher. It was written March 7, 1921, and was made available by the public-relations department of Knox College at the suggestion of Wade Arnold, Knox alumnus and Marquis enthusiast, who knew about it and everything else in the Don Marquis file in the efficient information service of that institution. The salutation reads, "My dear Mr. Whipple." Whipple attended Knox College, which is located at Galesburg, Illinois, at the time Marquis spent a few months there—before the turn of the century—and was editor of the paper published in Galesburg at the time Marquis wrote him. We find Marquis seeking Whipple's advice in the matter of squaring himself with Knox College, which was prevented from honoring him by Marquis's carelessness. Here is the part of the letter—a four-pager typewritten on the stationery of the New York *Sun*—that is pertinent at this point:

"I have a matter on my conscience. Last spring the President of Knox wrote me, and very kindly offered me the degree of Doctor of Literature. I was really quite touched by it; but I lost the letter. Then, when I found it again, I discovered that the date had passed—I had thought it June or July, and it was May or June. I didn't know what the hell to do; so I didn't do anything; it looked like an awful slam at the college. Then I told Albert Britt about it. He said he would write for me and fix it up—fix it so I could write and explain. He wrote, giving me another chance to square myself . . . but I never wrote. In July of last year I had a nervous smash, with heart trouble, and nearly died. I have been coming out of it slowly ever since; there has been illness and death in my family, and a part of the time I have had to do my work lying in bed and send the copy to the office; so I let everything else go. And those Knox College people aren't squared yet; I suppose they still think I am an ungrateful kind of boob.

"Queerly enough, I have a great deal of sentiment about Knox College; I was there only three or four months—maybe less than three months; I don't know. But for years previously I had been planning to go. And for five or six years after I clung to the hope that I would go back there. But that faded after a while.

"And then I said my son should go to that school that I had al-

ways wanted to go to. And that kept my sentiment for the place
alive. And now my son is dead. I planned to square myself with
the school, and go there and get the honorary degree, and maybe
take the little boy with me when I got it."

None of Marquis's surviving friends—including intimates of that
period—had any idea that he was seriously ill in 1920. It is known
that there was a time before and after his son's death when he found
it a struggle to write his column but a study of "The Sun Dial" as
published in those troubled days reveals no slackening of his "incorrigible mirth." This continuity of quality in a crisis was Marquis's
own contribution, conscious or unconscious, to the philosophy that
the show must go on.

Subsequently, in letters to Clive Weed—some of which are in
the fine collection in the Walter Hampden Memorial Library of the
Players Club—Marquis mentions disturbing medical reports but cau-
tions his friend not to repeat any of this information as "it would be
bad for business" if it got around that he wasn't well.

Marquis delayed in putting between covers the characters in his
columnar dramatis personae that have proved most durable over the
years. In 1927—almost fourteen years after his literary cockroach
and corybantic cat made their successful debut in the pre-Munsey
Evening Sun—archy and mehitabel was published. The book made
an instantaneous hit. It was the most enthusiastically received of
Marquis's humorous books and early sales indicated that it would outsell by a good margin anything he had previously published.

Marquis did not underrate his bizarre duo—he considered them
good characters—but he always seemed a little puzzled when they
were taken more seriously than his serious work. Invariably they
elicited the loudest and most prolonged applause and their creator
never quite understood it. Stories—a number of them—have been
handed down that stem from a Marquisism to the effect that "it
would be ironic if I'm remembered only, assuming I'm remembered
at all, as the creator of a goddam cockroach." This observation is
in much of the published biographical data. For instance, Louis
Untermeyer, in introducing archy and mehitabel to readers of his
A Treasury of Laughter, had this to say:

"Donald Robert Perry Marquis had more friends and was compared
to more famous figures than any other journalist of his day. Christopher Morley said that Marquis was 'a careful blend of Falstaff and

Napoleon III.' Benjamin De Casseres likened him to 'Shelley trying to lasso the Golden Calf.' The incongruities were ingrained in
Marquis's character. He was a schoolteacher, an actor, a reporter, a
rewrite man, a poet and playwright, always in revolt." Untermeyer
then suggests Marquis's disappointment over the response to "his
most ambitious work . . . whereas his lighthearted archy and mehitabel, a set of conversations between a cat and a cockroach, was
joyfully hailed. Marquis tried to be casual about it. . . . 'It would
be one on me if I should be remembered longest for creating a
cockroach character,' he said. Time has proved the wry statement a
truthful prediction."

Time, which has a way of changing its story, may yet accord Marquis's more serious efforts the recognition that Brander Matthews,
Stuart P. Sherman, Christopher Morley, Donn Byrne, William Mc-
Fee, Benjamin De Casseres, Frank Ward O'Malley, Franklin P.
Adams, Heywood Broun, and other of his contemporaries believed
they merited. In the meantime, the record supports Mr. Untermeyer.
The *archy and mehitabel* omnibus, published in 1950 with a lively
and perceptive introduction by E. B. White, has settled down to a
career as one of those perennial best-sellers, whereas Marquis's other
books are out of print.

It was interesting to learn that Marquis's cat and cockroach had
become well known in England in the late twenties and early
thirties, and that that hard-to-impress British editor, critic, and humorist E. V. Knox had devoted six pages to two archy and mehitabel
poems in his anthology of humorous verse published in London in
1950—a book which, though it covers less than three hundred pages,
goes as far back as Alexander Pope. Both pieces—"the spider and the
fly" and "cheerio my deario"—are from this first of Marquis's books
devoted to his celebrated duo. Marquis, though a modest man, liked
recognition, and would have enjoyed seeing these reminders of his
Evening Sun days, written in the hurly-burly of daily newspaper-
columning, in the pages of Knox's anthology in the company of
G. K. Chesterton, Hilaire Belloc, C. S. Calverley, Lewis Carroll,
W. S. Gilbert, Bret Harte, A. A. Milne, Mark Twain, and others
whose humorous verse he admired. He would have been excited by
the inclusion of Twain's "The Aged Pilot-Man," which he considered one of the great humorous ballads and which he thought was
not better known because the small amount of verse its famous

author had written was overshadowed by *Huckleberry Finn* and titles almost as celebrated. Having written that Tennyson lacked a sense of humor, Marquis would have been prepared to be spoofed by literary friends because of Knox's inclusion of a humorous passage from "Audley Court."

In the introduction to *Humorous Verse*, Knox, explaining his selections, described them as "excellent comedy." Since the judgments of critics and editors sometimes change, I decided to communicate with Mr. Knox and see how he felt about Don Marquis today. He promptly replied that he had no reason to alter his belief that Marquis was excellent comedy, then echoed a passage in his introduction conveying that he had originally found his selections "good company," and still did.

I am indebted to Mrs. Homer Croy for these additional British comments:

"Mehitabel is a divine creature." —Rebecca West in the *Daily Telegraph*, London.

"Mehitabel is the only cat I ever loved." —Gerald Gould, in the *Weekend Review*, London.

"It is inspired lunacy." —The *Herald*, Glasgow, Scotland.

"Don Marquis is a man of genius. . . . Archy rises to real greatness." —Edward Thompson, in the *Observer*, London.

That the interest in Marquis is still very much alive in England is evidenced by an advertisement in The London *Daily Telegraph* that appeared May 26, 1961, announcing the publication by the English house of Faber of an *archy and mehitabel* paperback.

The American reviewers of the first archy and mehitabel book had many favorites. One they especially liked was "mehitabel joins the navy," as recorded by her lower-case Boswell. Here are six of the nineteen stanzas that comprise this saga:

> a tom cat off a cruiser
> was seeing of the city
> says he between his whiskers
> hello my pretty kitty
>
> oh i am pure and careful
> in manner well instructed
> i ve seldom spoke to strangers
> and seldom been abducted

so i replied discreetly
ain t you the nervy guy
how dare you brace a lady
so innocent and shy

oh look he said our warships
have all their flags unfurled
oh come and join the navy
and we will see the world . . .

i would not desert the navy
nor leave it in the lurch
though each place that he took me
was less and less a church

and now the fleet is sailing
with all its flags unfurled
and five little kittens with anchor marks
are tagging me round through alleys and parks
but I have seen the world

In the peroration of this tour de force mehitabel ascribes her difficulties to her "maternal instinct." She tries to be a good sport about
the whole thing, her lone use of the word "church" being the only
hint (as she pours out her tale to her tiny biographer) that that tom-
cat might have had the decency to marry her.

That year—1927—Marquis had many projects on "the work-
bench," as he sometimes called his desk. One of them was *Out of
the Sea*, a poetic drama; another was *Everything's Jake*, a sequel to
The Old Soak. Nothing better illustrates "the incongruities ingrained in Marquis's character," to use Louis Untermeyer's phrase,
than his working simultaneously on a drama that stemmed from the
medieval romance of Tristan and Isolde (*Out of the Sea*) and one
that featured the humorous characters of *The Old Soak*. He gave
priority to the serious play, on which he had been working intermittently for over a year, and finished it early that spring.

Much of the news about Marquis that year is to be found in the
theater pages of the newspapers, where his name kept popping up
with regularity. He was now being referred to as "playwright and
humorist," whereas it had once been "humorist and playwright." Because he was being identified more and more with the theater, it
isn't surprising that he was asked by *Theatre Magazine* for a state-

ment for publication in a symposium on "the fundamental significance of the theatre." Here is Marquis's reply, dated October 10,
1927:

Mr. Perriton Maxwell, Editor,
Theatre Magazine,
2 West 45th Street,
New York City

Mr. Dear Mr. Maxwell:
Here are a few lines which I am glad to send you in response to your
letter of October 6th:

> The theatre has been, in all ages, one of the greatest of civilizing
> and cultural agencies. Indeed, it might almost be said that the era
> which has no theatre, or which has a dead theatre, is little better than
> dead itself intellectually. One of the most promising things about Amer-
> ica today is that it has a living theatre, a theatre that is liberated, a
> theatre that is open to experiment.

I'm afraid that isn't very much in the way of bulk but it is all I seem to
think of at the moment. If you can think of something really flossy that
I ought to say and that doesn't get me in bad with the Ku Klux Klan, the
Church of Rome, the Synagogue, the Masons, the Odd Fellows, the Baptists, Equity, and the Authors' League, just say it over my signature and I
will stand for it.

Yours cordially and sincerely,
Don Marquis

P.S. Dear Mr. Maxwell:
The above quotation is for publication; for your private ear I wish to remark—having two plays now ready to go into rehearsal and two producers
unable to cast them—that I think the American theatre is a lousy institution and I hope it chokes to death. —D.M.

The plays Marquis referred to in that postscript were *Out of
the Sea*, previously referred to, and *The Skinners*, a comedy
satirizing a then current craze which Marquis had used as a target
in his columning days: the wholesale quest for dukedoms—or what
have you?—by title-smitten wealthy Americans. Rich Mrs. Skinner,
having bought her daughter everything else, takes her receptive offspring on a title-shopping tour of Europe to look over the summer
and fall line of bluebloods—"not too second-hand or factory-dam-
aged"—from whose number she hopes to select the man best qualified to add "class" to the Skinner genealogical orchard by planting in
it a family tree of nobler lineage than the scrub maples with which
it is now overrun. Mr. Skinner, who claims he is color blind and

never could tell blue blood from red, reluctantly accompanies his wife and daughter and does his best—which isn't good enough—to thwart the title-mad duo. This theme was not a new one, Marquis having given it quite a workout in his column, and others having used it too, in one way or another. Nevertheless, William A. Brady, the producer, and his associates backed their judgment that Marquis had created something fresh by imparting to a familiar theme the stamp of his individuality.

The Skinners was given a tryout in The Playhouse, Mamaroneck, New York, where it was accorded program-billing as "a new comedy by America's great humorist." For reasons unrevealed, it closed after one performance, was not given another tryout, and never reached Broadway.

Marquis had alluded—humorously and more or less self-critically —to disagreements (which "hadn't helped" his career as a playwright) with producers in the interpretation of what he had written. Whether there was any such disagreement in the case of The Skinners has never been disclosed.

Out of the Sea was produced on December 5, 1927, and was unfavorably received by most of the critics. One of them dismissed it as "closet drama." Another praised the beauty of the text ("there was sweep and grandeur to much of the writing") but felt nevertheless that the components of Marquis's "poetic concept" did not add up to "a good evening in the theatre."

That ardent Don Marquis fan Franklin P. Adams made this entry in the section of his column he devoted to "The Diary of Our Own Samuel Pepys":

"With F. Sullivan to see 'Out of the Sea,' a Tristan and Isolde play done as of today by D. Marquis, but it had, I thought, only one interesting scene in it, and so I fell to thinking that many would say, 'Why does Don Marquis not stick to the humourous and satirickall manner he is so adept at?' and if he had written a comick play many would have said, 'Can he do nought but play upon his penny whistle?' Lord! let a man write what he himself likes, and the devil take what he thinks people will say of it!"

In those days Oliver M. Sayler wrote a weekly piece for the Saturday Review of Literature under the standing head "The Play of the Week." In a long review he defended Out of the Sea and attacked the direction of Walter Hampden. The following excerpts are typical:

"In the production of his first serious drama on the professional stage, Don Marquis has played in poorer luck than he did with his first comedy. While 'The Old Soak' had the advantage of the flexible and sympathetic stage direction of Arthur Hopkins, 'Out of the Sea,' a modern tragedy of the Cornish cliffs with subtle legendary implications, is the victim in the theatre of heavy hands, clumsy minds, and sterile imaginations. . . . 'Out of the Sea' . . . is a deplorable example of what happens to dramatic literature when the theatre falls short in performing its share of a sensitive and intricate collaboration.

"The play is not enough of a literary masterpiece to override inept interpretation and to register its intrinsic merit on the mind of the casual playgoer in despite of theatrical mayhem." Mr. Sayler then takes exception to "the verdict of a newspaper critic" that *Out of the Sea* is closet drama, and sums up as follows:

"The demand here . . . is for a supple recreative imagination . . . and a sure and fastidious instinct working by no rule except the pragmatic one of fulfilling the author's challenge at every step. . . . It is just that flexible stage direction that I find lacking in 'Out of the Sea.' Seemingly convinced that the play must be either out-and-out realism or supernaturalism, and apparently unable to make up his mind which, Walter Hampden has resorted to the most threadbare of clichés, now of one, now of the other. . . .

"The most disheartening aspect of such a theatrical casualty as this is its waste—waste of dramatic literature which truly lives only when the theatre rises to its challenge; and waste of acting talents, in this case talents of a superior order. Such waste is less frequent today than it used to be before we trained directors of skill, sympathy, and resourcefulness, but it is for that reason all the more inexcusable. When it happens, it points to the grave responsibility of the theatre toward dramatic literature. We have heard enough and to spare about the responsibility of literature to provide the theatre with worthy material. Why should it, so long as the theatre shirks its own responsibility?"

Sayler, in this unorthodox critique, did not hesitate to call attention to flaws he had found in the writing and structure of *Out of the Sea*. Having mentioned these, his verdict was that Marquis had written "a moving and authentic tragedy in poetic prose."

It was typical of Marquis that when asked whether he thought Hampden's direction had hurt the chances of his play, he should reply that he considered Hampden a great director and that he felt as he did when he gave William Weer "that interview." Among Marquis's papers—that part of the collection that reposes in the twenty-two large file boxes at Columbia University—I found the clipping of an interview with Mr. Weer dated November 22, 1927 (a few weeks before *Out of the Sea* opened). Unfortunately there is no identification on the clipping to indicate the newspaper in which it had appeared. Here are a few paragraphs from this story, which carried the headline WALTER HAMPDEN BECOMES DIRECTOR FOR DON MARQUIS TO KEEP HIM IN THEATRE, and totaled almost a thousand words:

". . . Don Marquis, the author, paid his respects to the magic of the most distinguished actor of the American stage in directing his play, the first time he had directed any production but his own.

"'When you have a play in script,' said Marquis, 'you have practically nothing. When you have the script in your hand and the cast on the stage, you still have nothing. It is then up to the director to make it all come to life, and that is what Walter has been doing, doing in many ways. If this is an artistic success, it will be because it has passed through the hands of Walter Hampden.' . . .

"Tall and spare, Mr. Hampden told why he had, in the midst of his own work in the star role of 'An Enemy of the People,' at the theatre named for him, undertaken to direct another man's play.

"'I did it for two reasons,' he said. 'Because, for one, it is a beautiful thing. There will be no play like it this year and there hasn't been anything like it for years. And, for the second reason, because this man Marquis is not only a genius, but an extraordinary man, with a beautiful deep quality underneath; and I want to keep him in the theatre. If he has a chance, he will do something enormous, and I don't want the theatre to lose him.'"

Marjorie Marquis, a dedicated Christian Scientist, persuaded her husband to attend church services with her and succeeded in convincing him that he should adopt C.S. as his faith. To this he agreed, devoting considerable time to reading and studying *Science and Health, Messages to the Mother Church*, and other writings of Mrs. Eddy, including articles that had appeared in the *Christian Science Journal*. This was at the time when Marquis was revising and editing the newspaper columns that became a book called *The Almost Perfect State*, in which he called for "more religion and fewer churches" and reaffirmed that creeds and denominations were not for him! In a situation of this kind the deciding factor invariably was his philosophy, "If she's fool enough to love you, treat her well, treat her well." His notion of treating Marjorie "well" was to do her bidding more or less blindly. Rollin Kirby thought his friend Don was meekly complying with too many things that didn't appeal to him and told his fellow Player, George Britt, that he considered Marquis "the most henpecked husband in New York." Britt, who was with the New York *World-Telegram* for years and wrote one of the most revealing of the Marquis interviews, reported Kirby's remark when I discussed Marquis with him. Another member of the Players reports that Marjorie made a practice of "editing" her husband's remarks when she considered them "unrefined," one of her favorite words, according to this informant. Fola La Follette and George Middleton, old friends of the Marquises, dispute this with vivid recollections of Marjorie responding to Don's Rabelaisianism with hearty laughter. Mildred Dilling recalls that when Marquis's language struck her friend as being too earthy she "toned him down" with a line that she kept handy for such purposes: "Remember, Don, you're not at the Players."

Since these clashing sources are all completely reliable, I believe— as do others—that Marjorie's reactions to her husband's earthiness varied, depending on whose company she was in. Where risqué language was acceptable, she accepted it; where it wasn't she did a little eyebrow-raising and protesting, her reproof being too mild to be branded as scolding.

This calls to mind Howard Lindsay's appraisal of the matrimonial situation in the Marquis household: "An Elizabethan married to a mid-Victorian."

Lindsay, without the slightest suggestion of religious bias, declared that Christian Science had had a tendency "to shrink Don's personality." It was "not his dish of tea."

Lindsay doesn't know how long Marquis hewed to the Mary Baker Eddy line but reports that when the humorist found that he couldn't quite adjust to Christian Science and gave it up, the twinkle returned to his eye and he was his old ebullient self again. A study of Marquis's correspondence and other papers, and conversations with some of his long-time friends, suggest that he was a practicing Christian Scientist for about a year.

Subsequently, in his egobiography, he describes his efforts "to find a religious label." In this chapter, written a few years after he had ceased to be a member of the Science church, he mentions that faith, in a discussion that embraces several. Here is an excerpt from that chapter:

"There are only two Christian denominations which Marquis has ever felt that he could connect himself with, the Roman Catholic and the Christian Scientist, and he grieves a good deal when he reflects how bitterly opposed these churches are to each other for he is so fond of both of them. M. does not see why he should not be a Roman Catholic and a Christian Scientist at the same time; but the fact is that if he joined one of these churches the other would not take him in. It is probable that their antagonism arises from the circumstance that they are 'working the same side of the street,' to put it vulgarly; they both traffic in miracle.

"For a good many years M. was prevented from attempting to join the Roman Catholic Church by the belief that when the wine and bread are blessed, in the celebration of the mass, they become actually, physically, and literally the blood and body of Jesus Christ, a miracle having taken place. It is not that M. finds it impossible to believe in the miracle; he likes to believe in miracles, and can make himself do it any time he wants to. The trouble is that it has always made him a little faint and qualmish when he thinks of actual blood and flesh being drunk and eaten like that; he believes too thoroughly in the possibility of this miracle, and shudders away from the cannibalism involved.

"And he never could be an out-and-out Christian Scientist on account of Mrs. Eddy's poetry; it is almost incredible that a woman so extraordinary in so many respects should have written such terribly bad verse, and should have been so contented with it. Wasn't there anyone connected with her church in its infancy who knew how bad it was, and could influence her to keep it out of print? Apparently not. It should be translated into Greek or Hebrew and printed in an appendix to her works, and left that way for a hundred years; and then it should be translated back into English by a real poet. Then it might be readable, and would not prevent earnest spiritual seekers such as Marquis from coming into the fold. The ideas in it are not original . . . just the kind of thing one finds in country weeklies in the South and Middle West, written by the local 'poetess' who probably sings in the church choir and teaches one of the lower grades in the village school.

"Of course, a more serious objection to Mrs. Eddy is her command to her followers not to use alcoholic liquor, tobacco, tea, or coffee; but apparently her followers have progressed beyond a serious consideration of these trivialities in the past quarter of a century; M. has drunk red liquor and smoked with a number of most agreeable followers of Mrs. Eddy, and has observed that women saints seem no more able to give up their tea than Episcopalians or Theosophists.

"M. was never much attracted to the Episcopalian Church, and he cannot for the life of him tell why; it has most of the forms that attract him to the Roman Catholic Church, and it grew out of the lust, fraud, carnality, hypocrisy, greed, and political necessities, superstitions, and conscientious scruples of Henry VIII. It should therefore be a very appealingly human institution; but to M. it seems never to have quite come off, somehow; perhaps it has always been so mixed up in politics that it has never had much chance to develop a spiritual side."

On July 10, 1927, Maud Marquis wrote her cousin Neeta in Los Angeles a letter which is remarkable for two things: its sustained inaccuracy in reporting what was going on; and her open hostility toward Marquis's second wife. Maud had never given Reina reason to believe that she could count on her, so Marquis's first wife never confided in her; but there had been little open hostility. Vis-à-vis his second wife, however, Maud wavered between a covert and an unconcealed antagonism.

That eventually Marjorie knew where she stood is supported by Miss Susan Prince, whose restaurant on 62nd Street and Lexington Avenue was patronized by the Marquises (whose brownstone at 125 East 62nd Street was just around the corner). This restaurant is at the same location today and is still operated by Miss Prince, who reports that when Don entertained his sisters there, Marjorie remained at home to minimize her exposure to Maud's snappishness.

Although the letter of July 10 is important since it illustrates one of Marquis's chief problems—the campaign his sister was conducting against Marjorie—there is no need of reproducing, describing, or analyzing *all* of it. In fact, to weigh and consider its entire content—more than eight closely written pages on fairly large sheets—would amount to spreading gossip which does not merit repetition. So I omit the letter's most lurid allegation and confine myself to examining Maud's secondary plaints. The following will do as a starter:

"I don't like to put myself down in black and white about Don's marriage but I am not the only one who thinks it was a calamity. They took Barbara in with them when they were married, a year ago last February. I went South and had nothing to do with their affairs nor knew how Barbara was getting along. Marjorie and her children had abundant opportunity to 'make good' with Barbara. Don was paying all the expenses of both the Vonnegut children, giving them an allowance for clothes and pleasure, seemingly they were all treated alike."

As to Maud's statement about her brother's second marriage, "I am not the only one who considers it a calamity," originally she *was*. Verbally and in letters she made her views known but she made only a few converts.

For some time a number of her brother's friends had thought it would be a *real* calamity for him to live under the same roof with the quarrelsome Maud much longer. One of them told me, "Some of us believed that Don had taken on too great a responsibility in marrying a woman with two children. But even so, our congratulations on his marriage were sincere as we knew it provided an escape hatch. The house on Wendover Road was too small to accommodate Marjorie and her children. It was Don's excuse for leaving Forest Hills and getting away from Maud, who ever since they began living together had had an upsetting effect on him. The lash of her tongue had thrown him off stride as a writer countless times. That statement of Maud's is crazy. Who were we to call the marriage a 'calamity?' Marjorie Vonnegut was an unusually attractive woman and she and Don were in love with each other. To describe a situation of that kind as a calamity would be pretty silly.

"If I wanted to undertake the role of Monday-morning quarterback, I would say that the chief thing wrong with that marriage was that neither party to it had any sense of money. Both were impractical. Don didn't have enough business savvy to point out to Marjorie the folly of buying a high-priced house in New York City without the advice and guidance of someone in the real-estate business. With all Don's contacts he could easily have turned up such a person. In a buyer's market they undertook to pay much more for the brownstone at 125 East 62nd Street than they needed have, assuming they needed the house at all. Apartments were plentiful at the time, and rentals were reasonable. Today it seems incredible yet it is a fact that in those days they offered you concessions of from one to three rent-free months to get you to move in. Marjorie's determination to have a house—her views on *that* subject couldn't have been firmer—made it necessary for Don to assume a heavier financial burden than he should have at a time when he was seeking freedom to write the things he really believed in and to do as little pot-boiling as possible. He should have been able to figure that out for himself; but, as you and I know, he was incapable of opposing one he loved."

Another friend of Marquis's asked that he be quoted anonymously (if at all) on the following: "The marriage of Don and Marjorie was a natural. He used to say that she was the only person he'd ever known who was more stage-struck than he; and what could be more fun than being married to a stage-struck wife? He was a stage-struck ham, she a stage-struck professional. Here was his chance to get free acting lessons. Don and Marjorie used to talk far, far into the night about plays, players, and the stage in general. He was enthusiastic about her views on how to impart a greater vitality to the American theater. She told him about the theater movement she and her ex-husband [Walter Vonnegut] had launched in Indianapolis. Walter's father, one of that city's leading merchants, had backed the venture, which Marjorie had originated, and a substantial financial loss had resulted. She was completely frank about that but expressed confidence that she could make a success of a similar undertaking— it was a sort of poor man's Theatre Guild—in a larger community.

"But there would have to be adequate backing. When she and Walter came to New York from Indianapolis they established a theatrical organization which they called 'The Stagers.' The idea was to put on several plays a year on a subscription basis—plays of a higher quality than the commercial theater presented. The Theatre Guild had established that the public would buy quality, Marjorie argued in defense of her venture, which was an early version of today's off-Broadway development. But the elder Mr. Vonnegut (then Indianapolis's leading hardware merchant) withdrew his support before the enterprise had a real chance and attempts to save it through backing from friends yielded insufficient capital. Don knew that part of the story as Marjorie's ex-husband had persuaded him to participate, though how much money he put up is not known. He agreed with Marjorie that the venture was a high-minded one and that it had died because of inadequate support, a philosophic view since it was known to have cost him several thousand dollars. Maud had got hold of this story somehow and had spread a wholly distorted version of it, her fictionized account investing certain aspects of 'The Stagers' with scandalous overtones.

"Frankly, my only concern about Don's marriage was based on his having promised to back Marjorie in another theatrical venture. There was no definite plan. Marjorie would wait for the right moment and Don would provide the cash. He spoke enthusiastically about this. His wife's two disastrous experiences in the theater didn't seem to faze him in the least. His reaction, as I recall it, was something like this: 'Now she knows what has to be done. Experience pays off. It's very much like the problems of an author. Because he happens to write a few books that don't sell, should he quit? Or should he, learning the lesson of his early mistakes, keep on writing? The answer is obvious. You've got to believe in yourself and give your luck a chance to change.' That was the gist of it except that he worked in some humorous touches.

"In those days Don's faith in Marjorie's knowledge of the theater —it subsequently changed—was complete. Once, in one of his clowning moments, he said that this talent of his wife's would be the road to liberation for him. As America's most successful producer, Marjorie would make the money that would enable him to sit home and write masterpieces, including a ten-volume sonneteer's history of the world. He figured this would take about 25,000 sonnets. It would, of course, be the world's longest sonnet-sequence, and would through sheer bulk so overpower the critics they would hail it as a deathless classic. Even through the clowning you could read Don's seeming belief that Marjorie's theatrical talents would meet with success some day. He never gave his faith lightly and when he did he stuck to his story.

"Frankly Don's attitude scared the hell out of me. Marjorie had no more business sense than he and didn't belong on the production side of the theater. Among other things, that takes a good business head, and Don and Marjorie didn't have one between them. She had shown promise as an actress and I was hopeful—as were other friends of Don's—that she would get over her impresario complex and confine herself to acting."

In that same letter of July 10, 1927, to her cousin Neeta, Maud Marquis wrote: "Barbara was the only one of the family who had an inside room, the rest had sunlight. She was on a court and away off to herself. Walter, Jr. (Marjorie's little boy) had his nurse and Barbara got the tag ends of care."

Barbara had been given first pick of the rooms and had selected the one she occupied because what Maud called a "court" was really a garden which the child preferred, as a view, to the street. Her father had advised her that this would be the best room for her. Now that she was a busy author—(she wrote poems and stories and sent them to *St. Nicholas Magazine*, which accepted one occasionally) —she needed a quiet room, Don reminded her. The room had as much exposure to the sun as the others but Maud had never been in it at the hour when that happened and had jumped to one of her typical conclusions. As to the nurse referred to, she looked after both Barbara and Walter, Jr.

Maud, in the same endless letter, tells of being "reviled for telling the truth" about the shabby treatment that was being accorded her niece. She does not say who did the "reviling."

All of which is by way of showing that while Marquis had improved his lot by putting a number of miles between himself and Forest Hills, his sister was still a problem and could be counted upon to foment trouble whenever the spirit moved her.

The pattern of Maud Marquis's letters and conversations—the ever-present chip on the shoulder, the willful distortion of facts, the permanent posture of maltreatment by a cruel, cruel world—aroused my curiosity. How does a woman get that way? What does it signify? I decided to seek a few psychiatric opinions. True, psychiatry cannot be regarded as an exact science, which the best men in the field are the first to concede; but ever since the twenties when I had the luck to meet and have a long conversation with one of Sigmund Freud's ablest interpreters, Alfred Adler, I have been impressed by the interpretations and recommendations of certain members of the psychiatric profession.

One of the psychiatrists consulted had approximately this to say: "Miss Marquis's letters, and the conversations you report as coming from reliable sources, suggest certain possibilities, some of them reliable, some not. One can arrive at a fairly clear conclusion as to the reason for this woman's hostility toward her brother's wives. She was a financial burden to Mr. Marquis during both his marriages. She seems to have been the type—at least the facts suggest it—who could have concluded that a wife would necessarily be hostile toward one who was cutting into the family income and have said to herself, 'Don's wife hates me, so I hate her.' Situations of this kind are not uncommon. It might never have occurred to Miss Marquis that there are plenty of wives who cheerfully accept a husband's decision to help a member, or members, of his family."

A second psychiatrist said, "As I try to piece the story together from these letters and conversations I see an emotionally disturbed woman, a paranoiac personality. Her own particular monomania stems from the constant belief that she is being deprived of something that is rightfully hers. For instance, let us take this passage from a letter in which Miss Marquis complains about Mr. Marquis's second marriage: 'So far as Barbara having gained a brother or agreeable companions, she has gotten two children foisted on to her father, thereby cutting in three parts her father's income. Whether he has awakened to what he has done I do not know.' If she had been genuinely concerned about little Barbara she would not have left for a winter-long vacation in Florida almost immediately after the sudden death of the child's mother. She would have changed her plans to enable her to help her brother—and a five-year-old child on the verge of collapse—through a devastating crisis.

"She expressed concern about the cost of supporting the children of her brother's second wife and the conviction that this was unfair to her niece. What she really meant was that it was unfair to *herself*. What she feared was that these new expenses her brother had assumed would make it difficult for him to provide her with as much money as he previously had for her various trips. Here was a woman who loved to travel, who felt she needed a change of scenery at regular intervals—you have described at least a dozen protracted vacations in Florida, California, and Europe—and who could easily have thought that what she considered rightfully hers was being jeopardized by the second Mrs. Marquis and her brood. Maud Marquis, a woman with a clearly indicated persecution complex, felt that she was being punished by a development—her brother's remarriage—that threatened the pleasures she had come to regard as routine."

I feel indebted to these psychiatrists—old friends—for their efforts to quicken me to thought on the antagonisms of Marquis's unmanageable sister. They became so interested in the problem that they kept requesting additional information about Miss Marquis; and eventually they had a completer picture of that tiresome woman than I have felt justified in inflicting on the reader.

To understand Marquis's problem in trying to make a living as a free-lance writer it is necessary to expose the reader to at least a generous sample of Maud Marquis's cantankerousness. When Don was on the *Herald Tribune* payroll at $20,000 a year, Maud's tantrums were not as serious as they were now when he was in his toughest battle against time. To meet his heavy expenses he had to get a certain amount of manuscript to the market place; and it was no secret that Maud's telephone calls—either of a whining or a combative nature—and the scenes she made in the role of Barbara's defender and champion, to the embarrassment of that poor child, who was doing her best to get along with her stepmother's children, frequently had a disastrous effect on her brother's work schedule.

Marjorie Marquis adopted a policy of avoiding Maud whenever this was feasible, a decision based on practical considerations. For one thing, in rough-and-tumble debate she was no match for her truculent sister-in-law. Disliking such exchanges, she virtually let Maud win by default (on those occasions when she could not avoid a confrontation). She regarded it as a waste of breath to defend herself against Maud's charge that she was not treating her husband's daughter fairly.

The intent here is not to present Mrs. Marquis as one who was "above the battle," or too saintly to have any of the familiar human frailties. Bernard Sobel, author of *The New Theatre Handbook, Oxford Companion to the Stage,* and other books about the theater, and who knew Marjorie (she was then Mrs. Walter Vonnegut) back in the days when she and her husband were in the throes of their theatrical venture in Indianapolis, recalls a situation in which, as he put it, "she wasn't quite herself." She and her husband, after their Indianapolis theatrical venture had failed, came to New York, where Sobel was visiting them in their apartment. Having previously seen only the gentler side of Mrs. Vonnegut, he was surprised to hear her criticize her husband sharply in his presence. That morning she had sent Mr. Vonnegut on a shopping mission—his assignment was to buy some sofa cushions—and when he returned she decided he hadn't done a good job. The cushions he had purchased, it developed, didn't quite match the sofa for which they were intended, and her displeasure was a bit too bluntly expressed, thought Sobel, an embarrassed observer of the scene.

(Sobel, by the way, recalls the then Mrs. Vonnegut as an excellent actress and an exceptionally good-looking woman.)

Homer Croy admits that he never felt "quite comfortable" in the presence of the second Mrs. Marquis. He found her "cold and distant."

On the other hand, George Middleton, Fola La Follette, Mildred Dilling, Edith McDonald, and others spoke glowingly to me of Marjorie Marquis. Middleton (and his wife, Miss La Follette, who always uses her maiden name) developed a great affection for her, describing her as kindly, capable, and the perfect mate for Don. Miss Dilling and Miss McDonald were as enthusiastic in their comments. A secretary who works for a man whose office is in his home, as Miss McDonald did, is in a position to appraise what is going on. She was outspoken in her admiration of her employer's wife. She had served as Marjorie's secretary before she took the job with Don, and had been treated so well that when Marjorie asked her to serve her husband in a similar capacity she undertook the assignment, which proved a long and pleasant association for all concerned.

After the failure of *Out of the Sea* there were rumors that Marquis planned to return to columning. It is known that some of his friends, notably Christopher Morley, had urged such a course. Marquis may have toyed with the idea but there is nothing to indicate that he took it seriously. The number and nature of his writing commitments at the time the rumors were being circulated would argue against it.

Morley reasoned that the reading public needed Don's column and that Don needed it too. He had been noticeably more cheerful as a columnist than he now was as a free-lance. Morley thought his friend needed the stimulation he derived from the knowledge that as a commentator on the current scene he was avidly followed by a loyal army of readers, as he tried to show in an article which later served as an introduction to one of Marquis's books. Morley believed that much that Don had written in his column would survive, although he admitted—and thought it didn't matter—that "in a daily column, necessarily a great deal of matter is of ephemeral reference."

Morley clung to his belief that if Marquis would learn to kick time-wasters out of his office he would enjoy columning as much as he did in the days before he had become famous. In appraising his friend as a commentator on the passing show, Morley had this to say in that article: "A proportion of Marquis's most brilliant work in those years (1913–1925) was oblique comment on public affairs. . . . When anything happened, I give you my word, most of us didn't consult the leading editorials to know what to think. The almost universal reflex, in New York at any rate, was Let's see what Don says about it. I'm not saying that I always agreed, then or now, with Don's notions; but every so often he would turn on some particular fog of hooey and cut it with a blade that would divide floating silk. With a magic that seemed like that of Alice going through the mirror, suddenly we saw the whole furniture of affairs from the other side. For instance, when President Wilson brusquely dismissed his Secretary of State, Mr. Lansing, and Marquis burlesqued it by dismissing archy. There had been no such commentator on public affairs since Mr. Dooley; they don't come often. But it is only too characteristic of the Solemn Skullworkers that because many of Marquis's pungent comments on the human comedy were put in the form of soliloquies by the Old Soak or archy the roach they could not recognize their high coefficient of seriousness."

Doubleday published *Out of the Sea* that same year—1927—and also *The Almost Perfect State*, generally regarded as one of Marquis's best books. Reviewing the latter in the New York *Herald Tribune*, Will Cuppy said:

"The trouble with most Utopias is that they aren't funny enough. Take Plato's Republic. Take, er—well, there must be lots of them, and probably the only one fit to live in is Don Marquis's Almost Perfect State."

Cuppy liked everything about Marquis's Elysium, notably the provision in the bylaws that "anyone who talks about self-improvement, uplift and so forth will be boiled in asphalt." He concluded his review with this statement: "I will affirm my own recognizance that 'The Almost Perfect State' is one of Don Marquis's very best books. Can anyone say more?"

The *Boston Transcript*, in an enthusiastic anonymous review, noted that, in addition to being a book about a new Promised Land, *The Almost Perfect State* was a mine of miscellaneous information. For instance, want to know where Cheops is? Then, answering his own question, the reviewer quoted:

> He lies in his sarcophagus,
> With sand in his esophagus.

The *Transcript* review concluded as follows:

"Mr. Marquis, realizing the fleeting condition of all earthly things, puts in a plea for Levity and Wings, for the Idle Rich, because the world needs less work and more riches, for prophets rather than priests, and religion rather than churches, for a little cooking sherry. . . .

"This is a delightfully whimsical and ridiculous book."

In an exchange of letters E. V. Knox, British humorist and critic, and an admirer of Marquis's, describes one of the Marquis techniques as "a mockery that achieves its effect by bathos. He blows up a balloon and then pricks it with a pin." This method is very much in evidence in *The Almost Perfect State*.

Twenty-three years after its publication, Bernard De Voto had some things to say in his "Easy Chair" department in *Harper's Magazine* about Marquis's picaresque Promised Land. Here is an excerpt:

"*The Almost Perfect State* . . . is the damnest book, but which of Don's isn't? You learn from it that the soul comes just down to the midriff. You run into superbly angry outcries against man's nature and man's fate, usually with topspin. . . . At least fifteen different ways of establishing the Almost Perfect State are explored in detail, but there are going to be no reformers in it for it is better to behead a man than to reform him, and the inhabitants are going to be equally divided between radicals and conservatives who will never work at either trade. At one point the Home Must Go but later on it has to come back again; and the same with the legal system: the State must have a lot of laws, for 'The progress of humanity consists in the violation of laws,' but on the other hand there are going to be very few, but anyone who wants to violate any of them will be free to do so but must 'withdraw to a distance from his fellow men, so that the violation will not interfere with them,' but also at any time a law may seem desirable anyone is free to make one up to fit. . . . Dialogues so exquisite and cockeyed that partial quotation would spoil them are scattered through the text, and so are bits of Don's verse, played on every instrument from a violin to a kazoo."

In those days Simeon Strunsky, editor, critic, and essayist, who wrote the popular "Topics of the Times" for the New York *Times*, was also represented in that newspaper's Sunday book-review section by a weekly page called, "About Books, More or Less." He selected a book and made it the theme of a rambling, discursive, unfailingly entertaining essay. The week he picked *The Almost Perfect State* as his subject he had this to say in his opening paragraphs:

"It is no reflection on the merits of Don Marquis's *The Almost Perfect State* to suggest that the most important message is contained

in the last five lines of the book. 'I'm planning to go back to the
newspaper business before long, and then I'll be in a position once
more to review what the reviewers say of my stuff. And if they don't
take these articles more seriously than I ever did, I'll rip hell out of
them.'

"There is primary news value in Don Marquis's return to journalism. . . . The newspapers need Don Marquis."

Marquis's statement that he planned to return to the newspaper
business was intended as a joke—as witness its removal from subsequent printings—but following rumors, it gave Strunsky reason to
believe that Don was in earnest. With this in mind, he wrote:

"Whether Mr. Marquis, returned to his newspaper desk, will proceed to carry out his threat is another matter. He is not really fero-
cious. Of all our columnists he was always the most impersonal.
When he gave up journalism to write for the theatre he picked up an
enormous handicap. To be quite frank about it, he is lamentably
deficient in one of the first prerequisites for conspicuous success in
present-day dramaturgy. His vigor, of which he is supposed to have
plenty, is not quite the punch of the theatre today. His forceful vocabulary, in which people have found pleasure, is insufficiently devastating. He will say hell and damn; but a careful search of the present
volume reveals that he has no command of those riper, fruitier,
hyphenated expletives which it is the triumph of the new art of the
theatre to have transplanted from the barroom to the stage. He
has a great deal to say of women, but almost nothing of Sex. Apparently he takes it for granted that people will know without
being told that women belong to one sex and men to another.
But in that case what does it leave him to write about for the
stage?

"On the whole, then, it is an excellent thing both for Mr. Marquis and his public that he is coming back to newspaper work. It
should not be difficult for him to start in without much loss of time
on renovating plant and equipment. He is under no necessity of
building up a new aggregation of 'contribs.' They never were a feature
of his column. He is under no necessity of bringing his information
up to date. Mr. Marquis's interests always were peculiarly timeless.
His concern lay with Marcus Aurelius, the Bible, men, women,
children, beans, good drink. When he touched upon contemporary
subjects it was from the timeless angle. He seldom spoke of the
Eighteenth Amendment or Wayne B. Wheeler. He spoke of liquor

and the Old Soak. He was, like Romain Rolland, above the melee. 'Let others defend liquor; we praise it.' . . . Mr. Marquis can take off his coat and start in where he left off. He will be fairly well at home in every world because he always conveyed the suggestion of not being perfectly at home in any world. In Don Marquis there is a great deal of the elf and the Platonist."

Strunsky was right. Up to 1927, the year he wrote his essay on *The Almost Perfect State*, Marquis's work was free of those "riper, fruitier, hyphenated expletives." He reserved the right to address Frank Sullivan, Clive Weed, and other friends as "you poor son-of-a-bitch"; and, conversationally, when the occasion seemed to demand it, he would draw upon his sizzling line of emergency language— "hair-curlers" and "air-bluers," Rollin Kirby used to call them. As I have said, he was definitely not a dirty-joke man; whatever discoloration he lent a yarn derived from the use of an occasional goddam or bastard or s.o.b., or something on that order. He had been known to clean up such a story—it didn't involve much editing—and tell it in the presence of children or Reina's or Marjorie's church friends.

With two exceptions—books published after Strunsky wrote his piece—whatever there is by way of the Rabelaisian or the sexy in Marquis's books, is achieved by subtleties. The books referred to are *Master of the Revels*, a play (to quote the author) "about that ribald, disreputable old hellion, Henry VIII"; and his posthumously published (and unfinished) novel, *Sons of the Puritans*, both of which, by the nature of their subject matter, demanded a more direct approach. In *Master of the Revels*, for instance, Marquis was able through diligent research to reproduce some of the oaths and expletives—and a mighty colorful brand of cussing it was, too—employed by the roistering monarch who served as his protagonist.

In designating Marquis as a Platonist, Strunsky was right again. There are passages in Marquis's poetry and in his letters to support this—overtones that indicate his belief that physical objects are but impermanent representations of unchanging ideas, and that only through the medium of these ideas does true knowledge emerge. But more important—and even stronger evidence of Strunsky's shrewdness as a critic—is the fact that Marquis had planned to write a play about Plato. I found a comprehensive outline of it—four pages of solid, single-space typing—among the Marquis papers in the twenty-two-box collection in the Butler Library at Columbia University.

In 1928 Marquis decided to buy himself a dog—not to be confused with the one he had previously bought his daughter Barbara. He wanted his own particular pet—"someone to curl up at my feet and console me whenever my typewriter grew stubborn and refused to yield wordage,—someone to whom I could tell my troubles without having to listen to *his*."

He decided on a Boston bull, which was a compromise between Yale and Harvard. Why should such a compromise be necessary? Well, two years earlier when Marquis had lectured at Yale he had been received by the student body as a conquering hero, so he thought that perhaps he should buy an English bulldog such as the Elis use as a mascot; then a Harvard friend reminded him that the *Boston Transcript* had for years reviewed his books enthusiastically, which suggested to Marquis (whose formal education had stopped at the age of fifteen) that the Boston bull would be the perfect compromise. The Boston part would represent Harvard and the bulldog part would keep Yale happy. So he bought a Boston bull and named him Pete because he didn't know any Yale or Harvard man named Pete; thus the name would not prove controversial.

Some of the Marquis milestones in 1928 were the publication of two books, *Love Sonnets of a Cave Man* and a collection of short stories entitled *When the Turtle Sings, and Other Unusual Tales*; the sale to magazines of enough stories and articles to pay the bills; and the acquisition of Pete, the aforementioned Boston bull.

It was also the year of his fiftieth birthday and the year Hollywood renewed its interest in him, neither of which excited him very much.

As to Hollywood, Marquis still had painful memories of the filming of *The Old Soak*, a low-budget "silent" that was released in 1926. When Universal bought the play Marquis volunteered to go to Hollywood as an unpaid consultant, if necessary—a typically quixotic gesture—to help preserve the flavor of the original. He feared the point of view that might not see in Clem Hawley anything more than a lush. His offer was rejected.

When Marquis saw a preview of *The Old Soak* in a New York projection room he had a bad time. It had been transformed into a melodramatic morality play about the evils of drink—an obvious bid for the support of the drys and the bluenoses whom he had kidded for years in his column. About all that was left of what he had originally written was the title. Not one of the Old Soak's salty sayings was retained—not even the famous line, "Heredity runs in our family," or the situation from which it stemmed.

Marquis had once said in his column that Hollywood couldn't possibly be as bad as it was painted. He didn't care much for its product but he predicted that that would improve as the industry, a comparatively new one—(this was before the advent of the talkies)— achieved maturity. He branded as "cry babies" those writers "who wept in public" about the mangling of their books and plays. After seeing a preview of *The Old Soak* he ruefully remarked that he thought he'd join the cry babies.

Because of the fame Marquis's character had achieved in the New York area, there was great interest on the part of the big exhibitors— until they saw the picture. None of the good theaters wanted it. It opened in one of the city's cheapest houses, the Stanley Theatre, described by *Variety* as "a 25¢ grind." The reviews could not have been worse, an ironic situation since the original stage production had been so enthusiastically received by the critics.

Some of the reviewers aimed their barbs at the company that had produced the picture, others took a fall out of Marquis. *Variety's* reviewer said:

"Somewhere between the stage play and the screen version of Don Marquis's *The Old Soak* all of the comedy that played so important a part in the play was lost. That is where Universal fell down. One would think that with a property as valuable as this they would have taken pains to put over a picture that would have clicked."

Specifically, *Variety* lamented the failure to make capital of the play's "many laugh lines" in the titling, which was considered a big factor in putting over a motion picture in those days of silent films when everything depended on a combination of effective pantomime and snappy titling. It was then the responsibility of a movie producer, when his assignment was the filming of a successful Broadway comedy, to see to it that his scenarist extracted the lines that got the biggest laughs when the play was originally produced and used them as titles in his script. The best source of information on this was the author of the play himself. Marquis was never consulted. Universal had decided either that *The Old Soak* was not a comedy or not to present it as one. You don't need laughs in a morality play.

The net result was that a movie based on a play that had established a new record for a run at New York's Plymouth Theatre—423 performances, which was considered sensational in 1922–23—was "yanked" after only one day at the aforementioned grind-house.

Before he had seen the preview Marquis had promised to take some friends to the opening but begged off. Somehow an "opening" at the Stanley Theatre seemed like a sorry joke. "There's a better show on the same street," he is reported to have said, "a flea circus. Let's go there instead."

It would require a long chapter to recount all of the stories that have reached me regarding Marquis's newly acquired pet, puppy Pete, the Boston bull. Joseph Cummings Chase, well-known portrait painter, at a party at the inevitable Players Club a few years ago, where there is now a full-scale Don Marquis legendry, told of the humorist's troubles in housebreaking Pete. The pup regarded the back yard—an enclosure which with its grass and bushes seemed like a kind of Elysian Field that must be kept immaculate—as a much more important place than the house. He could not be induced to relieve himself in this little garden, dashing indoors for such mundane purposes. Don, who had a way with dogs, decided to take over the job of housebreaking his new acquisition. He finally accomplished his purpose but not without some embarrassment.

Marquis, a man without inhibitions and frequently oblivious of his surroundings, led Pete into the garden one day, and, squatting on his haunches, demonstrated by pantomime the more important of the functions the dog was supposed to perform outdoors. Having done this, he took hold of the puppy, and, to make the lesson stick, manipulated him into the desired position. He then proceeded to Lesson Two, first lifting his right leg to illustrate what he meant, then upraising the animal's rear right leg to drive the point home.

Marquis was totally unaware that while these lessons in canine P.s and Q.s, as he appropriately called them, were in progress, he had picked up quite an audience. He was the most surprised man in town when, on hearing a laugh from an adjoining dwelling, he looked up and saw that there were people at most of the nearby windows. He retreated into the house in confusion, Pete at his heels. He remarked afterward that he never realized what a drawing card he was.

John C. King, a retired actor who has been a member of the Players since 1903, loves to tell about the day he was about to enter the Club when he came upon his friend Don, who was seated on the curb in front of the clubhouse at 16 Gramercy Park and sharing his lunch with his dog. It seems that when Don arrived at the Club that day he checked Pete in the coatroom and went upstairs to the dining room for lunch. When the waiter brought his order—chops, according to King—Marquis was seized by a sudden whim to share it with Pete, who had not yet been fed. Plate in hand, he left for the coatroom, got Pete, whose leash loop he had thrown over a coat hook, and led him outdoors where they were lunching together on the sidewalk when King came along. King says that as he approached the pair, Marquis, who seemed perfectly at home on the curbstone, was saying, "Now it's your turn, Petey," as he gave the dog a bite of one of his chops.

When Marquis told his daughter Barbara about Pete's visit to the Players she said she would like to see it too. So one day he took her to his Home Away from Home and showed her around, explaining that with the exception of the famous French actress Sarah Bernhardt she, Barbara, was the only "woman" who had ever been admitted to the Club.

Bernhardt's visit proved even more memorable than the Club's officials and the membership had expected. The elevator that was conveying her to the top floor, where a committee waited to show her the apartment of founder Edwin Booth, got stuck, inspiring member Gelett Burgess to write this quatrain:

> The elevator's in the wall,
> And no one uses it at all;
> Bernhardt was stuck in it, they say,—
> For all I know she's there today.

Some time later Marquis, hearing about Burgess's versified comment, decided to add one of his own:

> If she's still there I'll Sarah-nade her,
> And after that perhaps persuade her
> To have a drink (she's a friendly egg)
> And tap out a dance on her wooden leg.

Only those who corresponded with Marquis saw any change in him that year—1928. Outwardly he was as jaunty as ever—a spirited conversationalist and a much-sought-after luncheon and dinner companion. Those with whom he swapped letters noticed a marked change. Once an indefatigable correspondent, he was now writing fewer and fewer letters. And the ones he wrote didn't sound like the old Marquis.

Much of his joviality (as a correspondent) seemed to have vanished. If something gave him "a pain acute and localized," to use an F.P.A.-ism he had picked up, he said so. The new bluntness seemed as spontaneous as the old ebullience had. In the past his letters never mirrored his frustrations; now they did.

The old Marquis was a great pleaser. He did a great many things he didn't want to do simply to avoid hurting people's feelings. The new Marquis turned down the things he didn't want to do, courteously but firmly. A man sent him a letter saying he was collecting Marquis books and wanted them all. He enclosed a substantial check, and authorized Marquis to advertise for such of his books as were out of print or to acquire them from second hand dealers. He returned the check with a letter stating that unfortunately he did not have the time to devote to this request and hoped his correspondent would understand. The old Marquis would have turned himself inside out to comply with such a request.

The following, from Christopher Morley's introduction to *The Best of Don Marquis*, published a few years after Marquis's death, tells its own story:

"I cannot help thinking that Marquis had a very special message to younger artists, a message which was implicit in many of his seemingly jocular paragraphs. It was this: energy is not endless, better hoard it for your own work. Be intangible and hard to catch; be secret and proud and inwardly unconformable. Say yes and don't mean it; pretend to agree; dodge every kind of organization, and evade, elude, recede. Be about your own affairs, as you would also forbear from others at theirs, and thereby show your respect for the holiest ghost we know, the creative imagination. I read him wrong unless I see that cry in many a passage. Read, and perhaps be startled by, the angry trio of sonnets called *A Gentleman of Fifty Soliloquizes.* . . .

"By a natural association I think of a letter he wrote in 1928 when a group of friends had planned a fiftieth-birthday party for him, which was to be humorously called the Marquis Semi-Centennial. Quite unwittingly we had touched upon a secret phobia of his. I venture to quote a few bits from that letter because it is surely important, once in a while, to know what people actually think behind the mask they learn to wear. And I somehow feel that his unusual frankness, though due to momentary fatigue or discouragement, may be valuable to someone:

I simply could not go through with congratulations or a party or anything of the sort. If you are an institution you may not mind the idea of a semi-centennial; if you are a human being, the word itself is an acute toothache.

In my case, it means to me that half a dozen novels, which I planned in my thirties, will probably never be written now, as I find myself still potboiling.

I have never told anybody how deep and abiding my professional disappointments are. I have had for fifteen years the consciousness of rather unusual powers—I can say this to you and have no risk of it being misunderstood as mere egotism. Along with that has gone the consciousness that, except in brief and fragmentary things, I have never displayed the powers I have, or developed them.

Well, there has always been the hope that the stuff was coming through yet. I still have it, mixed with a lot of humility. But you cannot understand, nor won't until you get to be 47 or 48, the continual internal gasping hurrying sense that they are not started yet, the big things.

I fight continuously and desperately against the idea that being 50 or 60 makes any difference at all—and it takes a lot of fighting and a lot of kidding along and a good deal of guts to keep steadily to the resolve to do something yet—and an awful lot of determination to keep from slumping into the easy affirmation: I've done something already. It isn't the tenth of what I should have produced.

Merely to pay up present debts and obligations there are at least 18 months of desperate and continued potboiling. I have a schedule that calls for one short story or one article each week for 18 months. . . .

Let's have a party in September, and not mention my birthday at all. . . . Forty and forty-five are bad enough; fifty is simply hell to face; fifteen minutes after that you are sixty; and then in ten minutes more you are 85.

These ten years from forty to fifty are by before you know it. For the love of God, don't let them slip from you, as I did.

"And by 'the love of God' he meant, as every artist does, the joy of creation.

"Of this man, more than of any I have known, the great seventeenth-century words apply—words three centuries old and still the most expressive of masculine love and fellowship. I change only the name—O Rare Don Marquis."

Morley makes an important suggestion in the foregoing: "Read, and perhaps be startled by, the angry trio of sonnets called A Gentleman of Fifty Soliloquizes." In terms of the year 1928 this sonnet

sequence is pure autobiography. Moreover, because it effectively por-
trays a mood that finds expression nowhere else in Marquis's prose
or poetry, it is here appended:

I

Some ten or twelve old friends of yours and mine,
    If we spoke truly, are not friends at all,
They never were. That accident divine,
    A friendship, not so often may befall!

But as the dull years pass with dragging feet
    Within them waxes, in us wanes, esteem;
For weakly, and half conscious of deceit,
    We gave them cause an equal love to dream.

Could we have told some fool with haggard face
    Who bared his soul, so sure we'd understand,
His little tragedy was commonplace? . . .
    We lied. We stretched to him a brother's hand;

He loved us for it, and mere ruth has kept
Our jaws from yawning while he drooled and wept.

II

The valour cold to be ourselves we lack;
    And so from strands of kindness misconstrued
And lenient moments, careless threads and slack
    We're meshed within a web of habitude.

And often these are worthier men than we;
    But that itself, in time, becomes offense;
We're burdened with this damned nobility
    That's forced on us, which we must recompense.

We loathe ourselves for being insincere,
    And lavish generous deeds to hide the fact:
For who could wound these hearts? Thus we appear
    Thrice loyal friends in word and look and act!

And golden lies with which we save them pain
But serve to make their true regard more fain.

III

Should chance strike out of me some human heat,
    Leap not at that and think to grasp my soul!
I flee new bonds. My self must still retreat
    Down devious ways to keep me free and whole.

> Give me your mind, and I will give you mine.
> Then should it change no heart will bleed or burn.
> Give me your wits. I want no heart of thine.
> You'll ask too much of life-blood in return.
>
> There was a golden lad in years long gone. . . .
> We twain together left the ways of men
> And roamed the starry heights, the fields of dawn,
> In youth and gladness. This comes not again.
>
> Give me your mirth. It bores me when you weep.
> My loves you cannot touch. They're buried deep.

Marquis's letter is important for still another reason. It is the first indication we have that he was broke so soon after his second marriage. The year he married Marjorie—1926—he established a $30,000 trust fund for Barbara. He had made an irrevocable transfer of the money to the child as a safeguard against the temptation to withdraw it and spend it on something else. This would at least assure his daughter of an education. His plan was to add to Barbara's trust fund in 1927 but he was snowed under by expenses and was unable to do so.

Howard Lindsay quoted Patterson McNutt to the effect that at one time Don Marquis was supporting thirteen people. The two households—New York and Forest Hills—took in eleven, including the hired help. Who the others were, assuming McNutt was correct, is anybody's guess. There were other drains on Marquis—for instance, those who had grown accustomed to borrowing from him, and his brother Harry in Alaska, who occasionally needed financial assistance. The wonder is that Marquis didn't go broke sooner.

Though his savings had evaporated, Marquis's income from his magazine work was substantial. His articles and short stories were in constant demand and the big national magazines to which he was contributing were paying him top prices.

Those were the days when Don told his friend Clive Weed that the Marquis Loan Association was about to close its doors—and might even go in for borrowing instead of lending "if the dissolution of the firm doesn't start ugly rumors in financial circles and impair my credit rating."

It was during that same period—the late twenties—that Marquis notified his sister Maud that he would be compelled to make a reduction in the amount of money he sent her monthly. The checks were always made out to Maud, who had written her cousin Neeta in Los

Angeles, "You see, I am the 'boss' here . . . because my sister never enjoyed being an executive." There is something weird and pathetic about Maud Marquis proclaiming herself the "boss" and executive officer of the two-spinster establishment in Forest Hills.

As the executive officer at 51 Wendover Road, Maud, even with her familiarly unrealistic approach to things, saw the need for cutting expenses and agreed to do so. She accomplished this by putting her housemaid and nurse on a half-time basis. Nev, who loved to cook, cheerfully reassumed that responsibility. To anyone who showed the slightest interest, Maud explained that she disliked to cook and had no intention of learning. Apparently she did some work outdoors, though it is hard to say what this consisted of. Only a small parcel of land came with the house. This outdoor activity was one of her favorite talking points as it was "man's work." She had a strange quirk that caused her to put great emphasis on anything she did that she considered in the category of masculine labor. The woman's mind is hard to follow. Haven't there always been a great many women gardeners? Cooking she regarded as "too feminine."

Maud spent most of her time reading, keeping up with her correspondence, and puttering (this went on for years) with her movie version of *archy and mehitabel*. With the aid of Nev and the maid or the nurse—it usually took two people to make her comfortable— she would prop herself up on a sofa against what one doctor (who claims that in all the years he called on Maud he never once saw her on her feet) described as "a mountainous arrangement of cushions." From this command post she issued orders to her staff as she read, wrote her letters, or continued to go through the motions of writing that *archy and mehitabel* screenplay which never emerged as anything more than a jumble of meaningless notes.

For a time one of her favorite topics in her letters was a cocker spaniel she had bought, feeling the need of a pet around the house. There is an allusion to it as "adorable" and just as we are ready to applaud the humanizing effect of this dog on her, we read: "He has to be catered for, washed, manipulated! I don't know why I've dilated so on the dog problem unless it is that some one thing always assumes more prominence, seems to be the last straw." Eventually this cocker spaniel became the reason why Maud wasn't getting anywhere as a writer. And it is quite possible that the poor confused woman believed it.

14 *"These Shameless Orgies of Literary Exhibitionism"—"Poetry Is a Business"—Morley and Marquis Get Back at Maud—Was Something Wrong with Don's Second Marriage?—Charles Connolly Tells an Unusual Tale—William Rose Benét on Don Marquis—Snubbed Again by the Sun —Marquis in Hollywood*

In 1928 Marquis decided that he would never deliver another lecture. He had previously complied with some of the requests made by his publishers that he deliver talks designed to stimulate the sale of his books. Asked by his friend Lyman Beecher Stowe, one of the editors of Doubleday, Doran and Company, to make a series of talks at the Hotel Barbizon in New York, Marquis announced that he was through with lecturing. The tone of his reply, which follows, and its bluntness, provide further evidence of the change in Marquis that his letters—and *only* his letters up to that time—indicated:

"Dear Lyman: I am afraid I cannot do the Barbizon lecture thing.

"I am getting out of all lecturing entirely. When I do a stunt like this it takes me two or three days of preparation and I have such a distaste for it that I have a nervous reaction for two or three days and then the stunt itself always drains my nervous vitality and it takes me two or three days to get over it. In fact I lose just about a week over one stunt of this kind and just now I am in no financial condition to throw away a week. I have got a lot of magazine stuff to do and have to keep right on plugging at it and get the money which it brings in.

"I had a number of dates under Mr. Pond's auspices. I think that there are two or three of them which are still to be filled, one a short one of 15 or 20 minutes and the other a longer or entire program. After these are done I have asked Mr. Pond not to make any dates for me as the work is too hard on me considering what it brings in. I get $300 for a full program through Mr. Pond but that is not enough when the work takes as much out of me as it does.

"Speaking of Mr. Pond, I want to correct an impression which I gave you in my former letter. As a matter of fact, I had a dicker with Mr. Pond to this effect: my contract with him is designed to steer away the dozens and even hundreds of people who are asking me to speak for nothing all the time. It got to the place where no kind of explanation would be accepted by them. So I got into the habit of referring all of them to Mr. Pond and saying that the brutal Mr. Pond would not let me lecture except under his auspices. This, of course, was technically correct, but the fact was that it was not really Mr. Pond who was holding me away from these things; it was I who was using Mr. Pond as a convenient excuse for getting out of things I didn't want to do, so don't blame him for kicking over the Barbizon thing. The real reason is that I don't want to do it, and that I am quitting it whether I do it free or whether I do it for money. It simply works the devil out of me for too long a time and more than that I hate the atmosphere of these god-damned intellectual semi-idiotic women who crowd into these things and gush and linger around afterwards with a lot of half-baked hooey.

"I would rather become a male prostitute outright than have to make my living dishing out that kind of bunk for that sort of superficial well-dressed people who have no ideas about anything in the world. Now and then there is somebody there who has some sense but they come as a matter of curiosity to see a damn fool author make an idiot of himself. Never again, so help me Jesus Christ, will I ever speak at anything again or read any of my own junk when I once get through with the two or three engagements I have already made, for fear of hurting anyone's feelings. Hereafter I don't intend to give a good god-damn whose feelings I hurt. I simply will not do it.

"I never willingly went to one of these Christ-forgotten, shameless orgies of literary exhibitionism and why the hell anybody else should want to go I don't understand. The vaudeville stunt is different. You get real money there and you don't have to meet people.

"As far as helping the sale of my books is concerned, the sale of my books is so limited anyhow that it would have to be multiplied by five to become a financial factor worth any consideration. My own theory is that half of the people in an audience of this sort, once they hear an author face to face, make up their mind that they will never buy one of that damn slob's books if a ticket to the Celestial City was included in it. These affairs for fat and smirking authors to meet the idle talcum-powdered female public are for me too disgusting for public discussion. I have always hated them and I shall never again be trapped into one of them. They are no more interested in an author on account of his literary ability, if he has any, than they are in the current prize-fighter or the latest quack to discover a cancer cure.

"The general public has only one function in my scheme of life—to support the magazines which buy my junk. I don't like people in large masses—except as material for stories. I can weep over them when I write about them, if I am writing the kind of story in which one is supposed to weep over them, but when I meet them in bulk, whether they happen to be the great unwashed or the idle over-washed, I don't like them. The strain of having to pretend I like them is a nervous agony. The trouble with the public is that there is too much of it. What we need in publics is less quantity and more quality.

"These, very briefly, are some of the reasons why I do not wish to speak any more and why I do not intend to do it. I could elaborate this brief sketch into a really lengthy letter.

"As far as the sale of books is concerned, I would rather never sell another copy of any book again than speak for three minutes to a hall full of god-damned pseudo-intellectual morons who don't know anything about books to begin with and have very little curiosity even, to excuse their presence. If you could get a thousand of them together and sell real estate to each one of them it would be worth-while, or if you could sell real estate to 5% of them it would be worth-while, but what does selling a copy of a book to 5% of them amount to? If I have got to canvass to sell these piffling little volumes which I exude because I have no moral or intellectual continence I would rather canvass for something that has got some real money in it—sell bonds, for instance, or houses and lots, or something that means some-thing, or advertising. . . . The fact that other authors do it (lecture) and like to do it bears no weight with me whatever. I have met very few authors of any sort that I ever cared to have around me. You meet a good many authors yourself and you ought to know exactly how I feel about them.

"The only enjoyment that I take out of life is in writing and now and then sitting down and getting quietly stewed. My stomach and nervous system are such that I cannot get stewed as often as I would like to. In fact, if I get stewed at all any more I pay for it with two or three weeks of illness and depression, and yet I would rather get stewed and be ill for three weeks than put on a show at one of these literary gatherings. The liquor is not what it should be and if I ever get money enough to leave this god-damned prohibition country I am going to go and live in some country where the liquor is good and do nothing but write and stay stewed the rest of my life.

"These, briefly, are some of my reasons for not wanting to speak at the Barbizon, or anywhere else. I hope you will appreciate that there is nothing personal in this belch. I will read poetry to you by the hour. I will come out to Doubleday, Doran for lunch and read poetry all through lunch time to the editorial staff and the firm, but I will not get up any more before a crowd of strangers and read poetry. I would rather go into the moving picture business. Yours cordially and sincerely, Don"

Recipients of letters from Marquis in that vein differed as to what they signified. Some said, "The old boy is turning sour." Others viewed it this way: "Don is growing up."

Whichever is the case, the tone of that letter is a good indication of the change that had come over Marquis. It will be recalled that only a few years earlier he considered it a lark to deliver two lectures at Yale. He and his audience had a wonderful time.

Once Marquis took a tolerant view of the many groups and organizations—this was in the heyday of "The Sun Dial"—that wrote him requesting him to deliver lectures and/or give readings from his poetry. Almost invariably these letters contained a paragraph to the effect that while the XYZ Culture Club or the Flatbush Poetry Society could not pay him any money for his efforts they would make up for it by urging their membership to buy his books, etc., etc.

These requests gave Marquis an idea for a column to which he devoted a whole issue of "The Sun Dial." Subsequently he had it mimeographed and used it as a reply to the more persistent senders of begging letters asking him to lecture or give poetry readings for nothing. It saved him the trouble of answering these pestiferous missives. It is reprinted for the contrast it provides with the mood of the letter to Mr. Stowe and for the additional reason that it is typical of the kind of extravagant kidding that made Marquis's column so popular:

"It is not, as some of our friends believe, because of any excess of timidity that we refuse to read our poems at teas and similar soul and culture fights.

"It is because no one wants to pay us what it is worth to us. We are perfectly willing, if we get enough money for it, to read poems at Teas, Dinners, Pugilistic Contests, Clambakes, Football Games, Prayer Meetings of any Denomination, Clinics, Divorce Trials, Balls, Dedications, Lynchings, Launchings, Luncheons, Weddings, Jail Deliveries, Tonsil Removals, Ice Cream Socials, Legal Executions, Wrestling Matches, Tooth Pullings, Commencement Exercises, Operations for Appendicitis, Coming Out Parties, Taffy Pulls, Better Baby Contests, Dog Shows, Gambling House Raids, Sunday School Picnics, Pool Tournaments, Spelling Bees, Adenoid Unveilings, Murders, Church Suppers and Cremations. But money we must have.

"For while reading one's own poems to a gang of strangers need not, of course, be absolutely degrading, yet it is bound to be a silly sort of performance.

"And it is worth money. Poetry, with us, is a business; it takes time, muscular effort, nervous energy and, sometimes, thought, to produce a poem.

"People do not ask painters to go to places and paint pictures for nothing, but they are forever trying to graft entertainment off of poets.

"Our rates, henceforth, are as follows:

"For reading small, blond, romantic poems, thirty-five dollars per poem. Blond, dove-colored or pink lyrics prominently featuring the Soul, thirty-five dollars each.

"Humorous poems, not really very funny, twenty-five dollars each.

"Humorous poems, with slightly sentimental flavor, forty dollars each.

"Humorous poems, really quite funny, seventy-five dollars each.

"Dialect poems mentioning persons called 'Bill,' 'Jim,' 'Si,' etc., Southern dialect, fifty dollars each; middle Western, fifty-five dollars.

"Pathetic dialect verse charged for according to the quantity and quality of pathos desired. (See rates on Mother and Old Sweetheart poems.)

"Sonnets, ten dollars each. Not less than five sonnets served with any one order.

"Pash poems, one hundred dollars each. Pash poems, however, will only be read from the interior of a heavy wire cage.

"Free verse, any kind, one dollar a line.

"No matter how long or how short the lines actually are, for business purposes a line of free verse is to be considered as containing seven words.

"Serious poems, melancholy tone, fifty dollars each.

"For ten dollars additional persons not to exceed twelve in number will be permitted to file by and feel the poet's heart beat after reading sad poems; persons in excess of twelve in number charged for at the rate of two dollars each.

"Serious poems, optimistic in nature, fifty dollars each.

"Old Sweetheart poems, in which she dies, one hundred dollars each. Old Folks at Home poems, sad, fifty dollars each; each reference to angels five dollars additional; father killed, mother left living, sixty-five dollars; both parents killed, seventy-five dollars; with dialect, one hundred dollars. Both parents killed during Christmas holidays, any dialect wanted, angels, toys, etc., two hundred dollars. Auditors' tears guaranteed, and for thirty-five dollars additional poet also will cry while reading this old reliable line of family poetry.

"Religious poems, not more than five stanzas, one hundred dollars each.

"Agnostic poems, latest cut, one hundred thirty-five to one hundred seventy-five dollars each.

"These agnostic goods are for very exclusive circles, as are our radical and anarchistic poems, which come at two hundred dollars each.

"Tame revolutionary poems, usual Greenwich Village sort of thing, fifty dollars each; if read in Flatbush, sixty-five dollars each.

"Really quite shocking revolutionary poems, two hundred dollars each. A very modern line of goods.

"Write for special combination offers and rates on limericks. We have limericks listed in three categories:

"Limericks Where Ladies Are Present.

"Limericks Where Ladies Are Absent but Clergymen Are Present.

"Limericks.

"In the event that we are expected to Be Nice and Meet People, 20% added to above rates.

"If expected to Meet People, and Being Nice is left optional with us, only 5% added to above rates.

"Conversation on poetry or related topics charged for at rate of $75 an hour in addition to reading charges.

"Conversation on Rabindranath Tagore: Listened To, $750 an hour. Participated In, $1,000 the first hour and $350 for every additional ten minutes thereafter.

"Limericks composed on spot (discreet) twenty-five dollars each. Impromptu couplets, good, twenty dollars each; medium, twelve dollars and fifty cents each; quite bad impromptu couplets, five dollars each.

"Poetry written by host, hostess or any guest, listened to at rate of one hundred dollars per quarter hour.

"Compliments on same to author, ten dollars each additional.

"Compliments spoken so as to be overheard by more than eight persons, twenty dollars each.

"Compliments dashed off in little informal notes, forty dollars each if notes are initialed, one hundred dollars each if notes are signed with full name.

"For pretending to like Amy Lowell's work our rate is $1,000 an hour or any fraction thereof.

"No orders filled amounting to less than two hundred dollars for ninety minutes' work. Certified check must be mailed with orders.

"Prices quoted are f.o.b. Pennsylvania Station, N. Y. City.

"Patrons will always confer a favor by reporting any inattention on the part of the audience."

That piece—which with a slightly different beginning wound up in Marquis's book of prefaces, forewords, and introductions referred to—is a good example of the oblique approach to criticism the author sometimes employed. Note the references to Rabindranath Tagore and Amy Lowell and the fact that Marquis, in announcing his price list, proposes to charge his highest rates for reading *their* poems.

When Amy Lowell took charge of the Imagists, whose influence she hoped to make international, "she filled the air with battle cries announcing the liberation of poetry from the shackles," wrote Marquis in a less oblique moment, "that prevented Shakespeare, Keats, Shelley, Blake, Donne and other promising poets from ever amounting to anything." He proposed the erection of a monument to "the Amyable One," to be unveiled during her lifetime and to bear the inscription:

> Here once the embattled Amy stood,
> And fired the shot heard round the block.

When Tagore became the darling of Greenwich Village, and the Hermiones and Fothergil Finches who infested that capital of alleged bohemianism assayed his work as containing more Pure Soul per line than that of any contemporary, and when critics of standing were hailing the Hindu poet as enthusiastically—though more pontifically and polysyllabically—Marquis found himself in the minority that demurred. When one of the contributors to his column echoed Marquis's doubts, declaring that Tagore's poetry was no better than the vers libre that was being daily ground out by the ream in Greenwich Village, the columnist gave his "contrib" a mock spanking, expressing the belief that the Hindu's product was "quite possibly a tiny bit better."

For some time Don had made a ritual of visiting Maud and Nev at Forest Hills for Sunday dinner, taking Barbara with him. The child missed her Aunt Nev and that genial soul in turn missed her niece. This proved a satisfactory arrangement until Marquis, whose magazine commitments kept him in a ceaseless battle for time, suggested that his visits to Forest Hills be put on a monthly basis and that his sisters visit him every few weeks in New York. This they did, usually arriving at East 62nd Street in the afternoon so that they could have a good visit with the child before dinner. Maud's interest in Barbara was superficial by comparison with that of her sister, but she went through the motions of being a dutiful and solicitous aunt.

Usually when the sisters arrived at the Marquis brownstone, Marjorie was there to greet them, then she would find an excuse—usually something having to do with the theater—for leaving. Before these visits were put on a regular basis Maud had charged repeatedly that Marjorie's children were being treated better than Barbara, pointing a finger at Marjorie as the one responsible. There had also been a stormy scene—one that Marjorie vowed would never be repeated if she could possibly prevent it—when Maud criticized her for buying the house at 125 East 62nd Street. As Don pointed out in bringing the scene to a close, it was none of his sister's business. He might have added that Maud had been a drain on him since 1912, frequently letting him in for wholly needless expenses, but it would have been unlike him to do it.

For some reason Marquis had elected not to tell Maud and Nev about Barbara's trust fund. One of his friends believes the reason why he withheld the information was that he feared Maud might have demanded a similar fund for herself; but this is conjecture. No one seems to have any factual information as to what motivated him.

When the sisters visited the Marquises in New York their brother took them to dinner at Susan Prince's Restaurant. The party usually consisted of Nev, Maud, Don, and one or more friends. Marjorie was never present. She occasionally risked a scene with Maud in her own home but could not be induced to take a chance in a public restaurant. Don, in inviting friends to join these family gatherings, predicted they would have "a lousy time," adding that he was too tired and too cowardly to do battle with Maud any longer and that the presence of a friend or two usually had a deterrent effect on that rambunctious woman. At Susan Prince's Marquis used loaded dice, as he put it. He usually added a person or persons that Maud admired and enjoyed engaging in conversation. Of all Don's friends she admired Christopher Morley the most; so he was the most frequent outside addition to these family dinner parties. His presence was almost a guarantee of a peaceful evening.

The irony of Maud's admiration for Christopher Morley is that Morley, a man without too many strong dislikes, detested Maud Marquis. He considered her a troublemaker and a leech and Marquis's most serious problem.

But, if Morley had strong feelings about Maud, he was also a good sport, and there wasn't much he wouldn't do to help his friend Don. At these family dinner parties Morley usually asked to be seated next to Maud, showed great interest in her adaptation of *archy and mehitabel* for the screen, which he knew would never get anywhere, made suggestions about that project that fell on uncomprehending ears, and did everything he could think of to keep her so occupied that there was small likelihood of her becoming embroiled with anyone.

Once, before one of these evenings at Susan Prince's, Marquis and Morley decided to have a little fun with Maud, confiding their plan to Clive Weed, who was also present that night and whose role was to ask questions—the sillier the better—whenever the conversation lagged. By prearrangement Chris asked Don as they were being served, "How do you think our play is coming, Don?" Before he could say much more, Maud wanted to know *what* play.

Marquis apologized. He'd been so busy he completely forgot to tell her about it. He and Morley were dramatizing Bulfinch's *Age of Fable*.

Maud thought this was a splendid idea and wanted to hear all about it. Which of the characters were they using? There were so many in Mr. Bulfinch's book! She recalled that when she taught school in Chicago she used to tell the children stories out of Bulfinch and she could go on endlessly because there were so many wonderful characters in that great big dear book.

Morley, in his best deadpan manner, said that the play covered so much ground—sky, that is, because that's where the gods lived—it would take all night to describe all the action. Besides, he and her brother were still picking and choosing and hadn't decided finally on the dénouement. In fact, they were considering nineteen or twenty dénouements, all of them good. But, if she wished, he'd be glad to describe one of the major scenes. Maud said she'd love to hear it.

One of their main characters, said Morley, was Erato, the Greek muse of love poetry. A cynical god in the play who has been divorced from ten goddesses has a confrontation with Erato in which he gives her the back of his hand for recommending to his eleventh wife—a goddess he recently married and who has turned out to be a frigid woman—love poetry which instead of having the desired aphrodisiacal effect, serves only to make her colder. They have quite a row and insult each other. It is what is known in Broadway parlance as a Big Scene. The multimarried god tells Erato she is a blithering idiot and that her name ought to be Erratum because the kind of poetry she has recommended has proven a big mistake. A policeman who is patrolling the cloud bank on which this scene is being enacted overhears the remark and snorts, "Erratum, eh? By special decree Latin has been against the law since last Tuesday. This is Greek territory and the ban is gonna hold till the trouble blows over. Besides, that ain't no way to speak to a lady! You're under arrest! . . . What's that? . . . Tell it to the judge!"

It seems, continued Morley, there was feeling at that time between the Greek and Roman gods, with war threatening, each side making angry statements, doing everything they could to embarrass each other and threatening and carrying out many reprisals. For instance, the Greeks shut down all the night spots in their Latin Quarter, whereas in their section of the heavens the Latins padlocked all Greek restaurants.

Marquis and Morley went on and on, improvising until they had Maud groggy, their involved answers to Weed's questions contributing no little to her befuddlement. They ranged far and wide in the realms of mythology, and by the time they got through they had quite a cast of characters—Zeus, Venus, Medea, Circe, Electra, Cupid (who kept the love interest going), Cerberus, Hero and Leander, Apollo, Melpomene, Excalibur, Samson, Hercules, Sappho, Aphrodite, assorted druids and dryads, Narcissus, Scylla and Charybdis, etc., etc.

This story has a pretty good oral history. There are several versions of it, alike in essence, differing only as to detail. According to one version, Maud thought Mr. Morley wasn't quite himself that night. Usually his conversation was so lucid, whereas that night he was hard to follow. She wondered if the poor man wasn't tired after a hard day's work.

What Maud didn't know was that even in those days when the doctors had Marquis on the Water Wagon a good deal of the time, he never felt equal to one evening with her without a few shots of whisky. He, Weed, and Morley had had some drinks together before dinner that night and though reportedly all three were under control, they had put themselves in a mood to have some fun with the terror of Forest Hills—to tame her for an evening, if possible, by befuddling her.

From the standpoint of their objective, the evening was a big success.

One finds himself thinking of the Don Marquis who in "The Jesters" wrote:

> "We cannot help it, we are cursed
> With an incorrigible mirth. . . ."

It made him unhappy that when he sat down to dinner with his sisters it was necessary for his wife to absent herself. He could make light of it by joining friends in a joke at the expense of the Troublesome One, one of his designations for Maud, but he could not have derived much satisfaction from it. Later in that same poem he changes "incorrigible mirth" to "desperate mirth," which describes the Marquis of 1928. "Some perverse humor shakes us, and we laugh!"

These "perverse humors" provided only temporary surcease but they kept him going. He didn't attempt to conceal that once the incorrigible mirth had had its innings he would

> . . . Sink again with baffled wings.

Then once again this moody and unpredictable poet would have to find a counteractive for

> . . . the clouds that shadow
> The disconsolate Earth.

And we find him reporting:

> Some rebel mood will seize us, and we laugh!

It is all there in "The Jesters." He rated other of his poems above it, yet on those few occasions when he consented to read from his poetry at "the literary teas" he came to despise, he always included that one, possibly because it explains his moodiness better than anything else he ever wrote.

One day at lunch Clive Weed told me he thought there was "something wrong" with Marquis's second marriage. Clive seldom mentioned Marjorie by name. It was usually "Don's second wife," which had a strange sound.

In the days of Marquis's first marriage Reina figured largely in his conversation with intimates. He would be reminded of something she had said or done that had tickled him and he would comment enthusiastically. By contrast, two years after his marriage to Marjorie she had practically dropped out of his conversation. "He never mentioned her any more," reported Weed. With a few exceptions, Marjorie didn't like "the Players crowd." One of those she didn't like was Weed, who, after a few calls at 125 East 62nd Street, decided not to return.

Marquis confided to intimates that Marjorie thought he spent too much time at the Players. One of his favorite stories—which he undoubtedly improved in the telling—finds Marjorie telephoning him at the Club to remind him that he also had a home on 62nd Street —it was an old brownstone house, in case he'd forgotten what it looked like, and would he mind dropping in some time?

Clive Weed, whose companions were mainly inhibitionless painters and writers, was a salty conversationalist who sometimes, without realizing it, shocked the uninitiated. Whatever the reason, Marjorie made no effort to conceal her dislike for him. This had no effect on the Marquis-Weed friendship. The men saw each other at the Players and elsewhere. A checkup reveals that not many members of that Gramercy Park monument to *gemütlichkeit* ever saw the inside of the brownstone on East 62nd Street.

Among those who were not affected by Marjorie's censorship were the Homer Croys. (Homer had been instrumental in getting her a job as a radio actress with NBC and although the job didn't last long, Homer remained in good favor. Meanwhile Marjorie and Mrs. Croy had become good friends.)

In 1928, the year this chapter deals with, Marquis published an article in the *Saturday Evening Post*, mentioned earlier in these pages in another context, in which he paid a touching tribute to his first wife, to whom he alluded as "the gamest person that ever lived, man or woman." In another passage (dealing with 1912) he wrote: "When the New York *American* fired me . . . my wife sold a story (to a magazine) and we lived on that for a while. I couldn't sell anything; I couldn't get a job anywhere." It was Reina, he tells us, who pulled him through.

In other words, two years after his remarriage we find him extolling his first wife—in several moving passages—in an article in which he doesn't make a single reference to his second wife! The fact that it was a two-part article that totaled over twelve thousand words made it all the more noticeable. It is doubtful whether Marquis was aware that there was anything tactless about this. There is no indication that during all the years of their relationship he had ever done anything consciously to hurt Marjorie.

Yet certain questions inevitably arise. Was this a happy marriage? Consider the public tribute to Reina in a mass-circulation magazine in combination with the following, which are reprinted for effect from letters Marquis wrote that same year:

"The only enjoyment that I take out of life is in writing and now and then sitting down and getting quietly stewed"—from a letter to Lyman Beecher Stowe.

"Merely to pay up present debts and obligations there are at least 18 months of desperate and continued potboiling. I have a schedule that calls for one short story or one article each week for 18 months" —from a letter to Christopher Morley.

Other letters of that same period, reflecting even blacker moods, could be cited. So there was probably something to Weed's belief that something had gone wrong with Marquis's second marriage. No one seems to know the whole story. It *is* known that Marquis was chagrined by his inability to keep his promise to back Marjorie in a summer-theater venture. She had confidence in her ability to produce and direct, and he had complete faith that, with what she had learned from previous ventures, she would be successful if given another opportunity. He had plenty of money when he had originally made that promise; now the money was gone. A man of his word, Marquis made good on that promise years later but he had kept her waiting a long time and something happened to their relationship in the interim.

Despite his gloomy letters to Morley, Stowe, Weed, and others, the subsequent record provides ample evidence that Marquis's incorrigible mirth rescued him time and again from "the disillusions of the barren years," another line from "The Jesters." In fact, Marquis's whole life was a struggle between a natural gaiety and the despair of disappointment. In his stoutest defense of his incorrigible mirth—a term that comes as close to a shibboleth as he ever had —he points to it as his only recourse on those occasions when he wearied of what he found when he had

> . . . stolen cowering through the nethermost
> Dim crowded hells
> Where in the common terror of doomed multitudes
> The vague ghost cringes, huddling toward his neighbor ghost,
> And each finds each the mirror of his sins.

Once, quoting a line he had written years before for the *Evening Sun*, Marquis told Weed that happiness was the interval between periods of unhappiness. So a man was entitled to a good laugh when the time for that came. Yet he had developed some strange phobia about finding it necessary to explain those bursts of mirth when they seized him. "It's a hell of a thing," he said, "when you feel an impulse to apologize for your cheerful moments."

Many other examples of the introspective Marquis could be cited. Writing about this characteristic of his friend, Christopher Morley had this to say in *Letters of Askance*:

"There is always the doubt as to whether a man is the best judge of himself. And it is almost certain that he will not show the figure to the world that he sees in his bright moments of self-appreciation

—and Marquis is a queer mixture of flamboyant self-appreciation and really humble self-depreciation. I never knew a man who devoted more time to thinking about himself; I never knew a man who thought of himself more variously, or who was less capable of a steady clarity in looking at himself."

One of the most unusual of the Players personalities is Charles Connolly, for years the Club's chief steward and general factotum. Unobtrusively efficient and blessed with charm and affability, Charlie, if you draw him out, is a first-class storyteller; and to those who know him and knew Don Marquis it is no secret why the men became good friends and why Charlie was welcome in Don's home. One of Marquis's lifelong enthusiasms was Mark Twain and it was a joy to have a friend who had known the author of *Huckleberry Finn* and could tell stories about him. Connolly, who is over eighty, joined the staff of the Players in his youth and has vivid recollections of the days when Twain was a member. A bartender then, Charlie served drinks to the famous writer and Marquis frequently repeated odds and ends of Twainiana that he picked up from the Club's companionable steward, as for instance:

In the days when Mark Twain was a Player, the street cleaners of New York wore white uniforms and were known as White Wings. This made the humorist a special target for kidding when he stepped up to the bar in his inevitable (weather permitting) white suit. The gibes ranged all the way from the predictable, "Have you had a good day in the street?"—a *double-entendre* stemming from "the street" being synonymous with Wall Street in those days—to mock-serious notes handed to him by page boys reminding him that street cleaners were not eligible for membership.

Charlie, now an honorary member of the Club, recalled for Marquis's benefit (who used it in his column) that more often than not Mark Twain ordered a hot drink of some kind, a Scotch, bourbon, or rye toddy, according to his whim, and frequently regardless of the weather or the season. "In those days," said Connolly, "no self-respecting bar would think of operating without a kettle of steaming water handy to take care of the hot-toddy customers. Today it's ice, ice, ice. No one seems to realize how good a hot toddy can be. Mark Twain did."

Connolly also recalls that when Mark Twain played pool at the Club, which he frequently did when he was in New York—(to this day his cue is displayed like a horizontal halo directly over his portrait in the billiard room)—he smoked cigars incessantly. The billiard room adjoins the bar and when Twain—(no one called him Clemens, Charlie reports, his pen name having taken hold)—needed a fresh cigar he would signal Charlie to throw him one. Half the fun was seeing whether the bartender and the smoker could collaborate on a perfect pitch and catch. Anyone, Mr. Twain contended, could walk up to the bar and buy a cigar. Besides, it interrupted your pool-playing.

Connolly recollects that when he was a young bartender at the Players a little after the turn of the century none of the Club personnel seemed to realize how important Mark Twain was. The same was true of most of the members. "Members and staff alike knew he was a leading writer," observed Charlie, "but I didn't get the impression that anyone seemed to think he was any more important, for instance, than a young writer named Newton Booth Tarkington, who had written a book called *The Gentleman from Indiana* that everyone was talking about." Which reminded Connolly that at one time there was a rule requiring members to sign their full names to bar and dining-room checks. Tarkington, who had gotten into the habit of signing "Tark," told Charlie he thought Newton Booth Tarkington was too long; it was hard to get it on one line and it took too much time. Connolly suggested that he continue signing "Tark," which the novelist did, and he never received a complaint from the Club's office. This became one of Don Marquis's favorite anti-red-tape stories.

Connolly recalls the time—it was in the twenties but he isn't sure of the year—when he heard that Marquis and a group of friends had decided to form a company to put on a play they were enthusiastic about. He doesn't recall the name of the play. He had been impressed by the success of *The Old Soak* and had decided to ask Mr. Marquis if he could be permitted to invest a thousand dollars in the new production. "If it proved to be a hit," Charlie said, "I'd get my money back many times over. They agreed to let me participate."

The play was produced and Connolly recalls that although the critics were friendly, appraising it as a laudable effort to do something artistic in the theater, it didn't fare well at the box office. The run was brief and those who invested in it, including Marquis, lost their money.

"One day at the Players," said Charlie, "Mr. Marquis signaled to me and said he wanted to have a talk with me. Before much talking took place, he took an envelope out of his pocket and handed it to me. 'There's your money back, Charlie,' he said. I handed it back to him, saying I had taken a chance like everyone else and stood to make money if the play succeeded. He insisted on my keeping it, saying that I made my money the hard way and he wouldn't be able to sleep nights if he thought he'd cost me a thousand dollars. I repeated over and over again that I had made an investment, that I'd gone into the thing with my eyes open and he didn't owe me a cent. But he brushed my arguments aside. 'Count it,' he said, 'and see if it's all there.' It *was*—the full thousand dollars. I've become acquainted with some wonderful people in my time but I've never met anyone who was quite the equal of Mr. Marquis. It's hard to tell you what I mean because it was more than just kindness. Other people are kind too. There was something about Mr. Marquis that was different. You had the feeling he was personally interested in you and it sort of got under your skin. If I'd been a favorite member of his family he couldn't have been more interested in me. I knew how much sorrow Mr. Marquis had suffered in the twenties—first his little boy died, then his wife—and I knew he was a sad man even though he put up a good front. I thought it was great that anyone who was having such a rough time himself could take the time to think about the other fellow's problems. He was easily the most thoughtful man I ever knew."

When Marquis's *Love Sonnets of a Cave Man* was published, the Boston *Transcript*, then the most "literary" of New England's dailies, whose judgments commanded attention, published a review that likened the author to Charlie Chaplin, leading comedian of the silent-film era, who was tremendously popular at the time and very much in the news. Because of this unorthodox comparison in a highbrow paper—and for the additional reason that the *Transcript* foreshadowed a "true and lasting recognition" for Marquis—this review attracted considerable attention and was widely quoted.

The *Transcript* featured *Love Sonnets of a Cave Man* in a three-column spread, and because it is one of the most unusual reviews of a Marquis book, it is here reprinted in part:

"There is not very much that one can say to prove that Don Marquis is an artist. It has all been said already, and by this reviewer

himself. Perhaps in a generation or two the average reader will
become aware of this fact. For the present, Mr. Marquis must
be content to be considered in a trivial light as the author of those
'funny little things.' As a matter of fact his light, whimsical touch
approaches that of Charlie Chaplin. His is the same unobvious
method that seems outwardly to be working on a lot of low-comedy
gags, and really contributes the highest and most delicate bits
of technical resource. It takes someone interested in writing to appreciate a rhymed interview with Julius Caesar, which besides
being excruciatingly funny, makes mock in the lightest manner of
the maudlin interviewer of great personalities. Listen to but a single
verse:

> "Caesar," I said to him as I pulled out a pad of paper,
> "You've seen, no doubt, what Cassius says about your latest caper?"
> C. Julius smiled and coughed into his purple-hemmed bandanna,
> He gave your representative a very fine Havana,
> He clicked his sandals on the tiles, he trifled with his vesture—
> We interviewers never miss the smallest little gesture!
> In building up the characters, of statesmen or of wretches,
> It is these telling little strokes that vitalize our sketches: . . .

"And then with a smile Mr. Marquis tosses off such a gentle line as
'A brontosaurus heaved his sluggish girth.' He even makes such
words as pterodactyl and pleistocene fit into his measures and his
rhyme schemes. And then just to show that he can top anything,
he writes a long narrative poem about the Irish, mentioning at least
a hundred truly Gaelic names and still retaining his lilting patter
melody. He is throughout the rather wide limits of this small volume
of verse the consistent bad boy, who, like Charlie Chaplin, succeeds
in being funny and yet slipping his 'Art' over on us who wish only
to guffaw at the custard throwing and 'wise cracks.' A fellow like
William Shakespeare could appreciate Mr. Marquis, but we work-
aday souls merely accept him as one of us and let it go at that. It
is too bad.

"Mr. Marquis sets himself a large order in this volume. Not only
does he make museums supply him with mirth-provoking material,
but he also writes several delightfully tender and at moments wistful
love lyrics. He takes a fling at prohibition, American history and even
Biblical stories. The Old Soak returns to life with one or two
hilarious narrations. Mr. Marquis runs the gamut of inventive
ability. Through it all he remains a remarkably effective poet and a

humorist who can smile at life as well as merely say funny things. He sees life directly, as deeply as Charlie Chaplin. . . . He can be cleverly funny, as in 'The Primitive's the Mode,' or he can be as soundly a commentator on life in a dry way as in 'Reincarnated.' Thus in the latter poem:

> Lovers were we a million years agone;
> A dozen moons have fallen from the sky,
> A thousand empires laid them down to die,
> And still our amorous idyl carries on!
> When first we met, the roaring Mastodon
> Peered in our Cave and watched me black your eye;
> Today the roaring L-train rushes by
> Your flat—and I shall black your eye anon.
> Reincarnation once again, my Sweet,
> Brings us together o'er the waste of years!
> And once again I catch you by the ears,
> My Love, and slam your head against the door
> To show you that I love you as of yore—
> A love like ours can never grow effete!

"It is a pity, Mr. Marquis, that you must await the centuries to win a true and lasting recognition. Because you have conducted a column you are labeled as just a comic strip artist! . . .

"Mr. Marquis suffers, perhaps, because the ideas which shine through his buffooneries are not severe and pessimistic. He holds no dark thoughts upon the worthlessness of the universe and the men who dwell therein. . . .

"Mr. Marquis is an artist, and a subtle one. May his work be appreciated some day at its true worth!"

Many of the reviews in the Boston *Transcript* were anonymous. This one was signed "W.E.H."

"These sonnets start out uproariously," said William Rose Benét, writing about the same book in the *Saturday Review of Literature*. "They are tossed off with huge carelessness . . . and yet we are no further along than the third one when its two final lines bring us up short with a start:

> And the shag headlands shook and shrank beneath
> Tread of the thunder-footed Mastodon.

"Great gravy! Why, there might actually have been a great sonnet, ending with such lines!"

Benét liked "the gusto of 'A Chant of the Rum Banks.' . . . Then along comes the famous Old Soak, singing of King David and Samson; and this is good, highly individual stuff. It is in 'A Plea for Disarmament,' however, that Marquis bursts forth into his occasionally inimitable burlesque balladry at its best. His 'Abridged History of the U.S.,' with its intricate rhyming, is another excellent thing. The ballads of Prohibition that bring the volume to a close, we should like to learn by heart. . . . For the finale, the long-famous 'Noah an' Jonah an' Cap'n John Smith,' which is reprinted, we have, of course, nothing but the highest praise. We ourself should purchase the book if only for that epic scrimmage between the 'bull of great renown' and the 'rhino red with ire,' which ought to be sung to the trumpeting of tubas and the sough and swelling roar of some cosmic accordion!"

In that last paragraph Benét is referring to "A Plea for Disarmament," to which he had made an earlier allusion. This is one of the most meaningful pieces of nonsense Marquis ever wrote. The "bull of great renown" and the "rhino red with ire" symbolize in their six pages of metrical high jinks two irreconcilable forces spoiling for a fight. This ballad, originally written shortly after the termination of World War I, and first published in book form in 1928, is as timely today as when Marquis first pounded it out on his typewriter. It winds up as follows:

They met as if 'twere engines propelled by steam and fire,
For they were full of anger and they were full of ire—
Oh, the rollicky, bullocky Bullock and the Rhino red with ire! . . .

They met as two volcanoes both bent on damage fell,
Might butt each other, bursting, and scatter chunks of hell.
Oh, the ramping Rinktum Rhino and the Bullock full of hell! . . .

Two cataclysms clashing in cosmic counterpoint
Are apt to wry the keyboard a little out of joint—
Wagner sometimes wiggles the keyboard out of joint.

But only roaring Wagner with his blethering bellows full
Could have sung the maelstrom music when the Rhino met the Bull—
Oh, the ringtum, rangtum Rhino and the rollicky, bullocky Bull!

They met as haughty meteors, all raging and head on—
And presently the Rhino and the Bullock both were gone!
The ringtum, rangtum Rhino and the Bullock both were gone.

Two vacuums they lay there, deleted, side by side.
And it never need have happened but they both were full of pride,
Full of beaniness and bluster, full of emptiness and pride.

And you'll surely get my meaning, unless you're very dull,
Of the ringtum, rangtum Rhino and the rollicky, frollicky Bull!
Oh, the rinktum, ranktum Rhino and the rollicky, bullocky Bull!

In Marquis's free-lance days he joked constantly about his aches
and pains; but this was one time when his friends had no trouble
figuring out whether there was anything behind the clowning. He
didn't look well.

When Marquis found himself falling behind his promised delivery
dates he made a practice of working late, drinking more coffee to
keep awake than was good for him. After a long stretch of night
writing it was not unusual for him to be so stimulated by caffeine
that sleep became an impossibility.

Marquis, having jocularly announced early in his columning days
that the German government during World War I regarded him as
their most serious obstacle to victory, what with his constant chaff-
ing of the Kaiser, friends of the columnist and the reading public
wondered if there was anything behind the flippantly worded paragraphs to the effect that he was being threatened by German sympathizers. Few realized that the gibes had had a basis in fact until
they read in a *Post* article, published in December 1928:

"During 1915 and 1916 I got scores of letters from German
sympathizers, who used to threaten to bump me off if I didn't quit
writing against the godly Kaiser and his noble cohorts, and from
not a few persons who called themselves pacifists. I lost my neutrality,
early and often, in spite of President Wilson's fervid appeals for
no American to take sides in thought, word or deed. The only difference I could see between the pacifists and the pro-Germans was
that the former merely intimated that I ought to be suppressed, while
the latter promised to call some day soon and do it with their own
fair hands. After the letters that were written to me in those years,
nobody can really hurt my feelings about anything. . . . A Secret
Service man told me I was one of about thirty writers whom the
pro-Germans were trying to intimidate into silence at that time, with
no success whatever in any one instance. It was a deliberately planned
policy, but a very stupid one."

That *Post* article, which has proven so fine a source, also clears up a mystery about a piece of verse Theodore Roosevelt reportedly sent to Marquis as a contribution to "The Sun Dial." The following from Marquis's confessional (published that year, 1928) explains why efforts to find the poem have been fruitless:

"It was during the war that I had the dubious distinction of losing the only bit of verse the late Theodore Roosevelt was ever known to have written. He was writing for a New York magazine at the time, and he appended the verse in his own handwriting to a dictated letter—a rather jolly little jingle chiming in with some topic that was running in the column. I didn't know whether it was for my private consumption or whether he meant for me to print it. I asked him and he said to go ahead and print it. But by that time it had got mixed with the pile of contributions on one of my desks and was lost forever."

This magazine article also gives Don's own version of still another story that has taken its place in the Marquis archives. It has been varyingly told but the points of conflict are mere details, and the different renditions all add up to the same thing. The story has to do with Frank Munsey, owner of the New York *Sun* during several of Marquis's years on that paper, and a situation that developed from a discussion of Mr. Munsey's last will and testament. Wrote Marquis:

"When Munsey died, leaving I don't know how many millions to the Metropolitan Museum of Art, parts of his will were subjected to criticism. I remember being at a large confused dinner party one evening shortly after the terms of his will were published, when the subject came up.

"The lady whom I had taken in to dinner, and whose name I hadn't caught distinctly, did not join in the criticism, but spoke in warm appreciation of him. She turned to me a little later and said:

"'That donation to the Metropolitan was a wonderful thing for Mr. Munsey to do. But the terms of it have been making a little difficulty for me.' She explained that she was on some committee charged with the job of collecting money for the Metropolitan, but since the papers had published the news of his magnificent gift some of the regular yearly donors felt relieved of the necessity of contributing because of it. They didn't understand that it wasn't all to come to the Metropolitan at once in a lump; that it would be some time before its full benefits would be felt.

"'Leave it all to me,' I said easily, for I never know what to talk about at dinner parties and grab at any subject. 'I'll get the Metropolitan all the money it wants.'

" 'I thought you were some sort of writer,' she said, looking puzzled.

" 'Writing a column was a fad of mine for a while,' I said, 'but nothing more than a fad. I used to dictate a column every morning to one of my secretaries while I was shaving. My real interests are financial—oil, railroads, rubber, real estate, mines, insurance companies—all that sort of thing. I'll fix up some scheme so the Metropolitan won't have to worry or wait.'

" 'Really?' she said.

" 'Surely,' I rejoined. And outlined a plan—which flashed into my head just like that!—whereby the Metropolitan could get the entire benefit of Mr. Munsey's gift even before they got the gift itself.

" 'If you like,' I said, 'I'll give you an introduction to my own banker, which will get you all the credit you want.'

"I was just about to go on and tell the lady that she could do a good deal worse than put all her own business affairs into my hands, when I caught sight of the place card by her plate and ceased to give her financial advice, perceiving that it was Mrs. W. K. Vanderbilt."

That year also saw the publication of the revised edition of *The Story of the Sun* (from 1833 to 1928). Friends of Marquis's having protested the exclusion of the originator of "The Sun Dial" from the first edition—(it appeared when the column was at the peak of its popularity)—were eager to see how the revised version dealt with him. It was announced that the book had been brought up to date in all particulars and was "a definitive chronicle of the first ninety-five years of a great newspaper."

It didn't take these people long to find out. Again Don Marquis had been excluded! There was not a single reference to him from cover to cover.

To date approximately 350,000 copies of the archy and mehitabel books have been sold, including an omnibus which embraces the three volumes of these pieces that Marquis published and which has established itself as one of those perennial best-sellers. About 80 per cent of the contents of these books originally appeared in the *Sun*, about 15 per cent in the *Tribune* and the *Herald Tribune*, the rest in *Collier's*. So it is not surprising that the student assigned to write a paper on Marquis is perplexed to find not a scrap of information about him in what purports to be a definitive work.

One of the Poohbahs of the *Sun* is reported to have said, when confronted with this second failure to mention Marquis, "Hell! you can't mention everybody." Perhaps. But, if you try, you can mention *nearly* everybody, as Frank M. O'Brien, the author of the book, demonstrated. Among those to whom O'Brien alluded by name in his revised edition were: John Edgar Martin, production manager of the mechanical department and seventeen of the men who worked under him, all specifically identified; Charles E. Luxton, office manager; Hans Muller, manager of the general bookkeeping department; Samuel Wolfender, manager of the advertising bookkeeping department; Howard F. Rhoads, manager of the circulation bookkeeping department; Hilson Munsey, auditor; Emma André, cashier; John E. Dies, purchasing agent; Martha Dusseau, chief telephone operator.

With the lone exception of Marquis, all the people connected with the paper's editorial department were mentioned, including the society editor and his two assistants, the people who ran the school page, and the photographers.

Owner Munsey died three years before this revised edition was published. When the book was originally issued in 1918 it was a Munsey project and the policy of excluding Marquis may have been preserved in recognition of Munsey's anger—(the paper was now owned by Munsey's former associate and close friend William T. Dewart)—when Marquis left the *Sun* in 1922 to join the *Tribune*.

The Story of the Sun is loaded with so much information about Frank Munsey, a journalistic pigmy, that a full page in the index (beginning with "Munsey, Frank Andrew, remarkable career of") is required as a key to the many references!

How Marquis felt about being excluded a second time is not known, since he discouraged efforts to get him to comment. One is reminded of a philosophic comment in his column on what he called "the pleasures of the petty." Those who tried to reform the small-minded were guilty of cruelty since it was wrong to interfere with *anyone's* fun.

Marquis's daughter Barbara was ten at this point in our story. It will be recalled that as a tot she had been considered "a sickly child," a classification from which she had graduated. Now she was again showing signs that disturbed the family doctor. She complained of headaches and dizzy spells and was several pounds underweight for a girl who was nearing her eleventh birthday. A diet designed to increase her weight accomplished nothing because Barbara didn't have enough appetite to give it a fair trial. In fact, during the fall of 1928 she lost a little weight instead of gaining.

Marquis's health was none too good either. He had been in and out of bed with an assortment of complaints, mostly minor, that Dr. March ascribed to overwork. March urged a complete change for both Don and Barbara. The child had not quite adjusted to her new mother, sister, and brother. All three—Marjorie, Ruth, and Walter, Jr.—were kind and considerate, but Barbara, sensitive and introspective, still talked about the wonderful times she and her mother had had together. Although she was not yet six when her mother died, she remembered vividly the talks she had had with Reina, and tried to interpret those conversations in terms of her new life, even struggling to figure out what her mother would have wanted her to do under certain circumstances. These backward looks were not good for this overimaginative youngster who lived in a world of her own, one in which poetry and fantasy predominated.

Marquis decided to take Barbara to Hollywood. He had hoped that Marjorie would be able to accompany them but she did not find this practical. She would stay in New York and look after her children and perhaps join them later.

Marquis felt he would be able to fulfill his magazine commitments as well in Hollywood as anywhere else. It now made no difference where he worked. Several of his friends—playwrights and other writers —were working in Hollywood and he would be able to learn from them whether he should try to write for the movies. This was during the period when he had temporarily abandoned his plan to write "the Great American Something or Other" and was concentrating on the mundane business of "keeping his creditors happy." "Only General Motors, U. S. Steel, and a few others in that class," he had remarked, "have a bigger overhead."

One of Don's problems before leaving was to assign someone to look after Pete, his Boston bull. Marjorie's son Walter, then between seven and eight, assumed this responsibility, with Marjorie as his assistant. Marquis had become attached to Walter, by all accounts a lively, fun-loving mite who was liked by everyone who recalls him. Marquis found the boy first-rate company. One day he had come upon little Walter examining his chess set and studying the different pieces. And when the lad expressed a desire to learn the game Don had started teaching him, his pupil making satisfactory progress for one so young. Occasionally before the youngster's bedtime Don gave him a game. Never having overcome his love of play-acting, Don sought to amuse the lad by pretending to be stumped by moves the latter made, making gestures of despair and rumpling his hair as he studied the chessboard, and occasionally, for added emphasis, faking finger-nail biting to give the child a chance to remind him that such things were not permitted in that house.

Marquis had also offered to show Barbara how to play chess but she was too busy playing with words—writing poems and stories— to give it serious consideration. However, because it was fun to join her father and Walter in the laughter that inevitably resulted, she was an enthusiastic gallery of one during some of these contests.

In entrusting his dog to Walter Marquis was displaying real confidence in his chess pupil. For that little Boston bull had so endeared itself to its master that he had written poems and short stories about it. Four of these poems are to be found in Edwin Burtis's *All the Best Dog Poems*, along with contributions by T. S. Eliot, Louis Untermeyer, Dorothy Parker, Robert Browning, Rudyard Kipling, Carl Sandburg, Eugene Field, Thomas Hardy, Lord Byron, Shakespeare, Wordsworth, and Marquis's old friends Dana Burnet and Oliver Herford.

To Marquis, one of the most attractive features of the California trip was that it would put more distance between himself and Maud. As things worked out, Marquis had congratulated himself too soon on his contemplated escape to Hollywood. One of those unexpected developments that the fates seemed forever to have in store for him found him committed to an arrangement whose ramifications could not have been less to his liking.

Barbara had suggested that her Aunt Nev be asked to make the trip to the West Coast with them. No one except her father understood Barbara quite as well as the self-styled "homebody" who had accompanied her sister on so many trips that she was now a kind of contradiction, a *well-traveled* homebody, a split role she had accommodated herself to and seemed to enjoy. She would be delighted to make the journey and spend a few months in California, she told her brother, but she would be unable to leave the unpredictable Maud, whose behavior might approximate the normal for a week at a time and who, without any hint of what was coming, might then have several disturbingly erratic days in a row. It is not known how much of a factor at that time was her drug addiction.

So we are confronted by the irony of a man who thought he was about to leave Queens County, New York, far behind him being suddenly thrust into the position of taking the most troublesome feature of that county to California with him. This development didn't promise the "change" that Marquis needed. "Dump the medicines I've prescribed down the nearest sewer if you wish," March had pleaded, "but for God's sake get a complete change." The doctor was an unhappy man when he learned that Maud was accompanying her brother to California.

Late in November 1928 Marquis, his sisters, and Barbara moved into a house at 1919 Argyle Avenue, Hollywood, which had been recommended by friends.

In a few weeks Barbara was responding to the California climate and looking and feeling better. Her interest in writing returned and the poems began to bubble forth again. Once more she was carrying around with her the copy of selections from the poetry of William Blake which her mother had given her before she could read. It was from this book that Reina had read to her—and sometimes Don—before she had more than a glimmering of the meaning of *Songs of Innocence* and had captivated her parents with the observation that she liked "the way they sounded."

Now that Barbara could read, her father had come to regard this volume by Blake as a barometer. When, for instance, *she* insisted on reading to *him* one of the songs he was accustomed to recite to her from memory, or to read, he knew that she was herself again. Now she declared her intention of entering the newest poetry contest that *St. Nicholas Magazine* had announced and was occupying herself with the composition of possible entries.

The other writer in the family—her father—was finding it more difficult to get started. After a few days of staring futilely at his typewriter Marquis decided to follow the advice of Hollywood friends and take a good look at the movie colony and the rest of the Los Angeles area. He attended parties, met writers he knew who were working in the different studios, and tried to figure out from what he saw and heard whether there was an opportunity to do something of consequence for the movies. With this in mind he asked his friends to introduce him to some of the policy-makers, the executives who made the decisions that determined what pictures the movie-going public would see. He wanted to take soundings that conceivably could be helpful if he subsequently had occasion to sit down with any of these men in their offices and try to sell them ideas. For instance, what would the reaction be to a trial balloon designed to gauge the interest in an adaptation of Kipling's *Kim* for the screen? Marquis, it will be recalled, was unenthusiastic about the early Kipling but he admired much of that author's later work, including *Kim*. In fact, he considered *Kim* a classic and made the mistake of saying so to Hollywood executives. (He also took soundings on the possibility of selling adaptations of other books that were more familiarly classified as "classics.") In those days, before Hollywood realized the possibilities of good literature, the word "classic" was synonymous with dullness and the surest guarantee of a negative response was to propose filming one. Marquis expected too much of the moneybags who had drifted into the motion-picture industry and had to be told who had written *Kim* and what it was all about. He seems to have expected of the movie-makers, most of them hard-boiled businessmen who had originally come to Hollywood as participants in a gold rush that promised greater profits than their former businesses, some deep overwhelming appreciation of the motion picture as an art form. Since, almost without exception, these former enterprises of the major movie-makers had had nothing remotely to do with anything that could be labeled "art," perhaps Marquis had set his sights too high. The movie-makers did not claim much more in those days than that they were good businessmen who knew how to make a product that the public would buy. Having the viewpoint of the artist, it was natural that Marquis should have expected more of Hollywood than it was capable of producing.

Although disappointed in the unimaginative, uninformed types he found at or near the top of the motion-picture industry, Marquis's sortie into the Hollywood jungle was not entirely unproductive. It yielded some ideas for magazine fiction. He finally got down to work and just about the time his typewriter again began to produce salable words he developed a heavy cold. Despite a fever that clearly indicated that he belonged in bed, he continued to work in an effort to meet promises he had made for the delivery of short stories and articles to magazine editors and for the equally good reason that he needed the money those manuscripts would yield. One day he had a "seizure" that gave him the feeling he was "going to crack up and fall apart," and finding himself "without the strength to write another word," he took to his bed and sent for the doctor, who declared that his patient would have to remain quiet for three or four weeks, after which he would be able to work again on a limited schedule. The doctor who attended Marquis has since died and efforts to determine the precise nature of the "heart trouble" his patient reportedly had have proven unavailing.

Stories about Marquis's illness appeared in the press. No doctor is mentioned in any of them.

How the press learned of Marquis's illness is not known. Maud acted as spokesman for her brother, using her full name: Bernice Maud Marquis. None of the stories quoted Nev, who was usually pushed out of the picture by her aggressive sister (who was her junior by five years) in a situation involving contact with the outside world. Over the years Maud had made about a half-dozen statements to the press regarding her brother, some voluntary, some in answer to queries put to both sisters. Because Nev never once was quoted on anything involving her brother, it is possible that the sisters had an understanding that Maud was to do the talking. Maud also occasionally sent letters to the editors of newspapers and in one of them used a quotation from Marquis—not too logically, he thought—to establish a point she was making rather truculently. This proved an embarrassment to her brother and he asked her not to repeat the performance.

On January 19, 1929, the following appeared in the New York *Times*:

"Los Angeles—Don Marquis, New York humorist, columnist and playwright, spent his seventh day in bed today, recuperating from a severe heart attack resulting from influenza. His condition is not alarming but several weeks of complete rest will be necessary. According to his sister, Bernice Maud Marquis, the writer failed to take proper care of himself, trying to continue his work while ill.

"Marquis arrived in Hollywood on Nov. 23, accompanied by his two sisters, Miss Bernice M. and Miss Neva V. Marquis, and his 10-year-old daughter, Barbara. They came West, it was said, to benefit Barbara's health. She is said to be showing marked improvement. Prior to his illness Marquis was devoting his time to fiction writing. They plan to stay here until Spring and then return to New York by a leisurely trip around the Isthmus."

After communicating with Marjorie in New York, the *Times* added this to its story: "Mrs. Don Marquis authorized a statement last night denying that her husband was critically ill. His condition was not serious, she said."

As the person to whom Marquis most frequently wrote, Clive Weed was urged to suggest that Marjorie leave for Hollywood at once and see her husband through his illness. Weed demurred, fearing that if Maud picked a fight with her sister-in-law, which was not unlikely, the effect on Don would be bad. Weed also feared that Don would be subjected to Christian Science readings and doubted whether his friend was in the mood for this.

The last time Don had been ill—this was in New York—Marjorie herself had called in Dr. March and co-operated fully with him. She had also reserved the right to produce Christian Science nurses, who read selected passages from Mary Baker Eddy to her husband. There were times when Don wanted to be alone to read a book or take a nap but he submitted. He realized that his wife was trying to help him and therefore offered no resistance to these ministrations. But since he had tried, at his wife's urgent pleading, to become a Christian Scientist and had found that he could not live by Mrs. Eddy's code, he was puzzled by this insistence on reading to one with whom these readers had no "communication." But he let them drone on to avoid a quarrel.

If Marjorie was upset by her husband's illness, she didn't show it. She was praying for him, she had arranged for "absent treatment," and was confident he would recover.

There is nothing to indicate that Marquis was aware that his illness was receiving attention in the press. In the collection of letters written by Marquis—on the typewriter and by hand—in the Walter Hampden Memorial Library of the Players Club there are many, including long ones, that he wrote to Weed from Hollywood. In one of them, dated March 12, 1929, almost two months after that story appeared in the *Times*, we find him writing: "Don't tell anyone I'm sick— business reasons." In the same letter, which covers nine long pages, he writes:

". . . I'm out of bed in a chair a large part of the day, but I can't walk about much. It brings on another attack. It scares hell out of me. . . . I'm writing a novel. Don't tell anybody. . . .

"This country consists of great sunshiny stretches of Blah. It is a country that has *never been thought in*. You feel it. It never will be.

Nothing mental can ever take root here. I seriously believe that one thing the matter with the movies is that they are made here. . . . It is a great place for superficial religious cults, not only the pseudo-Christian, but pseudo-Buddhist, new-thoughtist, and all the Blah stuff. The beef is stringy, the chickens are tasteless and tough, the fish is bad, the houses are flimsy, the hills are ugly, there is little oxygen in the air, the natives are cheap and childish . . . with no finish to them, and crude, uninteresting liars; there is neither passion nor reality in this trashy civilization—except, possibly, among the Mexicans, Hawaiians, Japs, Chinese. . . .

"I have started a new religion myself; I will tell you about it, when I see you. You know it is impossible for me to get away entirely from the moralistic inhibitions which I inherited; I learned that 20 years ago, and quit trying. You can't get entirely away either, and it makes you unhappy; but they are in your blood and nerves; you insist, however, on repudiating them; it is an intellectual gesture with you, in order to keep your self-respect. You aspire to the amoral, but you can't quite make the grade with anything but your mind. Along with this, you have an exaggerated instinctive chivalry, which you are ashamed of, because it ties up with the old-fashioned traditions which you try to shuck; it bothers you because of its sentimental connotations, which (mentally) you despise. You interest me almost more than anyone else I know. You need a new religion, too—not mine, but one of your own.

"Here is a truth: getting a true religion for yourself is merely the discovery—the conscious appraisement—of the qualities in yourself which have hitherto influenced you unconsciously; the gain of the ages, humanly, has been merely a gain in individual self-consciousness,—I can't quite formulate it, but I'm on the track of something here.

"You may as well give up and be the sentimentalist you really are. This advice irritates you, of course. I intended it to. I love to irritate you; it always brings out a flash of reality. I discovered years ago that I could irritate you by accentuating the smug, bourgeois, self-complacent side of my own make-up, in your presence, and have practised it at times ever since. You are continually hoping, from me, for something a little more reckless and more quixotic than you ever find in me; it disappoints you because I am humdrum fundamentally, although I am able to assume a literary flamboyance when it costs me nothing.

"You must forgive me for all this stuff; it is because I am trying to write a novel—it sounds as if it might mean something—but if it does, what's the difference? Affectionately, old puke, Don"

When Don Marquis said to Clive Weed, "You interest me almost more than anyone else I know," he meant it. He revealed more of himself in his letters to Weed than in anything else he ever wrote except certain parts of his egobiography. This was because Weed knew how to draw him out, if necessary to make him angry enough to take a pot shot at his *provocateur*. When he did, Weed struck back even harder, and in the process, oddly enough, started Marquis thinking about things that found a place in something he wrote for publication.

For one of the Players Club yearbooks Marquis wrote a poem called "Weed!" To those who understood the real Don Marquis this was as fine a compliment as he had ever paid anyone:

> Burdock, pig-weed, bunch-grass, purslane, thistle, burrs,
> And poison-ivy posing as a passion flower,
> Stinging like mustard pungent from a shower,
> Horse-radish, bitter root, a weed with barbs,
> A mess of wholesome tonic-stringent "yarbs,"
> Which makes no claim to blossom, scorns perfume,
> And yet is somehow healthy in a room—
> A kind of weed whose essences and juice
> Cooked with the too-fat sentimental goose
> Give something well-corrective of its grease . . .
> Flaunting, with tattered fronds and uncouth mirth,
> His prickly edges at lawn-mowered earth.
> And when the Scythe shall reach him in the end
> There are a few who knew him well will say:
> "This Weed, by God, he was a tonic Friend—
> I'd rather have him back than all this Hay!"

Weed and Marquis lent each other money, both men seeming to sense when the time for slipping a check into an envelope had arrived—the recipient invariably excoriating his benefactor in mock insults. An example of Marquis acknowledging a loan from Weed in unprintable language is to be found in the Marquis-Weed letters in the Walter Hampden Memorial Library of the Players Club.

Five or six weeks after he wrote his long letter to Weed—(one of several he sent Clive in those days)—which was reprinted in part a few pages back, Marquis, Barbara, and his two sisters booked passage for New York, a two-week ocean voyage, with stops at Panama City and Havana. Barbara attended all the shipboard parties, including a children's masquerade, participated in deck sports, and won a prize for finishing first in one of those trick races designed to provoke the laughter of both participants and spectators. The child, well again, told her father that she was having "the best, best time of her whole, whole life," and for this reason alone he felt that the Hollywood excursion was worth all the headaches entailed, with special reference to the inevitable skirmishes with Maud.

Don spent a good deal of time on deck and benefited greatly by the trip. During the warmer days he stripped to the waist and sat in the sun on the top deck, which enabled him to get away from Maud and her incessant chatter about the dearth of green vegetables on a ship that left from California, a state that's loaded with them, and you'd think someone would have sense enough, etc., etc., etc. Maud didn't like to climb to the top deck, which was a break for Don. (Perhaps, after his heart attack, he should not have made this steep ascent himself but he probably figured that a few hours of peace was worth the risk.)

Maud, though unwilling to admit that *she* had enjoyed the trip, thought her brother had: ". . . He came to life socially and played chess in the lounge and seemed to enjoy himself."

Marquis did some light work on the trip, which consisted mainly of jotting down ideas for *Everything's Jake*, the proposed sequel to *The Old Soak*, in which he hoped to interest a Broadway producer. There were several theatrical people on board, including May Robson, a well-known actress of the time, whom Marquis found an engaging conversationalist. It was stimulating to discuss the theater with her and some of the others at a time when he was working on a playscript and trying to put himself in "a Broadway mood," as he expressed it.

Before leaving Hollywood Marquis got Marjorie (whom he hadn't seen in over four months) to agree to meet him at the pier in New York. This took a little doing as his wife, quite understandably, sought insofar as possible to avoid confrontations with the woman who had shown her so much antagonism. Don had to put on a campaign before Marjorie agreed to meet him at the dock.

15
"A Variety of People"—Marquis's
Impressions of Douglas Fairbanks and Charles
Chaplin—"The Greatest Autobiography Since
Cellini's"—Paris's Little Group of Serious Thinkers—
The McTavish Smith Letters—Everything's Jake—
The Big Novel—Marquis on Einstein—Tragedy in
Hollywood

In 1929 Marquis published a collection of short stories called *A Variety of People*, all of which had appeared in national magazines. A few of them were built around characters he had created in his columning days. Clem Hawley, better known as the Old Soak, and now established as a Marquis fiction prop, is the narrator of "In the Bulrushes," one of the best stories in the collection. In this yarn the O.S. returns to one of his favorite themes, "The thing I like about the Good Book is the way it keeps right on comin' true. . . . There ain't hardly a story in the Old Testament that I couldn't match up with a story that's happened right here in this village." (Since Marquis subsequently wove the theme of "In the Bulrushes" into the fabric of his last work, his posthumously published, unfinished autobiographical novel, *Sons of the Puritans*, it is clear that the phrase "right here in this village" is a reference to Walnut, Bureau County, Illinois, the author's birthplace.)

Marquis, in this story, set the stage by giving us another quick picture of the Old Soak, whom he described as "the only man I ever knew who chewed tobacco and smoked simultaneously." Among other things, the yarn is a satiric thrust at gossipy types and Marquis has his narrator introduce that phase of his theme as follows: "Mebby you remember readin' in the Good Book about Moses bein' found in the bulrushes, and all the gossip around Egypt as to how it was he got there? . . . It was Pharaoh's daughter that found him, and more'n likely she was a nice girl and everything; but the gossips don't care. You can't tell those wise birds anything good about anybody. And the gossips in this here town are just like they was in Egypt thousands of years ago."

In the same story Marquis seized upon the opportunity to poke fun at the worship of bigness that was reflected in the newspaper head-lines of the time (the tallest building, the longest ship, the world's biggest dance floor, etc.). This is a sample of how he handled it: "First and last, King Pharaoh of Egypt had a heap of trouble with Moses and the Children of Israel, which was descended direct off of the original Beegat tribes of the Bible. . . . The Children of Israel had been admitted into the land to build sepulchres and peerymids. If one king says he is going to have a peerymid the size of a barn, the next one says to watch his smoke, he will have one the size of two barns. And the next one would send for Uncle Hiram of Tyre and say, 'You seen what my ancestors has done? Well, expense is no object; you build me a sepulchre that will lay over all these past issues for size and style.' Well, this particular King Pharaoh says he is going to have the finest sepulchre, and at the least expense, and he tells the Children of Israel the straw they've been putting into the bricks runs up the expenses, and they gotta leave it out in the future."

Marquis was in the habit of dismissing his short stories as pot-boilers, which accurately described some of them but was unfair to others.

"Mr. Marquis is at his best," said the New York *Times* book review, "in the story of the glass eater. How this man took his first glass, how he went from bad to worse, from tumblers to glass eyes, and how he finally was no longer able to take a glass or leave it makes a tale delightfully silly and worthy of the Marquis tradition, culminating in the awful discovery, on the part of the now reformed glass eater, that his child had inherited his fondness for crockery."

The New York *World* liked best "The Strong Grasses," calling it "a notable short story."

The Doubleday files reveal some amusing side lights in con-nection with the publication of that collection of short stories, not the least of which was the author's uncertainty as to the make-up of his own table of contents. We find Marquis writing his publisher on April 8, 1929: "Just what stories are in 'A Variety of People'? Do you have the copy? You see, when you thought you would not use them so soon, the whole thing passed out of my mind. Can you forward the list? I want to make sure I got permission to reprint from all the magazines. . . . Enclosed is the signed contract. . . . With regard to serializing the novel: I have decided against it, and am now trying to make several chapters into short stories and sell them in that form instead."

The novel referred to is *Off the Arm*, in which the author's first stay in Hollywood is reflected. It was written in 1929, the year we have now reached in our chronology, and published in 1930. In this book he experimented with a technique he had never employed before, fiction sprinkled with fact. A more explicit way of putting it is to say that he has dropped into his novel a few short articles in which he gives his impressions in terms of actual people. For example, we read that the book's protagonist, presumably Marquis, has been invited to meet Douglas Fairbanks. He replies:

Gratified, I went. . . . Fairbanks was in the large office which adjoins his studio at the United Artists; it was that time of day between work and dinner, and he was just out of the swimming tank. I say office, but I never really determined what the room was. There was an office desk, but there was also a barber chair, in which Fairbanks sat in his bathrobe, shaving himself. One wall was covered by an immense blue chart, which was a cryptic diagram of the progress of the Iron Mask, which he was working on at the time—for he invents his own pictures—and there was a clutter of swords, foils, costumes and properties about the other walls and in the corners. In this respect, it was like a dressing room. Twelve or fifteen people lounged about—chauffeurs, directors, actors, menials, magnates—and they were all talking about the only thing (except the climate) I ever heard mentioned in Hollywood—moving pictures. And in this respect it was like a debating society. Some of them had got out of the tank; some of them were getting ready to go in; and in this respect it was like the locker room of a club.

"Have a swim?" invited Tommy Geraghty, and threw open a door which communicated with the tank itself, a large pool.

I saw in the pool what I first took for a particularly energetic seal engaged in joyous gambols. I looked again, and discovered it was Charlie Chaplin.

Tommy shed down an introduction upon Chaplin's sleek wet head, and Mr. Chaplin blew some intrusive water from his mouth and politely acknowledged it, sounding again immediately thereafter.

"When he comes up again, ask him what he thinks about the talkies," said Tommy, with a chuckle.

"Why?"

"He loathes 'em," said Tommy. So when Chaplin reappeared, I asked him.

The world's greatest pantomimist brushed the water from his tricky eyes, gave me a look in which heartbroken reproach was mingled with a kind of ironic humor, and with a gesture of upflung arms let himself sink again—the effect was as if the question had drowned him. It was a great artist conveying his comment without a word; for a moment, looking at the spot where he had sunk, I experienced the desolate feeling that all the art of all the centuries had gone down, irrevocably, to unplumbed depths, and that is exactly what he had wished me to feel. . . .

That year—1929—*St. Nicholas Magazine* published two of Barbara Marquis's poems, one in which she gave her impression of the Western desert as viewed from the window of a California-bound train:

> Oh, this desert! Oh, this plain!
> Oh, this cactus ranch,
> Oh, this unworldly branch
> Of the world!
> Oh, these mountains! Oh, these spaces,
> Not kept up with modern paces.
> Oh, this desert! Oh, this plain!
> And not a single drop of rain!

The foregoing was simply titled "Poem." Another, which the child called "Aspiration," won a prize—a silver badge—in the magazine's competition for children in the eleven-to-twelve age bracket. (Barbara was eleven at the time.) I am indebted to Mrs. Homer Croy for copies of these poems. The prize-winner read:

> I yearn to rise above the people who doubt me,
> And flash my glamor in their faces.
> But first I must work.
>
> I long for a life of brightness
> Sewn with threads of gold and joy.
> I wish for laughter, gaiety, beauty and love.

The way to greatness is not paved with firm cement,
But with mud and swamps where I would sink and sink.
My ideals would die.

People laugh at my childish idea of life.
Let them laugh.
It is not myself I yearn for
But the poor imprisoned hopes heaving in my breast—
Things that God put in me.

Barbara seldom wrote unless she was feeling well. During and immediately after her stay in California she "broke out in more poetic
rashes than ever," according to her father, and this was further proof
that she had benefited by her California vacation; but it also had its
disturbing side. The poet in Marquis was gladdened that there was
another poet in the family—there had been three before Reina died
—but it is known that he worried when Barbara spent hours at a
time in her room writing her little poems and stories. In an effort to
get her to spend more time outdoors he explained that her first duty
as a writer was to know many people and the world around her—
that she should become acquainted with more boys and girls and
participate increasingly in their activities. This would give her a
chance to exchange ideas with them and in the end she would
have more things to write about. He himself didn't get anywhere as
a writer, he told her as earnestly as if he were advising a contemporary, until he'd soaked up a certain amount of experience. This
was all part of a plan to get the child to spend less time in her room.
She had to be handled subtly and cautiously, this precocious little
dreamer who was sensitive to the point of touchiness. Though she
was maturer now in many ways, her nerves were still close to the
surface and she was easily upset when she thought her writing ambitions were not being taken seriously. Wise beyond her years in
that she could hold her own in many areas of adult conversation,
she was still a child and emotionally she had not developed beyond
the average child of her age.

Barbara responded to gaiety and could be drawn out of her over-
serious moods by those who understood her. But you had to know
how to do it. Don knew how; so did Nev. Marjorie, though not
from a lack of trying, did not; nor did Maud. Franklin P. Adams was
one of those who could bring out the fun in Barbara. His technique
was to find out what foods she didn't like, which, oddly enough,

turned out to be the ones *he* didn't like. Then they would enjoy a good laugh as they heaped scorn on the targets of their disdain.

Marquis's technique in handling the child was to switch to gaiety once he had gotten his serious ideas across; consequently, no matter what they discussed, they wound up on a note of laughter. More of a latent than an active quality, her sense of humor had to be rescued from her more serious side; and when her father recognized the need for it he appointed himself a committee of one charged with the responsibility of clowning until the youngster's inherent mirth came bubbling forth.

There is a difference of opinion as to how much time Marquis spent at the Players Club in those days. It is known, however, that he frequented it the most when he was working the hardest—to give himself a breathing spell between long stretches of writing. So his wife's increasing fear that the Club would interfere with his productivity was not well founded. She had other concerns, one of them having to do with "gambling." The quotation marks are essential to establishing the kind of gambling that took place at the Players, where a man played as determinedly to win twenty-five cents at Kelly pool as if big money was involved; and where the bridge and poker stakes were also inconsequential. So Marjorie's fears that her husband might drop the family fortune some day were not very realistic.

Some of Marquis's former playmates—men who still frequent the Players—recall a telephone call from Marjorie that was announced while he was playing poker for chicken feed. As he picked up the telephone they heard him say, "About even, dear," so they guessed he was being asked how he was faring. This he confirmed with a laugh as he returned to the table, observing that his wife seemed fearful that "the Marquis millions" might be in jeopardy. A few weeks later a similar call was announced under similar circumstances. He was about to pick up the phone when a mocking comrade called to him, "About even, dear!" And that's what Don again told her. "Thanks for reminding me," he said as he resumed playing. "I can't afford to admit I'm either winning or losing." And from then on that became his stock reply.

Was Marquis a henpecked husband or wasn't he? The subject is still good for an argument.

Not with the thought of settling this debate but in an effort to get a clearer picture of Mrs. Marquis, I had a second talk about her with Howard Lindsay, who played opposite her in summer stock.

"I found it impossible to create reality," said Mr. Lindsay, "when I played opposite Mrs. Marquis. She was a solo actress. I couldn't make contact with her. She kept staring at my forehead, never looked me in the eye. It is hard to give a good performance under such circumstances."

Lindsay recalled the night that Marjorie called Don at the Players and he declined to take the call. "Tell her I've left the Club," he said.

Insiders who knew what was going on considered it inevitable that Don would assert himself sooner or later. He had just renounced Christian Science and felt there was nothing further he could do to make Marjorie's religion work for him. *She* thought there *was*; and tried to get him to reconsider. This stiffened his resistance and for a time their relations were strained. It was an unfortunate situation since the conduct of both stemmed from deep convictions and neither had any desire to hurt the other. In time Don and Marjorie became reconciled to their religious differences and the breach was healed.

Having given his impressions of Marjorie Marquis as an actress, Lindsay found himself recalling the rapidity with which Don could formulate a quip. "Some years ago," he said, "he was visiting our home in Stanton, New Jersey, where we had an enormous fireplace, one of those huge affairs that they used to build over two hundred years ago. Don took one look at it and you could tell from his expression that something appropriate had occurred to him. 'Howard,' he said, 'a man could live a double life in that fireplace.'"

During the next few years Marquis was in and out of Hollywood several times. Ever since the success of *The Old Soak* efforts had been made to sign him to long-term contracts but he was not interested. To an agent who was prepared to produce several years of motion-picture work for him he wrote: "I don't want a long-term contract. . . . My fiction work, novels and short stories, will always be the thing I want to put my best efforts into, the thing that satisfies me, builds for me. I should like a short term job *now and then*. . . . Never more than three or four months. Intervals between these jobs. Nothing that ties me up for a long time. . . ."

Magazine editors who asked Marquis for biographical data seldom got what they wanted. Usually they received something irrelevant and immaterial, but at the same time entertaining, and the temptation to publish it was great. When in the fall of 1929 the *Saturday Evening Post* requested some information about himself for publication as a "Who's Who—And Why" page ("Serious and Frivolous Facts about the Great and the Near Great") he decided to concentrate on the "frivolous" and skip the "facts."

At that time two phenomena that irked Marquis were in the ascendency—the name-dropping autobiography, and ghost-writing—and with complete indifference to his assignment he wrote a piece that confined itself exclusively to taking pot shots at these special aversions of his. The editors of the *Post* published it because it was pure Marquis, at the risk of bewildering their vast audience. Bravely they titled it "Don Marquis," although it didn't contain a scrap of information about that gentleman. Robert Benchley, after reading it, described it to me as "the greatest autobiography since Benvenuto Cellini's," and that is one of several reasons for reprinting it here as it appeared in the November 9, 1929, issue of the *Post*:

"I was a very handsome child, and good. There are pictures of me in the old family album, with a Little Fauntleroy suit on, that show that to be true. But soon after, my parents moved; steam came in then, and the old sailing ships lay rotting at the wharves. I still struggled along, trying to keep my faith, but eventually I gave up the unequal fight, and, the day after Balfour was returned for the third time from Stoke-Pogis, the Queen herself sent for me.

"'Marquis,' said Her Majesty, 'are you willing to let bygones be bygones, and form a new government for me?'

"'There's always Winston, Your Majesty,' I demurred.

"'Yes, Winston.' I never knew exactly what was behind that remark. But Canterbury must have known.

"'Your Majesty——' he said warningly.

"'Who is this man?' I said, although I knew perfectly well. The archbishop tried to bluster it out, but I suddenly caught him by the arm, shook his lawn sleeve, and the ace of hearts dropped to the floor.

"The pip had been pierced by a pistol bullet.

"'Just a little pistol practice,' said the fellow, with a feeble grin.

"'Quite so,' said Her Majesty—and I never understood until that moment how Her Majesty's cultivated voice could carry such a mordant edge of sarcasm.

"Margot Asquith was dying to say something, but Isaac Marcosson held up an authoritative finger, and she mounted her horse and galloped out of the throne room, slashing down the Life Guards with her whip.

"I was too lenient as Prime Minister; and the opening of the Suez Canal changed everything. I quit school and took a position as oyster opener in a café; my father and grandfather needed every cent that I could earn. They were great pinochle players; for many years it had been their ambition to get enough ahead to start a pinochle salon of their own at Monte Carlo, and day and night they toiled toward that goal. But it was hard, for they played only with each other.

"These baffled old men! The pathos of it all! I shall never forget what Eugene O'Neill said when he saw them toiling at a table in the back room of a place in Hoboken; he said: 'These baffled old men! The pathos of it all!' And then turned away and hummed Whisky Johnnie to cover up his tears. Rough, honest 'Gene! I wanted to do something with my life; be something more than a waster. The Haymarket Riots came and went, and still I dully opened oysters. Life was all one drab, desert expanse, but I felt that our principles were winning. Here and there some Muzhik was learning to think for himself. It was during this winter that I saw a great deal of Lenin and Henry Van Dyke, the authors of Rab and His Friends, and Van Dyke used to say often to himself: 'They are learning to think for themselves.'

"Then the cotton gin was invented, and I soon saw that to keep up with the changed times the character of our business would have to be changed entirely

"Here is the place, I think, to present a letter which I received from Rutherford B. Hayes:

Dear Marquis: While you are in London, won't you be good enough to run around to Madame Tussaud's place, and give her my compliments, and take a look at the waxwork figure of me she has recently installed? I have heard it is really an effigy of Millard Fillmore. It should really be a duplicate of the one we have here in Eden Musée—but you know how the English are! Great colonizers, of course, but a little on the short side when it comes to sculpture, *n'est-ce pas?*

—Rutherford.

"After receiving this letter I retired to a Balkan monastery, where I began my literary career, becoming what is known as a Ghost Writer. That is to say, I write a good many things and sign other people's names to them, for which they pay me well.

"Last year I wrote *Jane Eyre, The World Almanac, The Origin of Species, The Hairy Ape, Tarzan* and *The Collected Verse of Rudyard Kipling;* and I am producing some copy this year under such pen names as Lord Beaverbrook—pronounced Baruch—Irvin S. Cobb, Doctor Cadman, John Milton, Edgar Guest, and Pelham Grenville Wodehouse—pronounced Paggle-Wuddus.

"This brings the story of my life down to the present moment, but I am scheduled for an operation for appendicitis next week, and many people are hoping and many people are fearing.

"I shall be opened with prayer."

Marquis had quite a following in undergraduate circles and not long after the foregoing appeared, there was an epidemic of imitations in college humorous magazines. A few burlesque autobiographies along the same line also appeared in book form.

Subsequently, when the editor of *Harper's Magazine* asked Marquis for a biographical sketch, he received the following:

DONALD ROBERT PERRY MARQUIS (PRONOUNCED MAR-KWIS)
He came from a small town in Ill.,
Which he left, and kept gypsying till
He decided to try
The town of N.Y.,
Where he's laboring fitfully still.

In 1930 Doubleday published Marquis's novel *Off the Arm,* a book that couldn't decide whether its purpose was to satirize Hollywood or what he called "Paris's Greenwich Village" (the cafés haunted by the Left Bank's pseudo-intellectuals), or to paint a full-length portrait—or perhaps only to sketch a caricature—of a wonderful literary poseur, Hugh Cass, a popular novelist who was "one-third genius and two-thirds faker" and who did all his writing "in the back seat of his car with a drawing board on his knees."

This book was referred to earlier in these pages in a prepublication context in which Marquis gave his impressions of Douglas Fairbanks and Charlie Chaplin. It is a tantalizing work in that it is an uneven mixture of brilliance and hasty writing that substantiates what Marquis said about some of his work in a self-critical letter to Harry E. Maule, then his editor at Doubleday, in which he alluded graphically to having "wasted tons of rich material . . . through rushing it rawly into print."

Not many years earlier Marquis had had some close-ups of young

Americans pursuing art with a capital "A" with grim determination in Paris. Of one such group he wrote in *Off the Arm*:

"Cass's satellites were the same in Paris as if they had never left Greenwich Village; they sat about at the Café du Dome, and La Rotonde, speaking bad French to waiters who understood English well enough, and acted superior to all creation on the strength of the fiction that they were great artists. But the sculptors never sculped, the painters never painted, the poets never poetized, the musicians were beyond all instruments, the novelists never produced novels; none of them ever worked. They talked, they theorized, they condemned; principally they condemned people who worked or were Americans. Perhaps some of them had ability, but they were too wise to employ it in any way that might give the measure of its quality. They had elected themselves and each other geniuses by acclamation; to doubt the genius of one of them was as great an insult as to impute conventional morality to him; they all held tightly to the dreary convention of unconventionality. But they were having a good time in their own fashion, and it is pleasant to see immaturity at play, even if it is playing with nothing more than the second-hand ideas which it cannot vitalize into fecundity.

" 'Walt Whitman,' one young fellow asserted—and he seemed quite serious when he said it—'was the great prophet who prepared the way for the splendid creative work of Henry L. Mencken.'

" 'Both Rotarians, my dear!' said Nancy, blowing Whitman and Mencken away in the same puff of smoke."

In the same scene the Russia-worship of those days is reflected in the comment of one of the saner characters on an exploit of another branch of this expatriate Little Group of Serious Thinkers: "They've got hold of a Russian now, and they're worshipping him because he's a Russian. . . . But the Russian doesn't know what it's all about, nor why he's being worshipped—he's used to Russians himself. . . . Some of them assumed he was a grand duke in exile while others assumed he was a Bolshevist agent; all assumed he must know everything about The Arts, being Russian. And they were happy—they had their Russian; no little group (in Paris) is complete unless it has its Russian."

And then there is a scene in which "an enameled blonde . . . is asking the Russian, Michael by name: 'Don't you think that the dynamically symmetrical rhythms which underlie the work of Artchipenko and Stravinsky also make themselves felt in the passionate architecture of the Kremlin and the strophes of the Third Internationale?'

"'Ah, *oui!*' said Michael, 'Oh, yes-s, a good deal!' And added, a little vaguely, 'It is the same with your Wall Street, *n'est-ce-pas?* Up and down—down and up—rhythmic! Yes-s?'" (Marquis may have been referring to the spectacular rise in U.S. stock-and-bond prices in the late 1920s, followed by the Wall Street crash of 1929.)

At this point the character in *Off the Arm* who represents the author's point of view has this to say about the captive Russian: "What Mike really wants is to get to New York and be a bond salesman. He keeps telling them so, but they won't believe him."

The grimness and irritability that characterized many of the letters Marquis wrote in the 1928–29 period is not in evidence in the batch of 1930 letters that have been recovered. He is his old jaunty self, for instance, in a letter written on June 21, 1930, to Harry E. Maule, Doubleday, Doran editor, who had asked him for the assignment of copyright from the *Saturday Evening Post* for the book just mentioned, which that magazine had previously published in its pages:

"Dear Harry: I have the assignment of copyright for OFF THE ARM somewhere on my desk, or in it. I am gradually working toward the place where it was last seen. It can't get away, for nothing is taken out of my room without my personal supervision. You should get it in a few days. The only harm that could happen to it is that it might catch fire; for there is an electric lumbago pad among the papers on my desk and the wires are exposed. It is plugged in on the baseboard. I use it to warm up fountain pens with so that the ink will flow better; and when I sleep on the desk it nestles in the small of my back.

"You mustn't try to hurry things too much about this, for I am armed. I used to have a secretary, but he disappeared about 18 months ago. I think when I dig a little deeper I may find him among the papers. The assignment of copyright is not that far down, by more than a year. It is safe so you needn't worry about it in the slightest. After I turn it over to you, of course I will have to have it back again if I sell the movie rights to the story. There is another assignment on the same sheet of paper.

"I feel we are making progress in this thing, and that it will work out all right if we don't get all flurried and excited over it. If your agents steal into the house at night and try to get at my desk

I may mistake them for burglars. I am armed, as I said. I sometimes think it rather impolitic to permit emotional persons such as myself to carry guns; but that seems to be a settled policy and I do not know enough about politics to have it changed; so I am obliged to keep on packing this gun. You just leave all this to me, and it will work out all right. Did you ever have the lumbago?"

The secretary Marquis refers to in the foregoing as having disappeared was Harold Winney.

I had heard about the so-called "McTavish Smith letters," in which Marquis wrote friends and signed that name as "secretary" or "confidential secretary." After a long and fruitless search, a few of these letters have come to light. One of them is addressed to Christopher Morley on the eve of his departure for London and reads as follows:

"My dear Mr. Morley:

"Mr. Don Marquis has insisted that I write you urging you, when you arrive in England, to 'lift one or two for him.' It is my conjecture that Mr. Marquis refers to some form of alcoholic beverage; but I have not cared to inquire too deeply into his meaning, as this is a habit of thought which I do not consider it advisable to encourage in Mr. Marquis.

"In accepting a position as Mr. Marquis's confidential secretary, I made it quite plain that I should expect to exercise a certain amount of wholesome supervision over his social contacts and his moral tendencies as well as over his literary endeavors and his business affairs. It is my hope that I can look forward to the cooperation of his familiars. I find in Mr. Marquis a constitutional disinclination to consistent industry, as well as an incalculable levity which must be disconcerting to his true friends. If I may say so without offence, Mr. Morley, your name has frequently been mentioned as one of his friends who has, to say the least, exhibited no inclination towards impressing upon him the advantages of unremitting application.

"Mr. Marquis can scarcely claim for himself talents of the first order, and, as you may know, he is somewhat deficient in formal education; therefore, his only salvation lies in unflagging toil and the development of a more serious attitude towards life and letters. There is a fantastic vein which runs through his work which I consider very detrimental to its general effect, and I hope that you will agree with me and assist me in discouraging this manifestation.

"Mr. Marquis has charged me with a further commission, which, believe me, I should not put upon paper, Mr. Morley, were it not his definite order. I am careful to quote his exact words, from my stenographic notes.

" 'Tell Kit (he dictated) not to bite any Piccadilly bubbies unless he can get his teeth out of them afterward.'

"While I do not know exactly what the word 'bubbies' signifies, yet there was a ribald look in Mr. Marquis's eye when he dictated the sentence above which gave me sufficient assurance that . . . that, in short, I should not want to know. I believe I am right in assuming, however, that the word 'bubby' (if that is the singular form) designates some portion of a woman's (I will not say lady's) anatomy. I merely carry out my instructions, Mr. Morley. He also said:

" 'If the Archbishop of Canterbury asks after me, give the fellow tuppence and tell him to go and——in his hat.'

"I do not write it all, Mr. Morley. I am a secretary, but I am, also, a gentleman; and I am writing to one who is (I trust) a gentleman.

"There is, I regret to say, a vein of coarseness in Mr. Marquis's nature; I hope that you will give me your aid, when you return, in my endeavors to mitigate some of its more public and more offensive demonstrations. Yours faithfully, McTavish Smith, Secretary"

Everything's Jake, Marquis's sequel to *The Old Soak*, opened June 16, 1930, at the Assembly Theatre (the old Princess) under the auspices of a production group known as the New York Theatre Assembly. In embarking on this venture Marquis ignored the message of his own various satiric commentaries on "a certain well known device for cashing in a second time on a former success." Or, as he had also put it—both are from "The Sun Dial"—"a sequel is an admission that you've been reduced to imitating yourself."

The reception of the new play was mixed. None of the reviews glowed with the enthusiasm *The Old Soak* had evoked. Only one, that of the New York *Times*, could be appraised as "good box office." The *Times* review carried the headline:

"EVERYTHING'S JAKE"
AN ENJOYABLE COMEDY

The subhead proclaimed that "Don Marquis's art flows nimbly" in the further adventures of Clem Hawley (the Old Soak) and his cronies. "Mr. Marquis is at his best," this *Times* piece—it was unsigned—declared, "when he is writing freely and unrestrainedly about the characters, unconcerned with the exactions imposed by play-building. His native wit flows nimbly, and from time to time he achieves scintillant lines which are packed with wise and felicitous observation. And he has written two scenes that are about as funny as any the town has to offer."

In this new play the Old Soak and Al the bartender are in Paris on the invitation of their old friend, Jake Smith, now a wealthy bootlegger. We find them ill-at-ease in the presence of a British blueblood, the Duchess of Billhorn, until they discover that the noblewoman is related to and part owner of Billhorn's Whisky. This leads, without much loss of time, to a deal for the transportation of vast quantities of the Duchess's product across the Atlantic for illegal consumption in the United States. The *Times* called this "one of the funniest scenes in the comedy." For laughs it was topped only by a sidewalk-café scene in which the antics of the Old Soak were described as "hilarious," "side-splitting," etc., even in the lukewarm reviews.

George Freedley, then an actor, now curator of the Theatre Collection of the New York Public Library and one of the most distinguished men in his field, was in the cast of *Everything's Jake*. He played the part of a chef. Freedley recalls that the comedy was doing well at the Assembly Theatre, where it opened, but that business fell off when it was moved to another house, where its life was automatically limited by the need of the Shuberts for this second theatre by a certain date for the opening of another play. He believes that this sequel to *The Old Soak* would have run for the duration of the season if it had been permitted to remain where it opened. In all, it ran for seventy-six performances.

From the standpoint of the collector of Marquisiana, the chief value of *Everything's Jake* lies in the lines it could contribute to a possible collection of Marquis aphorisms (most of which would be taken from the New York *Evening Sun*, the New York *Herald Tribune*, and *Collier's Weekly*).

Freedley also recalls that when the casting of *Everything's Jake* was still incomplete, the director, Walter Greenough, asked Marquis if he had any preferences as to players for the uncast roles. Marquis made only one suggestion: that a part be found for Walter Vonnegut, his wife's divorced husband. "This was typical of Don," said Freedley. "He had heard that Vonnegut was discouraged, having been un-

employed for some time, and he wanted to do something for him."
This has special significance in that Vonnegut had been unable to
live up to his divorce settlement with his former wife, now Mrs.
Marquis, which called for his contributing to the support of his
children. This had engendered bitterness in Marjorie but none in
Marquis, who was unfailingly understanding when a friend—he still
regarded Walter Vonnegut as such—was unable to meet a financial
obligation. He also expected people to be understanding when *he*
was broke, and he was to learn that it didn't always work out that
way.

Vonnegut was given the part of Hennery Withers, a favorite character of book critic Stuart P. Sherman, who in an article had imputed
Shakespearean stature to Hennery. In one of the reviews of *Everything's Jake* Hennery is described as "a man of wandering tendencies
and a desire to place wreaths on Voltaire's tomb." This is the kind
of humor that probably does better in the library than on the
stage. At any rate, the reviews would seem to indicate that Hennery's
crusade-like determination to honor appropriately, and frequently,
the memory of the author of *Candide*, who also happened to be
Marquis's favorite pamphleteer—(Don's incidental tribute to the
French satirist's struggle against official intolerance and ecclesiasti-
cism)—was lost in this production. The demands of the theater had
resulted in the Hennery Withers part being sharply cut and apparently
the playwright's intent did not emerge with sufficient clarity to be
quickly recognizable.

Actually Marquis's problem was that he had written *The Old
Soak* twice—first with an American background, then with a European. Though the plays were radically different in terms of the
mechanics and nuances of storytelling, they added up to the same
thing. The author did the same job of comic vivisection of Prohibition
in both, making the same thrusts at the same soul-savers, blue-noses,
and busybodies through the medium of the key characters who
supplied the point, purpose, and motivation of the two plays. If
Everything's Jake had been produced first the chances are that it
would have met with an immediate response from the public, and,
by the same token, if *The Old Soak* had been the sequel it might
well have had an uphill climb and might not have succeeded.

Marquis had counted on *Everything's Jake* to put him back on his
feet financially. And though only intimates, and not many of those,
were privy to his disappointments—and then only by resolutely

drawing him out—there are a few of his old companions who recall his stunned bewilderment when the Old Soak, the bread-and-butter character that had served him so well in his column, in a Broadway hit, and in highly remunerative short stories published in national magazines, failed him for the first time. He had completely rewritten the play since William A. Brady, the original producer, had tried it out on the road and relinquished his rights to it; and he felt he now had a property that would enable him to pay his debts—he had been borrowing money—and to increase Barbara's trust fund from $30,000 to $50,000, a goal he had set for himself.

In the meantime, two other Marquis characters—archy and mehitabel—were earning money for their creator, though not on the scale on which money is made in the theater. The first of the books featuring the popular pair had gone through several printings since it was published in 1927. And now Marquis received word from Doubleday, Doran and Company that the firm had decided to issue an illustrated edition, the drawings to be done by Herriman, creator of the famous comic strip, "Krazy Kat." Such an edition had been proposed in an article in *Vanity Fair*; Maule and his associates were alert to its possibilities and lost no time in putting it into effect. The author of the piece—an article that typified the suave jocularity that Editor Frank Crowninshield encouraged—was Corey Ford, whom Marquis had described as "that rare phenomenon, a humorist with a sense of humor."

Marquis enthusiastically endorsed the Herriman idea, which was no surprise, as he was known to be a "Krazy Kat" fan. His letter was dated June 29, 1930. Having expressed himself on the Herriman matter, Marquis, in the same letter, turned to other matters, in the process commenting revealingly on his health, his financial situation, and some aspects of his writing career. This letter, which I found in combing the old Doubleday, Doran files, is typewritten in typical Marquis fashion on a machine whose spacing mechanism was obviously not functioning and whose type faces were clogged and needed the ministrations of a brush. The typing is a combination of double-spacing, single-spacing and *no* spacing, with some of the lines running uphill and converging with the ones above. That typewriter had probably not seen a repairman in ages. Here is the letter:

"My dear Harry: I think the archy and mehitabel with pictures by Herriman is a swell idea. I hope it sells; I am anxious to cut down the advance from the firm. A year ago I was $14,000 in the red; have paid back $5000 of it, and lived, in spite of several relapses, and the fact that when I work a couple of hours I have to lie down a couple of hours afterwards.

"You must not think I have been loafing on the novel. I have rehandled it from the beginning, practically the whole 75,000 words. Have cut out a lot; introduced some stuff and blended it all; not any great bulky changes; but a hell of a lot of work.

"I had hoped to have it to you, and get it to work doing what it will in cutting down the overhead of advances. But I simply can't let this go out loose and sleazy. It is my current bid to amount to something—a sort of late autumnal ambition, I suppose.

"I seem to myself, looking back on my so-called literary career, to have missed coming through in the larger way that certain people expected. This has been because I have scattered my good stuff so widely, through such a variety of forms and mediums; there hasn't been the necessary concentration on one kind of thing. I put, for instance, ten years of fiction material into newspaper columns.

"This novel is really my bid to get started with the stuff that has some weight in people's minds. It may be too late, now, to do anything with the ability I have—especially as the potboiler problem is always present—but I'm giving myself a last fling at it with this novel before retiring permanently to the ranks of the superannuated hacks; so I want the novel to be as good as I can make it.

"You will perceive that I'm writing to you as an old friend rather than as a publisher.

"I suppose the real trouble has been that, while I have a very keen appreciation of the value of publicity, and have known pretty well how to get it when I made the effort, I have never had along with it any real continuing concern with what is called 'fame.' It has always seemed to have so much bunk in it. But now, very belatedly, I'd like to have some of it, rather than mere notoriety.

"Well, what the hell! Yrs, Don Marquis"

Marquis's "bid to amount to something, a sort of autumnal ambition," was to be an autobiographical novel in which his home town of Walnut, Illinois, would become a place called "Hazelton." Long afterward Christopher Morley, with whom Marquis had discussed the proposed work, wrote a piece telling how "Don had been planning and practising for this larger stroke in fiction, and pushing toward it under duress of taskwork."

Morley's "taskwork" was synonymous with Marquis's blunter "potboiling." The former columnist maintained that he had never consciously set out to write "junk," as he also designated his hastily written short stories and articles, postulating that frequently an idea that had larger possibilities became "blah stuff" when economic pressures prevented him from putting in more time on it.

Marquis's predicament amounted to this: a man whose health was none too good would, after he had finished his day's work on the quick-turnover stuff that paid the bills, start a second day's work dedicated to living up to the talents he felt he had been prostituting—that is, when he could rally the strength or stimulate his mind sufficiently by drinking quantities of coffee halfway through the night. More often than not, the self-styled potboiling of his daytime work schedule would exhaust him sufficiently to prevent his working as late as he wanted to.

It was an uneven fight: Marquis versus the endless stream of bills that accumulated in the maintenance of two households, their occupants, and the hired help. He frequently joked about being "on the treadmill," seldom complained. He didn't have to; what was happening to him was written in the deepening lines of his face, his ashen complexion, and the whitening, in spots, of what he used to describe as his "dove-colored" hair.

You would now expect that when his sister Maud interrupted his work to announce that she had overspent her allowance, which she did from time to time, that Marquis, his patience exhausted, would tell her to go to hell and hang up. But he didn't. He learned it was easier to listen and to say he would see what he could do.

The Big Book, the autobiographical novel!—that's what he tried to think of when his morale sagged and there was need to bolster himself. This was the book in which he would say all the things he had been dying to say—the things he couldn't get into his magazine stuff. His cast of characters would be fictionized versions of some of the people he remembered from his early days in "Hazelton,"—Mr. Splain, the town tinker; Emmeline Paisley, the obituary poet of the weekly paper; Miss Carson, the amorous evangelist who takes time off from her soul-saving to permit a moonlit night to have its way with her physiology; the likeable Henry Gage, who leads a double life, a circumstance Marquis would make understandable in terms of what Hazelton could drive a man to; the "swamp angels" who lived on the edge of town and would supply the motivation for some dramatically ironic moments; and the preachers of the two rival churches, grimly competitive emissaries of the Lord. And then there was the young man, Jack Stevens, who could safely be interpreted as Don Marquis himself; and the girl, one of the author's favorite characters, whom he had named Barbara, after his own daughter. And many, many others.

This was the book he liked so much he couldn't keep his hands off it; he would pile up a lot of copy, study it, tear it apart, make fresh starts. In addressing himself to this novel he seems to have forgotten a philosophic passage from "The Sun Dial" which attracted attention and was widely quoted when it was published some years earlier:

"If you try too hard to get a thing, you don't get it.

"If you sweat and strain and worry the other ace will not come—the little ball not settle upon the right number or the proper color—the girl will marry the other man—the public will cry, Be-damned to him! he can't write anyhow!—the cosmos will refuse its revelations of divinity—the Welsh rabbit will be stringy—you will find there are not enough rhymes in the language to finish your ballade—the primrose by the river's brim will be only a hayfever carrier—and your fountain pen will dribble ink upon your best trousers."

Which brings us back to something Christopher Morley said in his chapters on Don Marquis in *Letters of Askance*:

"There is always one more bit of hackwork to be ground out before we can get at the great masterpiece. More ironical still, when we deliberately sit down to tackle the annunciated masterpiece, how often it goes wooden in our hands. The journeyman job we drudged at day by day, and grimly estimated as potboiling, perhaps was the big thing after all."

Time and again when Marquis read one of his columns he didn't like, he was as rough on himself as he subsequently was when he undertook magazine writing and he dismissed *all* of it, including some first-rate work, as potboiling. Actually he seldom was pleased with what he wrote.

Only a few of the letters Marquis wrote in 1930 add any new information. One that does was written in the spring of that year—to Edward Caldwell, who had invited Marquis to attend a Knox dinner and had received the following reply:

"My dear Mr. Caldwell: I wish I could be present at the Knox dinner. . . .

"I have always had a very strong sentiment with regard to Knox College—an almost inexplicable sentiment, when you consider that I was never there more than a couple of months. I am, in fact, loyal to the college education I might have had if I had had one; loyal to the college I should have gone to if I had gone to college. As a youth of fifteen my then school teacher, Mr. John Wylie, fired me with an ambition to go to Knox College; and a few years later Albert Britt came through the village where I lived, singing a barber shop baritone, as I remember it, on something he called a Glee Club. If you don't think Britt can sing, ask him to at the dinner and—but I was never any judge of music. At any rate, Mr. Britt fired me once more with the ambition to go to Knox College. I took a lot of firing, it appears. Later, Mr. S. S. McClure, through the medium of his magazine, fired me once again; all I had to do was get a thousand subscriptions to the magazine, and I could go to Knox College. I was never any good selling books or magazines, however—to this day my books don't sell very well; and I left the McClure proposition flat, after I had put in six months getting twelve subscriptions. Then John Cleveland fired me with ambition to go to Knox College again, and this time I borrowed $20 and went.

"Twenty dollars was an immense sum to me in 1898—and, indeed, I've seen a lot of times since when I'd rather have twenty dollars than what I had at the moment—and I went down to Galesburg on a railroad pass (I knew some brakemen on the C., B. & Q.) and started to college.

"There were two things right at the start that bothered me. One was my appetite, and the other was a desire to play football. I never got any farther than an assistant substitute tackle on the second team, but I found I couldn't even do that and work my way through school. And if I didn't work I could not satisfy my appetite, which had dilated owing to contact with football. After coming out of a showerbath, my appetite was imperious. I spent enormous sums for food. I used to go to the 3-cent restaurant and put away as much as 27 cents worth of food at one meal, and you could get large quantities of food in 1898 in that lunch room for 27 cents. Any time I got away from being massacred in practice games and eating, I put in reading the romances of Walter Scott and Alexandre Dumas in the college library. The purely academic side of my college career was increasingly neglected.

"Before Thanksgiving I saw a showdown rapidly approaching. I would either have to give my time to manual labor and study, or inherit a fortune, or quit college. While I was still hesitating Dr. Finley sent for me—I suppose he had heard that I was a fellow who needed a job. At any rate, I was afraid of that; I was afraid that he had a job for me. I couldn't face it; I sold my books, laid away one final enormous meal in the 3-cent restaurant, and left Galesburg in an empty box car. For many years afterward I hoped that I would be able to get back there; my plan was to save enough money to put myself through Knox and have a fairly good time doing it. But in the thirty years since I have never been able to save the money. Perhaps by the time I am 75 years old I will be able to matriculate with some hope of getting through the whole academic course. If that ever comes to pass, I pledge myself to the matriculation. I am not as optimistic as I used to be, but I still have some hope.

"But what I am trying to get at is this: during all these years of frustration, my primary loyalty to the particular school has remained unimpaired. It has always been my college, though I have never been its—at least it has been my alma step-mater. And as I look about me in the world and see the men and women who have helped make the college, and who have been made by it, I grow increasingly prouder of this step-college of mine. I can, in a way, take a more detached point of view than any of the rest of you—in fact, mine has been rather a continuing detachment *from* than a continued connection *with*. But, seriously, this college and a few like it have done a great quiet work in the world which the world can ill afford to get along without, whether the world is aware of that fact or not.

"I hope you will continue to allow me to retain my sentiment for the college—my spiritual kinship—despite all my physical absences. Perhaps this sentiment may strike old Knox graduates as a little bit absurd under the circumstances—rather like a sentiment on the part of an old bachelor for the girl he never married. But the elusive character of these things does not mitigate their poignance, and I insist on keeping this feeling for the place I did not spend my youth at.

"Hoping you will pardon my multitudinous prepositional endings, and assuring all Knox people of my cordial regards, I am Sincerely yours, Don Marquis."

The Dr. Finley referred to in this letter was John Huston Finley, president of Knox College during Marquis's brief attendance there. Finley later became president of the College of the City of New York and subsequently editor of the New York *Times*.

Marquis continued his policy of taking short-term assignments in Hollywood. He needed the money but he avoided committing himself to contracts of more than three or four months' duration. His name was appearing often enough in national magazines to give it a certain recognizability among the motion-picture executives who signed up writers, but apparently nobody took the trouble to find out how to make effective use of his services.

Perhaps because, as he himself had pointed out, he had scattered his talents, his work did not stand out in bold enough relief to give him the quick identity some writers had. Much of what he had written had become well known but it was a conglomeration and no one had found a suitable tag-line for him, though some had tried. To Clive Weed he had reported a conversation he had heard at an extra-moist cocktail party at the home of a Hollywood bigwig at which two of the guests, their voices amplified by alcoholic exuberance, were trying to figure out who he was. One said he thought he was "some kind of a humorist" and would be used "to spot gags for laughs." The other chap had never heard of him. A third party, joining them, volunteered the information that he thought the subject of their speculation was "that guy who writes that stuff about Artie, the cockroach. Can you 'magine a guy writing about roaches? Name's Mar*kee*, I think."

Marquis couldn't figure out why there should be such wholesale miscasting of writers, that if the studio executives in handing out assignments would make an effort to keep in mind what writer A, B, C, or D was good at, the authors of books and plays who wound up in the film colony would have a much better chance of landing assignments in keeping with their background.

In *These Things Are Mine*, his spirited and informative autobiography, George Middleton gives an example of the type of miscasting of writers that he considered well-nigh inexplicable. "With sympathetic handling," wrote Middleton, "Don might have been the ideal man to compose enduring films. . . . I remember his laughter in recounting how he, for years a New York newspaper columnist, had been hired at $1000 a week to write a story of embassy life in Lisbon—to discover, in the next cubbyhole, a former American consul at Lisbon struggling over a scenario about a New York columnist!"

Once, before he had even reported, Marquis was detached from a motion picture whose screenplay he had been retained to write, and assigned to rewriting scripts that needed repairs before they could be filmed. On one of these occasions he had been asked to "fix up the love interest," and several times he was asked to supply new dialogue for certain scenes. He didn't fare well as a rewrite man. Two or three jobs in a row were returned with caustic comments.

These were not merry days for Marquis but there were few times in his career when his "incorrigible mirth," even when long dormant, did not come to his aid in a predicament of this kind. According to a story that he told Gilbert Gabriel, former drama reviewer of the New York *Evening Sun,* and which Gabriel told Newman Levy, who relayed it to me, Marquis, having got nowhere with his rewrite jobs, decided he must find some other way of making an impression. The motion-picture company for which he was working—at a handsome wage, incidentally—had a system that was employed in most of the studios at the time. Writers were supplied with typewriter paper of different colors, each hue signifying a different stage in the life of a script. For instance, a script on yellow paper, in some studios, meant that it was in its early stages, whereas other colors signified more advanced stages. Marquis had been submitting his rewrite jobs on paper indicative of intermediate stages and it occurred to him that this was probably bad psychology. Where he worked, blue paper connoted the finished product, and this gave him an idea. Taking one of his unsuccessful rewrites—it had been rejected with a note stating that it was "no damn good"—he typed it, without changing a word or a comma, on blue paper. For effect, he held it until over a week had elapsed since it had been turned down, then resubmitted it. A few days later Marquis was congratulated on having at last struck his stride. "This is just what we've been looking for!" was the enthusiastic comment of the chief factotum of an army of such who were masterminding this particular picture.

Old newspaper clippings reveal that for the next five years Marquis was in Hollywood a number of times in connection with an assortment of short-term contracts. One item is headed DON MARQUIS SIGNED BY FOX, and informs us that "Don Marquis has joined the writing staff at Fox Films and will soon start work on a story for Shirley Temple, which B. G. De Sylva will produce." Another conveys the information that he has signed a contract to write "special dialogue" for a "Skippy" picture. (Percy Crosby, the cartoonist, had popularized a comic-strip character by that name and Hollywood had undertaken to produce a "Skippy" picture.)

Playwright Howard Lindsay was in Hollywood in the early thirties as a writer when Marquis was there, and he and his wife, the well-known actress Dorothy Stickney, recall the days when one of the studios, finding nothing else for him to do, assigned Don to writing song lyrics. "Someone had heard he was a poet," said Miss Stickney, "so they teamed him up with a songwriter." Lindsay commented that writing verse to be read was one thing and writing words to be sung was quite another. Marquis had had no experience as a "lyric-writer" and knew none of the tricks of the trade. At any rate, none of the song lyrics he wrote ever got into a motion picture.

Once, when Marquis found himself on a Hollywood assignment that had sounded definite enough in the beginning but had turned nebulous, he decided that he ought to produce something tangible for the generous salary he was receiving. So he wrote several originals and "tried to give them away." The studio rejected them. He subsequently rewrote them and sold them to magazines as short stories. One of them, not long after publication, was bought by the company to which he had offered it for nothing.

Marquis's unhappiness in Hollywood is reflected in a fine sonnet he wrote and presented to Miss Stickney. Over the years most of the poems he composed and sent to friends eventually saw publication. The one he gave Miss Stickney, which she has graciously made available, has never before been published:

Sketch of a Poet

Once the wild rapture and the beating wing
Of Song were mine, the Sun, the climbing flight,
The storm's great fellowship upon the height—
Rider of winds that spin the worlds and fling
Space-wide the starry levities of Spring!
I falter now; there falls and blurs my sight
A drift of ashes down a dusty night,
Nor dull ears hark what magic bells may ring.
I should have striven for some faith whose heat

> Of burning hearts might set a planet flaming;
> Or fallen like great Lucifer, proclaiming
> Across the skies his splendor in defeat.
> —But meanly I sink down: wasting large powers
> On tavern satellites and sodden hours.

Marjorie accompanied her husband to Hollywood when she was able to make arrangements that freed her mind of worries about her children. A few of the trips he made alone.

Several times Maud had the urge to join these Hollywood excursions that took place in the 1930s, as she had previously done. Her brother vetoed her bids two or three times but twice gave his consent when Maud's persistence wore him down. This meant that Nev would also have to be included, as Maud was now depending on her sister more and more. And though the latter still maintained that she was the "executive" at Forest Hills, she was that strange contradiction, an executive whose sister did most of the planning.

As a result of these developments Don was twice in the fantastic position of maintaining four establishments!—two houses in Hollywood, one in New York, and one in Forest Hills. In Hollywood, Don, Marjorie, and Barbara occupied one house; the other was for Maud and Nev. Because of the ill-feeling between Maud and Marjorie, which neither bothered any longer to conceal, they had to live in separate dwellings. They were now past the arguing stage. When they met, which was seldom by design, they exchanged perfunctory greetings or there was a stony silence.

Small wonder that Marquis occasionally found himself

> . . . wasting large powers
> On tavern satellites and sodden hours.

But one must also not forget that, among Marquis's "large powers," was that of self-castigation. It will be recalled that he had written his friend Weed only a few years earlier: "It is impossible for me to get away entirely from the moralistic inhibitions which I inherited; I learned that 20 years ago and quit trying." As a young man he had said in a poem:

> I am mine own priest, and I shrive myself
> Of all my wasted yesterdays. . . .

In this poem he had spoken of "all the ill weeds" that "grew rank . . . and ugly" inside a man named Marquis, the weeds of "sin and

sloth and foolishness, of error, evil and neglect." At the time he
wrote that poem, which first appeared in "The Sun Dial" and in
1915 was published in book form in *Dreams and Dust*, he was so hob-
bled by "sloth" that he was writing six columns a week, getting his
first short stories published, writing a novel, and blocking out future
plays. Marquis was so inherently remorseful a personality that he
was capable of converting a few hangovers into enough self-reproach
to give those who didn't have the time or the inclination to study the
facts the impression that he spent most of his life boozing.

Another of Marquis's "large powers" was that of overdramatiza-
tion. In his projected autobiographical novel, young Jack Stevens
(Don Marquis) gets into trouble at college for offering the following in his freshman year as one of the original themes he is supposed
to submit in English class:

> God and His Son, Jesus,
> Were sitting up in heaven one day
> And Jesus asked:
> "Father, who made the Devil?"
> "My Son," replied Jehovah,
> "Don't bother yourself with questions of that sort—
> They will only worry you.
> It was Theology invented the Devil."
> "Yes, I can understand that,"
> Replied the Savior of the World,
> "I know what you mean about Theology,
> But who invented Theology?"
> "My Son," said the Father,
> "The Devil invented Theology!
> Now don't get yourself all tangled up with such questions!
> Remember that from where I sit
> Things look differently;
> I'm a good deal older than you are,
> And I'd never get anything done at all
> If I gave up my time to all these catch questions—
> I haven't the time for them."
> "Time?" said Jesus. "Time?
> Why, haven't we got Eternity, Father?"
> "Yes," said the Father,
> "But Eternity isn't any too long
> Considering that we also have Infinity on our hands too—
> They just about match up with each other."

"The English instructor, shocked to the very core of his soul," wrote Marquis, "scuttled off with this to the president of the college himself."

Marquis had tried this out (and other parts of his book) on friends, in manuscript form, and one of them had said to him half-kiddingly, "Come clean, Don—isn't that what got you kicked out of Knox College?" Marquis grinned and cryptically replied, "What do *you* think?"

It will be recalled that Marquis was quite serious, though his tone was not, when he admitted in a letter to Christopher Morley that he had been responsible for some of the fanciful stories about himself that were in circulation. He had not tried to stop them because he felt—at this point we quote him—"they were experiences which belonged to me by right of temperament and character."

I confess that when I wrote to Knox College I had hoped my letter would elicit the information that Marquis *had* been kicked out, with its promise of the inside story of young Donald Robert Perry Marquis battling it out with the authorities at Knox, with the town of Galesburg taking sides, and perhaps all of northern Illinois aroused by the issue, and possibly even the whole state of Illinois. It *was* an experience to which Marquis was entitled "by right of temperament and character." But actually he left because he had run out of money.

In Hollywood—usually when he had made the trip from New York alone—Marquis played bridge. It was the "conversational bridge" he played at the Players, a version of the game—a Marquis invention—that he hazarded only with friends whose patience he was reasonably sure he could count on. Businesslike bridge-players would never stand for his interrupting play to tell why something reminded him of the town spiritualist back home in Walnut, Illinois, a Mrs. Epperson, who for twenty-five cents would teach you how to excel at any and all card games by establishing contact with the spirit world. Nor would these more serious-minded players stand for the pantomime—another phase of the Marquis System— by means of which he flashed signals to his partner. Once while teamed up with playwright George Kelly (*The Show-Off, Craig's Wife*, etc.) against Fola La Follette and George Middleton, he started furiously scratching his head as he beamed admiringly at an imaginary gem on his ring finger. When Kelly registered bewilderment Marquis expressed disappointment in his partner's failure to realize he was signaling that he was "lousy with diamonds."

Marquis admitted in Hollywood what he had confessed in New York, that he hoped his adventures in the bridge world would yield something to write about. They did. He used the theme in fiction and in articles. In *Collier's* he subsequently wrote:

"My suspicion that bridge is something more than a pastime, that it is really a Cause, a Life Work, has lately been confirmed by a volume entitled, 'The Official Book of the New Standardized System.' It is issued by the Advisory Council of Bridge Headquarters. . . .

"To play good bridge, it seems, one must put himself In Tune with the Infinite, and Vibrate in Harmony with the Cosmic All. He must be careful about his diet, too. I quote from pages 260 and 261 of this official work:

"'Avoid hearty eating before play. Stick to a simple diet of whole grain breads, vegetables and fruits. . . .

"'When the strain of the game has irritated you, take time out to get to an open window. . . .'

". . . Some of the conventions I have heard expounded lately have gone so far beyond anything you would expect from a mere game that they ought to be catalogued under the head of statesmanship."

Marquis gravely announced in this article that he decided to be open-minded and give the official diet a fair trial. The next time he played, he and his partner were down 5200 points at the end of an hour. "I can't understand it," he remarked to his partner. "I've been eating nothing but fruit and vegetables all week."

Occasionally Marquis left Hollywood for a week of seclusion at some resort where he could put on a writing spurt when he had fallen behind the schedule of his commitments. At other times he sought the refuge of an out-of-the-way retreat so that he "could be ill without an audience."

When he wrote Morley from La Casa del Camino, Laguna, California, on February 4, 1931, he was in the unhappiest mood that any of his letters reveal to that date: "I have been miserably ill much of the time since I saw you last. So ill that if it were not for Barbara I should be very glad to die, but I must get her well, grown up, started in life." This is taken from a long letter—one of the longest he ever wrote—in which he ranges far and wide, raising such questions as, "Is there a spirit which controls life, to some purpose? Or is there only life?" He struggles to answer the questions he raises and speaks of a "craving to find purpose and intention in natural phenomena of all sorts." He sets forth the following proposition, discusses it pro and con, and wants to know what Morley thinks:

"The moral generosities and intellectual superiorities of certain human beings are such as to have inspired many persons with the idea that they are the direct endowments of a deity, or spirit, consciously controlling the universe. But examination and consideration inevitably incline one to the belief either that the gods are not entirely wise and beneficent in their intentions, or else that they do not possess the complete power to make their beneficence and wisdom effective towards human beings and through human beings in the relations of human beings to one another. This leads many persons to suppose that there is in the universe no spirit possessing a beneficent intention, and such qualities as love, justice, and so forth, outside of men themselves; that such qualities, when they appear in men, have been worked up, so to speak, by men in their racial life, developed, evolved, without any correspondence with, or derivation from, what has conveniently been called an 'oversoul,' or, if you please, a God; or gods."

The overtones of this lengthy, involved letter suggest a preoccupation with premonitions of death, this precipitating speculation on aspects of the proposition: is there a hereafter?

But that is merely an impression. Marquis explains these speculations as follows:

"This train of thought has been induced in me this morning by the agreeable juxtaposition of Prof. Einstein and the Pacific Ocean. Einstein is in Southern California now. I am impressed by the magnificence of both; by the prodigious and extensive mental activity of Prof. Einstein; by the enormous random physical activity of the Pacific Ocean. It is only charitable to give both of them a clue to what their activity is all about, and to reconcile them to each other, if possible, and to try to bring the restlessness of both into the bounds of a thinkable circumference.

"Prof. Einstein says that the universe—the billions of 'universes,' whatever that may mean except the billions of systems in one universe—is *limited*. Bounded!

"If I asked him what is *outside* the limits he would either break down and cry, or else answer me with a dogma disguised as a hypothesis.

"The basic condition of the cosmos defies mathematical statement because of the essential paradox coiled at its center, ready to bite with its positive fangs or sting with its negative tail; the double-ended serpent of our philosophic Edens. The mathematician always finds himself at the end in a conflict which he cannot understand. . . . So he breaks down into some generality such as the statement that all space is curved, or something of that sort, as Einstein has done.

"It is obvious that all space is curved—everything that God made is round, spherical.

"God made things that way so that they would roll a hell of a distance when he kicked them. You don't need to be a mathematician or a philosopher to know that. You just know it, because it is what you would do yourself.

"The Pacific Ocean is in the backyard. I am supposed to be writing a moving picture scenario. Like hell I am!

"The juxtaposition of Einstein and Southern California pleases me beyond words. They like each other, too. I suppose the liking proceeds from an aridity of nature in both of them, and a mutual preoccupation with the thought of *size* . . . just simply *size*, and nothing much else to go with it. Einstein seems never to have bothered much about the *quality* of the cosmos, its character, its smack, flavor, smell, and where to jab it to make it bleed, or how to drop it into a highball and drink it down; he thinks about its size and shape. You know damned well its size and shape are what you and I determine they are at lunch today, and that we will change them next Saturday if it happens to occur to us. . . .

"Prof. Einstein is magnificent, but arid. Southern California is big and beautiful, but dumb. (I should say, *dumm*.) The Pacific Ocean is impressive, enormous, but (here at least) it lacks salt, pep, its winds lack ozone; the moving picture industry is extensive, but imbecile. . . .

"Give my love to Stringbean Benét and to Ben De Casseres when you see them. Love to you. Yours for coin, crime and the cinema, Don."

There had been an improvement in Barbara's health; then, a few months before the end of 1930, she began losing ground again. She was experiencing a slow but steady loss of weight and complained

O RARE DON MARQUIS

of what can best be described as a feeling of general weakness. For instance, when she sat down to write a piece for the *California Sun*, the little magazine she had started, she wasn't always sure she would have the strength to finish. A physician was on call and whenever Don or Marjorie thought Barbara needed medical attention he was summoned. There was talk of operating on the child for the removal of her adenoids but it was decided to wait until she responded to medication designed to restore her vigor.

In the fall of 1931 Marquis was still working in Hollywood, having been compelled, for financial reasons, to renounce his plan to take only short-term engagements in the motion-picture colony. He, Marjorie, and Barbara were living at 810 North Crescent Drive, Beverly Hills. Maud and Nev had also made the trip to California and were living in a house in Hollywood.

Barbara's doctor never got a chance to find out whether the removal of the child's adenoids would improve her health. She died of pneumonia in the Beverly Hills house in October of that year. In the opinion of this medical man she had been "walking around with pneumonia," though he hesitated to say for how long.

Marquis, on the verge of collapse, asked Fola La Follette (who was in Hollywood with her husband, playwright George Middleton) to speak at the funeral services. No one except Marquis himself knew the delicate mechanism that was Barbara as she did. In what she wrote and read at the services we get the best recorded picture of the child, according to those who remember her and have seen the text of what Miss La Follette wrote. One of these friends of the Marquis family—a writer—said after reading Miss La Follette's piece, "It brings Barbara back to life with its perceptive close-ups of her activities and the insights into her character. I'd half-forgotten these things when you queried me. Now they all come back to me and I can almost see the child standing before me."

Here is the text of what Miss La Follette (author of the distinguished biography of her father, former United States Senator Robert M. La Follette) had written about her little friend:

"Poets have lived longer, but few in youth have sung more beautifully than Barbara Marquis, child of two poets.

"Here today we who knew and loved Barbara recall with new wonder her rare genius which we accepted so naturally: The subtlety of her perceptions; her true and penetrating reading of people; her generosity to grownups, none of whose weaknesses escaped her; her swift satire and delicate ironical humor; her exquisite appreciation of beauty in all its forms; her wit and magic gift of gaiety; her extraordinary wisdom and maturity of vision, which was so startling in one who had all the clear charm of childhood.

"In her thirteen years her sense of values had surpassed that of most who live to three score and ten.

"She had focused her gifts and found the direction of her life. Though exceptionally endowed, her being was harmonious and balanced.

"With an initiative and capacity for hard work often lacking in the artist, she organized and carried on her magazine, *The California Sun*. She edited and wrote most of the paper. Here she demonstrated that, true to the fine tradition from which she sprang, though poetry was always her first love, fine prose was equally her medium. She typed the stencil, mimeographed all the copies, wrapped and sent them out herself to her eighty subscribers.

"She danced and chanted her first poem when she was five. At thirteen she had written enough poems for a unique book.

"Measured in years her life is short. Measured in fulfillment her life is long.

"Her poems reveal her spirit as no word of ours can. We want to share with you who love Barbara a few of her many beautiful poems.

"We are mute and helpless before the mystery of death."

Here followed two of Barbara's poems, one of them written a few days before she died, and reportedly premonitory in its overtones, almost as if she knew what was happening to her. This one is missing. Here is the other poem Miss La Follette read:

A Lovely Day

The day is cool and gray and the trees are
    stretching up their branches to the misty clouds.
The hills are wrapped in purple fog.
The morning is full of spring, and you can
    smell the flowers in the air.

I have been in touch with Mrs. Sophia Stokes, the nurse who was in charge when Barbara died. Here are some excerpts from her letters:

"I am sure she always must have been a fragile-looking little thing, but of course she was very ill then.

"I talked to her doctor and was told just to keep her as quiet as possible. He sent over a very small dose of morphia to be given if necessary that night, and later in the afternoon he stopped to see her.

"She was in a light sleep or doze all that afternoon—easily roused for any care—but there could be no conversation beyond the few words necessary in caring for her.

"As I said, she was a very fragile little thing. A small, oval face, long dark lashes, so very pronounced. She had a flowerlike beauty. . . . And it was a very delicate flower—one grown in shade.

"Pardon my attempt. But it is the way anyone would think of her. After her death an autopsy was performed and it was found that she was one of those children with an enlarged thymus gland. The skin, lashes, and the flowerlike delicacy is peculiar to these children.

"They are also very susceptible to infections and anaesthesia. In this day they are recognized early and are treated, but then not enough was known.

"She probably had the infection—a virus pneumonia—and had been walking around with it. She was not a child to complain and really she was not a child. She was a very responsible adult. You knew that instinctively and treated her as such.

"There is very little to tell about that night. She was quiet until about 5 A.M. and then became restless.

"I fixed the hypo for her and then told her what I wanted to do. She wanted to know what it was for. I told her to make her easier and I wanted to give it in her arm. She said, 'All right,' and held out her tiny arm.

"I gave it, and I think about ten minutes later she just ceased to breathe. The morphia of course did not cause her death, but for me it was a horrible feeling. The infection, the filling up of the lungs, that big thymus and the morphia and she was gone.

"I called the doctor, Don, and his wife and the fire department inhalator squad. They are so fast and I had no oxygen. Of course nothing could be done. She was gone. . . .

"After the funeral Don was in a state of shock really and his doctor put him to bed. I stayed on to take care of him for a few days, I thought, but his agent came to me and asked me to stay longer because he could not bear to be there alone with Marjorie. . . .

"While I was there Don told me little things about Barbara. How she had come to him and said, 'Daddy, I want to get through with this growing up business. I am too young to be with the older girls and I cannot be with those of my age. They are too young for me and I am very lonely. I want to finish this growing up business just like that,' and she snapped her fingers. Well, she did."

Mrs. Stokes wrote a second letter dated December 30, 1959. Excerpts from this letter follow:

"I don't know what Marjorie did or where she went, but she was not there much. I was on duty in Don's room, going home at night. Then Marjorie was with him, I think. Well, after a couple of days Don started to talk. The story that seemed to be the real breaking point for him was the one about the dog.

"Marjorie, as you know, had two children, a girl in her teens and a little boy, perhaps six years old or maybe seven. Don had, just a short time before, bought two dogs. One for Barbara and one for the boy. Little Boston bulls. Well, one day Don came home from the studio, and he said it was a very cold damp day in the fall of the year, and found Marjorie out on the service porch with one of the little dogs lying on the cold cement floor with a broken back. He had been struck by a car. Marjorie was reading Mary Baker Eddy to the dog. That almost killed Don. He called the vet and had him come and take the little fellow away. . . .

"Then he told me how Barbara had gone all through 'Science and Health' and had come to him one day saying 'she could not go for it, it did not appeal to her reason.' Marjorie of course had wanted to make a convert. . . . And I am sure she went right on trying to make Don see things the Christian Science way."

A day later—December 31, 1959—Mrs. Stokes wrote:

"I want you to have the following poem which Don wrote and gave to me before I left there.

"Some explanations are due.

"Because it was very cheap I had gone to the Hollywood Studio Club to live. It was during Depression days and Prohibition days. The Hollywood Studio Club was run by the Y.W.C.A. for the benefit of young girls who came to Hollywood with stars in their eyes and not much else. Mrs. Cecil de Mille headed the Board and a number of other very fine women. It was a beautiful place, still is and, due to the occupants, highly entertaining. We always had interesting things going on, including gossip. Of course I used to tell Don about it. Once in a while someone would have a bottle and being twice forbidden that was fun. Of course no booze is served at the 'Y'.

"Peter was the darling little Boston bull.

"So here is the poem. [*Note*—Sophia Stokes was then Sophia Young, hence the first line.] Don preceded it with this heading:

> La Maison Marquis
> Beverly Depths
> Cali-goddam-fornia,

under which he had written:

> Dear Sophie Young: Herewith I send
> The cash I owe. Please go on a bend
> At the roaring Y where the inmates drink
> Till they all fall limp in the kitchen sink,
> Where the Mother Superior brings round the booze,
> And dances all night in her gilt-heeled shoes.
> And the little rough nuns from dusk to dawn
> Dance on the roof with pajamas on.
> Peter sends love, and the missus, too—
> But there is no love like my love for you!
> For you washed my ears and you poached my eggs
> And you piled hot-water bags over my legs,
> And you shaved my face and you lathered my eyes,
> And listened to all my favorite lies,
> And you combed the hair on my gray old poll,
> And you cheered my heart and you helped my soul,—
> And for all you did to my spirit and carkis
> I'm yours forever
>
> > With love,
> > D. Markis.

"Then under that he signed 'Don Marquis' in parentheses. Doesn't this give you a chuckle?"

In his autobiography, mentioned several times in these pages, George Middleton refers to Marquis's "one self-preserving quality: he had no repressions and could suffer through his many dark hours to release." This, Middleton believes, is what enabled him to withstand three shattering blows—the death of his young son and of Reina, his first wife (the great love of his life), and now Barbara's passing. Middleton speaks with feeling of the "depths Don dredged" before he was mentally and spiritually capable of facing his responsibilities again—but face them he did.

Ironically, Barbara's death eased the uncomfortable financial situation in which Marquis found himself at the time. The thirty thousand dollars in high-grade bonds that represented her trust fund now reverted to him. For a long time he couldn't bring himself to sell these bonds—as he told Weed, he had a feeling he couldn't put into words that they were still Barbara's—so he held them as long as he could and used them as collateral in borrowing money.

Before Barbara's death Marquis had found consolation, when pot-boiling depressed him, in thinking about his projected novel, "the big book," tentatively titled "The Boy Who Tried to Be Good." Now he dismissed it from his mind and didn't return to it for a few years. His explanation was that Barbara's death had "snapped the mood." Before that tragedy he replied enthusiastically to letters on the subject that he received from his editor at Doubleday, Doran, while now he avoided the subject as much as he could. The files reveal that Harry Maule had high hopes for this book and that he kept after Marquis tactfully but persistently. Here is part of a typical letter he addressed to Marquis in Hollywood a few months before Barbara died:

"I do hope things have been going well with you there in the land of the American Arabian Nights; and, most of all, I hope that your own health and that of your family has been good.

"Meanwhile another season has rolled around and we are beginning to plan the list for next fall. The question, of course, arises as to whether you will have 'The Boy Who Tried to Be Good' ready. You know how anxious we are to have it and you know how much enthusiasm we have for your work. This novel of yours ought to be a big thing and I am sure it will be. Can't you let me know about it?"

Here are some excerpts from a letter Don wrote Clive Weed on October 26, 1931, evidently in reply to a letter of condolence:

"This thing is worse than the others, because the others were summed up in Barb for me; and there are many complications in this thing full of the most exquisite torture; but I am not going to do anything melodramatic, for I have those two old ladies, my sisters, to look after. . . .

"The worst thing right now is that I can't think she's gone; I don't know it yet, I mean. I still think she is going to have that little operation for adenoids in a day or two. If I go to sleep I think she is coming into my room when I wake up. And then it all hits me fresh again. She said to me two weeks ago that she wished childhood was over, for she had gotten nothing out of it since her mother died.

. . . She said, 'Daddy, I think it is about time I was getting a
break.' . . .

"She wrote a poem a few days before she died asking God to tell
her what He meant by the way things in general turn out in this
world, and saying she did not want to live again after she died,
though she did want to live on this earth. . . . She felt well when
she wrote it—she told me she was well that day, and seemed well—
she did not know it was her last word to this world while leaving it.
I had Fola La Follette read it at her funeral. She and Fola understood each other.

"It was an agnostic poem. That child always bit the bullet and
carried on. I have only known the last year how much she kept
under and what her real thoughts were that she told to no one but
me. I thought the people who came to her funeral might as well
know what her honest thoughts were about life and death and how
she felt about it—and it was as if she smiled at them with a kind of
gentle irony and asked them what *they* knew about it, anyhow. Life
made her an adult too quickly—and forced all the complications
of the grown-up world upon her. And her poor tired little heart quit,
and that is how and why she died. And, in the last summing up,
it was I who did it myself, and I see now all the things I should
have done . . . the last four or five years, and that is her story . . .
that I, the person she worshipped as if I were a god, up to her last
breath, let her down, and she died of it. She died because my
character is what it is. She said she did not want anything but to
be with me all the time, and until lately she has not been, and now
I cannot get hold of her any more; she told me that all heaven
meant to her would be just to be with me. . . . With love, Don"

As to the poem by Barbara to which he alludes—(the one that is
missing)—Miss La Follette, who read it at the funeral, does not
recall it as "agnostic" but understands how her father, in his over-
wrought state, could have thought it so.

The assurances Marquis gave his friend that he would not "do
anything melodramatic" remind me of Weed's report of one of "the
great conversations," in which Marquis, who played the leading role,
discussed the topic of suicide far, far into the night. Marquis maintained that many a perfectly normal person had toyed with "the
dark impulse of self-destruction," as he had described it. You
didn't necessarily prove yourself a strong character by establishing
that you never had any such thoughts; the real test was whether

you knew how to laugh them out of being. He thought most writers were afraid of the subject; while a few were too preoccupied with it —A. E. Housman, for instance, whose poetry nevertheless he greatly admired.

As far back as 1915 Marquis had published in his column a piece of light verse called "The Determined Suicide." It occupied more than two-thirds of "The Sun Dial," and appeared six years later in his collection *Noah an' Jonah an' Cap'n John Smith* (pages 92–94). The opening lines read:

> Just as I raised a pistol to my head
> From somewhere came a voice that said:
> "Don't pull that trigger! Let that weapon fall!
> Perhaps it is not loaded, after all,
> And think how silly one appears
> Snapping unloaded firearms at one's ears."

There follows a passage in which he considers slashing his throat with his razor. This he abandons as "selfish." His wife depends on that razor to pare her corns and if he employed it to destroy himself, she, a woman of sentiment, would be incapable of using it again:

> Ah, brute, indeed!
> To rob a woman in her hour of need . . .

He considers and dismisses hanging:

> Some meddling fool might come and cut me down,
> And then the crass unsympathetic town
> Will laugh . . .
> I'm sensitive, I never could stand chaff.

After weighing other possible methods he makes his decision:

> Some sure way it must be; sure way, but slow,
> Some gradual way, since Fate has willed it so.
> Why not, through all the bitter years,
> Of disillusion, balked ambition, tears,
> With stern, set face and laboring breath,
> Eat . . . eat and eat . . . and eat myself to death?
> Titanic steak, Gargantuan chop and Brobdignagian pie,
> Each one succeeding each, until I die.
> Ah, eighty years are not too much to give
> To suicide, when one has sworn: "I will not live."

On November 9, 1931, Marquis wrote the following letter:

Beverly Hills, Calif.

To The Players:

Dear Friends,—I want to thank you for the flowers for Barbara. She was a Player at heart herself. I took her into the Club one day when she was a little thing—it was raining and I had to stop there—and told her she was the only woman who was ever let in, besides Sarah Bernhardt, except on Ladies' Day and the suppers after the annual play revivals; and she was always proud of it. I found when she died she had in her bank account $40 profit from the paper she started some months ago—the paper actually paid her a profit almost from the first number! So I am enclosing this $40 as Barbara's contribution to the John Drew Fund, for I am sure, if she knows anything about it, it would please her.

Love to all,
Don Marquis

16 *A Child's Resolutions—What Was Marquis Really Like as a Drinker?—The Locust Swarm at Locust Valley—The Dark Hours Is Produced—Director Marquis Disagrees with Playright Marquis—Views on Draft Beer, Samuel Johnson, Edgar Allen Poe, etc.—Marquis's Desk—Edith McDonald, Susan Prince, and Pete*

The mention of Barbara to an old friend of the Marquis family invariably evokes some remembered something about that unusual child. In discussing her with Homer Croy, Homer said, "You'll recall from our visit to the old Marquis house in Forest Hills [in the spring of 1960] that when you descend from the second floor you reach a midway point where you can see into the dining room. One night when the Marquises had dinner guests, Barbara, who had been put to bed—she was about five at the time—decided to say good night to her parents a second time. As naked as the day she was born, she came out of her room and called to them from the stairway. When Reina reminded her little daughter that it was not ladylike to appear in the nude, Barbara exclaimed, 'But you can't see me, mummy! I used your vanishing cream!'" When Don told Homer the story, Homer asked if it was fact or fancy or a little of each. Don insisted that "this one" had happened exactly as he had told it.

Malthe M. Hasselriis was another Forest Hills neighbor of the Marquises, as was a brother of his. A letter to the former as to his recollections of Barbara elicited some interesting information about the child, including the following: "My brother has a book which belonged to her [Barbara] and which showed it had been read many times. It was the poems of William Blake."

In his will, which was written when Barbara was eight years old, Marquis named George W. Seymour and Mell Daniel as executors and as "guardians of the person and property of my said daughter." One day (January 1961) Mr. Daniel graciously called on me, bringing with him a brief case containing documents having to do with the Don Marquis estate. At the first mention of Barbara he dug into his papers and came up with a little notebook of hers containing some resolutions she had made. On the opening page there is a pen-and-ink sketch of herself—said to be a good likeness—captioned "Me," and signed "B. Marquis." The next page announces that these are the thoughts of "B. Marquis, age 11." In her January entries she resolves:

1. To be patient.—2. To hold my temper.—3. To be kind.—4. To be thoughtful of what is most easy and convenient for others.

The February entries are a restatement of January. In March there are a few new notes. Under the heading "Resolutions," the following are listed:

1. To *not* be sarcastic to my aunts. —2. To pay more attention to the dog. —3. Do not be so ready to criticize. —4. To overlook others mistakes. And to let *them* look-over *mine*.

For the month of April she resolves:

1. To be more mindful of my duty. —2. To save more. —3. To be nicer to Aunt Nev. —4. To keep my temper when Aunt Maud peeves me so.

There are no resolutions beyond May. During that month she resolves:

1. To not be so conceited.
2. To not mind getting dirty so much.
3. To not be so fussy.
4. To not be such an old maid.

On February 8, 1932, Marquis wrote a long letter to Russell Doubleday. Here it is, minus passages that do not seem pertinent: "Dear Russell:

"Thanks for your letter and the statements. I note that Archy and Mehitabel sold in the regular edition 19,305 copies, and in the large illustrated edition 8,165, or 27,470; but I don't know the entire period. I mean, when the book was published, etc.

"As there is a movement on foot to put these characters in the moving pictures—as short subjects, something in the nature of Mickey Mouse, and that sort of thing—I'd like a complete, separate statement of the whole Archy and Mehitabel business. . . ."

The letter to Mr. Doubleday is interrupted to point out that twice in the foregoing Marquis capitalizes the names of his well-known pair. Which calls to mind a passage from E. B. White's introduction to *the lives and times of archy and mehitabel:*

"I feel obliged, before going any further, to dispose of one troublesome matter. The reader will have perhaps noticed that I am capitalizing the name Archy and the name Mehitabel. I mention this because the capitalization of Archy is considered the unforgivable sin by a whole raft of old Sun Dial fans who have somehow nursed the illogical idea that because Don Marquis's cockroach was incapable of operating the shift key of a typewriter, nobody else could operate it. This is preposterous. Archy himself wished to be capitalized—he was no e. e. cummings. In fact he once flirted with the idea of writing the story of his life all in capital letters, if he could get somebody to lock the shift key for him. Furthermore, I capitalize Archy on the highest authority: wherever in his columns Don Marquis referred to his hero, Archy was capitalized by the boss himself. What higher authority can you ask?"

And now to resume Marquis's letter to Russell Doubleday:

"I note with pleasure that the book business is doing well in spite of the depression; I guess that is a good deal more than most of the publishing firms could say right now.

"With regard to my own novel: There has not been a time during the past two years that I could not have finished it with a big push of six weeks work.

"But there has not been a time during that period that I have been able to work for six weeks steadily. During the last year especially I have had wretched ill health. I have been steadily ill, for instance, since October; out of bed about four weeks during that time. [Note— October was the month his daughter died.]

"I worked a total of nineteen weeks during the year 1931, but as I got $1500 a week when I did work in the movies it carried me through. Now the movies are shot; the best I am offered is $750 a week, and am too ill to take that.

"Just a year ago I was offered a three-year movie contract which averaged $70,000 a year, but was sick in bed. Six weeks later, when I was up again, I couldn't get it. There are no such things going now, as the movies are in a state of financial collapse. Now, as I say, the salaries are cut in half—if you can get them at all—and I couldn't get to a studio now if I had one.

"So I will have to pay income tax on 30-odd thousand dollars earned last year at a time when I can't make a dollar—which is a humorously recurring situation with me. Bonds for which I paid $30,000 for a trust fund for my daughter have returned to me with her death—with a borrowing value of $15,000, which I will have to take to live till I get over this accursed lingering illness.

"The book I will finish piecemeal when I can get in a couple of hours work at a time; but have not been worrying as I want it put out at a time when things in general begin to pick up in a business way.

"Personal affairs and business are so mixed up in this letter that it will probably bore you to death. But the cursed part of a writer's business is that personal affairs and business are so damnably intermingled. His real capital is ability plus health, and when one or the other goes he is in a devil of a fix."

Before Marquis decided to borrow money on the bonds referred to in the foregoing he made some loans from friends. Here is a quotation from a letter to George Middleton in which he enclosed a check in payment of the money he had borrowed and characteristically observed:

"While we are on the subject of checks, I cannot resist telling you a charming little anecdote I heard about Rudyard Kipling. It seems that so many people want his autograph that when he draws a check he never knows whether it will be cashed—people save them for the autograph.

"It would be nice if something of this sort were to get started with one of us, wouldn't it? It's merely a thought—scarcely a suggestion just a vague feeling, you might say, that it would be nice."

Middleton tells in his memoirs about a Hollywood assignment he tried to get for Marquis:

"Learning that Metro was to do *Kim*, and knowing that Don reread it and Shakespeare each year, I wired suggesting that he make the 'story treatment.' Only an inadequate pen keeps me from repeating his adjectives when they turned him down. No: he was not happy. But, as Don's experience in the film capital adds perspective to any estimate of it, I linger with one who was a most talented writer and a most lovable man. Though we both had long been members of the Players, I came to know him best in the admitted isolations of spirit he and I were often to experience in this state of mind called Hollywood."

Marquis, in his earliest days in Hollywood, had a laudable if naïve notion that if he persevered he'd be given a chance to work on stories in line with his capabilities and thus be able to contribute something toward a better type of motion-picture entertainment. Though he realized before long that this might never happen and came to regard his work in the movie studios as "pot-boiling de luxe," he still clung to the outside hope that the miracle might happen: the chance to do a big picture. It was not until three years later that he seemed fully aware that this opportunity would never come.

Probably only Kipling himself knew *Kim* better than Marquis; yet he had been unable to get close enough to that contemplated production to lay bare some ideas he had long had as to how that famous story should be treated on the screen. The frustrations stemming from Hollywood's insistence on miscasting him as a writer and his complete inability to get the kind of assignments for which he considered himself qualified caused him to explode in the largely unprintable, privately issued "Ode to Hollywood," from which the following stanzas have been rescued:

> City of sterile striving,
> Where brains have not begun,
> I sing thy idiot faces,
> Thy leaguèd commonplaces,
> Bright in thy silly sun.
>
> Fertile in naught but faking,
> Futile each season passes;
> And scrutiny discloses
> Thy most prodigious roses
> Are really horses' asses.
>
> Diffuse, wide desert reaches
> Where no mind ever wrought.—
> Peer from thy cloudless skies
> Demons with lidless eyes,
> Scorching the buds of thought.

But Marquis did not often permit himself to be that grim about the world of the motion picture in which he found himself. The following letter from Hollywood is more typical:

Master C. R. Weed
The Players
16 Gramercy Park
New York, N.Y.
My dear young friend:
I am sure you are a very bright boy and keep up with your studies; it gives me great pleasure to forward you herewith the autograph which you requested.

Yours sincerely,

In line with his belief that he was "part of a rubber-stamp operation," the author of the foregoing had had DON MARQUIS imprinted on a rubber stamp and the "autograph" he sent Clive Weed was a stamped impression of his name. To amuse himself during one of his illnesses, he sent similar letters to other friends, all purporting to be in reply to requests for the autograph of the world-famous screen writer, Donald Robert Perry Marquis.

By the beginning of spring—this was 1932—Marquis's health was much improved and his doctor permitted him to resume work on a limited schedule. He wrote and sold a few magazine pieces and was able to undertake the assignment of writing "special dialogue" for a picture that needed bolstering.

He was now eager to return to New York. Marjorie's renewed interest in The Dark Hours—she had reread her husband's drama of the Crucifixion and was more convinced than ever that it could be successfully produced on Broadway—had the effect of reviving his own interest in the play he had almost forgotten. At the time it was published in book form—1924—he considered it his best piece of writing but it had long since slipped out of his consciousness. Now Marjorie's enthusiasm communicated itself to him and it gave them both a new interest at a time when they badly needed one.

In the 1920s Eddie Dowling, who has won distinction in the theater as actor, writer, director, and producer, read The Dark Hours, pronounced it a "distinguished work, perhaps a great one," and decided it was something he wanted to produce if he possibly could. At the time he had a big hit on Broadway—Sally, Irene and Mary, a musical he had written, and directed, and was appearing in—and he was in a strong position financially. But he had a prior commitment, a play he had contracted to produce before he could undertake *The Dark Hours*. This play failed and Dowling dropped the money with which he had hoped to produce Marquis's.

Dowling told me this story at lunch one day, expressing regret that once that opportunity was lost, Marquis's drama of the last days of Christ had receded into the background and he never had a chance thereafter to give it adequate consideration.

Dowling also recalled the night Governor Al Smith of New York, Don Marquis, and others were his guests at a performance of *Sally, Irene and Mary*. When Dowling introduced Marquis to the Governor —this was in the heyday of archy and mehitabel—he referred to Don as "an authority on cockroaches." Pretending he thought Marquis was an exterminator, Smith remarked, "We could use a man like you where I live."

In earlier passages the writer referred to conversations about Don Marquis with Charles Connolly, for years a factotum at the Players— a combination of maître d., chief steward, and general overseer— and now an honorary member of the Club. In a subsequent conversation in which these discussions were resumed, Connolly added some thoughts to his previous observations of Marquis as a drinker, declaring he could recall occasions when Don, in his best tall-story mood, told tales about his feats as a tippler that were obviously designed to shock his listeners, an old practice of his. The reader will recall that Marquis, prior to delivering a lecture at Yale University, confided to Professor William Lyon Phelps that he drank a bottle of brandy daily and loved every drop of it. Phelps believed the story and often repeated it in awesome acknowledgment of Marquis's prowess as a toper. (Marquis had enjoyed pulling this hoax at a time when he was "suffering a doctor-induced temperance that was so restrictive it bordered on teetotalism.")

Marquis had done his important drinking before he was forty. He had some nights thereafter when he displayed his old-time form but they were widely scattered. He renounced all credit for these "conquests of his will power," pointing out that you lose interest in liquor "when it pulls you down instead of giving you a lift." It will be recalled that he wrote Clive Weed from Hollywood after Barbara's death, "I would be grateful if I could get soused and relax; but a spoonful of booze damn near kills me."

Connolly says there were times, although he can't remember or even guess at the dates, when he witnessed Marquis so engrossed in conversation that he forgot or paid scant attention to the drink he had ordered. On one such occasion Don had ordered a double Scotch highball, started telling stories, and walked away from the bar with at least half his drink still in the glass.

Connolly also recalls Marquis's drinking pattern during a Players party which he described as one of the most hilarious in the Club's history. The second floor had been converted into an old-time Western saloon for the occasion and a long bar installed, complete with simulated bullet holes. And at Marquis's request a heavy layer of sawdust was sprinkled on the floor. The Club had also provided swinging doors, through which those attending the affair entered.

The membership and their guests were in dinner jackets, excepting a few (including Frederic Dorr Steele) who were made up as ladies of the evening—those wild women of the wild and woolly era who made their modest (or immodest) contribution to the building of the West.

Marquis, recalling the days when Salvation Army lasses invaded Lipton's Bar on Park Row to save from hellfire and damnation the assembled journalistic sinners, suggested that a few members appear as tambourine-wielding soul-savers, and this was done. Their job was to thwart, with hymns and prayers, the trollops who were displaying a bit of bosom or leg in their efforts to entice their dinner-jacketed fellow members.

Marquis and Brian Hooker were the bartenders. And Don, to show respect for the traditions of a noble calling, affected a handle-bar mustache, parted his hair in the middle, barkeep style, and donned the time-honored badge of office, a white apron.

Marquis had often wistfully remarked that he would love to stand behind a bar and serve beer from the wood and he achieved his ambition that night, learning to wield the little stick that leveled off the foam with the skill of a lifelong tapman. Once during the evening his mustache fell off and landed in a mug of beer, but aside from this lapse (which was said to have been prearranged) the Bartenders' Union would have been proud of his performance that night—and of the skill displayed by Marquis's assistant, Brian Hooker, who is said to have shown great fortitude in the face of the inevitable and oft-repeated gag by the whisky drinkers present, "Another hooker, barkeep."

All in all it was a great evening, Connolly recalls. He'd never seen

Marquis livelier or more disposed to swap quips and stories with his fellow Players. "I couldn't help noticing that Mr. Marquis drank very little that evening," said Connolly, getting to the point of his story. "He sipped a little beer now and then and when the evening was over and it was time to go home he was cold sober."

There was one other thing that Connolly noticed. It was the transition from the Marquis who had been gaily tending bar and swapping banter with his friends to the serious man who, looking worn and dispirited, wearily waved a good night to his fellow members. "I wondered afterward," Connolly concluded, "if Mr. Marquis had not taken part in this affair just to be good sport. He was almost like an actor playing a part."

A different picture of Marquis as a drinker emerges in a letter from Upton Sinclair dated November 12, 1960. The old Doubleday, Doran files having revealed that Marquis had once requested his publishers to send Mr. Sinclair an advance copy of one of his books, I decided to investigate and learn how well the men had known each other. Here is Mr. Sinclair's reply:

"I recall meeting Don only once, in Hollywood; evening party. I've forgotten whose home. He had the usual glass in hand, and fell asleep in a big arm-chair. All the others were woozy at the end, so it was no offense. A teetotaler all my life, I went to three or four such literary gatherings, and then decided to stay in my Pasadena home. Best wishes, Upton Sinclair

"P.S. My wife supplies the host's name, the poet Samuel Hoffenstein. Nice dinner party, then he got drunk too!"

Marquis had speculated in his column as to whether, since he had written so often and so affectionately about the Old Soak and his boozy entourage, people meeting him for the first time didn't find themselves wondering if he wasn't an old lush himself. In this connection it is interesting to note that Sinclair, although he had met Marquis only once, reports that Don "had the *usual* glass in hand." Marquis would have understood the psychology of that allusion and would have been amused by it. (If a slight digression is permissible, Mr. Sinclair will be interested to know that Marquis, in letters to his friends, recommended the controversial novelist's *Upton Sinclair Presents William Fox* as the only completely realistic Hollywood biography he could recall.)

One of the spokesmen for Prohibition, in an attack on Marquis, presented him as "a man who would upset the law of the land to restore that breeding-place of wickedness, the saloon." This was typical of the attitude of many of the Dry leaders toward the creator of "that symbol of sin, the Old Soak."

In his serious moments Marquis made it plain that his anti-Prohibitionism had two main motivations: impatience with "that most stultifying of phenomena, Puritanism," and a horror of gangsterism. On May 24, 1931, in replying to a letter from a reader, E. H. Brownell of Newport, Rhode Island, he said, "This is getting to be a hell of a country." Then, with a vehemence that few Marquis fans are acquainted with, he declared that if the country didn't rise up and "free itself of the Al Capones, the crooked district attorneys, the grafting cops, etc., and return to decency and the open saloon, I think I shall become a British subject . . . not that I am crazy about the British."

Lapsing back to some semblance of his familiar jauntiness, he concluded: "What the hell other country could you join? The French are peevish, the Russians are nuts, and the trouble with the Irish Free State is that it is Irish. And if you become a South Sea Islander they dress you in a coconut fibre tunic and shoot you for the movies."

In 1925 Marquis had planned to take a cottage in England for the summer, according to a letter from his sister Maud to her cousin Neeta. This was to be a test to see how he enjoyed living in England; but after a few halfhearted inquiries about cottages he abandoned the idea.

After many delays Don left Hollywood by automobile during the summer of 1932. In the party, in addition to Don and Marjorie, were the latter's teen-age daughter Ruth, her young son Walter, Jr. and a friend—a young actor who had asked them for a lift to New York. Marquis told the story of this trip across the continent in an article in the *American Magazine*. For a few years prior to the publication of this piece, items containing references to "a heart ailment" had appeared occasionally in the press in connection with his various illnesses. It was the belief of intimates at the time that Marquis wanted to counteract the publicity that had built up a picture of him as a sick man. This could best be accomplished by means of an article in a mass-circulation national magazine in which he showed himself withstanding conditions that would be too much for a man in feeble health.

Here are some excerpts from this *American Magazine* article, which, like so many of the pieces in the periodicals of thirty years ago, was a lengthy one:

"I started out with a certain sense of adventure. For one doctor had said to me: 'In the present condition of your heart, excessive heat will probably kill you.' Another doctor had said: 'In the present condition of your heart, a great altitude could easily kill you.' A third doctor had said: 'In the present condition of your heart, any sudden shock will kill you.'

"So, as I said, I started out with a sense of adventure, not wholly unjustified by medical opinion, to drive the roadster section of a two-car family caravan over the continent from Los Angeles to New York. I took the little roadster across the Imperial Valley in southern California through 140 degrees of heat, and the heat didn't kill me. I took it to the top of a mountain nearly a mile high in Arizona, and the altitude didn't kill me. I turned it over on top of the mountain— the neatest somersault you ever saw—and pinned another young fellow and myself among the splinters, and the shock didn't kill me. . . .

"I should like to tell at great length and with elaborate detail to all within sound of my voice . . . just exactly what is the matter with my heart; but the narrative might make thousands of other patient sufferers take pen in hand and write letters to the editor. We Heart Cases are like that. We like publicity, even notoriety. When we get a Listener, we Tell All. . . . So I will only say that, in my case, my heart trouble is complicated by another disease called hypochondria. Heart trouble can be cured, but hypochondria is an incurable disease. Ask any doctor. What I have suffered—and made others suffer—with my hypochondria!

"Well, anyhow, we set forth in the two cars. In the sedan section rode my wife, The Leading Lady; her daughter, The Ingénue; and her nine-year-old son, known as Two-Gun Walt because of a predilection for toy pistols which look horridly real to me. In the roadster were the Leading Juvenile, a young actor of twenty-three who journeyed East with us, and myself, the Old Character Man. . . .

"July 28th—Arrived in San Diego from Los Angeles and started East about dusk. Had a blow-out. Went back to San Diego and jacked up the dealer who had sold that tire, and got a new one. Just to give the new tire a chance, the Old Character Man deserted the Leading Juvenile and went to ride with the Leading Lady, who was driving the sedan.

"Discovered nobody in the party had a watch. But it must have

been nearly midnight before we found ourselves climbing the mountains east of San Diego. . . . Two-Gun Walt stertorously asleep
somewhere with his head lower than his heels. Leading Lady driving
through mountain passes and at the same time giving a lecture on
Rhythm in the Theatre, with illustrations and gestures which sometimes take one hand from the steering apparatus, and sometimes
both hands, while the rear right wheel hovers and hesitates over
gorges and precipices which, to the Old Character Man beside her,
seem to have no bottom.

" 'Yes, my dear, I agree with you—rhythm is the foundation of
all the arts,' says the Old Character Man feebly, trembling and clutching his aspirin closer to his bosom. 'But I think it would be a good
idea if a definite majority of the four wheels were on the road
practically all the time.'

" 'Now, in the Russian theatre,' continues the Leading Lady . . .
but just then a roadside restaurant dashes into sight. The Old Character Man feigns starvation. Saved! . . .

"There was a sign near that restaurant which said it was 4,300 feet
high and that the United States Government had officially pronounced it the healthiest place in the United States, and when I
read that I felt better at once. . . .

"July 29th—El Centro, Calif. . . . I learned it was only about a
quarter of ten in the morning, but the heat! 'How hot is it here this
morning?' I asked the man who runs the auto camp.

" 'Only 120,' he replied. 'But it's probably pretty warm out in the
valley. Not as hot as it will be in a couple of hours, though. By
noon,' he said, 'it would be from 140 degrees to 160, out in the
valley.'

"About eleven o'clock we started for Yuma, with the Old Character Man back again at the wheel of the roadster. . . . I don't
remember the distance between El Centro and Yuma, but I learned
what real heat is for the first time in my life. But that drive—probably
it was not more than sixty or eighty miles—bears no relationship
in my mind to any such realities as time or space or tangible earth.
It was purely fantastic. Pretty soon we got beyond the irrigated and
cultivated part of the Imperial Valley and into a world that was all
blinding white sand against a background of purple mountains.
We passed hitch-hikers, three bums lying in a ditch that brought
water from the hills: a 'desert rat' with the rheumy eyes and dirty
beard of an oriental beggar, and two young men in khaki. And all

these, and ourselves, and the occasional cacti, were but little dark specks floating in a universe that was blinding white and incredible purple. And the white and purple floated, too, and were not solid . . . were not hard earth and painted rock, but colors floating and streaming as if in some monstrous effect of stage-lighting. . . .

"Next day. Tucson. Concrete auto camp in outskirts. Sandstorm. All doors and windows of the camp closed tightly. Sand gets in anyhow. Gets into everything. Baggage. Beds. Throats. Noses. Brushes the teeth. Grinds the lenses of the eyes. Scours the tonsils. Polishes the lungs. Probably very sanitary. Mixes with the gastric juices. Rubs off the skin and strokes the nerves. Until they explode. And everything shut up so tightly that you'd think even a flu germ or a rough word couldn't get into or out of the place. . . .

"When I struck the border between Arizona and New Mexico I struck it, as I have previously intimated, on my ear. The gravel road had been ridged all the way, but ridged in a straight-across, washboardy fashion, and naturally I was taking it slowly. The Leading Juvenile was in the roadster with me, as usual; the others were in the sedan. I hit a series of diagonal ridges, which tipped the car onto its two southern wheels; and just as I was getting through that, I met a series of other ridges, set in a reverse diagonal, which tripped up the wheels that were still on the ground. Into the air we went, and came down plunk on the car's top. Judge, Your Honor, I know the nature of an oath, and I swear I wasn't going a foot more than thirty-five miles an hour, if that.

"I remember, while the car was in the air and about to come down, thinking that probably I wasn't going to be hurt. And I wasn't. But I had fallen on the Leading Juvenile—I weigh 200 pounds—and both of us were pinned so we couldn't move. I thought his back was broken, and after a while I asked him if such was the case. He didn't answer, and I realized that he was unconscious. Pretty soon I asked him again; and this time he said calmly that he supposed so.

"'I'm sorry,' I said politely. I think we were both a little goofy for a moment, for he replied, with equal politeness:

"'Oh, it doesn't matter.'

"I managed to get my left hand loose, and put my thumb on the button of the horn and held it there until somebody came—a rancher who had seen the spill from the door of his house six or eight hundred yards away.

"It seemed to me a long time before anyone got there, however. Some liquid began to drip all over us; and I thought it was gasoline, and began to get scared, for I imagined there would be a burst of flame in a minute, which would be too bad. I remembered how, when I was a small boy in Illinois, I used to knock potato bugs off the vines into a tin can, and then pour kerosene into the can and set fire to it, to destroy the bugs; and I worked up quite a bit of sympathy for those bugs—belated, it is true, but genuine. I don't believe anyone has ever felt sorrier for potato bugs than I did for the next five minutes. The Leading Juvenile had been smoking a cigarette and I a pipe, and I had neglected to turn off the ignition while we were doing our loop in the air—a fellow told me later that was what I should have done. But it wasn't gas; it was acid water from the battery, which later ate off our golf knickers and stockings and parts of our shoes, and made little holes in our feet and legs.

"The rancher who had seen us go over stopped a bunch of cowmen who were going along in a flivver, and they righted the car. Splinters were all over our heads and faces—wood, iron, glass splinters—and yet we were scarcely scratched. The Leading Juvenile had some ligaments torn loose in his right shoulder. The sedan came back, having missed us, and the Leading Juvenile was taken to Lordsburg, thirty miles away, to a doctor. He had to wear the shoulder in a cast for a week or so; which threw all the heavy lifting onto the women of the party, as I can't lift things because of my Heart Disease and Hypochondria. But they are both strong women, and after a few days began to enjoy it; or such is my belief. . . .

"We went across Texas the longest way, from New Mexico to Arkansas, and it surprised me how small the other states seem when once Texas is behind you. . . . At Fort Worth, I should have mentioned, I autographed some opi in a bookstore, participated as leading man in something like a literary pink tea, and was interviewed by reporters. In telling them the history of my life, which I always like to do because it comes out so differently every time, I mentioned that I died in 1927 and was buried in Westminster Abbey . . . under an assumed name, I added hastily, lest research should fail to find me and they would be disappointed. I explained I was too modest, and hated publicity too much, to permit myself to be buried under my real name. . . .

"At Memphis and Nashville we stayed at hotels; and from then on. . . . And then suddenly, one night, before I had grasped mentally that I was there, New York burst on me again, from the middle of the new bridge across the Hudson, which I had never seen before—burst on me all afresh, as she has again and again for the last quarter of a century. I had half forgotten the prodigious, savage beauty of her violent architecture, when she lies between a summer night and the ocean, with the sea winds singing high among the lighted towers; and for my infidelity she stabbed me sharply in the throat with an unexpected pang of joy."

Back in New York at the brownstone at 125 East 62nd Street, Marquis resumed contact with the magazines for which he had been writing—*Collier's*, the *Saturday Evening Post*, and others— and began turning out more short stories and humorous articles. But his main interest now was the business of getting *The Dark Hours* transmitted to the stage. He recanvassed all the leading producers, again sending out copies of the play in book form as published by Doubleday, Doran and Company; but, although he stirred up considerable interest, none of the producing firms was willing to take a chance on a religious play during the Depression—one that called for a large cast, elaborate costuming, and would, for additional reasons, be expensive to stage. One producer told Marquis that although he thought his drama of the Crucifixion "had a lot of sock" and was "terrific" when you read it, he wasn't sure how it would play. Besides, the rigors of the Depression had put everyone in a gloomy frame of mind and what the public needed was some belly laughs such as *The Old Soak* had provided; they could get their religion free in church.

Marjorie thought Don should produce the play himself; and he agreed—to a point. He was strongly opposed to self-backed books and plays—he had, in fact, used both as targets in his columning days; but, because he considered *The Dark Hours* his best writing in any category—it had received critical acclaim when published as a book—he decided to go ahead if he could raise the money "without putting himself in hock for the rest of his life." Previously he had borrowed money against Barbara's trust fund when the bonds reverted to him on her death, but he still had a $20,000 equity in these bonds. It was estimated that he would need a minimum of $30,000 to ring up the curtain, a rock-bottom figure that would not give *The Dark Hours* much of a chance if it did not take hold immediately. Marquis's other proviso was that some distinguished producer, one with a known policy of identifying himself only with ventures in which he believed, would have to show enough enthusiasm for the project to lend his name to it. He found such a producer in Lodewick Vroom, and when he was able to raise the rest of the money he needed without too many entanglements, he decided to go ahead.

Vroom, in his talks with Marquis, placed a great deal of emphasis on direction. This play would require the services of an imaginative director, one sensitive to the nuances of Don's stirring drama. To manipulate the scenes in which there were many participants, and to achieve the requisite integration, flow, and naturalism would take great skill, imagination, and patience. There came to Vroom's mind the name of a director who had been identified with several Broadway successes and who was synonymous with the better type of production. Vroom considered this man the right combination of artistry and practical experience and urged that he be retained, declaring that as the producer of *The Dark Hours*, a play he greatly admired but whose genre was new to him, he would have more confidence if he could lean on a director who had demonstrated his versatility in the theater.

But Marjorie had previously asked that she be permitted to direct the play and Marquis had assented. So great was her enthusiasm for what her husband had written that he seemed to believe that this would communicate itself to her direction and result in an inspired production. And he succeeded in convincing Vroom of this.

Marjorie thought there had been too much emphasis on her husband's career and not enough emphasis on hers. This was the perfect approach to a man who never missed an opportunity for self-reproach. He readily agreed with Marjorie that she must be given more of an opportunity to emerge in her chosen field. He completely overlooked the fact that in her ambition to establish a theater of her own, and now to direct, she had passed up many opportunities to appear as an actress and in the process had herself neglected the talent that gave her her best chance to emerge importantly in the theater.

Marquis also appears to have forgotten or decided to overlook that only a few years before, he had backed Marjorie in a summer-theater venture at Locust Valley, New York. She had doubled as actress and director and it was the consensus of those familiar with the undertaking that she had made a contribution as a player but not

as a director. Her direction was considered "conventional." Before
the Retreat from Locust Valley, as Marquis had termed it, he had
lost $18,000 on this venture.

But that was only the *cash* loss. There was another which, though
less tangible, was just as real. Marjorie had taken a house in Locust
Valley near the theater. This she used as living quarters and as
headquarters for her stock company. She suggested that Don transfer his writing activities from East 62nd Street to Locust Valley. A
summer in the country was just what he needed. It would give
him new ideas and enable him to work in peace and quiet. New
York, she insisted, was no place for a writer during the summer
months.

Marjorie filled the house with young actors and actresses who
couldn't afford to stop at the local inns and nearby hotels, which
were largely vacation places. There were so many of these impromptu
boarders that, although the house was a large one, they overflowed
onto the porch and the lawn (where some of them slept, weather
permitting). It was quite a horde, including players for whom there
were no jobs, and a goodly complement slept on the living-room
floor and the floors of some of the other rooms, all neatly divided
by sexes. In fact, Marquis said, that was the only neat thing about
it.

It reminded him of his days as a youngster back home in Walnut,
Illinois, when the carnival came to town and he entered the obstacle
races. He became quite expert at treading over and between the
recumbent figures without disturbing any of the slumbering artists
who were helping his wife reshape the American theater to her
heart's desire. He admitted that when it flashed across his mind that
these "bodies" also had to be fed it took restraint not to step on
one here and there—not with his full weight, of course. But he realized it was unfair to the best interests of the theater to harbor any
such mean thoughts. Marjorie and her Not So Little Group of Serious Thinkers, like Hermione before her, was dedicated to doing
something for The Thespian Art and that, of course, was an objective that had to be encouraged. *Someone* had to save the American
theater.

Marquis admitted that there were times when he didn't think it
very funny. In a sense it was like being invaded. But these invaders
troubled him less when asleep than when awake. His main objection
was that they devoted the hours from a little before midnight until

about three in the morning or later to seminars on what he called
the Drama with a capital D—sessions that were as noisy as they were
enthusiastic. And he found he could get very little sleep in Locust
Valley. His writing suffered as a consequence and he was missing
deadlines. So he spent more and more time by himself in the big
house at 125 East 62nd Street, returning to Locust Valley mainly, he
said, to resume the little game of stepping over the reclining forms
of the young people who were helping Marjorie uplift the American
theater. He called it fine exercise and good training in foot-control.
Anyone can step *on* a sleeping actor; and, under certain circumstances, anyone might be tempted to. It took restraint, also
steady pedal nerves, to tread *between* the bodies; and if he ever
had to make a living as a six-day bike-rider this training, he confided to intimates, might well prove to be the making of him. The
best riders, he had been told, went to extraordinary lengths to develop leg muscles.

In the end all would work out for the best. In his time he had
written a lot of nonsense about the need for encouraging youth; he
would now devote the rest of his life to the reverse of that unfortunate proposition. This would make him a controversial figure,
resulting in an avalanche of publicity that would make him the
best-known writer in the land. Millions would hate him but no editor
would be able to ignore him. They would be compelled, because of
the competition for his services, to pay fantastic prices for his attacks
on the young and to feature him big on the covers of their magazines.

On September 27, 1932, this item appeared in the New York
Herald Tribune, and presumably in other New York papers: "Don
Marquis has taken a studio over the St. James Theatre in West Forty-
fourth Street, where he will be available for consultation in the casting of his forthcoming play, 'The Dark Hours.'"

Marquis had promised his wife a free hand in the direction of
his play and he meant to keep that promise. He would also keep
another promise, one he had made to Lodewick Vroom: to consult
with Marjorie and to give her the full benefit of what he had visualized when he originally wrote *The Dark Hours*. He would attend rehearsals and make suggestions but he would not interfere. One
person had to be in charge and that person's authority could not
be challenged or the result would merely be to confuse the cast.

Marquis and Vroom, it was decided, would do the casting. The latter knew the capabilities of practically every player in the theater, and Don, as a result of his experience with several productions, had some ideas on the subject himself. Where a choice narrowed down to a few players who seemed to fit the requirements, Vroom thought Marquis should select the one whose voice and bearing most nearly approximated the character in question as he had visualized it in writing his play.

The casting completed, the responsibility for directing the play was to be solely Marjorie's.

Herbert Ranson, a distinguished Shakespearean actor—(as recently as 1959 he appeared with Sir John Gielgud)—vividly recalls *The Dark Hours*, in which he played the part of Caiaphas. As the rehearsals progressed there developed a feeling among members of the cast that Mrs. Marquis did not grasp certain values in the script, that her direction was lacking in boldness and imagination. It was rather openly stated by some that her prosaic approach to a poetic work would imperil its chance of success. Conventional direction, it was felt, was not good enough for a drama that gave you a spinal tingle when you read it.

Ranson and others felt that somehow "the majestic sweep of Marquis's lines" had been lost by a too literal piecing together of the scenic entities, with the result that the drama, as transferred to the stage, became a "routine enactment" rather than the stirring experience it should have been. Somehow the spiritual juices had leaked out and the impact of the author's writing had been lost.

During one of the rehearsals Marjorie fired Hugh Miller (Judas) and Eleanor Goodrich (Mary Magdalene), charging both with "incompetence." Highly regarded in their profession, they represented her husband's visualization of the characters they depicted and were the joint selections of Marquis and Vroom. The Miller firing was of particular embarrassment to Marquis, who had gone out of his way to thank that talented actor for his fine reading of the Judas part.

Marjorie Marquis, after trying to find another actor for the Judas role, decided that she had made a mistake and notified Miller that he had been reinstated. Miller replied that he would not return unless madam director also reinstated Eleanor Goodrich, whose Mary Magdalene he considered first-rate. Miss Goodrich had been discharged, he stated, because Mrs. Marquis had failed to appreciate the quality of her performance, and his ultimatum was firm and uncompromising. Marjorie demurred, then yielded; and Mr. Miller and Miss Goodrich were both restored. In the meantime the cast had suffered a loss of morale.

Ranson reports that Charles Bryant (who had been cast for the role of Pilate) came to him and voiced his displeasure with the way things were going. Bryant thought that Ranson, as one who was close to the author and whose motives would not be misunderstood, should seek out Vroom and tell him that *The Dark Hours* was foredoomed to failure unless drastic changes were made in Mrs. Marquis's direction—changes that would enable the cast to bring to life on the stage what Don had written instead of his wife's interpretation thereof, which was something else again.

Ranson was as disturbed by the situation as Bryant—(he described Marjorie Marquis as "a nice enough woman but deficient in the arts"—but he thought it would be a mistake to intervene. Marquis had been attending rehearsals—not all of them but enough to know what was going on—and it was up to him, Ranson thought, to say anything to his wife that needed saying. "Don was captivated by her," Ranson recalls, and he believes that that could have been the deciding factor when he wondered, as he must have, whether his play was being misdirected.

Medical records—those of Dr. Harry A. March—reveal that Marquis was a sick man at the time *The Dark Hours* went into rehearsal. (He was suffering from the flare-up of an old kidney ailment.) This may explain his not attending *all* the rehearsals. Every cent of his own cash was in that production as well as money he had borrowed, there was a great deal at stake and under different circumstances it seems indicated that he would have haunted the theater and not missed a minute of what was taking place.

To what extent he challenged his wife on her interpretation of *The Dark Hours* is not known, but it *is* known that he resolutely stuck to his story when she disagreed with the following, from his introduction to the published text of his play:

"In the English-speaking countries there is a sentiment against the appearance of Jesus on the stage. When I first considered this play, several years ago, I was inclined to rebel against the restriction. But the more I thought about it, the less inclined I was to rebel. I finally recognized that the restriction arises not altogether and alone from religious feeling in the narrower sense; it derives also from a

sound (though perhaps unconscious) apprehension of dramatic
values and possibilities on the part of the great masses of humanity
dwelling in these countries. For you cannot show Divinity on the
stage; you cannot get an actor to impersonate Divinity. You may
show humanity in juxtaposition to Divinity, acted upon by Divinity
and responding in one way or another to the contact—but Divinity
itself: no! The thing is impossible.

"There is certain to be in the mind of every person who has
thought about Jesus some conception of how he looked when he was
on earth; these are ideas and ideals that would necessarily be dashed
by the appearance and manner of any actor attempting to play the
part."

Marjorie called attention to the fact that in the famous Passion
play presented every ten years in Oberammergau, Germany, Christ
was depicted on the stage throughout the performance. People came
from all over the world to witness this production, the most successful play of its kind ever presented. When Marquis reminded
her that in the English-speaking countries the feeling about depict-
ing Jesus on the stage was different, Marjorie promised to follow
her husband's wishes. While she had been given a free hand as
director, it was understood that her authority did not extend to
changing her husband's concept. The mood Marquis sought to
create could not be achieved by using the Oberammergau technique.
Christ's materialization would be a jarring note; it would snap the
spell.

Marquis had plenty of support for his point of view. For instance,
John W. Crawford, in reviewing *The Dark Hours* as a book in a
New York *Times* book review, had written: "The author has
chosen to respect the Anglo-Saxon sentiment against the representation of Jesus in the theatre. Although Christ is never seen, his voice
and his words are recorded by the little groups of watchers in the
various scenes, and by them transmitted to the presumptive larger
audience. The effect, oddly enough, is to heighten the passion of
the Savior. It is communicated to even the more casual observers,
to Peter and John, and, with supreme vividness and poignance, to
the betrayer, Judas Iscariot."

For several days prior to the scheduled opening of *The Dark Hours*
Marquis had not been feeling well. He continued to work but complained of "dragging himself around." To improve his morale he did

what he had done so many times before: he sought the companionship of friends at the Players.

Recalling those days, Dr. Richard H. Hoffmann, a member of the
Players since 1916, tells the following story in a letter dated September 16, 1959:

"In the club one evening I came upon Don playing pool. He
stopped for a moment, his cue erect, then bent over the table. As
he did he asked, 'Who put out the lights?' He was about to make a
great shot, he added, and he wanted the pleasure of seeing it.

"His speech was hesitant, faltering, his stance a little unsteady. I
walked over to him to support him and whispered, 'The lights are
on, Don, you have had an accident. This will be a temporary blindness.' Quietly I explained that a cerebral vessel had been blocked,
but that it was probably in an area where there would be no resulting
paralysis. I suggested that I had better take him home. On the way
home I explained what must have happened and assured him that
his sight would be restored.

"Don thought about his wife. She was a Christian Scientist and
did not like doctors. 'When you see Marjorie,' he said, 'tell her that
what I have is due to constipation—that is all she understands.'"

Dr. Hoffmann then drove Marquis to his home at 125 East 62nd
Street and led him up the brownstone steps. He had just opened the
door with a key that Don supplied when Pete, the Boston bull,
rushed out to lick his master's hand, his standard greeting. This was
the cue for Don to joke about the possibility of teaming up with
Pete in a little business venture. Their stock in trade would be a tin
cup, a lot of pencils, a nice busy street corner, and permanent
sorrowful expressions that he and the dog would have to cultivate if
they expected to do any business.

"When Marjorie joined us," Dr. Hoffmann continued, "I told her
that Don had a disturbance of vision due to constipation and that
he had better go to bed. She thanked me perfunctorily and said
she would take care of him.

"I then called Dr. Fred Tilney and told him that it would be essential to see Don on the following day. Dr. Tilney was the best-
known neurologist in New York, Chief of the Neurological Institute.

"The lesion was as I have described it and within two days half
vision returned to Don. He made an otherwise uneventful recovery
from his cerebral accident. I was deeply moved by Don's courageous

spirit. There was no hysteria, no expression of protest—just the philosophical attitude of a great man."

Hoffmann is convinced that Marquis had suffered a complete blackout of vision immediately following his "accident." In fact, Don thought some practical joker had turned off the lights in the Club and plunged the place into darkness for a laugh. While his blindness was of brief duration—a day or two at most—it was real while it lasted. For instance, Don's reactions were those of a sightless person as he was led out of the Club and taken home. Hoffmann's admiration for Marquis's composure stemmed from his belief that almost anyone in such a situation might have wondered whether, despite reassurances, he would ever be able to see again.

News stories began appearing about Marquis's "blindness" and "near-blindness." One carried the headline:

DON MARQUIS'S SIGHT
BELIEVED TO BE SAVED

Following the publication of these news items, ugly rumors began circulating. These are reflected in a letter written years afterward by Rodman Gilder, who was then working on a biography of Don Marquis. When Mr. Gilder died before he had a chance to do any actual writing, his sister, Rosamond Gilder, presented his papers to the Manuscript Division of the New York Public Library. Gilder's letter was addressed to the wife of Dr. Harry A. March, Marquis's physician and friend of long standing. The letter is dated April 20, 1940. (Dr. March was seriously ill at the time or it would have been addressed to him.) The pertinent passage follows:

"The question about Don's real state of health in November, 1932 is inspired by an idiotic rumor that I recently picked up (and I naturally denied it violently) among some young newspapermen who 'had heard' or 'had got the impression' that, when Don temporarily lost his eyesight on the eve of the production of his play 'The Dark Hours,' his illness was not as serious as was pretended—in other words, that it was exaggerated or even invented for press-agent purposes."

It is interesting to note that a canard that was first circulated in 1932 was still alive in 1940!

Gilder attached to his letter a blank sheet of paper at the very top of which he wrote:

"Dr. Harry A. March's professional and personal opinion as to

Don Marquis's real state of ill health in November, 1932: (What was the nature of the illness that struck him blind while he was shooting pool at the Players?)"

Gilder asked Mrs. March to fill in the answer when her husband was well enough to supply the information. The sheet was returned with this reply:

"Don Marquis's illness in November, 1932 was diagnosed by Dr. March as uremic poisoning, in which diagnosis other New York doctors concurred. His sight was subsequently restored to a certain degree.

"Harry March describes Don Marquis as 'a wonderful fellow who couldn't be anything but square—much loved by other men,'—so he refutes absolutely the rumor that the illness was not genuine."

A story published at the time in the New York *Times* mentions a consultation between Dr. March and Dr. Gordon M. Bruce, ophthalmologist, who had been called in to care for Marquis's eyes. A letter to Dr. Bruce, one of the most respected figures in his field, elicited the following:

"Don Marquis suffered a vascular episode along the course of his optic fibers so that he didn't see to one side. It would have been utterly impossible for him to have faked this, quite apart from the obvious fact that he was not that type of person. It was for this condition, which was really a small stroke, that he was being treated in Harkness Pavilion."

The old hospital records were not accessible, wrote Dr. Bruce, adding, "This information is being offered from my recollection of the matter."

I discussed Marquis's hospitalization with Dr. Bruce in his office at the Institute of Ophthalmology one day. Bruce described him as a man of great personal charm and a cheerful patient despite the "horrible headaches" which he reported. These headaches eventually responded to codeine, the doctor recalls. He also remembers that when Mrs. Marquis called on his patient she used to read to him from the Christian Science writings of Mary Baker Eddy. One day when Bruce asked Don how he was feeling, he responded, "Between Christ and codeine I believe I'll make it."

Dr. Bruce also recalls Marquis's reminiscences about the days when he was stage-struck and his friend Howard Lindsay graciously "gave him a chance to wreck his summer-theater venture in Maine." On reflection Marquis thought Lindsay must have recognized in him a potential greatness as an actor—else why didn't he fire him after he'd forgotten his lines several times and then compounded the crime by walking onstage with the fly of his trousers "almost exhibitionistically open?"

In an article published in the theater section of the Sunday New York *Times* on the eve of the opening of *The Dark Hours*—and dictated from his sickbed, according to a foreword—Marquis restated his position about the desirability of representing the Saviour in his drama by an offstage voice. In this article he said that since the publication of his play in 1924 he had "run across a passage in the preface to one of Bernard Shaw's plays in which he discusses the same thing. Shaw says that if you attempt to show Jesus on the stage you have simply a handsome actor. . . . The more I studied the more I understood and respected the prejudices against actually representing Him. The dramatic consciousness of the people would be offended—and justifiably."

The Dark Hours opened on November 14, 1932, in the New Amsterdam Theatre. Marquis, still hospitalized, was unable to attend. He got the surprise of his life the following morning when he learned from Percy Hammond's review in the New York *Herald Tribune* that his wife, using her authority as director, had elected to discard the aspect of his drama that he considered most basic, and about which he had written and said so much, in explanation of his unshakable belief that Jesus should not be depicted as an onstage character. Wrote Mr. Hammond:

"After waiting seven years Don Marquis's Passion play, 'The Dark Hours,' reached Broadway last evening, its poetry preserved, its dignity marred. . . .

"I had been told that it was Mr. Marquis's intention merely to hint at the Galilean's presence and represent Him by celestial sounds from offstage. The playbill indicated that such was his idea. But evidently he changed his mind, for Christ, in the person of an actor identified only by asterisks, was to be seen as well as heard. This appearance, I fear, was harmful to the play's nobility since its performer was but a waxen effigy in a blond wig and false whiskers . . . a small, feeble fellow with a silky voice. If, for a moment, I may be permitted to indulge in the vice of constructive criticism, I shall advise the author and his producer, Mr. Lodewick Vroom, to banish this desecrating counterfeit from their drama, and leave the Character unsullied to the pious imagination of their audiences."

Director Marjorie Marquis did not choose to follow Hammond's advice, so "this desecrating counterfeit" remained for the run of the play, which was mercifully brief—eight performances. That Marquis was released from the hospital in time to witness his play before it closed is confirmed by Edith McDonald, his former secretary, and by others.

The only clue as to why Marjorie, ignoring what her husband had written and what he had told her so many times, elected to present Christ as an onstage figure, is to be found in a little story that has a good oral history: she thought that her husband, in interpreting Christ through the medium of an offstage voice, was "trying to be too subtle"—that "when you were too subtle in the theater you lost your audience." What this story does not explain is why she made this decision after promising to abide by her husband's wishes.

Among those cited by Percy Hammond for giving good performances in "speaking Mr. Marquis's lovely sentences and those of the King James version of Holy Writ" were the two performers Mrs. Marquis had fired: "Mr. Hugo Miller (Judas) is finely and reticently theatrical as the cosmic traitor; and Miss Eleanor Goodrich is effective as the holy harlot."

The failure of *The Dark Hours* was a calamity for all concerned. Although some members of the cast had lost faith in their director, they all worked hard to please her. They hoped and prayed for both a prestige and a money success; those were the days of the Great Depression when money was hard to come by and the incentives were even greater than usual. It was as melancholy an experience for Marjorie as it was for the cast. She had worked herself to the point of near-exhaustion in an effort to make a success of her husband's play. Time and again she used questionable judgment but no one could question the zeal and determination with which she tackled her job. When, as usual, her haphazard estimates of costs got her into trouble—(Producer Vroom, a talented man of the theater, seems to have wound up as a figurehead)—and she discovered that she had not allowed enough money for a professional costuming job, she undertook to make the costumes herself! She did all the research herself, bought the fabrics, and designed and executed the costumes with the aid of her daughter, Ruth. Neither of these indefatigable workers got much sleep while this was going on. If Marjorie's judgment and sensitivity to artistic values had been equal to her courage, she would have made a great director. She did a resourceful job of turning out the costumes but unfortunately they lacked the professional touch, and some of them did not fit properly.

In a reminiscent article published a year later in the Fiftieth Anniversary Edition of his former paper, the Atlanta *Journal*, Marquis touches upon his experiences in trying to keep *The Dark Hours* alive.

"I had a play running on Broadway," he wrote, "which I had backed with my own money. 'Once a sucker, always a sucker,' as the saying is. . . . People were beginning to buy tickets, but I needed $5,000 to keep the show on the next week and give the public a chance to get there. It was a play with a particular appeal to the church people and they were beginning to come—in fact, the day after the show closed preachers all over New York and New Jersey were haranguing their congregations to go see it, and I took it off and slammed the door right in the face of a good many thousand dollars because I could not get hold of $5,000 quickly. . . . I wasn't very well at the time and so could not get around and high-jack the money out of any of my friends.

"While I was sitting thinking of the situation, I was called to the telephone.

"'Mr. Marquis,' said an unfamiliar voice, 'this is Jake.'

"'Jake who?' I asked. 'I know a lot of Jakes.'

"'Jake who used to be your office boy on The Atlanta Journal,' said the voice, 'years ago. I saw it in the papers where you have been pretty sick, and I wondered if I could do something for you. I hear you got a show on. There isn't anything I could do for you, is there?'

"'Jake,' I said, 'you could come over with a certified check for $5,000.'

"'Mr. Marquis,' said Jake, 'the coats ain't moving from the racks so fast this season.' He explained he was in the fur business now. 'Five thousand dollars would not be so easy to get hold of in the next hour or two, but I tell you what I will do for you. I will go right over to the synagogue and put up a special prayer for you right now, if you got no objections.'

"'Go to it, Jake,' I said, 'and good luck to both of us.'

"I had at that time two Catholic friends, a Methodist, and several others who were putting up special prayers for me and I thought I might as well take all the traffic would bear. Anyhow, about two hours later, I began to get better. I don't know whether it was the weight of Jake's petition added to the others that did the business or not. It is impossible to do any exact bookkeeping in these matters."

The failure of *The Dark Hours* was of course more of a tragedy for Marquis than for anyone else. In the past it did not bother him when he was broke. Now he was both broke and in dubious health, a combination he didn't like. In order to meet his many obligations he would have to embark on a campaign of overwork at a time when he didn't have any reserve energy to draw upon, when the doctors were urging him "to take it easy."

But though it was a gloomy prospect, Marquis had overcome gloomier ones. *Collier's*, some time earlier, had tried to interest him in writing a weekly page, at a figure he considered "impressive." He wanted to do it but his Hollywood work had prevented it. He wondered if they were still interested. It developed that they *were*. This was an important development to a man who had to keep two households going—(he still sent his sisters a monthly check and paid the taxes and other carrying charges of their home in Forest Hills).

Though financial considerations *had* to be a major factor in Marquis's thinking, the overwhelming reason why the failure of his drama of the Crucifixion had proven a crumpler—the severest blow his professional pride had ever suffered—was that, rightly or wrongly, he clung to the belief that if he had ever written anything of enduring value, it was *The Dark Hours*. Never had he approached a job of writing so reverently and never had he experienced such chagrin as when taxed with a lack of taste for presenting the Saviour in the flesh on the stage of the New Amsterdam Theatre. For Marquis, the veteran of a thousand anomalies, this was easily the most ironic situation in which he had ever found himself. He had not lost his faculty for laughing in the face of adversity but he admitted to intimates that this one "hurt"—that it was a fiasco in which he could find no consolation.

Much has been said by Marquis's friends about his unfailing thoughtfulness. Talk to almost anyone he knew and the chances are you'll hear something illustrative of that characteristic. It was typical that, at a time when he was so frankly unhappy over the failure of *The Dark Hours*, his mind could also accommodate worrisome thoughts about a suggestion he had made to his publishers that they issue a new edition of that play. On November 18, 1932, he wrote the following letter:

Mr. Russell Doubleday,
Doubleday, Doran and Company
Garden City, N.Y.

Dear Russell:

Unfortunately, my play (The Dark Hours) is not a financial success, and I am very sorry that in my enthusiasm I led you to publish a new edition. Perhaps you will find a sale for it just the same, because there have been stirrings of interest in it lately, and the $1.00 price may make it attractive—at any rate, I will be very sorry indeed if the firm loses money on it. . . .

I am sorry you were not able to see the play. It is closing tomorrow night.

Yours cordially and sincerely,

Don Marquis

Two days later, still concerned about the same matter, he sent Mr. Doubleday the following telegram, marking it "Deliver, don't phone," as an added precaution:

BETTER NOT START MANUFACTURE ON NEW EDITION AS PLAY HAS CLOSED UNLESS YOU THINK CHEAP EDITION JUSTIFIED ON OTHER GROUNDS STOP HOPE THIS REACHES YOU IN TIME TO SAVE FIRM NEEDLESS EXPENSE STOP WOULD BE GLAD IF YOU COULD DROP IN AT MY HOUSE SOME TIME WITHIN NEXT WEEK TO DISCUSS A BOOK WHICH I HAVE PRACTICALLY READY STOP SOME AFTERNOON ABOUT FOUR O'CLOCK GOOD TIME STOP AM RECOVERING MY SIGHT RAPIDLY CORDIAL REGARDS

DON MARQUIS

The dollar edition of *The Dark Hours* were never issued. The correspondence reveals that the transaction had reached the contract stage, Marquis having written Russell Doubleday, "As far as the royalty is concerned, the figure you named is O.K."

In his letter to Mr. Doubleday, just quoted, Marquis said of his play, "There have been stirrings of interest in it lately." By an odd coincidence, the day I decided to use that letter I received one from George Middleton calling attention to the program of a dramatic recital given at the Coolidge Auditorium, Library of Congress, Washington, on October 17 and 18, 1960, by Hugh Miller, Senior Director of the Royal Academy of Dramatic Art. Mr. Miller "depicted certain characters" from plays in different categories, including Sophocles' *Antigone*, Shakespeare's *Richard II* and *Hamlet*, Richard Brinsley Sheridan's *The School for Scandal*, George Bernard Shaw's *Man and Superman*, John Masefield's *England Beginning*, Sacha Guitry's

Don't Listen, Ladies!, and Don Marquis's *The Dark Hours*, so again there seem to be "stirrings of interest." The Doubleday files of recent years reveal a number of letters from theater and church groups— (some of them from foreign countries)—expressing interest in producing Marquis's Passion play and seeking information as to the securing of the necessary rights, the cost per performance, etc. If this interest stays alive, some day there may be another Broadway production, an adequate one.

Toward the end of that year—1932—the *Saturday Review of Literature* asked Marquis to write a weekly piece, to run anywhere from twenty-five lines—double measure—to a column, he to select his own topics, much as though he were running a brief weekly column. It didn't mean much revenue but he thought these oddments would be fun to write and he accepted. These pieces have never been collected. In selecting samples, an effort has been made to pick topics that enable us to get a little more information about the man who wrote them:

"I find a very serious error in 'Let There Be Beer,' by Bob Brown, published by Harrison Smith and Robert Haas. He refers to me as 'a big, bubbling beer-bibber' of the early part of the twentieth century and adds: 'Though Don Marquis slept in Brooklyn he had his beer being in Greenwich Village.'

"What we want in scientific research, above everything else, is absolute accuracy. And Mr. Brown's mistake is apt to give a wrong picture of the whole literary history of New York during that period. The fact is, that when I went to Greenwich Village in those days I drank wine; mostly dago red, with now and then some white wine. The wine of the country was what I was hunting for. My serious beer drinking of that period was largely done in a saloon which stood in the triangle where Nassau Street and Park Row came together; a wonderful place which was practically a newspaperman's club, and was known as 'Lipton's.' Ben De Casseres, Kit Morley, and I have solved most of the problems of the universe in that place, sitting in wooden booths under queer stained-glass windows.

"A good place for ale at that time was Farrish's Chop House, which used to stand at the corner of William Street and . . . and what? John? Or Fulton? I forget. I used to go there for the musty ale served in pewter mugs with glass bottoms, for the lush mutton chops, and now and then, following a substantial lunch with a quart or two of ale, a delicate dessert consisting of a Welsh rarebit poured over a wedge of hot mince pie.

"But the best ale served anywhere in the greater city in those days was set before you in the barroom of the old Clarendon Hotel, in Brooklyn, just across the street from the Post Office Building. It was Evans's Ale, and it was drawn from wooden casks, through wooden spigots. A great deal of it was sold there, so it was always running fresh and cool—never very cold, only cool. It was, to my mind, better than Bass's. I never got anything as good in the way of beer or ale anywhere in Manhattan, not even at the far-famed popular resorts; not even the imported German brews. That, of course, must be a matter of individual taste.

"Brooklyn, for the most part, working through the streets in a casual catch-as-catch-can spirit, always seemed to me to have better draught beer and ale than Manhattan. Perhaps there was some lingering sentiment from the old Dutch days on Long Island which worked into the brew.

"Before we leave beer and writers, here is a little note about the late James G. Huneker. I never met him, but about a year before he died he wrote me a letter asking me to have lunch with him. But towards the end of the letter he evidently grew a little melancholy, for he wound it up with a postscript which read: 'Oh, what the hell is the use of having lunch together—we can't get any good beer nowadays!' It was my impulse to get hold of a dozen bottles and hunt him up; but at just that period I couldn't find any decent beer anywhere. So I never saw him; and he was always one of my great admirations.

". . . I think it was Dr. Johnson who said that nobody would write at all, except for money. The Doctor could be an awful old ass at times; and yet, of course, professional writers know what he was driving at when he made that ill-considered remark. I have just been reading the Bible again, and I have run onto some awfully good stuff that probably never made a cent for the authors, although in the last couple of hundred years certain publishing houses have cashed in on it to an enormous extent. It isn't the money that makes people start writing, and stick to it; it is the hope of publication. The exhibition of the ego in public places means more to us writers than money. If I had a hundred million dollars I would go on writing; if I worked a sewing machine all day long in a sweatshop I would go on writing. In its highest phase the writing mania proceeds from the wish to break down, somehow, that awful barrier that exists between soul and soul, and share even bitterness, if there is neither knowledge nor joy to be shared; in its lower manifestations it may be merely exhibitionism, and yet, there, too, is the wistful hope of being understood. Those who write *only* for money, and who would cease to write if they had enough money without it, I don't consider writers at all. . . .

". . . A cult of the unintelligible in poetry has grown up, and actually flourishes and influences critics and public alike. A small army who resolutely defend the unintelligible—even argue that un-intelligibility is, somehow, an esthetic and artistic virtue—has come into existence; and verse that has something definite to say, and says it understandably and trenchantly, is currently unfashionable. . . .

". . . One of these days I am going to publish a book entitled: *Hell and How to Get There.*

"It will be a manual and guide book, with maps and other information for those interested . . . as so many of us are.

"All the hells will be included: Dante's, and Swedenborg's, and all the hells of all denominations and sects of all churches. The field of research is so vast, and the work of compiling materials is so great, that it may take me a dozen years more to get a good start on the book. . . . In fact I may quit the research work any time, and simply invent all the details I haven't looked up. . . .

". . . Poe is the American poet who is best known abroad. Poe's best things are wonderful, but his worst things are still the most popular, not his peculiar magic. There is possibly no worse poem in any language than *The Raven,*—cheap, gaudy, childishly sensational, and gaumed all over with sticky rhetoric. The Raven is like the red plush furniture in the parlor of an old-fashioned country hotel; and even when the hotel was new, it was red plush furniture. And you possibly remember the line from *Annabel Lee:* 'The moon never beams without bringing me dreaks,' etc. A tinkle which sinks to the level of the average popular song writer.

"But I suppose Europe will go on picking the worst stuff of American writers, and considering it the best, and judging of American writing in that way; in fact, some of my own worst things have attracted considerable attention over there, and at my worst I am pretty bad. . . ."

When Marjorie Marquis took over the direction of *The Dark Hours* she needed a secretary; and, on the recommendation of her neighbor Susan Prince, she retained Edith McDonald, who once served a bank official, a casualty of the 1929 Wall Street crash, in a similar capacity. Marquis had had glowing accounts from his wife of Miss McDonald's capabilities and devotion to her work, and retained her as his own secretary.

Miss McDonald said she found Marquis so friendly, likeable, and interesting, and so brimful of amusing quips, that she found it a joy to work for him, although she was frankly appalled by the state of his desk and the room in the house on East 62nd Street that served as his office.

Miss McDonald's description is reminiscent of a piece called "The Author's Desk" that Marquis once wrote with the aid of his famous collaborator, archy the cockroach—a piece that prompted an *Evening Sun* photographer to take a picture of the magnificent litter, practically a bushel of it, atop Don's desk when the confessional appeared in "The Sun Dial":

> i climbed upon my boss his desk
> to type a flaming ballad
> and there i found a heap grotesque
> of socks and songs and salad
>
> some swedenborgian dope on hell
> with modernistic hunches
> remnants of plays that would not jell
> and old forgotten lunches
>
> a plate once flushed with pride and pie
> now chill with pallid verses
> a corkless jug of ink hard by
> sobbed out its life with curses
>
> six sad bedraggled things lay there
> inertly as dead cats
> three sexless rhymes that could not pair
> and three discouraged spats
>
> the feet of song be tender things
> like to the feet of waiters
> and need when winter bites and stings
> sesquipadalian gaiters

i found a treatise on the soul
which bragged it undefeated
and a bill for thirteen tons of coal
by fate left unreceipted

books on the modern girl s advance
wrapped in a cutey sark
with honi soit qui mal y pense
worked for its laundry mark

mid broken glass the spider slinks
while memories stir and glow
of olden happy far off drinks
and bottles long ago

such is the litter at the root
of song and story rising
or noisome pipe or cast off boot
feeding and fertilizing

as lilies burgeon from the dirt
into the golden day
dud epic and lost undershirt
survive time s slow decay

still burrowing far and deep I found
a razor coldly soapy
and at the center of the mound
some most surprising opi

some modest pages chaste and shy
for pocket poke or sporran
written by archy published by
doubleday and doran

Marquis had written another piece along the same line that is
largely unprintable. It was a lengthy catalogue of things he claimed
he found in a desk he hadn't cleaned out in years. Here is a sample
of the tamer part:

A dispossess notice I somehow had gotten,
    A piece of old pot roast that once had been braised,
A sample of urine long since forgotten
    By doctor and patient, and never appraised.

Marquis had made an effort to set up a filing system but had given
up; and now *any* of the folders in his files could be the repository for

anything. He said it was a very simple system. When he wanted to find something badly he dug through all the file boxes, throwing papers on the floor as he pursued his quarry. Then, when he found what he wanted, he stuffed the papers on the floor back into the boxes.

Marquis couldn't be bothered filling out the stub when he wrote a check, consequently he never knew what his bank balance was. He explained that when he needed to know he could always call the bank. This had been his system years before and still was.

Miss McDonald, in a wry understatement, told me that she tried to convince Marquis that there was a better way of keeping track of one's money. He agreed with her ideas in principle but not always in practice.

Miss McDonald had made a rather lengthy series of miscellaneous jottings about her former boss in a notebook, which she graciously gave me with permission to use any or all of these notes. They add up to a kind of "Don Marquis As I Knew Him," and some of this material is appended:

"Mr. M. and his Boston bull Peter were together constantly at home and frequently when he left the house he took the dog with him. Dogs were not permitted at the Players Club but Peter was there often. Mr. M. left him on his leash on the street floor in the care of one of the pages. Once when Mr. M. had been to lunch there he came home greatly amused. He said Peter had lost himself at the club, and after a thorough search, was discovered, of all places, in Mr. Edwin Booth's bedroom, on the bed. [The Players was once the home of its founder, Edwin Booth, and to this day his bedroom is kept as it was when he lived in it.] I never could be sure whether Mr. Marquis was serious about this or whether he was inventing a story for the fun of it. Perhaps you could check at the club about it.

"Through his agent Mr. Marquis was offered a radio program which he was to write and deliver himself. He was enthusiastic about the job and accepted. As you know, he had a warm, clear speaking voice. When the day of the first program came, Mrs. Marquis, her children and I listened to it, and it was very good. His voice came over the air very well. When he came home, however, he seemed unhappy, saying he was afraid he would have to drop it. The sponsor wanted to dictate what he was to say and he would have to submit his copy in advance and agree to any changes the sponsor wanted to make. It was a disappointment to him as he liked the idea of a radio program, but said he couldn't let the sponsor put words in his mouth—that would spoil the fun—so he thought it best to quit the program before he became too involved, which he did.

"Mr. M. was a very charming person with a sparkling personality and gay wit. He had a wonderful vocabulary and could keep a room of people hanging on his words. But there was also a tragic side of his nature—days when he was aloof, quiet and wanted to be left alone. He had never entirely overcome the loss of his little boy and his daughter Barbara. He seldom mentioned them but when he did there were tears in his eyes.

"Once Mr. Marquis was shaken up by a telephone call that came through while he was dictating. A boy was calling his stepson Walter and he was almost speechless when he heard the voice. 'He sounded just like Bobby,' he explained, almost overcome by emotion.

"There is one thing that has always bothered me," Miss McDonald's notebook continues. "So many people who did not know Mr. M. personally seemed to believe that he was like his famous character, the Old Soak. In the four years I worked for Mr. M. I did not see him take a drink, I never smelled alcohol or saw him in the least under the influence.

"Mrs. Marquis was a beautiful woman,—fair skin, deep blue eyes, brown hair, and she wore practicallly no make-up. She was a charming person and a fine actress.

"Mr. Marquis liked to play chess. Often after dinner 'Colonel' (Mrs. Marquis's son) would challenge him and they played many a game together.

"Mr. Marquis fancied himself as an expert cook of certain dishes. One Thursday morning—(they had a colored cook named Pearl whose day off it was)—Mr. M. asked me to go to Bloomingdale's and buy him a bean pot as he was going to make some baked beans. Then he decided I should get two of them. When I came back with the two earthenware bean pots, he was in the kitchen working away getting his materials. All the ingredients had been checked. Later I came to give him a message. He was seated on the kitchen stool, in bathrobe and slippers, with a large spoon in his hand, and opening and shutting the oven door, having a wonderful time. It was practically an all-day job and when the beans were ready to be removed from the oven, Mr. Marquis succeeded in getting one pot out of the oven onto the table, but the second one slipped out of his hands and broke on the kitchen floor. He did have an enjoyable time that day, although I don't imagine many of the beans were eaten. And the next day Pearl (the cook) had quite a job restoring the kitchen to some semblance of order."

Miss McDonald's notes continue:

"Mr. Marquis had had the idea to write a play about Henry VIII for a number of years but did not start 'Master of the Revels,' his play on that subject, until 1933. He had discussed the idea with Arthur Hopkins, who produced 'The Old Soak,' and Mr. Hopkins was very much interested in putting on the play. As each act was finished it was taken to Mr. Hopkins to read and pass on, and it was practically a certainty that the play would be done that winter. Then came the announcement of the movie, 'Henry VIII,' with Charles Laughton in the title role. It was a great success. Mr. Hopkins felt that at that particular time a play on the same subject would not be successful. As the contract for the production of his play was about to be issued, Mr. Marquis was naturally very much disappointed."

Miss McDonald apparently believes that Marquis accepted the failure of *The Dark Hours* with greater resignation than his friends thought. After describing it as "a beautiful play, beautifully done," she writes: "Mr. Marquis was in the hospital when the play opened and was able to see only one performance. In spite of the money he lost—$32,000—I do not believe he regretted it. He had remarked, on announcing to a friend that he planned to back the production, 'I've always wanted to see it.'"

In 1932 and 1933 Marquis continued his free-lancing, as a supplement to his weekly page in *Collier's*, and made enough money to meet his responsibilities. He admitted to intimates that he was not feeling well and was finding it more and more of a struggle to "keep up production," as he put it. He no longer had the stamina to write halfway through the night, as he had done countless times in the past. Susan Prince reports that one night the electric percolator that he counted on to produce the brew that would keep him awake when he worked late had failed him. The next day his secretary found it on the floor where he had thrown it in annoyance. This was not like Marquis, the man who didn't have tantrums. His doctor took it as a sign that Don was overworking and showing the irritability so typical of an unwell man who was pushing himself too hard.

A favorite counteractive of Marquis's, when he found himself in a mood of mounting testiness, was to take his Boston bull for a stroll.

A few minutes "with that little clown," he both remarked and wrote, and his grouch was gone.

On those days when he worked and slept late, Marquis would stroll over to Susan Prince's, with Pete trotting beside him, for an afternoon meal of bacon and eggs. It was not until long afterward that Miss Prince learned that this dish had been forbidden her famous patron. (Marquis never paid any attention to medical instructions unless they were "firm and frightening." When he was told that bacon and eggs were "under suspicion" as possibly harmful to him he declared that he'd wait until the prosecutor brought in more evidence.)

Pete the Pup—(Marquis continued to call his dog a pup long after it had ceased to be one)—was a favorite at Susan Prince's; and as soon as his master sat down at a table, the animal headed for the restaurant's kitchen, where its frolicsomeness had made it popular and where it could always count on a friendly reception—and food. One day Pete received an extra dividend: a few chops that Miss Prince gave Marquis for his pet as he and the dog were leaving her establishment. A few days later Marquis left this note for the restaurant owner, which he claimed Pete had pounded out on the typewriter that morning:

deRe miz pRIncE
tHank yu fOre the ChoPPs   one of them i ETT rite off and Wropt the OtHer 1 upp in a peece of paPER & hiDD it but this Morning I cant find the Same   old Man Markis is goIng arounD with a gilty look toDAY he cant mete my EYE and meBBy he founD it DurING the nite and ett the saME   what do YOU tHinK of a old greY hared man would roBB a pore liTTle puPP   youRs till the dePRESSion is reeLy oveR
                                                        peTe the puPP

For added realism, the flap of the envelope containing this message shows Marquis's name crossed out, making the sender of record: Pete the Pup, 125 East 62nd Street, New York City.

It is interesting to find how many people have kept Marquis remembrances—fugitive notes like the foregoing, chits, bits of verse he scribbled at odd moments, etc. (not to mention those who jotted down remarks of his they didn't want to forget). One is not surprised that so many of the letters, especially the longer ones that are so characteristic, have been preserved; it is the survival of so many of the little odds and ends that one finds unusual.

One of Miss Prince's favorite Marquis souvenirs is a chair. Hearing that she was about to renovate and refurnish her restaurant, he pleaded with her to install chairs that would accommodate a "Bunyanesque bottom" like his. The chair she saved is one of the old narrow ones on which he frequently sat and from which he claimed he "overflowed." When she showed it to me I understood at a glance Don's appeal for something ampler.

Marquis continued to drop in at the Players whenever he could find the time. One day he startled some of the membership by appearing in a mixed suit, the pants of one color and the jacket of another. One of his friends accused him of trying to imitate a Brooks Brothers sportswear ad featuring a sports jacket worn with contrasting trousers. Don, who had never paid much attention to clothes, explained that on Lexington Avenue near where he lived there was a valet service that advertised that for thirty-five cents they would clean and press one of those two-pants suits that were born of the Depression. At the time he owned two suits of clothes, both of the two-pants type. He agreed with his secretary that this was a bargain he couldn't afford to miss. So one of the suits was dispatched to this cleaning and pressing establishment. Both pairs of trousers were lost and all Marquis got back was the jacket—and an apology. The day he was hailed at the Players as a fashion plate he had decided to give his one other jacket a rest and wear the one that survived his bargain in combination with a pair of trousers from his other two-pants suit. Someone cooked up a hoax that resulted in Marquis receiving a letter from one of the local newspapers asking if he would consider writing a weekly men's fashion column. Believing in keeping a prank alive, Marquis said he was interested and submitted some sample "fashion notes," including: "Pants will be worn this year of the Depression by those who can afford them."

17 A Return to Columning?—archy's life of mehitabel—A Triumph for Marjorie Marquis—"My Most Exciting Magazine Assignment"—Tenant John Dewey—On Being Fifty-five—Dark Doings of Byron and Shelley, as Revealed to Fola La Follette and George Middleton—The Bring-Your-Own-Dinner Plan—A Row with the Clergy

Marquis never considered consistency much of a virtue. There were times, he argued, when all it signified was that you were incapable of changing your mind; and, after all, how much of a virtue was inflexibility?

It was a subject he had treated in "The Sun Dial." Every man should have a maxim to support him on either side of a question. For instance, should you find yourself criticized for inconsistency the thing to do is to rush up the Emersonian dictum that consistency is the vice of small minds. When taxed with making all your thinking conform to a pattern, that should serve as your cue to look superior and announce that your philosophy, at that particular moment, is: "Consistency, thou art a jewel." Marquis said he'd lived by this double standard all his life and found it worked fine.

So Marquis's friends were not surprised when they learned, in 1933, that he planned to return to columning. It will be recalled that some years before in explaining why he had asked to be released from his contract as columnist for the New York *Herald Tribune* he had stated in a magazine article: "I got to seeing my column as a grave, twenty-three inches long, into which I buried a part of myself every day—a part that I tore, raw and bleeding, from my brain."

It was not Marquis's intention to return to a newspaper. His plan was to establish a four-page paper called *The Column,* to be written entirely by himself, and to be issued daily at five cents. The page size was to be ten by thirteen. There would be three pages of "column" to begin with, the fourth—the back page—to be devoted, in the early issues, to a message urging the reader to place an order with his newsdealer. (*"The Column* has no circulation department.") The three pages Marquis undertook to fill as a starter would require at least twice as much copy as one of his columns in the *Sun* or the *Herald Tribune.*

With the exception of two sonnets and a sprinkling of one-paragraph squibs, Marquis devoted his first issue to a statement of aims and policies, set forth in his characteristic style. Here are some quotes from that statement, which he wrote, according to Emily E. Connor, president of the Marchbanks Press, in the office of that printing establishment "with his dog on a leash beside him." First came the heading, then the declaration of objectives and policies:

THE COLUMN
New York City, February 15, 1933
Published daily at 114 East 13th Street
by The Marchbanks Press
The purpose of The Column *is to amuse,
to instruct and to astonish*

Several friends have asked me if The Column is going to be Free and Untrammeled.

Of course not. Complete freedom is a human impossibility, and a journalistic impossibility.

Nobody is free. We all have biases, inhibitions, fears, prejudices, whether we call ourselves capitalists or communists, Christians or atheists, and these condition everything we say, whether we are conscious of it or not, and everything we do.

I once wrote a play in which I had the heroine say that she was as free as a sea-gull. When I heard her pull the line in rehearsal I said to myself: "Oh, nerts!" For the sea-gull is looking for fish, and if it doesn't get them it starves to death . . . it will accept garbage on occasion, eat it, and continue to look beautiful afterward . . . but The Column is going to be too elegant for discussions of garbage: that is one of my inhibitions . . . in Life or Letters I must be elegant; it is a defect, but I am that way. I have been known too long as the best-dressed man in New York (with the possible exception of Heywood Broun) to be willing to give up my elegance without a struggle.

Will the editor of The Column always say what he thinks?

Not on your life! He doesn't want the paper barred from the mails, and he trusts that most of his readers are too decent and too well-brought-up even to understand the vocabulary he uses when he is intensely in earnest. He cannot even promise that he will still be thinking what he says a few hours after he has said it, for he has one of those minds which are apt to run around in circles just for the sake of the exercise.

Will the editor of The Column attempt to "debunk" (lovely word!) the world?

I don't know whether I want to start any of that stuff or not; so far as I can see, the rest of the world isn't any more hypocritical than I am. . . .

But what is the object of The Column?

Well, the first thing I want to do . . . is get some circulation. . . . If I can get enough people to buy it every day, my fortune is made. . . . I will be a rich man by the time the revolution gets to going good, and will be shot against a wall for a Capitalist. And the way I feel this morning, with taxes snarling at the door and bills floating through the windows and down the chimney, I can't think of anything I'd rather be shot for. I suppose the main thing is to get shot honorably for some worthy cause; and I've never seen the world at a time when it had more worthy causes . . . than now. I don't see how a person could go wrong, these days, about any cause he joined. Earnestness is so thick everywhere you could cut it into strips and fry it. . . .

But, seriously, what are you going to do with The Column?

Now, how the hell should I know? Possibly lose some money for the giddy optimist who is backing it; maybe get it going and do something rather interesting now and then; possibly make a little money and certainly have a lot of fun. . . .

Only that first issue of *The Column*—a fine example of typography—was printed; but it was not distributed. For a variety of reasons the plan collapsed. In the collection of Don Marquis papers at Columbia University I found the text intended for a subsequent issue. It began: "Mayor Fiorello La Guardia has disappointed me by favoring the notion of banishing hurdy-gurdies from the streets of New York City, on the plea that the hurdy-gurdy operators are beggars. I don't know Mayor La Guardia . . . but his name has always suggested to me something like a flower garden, and the syllables flow with an appealing Latin liquidity which is almost a guarantee of a lyric soul. Judging from the name alone, one would naturally think of him as a friend of song and sunshine; and judging from his record we know him to be an efficient and zealous public servant." Marquis then argued that the hurdy-gurdy man was a vendor, not a beggar—he sold something needed in New York, "a place, in some of its aspects, of bleak and barren efficiency; where people get from one uninteresting place of business to another with the least possible loss of time, their elbows abraded and their ears lacerated by all the grinding circumstance and raucous hullabaloo of traffic."

In the sign-off paragraph of what was apparently intended as his second issue, Marquis said:

"*The Column* is going to be just the cleanest damned thing! It will never print a word which would embarrass a waterfront dock-walloper or bring the blush of shame to the cheek of a Park Avenue super-flapper. Its author has never been one of the scandal-sniffing smut-snitchers of journalism, and doesn't care where you go when you leave the office nights, or who goes with you. He will take as his province everything from hell to breakfast; sometimes there will be an air of dignity about the publication which will make you think you have been left stranded at a highbrow lecture without a drink; and at other times it will be as crazy as a Hollywood movie director's ideas of Art. Politics, the stage, the screen, the revolution which is on the way, will be considered, as well as why don't more American women learn how to make decent coffee?"

In 1933 *archy's life of mehitabel* was published and received with huzzas and benisons. The reception of this, the second of the series, was even more enthusiastic than that accorded the first.

In the New York *Times*, C. G. Poore wrote: "archy has written one of the outstanding biographies of the year. It was not easy for him; as half the world knows, each word that this sapient cockroach types is accomplished only through gruelling labor as he butts his head against the keys of Don Marquis's typewriter. . . . Most of his chronicle of mehitabel, the incorrigible cat, is presented as it used to appear in The Sun and The Tribune when Don Marquis as a columnist added considerably to the gayety of the nation."

Mr. Poore quoted some of his favorite passages, including archy's "austere artistic code":

> i never think when i write
> nobody can do two things at the same time
> and do them both well

This proved to be one of Marquis's best-selling books. The edition I consulted bears this jacket notation, "This book has gone through seventeen editions and keeps on selling merrily from year to year." The only date indicated on the book itself is the year of publication— 1933—so it is hard to say when that particular printing appeared. The publisher's records did not yield this information; but they do reveal that by 1961 the total sales of the archy and mehitabel books—three were published, then an omnibus containing all three—was nearing the 350,000 mark and that the omnibus (with its brilliant introduction by E. B. White) was selling at a rate the publisher found "really astounding."

This paragraph from Marquis's introduction to the second archy and mehitabel book seems worth reprinting:

"I must suppose that these creatures have a kind of vitality. During the eight or ten years in which they appeared in the New York *Evening Sun*, and the several years succeeding in which they contaminated the pages of the New York *Herald Tribune* and the twenty-odd other journals throughout the country to which the material was syndicated, I tried to kill them off at least half a dozen times. But they would not stay dead. Every time I killed them, I got hundreds of letters from their devoted readers demanding an immediate resuscitation. It was easy enough to manage these resurrections; every time I stepped on Archy and slew him, his soul could transmigrate into another cockroach without missing a strophe. I finally began to understand that for some reason or other (or possibly for no reason at all) there was a certain public which wanted them. A few years ago I collected a number of Archy's communications into a book, and this volume surprised me by selling 30,000 copies at a time when 'books were not selling.' The characters appeared for two years in Collier's *Weekly* also, and they must have met with a response in that journal, for the editors insisted that I do them every week. For these reasons, it seems worth while to get out another book."

Marquis, it will be recalled, originally did not think Archy and Mehitabel worthy of book publication. Even when there was ample reason to believe that the reading public wanted these books, Marquis never seemed fully to understand the enthusiasm of the more ecstatic admirers of his cockroach-and-cat duo. Had he been alive to read it, he probably would have been a little puzzled (also pleased) by what Bernard De Voto said in *Harper's Magazine* in 1950 about the then just-published archy and mehitabel omnibus, with an introduction by

E. B. White, a book to which I have had occasion to refer three or four times. For De Voto was a prototype of the intellectuals who had failed to "certify" Marquis during his lifetime. For instance, Max East-man in "The Enjoyment of Laughter," which was accepted by typical spokesmen for the intelligentsia as a scholarly work, endorsed Amer-ican humorists whose work was appearing contemporaneously with Marquis's but made no mention of the latter. Here are some excerpts from what Mr. De Voto wrote:

"I am not going to risk competing with Mr. White. I am glad that . . . he muses about a metropolitan press that does not manage to climb this high any more. There has never been anything like Archy or Mehitabel and there never will be. Don Marquis got all his rich and strange talent into a cockroach who had the literary urge . . . and a cat . . . who was always a lady in spite of hell. Only fantasy was wide or versatile enough to contain him; his mind kept escaping through cracks in the sane, commonplace world out into dimensions that were loops and whorls and mazes of the unpredictable."

In an entertaining passage that covers over a column De Voto shows Archy's world "erupting with ribald, belly-shaking laughter," then goes on to say:

"You have to be as alert with this stuff as Archy in the roach-paste, for at any moment a thousand volts may hit you."

Many reviewers picked up E. B. White's now familiar line that Don Marquis "was never quite certified by intellectuals and serious critics of belles-lettres." It drew from De Voto a philosophic commentary on what constitutes Beautiful Letters, in which he said of Marquis's work:

"Simply, it was wonderful to read in those 'pleasantly preposterous' days and reads better now. I have difficulty in remembering the names and books of a good many writers of that time who got the right certificates with red wax seal and dangling ribbons, and my inability is pretty widespread. But no one who ever read Don Marquis has forgotten him. . . . The publisher's word that . . . the sale of *archy and mehitabel* remains 'really astounding' . . . is an omen of good fortune for the young who are coming up. Nobody is going to write that way for them.

"Let us avoid offense by calling it literature, which is a uniform substance that reacts dependably to standard tests, whereas Don Mar-quis is always slipping through your fingers. . . . There is a small bulk of writing . . . that people insist on reading for its own sake, regardless.

They have always held it more precious than rubies and if it isn't literature, then literature be damned. . . .

"*Eheu fugaces!* When last week I bought the book Mr. White has written a preface for, the clerk spoke of the author as Don Markee. The next evening I had dinner with a young professor of literature at Harvard. He carries easily the heavy scholarship of his trade and he is mellowed in light learning besides, but when I began to talk about Don Marquis he did some fast footwork and got off on Finley Peter Dunne. Clearly he had grown up in a barren time, and the next night an even younger instructor, finding me at my devotions, asked, 'Who in hell is this Marquis character anyway?' A tale so sad, so sad! . . .

"I wonder what books they read at Harvard now."

Marjorie Marquis's interest in the theater had not diminished but early in 1933 she heeded the advice of friends and decided to devote herself to acting. She had fared badly, beginning in Indianapolis, in her attempts to direct, produce, manage. There were about a half-dozen such ventures in all, including The Stagers, the Red Barn Theatre, and *The Dark Hours*. In these different enterprises she had not displayed the requisite business ability, acumen in the selection of plays, or—as in the case of her husband's Biblical drama—the capacity for bold, imaginative direction or the kind of leadership that inspires a cast. She *had* demonstrated skill as an actress, and if she could land a part that suited her she would demonstrate it again. Howard Lindsay was not being unkind when he described her as mid-Victorian; he was merely confirming what some of her friends knew: that she could not throw herself wholeheartedly into a love scene, her inhibitions acting as a brake.

The Theatre Guild was emerging in those days as the group more concerned with artistry in the theater—fine plays and fine productions—than any other producing unit. Marjorie admired the standards they had set for themselves and hoped some day to qualify for a major role in one of their productions. She had tried out for "fat parts" in two or three Guild presentations and had apparently made a good impression. The Guild encouraged her to keep trying, believing that eventually they would find the right thing for her. They meant it when they asked her to keep in touch with them, and she did.

Having heard that the Guild planned to produce a new play by Eugene O'Neill—*Ah, Wilderness!*—Marjorie acquainted herself with the casting needs and decided to make a bid for the important role of Essie Miller. She had two objectives in mind—to get back into the theater and to bolster the sagging financial position of her family.

Marjorie was selected for the Essie Miller part but she didn't stop there. She also found a place in the production for her son Walter and an understudy's role for her daughter Ruth. It was a good example of what Mrs. Marquis, a woman not lacking in resolution, could accomplish when sufficiently aroused.

Ah, Wilderness! was given an enthusiastic reception in Pittsburgh where it had its tryout. Marquis, in a letter to George Middleton, expressed doubt as to whether the Pittsburgh success could be repeated in New York, making this comment: "A little New England domestic comedy with a happy ending. . . . No incest in it at all, and no sex perversion. Well, I ask you!"

The opening night of *Ah, Wilderness!* in New York was a triumph for Eugene O'Neill, the Theatre Guild, George M. Cohan, Marjorie Marquis, and the supporting cast. The play, the players, and the producers were unanimously acclaimed by the critics.

George M. Cohan and Marjorie Marquis, as the parents of the rebellious young Richard, got the kind of reviews known in the trade as raves. In the New York *Herald Tribune* Percy Hammond wrote in part (October 3, 1933):

"In 'Ah, Wilderness!' a sentimental bantling (Elisha Cook, Jr.) is to be heard and seen wrestling pluckily with such foes as romance, poetry, sex and liquor. Observing the contest are his perplexed parents, played with conclusive art by Marjorie Marquis and George M. Cohan. . . . I thought last night that George M. Cohan was almost as perfect in his impersonation as was Mrs. Marquis, who played his wife and the mother of the wandering boy. . . . Mrs. Marquis is a fine player and her performance and that of Mr. Cohan will probably restore your waning faith in acting as an art."

The New York *Times* said: "Marjorie Marquis is excellent as a troubled, normal mother." Marjorie's son Walter—Marquis's chess companion who was nicknamed "the Colonel," also got good notices. Mr. Hammond in the *Herald Tribune*, for instance, spoke of "a shrewd little youngster's bit by Walter Vonnegut, Jr."

All in all, it was a great night for the Marquises, with Don leading his own little claque in vociferous applause. After seeing the play—(his earlier estimate of it had been based on hearsay)—Marquis pronounced it first-rate.

In "The Diary of Our Own Samuel Pepys" in the *Herald Tribune*, Franklin P. Adams wrote: "In the evening with Rose Feld to see E. O'Neill's 'Ah, Wilderness!', which I liked and enjoyed better than any O'Neill play ever I saw, and as well as any other play ever I saw, it being full of tenderness and humour and some of the heart-break-ingest scenes that ever I saw, and more than that, all parts acted so perfectly that even a less poignant play might have seemed good. I have never seen Mr. Cohan so good, and nobody else has either. And Marjorie Marquis and Elisha Cook and Gene Lockhart and all the others so excellent in their acting I could not imagine how any of them could have been better. So home and to bed, feeling that the play I had seen was worthy fifty Interludes and a dozen Electras, forasmuch as the story of the boy, with unimportant variations, is the story of almost every boy. . . ."

What Marquis described as his "most exciting magazine assignment" came when Sumner Blossom, editor of the *American Magazine*, asked him to write an article ("Do You Believe in a Future Life?") based on the following letter from a reader, James R. Young of Chicago:

"Can you print an article which will discuss this future-life business? For years I have been thinking about it and as yet have never seen a single shred of evidence that looks good to me. I have been told that not an atom of matter is ever lost. I have been told that if I would have faith in a life after the grave all I need to do is to look at the wonders of nature. But, some way or other, all the discussions seem to wind up in a single word—Faith.

"Now, I have lived the best life I know how to live. I have every desire in the world to believe that life goes on after death. I am not an obstinate unbeliever, but willing to believe, anxious and hopeful that I may learn. But always my thoughts come back to the speculation that, perhaps, after all, I am just a dynamo which, when the current is turned off, will be a dead and lifeless thing. There have been times, when I go out and look at the stars or when I read of scientists who discuss the infinity of space in terms of light-years, that I am sure of speedy and complete obliteration, so impressed am I with my own unimportance.

"Is there not among your writers one who can advance logical, convincing reasons to me and to thousands of others like me?"

For years Marquis had been preoccupied with the possibility of life after death and related mystical speculations. This preoccupation is reflected—sometimes casually, sometimes directly—in many a poem and prose piece he wrote. His egobiography is loaded with it, there is a generous sprinkling of it in his serious poetry—(British critics, even those who were otherwise friendly, accused him of overdoing it in their reviews of the London-published edition of *The Awakening and Other Poems*)—and there are even dashes of it, collaterally insinuated, in some of his humorous writings.

In *Dreams and Dust* Marquis had written:

> It shifts and shifts from form to form,
>   It drifts and darkles, gleams and glows;
> It is the passion of the storm,
>   The poignance of the rose;
> Through changing shapes, through devious ways,
>   By noon or night, through cloud or flame,
> My heart has followed all my days
>   Something I cannot name.

Marquis pursued that "something" throughout his life, at times defining his quarry as "love," "beauty," "God." More often than not, it developed that that "something" he sought was the answer—or answers—to questions he himself propounded, such as:

> Are we who breathe more quick than they
>   Whose bones are dust within the tomb?
>
> What lords of life and light hold sway
>   In the myriad worlds of the Milky Way?
>
> When morning skims with crimson wings
>   Across the meres of Mercury,
> What dreaming Memnon wakes and sings
>   Of miracles on Mercury?
> What Christs, what avatars,
> Claim Mars?
>
> Hath not man at his noblest
> An air of something more than man?—
> A hint of grace immortal,
> Born of his greatly daring to assist the gods
> In conquering these shaggy wastes,
> These desert worlds,
> And planting life and order in these stars?

When John Dewey was a tenant of Marquis's, occupying the second floor at 125 East 62nd Street, Don had long chats with the famous philosopher and tried more than once to get Dewey's views on the possibility of life after death. He told Clive Weed that he wound up learning a lot about the utilitarian and pragmatic schools of thought but that he couldn't draw out "that wonderful old gentleman" on any of the Great Mysteries. He called Dewey "the prince of the practical,—too sensible to waste his time on a spiritual wild goose chase." On reflection he thought that maybe if he could get George Santayana as a tenant he would fare better. Santayana rejected organized religion, while retaining "a sense of religion," which approximated Marquis's own position. Marquis accepted Santayana's belief that "religion is literally false but poetically true," though he did not accept his treatment of the life of Christ as a myth, "to be placed not with the heroes of history, but with those of legend, not with Alexander but with Achilles." In *The Dark Hours* Marquis had treated the life of Christ as history. But even so he felt sure that Santayana "was his man." For one thing, he was a poet and a good one, and he thought philosophers should be poets, and vice versa. Another thing that appealed to him was that Santayana was sometimes contradictory, which made him feel better about having that same characteristic. Yes, he thought Santayana would make a fine tenant. He was captivated by the Spanish-born philosopher's belief that one must have "faith in the unknowable" and would like to have a long talk with him about that.

Marquis's article in the *American Magazine* in reply to Mr. Young's letter is too long to reprint in full but some quotations are indicated, since Don had speculated on this question—survival after death—all his life. Here are his opening paragraphs:

"Mr. Young comes at once to the milk in this cosmic cocoanut when he says that discussions of this future-life business 'seem to wind up in a single word—Faith.'

"In short, if you believe in it, you believe in it; and your premise is your conclusion.

"This tallies with my own observation, that logic does not have much to do with attaining such a belief. The conviction floats into the consciousness out of the everywhere; afterwards logic is summoned to the support of the established conviction. . . .

"Our correspondent says he has lived as good a life as he knows how to live, and yet faith in a future life has not come to him.

"Personally, I don't believe that conduct or character has any direct connection with faith in a future life. Some of the most objectionable persons I have known have professed an unshakable faith in a future life. . . . And some of the loveliest persons in the world have not only doubted the existence of a future life, but have intimated that they did not find the prospect particularly desirable."

Marquis expressed the belief that too many people thought of survival after death in some such terms as this: "Will I meet Susie Jones in the hereafter; and will she be wearing the same checked gingham dress she wore the morning, forty years ago, when I carried her books to school, and gave her, along with my undying devotion, two sticks of chewing gum, afterwards cutting our initials, surrounded by the fat outline of a heart, in the bark of a slippery-ellum tree; and will I recognize Susie and will she recognize me?"

"Or," he adds, "something of that sort. It may be just like that, for all I know. But I don't feel strong enough, this morning, to commit myself to a whole scuttleful of such sentimental details and put up a battle for them. I am especially chary of committing myself to the theory that Susie will go along just like that forever, through all eternity, with the same china-blue eyes and blond curls. . . .

"Whether it disturbs us to acknowledge it or not, we shall have to recognize that it is the spiritual element in man—the element which thinks and acts, independently of the salts and gases which constitute his physical body—which is the seat and center of life. . . . Call it what you like—mind, or spirit, or soul—it has command of the body. . . . It commands man's destiny and justifies his existence. . . .

"I believe the mind of man will continue to exist as an entity, as an individual, after the death of the physical body; but as to whether it will exist 'forever', without undergoing further changes, I have no clear convictions. I doubt it very much. Forever is a long time. It is impossible for me to grasp the idea of eternity. And since the essential man has progressed through so many changes, I do not see why the final abandonment of his physical body—the abandonment of the last of his several successive physical bodies—might not be merely the prelude to many continuing changes; but I do not see how anyone could have the remotest guess as to the period of duration of such changes, if they do come.

"Nor do I see how anyone could be sure that the spirit which is man will carry the memory of one state and circumstance of existence into the next one—nor yet how anyone could be sure that he would *not!*"

Despite a few successive years of jolts and disappointments, Marquis in 1933, at the age of fifty-five, seems to have experienced a new surge of hope. The renascent Marquis is reflected in an article he wrote that year for *Harper's Magazine,* called "On Being Fifty-five," in which he said:

"I don't know how to account for it, or explain it, but I have suddenly got to feeling young again. From somewhere or other, and I don't care where or how, there has curiously drifted into my consciousness the conviction that I am getting a second start in life, a kind of second wind, that I am beginning all over again and that—damn it all!—fifty-five *isn't* so very old.

"I know very well the reasonable and logical arguments against this feeling. I know as well as you do that when a man is fifty-five he might as well be sixty . . . and that when a man is sixty he is practically seventy-five . . . and that when he is seventy-five he has only a moment to go until he is ninety . . . and that when he is ninety he is a hundred . . . and when he is a hundred he has been dead at least fifteen years. But somehow all that doesn't impress me.

"I am experiencing a kick of hope, an illusion of youth and a flush of self-confidence that is based upon nothing I could justify by any rational process. I even believe I may yet write something worth while. Oh, yes, I know—and thank you for the pretty speech and the nice thought behind it—but I know better than you do what I intended to write when I was thirty, and that I haven't written it. . . .

"Fifty-five is not, after all, the jumping-off place—if I remember to Wear My Rubbers, and don't overestimate my capacity for distilled and fermented beverages of a high alcoholic content. . . .

"As I said, at fifty-five I have suddenly had showered upon me the goofy conviction that I'm a young fellow starting out in life again. It's all boloney, of course. But I suppose the explanation of this kick of uplift I am experiencing lies in the fact that nothing much can happen to me that I haven't already been through. I have stuck around long enough to have acquired an immunity to violences; to the violences of sudden good luck and the violences of sudden bad luck. I've been vaccinated. . . .

"There was a period during which the phrase, 'Promising young

man,' used to get my goat. . . . But now it pleases me. I'm grateful
for it. After all, it is something to be a Promising Young Man for
thirty years. And, at fifty-five to feel, suddenly, that it is true once
more . . . that one is still (or again) a Promising Young Man!

"In fact, now that I think of it, *there* is an ambition for me to cultivate: To be a Promising Young Man at seventy-five."

In an extravagant moment Marquis told a newspaper interviewer
that he'd spent 1933 and 1934 writing letters. In the past, similar
exercises in letter-writing preceded bursts of creativity and those
who knew him best took it as a good omen when he "went on a correspondence jag."

In addition to writing letters Marquis published three books during those years—*Master of the Revels*, a play about Henry VIII;
Chapters for the Orthodox, a collection of satiric stories, some of
them interrelated, and *archy's life of mehitabel*, which was mentioned earlier. The assembling of an archy and mehitabel book always entailed considerable work, as Marquis had never trained himself
to save clippings and consequently these collections meant ransacking
the files of the *Evening Sun*, the *Tribune*, and the *Herald Tribune*.

He also wrote a number of articles and short stories for the magazines—more in 1934 than in 1933. He appears to have had more
physical stamina in '34 than the preceding year and to have produced more as a consequence.

The Marquis health picture is a confusing one. Such records as are
available reveal that physically he had been pretty much of an in-
and-outer for several years. The correspondence frequently adds to
the confusion. Whereas in a letter to friend "A" he might unburden
himself and announce that he was "about to fall apart like Oliver
Wendell Holmes's One-Horse Shay," in a letter to friend "B," written
at approximately the same time, he would either skip the question of
health or vaguely intimate that he was feeling well. In his strictly
reportorial moments he appraised his health as "erratic," once adding, "but I wonder how often I can afford to admit it or talk about
it. One could easily become a bore on the subject." Loved by many,
he was deluged with inquiries whenever anything got into the papers
about his being "laid up for repairs," as he put it. He was then faced
by the problem of confirming or playing down the reports; and in
this respect he seems to have had no consistent policy.

At a time (1929) when Marquis was getting nowhere in his efforts
to get a motion-picture company to give him less routine assign-

ments, he wrote his friend Charles J. Bayne, with whom he became acquainted in his Atlanta days, one of the most depressing letters he had ever composed. He was in ragged health at the time, his morale was worse, and the letter sounded as if he would not live out the year. A former associate of Marquis's, reading that letter, remarked, "He sounds like a dying man yet a little good news probably would have transformed him to the old exuberant Don."

George and Fola La Follette Middleton corresponded with Marquis in those days. This letter is one of their favorites:

"Dear Georgie and Fola: . . . Faust is a little less than half done. I am to see Hopkins tomorrow about Henry.

"Hopkins is now figuring on —— for Henry. I think —— has turned too soft and pudgy for it the last couple of years. Henry was fat, but he had a lot under his fat. I don't care about anything else except an actor who can act it; I rather doubt ——'s ability to put it across. Or, more properly, to see what there is to put across; he is a nice chap, but opinionated as hell about the theatre, and, to my notion, usually wrong. . . .

"My new play, which I am now working on, is about Bryon and Shelley in Pisa in 1821, and will have incest in it, so you see I am in the van of thought. The heroine, Clare Claremont, was the half-sister of Shelley's wife; the full sister of Shelley's Soul and the mother of Byron's bastard. Shelley laid them in rows, and called them the Sisters of his Soul. Byron planted little deeds of kindness between the rows, like beans between the rows of corn, and called them mistresses; on two or three occasions they were the same girls. Byron, however, remained Satan, and was very proud of being Satan; Shelley remained an Angel, and was very proud of being an ANGEL. It was really a case of non Angeli, sed Angli; the English being very prone to Shelley's kind of spiritual hypocrisy—be sure you're moral, then go ahead.

"I have a great scene in which somebody has told Byron that he is not a devil; and this hurts Byron so that he cries and cries; his mistress has to comfort him and pet him up, and her husband and her father have to help her; finally Byron's self-respect is restored. The setting is in Byron's palace at Pisa. On the ground floor are six peacocks, two bears, four monkeys; Leigh Hunt and his wife and the Hunts' six children. Two or three Shelley children, and Clare's bastard, wander in and out chased by bears and so forth. I think I shall show Byron throwing his bastards to the beasts, and Shelley the angel rescuing them. Bryon's official mistress at the moment, the Countess Broccoli, or something, has a husband who is wanted by the cops; Count Gamba, her father, is also wanted by the cops; everybody is wanted by the cops. The author will be wanted by the cops. What the hell, what can you do about it?

"Me, I am also wanted by women. On my 55th birthday a nineteen-year-old girl tried to make me. I don't know whether she really wanted me, or it was habit with her, or she sort of pitied me. Anyhow, it flattered me and I have been bragging about it ever since. I didn't fall, but that was principally so I could still have something to brag about, which I probably wouldn't have had if I had gone through with it. Well, what the hell, you can't have everything. When you can't have anything else you can have virtue, I guess. Not that I have crossed the Creek of Dead Desire, but laying a girl of nineteen would be a hell of a lot of trouble when she found you couldn't do it again in thirty minutes; you can talk them into it, but you can't talk them out of it.

"Well, I haven't got any money at all now; but my wife is working, my stepson is working, and my stepdaughter will have an understudy job next week; so why the hell work? I suppose some damned job will come along, now that everything is fixed comfortably, and I will feel I ought to take it, and quit writing plays which will never be produced. Well, what the hell; you can't have everything, nor even much of anything; all you can have is virtue. I never liked virtue, but if I've got to have it, I can take it. It's like spinach; it's good for you. The nearest I ever got to incest was a second cousin, and we were both so young we fumbled the job; really quite, quite young; and a second cousin isn't really incest anyhow. I have failed in living, and now I will have to write about it. What the hell, you can't have everything. Well, you can have virtue anyhow, and in this connection I wish to tell you what Christian Science has done for me. I had a heart attack the other night, and I got out Mrs. Eddy's little book —I rewrite it for the old dame as I go along with it, because she didn't know how to write—and it knocked the heart attack, and then I took up Ely Culbertson's bridge book, and read that a while, and then I went back to Mrs. Eddy, and then back to Culbertson, and so on; and about six in the morning I went to sleep and overheard myself saying—you know you catch yourself saying things as you drop off—that there was no life, truth, intelligence or reality in an opening one-bid unless the declarer had at least two and a half defensive honor tricks; that God is all-in-all, and when your partner takes you into two no trumps the bastard is probably trying to show you a bust hand; and I haven't had a bad attack with my heart since then. I can't understand all of Mrs. Eddy nor all of Ely Culbertson either, but they are a great comfort to have around. You got to have faith where you can't understand things. Well, you can't have everything, so what the hell. We're having a lot of fun, aren't we? . . .

"Byron, in my play, denies incest until it occurs to him that incest is splendidly, satanically wicked; and then he lets Shelley think he is guilty of it. Shelley is all for it on the very highest grounds; he thinks it is great, and it gives him an idea for a swell poem. Well, Byron and Shelley both did what they wanted to, often the same things, and Byron remained a devil and Shelley an angel. Each was that to himself and his friends, and it has imposed on their biographers to this day. Byron was a lord but not a gentleman. Shelley did a dozen caddish things, but remained really a gentleman. What the hell, you can't have everything. Two women, Harriet Shelley and Fanny Imlay, killed themselves over Shelley, and he really rather regretted it, even when Mary Shelley told him that things had worked out on the Highest Spiritual Plane. . . .

"But Byron is terribly jealous; no woman ever killed herself on account of him; he feels that he has missed something that would make him a real devil. But what the hell, you can't have everything. Poor Byron didn't have the consolation that Shelley and I have; that you can always fall back on virtue. It is the only thing you can get for nothing, so it's a wonder that more people don't go in for it. . . . But when people have it, it makes them uncomfortable, and they take a lot of trouble to get rid of it. I found some old Civil War veterans in the soldiers' home at Santa Monica, from 93 to 98 years old, who went off every time they got their pensions and spent it on tarts. But I am afraid it was just the persistence of lifelong habit, and did not proceed from any reasoned principle of life. The admirable thing about the human race is the persistence of the illusion of romance even to the point where one ghostly galosh is being splashed with water over the gunnels of Charon's skiff. . . .

"There's a lot to be said for wives . . . and I've always said it, especially where they could hear me. . . . I always say the mean things I have to say behind people's backs; because if you said them to their faces it would hurt their feelings and make trouble. Which is what I mean when I say I am virtuous. I went to a Baptist Sunday

School as a small boy, and it has stuck, and I know what virtue is
to this day. It is red and purple and golden Sunday School cards,
with Jacob sacrificing Isaac on a brush pile to God. . . .

"What you want to do is cheer up. The saloons are going to open
up again in a few months and the country will drink its way back
into prosperity, and then we will have another slump, and then they
will close the saloons again, being firmly convinced that there is
some basic network which takes in morality, economics and your
habits about liquor, and it is this faculty for adjusting everything
correctly which makes democracy what it is. What the hell, you can't
have everything; a good many people are getting tired of both
churches and political parties because they say you *can*. . . .

"I've never thought Culbertson was really conscious of all the evil
he brought into the world along with the approach forcing system.
The world was comparatively virtuous up to about 1927, and then
everyone took up the approach forcing system, and now show me a
virgin over fifteen. Just show her to me—I don't mean that I'm going
to do anything. Marjorie says I am senile when I talk this way;
just a dirty-minded old man. Hell, I've always been dirty-minded,
and always will be; you can't have everything. In fact, you can't have
much of anything. I don't give a damn how dirty-minded I am if
down underneath everything else I am really virtuous. . . . I've
seen the two things going together all my life. People resent being
forced to choose between dirty-mindedness and virtue; and if they
are absolutely compelled to choose they are naturally going to give
up virtue, insofar as they are able to give it up. *I* am handicapped in
giving it up by physical disabilities; I mean my heart. I don't want
to die right in the act of giving it up. Well, you can't have everything; I got to stick to virtue and I will tell you the truth, I DON'T
like being made to stick to it. It's all right as a whim if the choice is
open to you. Well, you can always take a risk with your heart now
and then, and there is quite an additional thrill to that, too. Well,
what the hell; if you were found dead in bed in your own home,
that is okay, that is respectable, and there's a little life insurance
money, and that's that, and everyone is happy. You got to be respectable. But suppose you were in bed with a tart and your boyish
enthusiasm was too much for your heart, then the poor tart has a dead
body on her hands. . . . What's she going to do with it? Or say about
it? It makes no end of trouble, cuts into her business hours, and
may end by ruining her position in the community; and she's prob-

ably got a lot of trouble anyhow. I never knew a tart that wasn't in trouble. Women have a hell of a time anyhow. If a woman is a nice old-fashioned, genuinely virtuous woman, everybody uses her as a doormat; if she turns tart everybody kicks the hell out of her one way or another. What's a woman going to do?

"I think it would be a nice start for a play—a woman with a dead body in the bed, and what's she going to do with it? Well, there's a preacher in this play, her spiritual adviser, and he loves her, but he is noble and he has never said a goddam lousy word about how he loves her, the son of a bitch, because he is fine and noble. She sends for him and his name is Gerald. And he sacrifices his reputation to save hers, the lousy bastard, because he is so noble. He gets into bed with the corpse, and the cops come and say there is a lot of that homosexual stuff going on among the Anglican clergy these days, and they never know he is a pure man, but he is happy because he has given all for love—and the woman says she loves him now, and would marry him, too, just to prove it, but he's got such a terrible reputation now that she can't afford to marry him. And Gerald says yes, he understands; he will bear his cross for her sake; you got to be noble, says Gerald. . . . Anyhow, he is only a curate . . . and she marries the vicar. And she tells the vicar, and the vicar says that louse Gerald is really homosexual, the bastard, and his nobility gives me a pain in the neck; why, he tried to make me again and again. But I have a morality as firm and sound as an oak. Didn't he know, says the poor woman, that only God can make a tree?

"Well, the play goes along like that for quite a while, and there is a lot of morality and honesty and nobility in it to satisfy the better element, and a good deal of sexual perversion in it to satisfy the plain unsophisticated toiling masses, and after a while the police stop it—come right onto the stage and stop it, like that. But there is an epilogue . . . and everybody goes home happy and uplifted, and they have laughed through their tears, and what I always say is that if you can't write plays that will make people better then the thing to do is write plays that they will pay money to see. What, I got a dirty mind and you can't wash it, for this stuff the laundries use nowadays has got some acid in it that eats holes in everything.

"Well, my wife is in Pittsburgh and I am going down to the club and play bridge, and I think she's got the best of it. She doesn't give me any excuse to run around with other women. That's the trouble with being married to a woman that is really virtuous; if she got up a flirtation with somebody else I would have an excuse for acting just as dirty as I feel; but I got to be virtuous. What the hell, you can't have everything. I'm in love with her, too, and don't want to hurt her feelings; but you could be in love with somebody and be dirty at the same time with somebody else, and if you were not caught it would not hurt her feelings. But I would get caught because I never have any luck.

"Well, between one thing and another, between being virtuous and at the same time having a dirty mind, I live a hell of a life; and the only thing that keeps me going is that I see how funny it is. . . . But that doesn't get you anywhere; though of course there's this: Where would you want to get to? The only place to get to is to get to be twenty-three years old and write lyric poetry and be in love with a girl, and want to lay her, and be too chivalrous to do it; and then she insists on it, and you then have the double satisfaction of being virtuous and getting what you want at the same time, for of course it is all the girl's fault and your conscience is clear and when you get tired of her you get rid of her because she is not moral; yours was a pure love and she seduced you, the bitch; and then there is another girl and you are pure and romantic about her too, and she does the same thing to you, and you get melancholy about life and enjoy yourself that way, and everything is always somebody's else or somebody else's fault, and you forgive them for it, and that makes you a Christian, and any lousy bastard who doesn't want to be a Christian can go to hell.

"That, in a nutshell, is what I think of Life. When I went to the Baptist Sunday School there was an old murderer by the name of Hank Williams who was prominent in the church; he had kicked his wife to death when she was pregnant, and my father, who was a doctor, was called in when Mrs. Williams was dying. He turned Hank in and Hank got imprisonment for life. But he turned Christian in prison and the Jesus crowd rallied round and his term was commuted to twelve years. Well, he came back to town, and the church crowd had to take his new-found Jesus stuff seriously, because he had repented and been saved; the old humorist had it on them and enjoyed being a murderer and being saved at the same time; their creed enjoined them to take him in; and he used to lead prayer meetings, etc., and mercy feasts; and that was my first impression of the Christian religion and I never have been comfortable about it since. I made up my mind then that if Jesus felt right about

old Hank I never could feel right about Jesus. I learned later that
the Baptist Church didn't know anything about Jesus; but it was a
long time before that occurred to me. Well, some of the dirtiest-
minded people I ever knew were Christians; I've got precedent
everywhere for being virtuous and dirty-minded at the same time.

"Well, the next letter I write I will try and tell you something
about myself. I know you want to know what I am thinking about
these days, and will try to overcome my native reticence. But what
the hell, you can't have everything. Love to both of you, Don"

Occasionally, as if to prove that he really wasn't "dirty-minded,"
Marquis slipped into an envelope containing one of his earthier
letters a mitigating splash of loveliness, as in the case of the following
dedicated to Fola La Follette:

> Give up the dream that love may trick the fates,
> To live again somewhere beyond the gleam
> Of dying suns, or shatter the strong gates
> Some god has builded high: call back the dream.
> Flame were not flame unless it met the dark,
> And half life's shaking ecstasy, and love's,
> Dwells in the transcience of the moving spark
> Which pricks oblivion's vastness as it moves;
> Let us not babble of eternity,
> Who stand upon this little ledge of time:
> A few more heartbeats and our hearts shall lie
> Dead to all beat of rapture, heat or rhyme—
>   Send we no vision down the vague abyss,
>   But rape these flashing moments of their bliss!

In a speech at the University of Michigan, Christopher Morley said:

"He [Marquis] was always infatuated with theology, and profoundly reverent in spirit, but united with this so potent a vein of
mother-of-pearl blasphemy and—shall we say—verbal frowardness,
that his private correspondence will remain mostly unquoted." The
quarter of a century that has elapsed since Morley made that statement has witnessed a liberalization that makes it possible to publish
today (with some editing) much that could not be published then.

Most of the holders of the so-called "unprintable" letters—the original recipients, descendants, or other members of their families—
believe they should not be published. I believe that a number of these
letters are publishable, and parts of others, but one is compelled to

respect the decision of the owners of this correspondence, whose position can be summed up in an impromptu statement by an old friend of the Marquis family which went approximately as follows: "I agree that in currently published literature there is much that goes beyond these letters—books that make Marquis's inelegances and seeming heresies sound mild by comparison. Nevertheless this correspondence might give the general public the wrong impression. It was as natural for Don to write ribald, irreverent-sounding stuff as it was for him to breathe and I regard his as a healthy kind of Rabelaisianism; but I don't want the responsibility for others picking up and using against him his own wry self-derogation—for instance, his oft-repeated and inaccurate designation of himself as 'dirty-minded.' Sorry I can't help you out. If I change my mind I'll let you know."

Dissenters from this point of view are George and Fola La Follette Middleton who believe that the reader who is not familiarized with the Marquisian indelicacies is being given a censored picture; that without a peek at this side of the man it is not possible to understand him fully. And, with this in mind, they have given me their permission to use anything in their letters from Marquis that the publishers do not find objectionable.

Middleton, hearing that one of the motion-picture companies planned to produce Kipling's *Kim*, recommended Marquis for the screenplay assignment and asked if he would be willing to go to India for two thousand dollars a week. Marquis replied: "I would go to Indiana for $2,000 a week; but it would cost them $4,000 a week if I went to India. I would succumb there. Why don't they get Kipling to do it? I had a good job all fixed up for Kipling a couple of years ago, writing a life of St. Paul for the movies. Wrote him through Russell Doubleday. The son-of-a-bitch was too proud to write me direct about it; he wrote through his secretary. He could have got $100,000 for nothing, and he needs the money. . . .

"I don't like the world; it is too worldly. I think I am getting ready to go to heaven in a fiery chariot. . . . Mentally, this morning, I have The Itch. Probably riding in a fiery chariot would be like having the itch. But St. Francis of Assisi, if I got to heaven with the itch, would drop everything else and scratch me. . . . I have tried very hard to be a Christian, and can't make the grade. . . . There is something about it I don't like. I started a sonnet, like this, about it:

> This Jesus had no Father but a Ghost,
> No Mother but a Virgin, had no Wife . . .

Couldn't get any further. . . . Then it occurred to me: Why get any further? That says it all. It takes away from his humanity. Or would, if it were true. It isn't true. That's what's the matter with official Christianity,—so much of the foundation isn't true. You don't know how you know it, but you just DO know it. I think I'll go on with the sonnet, and end it up by Jesus saying:

> 'Who ever told you that that stuff was true?' "

In a sense that is merely an adaptation of Santayana's belief that religion is literally false but poetically true.

In another letter to the Middletons Marquis wrote a ballade from which the following is taken:

> The world is too much with us, soon and late,
> Too full, too full, of lousy sons-of-bitches.
> Be careful or you'll wind up sorry, Kate,
> And wish you'd never taken down your britches.
> O Sonia of the Slav Stepanovitches,
> Say no, say no, reiterate it ever!—
> Be saintly, girls, in pure cool marble niches:
> Be good, sweet maid, and let who will be clever.

Marquis used to say that the Letters to the Editor columns in newspapers were a great comfort to him. When thoughts occurred to him "that didn't seem to belong anywhere else he would send them to some unsuspecting editor," more often than not the editor of the New York *Herald Tribune*, where his column once appeared. If it had to do with the theater he usually sent it to the Dramatic Editor of the New York *Times*. During those years of his recurrent letter-writing jag he sent a long letter to the editor of the *Herald Tribune* (April 19, 1934) from which the following is taken:

"I no longer keep up with the times. Frequently the items in your 'Twenty Years Ago Today' column seem like current news to me. I am not so young that I fight policemen just because spring is here. Believe it or not, I have seen the country Ruined, and have seen the country Saved, at least ninety-five times in the last forty years—and by the strangest things. I can remember back to the days when the participation of women in bicycle races Ruined the country. Then the Spanish War and Bill Bryan came along and Saved the country.

Horseless Carriages Ruined it again. Female Suffrage agitation
Saved it, Ruined it, and Saved it again.

"One Piece Bathing Suits, Hook Worm, the Federal Income Tax,
Sun Spots, Birth Control, Mark Hanna, Theodore Roosevelt, Swizzle
Sticks, Monkey Glands, Moving Pictures, Wall Street, Fallen Arches,
Starchy Diet, Burlesque Strip Acts, Daylight Saving, Cigarette Smoking by Women plunged it back into the nether gloom of irrevocable
Ruin; from which it was Saved once more by the discovery that every
farmer may have his own canning outfit and preserve his own
produce, and by William James's popularization of Pragmatism. . . .
Prohibition Saved the country, and then Ruined it again. . . . I
saved it myself once by the invention of the Old Soak, and Ruined it
immediately afterward by the creation of a Literary Cockroach who
made little midnight tracks across the leftovers in the iceboxes of the
Higher Life. The Rollo Stories and Woodrow Wilson Saved it, but
it was Ruined again by the introduction of Deuces Wild into a
game called the League of Nations. And then came Walter Lipp-
mann, who Saves it on Mondays and Wednesdays and Ruins it on
Tuesdays and Thursdays; the rest of the week belong to President
Roosevelt to do what he likes with. . . ."

Corey Ford, a friend of Don Marquis's, suggested that it would be
appropriate to provide in these pages an example of Marquis in the
unfamiliar role of the militant crusader. Mr. Ford supplied the clipping of a letter Marquis sent to Franklin P. Adams, and which on
January 2, 1934, occupied all but a few lines of Adams's famous
wide-measure column, "The Conning Tower," in the New York
Herald Tribune. Here are some excerpts:

". . . After sweating his brain to the bone to produce a book,
the writer learns that the government looks upon his royalties as
'unearned income,' and taxes him accordingly. . . .

"I have never been convinced that there is any justice in levying
any income tax at all upon the royalties received from books and
plays. This is essentially a levy against capital itself, rather than a
levy against income produced by capital. . . .

"The vital energy, skill, technical experience, which I bring to
the creation of a book or a play represent a definite expenditure
of capital; these things are my capital, my stock in trade. But the
government considers this disbursement of my capital to amount
to nothing at all; and what I receive in return for this outgo of my
capital to be unearned income. The government taxes the receipts

for the exchange of my principal as if it were increment from the *employment* of that principal, instead of reimbursement *for the expenditure of the principal itself.* . . .

"Let us say that the author of a play receives $100,000. That means that the play has grossed considerably more than a million dollars. Of that million the government gets 10% at once, right at the box office. Then it gets in taxes its cut of the producer's profit. Then it gets an income tax on the salaries of the actors, etc. . . . Then it gets an income tax on the author's royalties. Then, if the picture rights are sold to Hollywood, it treats the proceeds of this sale as unearned income also, and gets another cut at that. This latter is in itself an essential injustice, for in parting with his movie rights the author is selling a piece of property. . . . He gets no royalty from the movie company's sales to movie theatres; it is a straight-out, across-the-counter sale. The government goes on collecting, however. It collects from the film company, it collects from the film actors, it collects from the box office window again, it collects from the proprietors of the picture houses where the film is shown. It collects from the writers in Hollywood who fixed up the scenario for the camera. It collects from the camera men, supervisors, electricians, directors, etc., etc., to say nothing of tax collections from owners of theater real estate, agents, advertising media, etc.

"Altogether, when the original author bought sixty cents worth of yellow manila paper and two soft lead pencils, he started a train of industry which may bring in the government half a million dollars in taxes, one way and another. He ought to be pensioned by the government for stirring up business. . . . The politicians who put this stuff across would never be heard of, if it were not for writers. . . .

"Personally, I am in favor of an organized union of writers, something on the order of the unions connected with the A. F. of L., and possibly affiliated with it, to exercise political influence. The Authors' League is all very well, and has done good work; but it is a little too genteel, social, and inclined to recognize the existing order of things as permanent. The union should include all classes of writers, reporters, editors, novelists, playwrights, short-story writers, and it should be avowedly political and militant, and should raise hell till it gets what it wants. There is no system of government nor economy which it could not modify or overthrow in a few years, if it set itself steadily to work on a definite program."

There seems no end to the letters Marquis wrote in that 1933–34 period; a sampling of the different categories in which they fall is all that can be attempted. Here is Marquis's reply (dated July 6, 1934) to a letter from Homer Croy suggesting it was about time Don and Marjorie invited the Croys over for a meal:

"I note with a good deal of interest what you say about being open to luncheon, dinner, tea, buffet luncheon, and cold supper propositions. We have been having a good many people in to meals during the last year, and a nice little custom has grown up in our circle of acquaintances which adds an interesting feature to these meals. The guests, upon being assembled, are asked what they would like for supper, tea, luncheon, or dinner.

"If, perchance, a guest expresses a preference for pickled pigs' feet, he is sent at once to a nearby delicatessen, and, to do our guests justice, he seldom returns without the pickled pig's feet which he craves.

"If a guest should yearn for chocolate layer cake, there is a bakery nearby.

"I will not go into elaborate detail; you can see the principle of the thing.

"An engaging variation of this procedure has been furnished on several occasions when guests arrived with a complete dinner, piping hot and just out of the oven, and set it upon our dining room table all ready to serve. Two very nice young people brought in this manner several roast turkeys, all complete, with the stuffing, gravy and gadgets; they even insisted upon carving and serving. A good time was had by all.

"This is called our Number Two, or Deep Depression type of party.

"There are several other variations; but I should like to leave you the utmost liberty of choice.

"Come any time, Homer, and bring five or six friends with you. It would be a good thing to impress upon each one of these guests the desirability of bringing his own paper napkin with him, as we find that with the regular cloth type of napkin the laundry bills mount so high that they take the profit out of our percentage as hosts.

"One guest came and brought his food raw and cooked it in our kitchen, but we don't favor this method, as a general rule. In the first place, the guest might not be a good cook. In the second place, he might bring only enough for himself. In the third place, such seasoning matter as salt, pepper, mustard, butter, etc., runs into real money if the guests are not watched. Gas is also an item.

"We think, on the whole, that the proximity of the delicatessen shop solves most practical difficulties. Yours cordially and hospitably, Mister Marquis"

One of those who brought the Marquises a whole turkey, under Plan Two, was Mildred Dilling, famous harpist, who shared an apartment with Marjorie before she became Mrs. Marquis. Miss Dilling had never cooked a turkey before, and being unfamiliar with the secrets of roasting, had no success in her efforts to brown the bird. She finally gave up and brought the turkey as it was—thoroughly cooked, but the whitest-looking roast fowl ever to come out of an oven. Marquis examined the bird gravely as if trying to decide whether to reject it, thanked her, and proclaimed this "rather pale offering" acceptable provided she understood that the *next* one would have to be thoroughly browned if she expected to be permitted to present him and Marjorie with any more turkeys.

Miss Dilling also reports that when the hour grew late and she was ready to leave, Don told her it was established policy at 125 East 62nd Street not to permit guests to leave until the silverware had been checked. With which he had all the silver brought in, listed the different pieces as he counted them, pretended a few times to be disturbed by his arithmetic, finally said, "I guess it's all here," and told Miss Dilling she now had permission to leave the premises.

Among the most interesting Marquis letters of that period are some he seemingly never mailed. Among these is the unfinished draft of one addressed to Hugh Walpole. At times Marquis dictated to his secretary, at other times he composed letters on the typewriter, made his corrections, and then had his secretary make clean copies. The one addressed to Walpole, with its strikeovers and emendations, looks and sounds like a letter he never finished. At any rate, a hunt through the old Doubleday, Doran files and a combing of the papers that were once in his own files failed to yield a carbon copy of this letter, or a reply from Walpole. It has been established that Walpole (accompanied by Joseph Conrad) visited Marquis at Forest Hills some time in the twenties, the author of *Jeremy* and the columnist having originally been brought together by Christopher Morley. But this antedated by many years the matters on which Marquis sought Walpole's opinion in the unfinished letter which follows:

"Hugh Walpole, Esq.,
Metro-Goldwyn-Mayer Studios,
Culver City, California

"My dear Hugh:

"You have the galley proofs of 'Chapters for the Orthodox'
[a book by Marquis that Doubleday, Doran and Company was about
to publish] by this time, and have either thrown them into the
Pacific Ocean, or read them. Perhaps you read them and *then* threw
them in. I can't help wondering what slant you get on the stuff—
as the author of 'The Cathedral,' a bishop's son, and all that.

"I really hope that people aren't going to think that I am irreverent
where Jesus is concerned. I'm not, really. I think he has been lied on
by a lot of his so-called friends. I don't think he ever said or did some
of the things he is reported to have said and done in the Bible.

"How is anyone to be certain that he has formed a just estimate of
the character of Jesus? The only records of his sayings and doings
which we possess impress me as being liberally sprinkled with mistakes, exaggerations and misinterpretations; one reader is inclined to
accept this, another reader to accept that: in the end each individual
forms his own conception, builds his own idea of Jesus.

"To get at him one must peer and grope through the medium of
the minds which have presented him as he is in the Bible, must fight
with the thought that here or there or elsewhere he has been mis-
reported and misunderstood and misrepresented. For instance, I find
it easier to disbelieve than to believe that Jesus really uttered the
threats with regard to hellfire and eternal torture with which he is
credited in Matthew and Mark, because these threats are not con-
sonant with the spirit of the vast bulk of his teachings and actions.

"But if he really did utter such warnings, and believe in a place or
condition of ceaseless torture—not torture for a day or a week or a
year or a mere million years, but 'everlasting fire'—if he did believe
that certain sinners were actually to 'go into hell, into the fires that
shall never be quenched, where their worm dieth not, and the fire is
not quenched,' he believed something that the best modern minds
instinctively reject as barbarously impossible, and the most enlight-
ened pagans who preceded him never conceived of.

"Could the great genius that he was, the great teacher, the great
wit, the great prophet, the great lover of humanity, have had this
mental limitation? Could he really have held this savage conception, so relentless that the mind faints away from the thought of

the malignity which originated it—this truly fiendish idea of pain which must be consciously endured forever and forever? My instinct has always been to defend him against the imputation.

"Christianity has been, on the whole, and considered as any large alleviative of the lot of man, a failure. If it is possible that Jesus really held and preached the doctrine of hellfire everlasting imputed to him in the Bible, we need look no further than that for the cause. Not all the compassion and kindliness in the man who founded it, not all his courage and genuineness and spiritual appreciations and loving willingness to serve, could make themselves truly effective when contained in a nature which combined with them this fundamental cosmological misconception. The thought of everlasting torture, and the fear which it has given rise to among those who have held it, have been the chief things wrong with the world and humanity ever since Christianity attained its ascendancy in the occident in the fourth century.

"Even if Jesus did not believe it himself, his orthodox followers have believed it, and believed that he believed it, and it has left its cast and color in their minds, and affected their teachings and their administration of their organizations. No doubt Christians of a gentler mould and mood have always averted their eyes from it, and deliberately closed their minds and refused to speculate. But the belief dwells like a cancer among the vitals of organized Christianity, and its fibres have reached out (through the minds which have been influenced by the belief) to contaminate the whole body of civilization, as any cruel doctrine must do.

"My preference to believe, my wish to believe, that Jesus never thought nor said such a thing may be worth nothing at all. One may believe that he thought it and said it and that your Bible has not misrepresented him. Or one may believe that he merely reported a formalism of his time, somewhat rhetorically, without troubling himself to examine its frightful connotations and its real meaning.

"He was a man of his own time and place, in spite of the penetrating quality of his genius, and the constant escapes of his mind into a spiritual realm. And for that reason it is possible that the nature so fulfilled of love and compassion, so saturated with wisdom and good-will, had actually not been able to get rid of this belief, and that he did preach it, and that all the evils of a Christian civilization which are due to this belief proceed not from a misapprehension or

perversion of his doctrine, but more directly from the founder of
the Christian religion himself. Everlasting torture rings in the sermons reported as if it were something from which Jesus were passionately anxious to save the multitudes whom he loves and yearns
over; he is bringing them life and truth and love, and an insight
into the proper way of existence, according to the Bible reports, because he doesn't want them to be cast into this everlasting torture."

On July 2, 1934, Marquis said in a letter to Harry E. Maule, Doubleday editor: "I am depending on you to stir up some interest in
'Chapters for the Orthodox.' When I say *you*, I mean you personally
because you are my only cake of Ivory Soap left floating in the
bath-tub of despair. . . .

"I am depending on this book to make a bit of noise in the fall
and confirm that I can write like a ring-streaked son-of-a-bitch when
I get my elbows on the desk. . . ."

In subsequent letters he wrote his publisher asking that *Chapters
for the Orthodox* be sent to Bernard Shaw, adding: "If Shaw
doesn't like it . . . he will fall several degrees in my estimation as a
great writer." He also asked that the book be sent to Rudyard
Kipling, pointing out that the second chapter in the book has a certain resemblance to Kipling's poem "Tomlinson," a fact he thought
the British writer might find of interest. He adds: "Kipling sent me
word, through a mutual friend, that he was interested in my stuff
and wanted to see more of it. I don't know him and he may be a
polite liar. He is one of your authors. Why don't you see whether he
might be interested in this book? . . ." Marquis once wrote a piece
for his column about a plan he had for "dramatizing Shaw's plays."
He never learned whether it had been called to the famous Irish
playwright's attention.

Several members of the clergy had declared *Chapters for the
Orthodox* to be blasphemous. "Satan Goes to Church" was the
name of one of the stories that provoked criticism. One clergyman,
lifting the opening paragraphs of this story out of context, had
pronounced them "irreverent." The disputed paragraphs follow:

"Dr. David Bentley enjoyed a lucrative position as pastor of the
church to which belonged one of the richest men in the world,
Mr. Jefferson Pettigrew. One Sunday, during the Lenten season,
Mr. Pettigrew proceeded up the aisle arm in arm with no less a person
than the Devil himself, and they sat down side by side in the Pettigrew pew.

"Satan on this occasion had not even taken the trouble to disguise himself as an ordinary citizen, although he was considerate enough to hold his long spiked tail in such a position that it would not catch and snag the clothing of any of the other members of the congregation. He listened to the sermon in a decorous manner, and when the services were over lingered with Mr. Pettigrew to shake Dr. Bentley by the hand."

Marquis had a few churchmen on his side but there was only one, the Rev. Norman William Guthrie, who extended himself in his behalf.

In a letter to his publisher Marquis said:

"The Rev. William Norman Guthrie, Rector of St. Marks in the Bouwerie, is getting up a symposium on what constitutes reverence and irreverence, at his church in a couple of weeks. I am to speak at it, along with Heywood Broun, and other lit'ry guys. . . . Guthrie is enthusiastic about the book, and is inclined to help me answer kicks from preachers who are against it. Be sure that the editor of *The Churchman* gets a copy, with a special request that Guthrie be allowed to review it for that publication. He is going to get a rise out of some people through *The Churchman*, and have some fun generally. . . .

"If you get any more kicks from clergymen, send me copies of them right away. . . . If we can get the sky-pilots cussing out each other about this book, we can get some real interest stirred up, in a dignified way. To hell with anything as ain't dignified."

This was the kind of situation that Marquis enjoyed. It provided the excuse for several additional letters, in one of which he suggested that his publisher "send a man pronto to Atlantic City to do some dirty work with the new book at the Episcopal Conference down there. We might as well get a roar from a couple of bishops that would sell books. I don't wish to be too opportunist for dignity; but neither do I wish to be too dignified to grasp opportunities. Yours for Coin, Crime and Casanova, D.M."

That Marquis was hard up that year is established by several letters he wrote, including one dated February 9, 1934, and addressed to the Board of Directors of the Players Club:

125 E. 62 St., N.Y.C.

Gentlemen:

As I am busted, and don't feel easy spending anything that is not absolutely necessary until I get my debts paid, I am obliged to resign from the Club. When I get straightened out again financially, I shall apply for reinstatement. Please send any current bills to the above address, and have the office send mail there.

Cordially and sincerely,
Don Marquis

P.S. There's no silly peeve of any kind, but the plain statement is the true one. And for Christ's sake don't fish around for any special list for me to go on, like a deferred payment plan, or anything of that sort, which some clubs have, because I feel badly enough about getting out. If I stay away from the damned, dear old dive for six or eight months and get some real work done, I'll have money enough to come back in. —D.M.

At the next meeting of the Club's board of directors Marquis's resignation was submitted and unanimously rejected. The treasurer, David A. McKinlay, was instructed to "carry" him indefinitely.

But Marquis now seldom appeared at the Club. It was a matter of pride with him.

But, though Marquis was broke, he hadn't lost his spirit. On October 10, 1934—he was in financial difficulties throughout that year—he wrote his publisher regarding the latest requests from anthologists (there had been a steady stream of them for years) for permission to use humorous verses from his books. His contract called for his sharing with the publisher whatever fees accrued therefrom, although he had always thought such fees were not worth bothering with except where a short story or something of similar length was concerned. He forwarded the two latest requests with this comment:

"I am writing them giving my permission and I hope you will write giving the permission of Doubleday, Doran and Co. And I would be glad if D. D. & Co. would waive any fee in giving permission to reprint. I think these exchanges of courtesies among writing people and publishers amount to a damsite more than a few shekels from a reprint fee, having a tendency to impart health, love and joy vibrations, bring a sparkle to the eye, promote digestion, stabilize the industries of the world, and keep the grapes from souring on the vines."

A letter Marquis wrote George Middleton in August of that year tells in Marquis's own words the story of two collaborations that never eventuated and reveals that the author of the letter had not lost his love of ribaldry. Here are some excerpts:

"Dear George: Yes, I've been very much implicated in the theatre. I was supposed to be writing a play for George M. Cohan about Al

Smith, with a collaborator. But last week I looked at the damn thing, and said to myself, to hell with it. So I wrote a letter to the collaborator, saying, in effect, to hell with it. Finish it and you can have it.

"So that reminded me of another play I was supposed to be writing with a collaborator—a play about a racing character; with Damon Runyon. So I wrote a letter to Damon, and another to the producer, saying, in effect, to hell with it. I don't want to write it.

"I feel much better since I have kicked over these collaborations. I was afraid I might get rich, and that would destroy my sympathy with the downtrodden millions. You can't be too careful about these things. . . .

"If I could get hold of an enthusiast with money enough I would get him to start an independent producing company to do Nice Clean Movies here in New York. You rent a studio and some actors for five or six weeks, and get a little can of film. You can get releases nowadays. But I don't have much enthusiasm, myself; and it takes enthusiasm to inspire enthusiasts with money. I am selling quite a bit of stuff to magazines again—enough to keep my three-ring circus going—and I think I'd better stick to that, and let everything else go. It's a debased trade, of course, but what the hell—it's more honorable than hiring a bunch of girls and running a brothel. Besides, the massage parlors have that business pretty well sewed up. You ought to see their ads in the telephone book—the Red Book—with illustrations. They tell me the gigolo business has gone to hell, too. I did think of rounding up some personable young men and starting a gigolo parlor, a really refined one, where elderly ladies with money came to meet my young men. But the elderly ladies have lost their money. . . .

"I think I will stick to the magazines."

Marquis was agreeably surprised when the third archy and mehitabel book—*archy does his part*, published in 1935—showed how groundless were his fears that the critics would spank him for "overdoing" his now famous roach and cat characters. It will be recalled that originally he wondered whether this was book material at all—whether, in other words, the archy and mehitabel columns were worth collecting.

In his column "The Conning Tower," which had moved from the New York *World* to the New York *Herald Tribune*, Franklin P. Adams wrote: "Very gayly up and read Donald Perry Marquis's

archy does his part. . . . What a deeply humorous man Don is and
far closer to Mark Twain than anybody I know and am likely ever
to know." (Both Adams and Marquis had been kidded for running
one of those Mutual Admiration Societies but the facts do not support this, both men having praised and criticized each other's work,
as witness Adams's unfavorable comment on Marquis's version of
the Tristan and Isolde legend, *Out of the Sea*, which was produced
on Broadway in 1927.)

A favorite of the reviewers of the third archy book was a piece
(from which the following is taken) in which the insect philosopher
reviews the field of earthiness:

> coarse
> jocosity
> catches the crowd
> shakespeare
> and i
> are often
> lowbrowed

To show he could also be a highbrow—or, at least, sound like one
—archy wrote:

> the ant bear may be toothless
> but scorn not his capacity
> his appetite is ruthless
> his chief vice is edacity
> he boasts without apology
> his fad is entomology

A departure that pleased Marquis fans (and the reviewers) was
that Pete, his Boston bull, was represented in this book by a series of
poems that archy, the indefatigable spook, ghosted. Pete had appeared in articles and short stories, and in Marquis's weekly page in
Collier's, and had become a favorite with those who, no longer
able to follow Marquis in a daily column, were following his work
wherever they could; and were pleased to see their special enthusiasms
represented in this new book.

In Hollywood that year Marquis had an assortment of assignments—originals, adaptations, and special dialogue for screenplays
written by others. To a friend he wrote that this time he had invaded the film colony as a dedicated man—he was dedicated to
getting out of debt.

Marquis and Will Rogers, cowboy philosopher and comedian, had become friends and they had several animated talks about an idea of Marquis's that appealed to Rogers. The idea had been submitted to 20th Century-Fox, under the working title "The President's Husband," and Marquis had been told that if he could put together a story that Rogers and the studio liked, there would be a deal. There is said to have been considerable correspondence on this but only one letter has turned up. It is addressed to the story editor of 20th Century-Fox, Julian Johnson, and doesn't do much more than establish that such a project was under consideration.

Marquis's theme was that sooner or later there would be a woman President of the United States, and that her husband would find himself in a tough spot. Will Rogers was to play the role of the woman President's husband. Marquis saw him as a character "with a lot of shrewdness, a lot of humor, and a real grasp of public affairs." It was frankly designed as what Hollywood called a "vehicle." It would be studded with opportunities for Rogers to Save the Day with bits of Homely Philosophy and wisdom-laden quips designed to quicken his wife to thought on solutions of Presidential problems and to take her mind off the cares of office.

He must have been a little sad to be compelled to stop work on his egobiography, and on a novel for which he had high hopes, to devote himself to what he called "piffle."

Marquis told Weed and the other friends that the reason why he would never amount to anything as a screenwriter was that he didn't have the sense to confine himself to piffle when that was what a given situation called for. "You've got to know when to leave bad enough alone, Clive," was how he put it. He admitted succumbing to the temptation to interlard twaddle with something better, which resulted in a "bastard product that wasn't as good as pure piffle." Certain kinds of hokum, he argued, must be undiluted to amount to anything; otherwise you do not even have first-rate second-rate stuff. He knew these things to be true but nevertheless when it came time to strike those typewriter keys he would try to "elevate" a theme that could only be worsened by such treatment.

Meanwhile the Mohawk Drama Festival at Union College was rehearsing *Master of the Revels*, Marquis's play about Henry VIII, which it planned to produce "under the open sky" in Schenectady, New York, with direction by Karl Nielson and "supervision" by

Charles Coburn, who had undertaken the starring role, with Mrs. Coburn cast as Catherine of Aragon.

Brooks Atkinson, drama critic of the New York *Times* and a Don Marquis fan, attended the opening of *Master of the Revels* in which, he pointed out, the players competed with "the hum of August crickets."

The following excerpts are taken from Mr. Atkinson's review:

"Although it is a new play the period it explores is familiar ground to those itinerant classicists, Mr. and Mrs. Coburn, who have been improving the drama in the Mohawk Valley. . . . For Mr. Marquis is writing of Henry VIII, his wives, strumpets and his knavish ministers, and 1,400 of the neighborhood folks found it good stuff to hear in the summer time.

"It is good stuff at any rate for America's most ruminative humorist. In the published version Mr. Marquis dubs it 'a novel in play form' which is an acknowledgment of its dramatic infirmities. Let them pass for peccadilloes; they appear to be inherent in Mr. Marquis's bubbling frame of mind. Having discovered that Shakespeare's 'Henry VIII' is on the whole a bad play, he has felt encouraged to write one that is no great improvement in form. But Mr. Marquis has an infectious fondness for rogues, and he has treated himself to a rowdy portrait of a bibulous King and a parliament of shameless women. Mr. Coburn, who has cut it wisely, plays the part with robust swagger. . . .

"Put Mr. Marquis's drama down as uneven . . . but a good field day for prose, humor and revelry. . . ."

In Hollywood Marquis received a letter from his play agent telling him how unfortunate it was that he couldn't attend the opening. How nice it would have been if he could have responded to the enthusiastic cries of "Author! author!" that were heard everywhere in the audience at the conclusion of the performance, etc., etc.

In the same batch of papers in which I found the letter from Marquis's agent, I found a copy of the following letter to David A. McKinlay, treasurer of the Players, written early in 1935, or shortly before Marquis left on this, his last trip to Hollywood:

"My dear Dave: I have your letter in which you express the hope that Dame Fortune may be smiling upon me.

"She is, but it is the most sarcastic goddam smile I ever saw on anyone's face. Yours sincerely, Don Marquis

"P.S. Enclosed, a small payment on acct."

As previously pointed out, among Marquis's papers are drafts of letters he apparently never sent. The ones referred to are unfinished, sometimes ending in the middle of a sentence. At a certain point in these unsent missives Marquis seems to decide that he is asking too much of the addressees or that the questions he poses are ones that he should decide for himself.

I found in the Marquis Collection of Columbia University the unfinished draft of a letter addressed to Brooks Atkinson. The draft of this letter was written shortly after the tryout of *Master of the Revels* in Schenectady. Dated August 16, 1935 and written from the Hotel Hollywood, Hollywood, California, it reads in part:

"I am going to ask a great favor of you. I want your opinion as to whether it is worth while to let my *Master of the Revels* come into New York . . . and will of course keep your reply confidential. No one saw it except yourself, as far as I can find out, who knows anything about the theatre. And I seemed to feel in your criticism that you were being more kind and lenient towards the performance which you saw than it deserved. That you had said to yourself, 'Oh, what the hell!—it's only a little summer theatre production anyhow; let them get away with it for once.'

"What I want to know is the lowdown. I am surprised that they got away with it at all, with only a week's rehearsal. I don't know where or how they cut the show, or what they did to the tone of it. . . ."

Then he puts a series of queries designed to answer his earlier question: do you think this play about Henry VIII is good enough for Broadway?

"You see," he concludes, "all you have to do is say yes or no. . . . If you can conscientiously do this I will be very much"——

There the draft—a self-typed original—ends.

Midway in this unfinished letter Marquis interrupted himself to express shock and sorrow over a piece of news that reached him as he was pounding away at the typewriter. This passage begins: "Jesus, I just this instant heard that Will Rogers was killed." (The plane bearing Rogers and Wiley Post crashed near Point Barrow, Alaska, and both men were killed.)

A letter to Mr. Atkinson (enclosing a photostat of the unfinished draft of Marquis's letter) elicited the following reply:

"This may not be a copy of the letter that Don Marquis did send to me. But I remember receiving an inquiry from him identical with the inquiry he made in the enclosed letter. Maybe he wrote another letter, but my memory of the gist of it, dim after more than a quarter of a century, coincides with the one you have submitted. I forget what I answered. But again, trusting to memory . . . I hope I advised him not to bring it (*Master of the Revels*) to New York. . . . No, I never met Don Marquis. He was to me a happy legend, and one that is still bright in my mind."

There is also a long and interesting letter to Charles Coburn—four and a half pages of rather solid, single-spaced typing—written when Marquis's play about Henry VIII was still a live possibility for Broadway production. It covers a lot of ground, including Marquis's reply to Coburn's offer to invest some of his own money in the proposed production:

"It is a kind of damned circus parade, in one sense, this show; and *you* have got to be the big bass drum all the time. I can't imagine any part which calls for a more continuous, unrelenting exercise of personal vitality on the part of the leading actor, and that is enough for any actor on earth to saddle himself with, without worrying whether he is going to lose his shirt into the bargain. I want—speaking selfishly—all your guts and gumbo for the show; and I will put into the job of rewriting everything I have got, and that's all that should be asked of either one of us. Somebody else should take the financial risk. You must nick the backer for a good salary so that if it has a run you will be well heeled without risking anything financial of your own; you and I risk enough in risking our work and our reputation.

"I won't worry about your performance; it will be swell—and yet, frankly, I would worry about any man's performance if he personally were holding the financial bag on the kind of production I want. It is simply not in human nature to be the House of Morgan and David Garrick on the same evening. I have a good deal of hope about the whole thing."

In some ways the most interesting introduction Marquis ever wrote is the one he prepared when his publisher decided to issue *Master of the Revels* as a book. It covers more than thirteen printed pages and is much too long to quote entire, although the temptation to do so was hard to resist. This introduction takes the form of a "dedicatory letter" which Marquis addressed to "My Old Friend, Charles J. Bayne, Poet and Scholar."

Here are some excerpts:

"My dear Charlie:

"It has been a good many years since we worshipped together at the shrines of Keats, Shakespeare and Kit Marlowe, among the mingled fragrances of blossoming honeysuckle and spilled Bourbon whiskey,—both odors excellently aromatic in their way—wallowing in youth, springtime and poetry like a couple of pigs in paradise. I suppose we have changed. I no longer wake up of a Sunday morning in unfamiliar choir-lofts, queerly tangled in the mechanism of a pipe-organ, wondering how the devil I got poured in there, where I came from, and how I am going to trickle away again without disturbing a church service.

"And you I hope no longer, on your rambles among the red old hills of Georgia, flag down and stop fast express trains on the Southern Railroad to ask the engineer for a match for your pipe.

"It seems to be true that if you give almost any man time enough he will get a little older.

"It will be no news to you that I have always had a certain amount of sympathy for that ribald, disreputable old hellion, Henry VIII of England; and it was somewhere between twenty-five and thirty years ago that I mentioned to you that I intended to write a new play about him. But the project (like so many others) slumbered in the fat and indolent recesses of my mind. It might be sleeping there yet, but for two things. First, the performance of that very clever young woman, Miss Cornelia Otis Skinner, as each and all of the six wives of Henry, and for the biography of Henry by Mr. Francis Hackett. These reawakened it; in fact, they seem to have started a new cycle of interest in Henry. It has been more than three hundred years since the great hulk of his flesh was hoisted into the tomb, but Henry keeps coming back, with a limp in his leg and a look in his eye, and his cap tilted at a somewhat rakish angle, to remind the world that he had a good deal to do with making it what it is today, like it or not.

"I wrote the play, after intensive reading . . . and it was accepted for production on the stage, and the production announced for October. But the producer changed his plans when the motion picture starring Mr. Charles Laughton appeared in New York in

September. The author of the motion picture must have been at work on his script at about the same time I was working on my play. And now plays about Henry VIII are breaking loose in every direction. Possibly some of them which were written later will be produced on the stage earlier; will 'beat me in,' as the theatrical slang is. Which is 'the luck of the theater.' So I publish this, not to have too much the appearance of trailing in the rear of a popular movement. . . .

"Of the twenty-odd volumes which I consulted, the *Six Wives of Henry VIII*, by Martin Hume, and Mr. Hackett's biography, were the most interesting. Mr. Hackett's volume reads like a novel—in fact, a little too much like a novel, if it is not disgraceful to say so. I don't mean to imply that it is inaccurate, for it is anything but that; it is wonderfully documented, and should remain for a good many years the standard work on Henry. What I mean exactly is, that now and then Mr. Hackett tells us what Wolsey thought when he went to bed on a certain night, and what he thought when he got up the next morning, after a good night's rest, etc. I don't see how a biographer or historian could know such things; although I see how a novel writer is under the necessity of making his story more immediate and humanly interesting by the introduction of such inferences. But this is a very trivial criticism of a great, scholarly, and human book. . . .

"I discovered, when I read into the subject, a great diversity of opinion with regard to Henry himself. To James Anthony Froude he was a hero who could do no wrong. To Charles Dickens he was a blot of blood and grease upon the history of England and could do nothing right. . . .

"There is one character connected with these events who should have a separate play written about him. And that is George Boleyn, Anne's brother. George was so impolitic as to make the remark that the King lacked the virility to get a son. This was reported to Henry, and it hit him in one of his tenderest parts, his masculine vanity. Henry, all the time he was fulminating against Catherine of Aragon for not bearing him boys, princes that lived, was probably a little uneasy about his own virility; and this was one thing which made him so extensively amorous: he was always forcing himself to prove to himself that he *was* the capable male. When George Boleyn was on trial for his life, on the charge of incest with his sister, this other charge was brought up against him, that he had cast doubts upon the King's potency. The charge was written on a piece of paper, and handed to him, as the judges did not want it to become public property. George looked at the paper, laughed, and then, before he could be stopped, read the charge aloud, pleaded guilty to having said it, and averred in a loud voice that it was true. . . .

"Henry was a lecherous, treacherous, ribald, disgusting villain; but he was something more than that, too. He became a very clever politician, an astute statesman. And I think . . . that even if he had been born a commoner, he would have climbed and fought his way to power. . . .

"Of all the wives—I have introduced Anne of Cleves only as a sort of windy reminiscence—the one who appeals to me most is Katheryn Howard. Katheryn must have been a darling: king-hearted, handsome, and, poor girl, quite unable to say No and mean it. I confess to a great deal of pity for poor little Katheryn. She wanted to be kind to everybody, and she lost her head. As Henry says in the play: 'A whore, yes—but what a wonderful whore!' . . .

"I have heard, Charlie, that that train you stopped (to ask the engineer for a match) was rushing frantically from New Orleans to Atlanta filled with yellow fever refugees; and on account of the delay several of them did not get to the Georgia uplands in time to be saved. This is probably not the only disaster you have caused by your incorrigible levity; and it is something for you to think remorsefully about, as you sit on your vine-clad verandah in mid-Georgia, a mint julep at your elbow, listening to the mocking-birds whistle up a red-faced moon from the wide and breathing dusk. Or did they quit singing permanently when Frank Stanton died? I could cite other examples of your levity. I think you were connected with the gang of ruffians who threw me into a cellar excavation one night, and then threw thousands of Negro cab-drivers down on top of me, on the theory that being a dam-Yankee I must enjoy the association. And . . . and . . . but maybe you wouldn't like the details in print. I have become staid and sober myself. I go to dull dinners of committees for the advancement of everything worthy, and listen to serious thinkers boring each other with speeches, who have not enough sense of reality to know that they are being bored.

"You have probably caught me at it by this time! I am desperately trying by suggestion to refer this play to a period of my youth when nobody expected me to be dignified; and this is because it is such a bawdy thing that I feel a man of my sedate years and reputation for propriety should be ashamed of it. It really *has* some lousy language in it; but that is the way Henry and I have always spoken when we felt at ease. Don Marquis. New York, November, 1933"

A few weeks after the tryout of *Master of the Revels* in Schenectady, Ruth Vonnegut, Marjorie's daughter by her first marriage, was married in San Diego, California. The date was August 31, 1935.

Marquis had not been feeling well—he said that at fifty-seven he felt like eighty-seven and hoped someone would be thoughtful enough to give him a wheel chair for Christmas—but he was as fond of Marjorie's daughter as he was of her son, Walter, and he forgot his aches and pains sufficiently to be a helpful, enthusiastic stepfather of the bride. And to pay the bills, cheerfully for a man who was broke. (It should be noted that, although he was in debt at the time, his Hollywood salary was substantial.)

In a letter to a friend on the eve of the nuptials (Huntington Library Collection) Marjorie wrote that the wedding would take place in the San Diego garden of a friend. "This garden," she said, "has won several of the local Garden Club's prizes. It is on the slope of a hill with a magnificent view of the bay. Over the terrace where the ceremony will take place is a balcony where the harpist will sit. . . . There will be high tea in the house after the wedding and then a short harp concert. Daniel Carroll, Jr., of St. Paul is the groom,—Lieut. Jr. Grade on the U.S.S. Decatur.

"Don will give the bride away. . . .

"Lieutenants Osborne, Hughes, Douglas and Herring will perform the navy stunt—holding their crossed swords for the bride and groom to pass under.

"Ruth's gown is from Italy, fashioned by Mario Fortuny of Florence (a Greek design) and the gold head-dress will be by Bullock Wilshire. . . .

"Only intimate friends of the families will be there, among them some prominent San Diego people."

Comments in letters to friends indicate how pleased Marquis was that Ruth had made what he considered "a fine marriage." He had once written Clive Weed: "At the risk of seeming a Pollyanna, I'm always glad to have a seat down front where happiness is on display."

As Marquis gave the bride away it might have crossed his mind that if his daughter, Barbara, had lived she would be nearing her

eighteenth birthday and conceivably not too far from bridehood
herself.

Stage Magazine requested Marquis to write an article on how
the American theater looked to him in 1935. Fearful that, no matter
how hard he strove to avoid it, this assignment might result in a
certain amount of pontification, he said he would do the piece if
he could use archy the cockroach as his mouthpiece. What he would
say through this device would represent his views as definitely as a
serious article. If this approach was acceptable he would do the
piece; if not, he would have to decline.

The editor told him to go ahead, and this is in part what resulted:

                . . . i come of a long line
            of theatrical cockroaches
            my family has inhabited theatres
            for thousands of years
            one of our family traditions concerns
            the ancestor who stood up in one
            of the eye sockets of yoricks skull
            at a performance of hamlet and waved
            four of his six legs jovially at
            queen elizabeth
            she thought the skull was winking at her
            and was in doubt whether to be insulted
             or complimented but finally compromised
            by ordering the execution of the earl
            of essex that afternoon

            the theatre nowadays has lost most
            of its glamor and illusion
            that has all been kicked out doors
            and the motion pictures have picked it up
            and in their crude and bungling way
            are doing the best they can with it
            they are laboring in their dumb headed
            thumb handed manner to give the public
            an escape from the malevolent realities
            of existence and induct them into
            a fourth dimension . . .

In this piece Marquis publicly conceded, for the first time, that
Hollywood knew something about show business. He didn't pay

the movies any handsome compliments but clearly he seemed to believe that in the year 1935 the film-makers were a little smarter than
the Broadway producers.

When Rodman Gilder, who died in 1950, was beginning to organize his material for a biography of Don Marquis, he compiled
for the "American First Editions" series in *Publishers' Weekly* the
most comprehensive check list of Don Marquis's writing ever published. This list embraced most of the privately printed items. Some
of the latter were described by a friend of the author as "calculated
to bring a blush to the cheek of the most hardened Elizabethan,"
although I still cling to my belief that by today's liberal standards
most of it is publishable. There is another category of privately
printed Marquisiana which is not only publishable but *has* appeared
in the public prints. In the latter classification is *Her Foot Is on the
Brass Rail*, listed by Mr. Gilder as "privately printed in 1935 in an
edition of 500 numbered copies only." It is a slender volume in
which there appears a two-page illustration by James Thurber—one
of Mr. Thurber's best.

This little book—handsomely produced by the Marchbanks Press—
originally appeared as a letter to the editor of the New York *Herald
Tribune*, the last newspaper in which Marquis's column appeared.
Ever since he left the newspaper field, the ex-columnist, when the
spirit moved him, wrote a letter to the editor of the *Herald Tribune*.
They are all in the vein of columnist Marquis and amount to the
sort of thing he would have written if he were still producing
"The Lantern" for that newspaper.

Here is the letter that later emerged as the slender volume *Her
Foot Is on the Brass Rail*:

"I don't know what you think about it, but the Old Soak and I
are profoundly disappointed with the New Barroom. What we had
wanted, what we had hoped and prayed for, what we had fought,
bled, died and lied for, was the return of the Old Barroom. The
vision of its return, just as it used to be, cheered us and sustained us
through all these desert years of drought (mitigated by the speakeasy) known loosely as the 'prohibition era.' Well, we have repeal;
and we have a barroom. It is an Open Bar. But it is not the Old
Saloon.

"Open . . . yes, Heaven help us, open! Not even soap or whiting
on the windows—oh, abominably and inescapably Open! You can

see right into it, and right through it; it has no more secrets from the public than a sick man's innards under the X-ray or fluoroscope. It does not even have a decent privacy. Your wife, your sister, your maiden aunt, your little golden-haired daughter, your mother-in-law, the pastor of your church, the boss at your office, the wife of your boss and the wife of your pastor, the man you are trying to get a contract out of, your creditors, may look right through the window and count every drop of liquid damnation you dribble down your gullet.

"That is bad enough. But there is worse. Women come into this New Barroom. Not through a Family Entrance, but through the front door. They go right up to the bar. They put a foot on the brass railing. They order; they are served; they bend the elbow; they hoist; they toss down the feminine esophagus the brew that was really meant for men—stout and wicked men.

"The last barrier is down; the citadel has been stormed and taken. There is no longer any escape, no harbor of refuge, no haven, no sanctuary, no hiding place, no hole or corner, no burrow nor catacomb, no nook amongst the ruins of civilization, where the hounded male may seek his fellow and strut his stuff, safe from the atmosphere and presence of femininity. A man might as well do his drinking at home, with his wife and daughters; and there never was any fun in that. It was merely—drinking! It was merely a satisfaction of the physical appetite for alcohol.

"The spiritual essence of drinking—drinking as it was practised in the Old Saloon—is gone forever, killed by this invasion of women.

"You know the Talk—or maybe you don't. Perhaps no one connected with the editorial staff of the Herald Tribune, which is a home paper resolute for the conventions and respectabilities, was ever in the Old Saloon. The conversation was enjoyable. It was apt to be . . . Free. It was ripe, fruity; it verged, at times, on the rowdy. There were moments when Rabelais would have felt perfectly at home there. It was as masculine as an Andalusian bull or a Tuscan billygoat. It was conversation with whiskers on it. It ranged . . . from the nadir of the unprintable to the zenith of realistic poetry. It smote the welkin with the bung-starter of imagination till the cosmos rang again.

"It is not the occasional rowdiness, the semi-occasional bawdiness, of this barroom conversation which I chiefly regret. It is the philosophical admixture; the startling, first-hand, spontaneous appraisal of

everything in heaven, earth or hell which spouted forth with the removal of all inhibitions. The very presence of a woman—any woman,
any kind of woman—checks this. A man, whether in a drawing room
or a saloon, talking to other men, is not the same person when
there is a woman present. He adopts some sort of attitude, in spite
of himself. Perhaps he is old-fashioned enough to pull his punches
lest he offend her. Perhaps he exaggerates his own tendencies, deliberately seeking to offend her, shock her. He isn't the same; he
listens to himself. He might as well be at home. And it was home
that he came here to get away from. Not because he didn't like home
particularly, but because he wanted to exchange ideas with a lot
of other men who came here for the same reason he is here. Even if
he wanted to let women into this exclusively masculine atmosphere,
he couldn't do it. They can't come in. They can destroy it, but they
can't get into it. But here she is, in the New Barroom, and her foot
in on the brass railing. My observation of that foot is that once it
sets itself anywhere it never retreats. With all their superiorities to
men—and I am willing to admit their superiority in nine cases out
of ten—they won't know what I am talking about in this letter.

"I am a religious person, and the only hope I see is in the New
Jerusalem. I shall run a barroom in the hereafter, and there will be
no feet of feminine saints on the brass railing. (They'd demand a
gold railing if I let them in.) Kit Marlowe will be there, and Kit
Morley, too, and Shakespeare and John L. Sullivan and Frank
O'Malley and Benjamin De Casseres and Benvenuto Cellini. There
will be a good deal of Talk. And if they make me let women in, I'll
take my saloon to hell. If they invade those precincts, I suppose I'll
have to move to Hoboken. Don Marquis. P.S. There will be a
Back Room.—D. M."

Marquis made a reference to what was known in the days of the
Old Saloon as the Family Entrance. He had once said in "The
Sun Dial" that his ambition was to see a family entering a Family
Entrance. He had also observed, in one of "the great conversations"
reported by Weed, that tobacco-chewers would be accommodated
in any saloon he ever ran. A former tobacco-chewer himself (going
back to his near-hobo days) he would see that there were plenty of
shiny brass cuspittoons, a word he invented when one of the participants in that conversation complained that the word "spittoon" had
an inelegant ring and someone else argued that "cuspidor" sounded
"too refined."

18

Marquis and Will Rogers—"Bad Thoughts" about Summer Theaters—Marquis as Golf Instructor —How Do You Dictate a Novel?—Marjorie Marquis Dies—Don's Failing Health—The Old Soak Visits Forest Hills—"Like the Hero of a Greek Tragedy"— "Lines for a Gravestone"

Marquis once considered doing a book about the theater and the motion pictures. He had written several pieces for magazines on these subjects—including the gay confessional, "Stage-struck," for the *Saturday Evening Post*—and among his papers are bits and pieces of others he had written and seemingly planned to develop further. One of the most amusing in the latter category is called "The Golden Legend," in which he discusses a simple formula for writing plays and screenplays that was once his for the reading but, alas, he had not been attentive enough!

"On one of the movie lots in Hollywood is a wooden building inhabited almost entirely by writers and their secretaries—although I have seen a cockroach or two there, and supervisors and directors wander in and out at will, and little black slugs from the rose bushes outside occasionally crawl in under the screens. The raptures and roses of Hollywood, as Swinburne might have put it, foster innumerable slugs, as do its languors and lilies.

"This building, for slugs and writers, is in two sections; it is split by a concrete roadway, and the two sections are joined by an overhead arch which bridges the roadway.

"Over this arch, in large golden letters—if it were anywhere else, I should say gilt letters, but there is a possibility that the letters may be of solid gold, as they are in Hollywood—is a legend which tells what a play is, and how it should be written. I used to read this golden legend four times a day. Once when I was in the studio in the morning, again when I went out to lunch, once more when I returned from lunch, and finally when I left the studio in the evening.

"Therefore, I read it twenty-four times a week, or seventy-two times during the three weeks I worked in that studio last summer; and several years ago, when I was at the same studio for ten weeks, I read it at least two hundred and forty times.

"Having read it more than three hundred times, you would think I would know exactly what a play is, a picture play or a real play, and how it should be written. But the lamentable fact is that I never could remember it. I must be cursed with the kind of mind which resists such useful information, for the only vague recollection I have is that the word 'human,' or perhaps the word 'humanity,' appears in this golden legend once or twice, possibly three times. I think the sense of the admonition must be that a play, whether for the screen or the stage, should have some connection with humanity; a sentiment which, I believe, few will seek to controvert.

"I remember once reading it in company with the late Will Rogers.

"'Could you lasso that motto, Will,' I asked him, 'and drag it off the wall a letter at a time?'

"'Really, or for a picture?' asked Will. 'Of course, I could do it in a picture. You can do anything in a picture.'

"I was supposed at the time to be writing an original for Will; he liked it and I liked it—we thought it was 'human'—but nobody else did and so the masterpiece was never filmed. We continued to gaze at the golden legend for some moments, and then as we turned away to go to the lunch room, Mr. Rogers remarked meditatively: 'What a racket it is, this picture business!' . . .

"'You ain't havin' me make love to nobody in this picture, Don?' said Mr. Rogers, anxiously, one day.

"'No,' I said. 'I wouldn't do a mean thing like that, Will.'

"'I won't have the picture if you do,' he said. He waved his hand towards the semi-circle of hills which look down on Hollywood. 'Them hills are filled with the graves of reputations—the reputations of picture actors over fifty, who thought they could make love on the screen.'

"With all the chances I have had to learn about plays, especially the opportunity to spend countless hours standing in the sunkist roadway reading that golden legend at a pretty fair salary, I cannot complain that my education as a writer has been neglected. Every facility has been afforded me, and if I don't know yet exactly what should and what should not go into plays, it is obviously my own fault.

"The matter seems to me important—that is, if anything about the theatre is important. Producers, directors, editors, critics, college professors, social workers, press agents, actors, box office men, and even the bankers who occasionally back shows, to say nothing of the people who write prefaces to the collected works of Ibsen, are forever saying just what should, and what should not, go into a play. If I could only remember what I used to read on that building, I feel that I could always answer them all, pat and pertinently.

"I remember that one time I had a baby's shoe in a play which Mr. Arthur Hopkins produced. He made me take it out. I thought the way I had used it was in the best tradition of homely American pathos—it was the sort of thing that had been done a thousand times—and I cried every time I thought about it; but Mr. Hopkins had his way. Less than a year later, he produced a play, the scene of which was laid in Austria or Poland or Russia, or somewhere around that neck of the woods, in which there were *two* babies' shoes; and it made a hit with the audiences too. They sobbed.

"I went to Mr. Hopkins about it, and reproached him. He explained to me that a baby's shoe was hokum if I did it, or any other American writer, but an Austrian, or a Pole or a Russian could do it, and it was legitimate. I ran into a similar thing with regard to a mortgage one time; I gave a script to a producer, and he kicked because I had a mortgage in it. Later, I saw him at a performance of 'The Cherry Orchard,' in a glow of enthusiasm. And, as near as I could find out, 'The Cherry Orchard' is all about a mortgage—a mortgage on the Old Home Place—and the mortgage is foreclosed, and the cherry trees are cut down, and it is all very sad. It is Russian; and a Russian mortgage isn't hokum; it is just Russian.

"My own impulse is to think that you can have anything in a play that is interesting, whether it has been in a thousand plays before, or whether it has never been in a play before; that the one and only test is whether it really interests people who go to see the show. But I'm probably wrong about it; I am wrong about the theatre just as often as most other people—and that means an overwhelming proportion of the time.

"I will have to go back to Hollywood, I suppose, and read that golden legend three or four hundred times more, and make a real effort to remember it. Writing it down would do no good; I always lose the little slips of paper I write things down on. But there it is, in big gold letters, and it settles everything for all time, and it is just simply stupid that all the playwrights in the world haven't learned it by heart.

"I don't know whether the man who wrote the recipe ever wrote a play or not. I've heard it said that writing a play is a bit more difficult than writing recipes telling how to write plays; although you'd think writing a play ought to be easy enough, too, if a fellow just followed the recipes.

"I have been to several plays this year which I am sure must have been pretty easy to write; but they must have been rather difficult to act, and Heaven knows they were hard enough to look at and listen to. Everybody who writes should go out to Hollywood at once and read the golden legend—if there is anybody who isn't there now. . . ."

There was much puzzlement among Marquis's friends over his inability to produce an idea that Hollywood considered suitable for Will Rogers. Several of Marquis's ideas had Rogers's wholehearted approval, including a completed screenplay which the cowboy comedian liked because it departed from the pattern that had been established for him. But Hollywood was fearful of budging an inch from the formula that had proved successful and the more Marquis tried to bring his imagination into play the further he found himself from what the play-it-safe story editors, directors, and producers wanted. Hollywood regarded itself as a business and these men felt there was much to be said for the position they took. The Will Rogers pictures had been uniformly successful—Marquis thought the liveliest of the lot was the one based on Homer Croy's book *They Had To See Paris*—and it was not surprising to see Hollywood invoking its old injunction (based on a combination of box-office figures and superstition) against tampering with a winning recipe. So each new Will Rogers picture was essentially the *same* picture, with a new background and enough plot variation to give the impression of freshness.

A successful screen-writer of that period believes that Marquis's difficulties stemmed from his appraisal of Will Rogers as something more than an amiable cracker-barrel philosopher. Behind the façade of loose grammar and dropped "g's," Marquis, according to this informant, found a penetrating intelligence. Don had stated that, as an old editorial writer, he considered Will Rogers's daily "box" in the New York *Times* "the best editorial page in the country." He believed that Rogers frequently emerged as the deftest debunker of them all, sometimes accomplishing his purpose in a single pungent sentence, as many a political nonentity of the time could have attested.

Marquis thought that in the field of general humor Rogers was equally effective. In making his point he referred to a piece he had written in his columning days kidding beauty parlors. He thought it was a pretty good piece until Will Rogers "covered the whole subject in one sentence," as follows: "Most women leaving beauty parlors look as if they hadn't been waited on."

It was the mordant Rogers that Marquis tried to capture in a screenplay—the satirist who enjoyed deflating phonies—and he met with failure because Hollywood thought that if the lariat-wielding comic were permitted to put real bite into his "homely philosophy" the public would cease to find him "lovable." Marquis believed (and Rogers concurred) that his view of his friend Will was more accurate than the familiar one and that the public would welcome the change to a more piercing Rogers if his barbs were directed at plausible stuffed shirts. But Don, considered "impractical" by many studio executives, was unable to convince anyone in authority.

When Marquis was asked to handle the negative side of a pro-and-con article for *The Stage* on the summer-theater movement he decided to take the assignment if his wife had no objection. Marjorie, even after the Marquises had lost heavily in their summer-theater venture in Locust Valley, was enthusiastic about the movement, firmly convinced that it was making an important contribution to the American theater. That Marquis considered it necessary to discuss the matter with his wife had been cited in support of Rollin Kirby's contention that Marquis was "the most henpecked husband in New York."

Marjorie thought Don should express himself as he saw fit. His opposition to summer theaters merely amounted to "a bad thought." It would pass. Bad thoughts always do.

Here are some of Marquis's "bad thoughts" about the Haybarn Circuit, as published in *The Stage:*

"As for the Little Summer Theatres, they can turn them all back into stables and garages and woodsheds and lumber scows for all I care. . . .

"There is a curse upon them. I can't understand what happens to a show in Little Summer Theatres on any other hypothesis than that there is a curse upon them. Heaven has said: 'We can't let them get away with *that!* Go tell Satan they are delivered into his hands, and the details are left to him . . . !'

"I have seen Little Summer Theatres which employed as good actors as you can find on Broadway, and as good directors, too—in fact, the same actors and directors—and yet the net result was something amateurish. A show may go into a Little Summer Theatre as sleek and neat as an eel, attended by all the wisdom and experience of a corps of theatrical trained nurses, mounted and lighted with everything in the latest editions of the latest text-books, but when the curtain goes up (and sometimes it actually goes up the first time they try to put it up) that show comes forth treading amateurishly on its own feet, and stands there embarrassed, all covered with horse feathers, apple sauce and alibis. It's in a Little Summer Theatre, and it knows it and feels it, and wishes it were somewhere else. The 134 people in the 197 seats thank everybody connected with the theatre for the good time they have had, and say what a wonderful thing it is for the community to have a theatre like that in its midst, and the next night go to a good clean movie, or even a dirty one. . . .

"I think that maybe the main thing the matter with the Little Summer Theatres is that few of them ever make any money, and few of them expect to. . . .

"The backer . . . sees after a few weeks that he isn't going to get a break. . . . He goes and counts the seats in the auditorium. He figures that if every seat were filled every night, for five nights a week, at an average price of a dollar a seat, the total intake could not be more than a thousand dollars. Productions cost something, so does rent; there are electrical bills, actors' salaries, printing and the rest of it. Probably he hasn't thought of it before—but he couldn't make money if he filled every seat at every performance. There are a surprising number of Little Summer Theatres which innocently start out with this handicap, and the seats are counted later.

"I think, on the whole, that the Little Summer Theatre does more harm to the drama than good. In hundreds and hundreds of spots all over the country it pops up every summer, and tells thousands and thousands of people who have not had much experience as theatre-goers: '*This* is the theatre; *I* am the theatre.' And because they believe it is, it puts them off the theatre. It kills more audiences, by and large, than it makes. . . ."

Marjorie voiced 100 per cent dissent when her husband's views were published and predicted that some day Don would See the Light and have "a good thought" about the little summer playhouses.

That year—1936—saw the publication of *Sun Dial Time*, a collection of short stories by Marquis that had originally appeared in *Collier's*, the *Saturday Evening Post*, and other magazines. The reviews ranged from good to enthusiastic. Here is a quotation from the one that appeared in the New York *Times*:

"Engaging as they are, it would be a pity to identify Don Marquis exclusively with archy and mehitabel. He can write, when he puts his mind to it, as uproarious a short story as any American humorist. His fiction lacks the pitch and sting of Lardner's, is gayer, crazier, more farcical, but is equally alert to the nuances of the popular idiom. . . .

"Mr. Marquis is at his best when he relies most freely on his powers of cock-eyed invention. . . ."

Some years ago, in the bar of the Chatham Hotel in New York, Grantland Rice told Bill Corum of the New York *Journal American* and me that Don Marquis had written the two funniest golf stories he had ever read—"Rattlesnake Golf" and "The Rivercliff Golf Killings." (Both appeared in *Sun Dial Time*.) Rice mentioned that he had once urged Marquis to build another golf story around a speakeasy incident that had taken a place in the ex-columnist's storytelling repertoire. Here is the version told by Clive Weed, one of the two participants—the other was Marquis—in this little drama of the blind-tiger-turned-links:

During his last year as columnist for the New York *Herald Tribune* Marquis wrote that he had just learned that due to his having earned money by writing about golf he had automatically lost his amateur standing. He was now a professional!

One day he found himself in front of one of those Broadway

specialty shops, which, in those days, printed calling cards while you waited. Marquis stepped in and had a card printed which proclaimed:

DON MARQUIS
Golf Pro   Lessons Cheap

Unable to drum up business any other way he offered to give Clive Weed lessons for drinks. Weed accepted and they repaired to a speakeasy where they were well known. Marquis carried two golf clubs, one for his pupil and one for himself.

Marquis recalled that this particular grog-shop always had some edibles on the bar, hard-boiled eggs invariably among them; and for the purpose of instruction an egg would serve as well as a golf ball. They had a drink, Marquis having routed his will power that day, and sought the privacy of a back room that was reserved for private parties. Since there was none that day, pro-golfer Marquis and his pupil took it over as a classroom.

When Marquis teed up his hard-boiled egg he had no intention of hitting it. He would go through the motions of demonstrating his swing for the benefit of his one-man student body and bring his club around a few inches above the egg. Nevertheless, when he swung he hit the egg a resounding smack and it landed with authority against the forward wall. Marquis said it was a great day for science: he had discovered a new and swift way of de-shelling a hard-boiled egg. But an even more important discovery, he thought, was that the way to connect with a golf ball was to try not to. He said he had met that egg more squarely than he had ever hit a golf ball and now he was in possession of a great secret, one which at least applied to Don Marquis and would probably result in his winning all the major golf titles in the country: that you missed when you tried and connected when you didn't. This, he thought, had the makings of a good short story, the one Grant Rice tried to get him to write: how the author became the greatest golfer in the history of the game.

Marquis's last tour of duty in Hollywood had been more of a disappointment than his previous ones. He had thought that, profiting by his earlier experience, he would be able to help create an important motion picture—something that would be worth reviving for years to come because it would be timeless and eternally appropriate. He had talked about renewing his Hollywood activities merely for the pay checks; but this did not fool intimates who knew that he hoped to have a hand in producing at least one motion picture of enduring worth.

Back in New York at the brownstone on East 62nd Street, Marquis decided to turn his back on Hollywood forever. He would put most of his creative energy into *Sons of the Puritans*, the new title of the "big book" that he hoped would solidify his reputation as a writer and help solve his financial problems. He would write a good novel that would sell. Others had done it and he felt he could, too.

Much of the copy Marquis wrote in those days was characterized by the same gay unorthodoxy that typified his earlier work; so he was inherently the same person, with mirth and disillusion battling for possession of his mind. In the old days mirth came out on top—superficially, at least—no matter how troubled his spirit. Now disillusion was winning on all counts; and the reason, Dr. March thought, was that his patient was used up physically. Once he could make his typewriter "sing," as he put it, and "write himself out of a hole" in a few weeks. At the very least, he would be able to meet current expenses. Now he was getting deeper in debt because that amazing productivity of his, which he seemingly thought would continue endlessly, was now a thing of the past. It was an ordeal, for instance, to write a short story. Ideas were almost as plentiful as in his heyday but he was finding it more and more difficult to execute them. He complained of feeling exhausted from the time he rose to the time he retired.

Now that he was incapable of sustained creative work and had time to brood, his mind drifted back to "his dead," as he called them in several poems—Bobby, Reina, Barbara. In the final couplet of a sonnet sequence he had written:

> Give me your mirth. It bores me when you weep.
> My loves you cannot touch. They're buried deep.

Marquis no longer wanted anyone's mirth. He wanted to be left alone.

One day, in a moody moment, Marquis figured that if Bobby had lived he would be nearing his twenty-first birthday. Memories of Bobby had previously been revived by telephone calls for Marjorie's little boy Walter (who was nicknamed "Colonel") when Marquis thought the voices sounded like his yellow-haired son who had died in 1921 at the age of five. It will be recalled that Edith McDonald, Marquis's secretary, was present when he picked up the telephone and took one of these calls, reporting that it shook him up badly. Other things reminded him of Reina and of Barbara. He was having a bad time.

When he was convinced that he could no longer compose on the typewriter and "make the words come tumbling out," as he had once put it, he decided to try his hand at dictating the rest of his novel. Although he had misgivings about this method of writing he wanted to give it a fair trial. He was bogged down and had nothing to lose.

In 1932 when he was hospitalized at the Harkness Pavilion (in New York's Presbyterian Medical Center) after suffering what was described by Dr. Gordon M. Bruce as "a small stroke," he managed to dictate one of his *Collier's* pieces to Miss McDonald. But, by and large, he had not had much success at composition by the dictation method. In 1925 he had given it a trial when his then secretary, Harold Winney, had urged him to buy a Dictaphone and use it as a means of easing his burden. But in less than a week he had abandoned it and was back pounding out his column on the typewriter. In commenting on his experiment with this "modern efficiency device" he had this to say (March 13, 1925) in his column: "All I have been able to do with it is to foster a kind of copiousness of voice together with a sort of poverty of intellectual output."

When Marquis stopped using his Dictaphone he placed it on the floor of his office in the house on 62nd Street. After stumbling over it several times he kidded Winney about having talked him into buying that blankety-blank machine which had taken a dislike to him and was doing its best to trip him up and break his neck. Winney, a humorless young man, made an elaborate apology. Marquis decided to give the Dictaphone to Winney but before he had a chance to do so his secretary had utterly vanished. "Only the day before," Marquis told Weed, "we had been discussing the next day's work. In the morning Winney failed to report. He didn't telephone and I never heard from him again."

Getting back to 1936, Mrs. Marquis confided to Miss McDonald that her husband was having more and more "bad days." When he was not in the mood to dictate or seemed too weary to continue, she was not to press him; she was to busy herself with other tasks and wait for him to announce that he was ready to begin or to resume, as the case might be. (Miss McDonald reported for work daily at the Marquis home and operated on a nine-to-five schedule.)

When the words did not fall into place properly as he dictated passages of his novel, he would try to dictate parts of his egobiography—referring to it for the first time as "this autobiography"—and when he found himself stymied in that venture too, he made a few attempts to write direct on the typewriter as of old. But it didn't take him long to discover that he no longer had the stamina for that.

Miss McDonald pictures Marjorie Marquis as a thoughtful, understanding wife who was deeply concerned about her husband's now chronic moodiness. Sometimes he would sit for long minutes at a stretch and stare straight ahead, his face expressionless until some thought occurred to him that seemed worth recording, when a faint smile would register as he interrupted his immobility to make a note. The worst thing that could happen to him in such moments was a telephone call from his sister Maud.

The memorabilia-filled notebook that Miss McDonald turned over to me contains some interesting side lights on the business of recording the thoughts of a writer in the throes of dictating—or trying to dictate—a novel, as for instance:

"Once when Mr. Marquis was dictating new material for 'Sons of the Puritans' he seemed to be having trouble putting his thoughts together. He turned to me and said in distress, 'I can't make them do what I want them to.' The characters seemed to have become so real to him that they had taken the plot out of his hands."

"Good writing," Marquis had told an audience of Yale university students in 1926, "is an agony of effort." But in the old days, when the agonizing was over, "the words came tumbling out." Now he didn't have many words to show for his mental anguish.

On his bad days—that is, when he failed to accomplish anything on *Sons of the Puritans*, his overriding interest—Marquis made an effort, occasionally a successful one, to add to his egobiography, which since the days several years earlier when he had first started it had developed into a rather sizable manuscript. These passages took the form of miscellanies that he later planned to fit in where he thought they belonged. Here are some typical results as dictated in the third person to Miss McDonald:

"Notes, egobiography:

"The parts of this autobiography which sound the most utterly cuckoo are probably going to have the most sense in them . . . for instance, the discovery that if you quit looking at the Devil, and look long enough and steadily enough at God, the Devil vanishes, and with him the problem of evil in the universe. And that is good, sound, orthodox Christian Science, too; Marquis's secretary, who has just taken it down, says it is good Christian Science, and she ought to know, for she belongs to that church.

"Marquis's tendency towards orthodoxy, he has sometimes thought, is a little too strong. For he has, unfortunately, a tendency to embrace in turn *all* the orthodoxies . . . orthodox Buddhism, orthodox Moslemism, orthodox Shintoism, orthodox Judaism, as well as orthodox Christianity. Christopher Morley complained of it one time.

" 'You embrace too many doxies,' he said.

" 'Sir!' expostulated Marquis.

" 'Oh, I don't mean what *you* are thinking of,' said Kit. 'I mean orthodoxies.'

"But what is one to do when one sees value in all these things? Deny it? Stultify the instinct, the spirit, the intellect?

"Marquis's belief in so many different things would, under any circumstances, prevent him from being a martyr to any one of them. It would be absurd to die for six or eight different creeds, even if it could be managed.

"At the same time, the absurdity of any given cause has never seemed to keep people from dying for it. Willingness to die for an idea is not really good testimony as to its truth.

"Ask people to die for almost anything and, if you speak sufficiently like a trumpet, they will respond by thousands.

"Marquis has never been able to get away from a belief in miracles; not only the Jewish and Christian miracles narrated in the Bible and elsewhere, but miracles of all sorts, ancient and modern: Buddhist miracles, Hindu miracles, Mormon miracles, Persian miracles, Egyptian miracles, Chinese miracles, Afro-American miracles, Los Angeles miracles.

"If I am weak in my faith anywhere, it is with regard to Moslem miracles. I seem to remember reading that, on one occasion, Mahomet could not make a mountain come to him, so he had to go to the mountain. Contrast this with the utterance of Jesus to the effect that if one has faith only as a grain of mustard seed one may move mountains, and the superiority of the Christian religion over the Moslem religion is at once apparent.

"At the same time, one must not be too hard on Mahomet. It is possible that on the occasion when he tried to make the mountain come to him he was surrounded by people who had known him all his life and were, therefore, naturally incredulous of his powers. The Bible specifically states that Jesus had no great success with his miracles in the neighborhood of Nazareth, where he had grown up, because the inhabitants had so little faith in his ability. Mahomet may have encountered a similar incredulity. It seems to take at least two to make a miracle, the performer and a sympathetic subject or a sympathetic audience.

"The miracles of healing performed by Jesus and certain of his followers, in his own time on earth and even since, have Marquis's entire approbation. He only wishes there had been more of them. Why not a general blanket miracle, so to speak, removing all the ills of humanity with one large and generous gesture? . . .

"A miracle of which Marquis does *not* approve, although he cannot help believing in it, is related on the indisputable authority of St. Matthew:

Now in the morning as he returned to the city he hungered.

And when he saw a fig tree in the way, he came to it, and
found nothing thereon, but leaves only, and said to it,
Let no fruit grow on thee henceforward forever. And presently the fig tree withered away.

And when the disciples saw it, they marvelled, saying,
How soon is the fig tree withered away!

"Reflection: One would think that the creation of a world with enough faith in it so as to be saved by its faith would be easy enough for a beneficent and omnipotent God.

"But that sort of reflection is unprofitable. It can lead nowhere else except straight to another attempt to consider the problem of evil in the universe—and what do you get when you consider that? Only a headache. The best thing to do with a reflection such as that is just to leave it lie where it is, and walk round it and pretend you don't know it's there, and trust to some future inspiration, some divine revelation, to get rid of it . . . some bolt of white fire from the heavens to come slanting down and consume it. . . ."

Even though he considered material such as the foregoing publishable (once he got it organized and dropped each passage into the particular slot where it belonged) he didn't derive much satisfaction in those days from writing anything that did not contribute to the advancement of his novel. This was the book on which his reputation would ultimately depend, the one that would put him back on his feet financially. He figured that he had the equivalent of about 225 printed pages that had merit, followed by several inferior chapters that would have to be rewritten. There were three projected endings and he would not be able to decide which was best until he rewrote the unsound pages.

Marquis had an unhealthy look in those days—his face was described as "ashen and puffy"—and solicitous friends urged him to suspend work for a month or longer and take a vacation. But before they had a chance to sell the idea Marquis suffered a cerebral hemorrhage, his second.

There is reason to believe that, although he was disturbed when he was compelled to take to his bed, he doubted whether there was anything serious about this mishap since there was no impairment of his faculties. Somehow he had come by the notion that if you suffered a stroke and there was no resultant paralysis, it didn't amount to much. The doctors thought differently.

Mrs. Marquis did not deny her husband medical attention though she herself leaned so heavily on Christian Science that it never occurred to her to send for a doctor until something drastic happened and her husband asked for one, as in the case of this latest illness. Some of Marquis's intimates described his wife as anti-medic. Others, as recently as 1960, told me that it wasn't so much a case of her being "anti" as of living in a world of her own in which doctors did not exist.

Marquis, wrapped up in his work, was not doctor-conscious. In magazine articles he had proclaimed himself a hypochondriac and since editors liked the joke he gave them copious doses of it. It helped pay the bills. But actually he was not a good example of hypochondria. If there was work to be done he did it. How he happened to feel had little to do with it. If he could drag himself to a typewriter and find the keys, whatever had to be written was written. In the old days on the *Evening Sun* when Dana Burnet filled in for Marquis it was generally when the boss of "The Sun Dial" was too sick to drag himself out of bed, look a typewriter in the eye, and pound out a column.

A study of Marquis's medical history reveals that from 1921 on, when he was forty-three years old, he was plagued by an assortment of ailments. In view of this, his productivity was remarkable—thousands of newspaper columns, scores of magazine articles and short stories, and twenty-eight books (some of them collections on which he did considerable work, a few of them collections on which he did none).

In a letter to Gamaliel Bradford dated February 26, 1922, Marquis estimated—in explaining why he hadn't published more poetry—that he had written ten million words from 1902 to 1922, "most of it necessarily very bad stuff, for the newspapers," he characteristically hastened to add.

In February 1936 Marquis suffered a third stroke. "After this stroke," Miss McDonald wrote on June 27, 1960, "he was unable to do any work. His speech was affected and also his sense of locomotion. That was the end of my employment by Mr. Marquis.

"At that time Mrs. Marquis asked me to give up my room at 808 Lexington Ave. and take a room in their house. Her daughter Ruth had married the previous year, and after Mr. Marquis's third stroke, I believe she felt a great weight of responsibility. I paid the rental for my room and when Mrs. Marquis needed letters written or someone wanted a copy of a manuscript, she paid me by the particular piece of work. I had started doing free lance secretarial work and was out of the house most of the time, but could always find time to look through files or attend to details about things I had handled for Mr. Marquis.

"During early July, 1936 I visited my sister and her family in Georgia for about two weeks. On returning to New York, Mrs. Marquis told me she had leased an apartment at 276 Riverside Drive, and they moved very shortly afterwards. Mrs. Marquis asked me to go with them. . . ."

The move from midtown to Riverside Drive was explained as a health measure—Don would now be able to sun himself in a wheel chair near the river, etc., etc. Intimates, however, knew that there was more to the story than that. The brownstone on East 62nd Street

had become too much of a financial burden, the threat of fore-
closure having proven nerve-racking on several occasions.

Marquis's condition was said to be improving. This is reflected in
a letter from Mrs. Marquis's daughter, Ruth, to a West Coast cousin
of her stepfather's (in which she called Marquis "Uncle Don").
In her letter Ruth, now Mrs. Daniel Carroll, reported two communications from her mother conveying that "Uncle Don was recovering."

Mrs. Carroll mentioned that her mother was "so busy" that she
had not been able to write at length but that both her letters were
reassuring. Her mother was indeed busy. Don's incapacitation—she
had been told that he would be unable to work for at least a year—
had made an important decision for her. For some time she had
been considering the advisability of starting a dramatic school. She
had always wanted a connection with the dramatic arts that had
"continuity," as she had put it. Teaching had this characteristic and
she was confident that she would enjoy it.

Marjorie Marquis had been widely publicized during the thirty-
seven-week run of Eugene O'Neill's *Ah, Wilderness!*, in which George
M. Cohan had starred and she had been a featured player. The reviewers, it will be recalled, had unanimously praised her performance.
This publicity had made her reasonably well known in theatrical
circles, and would prove helpful, she thought, in getting her school
started. She had friends in the Theatre Guild and in the offices
of other producers and she was hopeful that they would have opportunities to recommend her.

Mildred Dilling, internationally known harpist and close friend
of Mrs. Marquis, recalls those days vividly. Miss Dilling remembers
the heavy responsibilities her friend Marjorie bore in 1936. With Don
incapable of working she was eager to get her acting school started
as a means of improving the family's financial position.

Miss Dilling also recalls being shocked by Marjorie Marquis's
appearance when she saw her prior to the move from the house on
East 62nd Street to Riverside Drive. "By any standard Marjorie was
a good-looking woman," Miss Dilling said, "but hers was an attrac-
tiveness that went beyond mere good looks. She had a magnificent
carriage. She was graceful, full of vitality. As she moved toward you
to greet you, you thought of an old but appropriate phrase: the
poetry of motion. Now, suddenly, all that was gone. She was bent,
listless, gaunt. She had lost considerable weight and that wonderful

carriage had vanished completely. Worry had taken its toll. It was shocking."

Marjorie had a partner in her proposed school of the dramatic arts, a woman who would be able to provide a certain amount of backing, though not enough to finance the venture. Marjorie and this associate hoped to interest others in investing in the enterprise.

The apartment at 276 Riverside Drive was a large one—eleven rooms. Some of these rooms would be pressed into service in the early stages of the school's development. The apartment would also serve, at the start, as headquarters for the operation.

There are pertinent references to this acting school in the following paragraph from Miss McDonald's memorandum of July 23, 1960:

"I would like to tell here about Mrs. Marquis's activities during the spring and summer of 1936. She had written a play,—I think a dramatic and very good play—which she was trying to sell. Also she had talked in person and exchanged letters with a woman friend—whose name after all these years I cannot recall—about starting a school for young actors, and I do remember that the plans for the school had really begun to take shape. . . . Mrs. Marquis was very much interested in the idea, and it was only after moving into the apartment that she did not seem to feel equal to going ahead with it."

For the next few months Marquis was an in-and-outer. He showed improvement one day, lost ground the next. One barometer was his speech. Some days he was incapable of speaking even a few words, or perhaps it was too much of an effort; at other times he was able to carry on a brief conversation. The fact that he was able to make notes—notes that indicated his mind was functioning—was encouraging to Marjorie and a few friends (members of the Players) who were permitted to call. But his long-time friend and physician, Dr. March, thought this note-taking was too much of a strain and discouraged it.

Rollin Kirby, one of the few who were allowed to call—(Dr. March said Kirby's calls had a tonic effect on his patient)—declared after one of these visits that some notes, abbreviated and hard to decipher, that Marquis asked him to read revealed that their author had not lost his sense of humor.

There is no clear evidence as to the significance of these notes; nor is there any way of verifying which, if any, of the many notes found among Marquis's papers were made during this particular period. An old friend of the family has produced two Marquis items which he believes were written early in 1936, some time between the third cerebral hemorrhage and the move to Riverside Drive. Here they are:

> I wish I did not fear you so much, Lord!
> It makes me such a hypocrite.
> Frequently
> The thunderous reverberations of your voice
> Terrify me so greatly
> That I fail to grasp the meaning of your words.
> I am willing to promise you anything when I am frightened,
> Just so we both thoroughly understand
> That I probably won't be able to live up to it
> When I get over being scared.

> > I am not one of those who wait,
> > Cowered in a corner, the last stroke of Fate.
> > Whether towards Dawn or into black eclipse,
> > Proudly I go with Song upon my lips.
> > Speak thus of me: nor Life nor Death could bind
> > The scornful pinions of his laughing mind.

The last two lines of the foregoing, with slight variations, appear in two or three places in Marquis's published work.

I found a copy of the first poem in the Don Marquis Collection at the Butler Library, Columbia University, where there are also several versions of the second—one that duplicates the foregoing and a few longer treatments of the same idea. But there are no clues as to when they were written.

Marquis, like many another poet, began writing about death as a young man—in fact, he once referred to the subject in "The Sun Dial" as "one of the standard props of the poetry business"—so, lacking specific proof, the second of these poems cannot confidently be described as premonitory. Our source, who has provided much helpful documentation in other areas, and many helpful suggestions, dissents, believing that Marquis wrote this poem—or fragment—on one of his bad days in 1936 when he despaired of recovering.

It is hard to gauge with accuracy what Marquis's condition actually was after that third stroke. We know it was serious but there is a difference of opinion as to whether it was hopeless.

In a letter to a relative dated February 22, 1936, Marquis's sister Maud wrote from her home in Forest Hills:

"On Feb. 2nd in the evening I talked to Don over the 'phone. He was cheerful, said he had a bad cold and dreaded to go out. I begged him not to try to come, although I had not seen him since New Year's Day. I did not hear from him again until Tuesday morning at 11 o'clock. Dr. Harry March, a long-time friend of Don's, called us saying Don had had a stroke. It might be a question of hours, he might linger along, might get up again.

"Nev got ready and went right in. She went all to pieces. I had to brace up and manage. I have not been on the ground since the middle of September. Not able to be out of bed at all until within the last month. I called a nurse and sent her off. After she was gone I got to thinking that he might go and I never see him again, like Barbara, only *then* we were not told she was in bed.

"I called a taxi, cannot climb stairs to trains. The nurse and I drove in (to New York) and I saw him for about ten minutes. He knew me and understood what I said but did not talk. . . .

"Dr. March says that he cannot do anything for him. He thinks the clot is absorbed. Thinks it a cerebral hemorrhage. We do not know. We are allowed to see him, but never alone. He is very glad to see Nev. Presses her arm and speaks a little. I do not feel satisfied but do not know what else to do. . . ."

Only twelve days later Marquis's stepdaughter, Ruth, wrote that letter in which she said, "Uncle Don is improving rapidly." This is quite a transition from the statement in Maud's fifth paragraph: "Dr. March says that he cannot do anything for him."

Marquis continued to be an in-and-outer. He had his good days and his bad ones. He did a little note-taking when he felt stronger and occasionally wrote a few lines of verse. He spent most of his time in his wheel chair looking out at the Hudson River. Occasionally a friend dropped in. Only a few callers were permitted and these were admonished not to discuss anything that might "excite" him or stir him into attempting more speech than was good for him. His speech impairment had not cleared up and some days it required too much of an effort to put words together clearly.

During that dismal period Marquis was cheered by letters from his old friend, the well-known playwright A. E. Thomas, who was in Hollywood writing the screenplay for the talking-picture version of *The Old Soak*, which had been produced some years before as a "silent."

Thomas was disturbed because of his inability to get MGM to stick to the original title. They insisted on changing it to *Good Old Soak*, arguing that the public was accustomed to having Wallace Beery's "goodness" accentuated. In this picture he played the bibulous Clem Hawley and, in line with the formula for Beery pictures, Thomas had been instructed to stress Clem's Heart of Gold by way of helping audiences overlook his weakness for liquor. The new title, *Good Old Soak*, began with the word that Beery fans, according to MGM, considered synonymous with their star.

Rollin Kirby reportedly got a laugh out of Marquis by pointing out on one of his visits to Riverside Drive that, if Don were still running a column, MGM's announcement of the forthcoming movie would have stimulated stacks of letters from contributors pointing out the appropriateness of a man named Beery playing the Old Soak (even though the Old Soak had once dismissed beer in "The Sun Dial" as "a soft drink").

The resale of *The Old Soak* to the movies was excellent for Marquis's morale. Metro paid a good price for it, the first important sale the ailing writer had made in some time. This whole development could not have been timelier. Marquis's physician thought his patient's condition had been worsened by worry over the fact that his indebtedness had been steadily growing, with little income to balance it.

In the meantime Doubleday, Doran and Company had a problem involving the incapacitated Marquis. After conferring with Dr. March they arrived at the conclusion that he would be unable to finish *Sons of the Puritans*, the "big book," which, as he had once put it, "I've been in training for all my life." Reluctantly Dr. March ventured the opinion that it would be dangerous for his patient to undertake the kind of sustained concentration and hard work which, as the matter was explained to him, the completion of this novel would entail. With luck, Marquis might be able to turn out some short stuff later on but the novel was out of the question.

Marquis's editor, Harry E. Maule, wrote Elmer Davis, former newspaperman and a friend of Marquis's who had achieved success in the 1920s and '30s with novels of a higher quality than most popular fiction. He explained the problem and asked Davis whether he could undertake the completion of *Sons of the Puritans*.

On July 13, 1936, Davis wrote Maule as follows from Mystic, Connecticut:

"Dear Harry: This is a matter calling for the most delicate consideration.

"In principle, I should be very happy to do the job if it could be done to the universal satisfaction, but that depends on a number of factors. For one thing, I couldn't do it right unless I got into the spirit of it and felt I could do it right. I am much involved at present and couldn't get at it for some time in any case, but I take it that this is not an immediate job. If you have several copies of the manuscript, perhaps you could mail one to me here (I can't come in town at present) with any notes on what Don's intentions were for the conclusion, and then I could see whether I could do it. But if you have only one copy, for God's sake keep it in the safe at Garden City.

"There is, however, another and even more serious aspect of the case. If somebody else finishes Don's big novel, it amounts to a public notice that Don is dead. I take it that the matter would be kept secret, but there is one person from whom it couldn't be kept secret—Don himself. You know how a writer feels about a novel, especially his big novel. . . . If it were done unsuccessfully he wouldn't like it, and perhaps might like it even less if it were done successfully. To let somebody else finish this particular novel is simply a notice to Don that the sooner he is buried the better.

"So it would depend first of all on how Don feels about it. If he understands the situation and is willing to sacrifice everything else to the need of making some money for his family—which is the way I imagine I'd feel in his case—then any friend of his would be willing to go ahead, naturally without charge. Provided of course he could do the job at all; it would be no use doing it badly. If you could find out positively about Don's feelings, and then let me look over a copy to see if I could get into it, perhaps by that time my own affairs may have cleared up so that I could take the time. Which at present I could not."

On receipt of this letter the matter was tactfully taken up with Marquis, who stated that Davis would be acceptable to him and that he would like to explain to him on one of his "good days" what he had in mind by way of bringing his novel to a close. Davis wanted to do the job but subsequently found that his own commitments would necessitate his deferring it indefinitely and suggested that someone else be given the assignment. Homer Croy—author of the successful novel *West of the Water Tower*—was approached but declined on the ground that he did not believe he could satisfactorily complete Marquis's book. Croy, offered a thousand dollars to do the job, took the position that he would undertake it for nothing if he thought he could write in a style that sounded like Marquis's or could simulate his friend's philosophy and individualism.

For further information on Marquis's condition we turn to a letter from Christopher Morley, dated July 24, 1936, to George Middleton:

"Dear George: The situation about poor Don seems to be pretty hopeless. I don't think there is anything any of us can do except try to ease the financial problem in any way possible and trust that time may show some improvement. I am keeping regularly in touch with Marjorie."

If the record means anything, at no time did Marjorie Marquis despair of her husband's "complete recovery." She responded to all inquiries—written and telephoned—with optimistic reports which seemed to be based largely on her faith in Christian Science. Her symbol of the healing powers of Mary Baker Eddy continued to be the clubfoot which a Christian Science practitioner had "cured" when she was in her teens. (In addition to having *Science and Health* read to him by Marjorie, Marquis was ministered to by Christian Science practitioners—referred to by Maud Marquis and others as "C.S. doctors"—and by Christian Science nurses.) "Everything is being done," Marjorie reported to Rollin Kirby.

Maud Marquis, who for the first time in her life seemed whole-heartedly concerned about her brother, addressed the following letter —on August 11, 1936—to New York City's Health Department:

"Would you please inform me what the law is in the following case: A man of 57 was stricken with paralysis last February. His wife is a Christian Scientist. Some time after he had this stroke his wife called a regular physician who diagnosed the case as cerebral hemorrhage. This physician aided her to get power of attorney to manage his property. After that she did not welcome the physician, who is an old friend of her husband, so that his calls have been infrequent.

"I am a sister of this man, our father was a regular physician. I do not believe in Christian Science, holding the opinion of Mark Twain, yet neither I nor my sister, my brother's only relatives, combat his wife having the Christian Science practitioner.

"My brother had enlargement of the heart while he was in California a few years ago. He was treated by Dr. John V. Barrow of Los Angeles. He has for many years been subject to spasmodic heart pains, whether nervous or anginal I do not know. He told me that when he had them he took codeine or called a doctor. After the pain was relieved he read Science and Health, presumably to keep peace in the family.

"My sister and I have been regimented, barred from seeing him except for long intervals, the door to his dwelling has been locked in our faces. He has not been allowed to see any of his friends. She alleges that this is by doctor's orders. As I told you above, he has no regular physician and neither the one whom I mentioned nor the C.S. practitioner has ever been present when we have been there. So that the statements are not supported by evidence.

"Some months ago when I went in to see him I found him alone for a few moments. The Christian Science nurse or his wife is always present all of the time when we see him. I found him clutching his heart and head with his left hand. I said, "Are you in pain?" He said, "Yes." I said, "Do you want a doctor?" He said, "Yes." I got as far as, "Shall I send ——" when his wife entered the room. He looked at her in a terrified manner and said, "No, no!" Every time she turned her back he made a horrible face at her.

"Through the instrumentality of a friend I succeeded in getting a physician from the Neurological Institute in to see him. This physician said he could not make a complete diagnosis in the short time he was permitted to see him but that he thought his recovery was doubtful but not impossible under proper care, in fact he should be in a hospital or some place where his care was under authorized medical treatment.

"Since that time his wife's animosity toward us has redoubled. We have not quarreled nor answered her allegations and have submitted to her regulations tactfully.

"Last Saturday we went to see him and found him very much worse. His right leg, of which he has no use, and his hands were swollen double, his foot was cold and discolored. He kept showing it to me like a wounded dog would.

"He had what the doctors called a stroke two years ago, was suddenly stricken blind. But he could then speak. His wife begged him not to go into a hospital but he did and recovered.

"Now to sum up—has any person the right to subject a man, even if he is her husband, to Christian Science treatment alone when he cannot tell what he wants or is prevented from telling it to anyone who should ask him? His mind is not so good as it was at the first but he understands what one says and answers decidedly yes or no. Should he not be allowed to say what he wants? Does not the law allow him this privilege?

"No one except the servants in the house and the Christian Scientist practitioner is allowed to see him, that is, none of his friends. We have hesitated about taking a stand in this matter for fear of his wife creating a disturbance and making him worse. But, now that his condition is most critical, he will die anyway.

"Must this man die without help? What is the law?

"The man in question is Don Marquis, whose writing you may be familiar with. My statements can be verified. I have lived in Forest Hills for over twelve years and I can cite you to well-known people who will vouch for my veracity and sanity.

"Please pardon me for my lack of brevity. Sincerely yours, Bernice Maud Marquis"

I have examined scores of letters written by Maud Marquis. Of those on controversial subjects this is the most restrained. It suggests consultation with a calmer mind—perhaps her sister Nev, whose advice she did not often seek. In a letter of apology to Christopher Morley, whom she had offended by rudely rebuffing his efforts to help her in a situation on which she had sought his aid, Maud confessed that her sister Nev had told her that usually her letters of apology were worse than the original offense and that therefore she was composing this one carefully. Morley continued to help her—financially, be it added—but through a third party, since he wanted no further direct contact with "the old eldritch."

When consulted, Nev exercised a restraining hand and it is quite possible that this was true in the case of the letter to the New York City Health Department, which sounded more like Nev than Maud. At any rate, it is the only letter of record by Maud in which she discusses the Christian Science complications affecting her ailing brother without subordinating the problem itself to lengthy, bitter fulminations. Efforts to learn what, if anything, the Health Department said in reply have been unavailing.

A pertinent supplement to the foregoing is to be found in a letter Nunnally Johnson sent me on June 5, 1961, from which I quote:

"After Don's [last] stroke, when he lay there like a vegetable, I received a telephone call at the Plaza Hotel, where I had just arrived from Hollywood for a few days, from one of Don's sisters . . . She asked if I could think of any way that she could get in to see Don. I had no idea what she was talking about. Her explanation then was that she and her sister thought that Don should receive proper medical attention. But as she went on to explain, Don's second wife was a Christian Scientist and the only attention Don was getting was a daily visit from a Christian Scientist reader . . .

"I learned then for the first time that there is no law compelling medical attention of any kind to anybody, once the authorities have satisfied themselves that the ailment is not infectious, contagious, or epidemic in any way. In other words, Mrs. Marquis was within her rights in taking no more orthodox care of Don than this Christian Science attention. It seemed barbaric to me, but there was nothing I could do about it. I didn't know the second Mrs. Marquis, and even if I had known her it seemed unlikely that I could alter her religious convictions in the matter. And so I was compelled to tell Don's sister that there was nothing I could do about it. The poor woman must have been desperate to come to me, for I knew her and her sister very slightly. She must have appealed to everybody else first."

On July 30, 1936, Marjorie Marquis sent the following letter to Maule:

"Enclosed is a copy of the letter from Mr. Cyril Clemens awarding Don the Mark Twain Medal for 1936. Also a list of the former 'holders of the title.' I am writing Mr. Clemens to ask him to produce the medal, if any, soon!—though not exactly in those words!"

Whether there had actually ever been a "bestowal," to use the Society's own word, cannot be determined. It does not appear so. A careful search of the Marquis clippings in newspaper morgues disclosed no information about this medal nor is there any further reference to it in the Doubleday, Doran files. Here is an explanation, from a source that has proved reliable in other areas, as to why Marquis apparently never received the award for which he had been named:

After his organization had named Marquis for the 1936 medal, Cyril Clemens is said to have been reminded by an associate that several years earlier he had tendered this same Don Marquis an "honorary vice-presidency" in the Society and that the latter had declined in an "ungentlemanly letter." Efforts to find a carbon copy of this letter proved unavailing. Told by a former associate of Marquis's that "someone had put it in an anthology of snappy retorts," I conducted a search and by a stroke of luck found it in *Insults*, published in 1941 by the Greystone Press, edited by Max Herzberg and described by him in his subtitle as "A Practical Anthology of Scathing Remarks and Acid Portraits." Here is the letter of declination Marquis sent to Cyril Clemens, as published in Mr. Herzberg's book:

"My dear Mr. Clemens: I am in receipt of your letter offering me an Honorary Vice-Presidency in the Mark Twain Society.

"I don't wish to appear unappreciative or ungrateful—but I notice that Premier Benito Mussolini is Honorary President; and if I can't also be an Honorary President I don't think I want to join.

"Is there any office higher than Honorary President? I mean, except President—I notice you are President yourself, and of course I don't expect that. But isn't there an office in between Mussolini's and yours that I could have; higher than Honorary President but not as high as President.

"If there is, put me down for it. But if there isn't, I'm afraid I can't join—it's not jealousy, really; it's a matter of principle not to let a foreigner like Mussolini have a higher office than mine, even if he is funnier than I am. Yours cordially and sincerely, Don Marquis."

Toward the end of September 1936 there were two sick people in the apartment at 276 Riverside Drive. Marjorie Marquis was the other. The many ramifications of the move from 62nd Street to the Drive had exhausted her. The sorting out and packing of Don's papers and manuscripts alone—the accumulation of over thirty-five years—was a big task, as was the bundling up of his countless books (many of them inscribed copies from fellow writers). . . . All this quite apart from the responsibility of dismantling a four-floor house—including basement—where the Marquises had lived for almost ten years, and removing its contents—furniture, general household furnishings, kitchenware, clothing, etc.—to an uptown address.

There had not been time to paint and decorate their new quarters before they moved in and Marjorie had the problem of unloading the family possessions in an apartment that was not ready for occupancy.

The suddenness of the move to Riverside Drive lends credence to the view of those who say that Don and Marjorie had to vacate the brownstone at 125 East 62nd Street by a certain date or make a payment on the house that represented far more money than they could scrape up at the time.

Marjorie, until her strength gave out, put in long hours trying to make their new home presentable. Until she could acquire the auditorium mentioned earlier in these pages, the apartment would have the added function of headquarters for the projected dramatic school. With an eye to business as well as good homemaking, she sought to make the premises as comfortable and attractive as possible.

It was not until she had worked herself into a state of near-collapse that Marjorie made the decision to postpone the school project indefinitely. She was so fagged out that she was compelled to take to her bed, an unusual proceeding for Marjorie Marquis, who did not believe in "giving in." In this instance she appears to have had no choice; the vigor, the tireless energy for which she was known had left her.

One day—the date was October 25, 1936—Marjorie Marquis was found dead in bed. She had died in her sleep while taking an afternoon nap.

A friend of the family who recalls that day says that when he called at the apartment he found Marquis "sobbing and babbling incoherently."

Dr. March, who was hastily summoned, found Marquis "in a state of dangerous excitement." He tried to make his patient realize that his frantic efforts to make himself understood merely accentuated his speech difficulties, made his words unintelligible, and sapped his waning vitality. But Marquis, too grief-stricken and too sick to be argued with, babbled on until he exhausted himself, when March gave him a sedative and put him to bed.

Later that day Dr. March ruled that the funeral service would be too much of an ordeal for Don and ordered him—through the nurse in attendance—not to attend. This edict upset Marquis, who indicated his intention of ignoring it.

It had been decided that the service for Marjorie was to be held in the commodious living room of the apartment on Riverside Drive which she had planned to use as a meeting place in connection with the contemplated dramatic school until such time as she could afford to make a deal for the building with the auditorium. It had been arranged with the nurse in charge that Marquis was to remain in his room until the rites were over. Mell Daniel, one of Don's closest friends who had been named many years before in Marquis's will as an executor, recalls visiting Don in his room not long before the services began. Don, in a state bordering on hysteria, prattled on disjointedly, his speech impediment obscuring his meaning, as it always did when he was overexcited. Daniel, moved but powerless to do anything, guessed that his friend was protesting the decision to confine him to his room.

And when the services started, Marquis was present, quietly sobbing. Dr. March was surprised to see his patient in the living room—no one seems to recall how he got there—but quickly decided it would be pointless to say anything further.

On October 26, 1936, the New York *Times* carried this story: "Mrs. Marjorie Potts Marquis, wife of Don Marquis, columnist and playwright, died yesterday at her home, 276 Riverside Drive, after an illness of several weeks. She was born forty-four years ago in Indianapolis, a daughter of Mr. and Mrs. A. F. Potts. In addition to her husband, she is survived by two children of her first marriage, Walter Vonnegut, Jr., and Mrs. Daniel Lynn Carroll, Jr. of San Diego, Calif.

"Mrs. Marquis was formerly an actress. She appeared in productions of The Stagers about ten years ago and later was with the Theatre Guild as the Queen in Shaw's 'The Apple Cart' and as Essie in Eugene O'Neil's 'Ah, Wilderness!' In 1926 she married Mr. Marquis, whose first wife died in 1923, after obtaining a divorce from Walter Vonnegut, actor."

In George Middleton's *These Things Are Mine,* "the autobiography of a journeyman playwright," the author alludes to the death of Marjorie, "Don's devoted second wife, an actress of talent and beauty, who had become a courageous, tragic figure in a domestic situation the Greek dramatists would have relished, inconceivable in its irony."

Middleton provides evidence of "the way Don's friends, quietly and sufficiently . . . expressed to a helpless comrade the affection and esteem in which all of his fellow writers and club mates held him. None more so than those who were about him during the Hollywood days of which I write.

"I am telling this as testimony of something else I was to learn of Hollywood. For that great sprawling, formless city, which made and crushed so many, was after all only a small town. Its heart, too, was as cruel. But it could also be as kind."

A letter has come to light that reveals that Marjorie Marquis was actively engaged in trying to establish her school of the dramatic arts only six weeks before her death. The letter is dated September 13, 1936, and addressed to Christopher Morley:

Dear Chris:

Do you or your son or Helen [Mrs. Morley] know of anyone interested to scout for pupils for my school on a 5% commission basis? There might be some prospects on the island. [The Morleys lived at Roslyn, Long Island.]

It's going to be a good school! Read the enclosed letter!

The pedagogy will be modern and stimulating rather than didactic. It's a splendid modern building too, with a restaurant, theatre and a museum and art gallery in it. Lot's doing.

We are also offering a scholarship to anyone bringing in five pupils!

Marjorie.

The "enclosed letter," to which Mrs. Marquis refers, has not been recovered. Presumably it was a prospectus—or the equivalent thereof—in which the advantages of the proposed school were described.

Marquis declined rapidly after Marjorie's death. His speech difficulty worsened, and only occasionally—and then by putting the words together a syllable at a time with painful deliberateness—was he able to make himself understood. On his really bad days, when he was incapable of communicating even a shred of his meaning, his frustration was pitiful to behold.

Mrs. Parry, the nurse who looked after Marquis, was an old friend of the family, capable and conscientious. She reported to Dr. March that the big apartment on Riverside Drive was now psychologically bad for his patient. It was full of reminders of Marjorie, and in his then emotional state these were bad for him. And there were also reminders from the outside. A few times Don overheard Mrs. Parry take telephone calls from people who apparently hadn't heard of Marjorie's death—once it was a tradesman calling, another time it was someone seeking information about the dramatic school. The effect of these calls on her patient, she reported, was "most unfortunate." Friends of Marquis's—members of the Players Club—began negotiating with the Sharp and Nassoit Management Corporation, through whom Marjorie had leased the apartment at 276 Riverside Drive, with the hope of working out a reasonable and amicable settlement that would release Marquis from the lonely bondage of an eleven-room apartment.

Not many days after Marjorie died, Norman W. Cook, Marquis's brother-in-law, and Mrs. Cook, Marjorie's sister, invited Marquis to take up residence with them in their home in Englewood, New Jersey. The idea appealed to him. He had found the Cooks kindly, considerate people, and he was sure he could get along with them.

At about the same time his sister Maud suggested that he move back to Forest Hills. Mrs. Parry reported at the time that Marquis had explained to her—and it took a lot of explaining because of his speech difficulties—that if the decision had involved going with the Cooks or with his sister Nev, he would have elected to join Nev, for he and the older of his two sisters had always hit it off. As Mell Daniel told the writer, "Don and Nev were cut from the same cloth. They understood, liked and respected each other." Maud was something else again.

One day Mrs. Parry, in the line of duty, informed Maud Marquis that Don had accepted the Cooks' invitation. Instead of viewing this as a gracious tender from friends whose only thought was to ease the plight of a stricken relative by marriage, Maud interpreted it as a challenge. These Cooks were meddlers. Implying ulterior motives, she took the position that they had exerted undue influence on her brother—or he would not have expressed a desire to take up residence with them instead of joining her and her sister, which was "the natural thing to do." It was merely a new version of a behavior pattern that had characterized Maud all her life. Rage had so clouded her judgment that she was incapable of recognizing the generosity of people who, in volunteering to look after a man as desperately sick as Don, were committing themselves to a program that would necessitate the reorganization of their household and their mode of living.

Maud, through Mrs. Parry, arranged a meeting with Mr. Cook at the Riverside Drive apartment. She lost no time in opening fire on that kindly gentleman and the discussion became acrimonious. She insisted that Don be present so that he could indicate by a nod of the head whether he wanted to live in Forest Hills or in Englewood. She was confident that her representations would cause him to change his mind. But it worked the other way. Maud's shocking rudeness to Cook made Don's decision for him; he indicated that he wanted to live with his brother-in-law. Infuriated, Maud stormed out of the apartment and returned with a policeman.

How Maud arrived at the conclusion that this was a police matter is anyone's guess. The policeman, who, of course, had no jurisdiction, decided nevertheless to do some enforcing; so, without benefit of authority, he assailed this busybody from Englewood who was trying "to bust up a family," ruling that Marquis should join his sisters in Forest Hills. Cook, having done his best to be helpful, then withdrew from the fray, having decided, according to Mrs. Parry, that it would only make things tougher for Don if he further contested the embattled Maud. According to the same source, Don looked on in horror while the struggle for possession of his paralyzed person was in progress. According to her, he kept waving his left arm at Maud—the right had been rendered useless by his last stroke—in an effort to get his sister to stop her shouted denunciation of Cook; but either because she did not understand her brother's gestures, or because she chose to ignore them, she continued her impassioned yipping. All in all, it was a bad day for Marquis.

When Don and Reina had occupied the house in Forest Hills they had enjoyed living there. In those days he made frequent references—once in print—to his "wonderful neighbors," the Burns Mantles, the John V. L. Hogans, the Homer Croys, the Lyman Beecher Stowes, Dr. Thompson Sweeney, the Malthe Hasselriises, the Dale Carnegies and others. His relations with Carnegie were put to the test when he burlesqued the Dale Carnegie success formula in his column. Carnegie enjoyed the joke and urged Marquis to make it a regular feature. It was good advertising for the D.C. enterprises, he thought, and only through repetition could advertising be expected to do a good job. The men became friends and that friendship was one of the reasons why Marquis once publicly proclaimed that Forest Hills had a sense of humor. The reader may be amused by a few passages from Marquis's mimicry of the Dale Carnegie success formula:

"Thrift cannot be too highly commended. Teach all those with whom you come in contact to be saving. You never know when you may need their savings to finance one of your ventures.

"Identify yourself publicly with some popular and sentimental form of charity, first being quite sure that its character is such that it will not disturb the foundations of the current social and economic system. You will find it a good investment. It will give you the air of being human and humane.

"Punctuality is one of the cardinal business virtues. Always insist on it in your subordinates and dependents."

In preparing to return to Forest Hills all Marquis could think of, he told Mrs. Parry through a combination of slow, deliberate, syllable-by-syllable speech and words printed out with his left hand, was that Maud was a quarrelsome woman who might prove even more so now that he had expressed a desire to live with the Cooks. She reassured him, declaring that his sister seemed eager to make amends for the past, an impression that proved correct.

With the advent of 1937 Marquis's condition was approximately what it had been during the last few months of 1936. He lay helpless in a second-floor bedroom of the house in Forest Hills. Directly to the left of the door was the bathroom where, fourteen years before, Reina had collapsed and died. When they brought him back to Forest Hills and carried him past this bathroom, he became excited and managed to put together enough words to indicate what had passed through his mind. His doctor pleaded with him not to speak of that tragic night again but of course no one could prevent him from *thinking* about it.

There is evidence that even in his helpless state Marquis occasionally had a return of that "incorrigible mirth" of which he had sometimes written semiapologetically, as if to explain his capacity for laughter when the gloom was thickest. "I remember one of his sisters telling me," wrote Christopher Morley in *Letters of Askance*, "that sometimes, during his long illness, he was heard laughing to himself. He was not able to communicate the matter of his mirth . . . but I like to think of that secret and unsharable communion. Gravity and levity were so mixed in Don's mind that it puzzled even himself, and certainly may have seemed shocking to many well-drilled citizens."

In a letter from Hollywood dated March 15, 1937, A. E. Thomas wrote his friend Marquis as follows:

"Dear Don: This is just to tell you that I have been having a swell time out here in Metro doing your Old Soak into a picture. It won't be as good as your play because, for one reason, the censors have lately become terribly booze-conscious on account of a lot of kicks from Methodists, Baptists and other Fundamentalist pests who complain that the pictures have been encouraging our young folks to drink likker. So we have had to struggle the best we could to keep them from sucking all the sap out of the show. However, Al is still in it and Nellie, too, and the parrot, though I am afraid you will find that a good deal of their guts have leaked out.

"Wallace Beery is playing the Old Soak and will be pretty good, I think. The picture is nearly completed and I am told that arrangements have been made so that you will be able to see it in your own home. And when that happens kindly remember what happened to you when you were out here in the studios and believe that I have done my darndest. Affectionately yours, A. E. Thomas

"P.S. I shall be back east in May and I shall come to see you if I am allowed."

Of the letters (many have been recovered) written at that time by Maud Marquis, one addressed on March 19, 1937, to a favorite cousin is the most informative. Among other things, it contains an allusion to the forthcoming special showing in the Marquis home in Forest Hills of *The Old Soak*—renamed *Good Old Soak* by MGM—which was mentioned by A. E. Thomas in his letter dated not many days earlier.

Here is Maud Marquis's letter, from which a number of passages that are not pertinent have been removed:

"Please do not think I have not wanted to write. If I enumerated all of the reasons why I have not done so my letter would have to go parcel post or express.

"I am superintendent of a small hospital, manager and part-time patient, a dishwasher, laundress, secretary, business manager of this small estate, litigant in the town house (at 125 E. 62 St., N.Y.C.), etc., etc. . . .

"This sounds egotistical, and it is. My ego is overworked,—as Don used to say, a Rolls Royce engine in a Ford body.

"Where is sister, where is she? *Always* on call, always patient, always slow, plodding along uncomplainingly. I couldn't keep up without her. . . . The only way I keep up my courage and driving power is to say,—'Self, get thee behind me.'

"The one and only thing is Don. He is in a sad condition, as you know, but the very fact that he has lived this long, over a year, nine months of which he had not the proper care, shows that there is both a physical and mental power yet.

"Beside the paralysis caused by the cerebral hemorrhage, he has bronchial trouble, myocorditis, hemorrhoids, and passed a small kidney or bladder stone. This you see calls for expert medical and nursing ability. Our physician has his home office here; he attended me two years. He is a man of sympathy and understanding. Besides him we have had specialists from the Neurological Institute, and others to make all sorts of tests. We keep two men nurses. These nurses have to be cooked for, waited on, etc.

"Don's greatest suffering is mental, his inability to talk, and there is where we have to come in. The nurses can figure out his physical needs but only we can minister to his spiritual. He is very difficult at times as he gets excited and provoked because we do not always understand but for the most part he is sweet and patient.

"We have had such wonderful friends, expressions of sympathy pour in every day and everyone wants to help in material ways. For a few months friends at the Players helped us . . . but, thank God, we got 50% of the sale of the Old Soak for the cinema. That does not mean royalties, but the selling price of the rights by Arthur Hopkins.

"Our expenses are enormous, do what we will. We have back taxes of three years on this place, had to pay heaped up back services bills. The furnace blew up, kitchen stove played out, roof leaked, etc., etc.

"The 'boys' at the Saturday Review of Literature gave Don a wheel-chair for Christmas, the American Academy of Arts and Letters have contributed $500.

"A letter just came from A. E. Thomas from L.A. telling Don about the progress of The Old Soak and saying his friends are going to arrange to show Don the picture here in the house! Isn't that glorious?

"A letter also came to me asking me to exhibit my work at the Pen and Brush and give a talk. I've had to submerge myself but I am going to try to do this. . . ."

At lunch one day in the spring of 1960 I showed the foregoing to John V. L. Hogan, a Forest Hills friend and neighbor of Marquis's, and a fellow Player. Hogan, a man with a sense of humor and constitutionally reluctant to criticize anyone, said he couldn't help chuckling over the second and third paragraphs of Maud's letter, as well as the fourth in which she patronizingly refers to her sister Nev as "always on call." Anyone who knew the workings of that house, he pointed out, was aware that Nev, not Maud, was the mainstay. One of the doctors in attendance during the period described in Maud's letter had told him that Nev, an early riser, usually had done two to four hours' work before her sister had "climbed out of bed." Hogan said that Nev, realizing Maud's need for appearing to be the "executive" who kept things running, submerged herself in the presence of others, giving some the impression that Maud *did* run the show. Maud was more active, Hogan added, than she had been during the previous two or three years (when she spent most of her days in bed) but it was Nev who "kept that household from falling apart."

Marquis saw the "talkie" version of *The Old Soak* from his wheel chair. The story is partially told in this advance news item from the New York *Herald Tribune* for May 29, 1937: "Don Marquis, playwright and author, who has been ill at his home in Forest Hills, L.I., will see the film version of his comedy, 'The Old Soak,' tonight at his home, through the courtesy of Loew theatres. The new title of the comedy is 'The Good Old Soak.'"

Some of Marquis's favorite scenes had to be dropped to please the censors but he was reportedly pleased with the inclusion of a scene that had been singled out for a special kind of favorable comment during the long run of *The Old Soak* on Broadway and had been provocative of much amused discussion in literary circles. Christopher Morley makes a reference to this scene in *Letters of Askance*, from which the following is taken:

"The Old Soak . . . always stood up for his trinity of fundamentals: the Bible, calomel, and straight whiskey. Mr. Marquis himself has been equally conservative in his choice of apostolic matter. It has come down to us by unbroken laying on of hands. The literary genealogy of Mr. Hawley was suggested with gorgeous impudence when Mrs. Quickly's death-watch for Falstaff was echoed in the hired girl's epitaph on the parrot. I'm ashamed to say I had

forgotten this colossal jape until I heard it again recently in the
talking picture. They've been trying Al's home-made hootch on the
parrot:

He's gone, Mr. Hawley. He's d-d-d-dead! Seriously dead! It happened a
half hour ago. I think it was his constitution undermined itself with that
hootch Al brought here the other night, and I never will forgive myself, I
won't. But he kept coaxin' and coaxin' for it that pretty that I couldn't
refuse him. . . . And he kept drinking of it till he deceased himself with
it. He called out to me a half hour ago, he did. 'Fair weather,' he says,
and then he laughed. Only he didn't laugh natural. Mr. Hawley, he
laffed kind of puny and feeble like there was somethin' furrin weighin'
onto his stomach. 'I can't give you any more, Peter,' I says to him, 'for
there ain't no more,' I says. And then he stretched his neck out and bit
the wire on his cage and squawked, for he says in a kind of sad voice:
'Nellie was a lady, she was,' he says. And them was the last words he ever
give utterings to. (*Exit Hired Girl, weeping.*)

While Pete the Parrot "died" in *The Old Soak,* he remained
very much alive in the 169 lines of "pete the parrot and shakespeare"
in *archy and mehitabel.* When this poem was published abroad in
the British edition of that book, Hilaire Belloc, long a Don Marquis fan, hailed it as a masterpiece.

The new film version of *The Old Soak* opened in New York on
April 22, 1937. The following day Marguerite Tazelaar had this
to say about it in the New York *Herald Tribune:* "The Good Old
Soak, in its present screen rendition, seems emasculated. Wallace
Beery does his best to personify red-nosed lovability, adding another
illustrious performance to his gallery of characters. . . . The word
'good' in the title may tip you off to the story's quality—alien . . .
to the original Marquis idea."

A study of the reviews, with special reference to the one in *Variety* which summed up the picture as "amiable, red-nosed slapstick,"
leaves one quite clearly with the impression that the critics, while
they seemed to consider the picture reasonably good fun, rejected
its "good" Old Soak as a counterfeit of the character Marquis had
popularized in his column, his books, and his play. The satire had
vanished, leaving an alcoholic do-gooder, an innocuous cracker-
barrel philosopher who didn't bear much resemblance to the salty
old tippler Marquis had created as a device for puncturing the sham
and hypocrisy of the Volstead Act which the Old Soak, with his
penchant for the Biblical, had renamed "the eighteenth command-

ment." Repeal having come in, there no longer was any need to kid Prohibition; but the Old Soak's gibes at the sanctimonious were as valid as ever, especially as the Dry organizations were now leveling their guns at licensed drinking places. But Hollywood had decided that Wallace Beery would be miscast in a satiric role, and A. E. Thomas, who wrote the screenplay, labored under this handicap.

The result was what amounted to a decision to miscast Don Marquis instead. Much to his distaste—for he loved the character his friend Don had created and wanted to stick to it—Thomas had to submit to sprinkling his script here and there with platitudes about the goodness to be found in the worst of us.

Marquis's good days became fewer and fewer. Toward the end of November of that year—1937—the doctors informed his sisters that there was no longer any hope. He might live another month or two or die suddenly within a few days.

Marquis, a voracious reader until he was incapacitated, was lost without books. No one knows for a certainty how much awareness he had the last few months but it is known that when he was brought to Forest Hills after Marjorie's death the year before he didn't lose much time making it known that he wanted to read. But one arm was paralyzed and he had found it difficult to handle a book even when it was propped up in front of him on a stand. When his nurse offered to turn pages for him this was tried but it didn't work. Once a rapid reader, his mental processes had slowed up markedly and he couldn't remember anything unless he read it slowly and with almost painful deliberation, and not always then. He became self-conscious about taking so long to finish a page. He found this laborious process exhausting and in time the doctors ordered it stopped.

Maud and Nev took turns reading to him but there were times when he couldn't follow the thought and he would indicate that he wanted a passage reread; and if he couldn't follow it the second time he became annoyed with himself and pointed to his head and shook it, seeking to convey, according to his sisters, that his mind was no longer any good.

So it was decided—just how long after his return to Forest Hills no one knows—to discontinue reading to him. And once again he spent his time staring at the ceiling or the walls.

In a letter dated July 14, 1960, Frank Sullivan writes:

"I knew Don and loved him but could not claim I ever was an intimate of his. His intimates were men like Chris Morley, and Rollin Kirby, and Donn Byrne, and you can't talk about Don with any of them because they have travelled the way he went and are now talking with him themselves. . . .

"Don was like the hero of a Greek tragedy, one of those on whom the gods piled misfortune after misfortune until it seemed unbelievable. I never knew anyone who had such tragedy in his life as Don, and he wasn't even spared at the end. Poverty, a long dreadful sickness, paralysis, loss of faculties. I went to see him once in those last days when he was at Forest Hills with his sisters. I went with Paul Wing and Alan Delano. His doctor had told us at the Players to come in twos and threes because he couldn't talk and whoever visited him had to do most of the talking. When we left he cried, in great sobs, and I tell you it was a long time before I got over that harrowing experience. . . .

"I can't bear to see anyone I like suffering and to see anyone as great as Don in such a state of physical and mental wreckage was almost too much to bear. The other two lads were as shocked as I was."

Marquis died on December 29, 1937, a few weeks after the last of his friends visited the sickroom at Forest Hills. Dr. March reported that even toward the end Marquis showed occasional flashes of awareness; and he and his medical colleagues wondered whether at such times their patient might not have suffered untold mental agonies. In his lucid moments before the power of speech had almost completely left him, Marquis showed deep concern about his heavy indebtedness and the financial future of his sisters; so, since there was no hope of recovery, March thought that death, when it came, was a blessed release for one who had already suffered overmuch.

Funeral services were held in the Church in the Gardens, Forest Hills, and conducted by the rector of the church, the Rev. John W. Rahill. Lyman Beecher Stowe recalls that when Marquis's drama of the Crucifixion, *The Dark Hours*, was published in book form some years earlier, a predecessor of Rahill's, the Rev. Silcox, preached a sermon on it from that same pulpit and also read a group of Don's poems that he considered "rich in spiritual values." The sermon consisted entirely of Marquis's writings and Silcox's comments thereon. Marquis was not present. "When I told him about it," Stowe told me, "he commented with mock dolefulness, 'Yes, isn't it too bad, Lyman? My works are gradually replacing the Scriptures.'"

Marquis's will contained the following stipulation: "It is my desire that the same disposition be made of my body as was made of the body of my deceased wife, Reina Melcher Marquis, and of my deceased son, Robert Stuart Donald Marquis, whose bodies were cremated and whose ashes were scattered upon the waters of New York Bay in front of the Statue of Liberty in New York Harbor, and I accordingly direct my executors hereinafter named to cause my body to be cremated as soon as practicable after my decease, and my ashes to be scattered upon the waters of New York Bay in front of the Statue of Liberty in said Harbor of New York, N.Y."

To be sure that there would be no publicity, Marquis had said nothing about the disposition of Robert's and Reina's remains until long afterward; and then only to a few intimates.

The "executors hereinafter named," also referred to in the same instrument as "my friends," were Mell Daniel and George W. Seymour. These gentlemen were placed in an awkward position when Marquis's sisters insisted on burial in nearby Maple Grove Cemetery, Queens County, New York. As Maud was known as a scrapper—some of whose previous dissents had been aired in the press—it was considered good policy not to make an issue of the matter. Marquis had always had a dread of publicity where anything of a highly personal nature was concerned, a factor that the executors had to take seriously.

Exclusive of the many editorials, hundreds of columns about Marquis's death appeared from coast to coast in the nation's press. Four New York papers alone—the *Herald Tribune*, the *Times*, the *World-Telegram*, and the Brooklyn *Daily Eagle*—carried ten columns; and if Marquis's ashes had been "scattered upon the waters of New York Bay in front of the Statue of Liberty in New York Harbor," there inevitably would have been a fresh burst of publicity—the news itself, plus Maud's protests. When Marquis signed his will—on June 21, 1926, over eleven years before he died—he seems to have had no awareness that his death would one day be big news. Which, of course, was characteristic; for he seemed unaware, at any time, that he was a "celebrity."

When the serious nature of Marquis's illness became known, the New York newspapers and the press associations prepared their obituaries well in advance. These comprehensive biographies reflect much digging and contain few inaccuracies. (I have examined them all and am in possession of many of them, including a printer's proof headed, "MARQUIS, Donald Robert Perry—set and hold for release.")

That distinguished batch of death notices contains anecdotes that have been handed down for years—for instance the following, which appeared in the *Herald Tribune* as a result of a conversation between Dr. March and the reporter who wrote the story:

"Dr. March said that during the last few months Marquis had built up a vocabulary of fifteen or twenty one-syllable words, including 'sure,' 'O.K.' and 'fine' for bedside conversation. When he developed a lusty 'damn!' a few weeks ago his friends said it sounded like the old Don Marquis and took new hope for his recovery.

"Marquis's last word, Dr. March said, sounded like 'pray,' an addition to his vocabulary which he had acquired on Christmas Day."

Before Marquis was buried in Maple Grove Cemetery a story involving Christopher Morley, which is in circulation to this day, gained currency. Morley, according to this story, had called at the Forest Hills undertaking establishment where his friend's body was on view, and, displeased with the shabby-looking necktie the corpse was wearing, removed it and replaced it with his own.

There is a letter among the Christopher Morley papers in the Library of the University of Texas which discloses the genesis of that anecdote. It is addressed to Lyman Beecher Stowe, previously identified as a Forest Hills neighbor of Marquis's and a good friend. In this letter, which is dated January 16, 1948, we find Morley trying to help Stowe identify a Marquis poem containing lines that had fixed themselves in his memory. Then Morley goes on to say:

"... At New Year's I thought, of course, of Don ... and of that strange New Year's Eve (just about ten years ago) when I made the accursed undertaker take him out of the dress suit (Don wouldn't have wanted to be buried like a head waiter; and it was too tight for him anyhow) and regarb him in that dear old brownish tweed suit he loved and always wore to The Players, and then I gave him my own favorite necktie, off my neck, and he went to his grave wearing it round his dear old burly neck, the saint and sweetheart. And then Bucky Fuller and I drove out to Roslyn and got plastered, in good company, as Don would have approved."

In that same letter Morley made an allusion to something that happened—or *almost* happened—at the Church in the Gardens, Ascan Avenue, Forest Hills, where the funeral service took place:

"You will remember how Maud started to try to put on an act at the service in Church (that church at the corner of Ashcan Avenue, as we always called it, in Forest Hills) but I gripped her and led her out, and everyone else kept gentlemanly silence. Don could have predicted all that. He didn't even raise one of those glorious bushy black-silver eyebrows; but he *would* have been sore, the death-tidying barber had trimmed them down."

Only a sampling of the obituaries, editorials, and syndicated columns that followed Marquis's death can be attempted. Some of these pieces were written by friends and contain information that belongs in the record—as for instance, this column by Heywood Broun:

"Don Marquis is gone with the old year, but he belongs to the new. Much has been written of him in newspapers, and these were not the usual obituaries. This was not material from the 'morgue' but the eloquent tribute of other reporters who knew him and loved him.

"There is little to be added, and I would not like to write a death notice on New Year's Eve but for the fact that I was among his ardent admirers. And I have a slight suspicion that in the case of such a magnificent person there is always the danger that he may be presented as too sweet for the good of his own eternal reputation.

"Don Marquis was a kindly man who did not fear enmities, but he was a satirist, among other things, and he could bring down a stuffed shirt on the wing with the best of them. And when he was of a mind he could and did land punishing punches behind the ear.

"And why not talk of Don on New Year's Eve, for like mehitabel, his famous lower case cat, he was 'toujours gai.'

"He was, I think, the worst poker player I have ever had the privilege of participating against. I do not want to press the theories of Dr. Freud too hard, but I am firmly convinced that Don must have had some unconscious urge not to take money from anybody.

"I hope that no one is going to try to draw any moral lesson from the fact that Don Marquis, after considerable success, died in straitened circumstances. The poker games were small, and he was not a man who blew himself to wild extravagances. He was too good to be syndicated much. The complete truth is that he sunk his savings in the production of 'The Dark Hours,' a serious play about the Crucifixion.

"As far as I know, Don was not a churchgoer or orthodox in any exact sense, but he was a mystic and deeply religious. Once around a table he told us, 'I've been trying to catch up with God all my life, but I've never quite made it. Often I've come into a room and had the strong feeling that God was there until just one second before I arrived. But I'm going to keep trying. I'll catch up with Him yet.'

"All my memories of Don are mixed up, as he was, in things grave and gay. I remember the time he swore off drinking for two weeks. It was to have been for a year. We were in a Park Row saloon which managed to persist through Prohibition. Don had ordered a brandy, and the waiter brought him a full bottle. He was talking earnestly, about religion I think, when the drink came, and with one sweep of his arm he hit the bottle and knocked it to the floor, where it smashed into a hundred bootleg pieces.

"The proprietor ran up and began to abuse the waiter. 'Don't blame him,' said Don. 'I did it. I hit it with my arm. I'll pay for the bottle.'

"Don smiled, but then he frowned. 'That bottle costs about $14,' he said. 'If he can afford to give me another I'm too good a customer. I'm going to swear off for a year.'

"Naturally he was not as stern as that. Don was a realist. He was a great newspaper man, a great artist, and what he wrote from day to day must not go down the sluiceways with the scrap paper. Some publisher ought to bring out a Marquis omnibus. Here was a fellow who could really write, and he ought to live. I'm sure he will."

(Such an omnibus—*The Best of Don Marquis*—was published in 1946. It has not enjoyed the spectacular sale of another Marquis collection—the three archy and mehitabel books published in one volume, with an introduction by E. B. White—but it continues to sell and the publisher believes it will stay in print indefinitely. The other goes gaily about its business as a perennial best-seller.)

The obituary editorial in the New York *Times* was said to have been written by Simeon Strunsky, the highly regarded philosophic essayist who for years wrote the entertaining "Topics of the Times" for that newspaper. This cannot be verified, although a few things point to the possibility. For instance, once Strunsky in discussing Marquis with me described him approximately as "a rarity for a good talker in that you never feel he's hogging a conversation." And the allusion to *The Almost Perfect State*, to which Strunsky once devoted a whole page in the Sunday *Times* book review, may be significant. This editorial, titled "Goodbye, Don," follows:

"Don Marquis was an Elizabethan born out of his time at Walnut, Bureau County, Ill. This, of course, made him an American, too, and all that he wrote or imagined was racy of the central prairies. But he could have been at home in the Mermaid Tavern raising a tankard to Ben Jonson, even rubbing elbows with Will Shakespeare, and quoting the profound Biblical misquotations of the Old Soak in praise of good liquor.

"There was something leonine about Don; yet he was as gentle as a child. He never seemed to monopolize a conversation, but somehow those who sat about a table with him preferred to listen. And how many thousands came to that broader table at which he presided when he was running his columns in The Sun and The Tribune, never to depart unsatisfied! No one in his day ever gave this city more rollicking fun or more good humor. There were deeper notes, too, such as the penetrating satire he unearthed in the agenda of The Almost Perfect State. . . .

"One morning Don found on his office typewriter a communication beginning 'dear boss' and signed 'archy.' The lack of capitals was explained by archy as due to his physical limitations as a rather small though willing cockroach; he could tap out the letters with his head, but couldn't shift the keyboard. Thereafter archy qualified as a regular contributor to Don's column, who, in his turn, dug up another companion of the night, mehitabel, the disreputable alley cat. Both became illustrious. Archy was not only a quaint philosopher in his own right but a faithful amanuensis for mehitabel, who, despite her flea-bitten and ribald adventures, managed to remain 'toujours gai.' Neither will ever be gay again.

"After a long, hard wait, Don himself has gone on a holiday with Noah an' Jonah an' Cap'n John Smith, his famous fishermen. He

will surely find something heady and invigorating in those wide
waters."

Speaking of fishermen, the tall stories for which some of them
were known had a fascination for Strunsky, who in 1931 wrote a
piece on the subject in "Topics of the Times" which opened as
follows: "Don Marquis's famous pet fish that took to a life on
land seems to leave no room for further flights of the imagination.
That remarkable bullhead, it will be remembered, grew so domes-
ticated that he used to sleep in the warm ashes of the kitchen stove,
and came to a violent end by accidental drowning."

Stanley Walker, former city editor of the New York *Herald Tribune*, and author of *City Editor* and other successful books, tells
a story about the editorial he wrote for his paper about Marquis's
passing. In a letter dated November 4, 1959, written from Lampasas,
Texas, and signed "S. Walker, Cattle Baron (third class)," he says:
"I did the best I could, but it was not quite enough to suit Geoffrey
Parsons, the chief editorial writer. He loved Don Marquis and insisted on recasting my last line. Somehow he managed to work in
the poetic word 'adown,' which is a word I would feel mighty
nervous about using in any circumstances. I don't mind editors
tinkering with my stuff with considerable freedom, but when they
spring such out-of-character words on me my feelings are hurt. For
a long time after this I addressed Parsons as Mr. Adown, or Good
Old Adown, or what not, until he finally begged me to stop."

Mr. Walker's editorial, complete with the hated word, follows:

"Death has come as a merciful release to one of the magnificent
men of our time. It was the fate of Don Marquis, the gay figure
and master of comedy, that his life was overlaid with tragedy. He
laughed much, but in his heart he was a mystic, a somber, brooding
poet. Nature gave him many talents. As a man he was full-blooded,
gregarious, friendly. His memory was phenomenal. No matter to
what he turned his hand—paragraphs, verse, satire, short stories,
plays—the product was received with respect and delight.

"Don Marquis was the product of an American small town, and
he remained in character all his life. He was as genuine as Mark
Twain. Out of his rich imagination sprang that long list of fanciful
and appealing characters which gave pleasure to millions—archy,
the philosophical cockroach; Captain Peter Fitzurse, the unquench-
able liar; Clem Hawley, the Old Soak; Hermione and her Little Group

of Serious Thinkers, mehitabel, the gallant but immoral cat, and so on. None but a first-rate mind touched with a sort of genius could have produced such a brave and charming company.

"He was a learned man and a wise man, but always there was something of the homespun about him. He had a roguish sense of fun. Money, to him, was something to be spent; he was totally innocent of what passes for financial acumen. The only thing he hated was meanness. He could be bitter against the pip-squeaks, the stuffed shirts and the mountebanks of this world. He understood, as nearly as any one can hope to understand, the wellsprings of tears and laughter. He had tolerance, sympathy and an understanding heart. He won the unanimous affection of all his friends and colleagues. By them he will be remembered above all else for his gayety. Wherever he happened to be, people were happier there. So, too, with his printed words—wherever they have gone or may go adown the years."

Homer Croy, lifelong friend of Marquis's, believes that a sentence in the first paragraph of the foregoing, "He laughed much, but in his heart he was a mystic, a somber, brooding poet," sums up Marquis as well as anything he has ever read.

Christopher Morley wrote a long obituary—actually it was a full-length article—which appeared in the *Saturday Review of Literature*. It opened with one of Marquis's favorite anecdotes, one that Frank E. Mason and others heard him tell at the Players. That anecdote follows, and also other passages from Morley's piece:

"Don Marquis used to tell, with his own complete gusto, of a time in Hollywood a few years ago when he was taken ill with a heart attack. According to his story—which I dare say he improved in the narration—it was urgent for him to be got to hospital at once; all the ambulances were in service, so a hearse was sent to fetch him. In this sombre glass-paned vehicle he was laid on a stretcher and rolled off toward the clinic. But on the way, halted in a traffic jam, the hearse pulled up next to a smart little roadster in which two frolicsome young women were gaily chattering. In the middle of their mirth they noticed the transparent chariot alongside; they piously withheld palaver, and glanced reverently through the glass panel where Don's burly figure lay decently composed under a blanket. At that moment he caught their gaze, and in spite of heartburn and syncope appalled them with a slow and magnificent wink. No one, may I add, was ever better furnished for that gesture of intimate apocalypse: he had a large and lustred eye, the heavy reef of eyebrow, which could make a wink seem as physically massive as a shrug. At any rate, Don always insisted, the damsels fell into a hysteric seizure, and as his carriage rolled away he saw them crash into someone else's car and attempt, with screams, to explain to a disbelieving policeman. 'I'll bet,' he used to add, 'they led better lives after that.'

"This may seem an odd salute to an old friend just gone, but I could not help thinking of it as we sat the other day at Don's own funeral service, and as some of his friends afterward repaired, for the ritual of affection, to the nearest inn. I should not have dared to look him in the face, in funeral state, for fear either of seeing that wink—or not seeing it. I wish our taboos were not so strong: it would have been a happy circumstance if some of his lighter madrigals might have been read at the service; for perhaps he was, above all, a really great writer of humorous verse. How rare these are, the study of any anthology will quickly show. *Noah an' Jonah an' Cap'n John Smith* is the best known of his ballads in easy vein, but there are many many others. There's *David and Bathsheba* ('Oh what the hell, it's spring') and *The Old Brass Railing* and the lyrics of *mehitabel* and the unsurpassed *Famous Love Affairs*. The best of these are sure of preservation for a long time to come. It is the rarest and scarcest of all literary talents—I don't mean just verse of wit and satiric precision; I mean the stuff of real midriff humor—and even its own creators are only too likely to belittle it. As Don himself once wrote—

> And so we raise superior eyebrows,
>   And scorn the lovely slapstick stuff;
> And so we pander to the highbrows—
>   We hate it, but we bluff.

". . . It used to annoy me that though universities annually bestow honorific degrees upon many solemnities and shirts of starch it never occurred to any of them to accredit Don in this way. How could it be, I used to wonder, that Columbia, here in the very city where Marquis's column ran for so many years, was not acute enough to recognize and salute his great quality? But I acquiesced in this eventually, realizing that awareness rarely originates inside a university but is forced on it from without, against its most obdurate struggles. The professors, very likely, will now be able to tell us *why* Don's stuff was good, and bracket it in some critical niche. But his fellow journalists always knew that it *was*. I recall the letter that Hilaire Belloc wrote to Marquis a few months ago, apropos the famous piece about the Mermaid Tavern parrot. Don was already too ill to read or understand this tribute, which said, 'It is a permanent addition to the furniture of my mind. It is a masterpiece and rare indeed.'"

Something else that used to annoy Christopher Morley was the attitude of Max Eastman and other "self-ordained high priests of literature." Morley put it this way: "It is only too characteristic of the Solemn Skullworkers that because many of Marquis's most pungent comments on the human comedy were put in the form of soliloquies by the Old Soak or by archy the roach, they could not recognize their high coefficient of seriousness. I was amazed to discover that Max Eastman's *Enjoyment of Laughter*, a book with a depressing picture on the jacket showing the author roaring with mirth, and including diagrams analyzing the various phases of a joke, made no mention whatever of the most philosophical humorist of our time. That was, to me, the biggest laugh in the book. . . .

"The fact that Don Marquis was, in his own circle, the best loved man of his time, makes it now all the more a point of honor to speak with judgment. He was, regardless of mediocre work done under pressure, a deeply mercurial intuitive artist and passionately concerned with the ardors and problems of art. A human being so largely and kindly planned moves always in widening rings of irony. It was tragic to realize that he, who uttered so many genial shouts in praise of idleness, was actually broken by overwork. He was, if I ever saw one, a victim of the constantly tightening strain and pressure of our present way of living. There was, in the last two years, nothing left of him but the look in his eyes, and it was grim to speculate how much he realized of what had happened. . . ."

Morley then tells at length how Marquis begged off when he and a group of friends tried to organize a fiftieth birthday party for Don, to be called the Marquis Semi-Centennial. Marquis, usually ready for a lark of this kind, was not in the mood, explaining: "Merely to pay up present debts and obligations there are at least 18 months of desperate and continued potboiling. I have a schedule

that calls for one short story or one article each week for 18 months.
. . . Let's have a party in September, and not mention my birthday at all. . . . These ten years from forty to fifty are by before
you know it. For the love of God, don't let them slip from you as
I did."

"And by the 'love of God,'" Morley continues, "he meant as
every artist does, the joy of creation.

"That outcry was, I hope and believe, a passing mood of over-
sensitized chagrin. There indeed spoke the true dreamer, who is
bound to exalt the undone"—Marquis had told Morley he wondered if he'd ever reach the books he really wanted to write—"at
the expense of the accomplished. But, as his friends agreed in the
barroom that gray New Year's Eve, there can be no sense of
sorrow at the escape of a winged thing after cruel imprisonment.
We have seen, in his own words,

> 'Beauty as a valiant wing
> Strike a white blow against a stormy sky.'

In the noble old phrase, 'Diuturnity to his relics!' Toward the end
of *The Almost Perfect State* is a poem he wrote which seemed perfect for that afternoon:

> Lines for a Gravestone
> Here the many lives I led,
> All my Selves, are lying dead:
> All they journeyed far to find
> Strawed by the dispersing wind:
> You that were my lovers true,
> That is neither sad nor new!
>
> Naught that I have been or planned
> Sails the seas nor walks the land:
> That is not a cause for woe
> Where the careless planets go!
> Naught that I have dreamed or done
> Casts a shadow in the sun:
> Not for that shall any Spring
> Fail of song or swallow's wing!
>
> Neither change nor sorrow stays
> The bright processional of days—
> When the hearts that grieved die, too,
> Where is then the grief they knew?

Speed, I bid you, speed the earth
Onward with a shout of mirth,
Fill your eager eyes with light,
Put my face and memory
Out of mind and out of sight.
Nothing I have caused or done,
But this gravestone, meets the sun:
Friends, a great simplicity
Comes at last to you and me!

What amounted to a felicitous postscript to the Marquis obituaries appeared years later in *The New Yorker*. Here is the opening paragraph:

"It surprised us not at all that when the *Sun* folded and the other papers wrote their obits and their tearful editorials about the foundering of a great ship that had held a true course, there was only one mention of the most distinguished *Sun* man of them all, Don Marquis. The fact that the *Sun* office was the place where the lower-case Archy, the bug with the soul of a poet, subsisted on stale paste and apple parings and performed his nightly labors on the typewriter keys proved not worth a passing notice. Ah, welladay! For many thousands of buyers of evening newspapers, there was one *Sun* man who outshone the Danas, the Munseys, the Arthur Brisbanes, the Richard Harding Davises, and the Frank Ward O'Malleys. For these people, the *Sun* died when Marquis left." Those last six words are an ironic commentary on the passing of a newspaper that failed to make a single mention of "the most distinguished *Sun* man of them all" in its official history.

On the 23rd of January, 1938, less than a month after Marquis died, there was held at the Ambassador Theatre in New York City— as a benefit for Marquis's sisters—what was described on the program as

DON MARQUIS NIGHT
An Evening in Praise of a Beloved Spirit
This program departs from the conventional memorial
and is given as Don's friends believe he would wish it to be

(Christopher Morley, as Chairman, will adapt his services
to the program, speaking at intervals upon the work,
humors and personal life of DON MARQUIS)

The talks by Otis Skinner, Walter Hampden, and Sam Forrest, and the interpolated comments of Chairman Morley, had their

serious moments but the emphasis was on the hedonistic Marquis,
the man who had written: "Give me your mirth, it bores me when
you weep."

Of Marquis's own compositions that played a part in the festivities,
"Noah an' Jonah an' Cap'n John Smith" was the hit of the evening.

Since this poem was Marquis's favorite of all his humorous writings, and as there are many allusions to it in this book, it seems
appropriate to make it available to the reader:

> Noah an' Jonah an' Cap'n John Smith,
> Mariners, travelers, magazines of myth,
> Settin' up in Heaven, chewin' and a-chawin'
> Eatin' their terbaccy, talkin' and a-jawin';
> Settin' by a crick, spittin' in the worter,
> Talkin' tall an' tactless, as saints hadn't orter,
> Lollin' in the shade, baitin' hooks and anglin',
> Occasionally friendly, occasionally wranglin'.

> Noah took his halo from his old bald head
> An' swatted of a hoppergrass an' knocked it dead,
> An' he baited of his hook, an' he spoke an' said:
> "When I was the Skipper of the tight lettle Ark
> I useter fish fer porpus, useter fish fer shark,
> Often I have ketched in a single hour on Monday
> Sharks enough to feed the fambly till Sunday—
> To feed all the sarpints, the tigers an' donkeys,
> To feed all the zebras, the insects an' monkeys,
> To feed all the varmints, bears an' gorillars,
> To feed all the camels, cats an' armadillers,
> To give all the pelicans stews for their gizzards,
> To feed all the owls an' catamounts an' lizards,
> To feed all the humans, their babies an' their nusses,
> To feed all the houn' dawgs an' hippopotamusses,
> To feed all the oxens, feed all the asses,
> Feed all the bison an' leetle hoppergrasses—
> Always I ketched, in half a hour on Monday
> All that the fambly could gormandize till Sunday!"

> Jonah took his harp, to strum and to string her,
> An' Cap'n John Smith teched his nose with his finger.
> Cap'n Smith, he hemmed some an' hawed some,
> An' he bit off a chaw, an' he chewed some an' chawed some:—
> "When I was to China, when I was to Guinea,

When I was to Java, an' also in Verginney,
I teached all the natives how to be ambitious,
I learned 'em my trick of ketchin' devilfishes.
I've fitten tigers, I've fitten bears,
I've fitten sarpints an' wolves in their lairs,
I have fit with wild men an' hippopotamusses,
But the perilousest varmints is the bloody octopusses!
I'd rub my forehead with phosphorescent light
An' plunge into the ocean an' seek 'em out at night!
I ketched 'em in grottoes, I ketched 'em in caves,
I used fer to strangle 'em underneath the waves!
When they seen the bright light blazin' on my forehead
They used ter rush at me, screamin' something horrid!
Tentacles wavin', teeth white an' gnashin',
Hollerin' an' bellerin', wallerin' an' splashin'!
I useter grab 'em as they rushed from their grots,
Ketch all their legs an' tie 'em into knots!"

Noah looked at Jonah and said not a word,
But if winks made noises, a wink had been heard.
Jonah took the hook from a mudcat's middle
An' strummed on the strings of his hallelujah fiddle;
Jonah give his whiskers a backhand swipe
An' cut some plug terbaccer an' crammed it in his pipe!
—(Noah an' Jonah an' Cap'n John Smith,
Fishermen an' travelers, narreratin' myth,
Settin' up in Heaven all eternity,
Fishin' in the shade, contented as could be!
Spittin' their terbaccer in the little shaded creek,
Stoppin' of their yarns fer ter hear the ripples speak!
I hope fer Heaven, when I think of this—
You folks bound hellward, a lot of fun you'll miss!)

Jonah, he decapitates that mudcat's head,
An' gets his pipe ter drawin'; an' this is what he said:
"Excuse me ef your stories don't excite me much!
Excuse me ef I seldom agitate fer such!
You think yer fishermen! I won't argue none!
I won't even tell yer the half o' what I done!
You has careers dangerous an' checkered!
All as I will say is: Go and read my record!
You think yer fishermen! You think yer great!
All I asks is this: Has one of ye been *bait*?
Cap'n Noah, Cap'n John, I heerd when ye hollered;
What I asks is this: Has one of ye been *swallered*?

It's mighty purty fishin' with little hooks an' reels.
It's mighty easy fishin' with little rods an' creels.
It's mighty pleasant ketchin' mudcats fer yer dinners.
But this here is my challenge fer saints an' fer sinners,
Which one of ye has v'yaged in a varmint's inners?
When I seen a big fish, tough as Methooslum,
I used for to dive into his oozly-goozlum!
When I seen the strong fish, wallopin' like a lummicks,
I useter foller 'em, dive into their stummicks!
I could v'yage an' steer 'em, I could understand 'em,
I useter navigate 'em, I useter land 'em!
Don't you pester *me* with any more narration!
Go git famous! Git a reputation!"

—Cap'n John he grinned his hat brim beneath,
Clicked his tongue of silver on his golden teeth;
Noah an' Jonah an' Cap'n John Smith,
Strummin' golden harps, narreratin' myth!
Settin' by the shallows forever an' forever,
Swappin' yarns an' fishin' in a little river!

On November 21, 1940—almost three years after her brother's
death—Maud Marquis wrote Christopher Morley that she and her
sister had found "Don's dictaphone and records." "Among them,"
she said, "is one where Don is reciting 'Noah an' Jonah an' Cap'n
John Smith.' . . . A dictaphone man came over with a new machine
and the voice came over wonderfully clear." Efforts to recover these
records have proven unavailing.

In an article published in *Harper's Magazine* in 1933, from
which the following is taken, Marquis expressed a philosophy that
became more and more typical of him in the final years of his life:

"The spectacle, the game, the drama of human existence fasci-
nates me more and more as the moment swiftly approaches when
I shall have to give up my seat in the theatre. *Swiftly* approaches—
for there is no use trying to blink the fact that when you get into
your fifties the speed with which time seems to pass is simply ap-
palling. . . .

"Life has lost the power to jolt me to any considerable extent,
although not the power to interest me. . . .

"Things happen so rapidly, come tumbling along upon the heels
of one another with such instancy that it seems scarcely worth while
to try to rush personally into the midst of these events and shout

and elbow for a place among them. I have lost the ambition to form a part of this speed and daunting mobility . . . but there is a part of me that rejoices in the rapid series of changes which shimmer over the surface of the world as little winds dart ruffling across a bay.

"I feel myself strangely unconcerned at what these changes may mean to me. . . . I am tired of trying to go in a different way from the way in which Fate has seemed to delight in kicking and hauling me. Perhaps this is the ignoble surrender of indolence. At least I do not want so many things as I used to, nor want those few things with such intensity, nor care so greatly when I get them or when I don't get them. . . . And whereas thinking, or trying to think, used to be a kind of coiled and knotted agony to me, now I actually take pleasure out of doing nothing at all but sitting down and thinking. The fact that the thoughts I think never get anywhere in particular doesn't bother me at all. . . .

"When I have to go, I hope I shall have the good manners to go without making too much fuss about the matter, realizing that the party is over and that it is time to get a little sleep."

INDEX

DATE DUE

PRINTED IN U.S.A.